THE BILL OF RIGHTS:
A DOCUMENTARY HISTORY

THE BILL OF RIGHTS:
A DOCUMENTARY HISTORY

BERNARD SCHWARTZ

Volume I

CHELSEA HOUSE PUBLISHERS in association with
McGRAW HILL BOOK COMPANY
New York, Toronto, London, Sydney
1971

MANAGING EDITOR: Leon Friedman

ASSISTANT EDITOR: Karyn Gullen Browne

EDITORIAL STAFF: Joan Tapper, Betsy Nicolaus, Christine Pinches, Jeanne Brody

NOTE: The original spelling, grammar and style have been retained in all documentary material.

PREFACE

In a broad sense, the history of the federal Bill of Rights is the history of freedom itself. To attempt a history of that subject, would, however, be as chimerical as the monumental history of freedom that Lord Acton was never able to write. What these volumes seek to do is to present the history of the federal Bill of Rights in documentary form. For that purpose, it is not enough to present the legislative history of the first ten amendments alone. The great documents of Anglo-American liberty which led up to the 1791 Bill of Rights must also be included, as well as explanatory material to show their significance. The arrangement is essentially chronological, covering 1) the English antecedents; 2) the Colonial period; 3) The Revolutionary Declarations and Constitutions; 4) developments under the Articles of Confederation; 5) the federal Constitution; 6) the state ratifying conventions; 7) the legislative history of the federal Bill of Rights, and 8) the ratification by the states.

Of one thing the reader can be certain: that all the materials used have been personally selected and analyzed by the editor. The noted French historian Fustel de Coulanges is said to have told a lecture audience, "Do not imagine you are listening to me: it is history itself that speaks." The same assertion could hardly be made of these volumes. They are presented from the editor's own point of view and emphasize those aspects in the development of the Bill of Rights which he considers of primary significance.

"Human history," says H. G. Wells, "is in essence a history of ideas." The federal Bill of Rights is the culmination of the idea of law as a check upon governmental power. If Americans live under a constitutional polity, it is only because we enjoy the fruits of a successful struggle to bridle public authority by constitutional guarantee. Our liberties today are based upon the words originally written into Colonial Charters and enactments, and, even earlier, into the great Charters of English history. From a historical point of view, the federal Bill of Rights is (paraphrasing Justice Holmes) a virtual magic mirror, wherein we see reflected not only our own lives, but the whole pageant of Anglo-American constitutional development and all that it has meant in the history of freedom. When one thinks on this majestic theme, his eyes dazzle. If only a part of his feelings on the matter are communicated to the reader, the editor will be amply rewarded for his labors.

Bernard Schwartz
Edwin D. Webb, Professor of Law
New York University

CONTENTS

Volume I

PART TWO
Colonial Charters and Laws

PART THREE
Revolutionary Declarations and Constitutions

PART FOUR
Confederation and Judicial Review

PART FIVE
United States Constitution

Volume II

PART SIX
State Ratifying Conventions

PART SEVEN
Federal Bill of Rights: Legislative History

PART EIGHT
Ratification by the States

PART ONE
ENGLISH ANTECEDENTS

ENGLISH ANTECEDENTS

Commentary

"You give me a credit to which I have no claim," wrote James Madison to a correspondent in 1834, "in calling me '*the* writer of the Constitution of the U.S.' This was not like the fabled goddess of wisdom the offspring of a single brain. It ought to be regarded as the work of many heads & many hands."

The Madison comment is equally appropriate to the federal Bill of Rights, even though Madison himself wrote the first draft of the ten amendments which became the Bill of Rights and his draft contained the substance and much of the phraseology of the final version. An attempt to write a declaration of fundamental rights on a *tabula rasa* may turn out favorably in Greek myth. In real life, the successful Constitution-maker must work upon an existing political and historical mold. Even a Madison could draft a Bill of Rights only because of the precedents furnished by centuries of Anglo-American constitutional development.

If Madison and his colleagues could draw up the classic inventory of basic rights, it was because they were the heirs of the constitutional struggles waged by their English forebears. All too few people in this country realize the extent to which our modern liberties are based upon the crucial battles waged against seventeenth-century Stuart tyranny. But the men who established the American constitutional system were fully aware of the vital importance of the Parliamentary victory over the Crown, as well as earlier efforts to curb royal power.

The roots of American freedom are thus to be found in English constitutional history. To understand the history of the federal Bill of Rights, one must understand the development of constitutional guarantees of liberty which led up to the 1791 document. For our purposes, this means a tracing of the Anglo-American antecedents of the Bill of Rights. The constitutional amendments proposed by Madison were the logical culmination of what had gone before in both English and American constitutional history. In particular, the federal Bill of Rights was based directly upon the great Charters of English liberty, which begin with the Magna Carta. Without the English development in this respect, it may be doubted that American colonists, revolutionaries, and Constitution-makers would (or indeed could) have acted as they did. We must consequently start our documentary history with the English antecedents of the federal Bill of Rights.

3

MAGNA CARTA, 1215

Commentary

To an American interested in the English antecedents of the federal Bill of Rights, the obvious starting point is the Magna Carta itself. For in it he sees for the first time in English history a written organic instrument exacted from a sovereign ruler by the bulk of the politically articulate community which purports to lay down binding rules of law that the ruler himself may not violate. In the Magna Carta is to be found the germ of the root principle that there are fundamental rights above the State, which the State— otherwise sovereign power that it is—may not infringe.

The traditional theory made the Magna Carta the direct descendant of the Coronation Charter issued by Henry I when he seized the throne on the death of his older brother William Rufus in 1100.

Yet, if the Charter secured at Runnymede in 1215 may thus be said to be derived from the Henry I Charter, its importance is to be found in the fact that it goes far beyond the earlier document both in its wording and implications. Most significant in this respect were the differing circumstances in which the two Charters were secured. Henry had issued his Coronation Charter to obtain support for his accession to the throne, but the instrument itself was a unilateral act on the part of the monarch—a promise by the King given as a matter of grace and not as the result of any external coercion.

John's Charter also, it is true, is in its terms only a grant by the sovereign to his subjects. "John, by the grace of God," it starts, and, after listing his titles and his formal greeting to his subjects, goes on to state "Know that . . . we have also granted to all free men of our kingdom, for us and our heirs forever, all the liberties hereinunder written, to be had and held by them and their heirs, of us and our heirs." And, after listing the different liberties granted, it concluded, with the traditional words of royal grant: "Given by our hand in the meadow that is called Runnymede between Windsor and Staines, June 15, in the seventeenth year of our reign." The actual giving, by John's hand, was effected by the imprint of his great seal.

But if the Magna Carta was thus cast in the form common to royal Charters of the period—announcing in the pious legal formula of the day that the King has been pleased to make certain unilateral grants, by the advice of certain counsellors who are named—how different was its reality! In actuality, John's Charter was anything but a unilateral act of grace on the part of that monarch. The promises made at Runnymede were exacted by the united arms of most of the kingdom. The reasons stated for the grant of the Charter were quaintly paraphrased by Lord Coke four centuries later: "Here be four notable causes of the making of this great charter rehearsed. 1. The honour of God. 2. For the health of the King's soul. 3. For the

4

exaltation of holy church, and fourthly, for the amendment of the King-dom." But the real reason is to be found in the army opposing the King. The true *quid pro quo* which John received for the grants made by him was the renewal by his opponents of the homage and fealty that they had solemnly renounced.

Seen in this light, what can we say is the true legal nature of the Great Charter? This is a question on which countless scholars have disagreed. As already indicated, the document's form as a unilateral grant—a mere act of grace—on the part of the Crown does not give the answer.

Stubbs's famous characterization of Magna Carta as "really a treaty between the King and his subjects" has been rejected by more recent historians. Yet it is not so far from the truth as they suppose—if we bear in mind that, unlike the usual treaty between independent States, this was a concord worked out between ruler and subjects of the same State.

From the point of view of the modern American, such an agreement, drawn up by the different estates of the realm, and accepted by the King as the price for their continued obedience—setting limits to the powers of government—has many of the earmarks of the constitutional documents with which he is familiar. Even the charter form—a grant of franchises freely made—does not seem out of place to one cognizant of the constitutional role played by documents cast in a similar form in the American colonies.

What is clear is that there took place at Runnymede what was essentially a bargain struck between the King and the nation. The result of this bargain was a document enumerating what were deemed the basic liberties of Englishmen of the day. Such enumeration may strike us as brief, contained as it is in 63 short chapters; for its date, nevertheless, it is a rather lengthy document. It was natural for the men of the day to resort to the legal form invariably used for all irrevocable grants—the feudal Charter authenticated by the grantor's seal. The analogy was that of a grant of land and much of the language employed was actually that appropriate to such a grant.

In a provocative passage, Maitland asks, "Have you ever pondered the form, the scheme, the main idea of Magna Charta? If so, your reverence for that sacred text will hardly have prevented you from using in the privacy of your own minds some such words as 'inept' or 'childish,' etc." Certainly, Magna Carta is an unrewarding document for the non-specialist. "If we set aside the rhetorical praise which has been so freely lavished upon the Charter," says Winston Churchill, "and study the document itself, we may find it rather surprising."

The Great Charter is drawn up as a feudal grant. It abounds in the technicalities of feudal law and, when these are out of the way, it seems to deal, in the main, with mundane and petty aspects of the relations between the King and his barons. There is in it no broad statement of principle or defined political theory. It is not what we would look for in a declaration of constitutional doctrine, but only a practical document to remedy current feudal abuses. Most surprising is that most of what we now consider the great safeguards of Anglo-American liberty are conspicuously absent from the first great Charter of English liberties.

Yet if we analyze the Magna Carta on its own terms, there is much that is notable. It is of great significance that the custom of feudal tenure is stated as a defined component of English law, with precise limits set to royal claims in strict terms of money, time, and space. The questions of scutage, feudal reliefs, wardship, and the like are regulated in legally enforceable terms against a King who had claimed to be all but a law unto himself.

More important is the fact that, though Magna Carta is primarily a feudal document directed against specific feudal abuses committed by the King against his tenants-in-chief, its important provisions are cast in broader terms. This is of crucial consequence, for it means that the key chapters of the Charter have been capable of construction to fit the needs of later ages which sought precedents to justify establishment of the liberties we now deem basic.

The barons were concerned with their own grievances against John; but, when the original Articles of the Barons were being refined, the words "any baron" were changed, in important provisions, to "any free man" (*liber homo*). This change in phraseology may have seemed of minor significance at the time (certainly "free man" was a technical feudal term with a far more restricted meaning than we should give to it), yet it turned out to be of momentous importance in giving the Charter the widest application in future centuries. The wrongs done to the barons may have been the direct cause of Magna Carta, but the language used was broad enough to protect the entire nation against governmental oppression.

This was particularly true of what history came to consider the two key provisions of the Great Charter: 1) Chapter 12, under which "Scutage or aid shall be levied in our kingdom only by the common counsel of our kingdom"; and 2) Chapter 39, which declares, "No free man shall be captured or imprisoned or disseised or outlawed or exiled or in any way destroyed . . . except by the lawful judgment of his peers and by the law of the land."

The first of these may have been intended by the barons only as an assertion of their right not to have their feudal obligations unilaterally altered by the King. But the language is more sweeping than a mere declaration of feudal right. Without undue stretching, it can readily be construed as an admission of the right of the nation to ordain taxation.

Chapter 39 has been even more consequential in the evolution of constitutional liberty. This is true although it was probably intended merely as a written confirmation of the baronial right, recognized by feudal custom, not to be tried by inferiors, but only by men of baronial rank. The breadth of the language used has made it serve a far wider purpose. Coke, in his seventeenth-century commentary on Magna Carta, could read it as a guarantee of trial by jury to all men; as absolutely prohibiting arbitrary arrest; and as solemnly undertaking to dispense to all full, free, and speedy justice—equal to all. Even more suggestive for an American, in Coke's commentary the crucial phrase at the end of the chapter, "by the law of the land," is read as equivalent to "due process of law" (a connotation it had begun to acquire as early as the time of Edward III)—thus providing the link between the Great Charter and the most important clause of the American Bill of Rights.

Of course, we read our own conceptions into the document sealed at Runnymede when we make of it an organic instrument designed, in Hallam's phrase, to "protect the personal liberty and property of all freemen by giving security from arbitrary imprisonment and arbitrary spoliation." Yet, intended so broadly or not by its framers, it can scarcely be doubted that Magna Carta has ultimately had such effect.

More important than the literal intent of the men of Runnymede is the meaning that future generations were able to read into their words. If, as Maitland has strikingly put it, it was possible for later men to worship such words only because it was possible to misunderstand them—the significant thing, after all, is that the words were written in a way that could be "misunderstood" so as to serve the needs of later ages. Because of this, to quote Maitland again, the "document becomes and rightly becomes a sacred text, the nearest thing to a 'fundamental statute' that England has ever had." In age after age, men will turn to the Charter as a continuing source of inspiration and authority in their struggles to bridle the "Johns" of their day.

For the truly great thing about the Magna Carta has been its ability to mean all things to all men—to project itself into the dreams and necessities of ages which the men of 1215 could not even dimly foresee. Thus it was that a document, which may itself have been only a product of feudal class selfishness, was able to serve as the basis for molding the foundations of a Parliamentary monarchy in the next two centuries, as the vehicle to enable the Parliamentary leaders to resist the misdeeds of Stuart Kings four centuries later, and even as the core of the rights of Englishmen asserted by American colonists against the England of the eighteenth century. Those who look at Magna Carta with only the pedantic rigor of the thirteenth-century specialist are bound to miss the mark so far as its ultimate significance in the history of freedom is concerned.

When all is said and done, indeed, the vital thing about the Great Charter is, not any specific provision contained in it, but its very coming into being—which alone has justified its continuing renown and significance. The mere existence of such a document, extorted from the King as it was, has been a standing condemnation of governmental absolutism. Instead, the Charter itself tells us that, in Winston Churchill's phrase, "here is a law which is above the King and which even he must not break. This reaffirmation of a supreme law and its expression in a general charter is the great work of Magna Carta; and this alone justifies the respect in which men have held it."

Magna Carta, 1215*

John, by the grace of God king of England, lord of Ireland, duke of Normandy and of Aquitaine, and count of Anjou, to his archbishops, bishops, abbots, earls, barons, justiciars, foresters, sheriffs, reeves, ministers, and all his bailiffs and faithful men, greeting. Know that, through the inspiration of God, for the health of our soul and [the souls] of all our ancestors and heirs, for the honour of God and the exaltation of Holy Church, and for the betterment of our realm, by the counsel of our venerable fathers . . . , of our nobles . . . , and of our other faithful men—

1. We have in the first place granted to God and by this our present charter have confirmed, for us and our heirs forever, that the English Church shall be free and shall have its rights entire and its liberties inviolate. And how we wish [that freedom] to be observed appears from this, that of our own pure and free will, before the conflict that arose between us and our barons, we granted and by our charter confirmed the liberty of election that is considered of prime importance and necessity for the English Church, and we obtained confirmation of it from the lord pope Innocent III—which [charter] we will observe ourself and we wish to be observed in good faith by our heirs forever. We have also granted to all freemen of our kingdom, for us and our heirs forever, all the liberties hereinunder written, to be had and held by them and their heirs of us and our heirs.

2. If any one of our earls or barons or other men holding of us in chief dies, and if when he dies his heir is of full age and owes relief, [that heir] shall have his inheritance for the ancient relief: namely, the heir or heirs of an earl £100 for the whole barony of an earl; the heir or heirs of a baron £100 for a whole barony; the heir or heirs of a knight 100s at most for a whole knight's fee. And let whoever owes less give less, according to the ancient custom of fiefs.

3. If, however, the heir of any such person is under age and is in wardship, he shall, when he comes of age, have his inheritance without relief and without fine.

4. The guardian of the land of such an heir who is under age shall not take from the land of the heir more than reasonable issues and reasonable customs and reasonable services, and this without destruction and waste of men or things. And if we entrust the wardship of any such land to a sheriff or to any one else who is to answer to us for its issues, and if he causes destruction or waste of [what is under] wardship, we will exact compensation from him; and the land shall be entrusted to two discreet and lawful men of that fief, who shall answer for the issues to us or the man to whom we may assign them. And if we give or sell the wardship of any such land to any one, and if he causes destruction or waste of it, he shall forfeit that wardship and

*C. Stephenson and F. G. Marcham, *Sources of English Constitutional History* (1937), pp. 115–26.

it shall be given to two discreet and lawful men of that fief, who likewise shall answer to us as aforesaid.

5. Moreover, the guardian, so long as he has wardship of the land, shall from the issues of that same land keep up the houses, parks, preserves, fish-ponds, mills, and other things belonging to that land. And to the heir, when he comes of full age, [the guardian] shall give all his land, stocked with ploughs and produce, according to what crops may be seasonable and to what the issues of the land can reasonably permit.

6. Heirs shall be married without disparagement; yet so that, before the marriage is contracted, it shall be announced to the blood-relatives of the said heir.

7. A widow shall have her marriage portion and inheritance immediately after the death of her husband and without difficulty; nor shall she give anything for her dowry or for her marriage portion or for her her inheritance—which inheritance she and her husband were holding on the day of that husband's death. And after his death she shall remain in the house of her husband for forty days, within which her dowry shall be assigned to her.

8. No widow shall be forced to marry so long as she wishes to live without a husband; yet so that she shall give security against marrying without our consent if she holds of us, or without the consent of her lord if she holds of another.

9. Neither we nor our bailiffs will seize any land or revenue for any debt, so long as the chattels of the debtor are sufficient to repay the debt; nor shall the sureties of that debtor be distrained so long as the chief debtor is himself able to pay the debt. And if the chief debtor, having nothing with which to pay, defaults in payment of the debt, the sureties shall be responsible for the debt; and, if they wish, they shall have the lands and revenues of the debtor until satisfaction is made to them for the debt which they previously paid on his behalf, unless the chief debtor proves that he is quit of such responsibility toward the said sureties.

10. If any one has taken anything, whether much or little, by way of loan from Jews, and if he dies before that debt is paid, the debt shall not carry usury so long as the heir is under age, from whomsoever he may hold. And if that debt falls into our hands, we will take only the principal contained in the note.

11. And if any one dies owing a debt to Jews, his wife shall have her dowry and shall pay nothing on that debt. And if the said deceased is survived by children who are under age, necessities shall be provided for them in proportion to the tenement that belonged to the deceased; and the debt shall be paid from the remainder, saving the service of the lords. In the same way let action be taken with regard to debts owed to others besides Jews.

12. Scutage or aid shall be levied in our kingdom only by the common counsel of our kingdom, except for ransoming our body, for knighting our

eldest son, and for once marrying our eldest daughter; and for these [purposes] only a reasonable aid shall be taken. The same provision shall hold with regard to the aids of the city of London.

13. And the city of London shall have all its ancient liberties and free customs, both by land and by water. Besides we will and grant that all the other cities, boroughs, towns, and ports shall have all their liberties and free customs.

14. And in order to have the common counsel of the kingdom for assessing aid other than in the three cases aforesaid, or for assessing scutage, we will cause the archbishops, bishops, abbots, earls and greater barons to be summoned by our letters individually; and besides we will cause to be summoned in general, through our sheriffs and bailiffs, all those who hold of us in chief—for a certain day, namely, at the end of forty days at least, and to a certain place. And in all such letters of summons we will state the cause of the summons; and when the summons has thus been made, the business assigned for the day shall proceed according to the counsel of those who are present, although all those summoned may not come.

15. In the future we will not grant to any one that he may take aid from his freemen, except for ransoming his body, for knighting his eldest son, and for once marrying his eldest daughter; and for these [purposes] only a reasonable aid shall be taken.

16. No one shall be distrained to render greater service from a knight's fee, or from any other free tenement, than is thence owed.

17. Common pleas shall not follow our court, but shall be held in some definite place.

18. Assizes of novel disseisin, of mort d'ancestor, and of darrein presentment shall be held only in their counties [of origin] and in this way: we, or our chief justice if we are out of the kingdom, will send two justices through each county four times a year; and they, together with four knights of each county elected by the county [court], shall hold the aforesaid assizes in the county, on the day and at the place [set for the meeting] of the county [court].

19. And if within the day [set for the meeting] of the county [court] the aforesaid assizes cannot be held, as many knights and free tenants shall remain of those present at the county [court] on that day as may be needed for holding the trials, according as the business is greater or less.

20. A freeman shall be amerced for a small offence only according to the degree of the offence; and for a grave offence he shall be amerced according to the gravity of the offence, saving his contenement. And a merchant shall be amerced in the same way, saving his merchandise; and a villein in the same way, saving his wainage—should they fall into our mercy. And none of the aforesaid amercements shall be imposed except by the oaths of good men from the neighbourhood.

21. Earls and barons shall be amerced only by their peers, and only according to the degree of the misdeed.

22. No clergyman shall be amerced with respect to his lay tenement except in the manner of those aforesaid, not according to the value of his ecclesiastical benefice.

23. Neither vill nor man shall be distrained to make bridges on river-banks, except such as by right and ancient custom ought to do so.

24. No sheriff, constable, coroner, or other bailiff of ours shall hold the pleas of our crown.

25. All counties, hundreds, wapentakes, and trithings shall remain at the ancient farms without any increment, with the exception of our demesne manors.

26. If any one holding a lay fee of us dies, and if our sheriff or bailiff shows our letters patent of summons concerning a debt that the deceased owed to us, our sheriff or bailiff shall be permitted, by view of lawful men, to attach and record such chattels of the deceased as are found on the lay fief to the value of that debt; so that, moreover, nothing shall thence be removed until a debt that is manifestly owed shall be paid to us. And the residue shall be left to the executors for carrying out the will of the deceased. And if nothing is owed us from it, all the chattels shall by yielded to [disposition by] the deceased, saving to his wife and children their reasonable portions.

27. If any freeman dies intestate, his chattels, under eccelesiastical inspection, shall be distributed by the hands of his near relatives and friends, saving to each [creditor] the debts that the deceased owed him.

28. No constable or other bailiff of ours shall take grain or other chattels of any one without immediate payment therefor in money, unless by the will of the seller he may secure postponement of that [payment].

29. No constable shall distrain any knight to pay money for castle-guard when he is willing to perform that service himself, or through another good man if for reasonable cause he is unable to perform it himself. And if we lead or send him on a military expedition, he shall be quit of [castle-]guard for so long a time as he shall be with the army at our command.

30. No sheriff or bailiff of ours, nor any other person, shall take the horses or carts of any freeman for carrying service, except by the will of that freeman.

31. Neither we nor our bailiffs will take some one else's wood for [repairing] castles or for doing any other work of ours, except by the will of him to whom the wood belongs.

32. We will hold the lands of those convicted of felony only for a year and a day, and the lands shall then be given to the lords of the fiefs [concerned].

33. All fish-weirs shall henceforth be entirely removed from the Thames and the Medway and throughout all England except along the sea-coasts.

34. Henceforth the writ called praecipe shall not be issued for any one concerning any tenement whereby a freeman may lose his court.

35. There shall be one measure of wine throughout our entire kingdom, and one measure of ale; also one measure of grain, namely, the quarter of London; and one width of dyed cloth, russet [cloth], and hauberk [cloth],

namely, two yards between the borders. With weights, moreover, it shall be as with measures.

36. Nothing henceforth shall be taken or given for the writ of inquisition concerning life and limbs, but it shall be issued gratis and shall not be denied.

37. If any one holding of us by fee-farm or by socage or by burgage holds land of some one else by military service, on account of that fee-farm or socage or burgage we are not to have the wardship of the heir or of the land that is another's fee, unless the said [land held by] fee-farm owes military service. By virtue of some little serjeanty held of us by the service of rendering knives or arrows or something of the sort, we are not to have wardship of any one's heir or of land that he holds of another by military service.

38. No bailiff shall henceforth put any one to his law by merely bringing suit [against him] without trustworthy witnesses presented for this purpose.

39. No freeman shall be captured or imprisoned or disseised or outlawed or exiled or in any way destroyed, nor will we go against him or send against him, except by the lawful judgment of his peers or by the law of the land.

40. To no one will we sell, to no one will we deny or delay right or justice.

41. All merchants may safely and securely go away from England, come to England, stay in and go through England, by land or by water, for buying and selling under right and ancient customs and without any evil exactions, except in time of war if they are from the land at war with us. And if such persons are found in our land at the beginning of a war, they shall be arrested without injury to their bodies or goods until we or our chief justice can ascertain how the merchants of our land who may then be found in the land at war with us are to be treated. And if our men are to be safe, the others shall be safe in our land.

42. Every one shall henceforth be permitted, saving our fealty, to leave our kingdom and to return in safety and security, by land or by water, except in the common interest of the realm for a brief period during wartime, and excepting [always] men imprisoned or outlawed according to the law of the kingdom and people from a land at war with us and merchants, who are to be treated as aforesaid.

43. If any one holds of any escheat—such as the honour of Wallingford, Nottingham, Boulogne, Lancaster, or the other escheats that are in our hands and are baronies—and if he dies, his heir shall give only such relief and shall render us only such service as would be due to the baron if that barony were in the hands of the baron; and we shall hold it in the same way that the baron held it.

44. Men dwelling outside the forest shall no longer, in consequence of a general summons, come before our justices of the forest, unless they are [involved] in a plea [of the forest] or are sureties of some person or persons who have been arrested for [offences against] the forest.

45. We will appoint as justiciars, constables, sheriffs, or bailiffs only such men as know the law of the kingdom and well desire to observe it.

46. All barons who have founded abbeys, concerning which they have charters from kings of England or [enjoy] ancient tenures, shall have the custody of those [abbeys] during vacancies, as they ought to have.

47. All forests that have been afforested in our time shall at once be disafforested; and the same shall be done with regard to riverbanks which in our time we have placed under ban.

48. Concerning all bad customs of forest and warrens, of foresters and warreners, of sheriffs and their officers, and of river-banks and their wardens, inquisition shall at once be made in each county through twelve knights of that same county placed under oath, who ought to be elected by the good men of the same county. And within forty days after the inquisition has been made, they shall be utterly abolished by the same [knights], so that they shall never be restored; in such fashion [however] that we may have prior notice, or our justiciar [may] if we are not in England.

49. We will immediately restore all hostages and charters which were delivered to us by Englishmen as security for the peace or for faithful service.

50. We will utterly remove from their offices the relatives of Gerard d'Athée, Engelard de Cigogné, Peter and Guy and Andrew de Chanceaux, Guy de Cigogné, Geoffrey de Martigny and his brothers, Philip Marc and his brothers and his nephew Geoffrey, togeher with all their adherents, so that henceforth they shall have no office in England.

51. And immediately after the restoration of peace we will remove from the kingdom all alien knights, crossbowmen, serjeants, and mercenaries, who have come with horses and arms to the injury of the kingdom.

52. If any one, without the lawful judgment of his peers, has been disseised or deprived by us of his lands, castles, liberties, or rights, we will at once restore them to him. And if a dispute arises in this connection, then let the matter be decided by the judgment of the twenty-five barons, concerning whom provision is made below in [the article on] security for the peace. With regard, however, to all those [possessions] of which any one, without lawful judgment of his peers, was disseised or deprived by King Henry, our father, or by King Richard, our brother—which possessions we have in our hands or which are held by others whose possession we are bound to warrant—we are to have respite for the ordinary term of crusaders, except those [possessions] concerning which suit was brought or inquest was made by our precept before we took the corss. Moreover, when we return from our journey, or if perchance we abandon our journey, we will at once administer full justice in such matters.

53. Moreover, we are to have similar respite and in the same way with regard to the disafforestation or retention of the forests which Henry, our father, or Richard, our brother, afforested; with regard to wardships over

lands of another's fee, which sort of wardships we have hitherto enjoyed on account of a fee that any one holds of us by military service, and with regard to abbeys which were founded in a fee other than our own, and over which the lord of the fee has asserted that he has the right. And when we return, or if we abandon our journey, we will at once give full justice to those making complaints in such matters.

54. No one shall be seized or imprisoned on the appeal of a woman for the death of any one but her husband.

55. All fines which have been made with us unjustly and contrary to the law of the land, and all amercements made unjustly and contrary to the law of the land, are to be entirely pardoned; or decision is thereon to be made by the judgment of the twenty-five barons concerning whom provision is made below in [the article on] security for the peace, or by the judgment of the majority of them, together with the aforesaid Stephen, archbishop of Canterbury, if he can be present, and other men whom he may wish to associate with himself for this purpose—and if he cannot be present, the business shall nevertheless proceed without him; yet so that, if any one or more of the twenty-five barons aforesaid are [involved] in a dispute of this kind, they shall be removed so far as this judgment is concerned, and others, elected and sworn for this purpose, shall be substituted in their places by the rest of the twenty-five.

56. If, without the lawful judgment of their peers, we have disseised or deprived Welshmen of their lands, liberties, or other things in England or in Wales, [the same] shall be immediately restored to them. And if a dispute arises in this connection, then decision is thereon to be made in the [Welsh] march by the judgment of their peers—according to the law of England for their tenements in England, according to the law of Wales for their tenements in Wales, and according to the law of the march for their tenements in the march. Welshmen shall act in the same way toward us and our men.

57. Moreover, with regard to those [possessions] of which any Welshman, without the lawful judgment of his peers, was disseised or deprived by King Henry, our father, or King Richard, our brother.

58. We will at once restore the son of Llewelyn and all the [other] hostages of Wales, together with the charters that were given us as security for the peace.

59. We will act toward Alexander, king of the Scots, in the matter of restoring his sisters and the [other] hostages, together with his liberties and rights in the same way as we act toward our other barons of England, unless by the charters which we have from his father William, one time king of the Scots, the action ought to be otherwise—and this shall be [determined] by the judgment of his peers in our court.

60. Now all these aforesaid customs and liberties, which we have granted, in so far as concerns us, to be observed in our kingdom toward our men, all men of our kingdom, both clergy and laity, shall, in so far as concerns them, observe toward their men.

61. Since moreover for [the love of] God, for the improvement of our kingdom, and for the better allayment of the conflict that has arisen between us and our barons, we have granted all these [liberties] aforesaid, wishing them to enjoy those [liberties] by full and firm establishment forever, we have made and granted them the following security: namely, that the barons shall elect twenty-five barons of the kingdom, whomsoever they please, who to the best of their ability should observe, hold, and cause to be observed the peace and liberties that we have granted to them and have confirmed by this our present charter; so that, specifically, if we or our justiciar or our bailiffs or any of our ministers are in any respect delinquent toward any one or trangress any article of the peace or the security, and if the delinquency is shown to four barons of the aforesaid twenty-five barons, those four barons shall come to us, or to our justiciar if we are out of the kingdom, to explain to us the wrong, asking that without delay we cause this wrong to be redressed. And if within a period of forty days, counted from the time that notification is made to us, or to our justiciar if we are out of the kingdom, we do not redress the wrong, or, if we are out of the kingdom, our justiciar does not redress it, the four barons aforesaid shall refer that case to the rest of the twenty-five barons, and those twenty-five barons, together with the community of the entire country, shall distress and injure us in all ways possible—namely, by capturing our castles, lands, and possessions and in all ways that they can—until they secure redress according to their own decision, saving our person and [the person] of our queen and [the persons] of our children. And when redress has been made, they shall be obedient to us as they were before. And any one in the land who wishes shall swear that, for carrying out the aforesaid matters, he will obey the commands of the twenty-five barons aforesaid and that he, with his men, will injure us to the best of his ability; and we publicly and freely give licence of [thus] swearing to every one who wishes to do so, and to no one will we ever prohibit [such] swearing. Moreover, all those of the land who of themselves and by their own free will are unwilling to take the oath for the twenty-five barons, with them to distress and injure us, we will by our mandate cause to swear [such an oath] as aforesaid. And if any one of the twenty-five barons dies or departs from the land, or in any other way is prevented from carrying out these aforesaid matters, the rest of the twenty-five barons aforesaid shall by their own decision choose another in his place, who is to be sworn in the same way as the others. Moreover, in all the matters entrusted to those twenty-five barons for execution, if perchance the same twenty-five are present and disagree among themselves in some respect, or if certain of those summoned are unwilling or unable to be present, that which the majority of those present may provide or command shall be held as settled and established, just as if all twenty-five had agreed to it. And the aforesaid twenty-five shall swear that they will faithfully observe all that has been set forth above. And neither of ourself nor through others will we procure from any one anything whereby any of these concessions and liberties may be revoked or dimin-

ished; and should anything of the sort be procured, it shall be null and void, and we will never make use of it either of ourself or through others.

62. And to all we freely pardon and condone all the ill-will, indignation, and rancour that from the beginning of the conflict have arisen between us and our men, both clergy and laity. Furthermore, to all, whether clergy or laity, we fully pardon and condone, in so far as pertains to us, all trespasses committed on account of the said conflict since Easter in the sixteenth year of our reign until the reestablishment of peace. And besides we have caused to be drawn up for them letters patent of the lord Stephen, archbishop of Canterbury, of the lord Henry, archbishop of Dublin, of the bishops afore-said, and of Master Pandulf, in witness of that security and the concessions aforesaid.

63. Wherefore we wish and straitly enjoin that the English Church shall be free and that the men in our kingdom shall have and hold all the aforesaid liberties, rights, and grants well and in peace, freely and quietly, fully and completely, for themselves and their heirs from us and our heirs, in all things and in all places forever, as aforesaid. Moreover, it has been sworn both on our part and on the part of the barons that all the aforesaid [provisions] shall be observed in good faith and without malicious intent.

By the witness of the aforesaid men and of many others. Given by our hand in the meadow that is called Runnymede between Windsor and Staines, June 15, in the seventeenth year of our reign.

PETITION OF RIGHT, 1628

Commentary

The second great Charter of English liberty is the Petition of Right. As such, it too is a vital antecedent of the American Bill of Rights. This is particularly true because of the part played by Sir Edward Coke in the enactment of the 1628 Petition. In many ways, Coke was to become the juristic progenitor of the men who were to make the American Revolution. James Otis, Patrick Henry, John Adams—to name but a few—were all nurtured upon Coke's writings and the example of his career. Coke himself had a three-fold career in the law, of which each part left its imprint on both the English and American Constitutions. As a writer and judge, Coke furnished a doctrinal foundation for the constitutional edifice which, starting with Otis' landmark 1761 argument against general writs of assistance (*infra* p. 184), Americans have erected. As a parliamentary leader, Coke's influence was the catalyst that led to the Petition of Right—itself to be a guiding precedent for the American colonists in their struggle with the British Crown.

In 1616, Coke had been discharged from his position as the highest judge of the realm, Chief Justice of King's Bench. He had been removed directly because of his consistent judicial efforts to frustrate the royal attempts to place the power of the Crown above the law. Now, at the age of 65, Coke appeared to be at the virtual end of his public career. In 1620, however, he was elected to the House of Commons. Now came the third, and in some ways the most admirable part of his career.

In Parliament, Coke gravitated naturally toward the growing opposition to the Crown. His reputation, learning, and passionate belief in the common law and a balanced Constitution—weighted with age and prestige, he was termed that great "*Monarcha Juris*" by no less a Parliament man than John Selden—all combined to give him an influence second to none among the people's representatives.

Coke's reappearance in public life as a Parliamentary leader was a natural development in one who had been so conspicuous in his refusal to accede to the Stuart theory of government. For the struggle against such theory was to shift, with Coke's removal from the bench, from the law courts to the Parliament. Thenceforth, the opposition to the concept of absolute prerogative was to be centered almost entirely in the House of Commons, which was ultimately forced to lead the nation in arms to vindicate the principle that even the Crown was subject to law.

Coke's emergence as a Parliament man was of primary significance in channelling the conflict with the Crown along legal lines. It was, in fact, the union of the common lawyers of the day with the Parliamentary leaders that made possible the successful resistance to the Stuart claims. This was true in

17

more than a mere material sense. Without the support of the lawyers, the Parliament would have appeared only as revolutionaries, seeking to tear down the established order. Instead, Coke and his confreres in the common law were able to enlist for the opposition that almost superstitious reverence which Englishmen felt for their law and to give to their struggle that note of legal conservatism that is at once its distinguishing characteristic and the cause of its successful issue. "Learned in the law . . . ," Winston Churchill tells us, "they gradually built up a case on which Parliament could claim with conviction that it was fighting, not for something new, but for the traditional lawful heritage of the English people."

In the Parliaments in which Coke sat, there was a growing struggle between the legislators and the pretensions of the Crown. This was especially the case in the Parliament of 1628. According to Holdsworth's monumental *History of English Law*, Coke's "labours in that parliament were destined to be a fitting conclusion to his career. They were to result in adding to the statute book the first of those great constitutional documents since Magna Carta, which safeguard the liberties of the people by securing the supremacy of the law."

Much had happened since Charles I had acceded to the throne in 1625. Under Charles, in fact, the Stuart theory of prerogative was quickly pushed to the extreme. By 1628, Englishmen had suffered the most serious attacks upon their personal liberties. In the two years that had intervened since the dissolution of the previous Parliament, a forced loan had been demanded; men who refused to pay had been punished, and judges who refused to enforce it had been dismissed. Soldiers had been billeted on the people and men committed to prison by the mere command of the King, with bail refused. Well might Coke plaintively ask the 1628 session, "Shall I be made a tenant-at-will for my liberties, having property in my own house, but not liberty in my person?"

The members of the 1628 Commons were confronted with the basic question of what they should do about the situation. Coke it was who rose to declare that it was the law of the realm that counted, not mere gracious promises from the throne. "Messages of love," he urged, "never came into a Parliament. Let us put up a Petition of Right! Not that I distrust the King; but that I cannot take his trust but in a Parliamentary way."

The Petition of Right, passed in response to Coke's plea, was enacted as a statute. It declared the fundamental right of Englishmen as positive law. Nor was the declaration weakened by any ambiguous saving of prerogative right. The Lords had proposed an amendment which provided that the Petition "leave intire that Sovereign Power, wherewith your Majesty is trusted for the Protection, safety, and happiness of the People." But Coke and the Parliamentary leaders saw that the Lords amendment would virtually nullify their Petition. "To speak plainly," said Coke, "it will overthrow all our Petition. . . And shall we now add it, we shall weaken the foundation of law, and then the building must needs fall; let us take heed what we yield unto; Magna Charta is such a fellow, that he will have no sovereign. I wonder this sovereign was not in Magna Charta. . . . : If we grant this by implication we give a sovereign power above all these laws."

Over a century later, men on the western side of the Atlantic who also sought to vindicate the rights of Englishmen would follow Coke, both in theory and practice. Again and again, the colonists would rely upon the authority of my Lord Coke to demonstrate the invalidity of acts of the mother country which restricted their rights.

And then, when the conflict over the Stamp Act increased in intensity, the colonists followed Coke's example in the 1628 Parliament. They, too, acted through a measure declaring the rights of Englishmen, as they were conceived to apply in the American colonies. The 1765 Declaration of Rights and Grievances passed by the Stamp Act Congress (*infra* p. 196) was the natural response of men familiar with the constitutional history of Stuart England. As such, it was the direct descendant of the Coke-inspired Petition of Right.

Petition of Right, 1628*

The petition exhibited to his majesty by the lords spiritual and temporal, and commons in this present parliament assembled, concerning divers rights and liberties of the subjects, with the king's majesty's royal answer thereunto in full parliament.

To the king's most excellent majesty: Humbly show unto our sovereign lord the king the lords spiritual and temporal, and commons in parliament assembled, that, whereas it is declared and enacted by a statute made in the time of the reign of King Edward the First, commonly called *Statutum de Tallagio non Concedendo,* that no tallage or aid should be laid or levied by the king or his heirs in this realm without the goodwill and assent of the archbishops, bishops, earls, barons, knights, burgesses, and other the freemen of the commonalty of this realm; and, by authority of parliament holden in the five-and-twentieth year of the reign of King Edward III, it is declared and enacted that from thenceforth no person should be compelled to make any loans to the king against his will, because such loans were against reason and the franchise of the land; and by other laws of this realm it is provided that none should be charged by any charge or imposition, called a benevolence, or by such like charge; by which the statutes before mentioned, and other the good laws and statutes of this realm, your subjects have inherited this freedom, that they should not be compelled to contribute to any tax, tallage, aid, or other like charge not set by common consent in parliament:

*Statutes of the Realm, V, p. 23.

yet, nevertheless, of late divers commissions directed to sundry commissioners in several counties with instructions have issued, by means whereof your people have been in divers places assembled and required to lend certain sums of money unto your majesty; and many of them, upon their refusal so to do, have had an oath administered unto them, not warrantable by the laws or statutes of this realm, and have been constrained to become bound to make appearance and give attendance before your privy council and in other places; and others of them have been therefor imprisoned, confined, and sundry other ways molested and disquieted; and divers other charges have been laid and levied upon your people in several counties by lord lieutenants, deputy lieutenants, commissioners for musters, justices of peace, and others, by command or direction from your majesty or your privy council, against the laws and free customs of the realm.

And where also, by the statute called the Great Charter of the Liberties of England, it is declared and enacted that no freeman may be taken or imprisoned, or be disseised of his freehold or liberties or his free customs, or be outlawed or exiled or in any manner destroyed, but by the lawful judgment of his peers or by the law of the land; and in the eight-and-twentieth year of the reign of King Edward III it was declared and enacted by authority of parliament that no man, of what estate or condition that he be, should be put out of his land or tenements, nor taken, nor imprisoned, nor disherited, nor put to death, without being brought to answer by due process of law: nevertheless, against the tenor of the said statutes and other the good laws and statutes of your realm to that end provided, divers of your subjects have of late been imprisoned without any cause showed; and when for their deliverance they were brought before your justices by your majesty's writs of *habeas corpus*, there to undergo and receive as the court should order, and their keepers commanded to certify the causes of their detainer, no cause was certified, but that they were detained by your majesty's special command, signified by the lords of your privy council; and yet were returned back to several prisons, without being charged with anything to which they might make answer according to the law.

And whereas of late great companies of soldiers and mariners have been dispersed into divers counties of the realm, and the inhabitants against their wills have been compelled to receive them into their houses, and there to suffer them to sojourn, against the laws and customs of this realm, and to the great grievance and vexation of the people: and whereas also, by authority of parliament in the five-and-twentieth year of the reign of King Edward III, it is declared and enacted that no man should be forejudged of life or limb against the form of the Great Charter and the law of the land; and, by the said Great Charter and other the laws and statutes of this your realm, no man ought to be adjudged to death but by the laws established in this your realm, either by the customs of the same realm or by acts of parliament; and whereas no offender of what kind soever is exempted from the proceedings to be used, and punishments to be inflicted by the laws and statutes of this your realm: nevertheless of late divers commissions under your majesty's great seal have issued forth, by which certain persons have been assigned and appointed commissioners, with power and authority to proceed within the land according to the justice of martial law against such soldiers or mariners, or other dissolute persons joining with them, as should commit any murder, robbery, felony, mutiny, or other outrage or misdemeanour whatsoever, and by such summary course and order as is agreeable to martial law and as is used in armies in time of war, to proceed to the trial and condemnation of such offenders, and them to cause to be executed and put to death according to the law martial; by pretext whereof some of your majesty's subjects have been by some of the said commissioners put to death, when and where, if by the laws and statutes of the land they had deserved death, by the same laws and statutes also they might, and by no other ought to have been, adjudged and executed; and also sundry grievous offenders, by colour thereof claiming an exemption, have escaped the punishments due to them by the laws and statutes of this your realm, by reason that divers of your officers and ministers of justice have unjustly refused or forborne to proceed against such offenders according to the same laws and statues, upon pretence that the said offenders were punishable only by martial law and by authority of such commissions as aforesaid; which commissions and all other of like nature are wholly and directly contrary to the said laws and statutes of this your realm.

They do therefore humbly pray your most excellent majesty that no man hereafter be compelled to make or yield any gift, loan, benevolence, tax, or such like charge without common consent by act of parliament; and that none be called to make answer, or take such oath, or to give attendance, or be confined, or otherwise molested or disquieted concerning the same, or for refusal thereof; and that no freeman, in any such manner as is before mentioned, be imprisoned or detained; and that your majesty would be pleased to remove the said soldiers and mariners; and that your people may not be so burdened in time to come; and that the foresaid commissions for proceeding by martial law may be revoked and annulled; and that hereafter no commissions of like nature may issue forth to any person or persons whatsoever, to be executed as aforesaid, lest by colour of them any of your majesty's subjects be destroyed or put to death, contrary to the laws and franchise of the land (all of which they most humbly pray of your most excellent majesty as their rights and liberties according to the laws and statutes of this realm); and that your majesty would also vouchsafe and declare that the awards, doings, and proceedings to the prejudice of your people in any of the premises shall not be drawn hereafter into consequence or example; and that your majesty would be also graciously pleased, for the further comfort and safety of your people, to declare your royal will and pleasure that in the things aforesaid all your officers and ministers shall serve you according to the laws and statutes of this realm, as they tender the honour of your majesty and the prosperity of this kingdom.

AGREEMENT OF THE PEOPLE, 1649

Commentary

The brief period (1649–1660) during which Britain, for the first and only time in her history, possessed a republican polity was one of vigorous speculation and experiment throughout the areas of political, legal, and social life. All the ferment in these areas, particularly in that of governmental experimentation, was directly to influence American constitutional development a century and more later, though it played no comparable part in Britain, when once the old institutions were restored with the accession of Charles II.

One who looks at the republican period that followed the death of Charles I through the lenses of American constitutional experience is bound to find striking parallels between the situation of Englishmen who had executed their King and that of the colonists almost a century and a half later who had declared their independence. In both cases, there was the overriding need to reconstruct the fabric of government which had been destroyed. In both cases, too, the need was met in similar fashion. When, in May, 1776, the Second Continental Congress adopted a resolution urging the various colonies to set up governments of their own, the latter acted by drawing up written constitutions establishing the new governments which had been called for. In so doing, they were following the example of Englishmen who had acted in a like manner to fill the constitutional vacuum caused by the death of Charles I.

Even before the execution of the King, in contemplation of such an event, the Council of the Army had presented, in January, 1649, a sketch of a republican Constitution known as the *Agreement of the People.* This document has well been characterized as a landmark in the history of constitutional theory. As the first written organic instrument in Anglo-American history, it suggestively anticipated many of the fundamentals of later American Constitutions. In particular, it was based upon the essential notion of a Constitution as laying down significant checks upon the power of government itself.

With the disappearance of the monarchy, it was realized that the chief danger to be feared was the misuse of power by a legally omnipotent legislature. To meet that danger, the solution was proposed of a written Constitution which would lay down limits which the Parliament itself would legally be powerless to violate. Such limits were laid down expressly in the *Agreement* in a manner that anticipated directly the prohibitory provisions of American Constitutions—notably the Bill of Rights of the federal Constitution.

The *Agreement of the People*, after providing for a Parliament of one House and a system of election based upon an expanded franchise and a

22

more equal apportionment of legislative seats (in both respects, the suggested electoral reform was not to be accomplished in Britain until the nineteenth century), went on to set forth six fundamental "points in the Reserve." These were to be matters beyond the power of the Parliament itself to alter. They included matters of religion (setting forth a principle of freedom of religion, except for "Popery or Prelacy"); military conscription; indemnity "for any thing said or done in relation to the late wars or public differences"; sanctity of the public debt; no punishment "where no law hath before provided"; and equality before the law.

In addition, during the debates which were held by the army officers before the final draft of the *Agreement* was submitted, other "Particulars were offered to be inserted in the Agreement" as additions to the reserved points beyond the power of Parliament. They included guarantees of the right against self-incrimination, against imprisonment for debt, against restraints of trade, of "punishments equal to offences," of trial by jury, against usury, and against religious disabilities. Though these guarantees were not included in the *Agreement,* they do show the type of radical (in the literal sense of that adjective) thinking on the matter that was then current. Too far advanced for its own day, it was to bear fruit in the American Bill of Rights.

It should not, however, be thought that the later American achievement in this respect was no more than the mere refurbishing of a constitutional edifice erected by Interregnum Englishmen. One must, in the first place, emphasize the crucial fact that the framers of American Constitutions and Bills of Rights were the first to put the notion of a written fundamental law which limits the power of the people and their political delegates into practical operation (the *Agreement of the People* itself was quietly shelved by the Rump Parliament to which it had been presented and the *Instrument of Government,* the written Constitution adopted in 1653, contained no real limitations upon the government provided for by it).

Even apart from the point just stressed, it should be realized that the concept of constitutionalism embodied in the *Agreement of the People* was at most rudimentary compared to that upon which American Constitution-makers were to act. Covenants without the sword, says Hobbes, are but empty words. The same is true of a Constitution written merely in hortatory terms. The American framers well knew that it was not enough only to declare fundamental rights and limitations in an organic document; just as important was the provision of machinery to ensure the enforcement of such document's provisions. The great contribution of the framers was to establish a polity based upon a system of checks and balances as well as power in the courts to control the constitutionality of governmental action. Thus there was the essential machinery by means of which the fundamental rights and restrictions provided for in the Constitution might be enforced. No comparable enforcement machinery was provided for in the comparatively crude constitutional documents drawn up in Interregnum England.

As already indicated, the *Agreement of the People* itself never went into effect as a working Constitution. In 1653, Cromwell announced his intention of ruling according to an organic document known as the *Instrument of Government*. It provided for a constitutional government carried on by a Lord Protector and a single House, as well as a Council of State to advise the Protector. It sought to apportion governmental power between the executive and legislative branches and in effect established a limited monarchy without a King in name. In practice, however, the *Instrument* in operation quickly revealed the basic defect referred to above—the lack of machinery to ensure its effective enforcement. Thus, a key provision of the *Instrument* provided that legislative acts were to "contain nothing in them contrary to the matters contained in these presents." But there was no institution to ensure that this provision itself would be adhered to.

When the Parliament elected under the *Instrument* met in 1654, it immediately refused to accept the binding force of the *Instrument* itself. Instead, it sought to enact a wholly new constitutional scheme, imposing legislative control far greater than that provided for in the *Instrument*. The result was a speedy dissolution of the House by the Protector. Cromwell then governed by naked military force, setting up a system of military government by Majors-General throughout the country. Funds were obtained by vote of the Council of State alone, including the arbitrary imposition of a tithe on the property of royalists. All this was, of course, wholly contrary to the scheme of government set up by the *Instrument of Governments* and, in the modern American sense, plainly unconstitutional. Yet there was no legal method provided by which the question of constitutionality could be determined and hence nothing to prevent first the legislature and then the executive from violating the organic document with impunity.

We can consequently say that the English age of written Constitutions, which began with so striking an anticipation of the American conception of government by law, ended in the very negation of that vital concept. Though Cromwell's wish may have been, in Macaulay's phrase, "to govern constitutionally, and to substitute the empire of the laws for that of the sword," he himself soon saw that it was only by the latter that he could govern effectively. The result was that (to quote Macaulay again) "the government, though in form a republic, was in truth a despotism, moderated only by the wisdom, the sobriety, and the magnanimity of the despot."

Agreement of the People, 1649*

An agreement of the people of England and the places therewith incorporated for a secure and present peace upon grounds of common right, freedom, and safety. Having, by our late labours and hazards, made it appear to

Sources of English Constitutional History, pp. 511–16.

the world at how high a rate we value our just freedom, and God having so far owned our cause as to deliver the enemies thereof into our hands, we do now hold ourselves bound, in mutual duty to each other, to take the best care we can for the future to avoid both the danger of returning into a slavish condition and the chargeable remedy of another war. For, as it cannot be imagined that so many of our countrymen would have opposed us in this quarrel if they had understood their own good, so may we hopefully promise to ourselves that, when our common rights and liberties shall be cleared, their endeavours will be disappointed that seek to make themselves our masters. Since, therefore, our former oppressions and not-yet-ended troubles have been occasioned, either by want of frequent national meetings in council, or by the undue or unequal constitution thereof, or by rendering those meetings ineffectual, we are fully agreed and resolved, God willing, to provide that hereafter our representatives be neither left to an uncertainty for times nor be unequally constituted, nor made useless to the ends for which they are intended. In order whereunto we declare and agree:

First, that, to prevent the many inconveniences apparently arising from the long continuance of the same persons in supreme authority, this present parliament end and dissolve upon or before the last day of April, 1649.

Secondly, that the people of England—being at this day very unequally distributed by counties, cities, and boroughs for the election of their representatives—be indifferently proportioned; and, to this end, that the representative of the whole nation shall consist of 400 persons, or not above; and in each country and the places thereto subjoined there shall be chosen, to make up the said representative at all times, the several numbers here mentioned. . . . Provided that the first or second representative may, if they see cause, assign the remainder of the 400 representers, not hereby assigned, or so many of them as they shall see cause for, unto such counties as shall appear in this present distribution to have less than their due proportion. Provided also that, where any city or borough, to which one representer or more is assigned, shall be found in a due proportion not competent alone to elect a representer or the number of representers assigned thereto, it is left to future representatives to assign such a number of parishes or villages near adjoining to such city or borough, to be joined therewith in the elections, as may make the same proportionable.

Thirdly, that the people do of course choose themselves a representative once in two years, and shall meet for that purpose upon the first Thursday in every second May, by eleven in the morning; and the representatives so chosen [are] to meet upon the second Thursday in the June following at the usual place in Westminster, or such other place as, by the foregoing representative or the council of state in the interval, shall be from time to time appointed and published to the people, at the least twenty days before the time of election; and [are] to continue their sessions there or elsewhere until the second Thursday in December following, unless they shall adjourn or

dissolve themselves sooner, but [are] not to continue longer. The election of
the first representative [is] to be on the first Thursday in May, 1649; and
that and all future elections [are] to be according to the rules prescribed for
the same purpose in this agreement, *viz.* : (1) That the electors in every
division shall be natives or denizens of England; not persons receiving alms,
but such as are assessed ordinarily towards the relief of the poor; not
servants to, and receiving wages from, any particular person; and in all
elections, except for the universities, they shall be men of twenty-one years
of age or upwards and housekeepers, dwelling within the division for which
the election is. . . . (4) That, to the end all officers of state may be certainly
accountable and no factions made to maintain corrupt interests, no member
of a council of state, nor any officer of any salary-forces in army or garrison,
nor any treasurer or receiver of public money, shall, while such, be elected to
be of a representative; and in case any such election shall be, the same [is] to
be void; and in case any lawyer shall be chosen into any representative or
council of state, then he shall be incapable of practice as a lawyer during
that trust. (5) For the more convenient election of representatives, each
county wherein more than three representers are to be chosen, with the
towns corporate and cities . . . within the compass thereof to which no
representers are herein assigned, shall be divided by a due proportion into so
many and such parts as each part may elect two, and no part above three
representers. . . .

Fourthly, that 150 members at least be always present in each sitting of
the representative, at the passing of any law or doing of any act whereby the
people are to be bound; saving that the number of 60 may make a house for
debates or resolutions that are preparatory thereunto.

Fifthly, that each representative shall, within twenty days after their first
meeting, appoint a council of state for the managing of public affairs until
the tenth day after the meeting of the next representative, unless that next
representative think fit to put an end to that trust sooner. And the same
council [is] to act and proceed therein according to such instructions and
limitations as the representative shall give, and not otherwise.

Sixthly, that in each interval betwixt biennial representatives the council
of state, in case of imminent danger or extreme necessity, may summon a
representative to be forthwith chosen and to meet; so as the session thereof
continue not above eighty days, and so as it dissolve at least fifty days before
the appointed time for the next biennial representative. And upon the fiftieth
day so preceding it shall dissolve of course, if not otherwise dissolved sooner.

Seventhly, that no member of any representative be made either receiver,
treasurer, or other officer during that employment, saving to be a member of
the council of state.

Eighthly, that the representatives have . . . the supreme trust in order to the
preservation and government of the whole; and that their power extend,
without the consent or concurrence of any other person or persons, to the

erecting and abolishing of courts of justice and public offices, and to the enacting, altering, repealing, and declaring of laws, and the highest and final judgment concerning all natural or civil things, but not concerning things spiritual or evangelical. Provided that, even in things natural and civil, these six particulars next following are . . . excepted and reserved from our representatives, *viz.*: (1) We do not empower them to impress or constrain any person to serve in foreign war, either by sea or land, nor for any military service within the kingdom; save that they may take order for the forming, training, and exercising of the people in a military way, to be in readiness for resisting of foreign invasions, suppressing of sudden insurrections, or for assisting in execution of the laws. And [they] may take order for the employing and conducting of them for those ends, provided that, even in such cases, none be compellable to go out of the county he lives in, if he procure another to serve in his room. (2) That, after the time herein limited for the commencement of the first representative, none of the people may be at any time questioned for anything said or done in relation to the late wars or public differences, otherwise than in execution or pursuance of the determinations of the present house of commons, against such as have adhered to the king or his interest against the people; and saving that accountants for public moneys received, shall remain accountable for the same. (3) That no securities given or to be given by the public faith of the nation, nor any engagements of the public faith for satisfaction of debts and damages, shall be made void or invalid by the next or any future representatives; except to such creditors as have or shall have justly forfeited the same: and saving that the next representative may confirm or make null, in part or in whole, all gifts of lands, moneys, offices, or otherwise, made by the present parliament to any member or attendant of either house. (4) That, in any laws hereafter to be made, no person, by virtue of any tenure, grant, charter, patent, degree, or birth, shall be privileged from subjection thereto, or from being bound thereby, as well as others. (5) That the representative may not give judgment upon any man's person or estate, where no law hath before provided; save only in calling to account and punishing public officers for abusing or failing in their trust. (6) That no representative may in any wise render up or give or take away any of the foundations of common right, liberty, and safety contained in this agreement, nor level men's estates, destroy property, or make all things common; and that, in all matters of such fundamental concernment, there shall be a liberty to particular members of the said representatives to enter their dissents from the mayor vote.

Ninthly, concerning religion, we agree as followeth: (1) It is intended that the Christian religion be held forth and recommended as the public profession in this nation; which we desire may, by the grace of God, be reformed to the greatest purity in doctrine, worship, and discipline, according to the word of God. The instructing the people thereunto in a public way, so it be not compulsive, as also the maintaining of able teachers for that end and for the confutation or discovery of heresy, error, and whatsoever is contrary to sound doctrine, is allowed to be provided for by our representatives; the maintenance of which teachers may be out of a public treasury, and, we desire, not by tithes—provided that popery or prelacy be not held forth as the public way or profession in this nation. (2) That to the public profession so held forth, none be compelled by penalties or otherwise, but only may be endeavoured to be won by sound doctrine and the example of a good conversation. (3) That such as profess faith in God by Jesus Christ, however differing in judgment from the doctrine, worship, or discipline publicly held forth, as aforesaid, shall not be restrained from, but shall be protected in, the profession of their faith and exercise of religion according to their consciences in any place except such as shall be set apart for the public worship—where we provide not for them, unless they have leave—so as they abuse not this liberty to the civil injury of others or to actual disturbance of the public peace on their parts. Nevertheless, it is not intended to be hereby provided that this liberty shall necessarily extend to popery or prelacy. (4) That all laws, ordinances, statutes, and clauses in any law, statute, or ordinance to the contrary of the liberty herein provided for, in the two particulars next preceding concerning religion, be and are hereby repealed and made void.

Tenthly, it is agreed that whosoever shall by force of arms resist the orders of the next or any future representative—except in case where such representative shall evidently render up, or give, or take away the foundations of common right, liberty, and safety contained in this agreement—he shall forthwith . . . lose the benefit and protection of the laws and shall be punishable with death as an enemy and traitor to the nation. Of the things expressed in this agreement—the certain ending of this parliament, as in the first article; the equal or proportionable distribution of the number of the representers to be elected, as in the second; the certainty of the people's meeting to elect for representatives biennial, and their freedom in elections, with the certainty of meeting, sitting, and ending of representatives so elected, which are provided for in the third article; as also the qualifications of persons to elect or be elected, as in the first and second particulars under the third article; also the certainty of a number for passing a law or preparatory debates, provided for in the fourth article; the matter of the fifth article, concerning the council of state; and of the sixth, concerning the calling, sitting, and ending of representatives extraordinary; also the power of representatives to be, as in the eighth article, and limited, as in the six reserves next following the same; likewise the second and third particulars under the ninth article concerning religion; and the whole matter of the tenth article—all these we do account and declare to be fundamental to our common right, liberty, and safety; and therefore do both agree thereunto and resolve to maintain the same, as God shall enable us. The rest of the matters in this agreement we account to be useful and good for the public. And the particular circumstance of numbers, times, and places expressed in the several articles we account not fundamental; but we find them necessary to be here determined for the making the agreement certain and practicable, and do hold these most convenient that are here set down, and therefore do positively agree thereunto. By the appointment of his excellency the lord general and his general council of officers.

A HEALING QUESTION, 1656
BY SIR HENRY VANE

Commentary

Sir Henry Vane was one of the remarkable men who led the Parliamentary party in the overthrow of Charles I. He is known to Americans as a Colonial Governor of Massachusetts, but his main role was in English politics where (in Richard Baxter's phrase) "he was that within the House [of Commons] that Cromwell was without." Though an early leader of the Commonwealth government, he broke with Cromwell over the forcible dissolution of the Rump Parliament. On that occasion Cromwell is said to have exclaimed, "O Sir Henry Vane, Sir Henry Vane, the Lord deliver me from Sir Henry Vane!" His conflict with Cromwell did not prevent Vane from being executed for treason after the Restoration.

In his pamphlet, *A Healing Question,* Vane sought to expound the basic principles of civil and religious liberty. In it, he proposed the method of drawing up a Constitution through a Convention called by the people for the purpose. This was, of course, precisely the method to be used by Americans during the Revolution, when Conventions in many of the newly independent states enacted Constitutions and Bills of Rights. Vane thus drew the distinction, so fundamental in American constitutional history, between the legislative and the constituent power. Exercise of the latter through a "convention of faithful, honest, and discerning men, chosen for that purpose by the free consent of the whole body" of the people would enable the "fundamental constitutions [to] be laid and inviolably observed as the conditions upon which the whole body so represented doth consent to cast itself into a civil and politic incorporation." Here was stated (apparently for the first time) the fundamental conception which was to underlie modern American constitutional documents, including both the federal Constitution and Bill of Rights.

A Healing Question, 1656*

By Sir Henry Vane

A Healing Question propounded and resolved, upon occasion of the late public and seasonable call to humiliation, in order to love and union among the honest party, and with a desire to apply balm to the wound before it become incurable.

Harvard Classics (1910), Vol. 43, pp. 126–43.

The question propounded is, What possibility doth yet remain (all things considered) of reconciling and uniting the dissenting judgments of honest men within the three nations, who still pretend to agree in the spirit, justice, and reason of the same good cause and what is the means to effect this?

Answer:
If it be taken for granted (as, on the magistrate's part, from the ground inviting the people of England and Wales to a solemn day of fasting and humiliation, may not be despaired of) that all the dissenting parties agree still in the spirit and reason of the same righteous cause, the resolution seems very clear in the affirmative; arguing not only for a possibility, but a great probability hereof; nay, a necessity daily approaching nearer and nearer to compel it, if any or all of the dissenting parties intend or desire to be safe from the danger of the common enemy, who is not out of work, though at present much out of sight and observation.

The grounds of this are briefly these: First, the cause hath still the same goodness in it as ever, and is, or ought to be, as much in the hearts of all good people that have adhered to it: it is not less to be valued now, than when neither blood nor treasure were thought too dear to carry it on, and hold it up from sinking; and hath the same omnipotent God, whose great name is concerned in it, as well as his people's outward safety and welfare; who knows, also, how to give a revival to it when secondary instruments and visible means fail or prove deceitful.

Secondly, The persons concerned and engaged in this cause are still the same as before, with the advantage of being more tried, more inured to danger and hardship, and more endeared to one another, by their various and great experiences, as well of their own hearts as their fellowbrethren. These are the same still in heart and desire after the same thing, which is, that, being freed out of the hands of their enemies, they may serve the Lord without fear, in holiness and righteousness all the days of their life.

*   *   *

A serious discussion and sober enlarging upon these grounds will quickly give an insight into the state of the question, and naturally tend to a plain and familiar resolution thereof.

That which is first to be opened is the nature and goodness of the cause; which, had it not carried in it its own evidence, would scarce have found so many of the people of God adherers to it within the three nations, contributing either their counsels, their purses, their bodily pains, or their affections and prayers, as a combined strength; without which, the military force alone would have been little available to subdue the common enemy, and restore to this whole body their just natural rights in civil things, and true freedom in matters of conscience.

The two last-mentioned particulars, rightly stated, will evidence sufficiently the nature and goodness of this cause.

For the first of these, that is to say, the natural right, which the whole party of honest men adhering to this cause are by success of their arms restored unto, fortified in, and may claim as their undeniable privilege, that righteously cannot be taken from them, nor they debarred from bringing into exercise, it lies in this:

They are to have and enjoy the freedom (by way of dutiful compliance and condescension from all the parts and members of this society) to set up meet persons in the place of supreme judicature and authority among them, whereby they may have the use and benefit of the choicest light and wisdom of the nation that they are capable to call forth, for the rule and government under which they will live; and through the orderly exercise of such measure of wisdom and counsel as the Lord in this way shall please to give unto them, to shape and form all subordinate actings and administrations of rule and government so as shall best answer the public welfare and safety of the whole.

This, in substance, is the right and freedom contained in the nature and goodness of the cause wherein the honest party have been engaged; for in this all the particulars of our civil right and freedom are comprehended, conserved in, and derived from their proper root; in which, while they grow, they will ever thrive, flourish, and increase; whereas, on the contrary, if there be never so many fair branches of liberty planted on the root of a private and selfish interest, they will not long prosper, but must, within a little time, wither and degenerate into the nature of that whereinto they are planted: and hence, indeed, sprung the evil of that government which rose in and with the Norman Conquest.

*   *   *

Having thus showed what the true freedom is, in both the branches of it, that shines forth in the righteous cause, wherein the good people of these nations have so deeply engaged, it will not be improper, in the next place, to consider two particulars more that give still farther light into the matter in question, as, first, the qualifications of the persons that have adhered to this cause; secondly, the capacity wherein they have been found from time to time carrying it on.

As to their qualification, they have, in the general, distinguished themselves and been made known by a forwardness to assist and own the public welfare and good of the nation, for the attaining and preserving the just rights and liberties thereof, asserted and witnessed unto in the true stating of this cause, according to the two branches thereof already spoken to. They have showed themselves, upon all occasions, desirers and lovers of true freedom, either in civils or in spirituals, or in both. To express their value thereof, and faithfulness to the same, they have largely contributed, in one kind or other, what was proper to each in his place to do; which actions of theirs proceeding from hearts sincerely affected to the cause, created in them a right to be of an incorporation and society by themselves, under the name of the good party, having been from the beginning unto this day publicly and commonly so acknowledged, by way of distinction from all neuters, close and open enemies, and deceitful friends or apostates. These, in order to the maintaining of this cause, have stood by the army, in defence and support thereof, against all opposition whatever, as those that, by the growing light of these times, have been taught and led forth in their experiences to look above and beyond the letter, form, and outward circumstances of govern-ment, into the inward reason and spirit thereof, herein only to fix and terminate, to the leaving behind all empty shadows that would obtrude themselves in the place of true freedom.

Secondly, as to the capacity wherein these persons, thus qualified, have acted, it hath been very variable, and subject to great changes: sometimes in one form, and sometimes in another, and very seldom, if ever at all, so exactly and in all points consonant to the rule of former laws and constitu-tions of government as to be clearly and fully justified by them any longer than the law of success and conquest did uphold them who had the inward warrant of justice and righteousness to encourage them in such their actings.

The utmost and last reserve, therefore, which they have had, in case all other failed, hath been their military capacity, not only strictly taken for the standing army, but in the largest sense, wherein the whole party may (with the army, and under that military constitution and conduct which, by the providence of God, they shall then be found in) associate themselves in the best order they can for the common defence and safety of the whole; as not ignorant that when once embodied in this their military posture, in such manner as by common consent shall be found requisite for the safety of the body, they are most irresistible, absolute, and comprehensive in their power, having that wherein the substance of all government is contained, and under the protection whereof, and safety that may be maintained thereby, they can contrive and determine in what manner this irresistible, absolute, and bound-less power, unto which they are now arrived in this their military capacity, shall have just and due limits set unto it, and be drawn out in a meet and orderly way of exercise for the commonweal and safety of the whole body, under the rule and oversight of a supreme judicature, unto the wisdom of whose laws and orders the sword is to become most entirely subject and subservient; and this without the least cause of jealousy or unsafety, either to the standing army, or any member thereof, or unto the good people adhering to this cause, or any of them, since the interest of both, by this mutual action of either, will be so combined together in one (even in that wherein before they were distinct), that all just cause of difference, fear, animosity, emula-tion, jealousy, or the like, will be wholly abolished and removed.

For when once the whole body of the good people find that the military interest and capacity is their own, and that into which necessity at the last may bring the whole party (whereof, of right, a place is to be reserved for them), and that herein they are so far from being in subjection or slavery, that in this posture they are most properly sovereign, and possess their right of natural sovereignty, they will presently see a necessity of continuing ever one with their army, raised and maintained by them for the promoting this cause against the common enemy, who in his next attempt will put for all with greater desperateness and rage than ever.

Again, when once the standing army and their governors shall also find that, by setting and keeping up themselves in a divided interest from the rest of the body of honest men, they withhold from themselves those contributions in all voluntary and cheerful assistances, by the affections and prayers, by the persons and purses of the good party, to the weakening themselves thereby, as to any vigorous support from them, in the times of most imminent danger (whereof the late king had an experience, that will not suddenly be out of memory, when he undertook the war, in the beginning of these troubles, against the Scots, and was, in a manner, therein deserted by all the good party in England), they will then find (if they stay not till it be too late) that, by espousing the interest of the people, in submitting themselves with their fellow-adherents to the cause, under the rule and authority of their own supreme judicature, they lose not their power or sovereignty, but, becoming one civil or politic incorporation with the whole party of honest men, they do therein keep the sovereignty, as originally seated in themselves, and part with it only but as by deputation and representation of themselves, when it is brought into an orderly way of exercise, by being put into the hands of persons chosen and intrusted by themselves to that purpose.

By this mutual and happy transition, which may be made between the party of honest men in the three nations virtually in arms, and those actually so now in power at the head of the army; how suddenly would the union of the whole body be consolidated, and made so firm as it will not need to fear all the designs and attempts of the common enemy, especially if herein they unite themselves in the first place to the Lord, as willing to follow his providence, and observe his will in the way and manner of bringing this to pass! in which case we shall not need to fear what all the gates of hell are able to do in opposition thereunto.

It is not, then, the standing and being of the present army and military forces in the three nations that is liable to exception of offence from any dissenting judgments at this time among the honest, well-affected party. In and with them, under God, stand the welfare and outward safety of the whole body; and to be enemies to them, or wish them hurt, were to do it to themselves; and, by trying such conclusions, to play the game of the common enemy, to the utter ruin and destruction, not only of the true freedom aimed at and contended for in the late wars, but of the very persons themselves that have been in any sort active or eminent promoters thereof.

The army, considered as it is in the hands of an honest and wise general, and sober, faithful officers, embodied with the rest of the party of honest men, and espousing still the same cause, and acting in their primitive simplicity, humility, and turst, in reference to the welfare and safety of the whole body, is the only justifiable and most advantageous posture and capacity that the good party at present can find themselves in, in order to the obtaining that true freedom they have fought for, and possessing of it in the establishment thereof upon the true basis and foundation, as hath been showed, of right government.

That wherein the offence lies, and which causes such great thoughts of heart among the honest party (if it may be freely expressed, as sure it may, when the magistrate himself professes he doth but desire and wait for conviction therein), is, in short, this:

That when the right and privilege is returned, nay, is restored by conquest unto the whole body (that forfeited not their interest therein), of freely disposing themselves in such a constitution of righteous government as may best answer the ends held forth in this cause; that, nevertheless, either through delay they should be withheld as they are, or through design they should come at last to be utterly denied the exercise of this their right, upon pretence that they are not in capacity as yet to use it, which, indeed, hath some truth in it, if those that are now in power, and have the command of the arms, do not prepare all things requisite thereunto, as they may, and, like faithful guardians to the Commonwealth, admitted to be in its nonage, they ought.

But if the bringing of true freedom into exercise among men, yea, so refined a party of men, be impossible, why hath this been concealed all this while? and why was it not thought on before so much blood was spilt, and treasure spent? Surely such a thing as this was judged real and practicable, not imaginary and notional.

Besides, why may it not suffice to have been thus long delayed and withheld from the whole body, at least as to its being brought by them into exercise now at last? Surely the longer it is withheld, the stronger jealousies do increase, that it is intended to be assumed and engrossed by a part only, to the leaving the rest of the body (who, in all reason and justice, ought to be equally participants with the other in the right and benefit of the conquest, for as much as the war was managed at the expense and for the safety of the whole) in a condition almost as much exposed, and subject to be imposed upon, as if they had been enemies and conquered, not in any sense conquerors.

If ever such an unrighteous, unkind, and deceitful dealing with brethren should happen, although it might continue above the reach of question from human judicature, yet can we think it possible it should escape and go unpunished by the immediate hand of the righteous Judge of the whole world, when he ariseth out of his place to do right to the oppressed.

*   *   *

The matter which is in question among the dissenting parts of the whole body of honest men is not so trival and of such small consequence as some would make it. 'Tis, in effect, the main and whole of the cause; without which all the freedom which the people have or can have is in comparison but shadow and in name only, and therefore can never give that peace and satisfaction to the body which is requisite unto a durable and solid settlement. This is that which makes all sound and safe at the root, and gives the right balance necessary to be held up between sovereignty and subjection in the exercise of all righteous government; applying the use of the sword to the promoting and upholding the public safety and welfare of the whole body, in preference, and, if need be, in opposition unto any of the parts; while yet, by its equal and impartial administration in reference unto each, it doth withal maintain the whole body in a most delightful harmony, welfare, and correspondency. The sword never can, nor is it to be expected ever will do this, while the sovereignty is admitted and placed anywhere else than in the whole body of the people that have adhered to the cause, and by them be derived unto their successive representatives, as the most equal and impartial judicature for the effecting hereof.

Where there is, then, a righteous and good constitution of government, there is first, an orderly union of many understandings together, as the public and common supreme judicature or visible sovereignty, set in a way of free and orderly exercise, for the directing and applying the use of the ruling power or the sword, to promote the interest and common welfare of the whole, without any disturbance or annoyance from within or from without; and then, secondly, there is a like union and readiness of will in all the individuals, in their private capacities, to execute and obey (by all the power requisite, and that they are able to put forth) those sovereign laws and orders issued out by their own deputies and trustees.

A supreme judicature, thus made the representative of the whole, is that which, we say, will most naturally care, and most equally provide for the common good and safety. Though by this it is not denied but that the supreme power, when by free consent 'tis placed in a single person or in some few persons, may be capable also to administer righteous government; at least, the body that gives this liberty, when they need not, are to thank themselves if it prove otherwise. But when this free and natural access unto government is interrupted and declined, so as a liberty is taken by any particular member, or number of them, that are to be reputed but a part in comparison of the whole, to assume and engross the office of sovereign rule and power, and to impose themselves as the competent public judge of the safety and good of the whole, without their free and due consent, and to lay claim unto this, as those that find themselves possessed of the sword (and that so advantageously as it cannot be recovered again out of their hands without more apparent danger and damage to the whole body than such attempts are worth), this is that anarchy that is the first rise and step to tyranny, and lays grounds of manifest confusion and disorder, exposing the ruling power to the next hand that on the next opportunity can lay hold on the sword, and so, by a kind of necessity, introduces the highest imposition and bondage upon the whole body, in compelling all the parts, though never so much against the true public interest, to serve and obey, as their sovereign rule and supreme authority, the arbitrary will and judgment of those that bring themselves into rule by the power of the sword, in the right only of a part that sets up itself in preference before, or at least in competition with, the welfare of the whole.

And if this, which is so essential to the wellbeing and right constitution of government, were once obtained, the disputes about the form would not prove so difficult, nor find such opposition, as to keeping the bone of contention and disunion, with much danger to the whole; for if, as the foundation of all, the sovereignty be acknowledged to reside originally in the whole body of adherents to this cause (whose natural and inherent right thereunto is of a far ancienter date than what is obtained by success of their arms, and so cannot be abrogated even by conquest itself, if that were the case), and then if, in consequence hereof, a supreme judicature be set up and orderly constituted, as naturally arising and resulting from the free choice and consent of the whole body taken out from among themselves, as flesh of their flesh and bone of their bone, of the same public spirit and nature with themselves, and the main be by this means secured, what could be propounded afterward as to the form of administration that would much stick?

Would a standing council of state, settled for life, in reference to the safety of the Commonwealth, and for the maintaining intercourse and commerce with foreign states, under the inspection and oversight of the supreme judicature, but of the same fundamental constitution with themselves—would this be disliked? admitting their orders were binding, in the intervals of supreme national assemblies, so far only as consonant to the settled laws of the Commonwealth, the vacancy of any of which, by death or otherwise, might be supplied by the vote of the major part of themselves: nay, would there be any just exception to be taken if (besides both these) it should be agreed (as another part of the fundamental constitution of the government) to place that branch of sovereignty which chiefly respects the execution of laws in a distinct office from that of the legislative power (and yet subordinate to them and to the laws), capable to be intrusted into the hands of one single person, if need require, or in a greater number, as the legislative power should think fit; and, for the greater strength and honour unto this office, that the execution of all laws and orders (that are binding) may go forth in his or their name, and all disobedience thereunto, or contempt thereof, be taken as done to the people's sovereignty, whereof he or they bear the image or representation, subordinate to the legislative power, and at their will to be kept up and continued in the hands of a single person or more, as the experience of the future good or evil of it shall require?

Would such an office as this, thus stated, carry in it any inconsistency with a free state? Nay, if it be well considered, would it not rather be found of excellent use to the wellbeing of magistracy, founded upon this righteous bottom, that such a lieutenancy of the people's sovereignty in these three nations may always reside in some one or more person, in whose administration that which is reward and punishment may shine forth?

And if now it shall be objected that (notwithstanding all these cautions), should once this sovereignty be acknowledged to be in the diffused body of the people (though the adherents to this cause, not only as their natural, but as their acquired right by conquest), they would suddenly put the use and exercise of the legislative power into such hands as would, through their ill qualifiedness to the work, spoil all by mal-administration thereof, and hereby lose the cause instead of upholding and maintaining it,

The answer unto this is, first, that God, by his providence, hath eased our minds much in this solicitude by the course he hath already taken to fit and prepare a choice and selected number of the people unto this work, that are tried and refined by their inward and outward experiences in this great quarrel, and the many changes they have passed through; in respect whereof well qualified persons are to be found, if due care be but taken in the choice of them. And if herein this people of the Lord shall be waiting upon him for his guidance and presence with them, we may have grounds and hope that God (whose name hath all along been called upon in the maintaining of this cause) will pour out so abundantly of his spirit upon his people attending on him in righteous ways, and will also move their hearts to choose persons bearing his image into the magistracy, that a more glorious product may spring up out of this than at first we can expect, to the setting up of the Lord himself as chief judge and lawgiver among us. And unto this the wisdom and honesty of the persons now in power may have an opportunity eminently to come into discovery; for in this case, and upon the grounds already laid, the very persons now in power are they unto whose lot it would fall to set about this preparatory work, and by their orders and directions to dispose the whole body, and bring them into the meetest capacity to effect the same, the most natural way for which would seem to be by a general council, or convention of faithful, honest, and discerning men, chosen for that purpose by the free consent of the whole body of adherents to this cause in the several parts of the nations, and observing the time and place of meeting appointed to them (with other circumstances concerning their election) by order from the present ruling power, but considered as general of the army:

Which convention is not properly to exercise the legislative power, but only to debate freely, and agree upon the particulars that by way of fundamental constitutions shall be laid and inviolably observed as the conditions upon which the whole body so represented doth consent to cast itself into a civil and politic incorporation, and under the visible form and administration of government therein declared, and to be by each individual member of the body subscribed in testimony of his or their particular consent given thereunto: which conditions so agreed (and among them an Act of Oblivion for one) will be without danger of being broken or departed from, considering of what it is they are the conditions, and the nature of the convention wherein they are made, which is of the people represented in their highest state of sovereignty, as they have the sword in their hands unsubjected unto the rules of civil government, but what themselves orderly assembled for that purpose do think fit to make. And the sword, upon these conditions, subjecting itself to the supreme judicature thus to be set up, how suddenly might harmony, righteousness, love, peace, and safety unto the whole body follow hereupon, as the happy fruit of such a settlement, if the Lord have any delight to be among us!

And this once put in a way, and declared for by the general and army (as that which they are clearly convinced, in the sight of God, is their duty to bring about, and which they engage accordingly to see done) how firmly and freely would this oblige the hearts and persons, the counsels and purses, the affections and prayers, with all that is in the power of this whole party to do, in way of assistance and strengthening the hands of those now in power, whatever straits and difficulties they may meet with in the maintenance of the public safety and peace!

This, then, being the state of our present affairs and differences, let it be acknowledged on all hands, and let all be convinced that are concerned, that there is not only a possibility, but a probability, yea, a compelling necessity, of a firm union in this great body, the setting of which in joint and tune again, by a spirit of meekness and fear of the Lord, is the work of the present day, and will prove the only remedy under God to uphold and carry on this blessed cause and work of the Lord in the three nations, that is already come thus far onward in its progress to its desired and expected end of bringing in Christ, the desire of all nations, as the chief Ruler among us.

*   *   *

BILL OF RIGHTS, 1689

Commentary

The Bill of Rights of 1689 may well be considered, after Magna Carta and the Petition of Right, the third great Charter of English liberty. As a statement of the basic rights of Englishmen, as well as of the limitations upon government that make such rights effective, it is the direct ancestor of the American Bill of Rights. Its technical title is "An act declaring the rights and liberties of the subject and settling the succession of the crown." In order to understand the popular title by which it has always been known and which has furnished the standard (as well as the name) for American Bills of Rights, one must know something of the background which led to the 1689 enactment.

The Bill of Rights was the culmination of what has ever since been termed the Glorious Revolution of 1688. The mildness of that event may lead modern observers to find hyperbole in the characterization of it as a revolution. From a constitutional point of view, however, it may not be doubted that the events which terminated in the Bill of Rights did constitute a true revolution—even though (in Macaulay's phrase) "of all revolutions the least violent" and "the most beneficent."

When James II ignominiously fled from his kingdom to spend the rest of his days (after a brief incursion into Ireland) as the pathetic figure we meet in the pages of Saint-Simon, he did what he could to disrupt civil government and plunge the realm into anarchy. Even the Great Seal—that almost mystic symbol of constitutional continuity—he cast into the Thames on December 11, 1688 (from which date, by legal reckoning, the reign of the last Stuart King has since been deemed ended).

The constitutional difficulty was that, from the day when the Great Seal was cast away until February 13, 1689, when William and Mary accepted the Crown, there was no legal government in England. Not only was there no King, but no Parliament either, since James's only Parliament had been finally dissolved in July, 1688. Without a King, it was impossible to assemble a lawfully-constituted Parliament and, without the Houses, a legal solution of the problem posed by James's flight seemed just as impossible.

The dilemma was resolved, as it had to be, by extra-legal methods. Recourse was had to the calling by William of an assembly composed of the peers and members of the Commons during the reign of Charles II, as well as the magistrates of London. From a legal point of view, this assembly was quite irregular. Yet even the lawyers recognized that this was an occasion on which the legal niceties had to yield. The assembly called by William advised him to summon a Convention Parliament. It met on January 22, 1689, and soon thereafter passed its celebrated resolution that James II had abdicated "and that the throne is thereby vacant." After the Crown was settled on

William and Mary, the Convention passed an act declaring itself to be a true Parliament, notwithstanding the want of proper writs of summons.

The throne had been offered to William and Mary subject to the conditions laid down in an instrument known as the Declaration of Right, which had been drawn up by a committee of the Convention. After that body had declared itself to be a Parliament, it turned its Declaration into a regular act of the legislature enacted as a statute in 1689. Hence, the name Bill of Rights itself is the result of the fact that the original Declaration was introduced as a bill (i.e., the first step in enactment of a statute) in the new Parliament.

The 1689 Bill of Rights sought first of all to eliminate the various methods by which the last two Stuart Kings had sought to influence Parliament and to suppress opposition therein. It declares that the election of members of Parliament ought to be free; that freedom of speech and debates in Parliament ought not to be questioned in any court or other place; and that Parliaments ought to be held frequently (a provision made more specific by the Triennial Act, 1694, which prohibited the intermission of Parliament for more than three years).

In addition, the Bill of Rights specifically condemned the abuses of the prerogative by James II. It expressly declared "that the pretended power of suspending of laws or the execution of laws by regal authority without consent of the parliament is illegall." A similar provision outlawed the dispensing power "as it hath been assumed and exercised of late." Thus (to quote Macaulay again), "by the Bill of Rights the anomalous prerogative which had caused so many fierce disputes was absolutely and forever taken away." Another royal abuse was dealt with by a provision prohibiting the raising or keeping of an army in time of peace, "unless it be with consent of Parliament," and there is a rudimentary statement of the right of the people to bear arms, as well as a complaint against the quartering of soldiers.

Of particular interest to an American are those sections of the Bill of Rights which deal with the perversions of justice by the last Stuart Kings, for they were to serve as the models for like provisions in the American Bill of Rights. Such sections provide that "excessive bail ought not to be required, nor excessive fines imposed, nor cruel and unusual punishments inflicted" (the direct ancestor of the Eighth Amendment to the Federal Constitution); that jurors should be duly impanelled; and that grants and promises of fines and forfeitures of particular persons before conviction are illegal.

Bill of Rights, 1689*

An act declaring the rights and liberties of the subject and settling the succession of the crown. Whereas the lords spiritual and temporal and

*Statutes of the Realm, VI, p. 142.

commons assembled at Westminster, lawfully, fully, and freely representing all the estates of the people of this realm, did upon the 13th day of February, in the year of our Lord 1688, present unto their majesties, then called and known by the names and style of William and Mary, prince and princess of Orange, being present in their proper persons, a certain declaration in writing made by the said lords and commons in the words following, *viz.*:

Whereas the late King James II, by the assistance of divers evil counsellors, judges, and ministers employed by him, did endeavour to subvert and extirpate the Protestant religion and the laws and liberties of this kingdom by assuming and exercising a power of dispensing with and suspending of laws and the execution of laws without consent of parliament, by committing and prosecuting divers worthy prelates for humbly petitioning to be excused from concurring to the said assumed power, by issuing and causing to be executed a commission under the great seal for erecting a court called the court of commissioners for ecclesiastical causes, by levying money for and to the use of the crown by pretence of prerogative for other time and in other manner than the same was granted by parliament, by raising and keeping a standing army within this kingdom in time of peace without consent of parliament and quartering soldiers contrary to law, by causing several good subjects being Protestants to be disarmed at the same time when papists were both armed and employed contrary to law, by violating the freedom of election of members to serve in parliament, by prosecutions in the court of king's bench for matters and causes cognizable only in parliament, and by divers other arbitrary and illegal courses;

And whereas of late years partial, corrupt, and unqualified persons have been returned and served on juries in trials, and particularly divers jurors in trials for high treason, which were not freeholders, and excessive bail hath been required of persons committed in criminal cases to elude the benefit of the laws made for the liberty of the subjects, and excessive fines have been imposed, and illegal and cruel punishments inflicted, and several grants and promises made of fines or forfeitures before any conviction or judgment against the persons upon whom the same were to be levied, all which are utterly and directly contrary to the known laws and statutes and freedom of this realm;

And whereas the said late King James II having abdicated the government, and the throne being thereby vacant, his highness the prince of Orange (whom it hath pleased Almighty God to make the glorious instrument of delivering this kingdom from popery and arbitrary power) did, by the advice of the lords spiritual and temporal and divers principal persons of the commons, cause letters to be written to the lords spiritual and temporal being Protestants, and other letters to the several counties, cities, universities, boroughs, and Cinque Ports for the choosing of such persons to represent them as were of right to be sent to parliament to meet and sit at Westminster

. . . , in order to [provide] such an establishment as that their religion, laws, and liberties might not again be in danger of being subverted, upon which letters elections having been accordingly made:

And thereupon the said lords spiritual and temporal and commons, pursuant to their respective letters and elections being now assembled in a full and free representative of this nation, taking into their most serious consideration the best means for attaining the ends aforesaid, do in the first place (as their ancestors in like case have usually done) for the vindicating and asserting their ancient rights and liberties, declare that the pretended power of suspending of laws or the execution of laws by regal authority without consent of parliament is illegal; that the pretended power of dispensing with laws or the execution of laws by regal authority, as it hath been assumed and exercised of late, is illegal; that the commission for erecting the late court of commissioners for ecclesiastical causes and all other commissions and courts of like nature are illegal and pernicious; that levying money for or to the use of the crown by pretence of prerogative without grant of parliament, for longer time or in other manner than the same is or shall be granted, is illegal; that it is the right of the subjects to petition the king, and all commitments and prosecutions for such petitioning are illegal; that the raising or keeping a standing army within the kingdom in time of peace, unless it be with consent of parliament, is against law; that the subjects which are Protestants may have arms for their defence suitable to their conditions and as allowed by law; that election of members of parliament ought to be free; that the freedom of speech and debates or proceedings in parliament ought not to be impeached or questioned in any court or place out of parliament; that excessive bail ought not to be required, nor excessive fines imposed, nor cruel and unusual punishments inflicted; that jurors ought to be duly impanelled and returned, and jurors which pass upon men in trials for high treason ought to be freeholders; that all grants and promises of fines and forfeitures of particular persons before conviction are illegal and void; and that, for redress of all grievances and for the amending, strengthening, and preserving of the laws, parliaments ought to be held frequently.

And they do claim, demand, and insist upon all and singular the premises as their undoubted rights and liberties, and that no declarations, judgments, doings, or proceedings to the prejudice of the people in any of the said premises ought in any wise to be drawn hereafter into consequence or example. To which demand of their rights they are particularly encouraged by the declaration of his highness the prince of Orange, as being the only means for obtaining a full redress and remedy therein. Having therefore an entire confidence that his said highness the prince of Orange will perfect the deliverance so far advanced by him and will still preserve them from the violation of their rights which they have here asserted and from all other attempts upon their religion, rights, and liberties, the said lords spiritual and temporal and commons assembled at Westminster do resolve that William and Mary, prince and princess of Orange, be and be declared king and queen of England, France, and Ireland, and the dominions thereunto belonging, to hold the crown and royal dignity of the said kingdoms and dominions to them, the said prince and princess, during their lives and the life of the survivor of them; and that the sole and full exercise of the regal power be only in and executed by the said prince of Orange in the names of the said prince and princess during their joint lives, and after their deceases the said crown and royal dignity of the said kingdoms and dominions to be to the heirs of the body of the said princess, and for default of such issue to the princess Anne of Denmark and the heirs of her body, and for default of such issue to the heirs of the body of the said prince of Orange. And the lords spiritual and temporal and commons do pray the said prince and princess to accept the same accordingly; and that the oaths hereafter mentioned be taken by all persons, of whom the oaths of allegiance and supremacy might be required by law, instead of them; and that the said oaths of allegiance and supremacy, be abrogated:

> I, A. B., do sincerely promise and swear that I will be faithful and bear true allegiance to their majesties King William and Queen Mary. So help me God.
>
> I, A. B., do swear that I do from my heart abhor, detest, and abjure as impious and heretical this damnable doctrine and position, that princes excommunicated or deprived by the pope or any authority of the see of Rome may be deposed or murdered by their subjects or any other whatsoever. And I do declare that no foreign prince, person, prelate, state, or potentate hath or ought to have any jurisdiction, power, superiority, pre-eminence, or authority ecclesiastical or spiritual within this realm. So help me God.

Upon which their said majesties did accept the crown and royal dignity of the kingdoms of England, France, and Ireland and the dominions thereunto belonging, according to the resolution and desire of the said lords and commons contained in the said declaration; and thereupon their majesties were pleased that the said lords spiritual and temporal and commons, being the two houses of parliament, should continue to sit and, with their majesties' royal concurrence, make effectual provision for the settlement of the religion, laws, and liberties of this kingdom, so that the same for the future might not be in danger again of being subverted; to which the said lords spiritual and temporal and commons did agree and proceed to act accordingly:

Now, in pursuance of the premises, the said lords spiritual and temporal and commons in parliament assembled, for the ratifying, confirming, and establishing the said declaration and the articles, clauses, matters, and things therein contained by the force of a law made in due form by authority of parliament, do pray that it may be declared and enacted that all and singular the rights and liberties asserted and claimed in the said declaration are the true, ancient, and indubitable rights and liberties of the people of this kingdom and so shall be esteemed, allowed, adjudged, deemed, and taken to be; and that all and every the particulars aforesaid shall be firmly and strictly holden and observed as they are expressed in the said declaration, and all officers and ministers whatsoever shall serve their majesties and their successors according to the same in all times to come. And the said lords spiritual and temporal and commons, seriously considering how it hath pleased Almighty God, in His marvellous providence and merciful goodness to this nation, to provide and preserve their said majesties' royal persons most happily to reign over us upon the throne of their ancestors . . . , do truly, firmly, assuredly, and in the sincerity of their hearts think, and do hereby recognize, acknowledge, and declare that King James II, having abdicated the government and their majesties having accepted the crown and royal dignity as aforesaid, their said majesties did become, were, are, and of right ought to be by the laws of this realm our sovereign liege lord and lady, king and queen of England, France, and Ireland, and the dominions thereunto belonging; in and to whose princely persons the royal state, crown, and dignity of the said realms with all honours, styles, titles, regalities, prerogatives, powers, jurisdictions, and authorities to the same belonging and appertaining are most fully, rightly, and entirely invested and incorporated, united and annexed.

And for preventing all questions and divisions in this realm by reason of any pretended titles to the crown, and for preserving a certainty in the succession thereof, in and upon which the unity, peace, tranquillity, and safety of this nation doth under God wholly consist and depend, the said lords spiritual and temporal and commons do beseech their majesties that it may be enacted, established, and declared that the crown and regal government of the said kingdoms and dominions, with all and singular the premises thereunto belonging and appertaining, shall be and continue to their said majesties and the survivor of them during their lives and the life of the survivor of them; and that the entire, perfect, and full exercise of the regal power and government be only in and executed by his majesty in the names of both their majesties during their joint lives; and after their deceases the said crown and premises shall be and remain to the heirs of the body of her majesty, and, for default of such issue, to her royal highness the princess Anne of Denmark and the heirs of her body and, for default of such issue, to the heirs of the body of his said majesty. And thereunto the lords spiritual and temporal and commons do, in the name of all the people aforesaid, mostly humbly and faithfully submit themselves, their heirs, and posterities forever; and do faithfully promise that they will stand to maintain and defend their said majesties, and also the limitation and succession of the crown herein specified and contained, to the utmost of their powers with their lives and estates against all persons whatsoever that shall attempt anything to the contrary.

And whereas it hath been found by experience that it is inconsistent with the safety and welfare of this Protestant kingdom to be governed by a popish prince or by any king or queen marrying a papist, the said lords spiritual and temporal and commons do further pray that it may be enacted that all and every person and persons that is, are, or shall be reconciled to, or shall hold communion with, the see or Church of Rome, or shall profess the popish religion, or shall marry a papist shall be excluded and be forever incapable to inherit, possess, or enjoy the crown and government of this realm and Ireland and the dominions thereunto belonging or any part of the same, or to have, use, or exercise any regal power, authority, or jurisdiction within the same. And in all and every such case or cases the people of these realms shall be and are hereby absolved of their allegiance. And the said crown and government shall from time to time descend to and be enjoyed by such person or persons, being Protestants, as should have inherited and enjoyed the same in case the said person or persons . . . were naturally dead. And . . . every king and queen of this realm, who at any time hereafter shall come to and succeed in the imperial crown of this kingdom, shall on the first day of the meeting of the first parliament next after his or her coming to the crown—sitting in his or her throne in the house of peers, in the presence of the lords and commons therein assembled, or at his or her coronation before such person or persons who shall administer the coronation oath to him or her . . . make, subscribe, and audibly repeat the declaration mentioned in the statute made in the thirtieth year of the reign of King Charles II. . . . But if it shall happen that such king or queen upon his or her succession to the crown shall be under the age of twelve years, then every such king or queen shall make, subscribe, and audibly repeat the said declaration at his or her coronation, or the first day of the meeting of the first parliament as aforesaid which shall first happen after such king or queen shall have attained the said age of twelve years.

All which their majesties are contented and pleased shall be declared, enacted, and established by authority of this present parliament; and shall stand, remain, and be the law of this realm forever. And the same are by their said majesties, by and with the advice and consent of the lords spiritual and temporal and commons in parliament assembled and by the authority of the same, declared, enacted, and established accordingly. And be it further declared and enacted by the authority aforesaid that, from and after this present session of parliament, no dispensation . . . of or to any statute, or any part thereof, shall be allowed; but that the same shall be held void and of no effect—except a dispensation be allowed of in such statute, and except in such cases as shall be specially provided for by one or more bill or bills to be passed during this present session of parliament. Provided that no charter or grant or pardon granted before the three-and-twentieth day of October, in the year of our Lord 1689, shall be anyways impeached or invalidated by this act; but that the same shall be and remain of the same force and effect in law and no other than as if this act had never been made.

PART TWO
COLONIAL CHARTERS AND LAWS

COLONIAL CHARTERS AND LAWS

Commentary

Even more important than the three great Charters of English liberty in the historical background of the federal Bill of Rights was the experience in the American colonies themselves. The colonists could build upon the foundation laid by the baronial opponents of King John and their successors through the centuries only because their prior history had brought them to a stage where they were able to do so.

The most important thing to bear in mind in considering the impact of Colonial history upon the Bill of Rights is that it is a history of *British* colonies. From a constitutional point of view, the colonies settled by Great Britain were unique—utterly unlike those of Spain or France or the nations of antiquity. When Englishmen migrated they took with them, in the words of a Parliamentary debate, "all of the first great privileges of Englishmen on their backs." Let an Englishman go where he would, said the counsel to the Board of Trade in 1720, in lands claimed by England, he carried as much of law and liberty with him as the nature of things would bear. It was because of this that Patrick Henry could claim, in the first of his 1765 resolves passed by the Virginia assembly, that the people of that Colony possessed "all the Liberties, Privileges, Franchises and Immunities that at any Time have been held, enjoyed and possessed by the People of *Great Britain.*" A similar claim could hardly have been asserted by Frenchmen, Spaniards, or Romans who settled overseas.

According to Thomas Pownall, perhaps the best of the Massachusetts Colonial Governors, the rights of Englishmen were preserved to the American colonists because of the fact that the Island of Jersey had, by its constitution, "a shadow and semblance of an English parliament." This precedent, he said, made it easy to put the same idea into early American Charters. Certainly, the Colonial Charters played an important part in the constitutional training of Americans. The grant of the Charters themselves was a natural development in an age when grants of property, powers, and immunities were commonly made through such instruments. When the first colonists came to Virginia, they came armed with a Charter granted by James I (*infra* p. 54) authorizing them "to make Habitation, Plantation, and to deduce a Colony of sundry of our People into that part of America, commonly called Virginia." This Charter called for the setting up of local government and expressly reserved to those who should live in the new Colony "all Liberties, Franchises, and Immunities . . . to all Intents and Purposes, as if they had been abiding and born, within this our Realm of England."

Along with Charters went the policy of establishing representative institutions in the colonies. "For in the Governments, where there are Charters," wrote Jeremiah Dummer in his early eighteenth-century *Defence of the New England Charters*, ". . . all Officers Civil and Military are elected by the People." This was to overstate the extent of popular control, but it is a fact that local legislatures did quickly develop in all of the colonies. The Virginia Colony was in existence little over a decade when London ordered the setting up of a representative assembly, the House of Burgesses, whose members were duly chosen in 1619.

A similar development occurred as the other colonies came to be settled—either, as in the case of Virginia, through decrees from London or through the voluntary action of the colonists themselves. Almost from the beginning the colonists became endowed with the two essentials of the English Constitution: a representative legislative assembly and a recognition of the basic rights of Englishmen. More than that, the establishment of such essentials in written fundamental laws or documents in the form of Charters granted from London had a profound influence on American constitutional ideas.

It may be true that, from a strictly legal point of view, all such Colonial organic instruments hardly possessed anything like the status attained by later American Constitutions. The Charters received from London were accorded as a matter of privilege and grace. They could be amended or revoked at the will of the grantor. In law, they remained only medieval grants, subject to the will of the grantor, though they regulated the lives and property of ever-increasing thousands of Americans.

The same was clearly true—with regard to control from London—of the fundamental laws drawn up by the colonists themselves. These, too, were legally subject to the overriding authority of the British government. So far as the law was concerned, then, the Charters and fundamental laws of the colonies were weak bulwarks behind which to defend the rights of Americans against the mother country. In the law, there was no answer to Lord Mansfield's assertion that the American governments set up by charter were "all on the same footing as our great corporations in London."

More important, nevertheless, than the letter of the law with regard to the Colonial Charters was the manner in which those instruments were viewed by the bulk of Americans. "Who, then," asked John Adams in 1818, "was the author, inventor, discoverer of independence? The only true answer must be the first emigrants, and the proof of it is the charter of James I." The strict legal rule might make of the Charters mere matters of royal grace. But the colonists looked upon them as much more. The very first Charter, that of James I to Virginia, said Adams, "is more like a treaty between independent sovereigns than like a charter or grant of privileges from a sovereign to his subjects."

Americans looked upon their Charters as the written source of their basic institutions and freedoms and were quick to oppose any infringements upon their Charter rights. As early as 1664, the men of Massachusetts resisted an attempt to replace their Charter by commissioners sent from London to "regulate" New England. The colonists, we are told, put their Charter in safe hands, manned the harbor fort, and petitioned the King to let their "laws and liberties live." When, in 1681, their Charter rights were again attacked, they asserted that it was their undoubted duty "to abide by what rights and privileges the Lord our God in his merciful providence hath bestowed upon us."

In 1684, to be sure, the Massachusetts Charter was actually withdrawn and the Dominion of New England governed in accordance with Sir Edmund Andros' notions of Stuart prerogative. But the resistance of the colonists led to the granting of a new Charter in 1691. In the other Colonies, the situation was similar. The Charters were regarded as the fundamental basis of rights and liberties. When the Charters were restricted or modified, the colonists, felt the loss as Englishmen might have mourned the loss of Magna Carta. The attachment to the Charters continued until almost the end of the Colonial period. When the Massachusetts judges were impeached by that Colony's House of Representatives in 1774, they were charged with "high crimes and misdemeanors, and . . . a conspiracy against the charter liberties of the people."

Just as significant as the way in which the colonists conceived of their Charters was the training in self-government which they received in operating the institutions provided for under those instruments. "Englishmen hate an arbitrary power," wrote John Wise of Massachusetts in 1710, ". . . as they hate the devil." The political history of the colonies shows that such hatred was not diminished among those Englishmen who had migrated to North America.

From the beginning of their existence, the Colonial legislatures looked upon themselves as the direct descendants of the House of Commons, vested with the privileges and powers won by that body in its struggle against executive absolutism. This was apparent at the very first sitting of the first Colonial assembly, the Virginia House of Burgesses. When the Speaker took exception to the qualifications of two members, the House, in direct imitation of the English Commons, proceeded to exercise the right to judge the qualifications of its own members.

In many ways, the constitutional history of the colonies in the century before the Revolution was a miniature copy of that which had occurred in seventeenth-century England. The claim for which one Stuart King lost his life and another his throne was put forward in lesser form by the royal Governors. The result was constant conflict between the popular assemblies and the Governors. Although the Governors themselves were in the main hardly the "men of vicious characters" described by Franklin, they were direct agents of the prerogative, with commissions and instructions which made them autocrats not beholden to those whom they governed. In England itself, the prerogative had been completely bridled by the revolutions which overthrew Stuart tyranny. In the colonies, on the other hand, the royal prerogative continued, in theory at least, without diminution, and the Governors were expected to be agents of Whitehall's will. It was inevitable that such agents would be opposed by the provincial assemblies.

From a constitutional point of view, the colonists remained more Englishmen of the seventeenth century than those of the eighteenth century. In England, the seventeenth century was the great age of struggle against government by prerogative. That struggle was definitively concluded with the final expulsion of the Stuart Kings. Thenceforth, the English executive was to be completely subordinate to the representatives of the people.

In North America the basic contention between the legislative and executive branches continued, for the blessings which 1688 brought to the mother country (so signally commemorated in Locke's writings) were not extended across the Atlantic. If anything, indeed, the establishment of Parliamentary supremacy, with the accession of William and Mary, was to make a sharpening of the constitutional conflict in the colonies inevitable.

Looked at in this manner, it is not mere hyperbole to characterize the constitutional history of the colonies as a chapter torn from the constitutional history of Stuart England. The battles between Crown and Parliament were all fought out, on a smaller scale, on the western side of the Atlantic. And, in America, too, the theme was that of gradual triumph of the popular assembly. Many of Parliament's hard-won privileges—control over its own procedure, freedom of debate, determination of election disputes and the qualifications of members—were also secured by the Colonial legislatures. Even more important was the successful assertion by the assemblies of that power which was the very keystone of the arch of Parliamentary authority itself, namely, the power of the purse. That power alone, coupled as it was with the failure of the British government to provide a permanent civil list in any of the colonies (in most colonies, the salary of the governor himself had become dependent upon appropriations by the local legislature), led to the dominance of the assemblies in most Colonial governments by the end of the French and Indian War.

Had the mother country continued to treat the colonies with "a wise and salutary neglect," it is possible that Colonial institutions would have taken their own way to the "perfection" of which Burke speaks—thereby anticipating by a century the modern development of the British Commonwealth. Such peaceful development within the British Empire was, however, made impossible with the assertion by London of an entirely new theory of imperial power after the successful expulsion of the French from North America. It is in this sense that there is constitutional truth in Francis Parkman's well-known statement, "With the fall of Quebec began the history of the United States."

FIRST CHARTER OF VIRGINIA, 1606

Commentary

The royal Colonial Charters are the oldest documents in American constitutional history, for the earliest English settlements were created under them. The first such Charter was the Virginia Charter granted in 1606. The vital thing to note about this document is that it states (at the very beginning of colonization) the fundamental principle that the colonists take with them all the rights and liberties of Englishmen; they are to "Have and enjoy all Liberties, Franchises, and Immunities. . . , to all Intents and Purposes, as if they had been abiding and born, within this our Realm of England."

The Virginia Charter thus established the vital precedent that the colonists were entitled to all the "rights of Englishmen." Had that principle not been so established, it may be doubted that the history of the American Colonies would have developed as it did. As already pointed out, when Patrick Henry made his famous 1765 speech in the Virginia House of Burgesses, he relied directly upon the 1606 Charter provision which, he said, gave Virginians "all the Liberties, Privileges, Franchises, and Immunities that have at any Time been held, enjoyed, and possessed, by the people of *Great Britain.*"

In this respect, the 1606 Virginia Charter was but the first of a series of Colonial organic documents which guaranteed the colonists all the rights of Englishmen. The same guaranty was repeated in the Charter of New England, 1620; the Charter of Massachusetts Bay, 1629; the Charter of Maryland, 1632; the Charter of Connecticut, 1662; the Charter of Rhode Island, 1663; the Charter of Carolina, 1663; and the Charter of Georgia, 1732.

The 1606 Virginia Charter was thus the first step in the American development which ultimately led to the federal Bill of Rights. It must, however, be emphasized that it was only a first step, since it did nothing more than declare that the colonists were entitled to the rights of Englishmen. All constitutional history tells us that a mere declaration of rights in a fundamental law—though written in letters of gold upon the most imperishable tablets—is not enough of itself to secure vindication of the rights declared in practice. Even more important than declaration is implementation.

As already noted, the first Virginia Charter contained only the bare declaration that the colonists possessed all the rights of Englishmen. Before that declaration could develop into the federal Bill of Rights, three steps were required. First of all, it was necessary for the rights protected to be defined. The 1606 Charter made no attempt to define what the rights of Englishmen were, even in rudimentary form. At the beginning of the seventeenth century, such definition would have been premature. It took the constitutional struggles of the seventeenth and eighteenth centuries on both

53

sides of the Atlantic to give specific content to the notion of fundamental rights, of which the federal Bill of Rights itself was to become the classic inventory

A second essential development was the establishment of representative government on the western side of the Atlantic. The right of self-government was not considered one of the "rights of Englishmen" secured under the first Virginia Charter. The government provided by that instrument was under a Royal Council of Virginia, whose 13 members were appointed by the Crown, and sat in London. In Virginia itself, there was to be a Colonial Council appointed by the Royal Council and under the direction of that body. It soon became clear, however, that government wholly under the control of London was not proving effective. In 1618, Ordinances for Virginia were issued which provided for direct participation by the colonists in their government through a representative legislative assembly. The House of Burgesses, first elected in 1619, was the first American legislature and the progenitor of similar assemblies in all the colonies. Without the training in self-government received by the colonists, it is doubtful that there ever would have been any Revolution, much less the Bill of Rights itself as the climax of the struggle for independence.

But more than representative government was necessary before the colonial experience could ripen into the constitutional guarantee of individual rights contained in the Bill of Rights. What makes the Bill of Rights more than a compendium of maxims of political morality is the fact that the rights enumerated in it are enforceable by the courts. At the time of the first Virginia Charter, of course, the doctrine of judicial review had not even begun to develop. That development was to come during the latter part of the Colonial period and to culminate in the movement to set up enforceable Constitutions that characterized the Revolutionary period.

First Charter of Virginia, 1606*

James, by the Grace of God, King of England, Scotland, France and Ireland, Defender of the Faith, &c. Whereas our loving and well-disposed Subjects, Sir Thomas Gates, and Sir George Somers, Knights, Richard Hackluit, Clerk, Prebendary of Westminster, and Edward-Maria Wingfield, Thomas Hanham, and Ralegh Gilbert, Esqrs. William Parker, and George Popham, Gentlemen, and divers others of our loving Subjects, have been humble Suitors unto us, that We would vouchsafe unto them our Licence, to make Habitation, Plantation, and to deduce a colony of sundry of our People into that part of America commonly called Virginia, and other parts and

*B. P. Poore, *The Federal and State Constitutions, Colonial Charters and Other Organic Laws of the United States* (1878), Vol. 2, pp. 1888–93.

Territories in America, either appertaining unto us, or which are not now actually possessed by any Christian Prince or People, situate, lying, and being all along the Sea Coasts, between four and thirty Degrees of Northerly Latitude from the Equinoctial Line, and five and forty Degrees of the same Latitude, and in the main Land between the same four and thirty and five and forty Degrees, and the Islands thereunto adjacent, or within one hundred Miles of the Coast thereof;

And to that End, and for the more speedy Accomplishment of their said intended Plantation and Habitation there, are desirous to divide themselves into two several Colonies and Companies; the one consisting of certain Knights, Gentlemen, Merchants, and other Adventurers, of our City of London and elsewhere, which are, and from time to time shall be, joined unto them, which do desire to begin their Plantation and Habitation in some fit and convenient Place, between four and thirty and one and forty Degrees of the said Latitude, alongst the Coasts of Virginia, and the Coasts of America aforesaid: And the other consisting of sundry Knights, Gentlemen, Merchants, and other Adventurers, of our Cities of Bristol and Exeter, and of our Town of Plimouth, and of other Places, which do join themselves unto that Colony, which do desire to begin their Plantation and Habitation in some fit and convenient Place, between eight and thirty Degrees and five and forty Degrees of the said Latitude, all alongst the said Coasts of Virginia and America, as that Coast lyeth:

We, greatly commending, and graciously accepting of, their Desires for the Furtherance of so noble a Work, which may, by the Providence of Almighty God, hereafter tend to the Glory of his Divine Majesty, in propagating of Christian Religion to such People, as yet live in Darkness and miserable Ignorance of the true Knowledge and Worship of God, and may in time bring the Infidels and Savages, living in those parts, to human Civility, and to a settled and quiet Government: Do, by these our Letters Patents, graciously accept of, and agree to, their humble and well-intended Desires;

And do therefore, for Us, our Heirs, and Successors, grant and agree, that the said Sir Thomas Gates, Sir George Somers, Richard Hackluit, and Edward-Maria Wingfield, Adventurers of and for our City of London, and all such others, as are, or shall be, joined unto them of that Colony, shall be called the first Colony; And they shall and may begin their said first Plantation and Habitation, at any Place upon the said Coast of Virginia or America, where they shall think fit and convenient, between the said four and thirty and one and forty Degrees of the said Latitude; And that they shall have all the Lands, Woods, Soil, Grounds, Havens, Ports, Rivers, Mines, Minerals, Marshes, Waters, Fishings, Commodities, and Hereditaments, whatsoever, from the said first Seat of their Plantation and Habitation by the Space of fifty Miles of English Statute Measure, all along the said Coast of Virginia and America, towards the West and Southwest, as the Coast lyeth, with all the Islands within one hundred Miles directly over against the same Sea Coast; And also all the Lands, Soil, Grounds, Havens, Ports, Rivers, Mines, Minerals, Woods, Waters, Marshes, Fishings, Commodities, and Hereditaments, whatsoever, from the said Place of their first Plantation and Habitation for the space of fifty like English Miles, all alongst the said Coasts of Virginia and America, towards the East and Northeast, or towards the North, as the Coast lyeth, together with all the Islands within one hundred Miles, directly over against the said Sea Coast; And also all the Lands, Woods, Soil, Grounds, Havens, Ports, Rivers, Mines, Minerals, Marshes, Waters, Fishings, Commodities, and Hereditaments, whatsoever, from the same fifty Miles every way on the Sea Coast, directly into the main Land by the Space of one hundred like English Miles; And shall and may inhabit and remain there; and shall and may also build and fortify within any the same, for their better Safeguard and Defence, according to their best Discretion, and the Discretion of the Council of that Colony; And that no other of our Subjects shall be permitted, or suffered, to plant or inhabit behind, or on the Backside of them, towards the main Land, without the Express License or Consent of the Council of that Colony, thereunto in Writing first had and obtained.

And we do likewise, for Us, our Heirs, and Successors, by these Presents, grant and agree, that the said Thomas Hanham, and Ralegh Gilbert, William Parker, and George Popham, and all others of the Town of Plimouth in the County of Devon, or elsewhere, which are, or shall be, joined unto them of that Colony, shall be called the second Colony; And that they shall and may begin their said Plantation and Seat of their first Abode and Habitation, at any Place upon the said Coast of Virginia and America, where they shall think fit and convenient, between eight and thirty Degrees of the said Latitude, and five and forty Degrees of the same Latitude; And that they shall have all the Lands, Soils, Grounds, Havens, Ports, Rivers, Mines, Minerals, Woods, Marshes, Waters, Fishings, Commodities, and Hereditaments, whatsoever, from the first Seat of their Plantation and Habitation by the Space of fifty like English Miles, as is aforesaid, all alongst the said Coasts of Virginia and America, towards the West and Southwest, or towards the South, as the Coast lyeth, and all the Islands within one hundred Miles, directly over against the said Sea Coast; And also all the Lands, Soils, Grounds, Havens, Ports, Rivers, Mines, Minerals, Woods, Marshes, Waters, Fishings, Commodities, and Hereditaments, whatsoever, from the said Place of their first Plantation and Habitation for the Space of fifty like Miles, all alongst the said Coast of Virginia and America, towards the East and Northeast, or towards the North, as the Coast lyeth, and all the Islands also within one hundred Miles directly over against the same Sea Coast; And also all the Lands, Soils, Grounds, Havens, Ports, Rivers, Woods, Mines, Minerals, Marshes, Waters, Fishings, Commodities, and Hereditaments, whatsoever, from the same fifty Miles every way on the Sea Coast, directly into the main Land, by the Space of one hundred like English Miles; And shall and may inhabit and remain there; and shall and may also build and fortify within any the same for their better Safeguard, according to their best Discretion, and the Discretion of the Council of that Colony; And that none of our Subjects shall be permitted, or suffered, to plant or inhabit behind, or on the back of them, towards the main Land, without express Licence of the Council of that Colony, in Writing thereunto first had and obtained.

Provided always, and our Will and Pleasure herein is, that the Plantation and Habitation of such of the said Colonies, as shall last plant themselves, as aforesaid, shall not be made within one hundred like English Miles of the other of them, that first began to make their Plantation, as aforesaid.

And we do also ordain, establish, and agree, for Us, our Heirs, and Successors, that each of the said Colonies shall have a Council, which shall govern and order all Matters and Causes, which shall arise, grow, or happen, to or within the same several Colonies, according to such Laws, Ordinances, and Instructions, as shall be, in that behalf, given and signed with Our Hand or Sign Manual, and pass under the Privy Seal of our Realm of England; Each of which Councils shall consist of thirteen Persons, to be ordained, made, and removed, from time to time, according as shall be directed and comprised in the same instructions; And shall have a several Seal, for all Matters that shall pass or concern the same several Councils; Each of which Seals, shall have the King's Arms engraven on the one Side thereof, and his Portraiture on the other; And that the Seal for the Council of the said first Colony shall have engraven round about, on the one Side, these Words; Sigillum Regis Magnae Britanniae, Franciae, & Hiberniae; on the other Side this Inscription round about; Pro Concilio primae Coloniae Virginiae. And the Seal for the Council of the said second Colony shall also have engraven, round about the one Side thereof, the aforesaid Words; Sigillum Regis Magnae Britanniae, Franciae, & Hiberniae; and on the other Side; Pro Concilio secundae Coloniae Virginiae:

And that also there shall be a Council, established here in England, which shall, in like Manner, consist of thirteen Persons, to be, for that Purpose, appointed by Us, our Heirs and Successors, which shall be called our Council of Virginia; And shall, from time to time, have the superior Managing and Direction, only of and for all Matters that shall or may concern the Government, as well of the said several Colonies, as of and for any other Part or Place, within the aforesaid Precincts of four and thirty and five and forty Degrees abovementioned; Which Council shall, in like manner, have a Seal, for Matters concerning the Council or Colonies, with the like Arms and Portraiture, as aforesaid, with this inscription, engraven round about on the one Side; Sigillum Regis Magnae Britanniae, Franciae, & Hiberniae; and round about on the other Side, Pro Concilio fuo Virginiae.

And moreover, we do grant and agree, for Us, our Heirs and Successors; that the said several Councils of and for the said several Colonies, shall and lawfully may, by Virtue hereof, from time to time, without any Interruption of Us, our Heirs or Successors, give and take Order, to dig, mine, and search for all Manner of Mines of Gold, Silver, and Copper, as well within any Part of their said several Colonies, as of the said main Lands on the Backside of the same Colonies; And to have and enjoy the Gold, Silver, and Copper, to be gotten thereof, to the Use and Behoof of the same Colonies, and the Plantations thereof; yielding therefore to Us, our Heirs and Successors, the fifth Part only of all the same Gold and Silver, and the fifteenth Part of all the same Copper, so to be gotten or had, as is aforesaid, without any other Manner of Profit or Account, to be given or yielded to Us, our Heirs, or Successors, for or in Respect of the same:

And that they shall, or lawfully may, establish and cause to be made a Coin, to pass current there between the people of those several Colonies, for the more Ease of Traffick and Bargaining between and amongst them and the Natives there, of such Metal, and in such Manner and Form, as the said several Councils there shall limit and appoint.

And we do likewise, for Us, our Heirs, and Successors, by these Presents, give full Power and Authority to the said Sir Thomas Gates, Sir George Somers, Richard Hackluit, Edward-Maria Wingfield, Thomas Hanham, Ralegh Gilbert, William Parker, and George Popham, and to every of them, and to the said several Companies, Plantations, and Colonies, that they, and every of them, shall and may, at all and every time and times hereafter, have, take, and lead in the said Voyage, and for and towards the said several Plantations, and Colonies, and to travel thitherward, and to abide and inhabit there, in every the said Colonies and Plantations, such and so many of our Subjects, as shall willingly accompany them or any of them, in the said Voyages and Plantations; With sufficient Shipping, and Furniture of Armour, Weapons, Ordinance, Powder, Victual, and all other things, necessary for the said Plantations, and for their Use and Defence there: Provided always, that none of the said Persons be such, as shall hereafter be specially restrained by Us, our Heirs, or Successors.

Moreover, we do, by these Presents, for Us, our Heirs, and Successors, give and grant Licence unto the said Sir Thomas Gates, Sir George Somers, Richard Hackluit, Edward-Maria Wingfield, Thomas Hanham, Ralegh Gilbert, William Parker, and George Popham, and to every of the said Colonies, that they, and every of them, shall and may, from time to time, and at all times forever hereafter, for their several Defences, encounter, expulse, repel, and resist, as well by Sea as by Land, by all Ways and Means whatsoever, all and every such Person and Persons, as without the especial Licence of the said several Colonies and Plantations, shall attempt to inhabit within the said several Precincts and Limits of the said several Colonies and Plantations, or any of them, or that shall enterprise or attempt, at any time hereafter, the Hurt, Detriment, or Annoyance, of the said several Colonies or Plantations:

Giving and granting, by these Presents, unto the said Sir Thomas Gates, Sir George Somers, Richard Hackluit, Edward-Maria Wingfield, and their Associates of the said first Colony, and unto the said Thomas Hanham, Ralegh Gilbert, William Parker, and George Popham, and their Associates of the said second Colony, and to every of them, from time to time, and at all times for ever hereafter, Power and Authority to take and surprise, by all Ways and Means whatsoever, all and every Person and Persons, with their Ships, Vessels, Goods, and other Furniture, which shall be found trafficking, into any Harbour or Harbours, Creek or Creeks, or Place, within the Limits or Precincts of the said several Colonies and Plantations, not being of the same Colony, until such time, as they, being of any Realms, or Dominions under our Obedience, shall pay, or agree to pay, to the Hands of the Treasurer of that Colony, within whose Limits and Precincts they shall so traffick, two and a half upon every Hundred, of any thing, so by them trafficked, bought, or sold; And being Strangers, and not Subjects under our Obeysance, until they shall pay five upon every Hundred, of such Wares and Merchandises, as they shall traffick, buy, or sell, within the Precincts of the said several Colonies, wherein they shall so traffick, buy, or sell, as aforesaid; which Sums of Money, or Benefit, as aforesaid, for and during the Space of one and twenty Years, next ensuing the Date hereof, shall be wholly emploied to the Use, Benefit, and Behoof of the said several Plantations, where such Traffick shall be made; And after the said one and twenty Years ended, the same shall be taken to the Use of Us, our Heires, and Successors, by such Officers and Ministers as by Us, our Heirs, and Successors, shall be thereunto assigned or appointed.

And we do further, by these Presents, for Us, our Heirs and Successors, give and grant unto the said Sir Thomas Gates, Sir George Somers, Richard Hackluit, and Edward-Maria Wingfield, and to their Associates of the said first Colony and Plantation, and to the said Thomas Hanham, Ralegh Gilbert, William Parker, and George Popham, and their Associates of the said second Colony and Plantation, that they, and every of them, by their Deputies, Ministers, and Factors, may transport the Goods, Chattels, Armour, Munition, and Furniture, needful to be used by them, for their said Apparel, Food, Defence, or otherwise in Respect of the said Plantations, out of our Realms of England and Ireland, and all other our Dominions, from time to time, for and during the Time of seven Years, next ensuing the Date hereof, for the better Relief of the said several Colonies and Plantations, without any Customs, Subsidy, or other Duty, unto Us, our Heirs, or Successors, to be yielded or payed for the same.

Also we do, for Us, our Heirs, and Successors, declare, by these Presents, that all and every the Persons being our Subjects, which shall dwell and inhabit within every or any of the said several Colonies and Plantations, and every of their children, which shall happen to be born within any of the

Limits and Precincts of the said several Colonies and Plantations, shall have and enjoy all Liberties, Franchises, and Immunities, within any of our other Dominions, to all Intents and Purposes, as if they had been abiding and born, within this our Realm of England, or any other of our said Dominions.

Moreover, our gracious Will and Pleasure is, and we do, by these Presents, for Us, our Heirs, and Successors, declare and set forth, that if any Person or Persons, which shall be of any of the said Colonies and Plantations, or any other, which shall traffick to the said Colonies and Plantations, or any of them, shall, at any time or times hereafter, transport any Wares, Merchandises, or Commodities, out of any of our Dominions, with a Pretence to land, sell, or otherwise dispose of the same, within any the Limits and Precincts of any of the said Colonies and Plantations, and yet nevertheless, being at Sea, or after he hath landed the same within any of the said Colonies and Plantations, shall carry the same into any other Foreign Country, with a Purpose there to sell or dispose of the same, without the Licence of Us, our Heirs, and Successors, in that Behalf first had and obtained; That then, all the Goods and Chattels of such Person or Persons, so offending and transporting, together with the said Ship or Vessel, wherein such Transportation was made, shall be forfeited to Us, our Heirs, and Successors.

Provided always, and our Will and Pleasure is, and we do hereby declare to all Christian Kings, Princes, and States, that if any Person or Persons which shall hereafter be of any of the said several Colonies and Plantations, or any other, by his, their, or any of their Licence and Appointment, shall, at any Time or Times hereafter, rob or spoil, by Sea or Land, or do any Act of unjust and unlawful Hostility to any the Subjects of Us, our Heirs, or Successors, or any the Subjects of any King, Prince, Ruler, Governor, or State, being then in League or Amitie with Us, our Heirs, or Successors, and that upon such Injury, or upon just Complaint of such Prince, Ruler, Governor, or State, or their Subjects, We, our Heirs, or Successors, shall make open Proclamation, within any of the Ports of our Realm of England, commodious for that purpose, That the said Person or Persons, having committed any such robbery, or Spoil, shall, within the term to be limited by such Proclamations, make full Restitution or Satisfaction of all such Injuries done, so as the said Princes, or others so complaining, may hold themselves fully satisfied and contented; And, that if the said Person or Persons, having committed such Robery or Spoil, shall not make, or cause to be made Satisfaction accordingly, within such Time so to be limited, That then it shall be lawful to Us, our Heirs, and Successors, to put the said Person or Persons, having committed such Robbery or Spoil, and their Procurers, Abettors, and Comforters, out of our Allegiance and Protection; And that it shall be lawful and free, for all Princes, and others to pursue with hostility the said offenders, and every of them, and their and every of their Procurers, Aiders, abettors, and comforters, in that behalf.

And finally, we do for Us, our Heirs, and Successors, grant and agree, to and with the said Sir Thomas Gates, Sir George Somers, Richard Hackluit, Edward-Maria Wingfield, and all others of the said first colony, that We, our Heirs and Successors, upon Petition in that Behalf to be made, shall, by Letters Patent under the Great Seal of England, give and grant, unto such Persons, their Heirs and Assigns, as the Council of that Colony, or the most part of them, shall, for that Purpose, nominate and assign all the Lands, Tenements, and Hereditaments, which shall be within the Precincts limited for that Colony, as is aforesaid, To be holden of Us, our heirs and Successors, as of our Manor at East-Greenwich, in the County of Kent, in free and common Soccage only, and not in Capite:

And do in like Manner, Grant and Agree, for Us, our Heirs and Successors, to and with the said Thomas Hanham, Ralegh Gilbert, William Parker, and George Popham, and all others of the said second Colony, That We, our Heirs, and Successors, upon Petition in that Behalf to be made, shall, by Letters-Patent, under the Great Seal of England, give and grant, unto such Persons, their Heirs and Assigns, as the Council of that Colony, or the most Part of them, shall for that Purpose nominate and assign, all the Lands, Tenements, and Hereditaments, which shall be within the Precincts limited for that Colony, as is aforesaid, To be holden of Us, our Heires, and Successors, as of our Manor of East-Greenwich, in the County of Kent, in free and common Soccage only, and not in Capite.

All which Lands, Tenements, and Hereditaments, so to be passed by the said several Letters-Patent, shall be sufficient Assurance from the said Patentees, so distributed and divided amongst the Undertakers for the Plantation of the said several Colonies, and such as shall make their Plantations in either of the said several Colonies, in such Manner and Form, and for such Estates, as shall be ordered and set down by the Council of the said Colony, or the most part of them, respectively, within which the same Lands, Tenements, and Hereditaments shall lye or be; Although express Mention of the true yearly Value or Certainty of the Premisses, or any of them, or of any other Gifts or Grants, by Us or any of our Progenitors or Predecessors, to the aforesaid Sir Thomas Gates, Knt. Sir George Somers, Knt. Richard Hackluit, Edward-Maria Wingfield, Thomas Hanham, Ralegh Gilbert, William Parker, and George Popham, or any of them, heretofore made, in these Presents, is not made; Or any Statute, Act, Ordinance, or Provision, Proclamation, or Restraint, to the contrary hereof had, made, ordained, or any other Thing, Cause, or Matter whatsoever, in any wise notwithstanding. In Witness whereof we have caused these our Letters to be made Patents; Witness Ourself at Westminster, the tenth Day of April, in the fourth Year of our Reign of England, France, and Ireland, and of Scotland the nine and thirtieth.

Lukin
Per breve de privato Sigillo

FUNDAMENTAL ORDERS OF CONNECTICUT, 1639

Commentary

Strictly speaking, the Fundamental Orders of Connecticut did not play a part in the history of the federal Bill of Rights, since the Connecticut enactment did not contain any guarantees of individual rights. The Fundamental Orders is, nevertheless, most relevant in a documentary history of the Bill of Rights, for it constitutes what James Bryce characterized as "The oldest truly political Constitution in America." The Fundamental Orders was framed by the inhabitants who left Massachusetts in 1635 and founded settlements at Hartford, Windsor, and Wethersfield along the Connecticut River. Those settlers, led by Reverend Thomas Hooker, had, from the beginning, provided for their own self-government, setting up a General Court modelled upon that of Massachusetts which first met in 1637. The Fundamental Orders was drawn up as an instrument to set forth and define the organs of government and their powers. As such, it was based upon the Puritan principle of a covenant designed to govern religious and civil affairs. However, it went far beyond the earlier covenant concept, for it laid down details with regard to the government formed. In this respect, it bears a closer resemblance to later Constitutions than to earlier models like the Mayflower Compact.

Though, as already stressed, the Connecticut enactment did not contain any guarantees of individual liberties, its adoption was an important step in the development that culminated in the Bill of Rights. A basic foundation of that document was the notion of an enforceable, written Constitution drawn up by the people to be governed. The Fundamental Orders was the first such constitutional document in the American Colonies. To be sure, compared with later organic instruments it was a rudimentary document, and did not provide any enforcement machinery. Still, it was of fundamental significance as a first step, one which applied the principles developed in covenants, Charters, and practice to the conscious organization of a new government.

Fundamental Orders of Connecticut, 1639*

Forasmuch as it hath pleased the Allmighty God by the wise disposition of his diuyne pruidence so to Order and dispose of things that we the Inhabitants and Residents of Windsor, Harteford and Wethersfield are now cohabiting and dwelling in and vppon the River of Conectecotee and the Lands

*F. N. Thorpe, *The Federal and State Constitutions, Colonial Charters, and Other Organic Laws* (1909), Vol. 1, pp. 519–23.

thereunto adoiyneing; And well knowing where a people are gathered to-gather the word of God requires that to mayntayne the peace and vnion of such a people there should be an orderly and decent Gouerment established according to God, to order and dispose of the affayres of the people at all seasons as occation shall require; doe therefore assotiate and conioyne our selues to be as one Publike State or Comonwelth; and doe, for our selues and our Successors and such as shall be adioyned to vs att any tyme hereafter, enter into Combination and Confederation togather, to mayntayne and prsearue the liberty and purity of the gospell of our Lord Jesus wch we now prfesse, as also the disciplyne of the Churches, wch according to the truth of the said gospell is now practised amongst vs; As also in or Ciuell Affaires to be guided and gouerned according to such Lawes, Rules, Orders and decrees as shall be made, ordered & decreed, as followeth:

1. It is Ordered, sentenced and decreed, that there shall be yerely two generall Assemblies or Courts, the on the second thursday in Aprill, the other the second thursday in September, following; the first shall be called the Courte of Election, wherein shall be yerely Chosen fro tyme to tyme soe many Magestrats and other publike Officers as shall be found requisitte: Whereof one to be chosen Gouernour for the yeare ensueing and vntill another be chosen, and noe other Magestrate to be chosen for more then one yeare; pruided allwayes there be six chosen besids the Gouernour; wch being chosen and sworne according to an Oath recorded for that purpose shall haue power to administer iustice according to the Lawes here estab-lished, and for want thereof according to the rule of the word of God; wch choise shall be made by all that are admitted freemen and haue taken the Oath of Fidellity, and doe cohabitte wthin this Jurisdiction, (hauing beene admitted Inhabitants by the maior prt of the Towne wherein they liue,) or the mayor prte of such as shall be then prsent.

2. It is Ordered, sentensed and decreed, that the Election of the aforesaid Magestrats shall be on this manner: euery prson prsent and quallified for choyse shall bring in (to the prsons deputed to receaue the) one single papr wth the name of him written in yt whom he desires to haue Gouernour, and he that hath the greatest nuber of papers shall be Gouernor for that yeare. And the rest of the Magestrats or publike Officers to be chosen in this manner: The Secretary for the tyme being shall first read the names of all that are to be put to choise and then shall seuerally nominate them distinct-ly, and euery one that would haue the prson nominated to be chosen shall bring in one single paper written vppon, and he that would not haue him chosen shall bring in a blanke and euery one that hath more written papers than blanks shall be a Magistrat for that yeare; wch papers shall be receaued and told by one or more that shall be then chosen by the court and sworne to be faythfull therein; but in case there should not be six chosen as aforesaid, besids the Gouernor, out of those wch are nominated, then he or they wch

haue the most written paprs shall be a Magestrate or Magestrats for the ensueing yeare, to make vp the aforesaid nuber.

3. It is Ordered, sentenced and decreed, that the Secretary shall not nominate any prson, nor shall any prson be chosen newly into the Magestracy wch was not prpownded in some Generall Courte before, to be nominated the next Election; and to that end yt shall be lawfull for ech of the Townes aforesaid by their deputyes to nominate any two who they conceaue fitte to be put to election; and the Courte may ad so many more as they judge requisitt.

4. It is Ordered, sentenced and decreed that noe prson be chosen Gouernor aboue once in two yeares, and that the Gouernor be always a meber of some approved congregation, and formerly of the Magestracy wthin this Jurisdiction; and all the Magestrats Freemen of this Comonwelth: and that no Magestrate or other publike officer shall execute any prte of his or their Office before they are seuerally sworne, wch shall be done in the face of the Courte if they be prsent, and in case of absence by some deputed for that purpose.

5. It is Ordered, sentenced and decreed, that to the aforesaid Courte of Election the seurall Townes shall send their deputyes, and when the Elections are ended they may prceed in any publike searuice as at other Courts. Also the other Generall Courte in September shall be for makeing of lawes, and any other publike occation, wch conserns the good of the Comonwelth.

6. It is Ordered, sentenced and decreed, that the Gournor shall, ether by himselfe or by the secretary, send out sumons to the Constables of eur Towne for the cauleing of these two standing Courts, on month at lest before their seurall tymes: And also if the Gournor and the gretest prte of the Magestrats see cause vppon any spetiall occation to call a generall Courte, they may giue order to the secretary soe to doe wthin fowerteene dayes warneing; and if vrgent necessity so require, vppon a shorter notice, giueing sufficient grownds for yt to the deputyes when they meete, or els be questioned for the same; And if the Gournor and Mayor prte of Magestrats shall ether neglect or refuse to call the two Generall standing Courts or ether of the, as also at other tymes when the occations of the Comonwelth require, the Freemen thereof, or the Mayor prte of them, shall petition to them soe to doe: if then yt be ether denyed or neglected the said Freemen or the Mayor prte of them shall haue power to giue order to the Constables of the seuerall Townes to doe the same, and so may meete togather, and chuse to themselues a Moderator, and may prceed to do any Acte of power, wch any other Generall Courte may.

7. It is Ordered, sentenced and decreed that after there are warrants giuen out for any of the said Generall Courts, the Constable or Constables of ech Towne shall forthwth give notice distinctly to the inhabitants of the same, in some Publike Assembly or by goeing or sending fro howse to howse, that at a place and tyme by him or them lymited and sett, they meet and assemble the

selues togather to elect and chuse certen deputyes to be att the Generall Courte then following to agitate the afayres of the comonwelth; wch said Deputyes shall be chosen by all that are admitted Inhabitants in the seurall Townes and haue taken the oath of fidellity; pruided that non be chosen a Deputy for any Generall Courte wch is not a Freeman of this Comonwelth.

The a-foresaid deputyes shall be chosen in manner following: euery prson that is prsent and quallified as before exprssed, shall bring the names of such, written in seurrall papers, as they desire to haue chosen for that Imployment, and these 3 or 4, more or lesse, being the nuber agreed on to be chosen for that tyme, that haue greatest nuber of papers written for the shall be deputyes for that Courte; whose names shall be endorsed on the backe side of the warrant and returned into the Courte, wth the Constable or Constables hand vnto the same.

8. It is Ordered, sentenced and decreed, that Wyndsor, Hartford and Wethersfield shall haue power, ech Towne, to send fower of their freemen as deputyes to euery Generall Courte; and whatsoeuer other Townes shall be hereafter added to this Jurisdiction, they shall send so many deputyes as the Courte shall judge meete, a resonable prportion to the nuber of Freemen that are in the said Townes being to be attended therein; wch deputyes shall have the power of the whole Towne to giue their voats and alowance to all such lawes and orders as may be for the publike good, and unto wch the said Townes are to be bownd.

9. It is ordered and decreed, that the deputyes thus chosen shall haue power and liberty to appoynt a tyme and a place of meeting togather before any Generall Courte to aduise and consult of all such things as may concerne the good of the publike, as also to examine their owne Elections, whether according to the order, and if they or the gretest prte of them find any election to be illegall they may seclud such for prsent fro their meeting, and returne the same and their resons to the Courte; and if yt proue true, the Courte may fyne the prty or prtyes so intruding and the Towne, if they see cause, and giue out a warrant to goe to a newe election in a legall way, either in whole or in prte. Also the said deputyes shall haue power to fyne any that shall be disorderly at their meetings, or for not coming in due tyme or place according to appoyntment; and they may returne the said fynes into the Courte if yt be refused to be paid, and the tresurer to take notice of yt, and to estreete or levy the same as he doth other fynes.

10. It is Ordered, sentenced and decreed, that euery Generall Courte, except such as through neglecte of the Gournor and the greatest prte of Magestrats the Freemen themselves doe call, shall consist of the Gouernor, or some one chosen to moderate the Court, and 4 other Magestrats at lest, wth the mayor prte of the deputyes of the seuerall Townes legally chosen; and in case the Freemen or mayor prte of the through neglect or refusall of the Gouernor and mayor prte of the magestrats, shall call a Courte, that yt shall consist of the mayor prte of Freemen that are prsent or their deputyes,

wth a Moderator chosen by the: In wch said Generall Courts shall consist the supreme power of the Comonwelth, and they only shall haue power to make laws or repeale the, to graunt leuyes, to admitt of Freemen, dispose of lands vndisposed of, to seuerall Townes or prsons, and also shall haue power to call ether Courte or Magestrate or any other prson whatsoeuer into question for any misdemeanour, and may for just causes displace or deale otherwise according to the nature of the offence; and also may deale in any other matter that concerns the good of this comon welth, excepte election of Magestrats, wch shall be done by the whole boddy of Freemen: In wch Courte the Gouernour or Moderator shall haue power to order the Courte to giue liberty of spech, and silence vnceasonable and disorderly speakeings, to put all things to voate, and in case the vote be equall to haue the casting voice. But non of these Courts shall be adiorned or dissolued wthout the consent of the maior prte of the Court.

11. It is ordered, sentenced and decreed, that when any Generall Courte vppon the occations of the Comonwelth haue agreed vppon any sume or somes of mony to be leuyed vppon the seuerall Townes wthin this Jurisdiction, that a Comittee be chosen to sett out and appoynt wt shall be the prportion of euery Towne to pay of the said leuy, prvided the Comittees be made vp of an equall nuber out of each Towne.

14th January, 1638, the 11 Orders abouesaid are voted.

The Oath of the Gournor, for the [*Prsent*]

I N. M. being now chosen to be Gournor wthin this Jurisdiction, for the yeare ensueing, and vntil a new be chosen, doe sweare by the greate and dreadfull name of the everliueing God, to prmote the publicke good and peace of the same, according to the best of my skill; as also will mayntayne all lawfull priuiledges of this Comonwealth; as also that all wholsome lawes that are or shall be made by lawfull authority here established, be duly executed; and will further the execution of Justice according to the rule of Gods word; so helpe me God, in the name of the Lo: Jesus Christ.

The Oath of a Magestrate, for the Prsent

I, N. M. being chosen a Magestrate wthin this Jurisdiction for the yeare ensueing, doe sweare by the great and dreadfull name of the euerliueing God; to prmote the publike good and peace of the same, according to the best of my skill, and that I will mayntayne all the lawfull priuiledges thereof according to my vnderstanding, as also assist in the execution of all such wholsome lawes as are made or shall be made by lawfull authority heare established, and will further the execution of Justice for the tyme aforesaid according to the righteous rule of Gods word; so helpe me God, etc.

MARYLAND ACT FOR THE LIBERTIES
OF THE PEOPLE, 1639

Commentary

The Charters granted after the right of representative government was recognized in Virginia provided for self-government through elected legislatures. This was true for example, of the Charter of Massachusetts Bay, 1629 (though it took some years before the colonists established fully their right to participate in the Massachusetts legislative process), and the Charter of Maryland, 1632. Those two Charters created the second and third self-governing assemblies in the colonies, and set the pattern which prevailed until the Revolution itself (with the brief interruption of the attempt at Stuart autocracy from 1684-1688). In Maryland particularly, the Charter provided directly for the setting up of a legislative assembly and the settlers were immediately able to participate in the political process.

The next step was for the settlers themselves, acting through their elected legislators to go beyond the bare statement in the early Charters that they were entitled to the rights of Englishmen, and begin the process of giving those rights specific content. They did this by the enactment of statutes which sought to define the basic rights to which the colonists were entitled. As such, these statutes were the direct American ancestors of the federal Bill of Rights. The most famous of these statutes was the Massachusetts Body of Liberties, 1641 (*infra* p. 71). It is not however, usually realized that before that law was enacted, the Maryland General Assembly approved the 1639 Act for the Liberties of the People. Elementary though it was, that document may rightly be considered the first American Bill of Rights.

The 1639 Maryland Act was a product of the struggle for popular government which was a feature of political life in all the colonies. Lord Baltimore, the Proprietor of Maryland, intended the primary role in legislation to remain with himself, with the popular Assembly limited to approving laws proposed by him. Assemblies (as Baltimore put it in instructions to his son, Charles) were to be called "for the giving of the advice, assent and approbation by the freemen to such acts as shall be by us att any time ordayned made and enacted." The very first Assembly rejected such a restricted role and drew up laws of its own to govern the Colony. By 1639, Baltimore had acceded to the desires of the colonists. The Assembly was thus able to vote the 1639 Act for the Liberties of the People on its own initiative.

Magna Carta was, of course, the direct source of the 1639 Maryland statute, which starts by reaffirming the principle that the inhabitants of the Colony are entitled to all the rights which Englishmen enjoy by virtue of

67

English law. It makes the important point that the common law is part of the English heritage in this respect. It then goes on to state what is essentially a paraphrase of the most important provision of Magna Carta, providing that no colonist is to be adversely affected in his person or property except "according to the Laws of this province." This phrase provides an American link between the original language of Magna Carta and the Due Process Clause that exists in modern American Constitutions.

We should not underestimate the significance of the 1639 Act, particularly in a Proprietary Colony like Maryland. To us, it may seem only a truistic restatement of Chapter 39 of Magna Carta. Yet even such a restatement was an act of consequence at a time when Charles I was pushing his theory of Stuart absolutism to its virtual breaking point. A later attempt by the Maryland Assembly to adopt Magna Carta was disallowed by the Crown because the liberties of the Great Charter might be inconsistent with the King's prerogative. And that, it should be noted, was true even though the attempt was made after the Revolution of 1688 itself.

Maryland Act for the Liberties of the People, 1639*

Be it Enacted By the Lord Proprietarie of this Province of and with the advice and approbation of the ffreemen of the same that all the Inhabitants of this Province being Christians (Slaves excepted) Shall have and enjoy all such rights liberties immunities priviledges and free customs within this Province as any naturall born subject of England hath or ought to have or enjoy in the Realm of England by force or vertue of the common law or Statute Law of England (saveing in such Cases as the same are or may be altered or changed by the Laws and ordinances of this Province)

And Shall not be imprisoned nor disseissed or dispossessed of their freehold goods or Chattels or be out Lawed Exiled or otherwise destroyed fore judged or punished then according to the Laws of this province saveing to the Lord proprietarie and his heirs all his rights and prerogatives by reason of his domination and Seigniory over this Province and the people of the same This Act to Continue till the end of the next Generall Assembly

---

*W. H. Browne, ed., *Archives of Maryland: Proceedings and Acts of the General Assembly of Maryland, 1637–1664* (1883), Vol. 1, p. 41.

MASSACHUSETTS BODY OF LIBERTIES, 1641

Commentary

If the Maryland Act for the Liberties of the People was but a rudimentary reaffirmation of the basic principle of the first Virginia Charter and Chapter 39 of Magna Carta, the same was not true of the second Colonial enactment safeguarding the rights of the people: the 1641 Massachusetts Body of Liberties. That enactment was the first detailed American Charter of Liberties and, bearing in mind its early date, was amazingly detailed in its provisions. It served as the model for other colonies, notably for the New York Charter of Liberties, 1683 (*infra* p. 163) and the Pennsylvania Charter of Privileges, 1701 (*infra* p. 170). Of the documents discussed thus far, there is no doubt that the 1641 Massachusetts Act was the most important as a forerunner of the federal Bill of Rights.

Americans today tend to adopt a denigrating attitude toward their Puritan forebears. We forget what it meant to our development to have New England settled by a people who, however stiff-necked they were in their moral attitude, could call on the limitless resources of religious fervor to plant the seeds of colonization in a forbidding environment. It is all too easy to look through twentieth-century spectacles at the harshness of rule and narrow-mindedness of the men who settled Massachusetts. But they produced a polity which was exactly what may have been needed in the bleak New England of the seventeenth century. A government which produced a landmark of liberty as fundamental as the 1641 Body of Liberties has every claim to the gratitude of its descendants.

The Mayflower Compact of 1620 itself indicates clearly the intent of the first New England colonists to establish a government in their own words, "a civil Body Politick," with "such just and equal Laws, Ordinances, Acts, Constitutions, and Officers, from time to time, as shall be thought most meet and convenient for the general Good of the Colony." In 1629, the Charter of Massachusetts Bay provided for the settlement of the Colony by a Company similar to that which had received the Virginia Charter. The patentees themselves were joint Proprietors, who were given combined rights of both ownership and government. The Massachusetts Charter repeated the Virginia guarantee of the rights of Englishmen for the colonists and provided for the second self-governing assembly in the colonies.

Most important in the development of government in the Colony was the so-called Cambridge Agreement concluded by the patentees soon after the grant of the Charter. By it, they agreed to transfer control of the government to those who were to emigrate to the Colony, instead of remaining in England. Local government was thus transferred at the outset "to remain with us and others which shall inhabit upon the said plantation." Thus was instituted the fundamental policy of permitting the Colonial governments to reside in the colonies themselves.

In the summer of 1630, a large group of emigrants was transported to Massachusetts Bay, including John Winthrop as Governor. Winthrop and the other leaders resisted popular government and a struggle ensued which led to the institution of a system of representative government. The result was stated by Winthrop in a 1634 letter to Sir Nathaniel Rich: "Our Civill Government is mixt: The freemen choose the magistrates everye year . . . and at four Courts in the yeare three out of each towne (there being eight in all) doe assist the magistrates in making of lawes, imposing taxes, and disposing of lands: our Juries are chosen by the freemen of everye towne." As Winthrop stated in his *Journal* in 1646, the colonists possessed "power to make laws, to erect all sorts of magistracy, to correct, punish, pardon, govern and rule."

The enactment of the Body of Liberties was one of the results of the movement to replace the oligarchy established by the Company with a representative system of government. The development in this respect may be seen in the contemporary account contained in Winthrop's *Journal*—the relevant portions of which are printed following this Commentary. The people, says Winthrop, "had long desired a body of laws, and thought their condition very unsafe while so much powere rested in the discretion of magistrates." This is the typical complaint of men when a legal system is first being formed; the need is for a fixed body of law reduced to writing, so that the rights of the people will not be at the whim of magisterial discretion.

What the Massachusetts colonists called for (as Winthrop put it) was a code of laws which would guarantee "such liberties Immunities and priveledges as humanitie, Civilitie, and Christianitie call for as due to every man in his place and proportion." To give effect to the colonists' desire, a committee consisting of Winthrop and three others was appointed in 1635 to frame "a body of . . . fundamental laws." This committee did not produce the required code and a year later, another committee was appointed "to make a draught of laws . . . which may be the Fundamentals of this Commonwealth." A member of this committee prepared a draft code which Winthrop termed "a model of Moses his judicials." This draft was never voted on, but it led directly to the drafting of the code which was approved by the General Court in 1641, after it had been fully debated both in the legislature and by the different town meetings of the Colony.

The present-day observer can only wonder at the boldness of the Massachusetts men in their pioneering efforts at codifying and providing statutory protection for individual rights and liberties. That they well realized the fundamental nature of what they were doing is shown by the fact that, in Winthrop's words, they were acting "to frame a body of grounds of laws, in resemblance to a Magna Carta." The document they produced was (as Richard L. Perry tells us) a blend of Magna Carta itself, the common law, and the principles of Puritan theology—all molded by the experiences and circumstances of the colonists themselves.

When we bear in mind the date of its enactment, both the scope and specific provisions of the Body of Liberties are startling. Merely to provide for the liberties of women, children, servants, aliens, and dumb animals, as well as those of free men, and to go as far as to outlaw slavery as well was virtually unique in so early a code. In addition, to recognize that individual liberty depended, in the last resort, upon the courts, and to provide in detail for the rights of litigants and accused in judicial proceedings was as far-seeing as it was unprecedented at that time.

Many of the fundamental liberties later to be protected in the federal Bill of Rights were either safeguarded or anticipated in the 1641 Massachusetts statute. These include guarantees covering taking of property without just compensation (section 8), freedom of speech and petition at public meetings (section 12), bail (section 18), right of counsel (section 26), trial by jury (sections 29, 30, 31, 49, 50, 76), double jeopardy (section 42), and cruel and inhuman punishments (sections 43, 46).

In addition, the Body of Liberties contained provisions protecting life, liberty, and property in language derived from section 39 of Magna Carta (section 1); guaranteeing that every person "shall enjoy the same justice and law" (section 2) (anticipating by over two centuries the Equal Protection Clause of the Fourteenth Amendment); forbidding monopolies (section 9); outlawing imprisonment for debt (section 33); prohibiting torture (section 45); requiring at least two witnesses for the death penalty (section 47); as well as a right of free access to public records (section 48) (anticipating the Freedom of Information Act of 1966).

Most important was the fact that the Massachusetts Body of Liberties was the first American attempt to give effect to the basic notion that fundamental rights should be contained in a written instrument enacted by the people's representatives—and that at a time when England had only Magna Carta itself and the Petition of Rights as legislative foundations of freedom. The Massachusetts act came only two years later than the Maryland Act for the Liberties of the People. The 1641 Body of Liberties, however, constituted a quantum leap forward from the 1639 Maryland Act. With it, the American legislator was well on the way toward the conceptions of law and liberty that were ultimately to be embodied in the federal Bill of Rights.

Massachusetts Body of Liberties, 1641*

*A Coppie of the Liberties of the
Massachusets Colonie in New England*

The free fruition of such liberties Immunities and priveledges as humanitie, Civilitie, and Christianitie call for as due to every man in his place and proportion without impeachment and Infringement hath ever bene and ever

*W. H. Whitmore, *The Colonial Laws of Massachusetts, 1672* (1890), pp. 33–46.

will be the tranquillitie and Stabilitie of Churches and Commonwealths. **And** the deniall or deprivall thereof, the disturbance if not the ruine of both.

We hould it therefore our dutie and safetie whilst we are about the further establishing of this Government to collect and expresse all such freedomes as for present we foresee may concerne us, and our posteritie after us, And to ratify them with our sollemne consent.

We doe therefore this day religiously and unanimously decree and confirme these following Rites, liberties and priveledges concerneing our Churches, and Civill State to be respectively impartiallie and inviolably enjoyed and observed throughout our Jurisdiction for ever.

1. No mans life shall be taken away, no mans honour or good name shall be stayned, no mans person shall be arested, restrayned, banished, dismembred, nor any wayes punished, no man shall be deprived of his wife or children, no mans goods or estaite shall be taken away from him, nor any way indammaged under coulor of law or Countenance of Authoritie, unlesse it be by vertue or equitie of some expresse law of the Country waranting the same, established by a generall Court and sufficiently published, or in case of the defect of a law in any parteculer case by the word of god. And in Capitall cases, or in cases concerning dismembring or banishment, according to that word to be judged by the Generall Court.

2. Every person within this Jurisdiction, whether Inhabitant or forreiner shall enjoy the same justice and law, that is generall for the plantation, which we constitute and execute one towards another without partialitie or delay.

3. No man shall be urged to take any oath or subscribe any articles, covenants or remonstrance, of a publique and Civill nature, but such as the Generall Court hath considered, allowed, and required.

4. No man shall be punished for not appearing at or before any Civill Assembly, Court, Councell, Magistrate, or Officer, nor for the omission of any office or service, if he shall be necessarily hindred by any apparent Act or providence of God, which he could neither foresee nor avoid. Provided that this law shall not prejudice any person of his just cost or damage, in any civill action.

5. No man shall be compelled to any publique worke or service unlesse the presse be grounded upon some act of the generall Court, and have reasonable allowance therefore.

6. No man shall be pressed in person to any office, worke, warres or other publique service, that is necessarily and suffitiently exempted by any naturall or personall inpediment, as by want of yeares, greatnes of age, defect of minde, fayling of sences, or impotencie of Lymbes.

7. No man shall be compelled to goe out of the limits of this plantation upon any offensive warres which this Commonwealth or any of our freinds or confederats shall volentarily undertake. But onely upon such vindictive and defensive warres in our owne behalfe or the behalfe of our freinds and confederats as shall be enterprized by the Counsell and consent of a Court generall, or by Authority derived from the same.

8. No mans Cattel or goods of what kinde soever shall be pressed or taken for any publique use or service, unlesse it be by warrant grounded upon some act of the generall Court, nor without such reasonable prices and hire as the ordinarie rates of the Countrie do afford. And if his Cattle or goods shall perish or suffer damage in such service, the owner shall be suffitiently recompenced.

9. No monopolies shall be granted or allowed amongst us, but of such new Inventions that are profitable to the Countrie, and that for a short time.

10. All our lands and heritages shall be free from all fines and licences upon Alienations, and from all hariotts, wardships, Liveries, Primerseisins, yeare day and wast, Escheates, and forfeitures, upon the deaths of parents or Ancestors, be they naturall, casuall or Juditiall.

11. All persons which are of the age of 21 yeares, and of right understanding and meamories, whether excommunicate or condemned shall have full power and libertie to make there wills and testaments, and other lawfull alienations of theire lands and estates.

12. Every man whether Inhabitant or fforreiner, free or not free shall have libertie to come to any publique Court, Councel, or Towne meeting, and either by speech or writing to move any lawfull, seasonable, and materiall question, or to present any necessary motion, complaint, petition, Bill or information, whereof that meeting hath proper cognizance, so it be done in convenient time, due order, and respective manner.

13. No man shall be rated here for any estaite or revenue he hath in England, or in any forreine partes till it be transported hither.

14. Any Conveyance or Alienation of land or other estaite what so ever, made by any woman that is married, any childe under age, Ideott or distracted person, shall be good if it be passed and ratified by the consent of a generall Court.

15. All Covenous or fraudulent Alienations or Conveyances of lands, tenements, or any hereditaments, shall be of no validitie to defeate any man from due debts or legacies, or from any just title, clame or possession, of that which is so fraudulently conveyed.

16. Every Inhabitant that is an howse holder shall have free fishing and fowling in any great ponds and Bayes, Coves and Rivers, so farre as the sea ebbes and flowes within the presincts of the towne where they dwell, unlesse the free men of the same Towne or the Generall Court have otherwise appropriated them, provided that this shall not be extended to give leave to any man to come upon others proprietie without there leave.

17. Every man of or within this Jurisdiction shall have free libertie, notwithstanding any Civill power to remove both himselfe, and his familie at their pleasure out of the same, provided there be no legall impediment to the contrarie.

Rites Rules and Liberties concerning Juditiall proceedings

18. No mans person shall be restrained or imprisoned by any Authority

whatsoever, before the law hath sentenced him thereto, If he can put in sufficient securitie, bayle or mainprise, for his appearance, and good behaviour in the meane time, unlesse it be in Crimes Capital, and Contempts in open Court, and in such cases where some expresse act of Court doth allow it.

19. If in a generall Court any miscariage shall be amongst the Assistants when they are by themselves that may deserve an Admonition or fine under 20 sh. it shall be examined and sentenced among themselves, If amongst the Deputies when they are by themselves, It shall be examined and sentenced amongst themselves, If it be when the whole Court is togeather, it shall be judged by the whole Court, and not severallie as before.

20. If any which are to sit as Judges in any other Court shall demeane themselves offensively in the Court, the rest of the Judges present shall have power to censure him for it, if the cause be of a high nature it shall be presented to and censured at the next superior Court.

21. In all cases where the first summons are not served six dayes before the Court, and the cause breifly specified in the warrant, where appearance is to be made by the partie summoned, it shall be at his libertie whether he will appeare or no, except all cases that are to be handled in Courts suddainly called, upon extraordinary occassions, In all cases where there appeares present and urgent cause Any Assistant or officer appointed shal have power to make out Attaichments for the first summons.

22. No man in any suit or action against an other shall falsely pretend great debts or damages to vex his Adversary, if it shall appeare any doth so, The Court shall have power to set a reasonable fine on his head.

23. No man shall be adjudged to pay for detaining any debt from any Crediter above eight pounds in the hundred for one yeare, And not above that rate proportionable for all somes what so ever, neither shall this be a coulour or countenance to allow any usurie amongst us contrarie to the law of god.

24. In all Trepasses or damages done to any man or men, If it can be proved to be done by the meere default of him or them to whome the trespasse is done, It shall be judged no trespasse, nor any damage given for it.

25. No Summons pleading Judgement, or any kinde of proceeding in Court or course of Justice shall be abated, arested or reversed upon any kinde of cercumstantiall errors or mistakes, If the person and cause be rightly understood and intended by the Court.

26. Every man that findeth himselfe unfit to plead his owne cause in any Court shall have Libertie to imploy any man against whom the Court doth not except, to helpe him, Provided he give him noe fee or reward for his paines. This shall not exempt the partie him selfe from Answering such Questions in person as the Court shall thinke meete to demand of him.

27. If any plantife shall give into any Court a declaration of his cause in writeing, The defendant shall also have libertie and time to give in his

answer in writeing, And so in all further proceedings betwene partie and partie, So it doth not further hinder the dispach of Justice then the Court shall be willing unto.

28. The plantife in all Actions brought in any Court shall have libertie to withdraw his Action, or to be nonsuited before the Jurie hath given in their verdict, in which case he shall alwaies pay full cost and chardges to the defendant, and may afterwards renew his suite at an other Court if he please.

29. In all Actions at law it shall be the libertie of the plantife and defendant by mutual consent to choose whether they will be tryed by the Bench or by a Jurie, unlesse it be where the law upon just reason hath otherwise determined. The like libertie shall be granted to all persons in Criminall cases.

30. It shall be in the libertie both of plantife and defendant, and likewise every delinquent (to be judged by a Jurie) to challenge any of Jurors. And if his challenge be found just and reasonable by the Bench, or the rest of the Jurie, as the challenger shall choose it shall be allowed him, and tales de cercumstantibus impaneled in their room.

31. In all cases where evidence is so obscure or defective that the Jurie cannot clearly and safely give a positive verdict, whether it be a grand or petit Jurie, It shall have libertie to give a non Liquit, or a spetiall verdict, in which last, that is in a spetiall verdict, the Judgement of the cause shall be left to the Court, and all Jurors shall have libertie in matters of fact if they cannot finde the maine issue, yet to finde and present in their verdict so much as they can, If the Bench and Jurors shall so differ at any time about their verdict that either of them cannot proceede with peace of conscience the case shall be referred to the Generall Court, who shall take the question from both and determine it.

32. Every man shall have libertie to replevy his Cattell or goods impounded, distreined, seised, or extended; unlesse it be upon execution after Judgement, and in paiment of fines. Provided he puts in good securitie to prosecute his replevin, And to satisfie such demands as his Adversary shall recover against him in Law.

33. No mans person shall be Arrested, or imprisoned upon execution or judgment for any debt or fine, If the law can finde competent meanes of satisfaction otherwise from his estaite, and if not his person may be arrested and imprisoned where he shall be kept at his owne charge, not the plantife's till satisfaction be made: unlesse the Court that had cognizance of the cause or some superior Court shall otherwise provide.

34. If any man shall be proved and Judged a commen Barrator vexing others with unjust frequent and endlesse suites, It shall be in the power of Courts both to denie him the benefit of the law, and to punish him for his Barrantry.

35. No mans Corne nor hay that is in the feild or upon the Cart, nor his

garden stuffe, nor any thing subject to present decay, shall be taken in any distresse, unles he that takes it doth presently bestow it where it may not be imbesled nor suffer spoile or decay, or give securitie to satisfie the worth thereof if it comes to any harme.

36. It shall be in the libertie of every man cast condemned or sentenced in any cause in any Inferior Court, to make their Appeale to the Court of Assistants, provided they tender their appeale and put in securitie to prosecute it before the Court be ended wherein they were condemned, And within six dayes next ensuing put in good securitie before some Assistant to satisfie what his Adversarie shall recover against him; And if the cause be of a Criminall nature, for his good behaviour, and appearance, And everie man shall have libertie to complaine to the Generall Court of any Injustice done him in any Court of Assistants or other.

37. In all cases where it appeares to the Court that the plantife hath wilingly and witingly done wronge to the defendant in commenceing and prosecuting any action or complaint against him, They shall have power to impose upon him a proportionable fine to the use of the defendant, or accused person, for his false complaint or clamor.

38. Everie man shall have libertie to Record in the publique Rolles of any Court any Testimony given upon oath in the same Court, or before two Assistants, or any deede or evidence legally confirmed there to remaine in perpetuam rei memoriam, that is for perpetuall memoriall or evidence upon occasion.

39. In all actions both reall and personall betweene partie and partie, the Court shall have power to respite execution for a convenient time, when in their prudence they see just cause so to doe.

40. No Conveyance, Deede, or promise whatsoever shall be of validitie, If it be gotten by Illegal violence, imprisonment, threatenings, or any kinde of forcible compulsion called Dures.

41. Everie man that is to Answere for any Criminall cause, whether he be in prison or under bayle, his cause shall be heard and determined at the next Court that hath proper Cognizance thereof, And may be done without prejudice of Justice.

42. No man shall be twise sentenced by Civill Justice for one and the same Crime, offence, or Trespasse.

43. No man shall be beaten with above 40 stripes, nor shall any true gentleman, nor any man equall to a gentleman be punished with whipping, unles his crime be very shamefull, and his course of life vitious and profligate.

44. No man condemned to dye shall be put to death within fower dayes next after his condemnation, unles the Court see spetiall cause to the contrary, or in case of martiall law, nor shall the body of any man so put to death be unburied 12 howers, unlesse it be in case of Anatomie.

45. No man shall be forced by Torture to confesse any Crime against himselfe nor any other unlesse it be in some Capitall case where he is first fullie convicted by cleare and suffitient evidence to be guilty, After which if the cause be of that nature, That it is very apparent there be other conspiratours, or confederates with him, Then he may be tortured, yet not with such Tortures as be Barbarous and inhumane.

46. For bodilie punishments we allow amongst us none that are inhumane Barbarous or cruel.

47. No man shall be put to death without the testimony of two or three witnesses or that which is equivalent thereunto.

48. Every Inhabitant of the Country shall have free libertie to search and veewe any Rooles, Records, or Regesters of any Court or office except the Councell, And to have a transcript or exemplification thereof written examined, and signed by the hand of the officer of the office paying the appointed fees therefore.

49. No free man shall be compelled to serve upon Juries above two Courts in a yeare, except grand Jurie men, who shall hould two Courts together at the least.

50. All Jurors shall be chosen continuallie by the freemen of the Towne where they dwell.

51. All Associates selected at any time to Assist the Assistants in Inferior Courts shall be nominated by the Townes belonging to that Court, by orderly agreement amonge themselves.

52. Children, Idiots, Distracted persons, and all that are strangers, or new commers to our plantation, shall have such allowances and dispensations in any Cause whether Criminall or other as religion and reason require.

53. The age of discretion for passing away of lands or such kinde of herediments, or for giveing of votes, verdicts or Sentence in any Civill Courts or causes, shall be one and twentie yeares.

54. Whensoever anything is to be put to vote, any sentence to be pronounced, or any other matter to be proposed, or read in any Court or Assembly, If the president or moderator thereof shall refuse to performe it, the Major parte of the members of that Court or Assembly shall have power to appoint any other meete man of them to do it, And if there be just cause to punish him that should and would not.

55. In all suites or Actions in any Court, the plaintife shall have libertie to make all the titles and claims to that he sues for he can. And the Defendant shall have libertie to plead all the pleas he can in answere to them, and the Court shall judge according to the entire evidence of all.

56. If any man shall behave himselfe offensively at any Towne meeting, the rest of the freemen then present, shall have power to sentence him for his offence. So be it the mulct or penaltie exceede not twentie shilings.

57. Whensoever any person shall come to any very suddaine untimely and

unnaturall death, Some assistant, or the Constables of that Towne shall forthwith sumon a Jury of twelve free men to inquire of the cause and manner of their death, and shall present a true verdict thereof to some neere Assistant, or the next Court to be helde for that Towne upon their oath.

Liberties more peculiarlie concerning the free men

58. Civill Authoritie hath power and libertie to see the peace, ordinances and Rules of Christ observed in every church according to his word. so it be done in a Civill and not in an Ecclesiastical way.

59. Civill Authoritie hath power and libertie to deale with any Church member in a way of Civill Justice, notwithstanding any Church relation, office or interest.

60. No church censure shall degrad or depose any man from any Civill dignitie, office, or Authoritie he shall have in the Commonwealth.

61. No Magestrate, Juror, Officer, or other man shall be bound to informe present or reveale any private crim or offence, wherein there is no perill or danger to this plantation or any member thereof, when any necessarie tye of conscience binds him to secresie grounded upon the word of god, unlesse it be in case of testimony lawfully required.

62. Any Shire or Towne shall have libertie to choose their Deputies whom and where they please for the Generall Court. So be it they be free men, and have taken there oath of fealtie, and Inhabiting in this Jurisdiction.

63. No Governor, Deputy Governor, Assistant, Associate, or grand Jury man at any Court, nor any Deputie for the Generall Court shall at any time beare his owne chardges at any Court, but their necessary expenses shall be defrayed either by the Towne or Shire on whose service they are, or by the Country in generall.

64. Everie Action betweene partie and partie, and proceedings against delinquents in Criminall causes shall be briefly and destinctly entered on the Rolles of every Court by the Recorder thereof. That such actions be not afterwards brought againe to the vexation of any man.

65. No custome or prescription shall ever prevaile amongst us in any morall cause, our meaneing is maintaine anythinge that can be proved to bee morallie sinfull by the word of god.

66. The Freemen of every Towneship shall have power to make such by laws and constitutions as may concerne the wellfare of their Towne, provided they be not of a Criminall, but onely of a prudentiall nature, And that their penalties exceede not 20 sh. for one offence. And that they be not repugnant to the publique laws and orders of the Countrie. And if any Inhabitant shall neglect or refuse to observe them, they shall have power to levy the appointed penalties by distresse.

67. It is the constant libertie of the free men of this plantation to choose yearly at the Court of Election out of the freemen all the General officers of this Jurisdiction. If they please to dischardge them at the day of Election by

way of vote. They may do it without shewing cause. But if at any other generall Court, we hould it due justice, that the reasons thereof be alleadged and proved. By Generall officers we meane, our Governor, Deputy Governor, Assistants, Treasurer, Generall of our warres. And our Admirall at Sea, and such as are or hereafter may be of the like genrall nature.

68. It is the libertie of the freemen to choose such deputies for the Generall Court out of themselves, either in their owne Townes or elsewhere as they judge fitest. And because we cannot foresee what varietie and weight of occasions may fall into future consideration, And what counsells we may stand in neede of, we decree. That the Deputies (to attend the Generall Court in the behalfe of the Countrie) shall not any time be stated or inacted, but from Court to Court, or at the most but for one yeare, that the Countrie may have an Annuall libertie to do in that case what is most behoofefull for the best welfaire thereof.

69. No Generall Court shall be desolved or adjourned without the consent of the Major parte thereof.

70. All Freemen called to give any advise, vote, verdict, or sentence in any Court, Counsell, or Civill Assembly, shall have full freedome to doe it according to their true Judgements and Consciences, So it be done orderly and inofensively for the manner.

71. The Governor shall have a casting voice whensoever an Equi vote shall fall out in the Court of Assistants, or generall assembly, So shall the presedent or moderator have in all Civill Courts or Assemblies.

72. The Governor and Deputy Governor Joyntly consenting or any three Assistants concurring in consent shall have power out of Court to reprive a condemned malefactour, till the next quarter or generall Court. The generall Court onely shall have power to pardon a condemned malefactor.

73. The Generall Court hath libertie and Authoritie to send out any member of this Comanwealth of what qualitie, condition or office whatsoever into forreine parts about any publique message or Negotiation. Provided the partie sent be acquainted with the affaire he goeth about, and be willing to undertake the service.

74. The freemen of every Towne or Towneship, shall have full power to choose yearly or for lesse time out of themselves a convenient number of fitt men to order the planting or prudentiall occasions of that Town, according to Instructions given them in writeing, Provided nothing be done by them contrary to the publique laws and orders of the Countrie, provided also the number of such select persons be not above nine.

75. It is and shall be the libertie of any member or members of any Court, Councell or Civill Assembly in cases of makeing or executing any order or law, that properlie concerne religion, or any cause capitall, or warres, or Subscription to any publique Articles or Remonstrance, in case they cannot in Judgement and conscience consent to that way the Major vote or suffrage goes, to make their contra Remonstrance or protestation in speech or

writeing, and upon request to have their dissent recorded in the Rolles of that Court. So it be done Christianlie and respectively for the manner. And their dissent onely be entered without the reasons thereof, for the avoiding of tediousness.

76. Whensoever any Jurie of trialls or Jurours are not cleare in their Judgements or consciences conserneing any cause wherein they are to give their verdict, They shall have libertie in open Court to advise with any man they thinke fitt to resolve or direct them, before they give in their verdict.

77. In all cases wherein any freeman is to give his vote, be it in point of Election, makeing constitutions and orders, or passing sentence in any case of Judicature or the like, if he cannot see reason to give it positively one way or an other, he shall have libertie to be silent, and not pressed to a determined vote.

78. The Generall or publique Treasure or any parte thereof shall never be exspended but by the appointment of a Generall Court, nor any Shire Treasure, but by the appointment of the freemen thereof, nor any Towne Treasurie but by the freemen of that Towneship.

Liberties of Woemen

79. If any man at his death shall not leave his wife a competent portion of his estaite, upon just complaint made to the Generall Court she shall be relieved.

80. Everie marryed woeman shall be free from bodilie correction or stripes by her husband, unlesse it be in his owne defence upon her assalt. If there be any just cause of correction complaint shall be made to Authoritie assembled in some Court, from which onely she shall receive it.

Liberties of Children

81. When parents dye intestate, the Elder sonne shall have a doble portion of his whole estate reall and personall, unlesse the Generall Court upon just cause alleadged shall Judge otherwise.

82. When parents dye intestate haveing noe heires males of their bodies their Daughters shall inherit as copartners, unles the Generall Court upon just reason shall judge otherwise.

83. If any parents shall wilfullie and unreasonably deny any childe timely or convenient mariage, or shall exercise any unnaturall severitie towards them, such childeren shall have free libertie to complaine to Authoritie for redresse.

84. No Orphan dureing their minoritie which was not committed to tuition or service by the parents in their life time shall afterwards be absolutely disposed of by any kindred, freind, Executor, Towneship, or Church, nor by themselves without the conseut of some Court, wherein two Assistants at least shall be present.

Liberties of Servants

85. If any servants shall flee from the Tiranny and crueltie of their masters to the howse of any freeman of the same Towne, they shall be there protected and susteyned till due order be taken for their relife. Provided due notice thereof be speedily given to their maisters from whom they fled. And the next Assistant or Constable where the partie flying is harboured.

86. No servant shall be put of for above a yeare to any other neither in the life time of their maister nor after their death by their Executors or Administrators unlesse it be by consent of Authoritie assembled in some Court or two Assistants.

87. If any man smite out the eye or tooth of his man-servant, or maid servant, or otherwise mayme or much disfigure him, unlesse it be by meere casualtie, he shall let them goe free from his service. And shall have such further recompense as the Court shall allow him.

88. Servants that have served deligentlie and faithfully to the benefitt of their maisters seaven yeares, shall not be sent away emptie. And if any have bene unfaithfull, negligent or unprofitable in their service, notwithstanding the good usage of their maisters, they shall not be dismissed till they have made satisfaction according to the Judgement of Authoritie.

Liberties of Forreiners and Strangers

89. If any people of other Nations professing the true Christian Religion shall flee to us from the Tiranny or oppression of their persecutors, or from famyne, warres, or the like necessary and compulsarie cause, They shall be entertayned and succoured amongst us, according to that power and prudence god shall give us.

90. If any ships or other vessels, be it freind or enemy, shall suffer shipwrack upon our Coast, there shall be no violence or wrong offerred to their persons or goods. But their persons shall be harboured, and relieved, and their goods preserved in safety till Authoritie may be certified thereof, and shall take further order therein.

91. There shall never be any bond slaverie, villinage or Captivitie amongst us unles it be lawfull Captives taken in just warres, and such strangers as willingly selle themselves or are sold to us. And these shall have all the liberties and Christian usages which the law of god established in Israell concerning such persons doeth morally require. This exempts none from servitude who shall be Judged thereto by Authoritie.

Off the Bruite Creature

92. No Man shall exercise any Tirranny or Crueltie towards any bruite Creature which are usuallie kept for man's use.

93. If any man shall have occasion to leade or drive Cattel from place to place that is far of, so that they be weary, or hungry, or fall sick, or lambe, It shall be lawfull to rest or refresh them, for a competent time, in any open place that is not Corne, meadow, or inclosed for some peculiar use.

Capitall Laws

94. a. If any man after legall conviction shall have or worship any other god, but the lord god, he shall be put to death.

Dut. 13. 6, 10.
Dut. 17. 2, 6.
Ex. 22. 20.

b. If any man or woeman be a witch, (that is hath or consulteth with a familiar spirit,) They shall be put to death.

Ex. 22. 28.
Lev. 20. 27.
Dut. 18. 10.

c. If any man shall Blaspheme the name of god, the father, Sonne or Holie ghost, with direct, expresse, presumptuous or high handed blasphemie, or shall curse god in the like manner, he shall be put to death.

Lev. 24. 15, 16.

d. If any person committ any wilfull murther, which is manslaughter, committed upon premeditated mallice, hatred, or Crueltie, not in a mans necessarie and just defence, nor by meere casualtie against his will, he shall be put to death.

Ex. 21. 12.
Numb. 35. 13, 14, 30, 31.

e. If any person slayeth an other suddaienly in his anger or Crueltie of passion, he shall be put to death.

Numb. 25. 20, 21.
Lev. 24. 17.

f. If any person shall slay an other through guile, either by poysoning or other such divelish practice, he shall be put to death.

Ex. 21. 14.

g. If any man or woeman shall lye with any beaste or bruite creature by Carnall Copulation, They shall surely be put to death. And the beast shall be slaine and buried and not eaten.

Lev. 20. 15, 16.

h. If any man lyeth with mankinde as he lyeth with a woeman, both of them have committed abhomination, they both shall surely be put to death.

Lev. 20. 13.

i. If any person committeth Adultery with a maried or espoused wife, the Adulterer and Adulteresse shall surely be put to death.

Lev. 20. 19, and 18, 20.
Dut. 22. 23, 24.

j. If any man stealeth a man or mankinde, he shall surely be put to death.

Ex. 21. 16.

k. If any man rise up by false witnes, wittingly and of purpose to take away any mans life, he shall be put to death.

Deut. 19. 16, 18, 19.

l. If any man shall conspire and attempt any invasion, insurrection, or publique rebellion against our commonwealth, or shall indeavour to surprize any Towne or Townes, fort or forts therein, or shall treacherously and perfediouslie attempt the alteration and subversion of our frame of politie or Government fundamentallie, he shall be put to death.

A Declaration of the Liberties the Lord Jesus hath given to the Churches

95. a. All the people of god within this Jurisdiction who are not in a church way, and be orthodox in Judgement, and not scandalous in life, shall have full libertie to gather themselves into a Church Estaite. Provided they doe it in a Christian way, with due observation of the rules of Christ revealed in his word.

b. Every Church hath full libertie to exercise all the ordinances of god, according to the rules of scripture.

c. Every Church hath free libertie of Election and ordination of all their officers from time to time, provided they be able, pious and orthodox.

d. Every Church hath free libertie of Admission, Recommendation, Dismission, and Expulsion, or deposall of their officers and members, upon due cause, with free exercise of the Discipline and Censures of Christ according to the rules of his word.

e. No Injunctions are to be put upon any Church, Church officers or member in point of Doctrine, worship or Discipline, whether for substance or cercumstance besides the Institutions of the lord.

f. Every Church of Christ hath freedome to celebrate dayes of fasting and prayer, and of thanksgiveing according to the word of god.

g. The Elders of Churches have free libertie to meete monthly, Quarterly, or otherwise, in convenient numbers and places, for conferences and consultations about Christian and Church questions and occasions.

h. All Churches have libertie to deale with any of their members in a church way that are in the hand of Justice. So it be not to retard or hinder the course thereof.

i. Every Church hath libertie to deale with any magestrate, Deputie of Court or other officer what soe ever that is a member in a church way in case of apparent and just offence given in their places, so it be done with due observance and respect.

j. Wee allowe private meetings for edification in religion amongst Christians of all sortes of people. So it be without just offence for number, time, place, and other cercumstances.

k. For the preventing and removeing of errour and offence that may grow and spread in any of the Churches in this Jurisdiction, and for the preserveing of trueith and peace in the several churches within themselves, and for the maintenance and exercise of brotherly communion, amongst all the churches in the Countrie, It is allowed and ratified, by the Authoritie of this Generall Court as a lawfull libertie of the Churches of Christ. That once in every month of the yeare (when the season will beare it). It shall be lawfull for the minesters and Elders, of the Churches neere adjoyneing together, with any other of the breetheren with the consent of the churches to assemble by course in each severall Church one after an other. To the intent after the preaching of the word by such a minister as shall be requested thereto by the Elders of the church where the Assembly is held, The rest of the day may be spent in publique Christian Conference about the discussing and resolveing of any such doubts and cases of conscience concerning matter of doctrine or worship or government of the church as shall be propounded by any of the Breetheren of that church, with leave also to any other Brother to propound his objections or answeres for further satisfaction according to the word of god. Provided that the whole action be guided and moderated by the Elders of the Church where the Assemblie is helde, or by such others as they shall appoint. And that no thing be concluded and imposed by way of Authoritie from one or more Churches upon an other, but onely by way of Brotherly conference and consultations. That the trueth may be searched out to the satisfying of every mans conscience in the sight of god according his worde. And because such an Assembly and the worke theirof can not be duely attended to if other lectures be held in that same weeke. It is therefore agreed with the consent of the Churches. That in that weeke when such an Assembly is held, All the lectures in all the neighbouring Churches for that weeke shall be forborne. That so the publique service of Christ in this more solemne Assembly may be transacted with greater deligence and attention.

96. Howsoever these above specified rites, freedomes, Immunities, Authorities and priveledges, both Civill and Ecclesiastical are expressed onely under the name and title of Liberties, and not in the exact form of Laws or Statutes, yet we do with one consent fullie Authorise, and earnestly intreate all that are and shall be in Authoritie to consider them as laws, and not to faile to inflict condigne and proportionable punishments upon every man impartiallie, that shall infringe or violate any of them.

97. Wee likewise give full power and libertie to any person that shall at any time be denyed or deprived of any of them, to commence and prosecute their suite, Complaint or action against any man that shall so doe in any Court that hath proper Cognizance or judicature thereof.

98. Lastly because our dutie and desire is to do nothing suddainlie which fundamentally concerne us, we decree that these rites and liberties, shall be Audably read and deliberately weighed at every Generall Court that shall be held, within three yeares next insueing. And such of them as shall not be altered or repealed they shall stand so ratified, That no man shall infringe them without due punishment.

And if any Generall Court within these next thre yeares shall faile or forget to reade and consider them as abovesaid. The Governor and Deputy Governor for the time being, and every Assistant present at such Courts shall forfeite 20sh. a man, and everie Deputie 10sh. a man for each neglect, which shall be paid out of their proper estate, and not by the Country or the Townes which choose them, and whensoever there shall arise any question in any Court amonge the Assistants and Associates thereof about the explanation of these Rites and liberties, The Generall Court onely shall have power to interprett them.

John Winthrop's Journal, 1635-1646*

[1635] The deputies having conceived great danger to our state, in regard that our magistrates, for want of positive laws, in many cases, might proceed according to their discretions, it was agreed that some men should be appointed to frame a body of grounds of laws, in resemblance to a Magna Charta, which, being allowed by some of the ministers, and the general court, should be received for fundamental laws.

* * *

[1636] Mr. Cotton, being requested by the general court, with some other ministers, to assist some of the magistrates in compiling a body of fundamental laws, did this court, present a model of Moses his judicials, compiled in an exact method, which were taken into further consideration till the next general court.

* * *

[1639] The people had long desired a body of laws, and thought their condition very unsafe, while so much power rested in the discretion of magistrates. Divers attempts had been made at former courts, and the matter referred to some of the magistrates and some of the elders; but still it came to no effect; for, being committed to the care of many, whatsoever was done by some, was still disliked or neglected by others. At last it was referred to Mr. Cotton and Mr. Nathaniel Warde, etc., and each of them framed a model, which were presented to this general court, and by them committed to the governor and deputy and some others to consider of, and so prepare it for the court in the 3d month next. Two great reasons there were, which caused most of the magistrates and some of the elders not to be very forward in this matter. One was, want of sufficient experience of the nature and disposition of the people, considered with the condition of the country and other circumstances, which made them conceive, that such laws would be fittest for us, which should arise pro re nata upon occasions, etc., and so the laws of England and other states grew, and therefore the fundamental laws of England are called customs, consuetudines. 2. For that it would professedly transgress the limits of our charter, which provide, we shall make no laws repugnant to the laws of England, and that we were assured we must do. But to raise up laws by practice and custom had been no transgression; as in our church discipline, and in matters of marriage, to make a law, that marriages should not be solemnized by ministers, is repugnant to the laws of England; but to bring it to a custom by practice for the magistrates to perform it, is no law made repugnant, etc. At length (to satisfy the people) it proceeded, and

*J. K. Hosmer, ed., *Winthrop's Journal* (1908), Vol. 1, pp. 151, 196, 323–24; Vol. 2, pp. 48–49, 290–304.

the two models were digested with divers alterations and additions, and abbreviated and sent to every town, (12,) to be considered of first by the magistrates and elders, and then to be published by the constables to all the people, that if any man should think fit, that any thing therein ought to be altered, he might acquaint some of the deputies therewith against the next court.

*   *   *

[1641] This session continued three weeks, and established 100 laws, which were called the Body of Liberties. They had been composed by Mr. Nathaniel Ward, (sometime pastor of the church of Ipswich: he had been a minister in England, and formerly a student and practiser in the course of the common law,) and had been revised and altered by the court, and sent forth into every town to be further considered of, and now again in this court, they were revised, amended, and presented, and so established for three years, by that experience to have them fully amended and established to be perpetual.

*   *   *

[1646] Then it was propounded to consideration, in what relation we stood to the state of England; whether our government was founded upon our charter, or not; if so, then what subjection we owed to that state. The magistrates delivered their minds first, that the elders might have the better light for their advice. All agreed that our charter was the foundation of our government, and thereupon some thought, that we were so subordinate to the parliament, as they might countermand our orders and judgments, etc., and therefore advised, that we should petition the parliament for enlargement of power, etc. Others conceived otherwise, and that though we owed allegiance and subjection to them, as we had always professed, and by a copy of a petition which we presented to the lords of the privy council when they sent for our charter anno [blank] then read in the court, did appear, yet by our charter we had absolute power of government; for thereby we have power to make laws, to erect all sorts of magistracy, to correct, punish, pardon, govern, and rule the people absolutely, which word implies two things, 1. a perfection of parts, so as we are thereby furnished with all parts of government. 2. it implies a self-sufficiency, quoad subjectam materiam, and ergo should not need the help of any superior power, either general governor, or, etc., to complete our government; yet we did owe allegiance and subjection, 1. because our commonwealth was founded upon the power of that state, and so had been always carried on, 2. in regard of the tenure of our lands, of the manor of East Greenwich, 3. we depended upon them for protection, etc., 4. for advice and counsel, when in great occasions we should crave it, 5. in the continuance of naturalization and free liegeance of ourselves and our posterity. Yet we might be still independent in respect of government, as

Normandy, Gascoyne, etc., were, though they had dependence upon the crown of France, and the kings of England did homage, etc., yet in point of government they were not dependent upon France. So likewise Burgundy, Flanders, etc. So the Hanse Towns in Germany, which have dependence upon the empire, etc. And such as are subject to the imperial chamber, in some great and general causes, they had their deputies there, and so were parties to all orders there.

And for that motion of petitioning, etc., it was answered, 1. that if we receive a new charter, that will be (*ipso facto*) a surrender of the old, 2. the parliament can grant none now, but by way of ordinance, and it may be questioned, whether the king will give his royal assent, considering how he hath taken displeasure against us, 3. if we take a charter from the parliament, we can expect no other than such as they have granted to us at Narragansett, and to others in other places, wherein they reserve a supreme power in all things.

The court having delivered their opinions, the elders desired time of consideration, and the next day they presented their advice, which was delivered by Mr. Allen, pastor of the church in Dedham, in divers articles, which (upon request) they delivered in writing as followeth.

*   *   *

The advice of the elders was as follows.

Concerning the question of our dependence upon England, we conceive,

1. That as we stand in near relation, so also in dependence upon that state, in divers respects, viz. 1. We have received the power of our government and other privileges, derived from thence by our charter. 2. We owe allegiance and fidelity to that state. 3. Erecting such a government as the patent prescribes and subjecting ourselves to the laws here ordained by that government, we therein yield subjection to the state of England. 4. We owe unto that state the fifth part of gold and silver ore that shall, etc. 5. We depend upon the state of England for protection and immunities of Englishmen, as free denization, etc.

2. We conceive, that in point of government we have granted by patent such full and ample power of choosing all officers that shall command and rule over us, of making all laws and rules of our obedience, and of a full and final determination of all cases in the administration of justice, that no appeals or other ways of interrupting our proceedings do lie against us.

3. Concerning our way of answering complaints against us in England, we conceive, that it doth not well suit with us, nor are we directly called thereto, to profess and plead our right and power, further than in a way of justification of our proceedings questioned, from the words of the patent. In which agitations and the issues thereof our agents shall discern the mind of the parliament towards us, which if it be propense and favorable, there may be a fit season to procure such countenance of our proceedings, and confirmation

of our just power, as may prevent such unjust complaints and interruptions, as now disturb our administrations. But if the parliament should be less inclinable to us, we must wait upon providence for the preservation of our just liberties.

*   *   *

The court conferred with the elders about the petition of Dr. Child, etc., also, for it had given great offence to many godly in the country, both elders and others, and some answers had been made to it, and presented to the court.

*   *   *

Their petition being read, and this charge laid upon them, in the open court, before a great assembly, they desired time to make answer to it, which was granted. And giving the court notice that their answer was ready, they assembled again, and before all the people caused their answer to be read, which was large, and to little purpose, and the court replied to the particulars extempore, as they were read. The substance both of the answer and reply was, as followeth.

*   *   *

Answer: To the fourth they answer as in their petition, and a reason they give of their fear of arbitrary government is, that some speeches and papers have been spread abroad for maintenance thereof, etc., and that a body of English laws have not been here established, nor any other not repugnant thereto.

Reply: To this it was replied, 1. that the constant care and pains the court hath taken for establishing a body of laws, and that which hath been effected herein beyond any other plantation, will sufficiently clear our government from being arbitrary, and our intentions from any such disposition, 2. for the laws of England (though by our charter we are not bound to them, yet) our fundamentals are framed according to them, as will appear by our declaration, which is to be published upon this occasion, and the government of England itself is more arbitrary in their chancery and other courts than ours is, 3. because they would make men believe, that the want of the laws of England was such a grievance to them, they were pressed to show, what laws of England they wanted, and it was offered them, (before all the assembly, who were desired to bear witness of it,) that if they could produce any one law of England, the want whereof was a just grievance to them, the court would quit the cause, whereupon one of them instanced in a law used in London, (where he had been a citizen,) but that was easily taken away, by showing that that was only a bye-law, or peculiar custom of the city, and none of the common or general laws of England.

Answer: They answer negatively to the fifth, alleging that they only commend the laws of England as those they are best accustomed unto, etc., and therein they impudently and falsely affirm, that we are obliged to those laws by our general charter and oath of allegiance, and that without those laws, or others no way repugnant to them, they could not clearly see a certainty of enjoying their lives, liberties, and estates, etc., according to their due natural rights, as freeborn English, etc.

Reply: To this it was replied, that they charge us with breach of our charter and of our oaths of allegiance, whereas our allegiance binds us not to the laws of England any longer than while we live in England, for the laws of the parliament of England reach no further, nor do the king's writs under the great seal go any further; what the orders of state may, belongs not in us to determine. And whereas they seem to admit of laws not repugnant, etc., if by repugnant they mean, as the word truly imports, and as by the charter must needs be intended, they have no cause to complain, for we have no laws diametrically opposite to those of England, for then they must be contrary to the law of God and of right reason, which the learned in those laws have anciently and still do hold forth as the fundamental basis of their laws, and that if any thing hath been otherwise established, it was an error, and not a law, being against the intent of the law-makers, however it may bear the form of a law (in regard of the stamp of authority set upon it) until it be revoked.

*   *   *

I should also have noted the Doctor's logic, who undertook to prove, that we were subject to the laws of England. His argument was this, every corporation of England is subject to the laws of England; but this was a corporation of England, ergo, etc.

To which it was answered, 1. that there is a difference between subjection to the laws in general, as all that dwell in England are, and subjection to some laws of state, proper to foreign plantations, 2. we must distinguish between corporations within England and corporations of but not within England; the first are subject to the laws of England in general, yet not to every general law, as the city of London and other corporations have divers customs and by-laws differing from the common and statute laws of England. Again, though plantations be bodies corporate, (and so is every city and commonwealth,) yet they are also above the rank of an ordinary corporation. If one of London should say before the mayor and aldermen, or before the common council, you are but a corporation, this would be taken as a contempt. And among the Romans, Grecians, and other nations, colonies have been esteemed other than towns, yea than many cities, for they have been the foundations of great commonwealths. And it was a fruit of much pride and folly in these petitioners to despise the day of small things.

MARYLAND ACT CONCERNING RELIGION, 1649

Commentary

Living in a secular century, we tend to minimize the importance of the freedom of religion guaranteed in the very first clause of the federal Bill of Rights. The men who made the American polity could make no such mistake, for the colonies themselves were, in large part, a product of the religious intolerance of seventeenth-century England. The great constitutional struggles in Stuart days were both political and religious struggles. It was religious strife that aggravated the political controversies of the time and made their resolution possible only by the sword. In the end, in fact, during the reign of the last Stuart King, the royal attempt to subvert the Constitution was made solely for religious ends.

Though many of the colonists fled to the New World to escape the religious discrimination of the mother country, that did not lead most of them to practise toleration. It is an unfortunate fact of history that when some of the very groups which had been most strongly persecuted by the established Church of England found themselves in control of Colonial governments, they immediately turned from oppressed into oppressors so far as those of other religious beliefs were concerned. We need only evidence the zeal of the Puritans of New England to enforce conformity to *their* beliefs and keep their Commonwealth free of anything that smacked of heresy.

Not all of the colonies were, however, dominated by the intolerance of the mother country. Some of them were, indeed, specifically founded as refuges of toleration. Notable among them were Maryland and Rhode Island. The first Lord Baltimore may have intended Maryland to serve as a haven for his Catholic coreligionists. He was, however, wise enough to realize that he could not get enough settlers without attracting immigrants of other religions. In addition, he knew that, as a Catholic Proprietor in a Protestant Empire, he would have to proceed very carefully. The result was a policy of religious toleration, which attracted many of the early settlers. The importance of this policy is well shown by a 1678 letter of the third Lord Baltimore which concedes that, without it, "in all probability this province had never been planted."

The right of toleration was expressly provided for in the 1649 Act Concerning Religion. This law (usually known as the Toleration Act) was a pioneer statute and gives Maryland the distinction of being the first American colony to recognize a measure of freedom of conscience. The Act provided that all professed Christians (Catholics and Protestants alike) should have freedom of conscience and worship containing in this respect a guarantee similar in terms to the Free Exercise Clause of the First Amendment itself: "noe person. . . professing to believe in Jesus Christ, shall from

90

henceforth bee any waies troubled, Molested or discountenanced for or in respect of his or her religion nor in the free exercise thereof." Although the Toleration Act was limited in its protection to Christians, there was not, so far as we know, any persecution of Jews or others in the colony. What the 1649 Act meant in practice is shown by what happened when the Puritans obtained control of the colony during the Interregnum. In 1654, the Act of Toleration was repealed and both Catholics and Anglicans were deprived of religious freedom. In 1658, the Lord Proprietor regained his authority and the Act of Toleration revived. Ultimately, in 1692, Maryland became a royal province and the Church of England was officially established in 1702. Even so, the religious toleration that had gained a foothold under the Baltimores was continued ultimately to become one of the cornerstones of the American system.

Maryland Act Concerning Religion, 1649*

Afforasmuch as in a well governed and Xpian Comon Weath matters concerning Religion and the honor of God ought in the first place to bee taken, into serious consideracon and endeavoured to bee settled. Be it therefore ordered and enacted by the Right Hoble Cecilius Lord Baron of Baltemore absolute Lord and Proprietary of this Province with the advise and consent of this Generall Assembly. That whatsoever pson or psons within this Province and the Islands thereunto belonging shall from henceforth blaspheme God, that is Curse him, or deny our Saviour Jesus Christ to bee the sonne of God, or shall deny the holy Trinity the ffather sonne and holy Ghost, or the God-head of any of the said Three psons of the Trinity or the Vnity of the Godhead, or shall use or utter any reproachfull Speeches, words or language concerning the said Holy Trinity, or any of the said three psons thereof, shalbe punished with death and confiscaton or forfeiture of all his or her lands and goods to the Lord Proprietary and his heires, And bee it also Enacted by the Authority and with the advise and assent aforesaid. That whatsoever pson or psons shall from henceforth use or utter any reproachfull words or Speeches concerning the blessed Virgin Mary the Mother of our Saviour or the holy Apostles or Evangelists or any of them shall in such case for the first offence forfeit to the said Lord Proprietary and his heirs Lords and Proprietaries of this Province the sume of ffive pound Sterling or the value thereof to be Levyed on the goods and chattells of every such pson soe offending, but in case such Offender or Offenders, shall not then have goods and chattells sufficient for the satisfyeing of such forfeiture, or that the same bee not otherwise speedily satisfyed that then such Offender or Offenders shalbe publiquely whipt and bee ymprisoned during the pleasure of the Lord

*Archives of Maryland: Proceedings and Acts of the General Assembly of Maryland, 1637–1664, Vol. 1, pp. 244–47.

Proprietary or the Leivet or cheife Governor of this Province for the time being. And that every such Offender or Offenders for every second offence shall forfeit tenne pound sterling or the value thereof to bee levyed as aforesaid, or in case such offender or Offenders shall not then haue goods and chattells within this Province sufficient for that purpose then to bee publiquely and severely whipt and imprisoned as before is expressed. And that every pson or psons before mentioned offending herein the third time, shall for such third Offence forfeit all his lands and Goods and bee for ever banished and expelled out of this Province. And be it also further Enacted by the same authority advise and assent that whatsoever pson or psons shall from henceforth vppon any occasion of Offence or otherwise in a reproachful manner or Way declare call or denominate any pson or psons whatsoever inhabiting residing traffiqueing trading or comerceing within this Province or within any the Ports, Harbors, Creeks or Havens to the same belonging an heritick, Scismatick, Idolator, puritan, Independant, Prespiterian popish prest, Jesuite, Jesuited papist, Lutheran, Calvenist, Anabaptist, Brownist, Antinomian, Barrowist, Roundhead, Sepatist, or any other name or terme in a reproachfull manner relating to matter of Religion shall for every such Offence forfeit and loose the some or terne shillings sterling or the value thereof to bee levyed on the goods and chattells of every such Offender and Offenders, the one half thereof to be forfeited and paid unto the person and persons of whom such reproachfull words are or shalbe spoken or vttered, and the other half thereof to the Lord Proprietary and his heires Lords and Proprietaries of this Province, But if such pson or psons who shall at any time vtter or speake any such reproachfull words or Language shall not have Goods or Chattells sufficient and overt within this Province to bee taken to satisfie the penalty aforesaid or that the same bee not otherwise speedily satisfyed, that then the pson or persons soe offending shalbe publickly whipt, and shall suffer imprisonmt without baile or maineprise vntill hee shee or they respectively shall satisfy the party soe offended or greived by such reproachfull Language by asking him or her respectively forgivenes publiquely for such his Offence before the Magistrate or cheife Officer or Officers of the Towne or place where such Offence shalbe given. And be it further likewise Enacted by the Authority and consent aforesaid That every person and persons within this Province that shall at any time hereafter pphane the Sabbath or Lords day called Sunday by frequent swearing, drunkennes or by any uncivill or disorderly recreacon, or by working on that day when absolute necessity doth not require it shall for every such first offence forfeit 2s. 6d sterling or the value thereof, and for the second offence 5s sterling or the value thereof, and for the third offence and soe for every time he shall offend in like manner afterwards 10s sterling or the value thereof. And in case such offender and offenders shall not have sufficient goods or chattells within this Province to satisfy any of the said Penalties respectively hereby

imposed for prophaning the Sabbath or Lords day called Sunday as aforesaid, That in Every such case the ptie soe offending shall for the first and
second offence in that kinde be imprisoned till hee or shee shall publickly in
open Court before the cheife Commander Judge or Magistrate, of that
County Towne or precinct where such offence shalbe committed acknowledg
the Scandall and offence he hath in that respect given against God and the
good and civill Governemt of this Province And for the third offence and for
every time after shall also bee publickly whipt. And whereas the inforceing
of the conscience in matters of Religion hath frequently fallen out to be of
dangerous Consequence in those commonwealthes where it hath been practised, And for the more quiett and peaceable governemt of this Province,
and the better to pserve mutuall Love and amity amongst the Inhabitants
thereof. Be it Therefore also by the Lo: Proprietary with the advise and
consent of this Assembly Ordeyned & enacted (except as in this psent Act is
before Declared and sett forth) that noe person or psons whatsoever within
this Province, or the Islands, Ports, Harbors, Creekes, or havens thereunto
belonging professing to beleive in Jesus Christ, shall from henceforth bee any
waies troubled, Molested or discountenanced for or in respect of his or her
religion nor in the free exercise thereof within this Province or the Islands
thereunto belonging nor any way compelled to the beleife or exercise of any
other Religion against his or her consent, soe as they be not unfaithfull to the
Lord Proprietary, or molest or conspire against the civill Governemt established or to bee established in this Province vnder him or his heires. And
that all & every pson and psons that shall presume Contrary to this Act and
the true intent and meaning thereof directly or indirectly either in person or
estate willfully to wrong disturbe trouble or molest any person whatsoever
within this Province professing to beleive in Jesus Christ for or in respect of
his or her religion or the free exercise thereof within this Province other than
is provided for in this Act that such pson or psons soe offending, shalbe
compelled to pay trebble damages to the party soe wronged or molested, and
for every such offence shall also forfeit 20s sterling in money or the value
thereof, half thereof for the vse of the Lo: Proprietary, and his heires Lords
and Proprietaries of this Province, and the other half for the vse of the party
soe wronged or molested as aforesaid, Or if the ptie soe offending as
aforesaid shall refuse or bee vnable to recompense the party soe wronged, or
to satisfy such ffyne or forfeiture, then such Offender shalbe severely punished by publick whipping & imprisonmt during the pleasure of the Lord
Proprietary, or his Leivetenat or cheife Governor of this Province for the
tyme being without baile or maineprise And bee it further alsoe Enacted by
the authority and consent aforesaid That the Sheriff or other Officer or
Officers from time to time to bee appointed & authorized for that purpose, of
the County Towne or precinct where every particular offence in this psent
Act conteyned shall happen at any time to bee comitted and wherevppon

there is hereby a fforfeiture ffyne or penalty imposed shall from time to time distraine and seise the goods and estate of every such pson soe offending as aforesaid against this psent Act or any pt thereof, and sell the same or any part thereof for the full satisfaccon of such forfeiture, ffine, or penalty as aforesaid, Restoring vnto the ptie soe offending the Remainder or overplus of the said goods or estate after such satisfaccon soe made as aforesaid

The ffreemen haue assented. Tho: Hatton
Enacted by the Governor Willm Stone

CHARTER OF RHODE ISLAND AND
PROVIDENCE PLANTATIONS, 1663

Commentary

When we think of the origins of the right to religious liberty which was ultimately enshrined in the first guarantee of the federal Bill of Rights, we think primarily of Roger Williams and Rhode Island. It was the 1663 Charter of Rhode Island that first provided for religious liberty in the organic law of a Colony. Important though the Maryland Act of Toleration had been, it was only an ordinary statute of the legislature, which could be repealed at will by the colonists themselves. The Rhode Island guarantee was contained in the Colony's Charter itself, which was (in the terms used by the Massachusetts General Court in 1661) "the first and maine foundation of our civil politye." That the Rhode Island Charter did in fact have virtually the status of a Constitution is shown by the fact that it was kept in force after the Revolution (when the other states had drawn up their own Constitutions), remaining as the fundamental law of Rhode Island until it was finally replaced by a Constitution in 1842 (and it took a mini-Revolution, the so-called Dorr Rebellion, to accomplish that).

That Rhode Island was founded upon the doctrine of religious liberty was due, in large measure, to the character of its founder, Roger Williams. When Reverend Williams arrived in Massachusetts in 1631, he proved a sore trial to his Puritan brethren because of his unorthodox ideas. To cleanse the Colony of heresy, the Saints banished him at the end of 1635 and he fled to the sanctuary of the Rhode Island Indians, and there founded the settlement of Providence. From the beginning, toleration was the cornerstone of the new Colony in accordance with Williams' own tenet that "none bee accounted a Delinquent for *Doctrine.*" At the very outset, in 1636, the Rhode Island settlers agreed that the authority of government would extend "only in civil things." The plantation agreement of 1640 expressly declared: "We agree, as formerly hath bin the liberties of the town, so still, to hould forth liberty of Conscience." Thus, freedom of religion was the basis of the Colony even before it was expressly stated in its fundamental law. Even Quakers and Jews were permitted to believe and worship as they chose.

Upon the accession of Charles II, it became necessary for Rhode Island to secure a Royal Charter to replace the Parliamentary Patent obtained during the Interregnum. The Charter secured in 1663 made religious liberty a part of American constitutional law. The language was broad enough to satisfy even a Roger Williams. It declared that "noe person within the sayd colonye, at any tyme hereafter, shall bee any wise molested, punished, disquieted, or called in question, for any differences in opinione in matters of religion" so long as he did "not actually disturb the civil peace of our sayd colony."

Further, the right thus guaranteed was to prevail, "any lawe, statute or clause. . . usage or custome of this realme, to the contrary hereof, in any wise, notwithstanding."

The Rhode Island Charter was really the first to contain a grant of religious freedom in the all-inclusive terms which have become familiar in modern American Constitutions. It served as the model for similar declarations in other Charters and Colonial enactments, as well as for Revolutionary Constitutions and ultimately for the First Amendment itself. For the first time, the present-day observer finds in a historical document an expression of his own belief in the limits which must be placed on the governmental power to interfere with the individual conscience.

Charter of Rhode Island and Providence Plantations, 1663*

Charles the Second, by the grace of God, King of England, Scotland, France and Ireland, Defender of the Faith, &c., to all to whome these presents shall come, greeting: Whereas wee have been informed, by the humble petition of our trustie and well beloved subject, John Clarke, on the behalf of Benjamine Arnold, William Brenton, William Codington, Nicholas Easton, William Boulston, John Porter, John Smith, Samuell Gorton, John Weeks, Roger Williams, Thomas Olnie, Gregorie Dexter, John Cogeshall, Joseph Clarke, Randall Holden, John Greene, John Roome, Samuell Wildbore, William Ffield, James Barker, Richard Tew, Thomas Harris, and William Dyre, and the rest of the purchasers and ffree inhabitants of our island, called Rhode-Island, and the rest of the colonie of Providence Plantations, in the Narragansett Bay, in New-England, in America, that they, pursueing, with peaceable and loyall mindes, their sober, serious and religious intentions, of godlie edifieing themselves, and one another, in the holie Christian ffaith and worshipp as they were perswaded; together with the gaineing over and conversione of the poore ignorant Indian natives, in those partes of America, to the sincere professione and obedienc of the same ffaith and worship, did, not onlie by the consent and good encouragement of our royall progenitors, transport themselves out of this kingdome of England into America, but alsoe, since their arrivall there, after their first settlement amongst other our subjects in those parts, ffor the avoideing of discorde, and those manie evills which were likely to ensue upon some of those oure subjects not beinge able to beare, in these remote parties, theire different apprehensiones in religious concernements, and in pursueance of the afforesayd ends, did once againe leave theire desireable stationes and habitationes, and with excessive labour and travell, hazard and charge, did transplant themselves into the middest of the Indian natives, who, as wee are

*Poore, *The Federal and State Constitutions, Colonial Charters and Other Organic Laws of the United States,* Vol. 2, pp. 1595–1603.

infformed, are the most potent princes and people of all that country; where, by the good Providence of God, from whome the Plantationes have taken their name, upon theire labour and industrie, they have not onlie byn preserved to admiration, but have increased and prospered, and are seized and possessed, by purchase and consent of the said natives, to their ffull content, of such lands, islands, rivers, harbours and roades, as are verie convenient, both for plantationes and alsoe for buildinge of shipps, suplye of pypestaves, and other merchandize; and which lyes verie commodious, in manie respects, for commerce, and to accommodate oure southern planta-tiones, and may much advance the trade of this oure realme, and greatlie enlarge the territories thereof; they haveinge, by neare neighbourhoode to and friendlie societie with the greate bodie of the Narragansett Indians, given them encouragement, of theire owne accorde, to subject themselves, theire people and landes, unto us; whereby, as is hoped, there may, in due tyme, by the blessing of God upon theire endeavours, bee layd a sure ffoundation of happinesse to all America: And whereas, in theire humble addresse, they have ffreely declared, that it is much on their hearts (if they may be permitted), to hold forth a livelie experiment, that a most flourishing civill state may stand and best bee maintained, and that among our English subjects, with a full libertie in religious concernements; and that true pietye rightly grounded upon gospell principles, will give the best and greatest security to sovereignetye, and will lay in the hearts of men the strongest obligations to true loyaltye: Now know yee, that wee beinge willinge to encourage the hopefull undertakeinge of oure sayd loyall and loveinge subjects, and to secure them in the free exercise and enjoyment of all theire civill and religious rights, appertaining to them, as our loveing subjects; and to preserve unto them that libertye, in the true Christian ffaith and worshipp of God, which they have sought with soe much travaill, and with peaceable myndes, and loyall subjectione to our royall progenitors and ourselves, to enjoye; and because some of the people and inhabitants of the same colonie cannot, in theire private opinions, conforme to the publique exercise of religion, according to the litturgy, formes and ceremonyes of the Church of England, or take or subscribe the oaths and articles made and established in that behalfe; and for that the same, by reason of the remote distances of those places, will (as wee hope) bee noe breach of the unitie and unifformi-tie established in this nation: Have therefore thought ffit, and doe hereby publish, graunt, ordeyne and declare, That our royall will and pleasure is, that noe person within the sayd colonye, at any tyme hereafter, shall bee any wise molested, punished, disquieted, or called in question, for any differences in opinione in matters of religion, and doe not actually disturb the civill peace of our sayd colony; but that all and everye person and persons may, from tyme to tyme, and at all tymes hereafter, freelye and fullye have and enjoye his and theire owne judgments and consciences, in matter of religious concernments, throughout the tract of lande hereafter mentioned; they behaving

themselves peaceablie and quietlie, and not useing this libertie to lycentiousnesse and profanenesse, nor to the civill injurye or outward disturbeance of
others; any lawe, statute, or clause, therein contayned, or to bee contayned, usage
or custome of this realme, to the contrary hereof, in any wise, notwithstanding.
And that they may bee in the better capacity to defend themselves, in theire
just rights and libertyes against all the enemies of the Christian ffaith, and
others, in all respects, wee have further thought fit, and at the humble
petition of the persons afosesayd are gratiously pleased to declare, That they
shall have and enjoye the benefitt of our late act of indempnity and ffree
pardon, as the rest of our subjects in other our dominions and territoryes
have; and to create and make them a bodye politique or corporate, with the
powers and priviledges hereinafter mentioned. And accordingely our will and
pleasure is, and of our especiall grace, certaine knowledge, and meere
motion, wee have ordeyned, constituted and declared, and by these presents,
for us, our heires and successors, doe ordeyne, constitute and declare, That
they, the sayd William Brenton, William Codington, Nicholas Easton,
Benedict Arnold, William Boulston, John Porter, Samuell Gorton, John
Smith, John Weekes, Roger Williams, Thomas Olneye, Gregorie Dexter,
John Cogeshall, Joseph Clarke, Randall Holden, John Greene, John Roome,
William Dyre, Samuell Wildbore, Richard Tew, William Ffeild, Thomas
Harris, James Barker,—Rainsborrow,—Williams, and John Nickson, and all
such others as now are, or hereafter shall bee admitted and made ffree of the
company and societie of our collonie of Providence Plantations, in the
Narragansett Bay, in New England, shall bee, from tyme to tyme, and
forever hereafter, a bodie corporate and politique, in ffact and name, by the
name of The Governor and Company of the English Colony of Rhode-Island
and Providence Plantations, in New-England, in America; and that, by the
same name, they and their successors shall and may have perpetuall succession, and shall and may bee persons able and capable, in the lawe, to sue
and bee sued, to pleade and be impleaded, to answeare and bee answeared
unto, to defend and to be defended, in all and singular suites, causes,
quarrels, matters, actions and thinges, of what kind or nature soever; and
alsoe to have, take, possesse, acquire and purchase, lands, tenements or
hereditaments, or any goods or chattels, and the same to lease, graunt,
demise, aliene, bargaine, sell and dispose of, at their owne will and pleasure,
as other our liege people of this our realme of England, or anie corporation
or bodie politique within the same, may lawfully doe: And further, that
they the sayd Governor and Company, and theire successors, shall and may,
forever hereafter, have a common seale, to serve and use for all matters,
causes, thinges and affaires, whatsoever, of them and their successors; and
the same seale to alter, change, breake, and make new, from tyme tyme, at
their will and pleasure, as they shall thinke ffitt. And further, wee will and
ordeyne, and by these presents, for us, oure heires and successours, doe
declare and apoynt that, for the better ordering and managing of the affaires

and business of the sayd Company, and theire successours, there shall bee one Governour, one Deputie-Governour and ten Assistants, to bee from tyme to tyme, constituted, elected and chosen, out of the freemen of the sayd Company, for the tyme beinge, in such manner and fforme as is hereafter in these presents expressed; which sayd officers shall aplye themselves to take care for the best disposeinge and orderinge of the generall businesse and affairs of, and concerneinge the landes and hereditaments hereinafter mentioned, to be graunted, and the plantation thereof, and the government of the people there. And, for the better execution of oure royall pleasure herein, wee doe, for us, oure heires and successours, assign, name, constitute and apoynt the aforesayd Benedict Arnold to bee the first and present Governor of the sayd Company, and the sayd William Brenton to bee the Deputy-Governor, and the sayd William Boulston, John Porter, Roger Williams, Thomas Olnie, John Smith, John Greene, John Cogeshall, James Barker, William Ffeild, and Joseph Clarke, to bee the tenn present Assistants of the sayd Companye, to continue in the sayd severall offices, respectively, untill the first Wednesday which shall bee in the month of May now next comeing. And further, wee will, and by these presents, for us, our heires and successessours, doe ordeyne and graunt, that the Governor of the sayd Company, for the tyme being, or, in his absence, by occasion of sicknesse, or otherwise, by his leave and permission, the Deputy-Governor, ffor the tyme being, shall and may, ffrom tyme to tyme, upon all occasions, give order ffor the assemblinge of the sayd Company and callinge them together, to consult and advise of the businesse and affaires of the sayd Company. And that forever hereafter, twice in every year, that is to say, on every first Wednesday in the month of May, and on every last Wednesday in October, or oftener, in case it shall bee requisite, the Assistants, and such of the ffreemen of the Company, not exceedinge six persons ffor Newport, ffoure persons ffor each of the respective townes of Providence, Portsmouth and Warwicke, and two persons for each other place, towne or city, whoe shall bee, from tyme to tyme, thereunto elected or deputed by the majour parte of the ffreemen of the respective townes or places ffor which they shall bee so elected or deputed, shall have a generall meetinge, or Assembly then and there to consult, advise and determine, in and about the affaires and businesse of the said Company and Plantations. And further, wee doe, of our especiall grace, certayne knowledge, and meere motion, give and graunt unto the sayd Governour and Company of the English Colonie of Rhode-Island and Providence Plantations, in New-England, in America, and theire successours, that the Governour, or, in his absence, or, by his permission, the Deputy-Governour of the sayd Company, for the tyme beinge, the Assistants, and such of the ffreemen of the sayd Company as shall bee soe as aforesayd elected or deputed, or soe many of them as shall bee present att such meetinge or assemblye, as afforesayde, shall bee called the Generall Assemblye; and that they, or the greatest parte of them present, whereof the

Governour or Deputy-Governour, and sixe of the Assistants, at least to bee seven, shall have, and have hereby given and graunted unto them, ffull power authority, ffrom tyme tyme, and at all tymes hereafter, to apoynt, alter and change, such dayes, tymes and places of meetinge and Generall Assemblye, as theye shall thinke ffitt; and to choose, nominate, and apoynt, such and soe manye other persons as they shall thinke ffitt, and shall be willing to accept the same, to bee ffree of the sayd Company and body politique, and them into the same to admitt; and to elect and constitute such offices and officers, and to graunt such needfull commissions, as they shall thinke ffitt and requisite, ffor the ordering, managing and dispatching of the affaires of the sayd Governour and Company, and their successours; and from tyme to tyme, to make, ordeyne, constitute or repeal, such lawes, statutes, orders and ordinances, fformes and ceremonies of government and magistracye as to them shall seeme meete for the good and wellfare of the sayd Company, and ffor the government and ordering of the landes and hereditaments, hereinafter mentioned to be graunted, and of the people that doe, or att any tyme hereafter shall, inhabitt or bee within the same; soe as such lawes, ordinances and constitiones, soe made, bee not contrary and repugnant unto, butt, as neare as may bee, agreeable to the lawes of this our realme of England, considering the nature and constitutione of the place and people there; and alsoe to apoynt, order and direct, erect and settle, such places and courts of jurisdiction, ffor the heareinge and determininge of all actions, cases, matters and things, happening within the sayd collonie and plantatione, and which shall be in dispute, and depending there, as they shall thinke ffitt; and alsoe to distinguish and sett forth the severall names and titles, duties, powers and limitts, of each court, office and officer, superior and inferior; and alsoe to contrive and apoynt such formes of oaths and attestations, not repugnant, but, as neare as may bee, agreeable, as aforesayd, to the lawes and statutes of this oure realme, as are conveniente and requisite, with respect to the due administration of justice, and due execution and discharge of all offices and places of trust by the persons that shall bee therein concerned; and alsoe to regulate and order the waye and manner of all elections to offices and places of trust, and to prescribe, limitt and distinguish the numbers and boundes of all places, townes or cityes, within the limitts and bounds herein after mentioned, and not herein particularlie named, who have, and shall have, the power of electing and sending of ffreemen to the sayd Generall Assembly; and alsoe to order, direct and authorize the imposing of lawfull and reasonable ffynes, mulcts, imprisonments, and executing other punishments pecuniary and corporal, upon offenders and delinquents, according to the course of other corporations within this oure kingdom of England; and agayne to alter, revoke, annull or pardon, under their common seale or otherwyse, such ffynes, mulcts, imprisonments, sentences, judgments and condemnations, as shall bee thought ffitt; and to direct, rule, order and dispose of, all other matters and things, and particularly that which relates to the mankinge of purchases of the native Indians, as to them shall seeme meete; whereby oure sayd people and inhabitants, in the sayd Plantationes, may be soe religiously, peaceably and civilly governed, as that, by theire good life and orderlie conversatione, they may win and invite the native Indians of the countrie to the knowledge and obedience of the onlie true God, and Saviour of mankinde; willing, commanding and requireing, and by these presents, for us, oure heires and successours, ordeyneing and apoynting, that all such lawes, statutes, orders and ordinances, instructions, impositions and directiones, as shall bee soe made by the Governour, deputye-Governour, Assistants and ffreemen, or such number of them as aforesayd, and published in writinge, under theire common seale, shall bee carefully and duely observed, kept, performed and putt in execution, accordinge to the true intent and meaning of the same. And these our letters patent, or the duplicate or exempliffication thereof, shall bee to all and everie such officer, superiour or inferiour, ffrom tyme to tyme, for the putting of the same orders, lawes, statutes, ordinances, instructions and directions, in due execution, against us, oure heires and successours, a sufficient warrant and discharge. And ffurther, our will and pleasure is, and wee doe hereby, for us, oure heires and successours, establish and ordeyne, that yearelie, once in the yeare, forever hereafter, namely, the aforesayd Wednesday in May, and at the towne of Newport, or elsewhere, if urgent occasion doe require, the Governour, Deputy-Governour and Assistants of the sayd Company, and other officers of the sayd Company, or such of them as the Generall Assemblye shall thinke ffitt, shall bee, in the sayd Generall Court or Assembly to bee held from that daye or tyme, newely chosen for the year ensueing, by such greater part of the sayd Company, for the tyme beinge, as shall bee then and there present; and if itt shall happen that the present Governour, Deputy-Governour and Assistants, by these presents apoynted, or any such as shall hereafter be newly chosen into their roomes, or any of them, or any other the officers of the sayd Company, shall die or bee removed ffrom his or their severall offices or places, before the sayd generall day of election, (whom wee doe hereby declare, for any misdemeanour or default, to be removeable by the Governour, Assistants and Company, or such greater parte of them, in any of the sayd publique courts, to bee assembled as aforesayd), that then, and in every such case, it shall and may bee lawfull to and ffor the sayd Governour, Deputy-Governour, Assistants and Company aforesayde, or such greater parte of them, soe to bee assembled as is aforesayde, in any theire assemblyes, to proceede to a new election of one or more of their Company, in the roome or place, roomes or places, of such officer or officers, soe dyeinge or removed, according to theire discretiones; and immediately upon and after such electione or elections made of such Governour, Deputy-Governour or Assistants, or any other officer of the sayd Company, in manner and forme aforesayde, the authoritie, office and power, before given to the fformer

Governour, Deputy-Governour, and other officer and officers, soe removed, in whose steade and place new shall be chosen, shall, as to him and them, and every of them, respectively, cease and determine: Provided, allwayes, and our will and pleasure is, that as well such as are by these presents apoynted to bee the present Governour, Deputy-Governour and Assistants, of the sayd Company, as those that shall succeede them, and all other officers to bee apoynted and chosen as aforesayde, shall, before the under-takeinge the execution of the sayd offices and places respectively, give theire solemn engagement, by oath, or otherwyse, for the due and faythfull per-formeance of theire duties in their severall offices and places, before such person or persons as are by these presents hereafter apoynted to take and receive the same, that is to say: the sayd Benedict Arnold, whoe is hereinbe-fore nominated and apoynted the present Governour of the sayd Company, shall give the aforesayd engagement before William Brenton, or any two of the sayd Assistants of the sayd Company; unto whome, wee doe by these presentes give ffull power and authority to require and receive the same; and the sayd William Brenton, whoe is hereby before nominated and apoynted the present Deputy-Governour of the sayd Company, shall give the afore-sayed engagement before the sayd Benedict Arnold, or any two of the Assistants of the sayd Company; unto whome wee doe by these presents give ffull power and authority to require and receive the same; and the sayd William Boulston, John Porter, Roger Williams, Thomas Olneye, John Smith, John Greene, John Cogeshall, James Barker, William Ffeild, and Joseph Clarke, whoe are hereinbefore nominated apoynted the present As-sistants of the sayd Company, shall give the sayd engagement to theire offices and places respectively belongeing, before the sayd Benedict Arnold and William Brenton, or one of them; to whome, respectively wee doe hereby give ffull power and authority to require, administer or receive the same: and ffurther, our will and pleasure is, that all and every other future Governour or Deputy-Governour, to bee elected and chosen by vertue of these presents, shall give the sayd engagement before two or more of the sayd Assistants of the sayd Company ffor the tyme beinge; unto whome wee doe by these presents give ffull power and authority to require, administer or receive the same; and the sayd Assistants, and every of them, and all and every other officer or officers to bee hereafter elected and chosen by vertue of these presents, from tyme to tyme, shall give the like engagements, to their offices and places respectively belonging, before the Governour or Deputy-Governour for the tyme being; unto which sayd Governour, or Deputy-Governour, wee doe by these presents give full power and authority to require, administer or receive the same accordingly. And wee doe likewise, for vs, oure heires and successours, give and graunt vnto the sayd Governour and Company and theire successours by these presents, that, for the more peaceable and orderly government of the sayd Plantations, it shall and may bee lawfull ffor the Governour, Deputy-Governor, Assistants, and all other officers and ministers of the sayd Company, in the administration of justice, and exercise of government, in the sayd Plantations, to vse, exercise, and putt in execution, such methods, rules, orders and directions, not being contrary or repugnant to the laws and statutes of this oure realme, as have byn heretofore given, vsed and accustomed, in such cases respectively, to be putt in practice, untill att the next or some other Generall Assembly, special provision shall be made and ordeyned in the cases aforesayd. And wee doe ffurther, for vs, oure heires and successours, give and graunt vnto the sayd Governour and Company, and theire successours, by these presents, that itt shall and may bee lawfull to and for the sayd Governour, or in his absence, the Deputy-Governour, and majour parte of the sayd Assistants, for the tyme being, att any tyme when the sayd Generall Assembly is not sitting, to nominate, apoynt and constitute, such and soe many commanders, governours, and military officers, as to them shall seeme requisite, for the leading, conductinge and trayneing vpp the inhabitants of the sayd Plantations in martiall affaires, and for the defence and safeguard of the sayd Plantations; and that itt shall and may bee lawfull to and for all and every such commander, governour and military officer, that shall bee soe as aforesayd, or by the Governour, or, in his absence, the Deputy-Governour, and six of the sayd Assistants, and majour parte of the ffreemen of the sayd Company present att any Generall Assemblies, nominated, apoynted and constituted accordinge to the tenor of his and theire respective commissions and directions, to assemble, exercise in arms, martiall array, and putt in warlyke posture, the inhabitants of the sayd collonie, ffor theire speciall defence and safety; and to lead and conduct the sayd inhabitants, and to encounter, expulse, expell and resist, by force of armes, as well by sea as by lande; and alsoe to kill, slay and destroy, by all fitting wayes, enterprizes and meanes. whatsoever, all and every such person or persons as shall, att any tyme hereafter, attempt or enterprize the destruction, invasion, detriment or annoyance of the sayd inhabitants or Plantations; and to vse and exercise the lawe martiall in such cases only as occasion shall necessarily require; and to take or surprise, by all wayes and meanes whatsoever, all and every such person and persons, with theire shipp or shipps, armor, ammunition or other goods of such persons, as shall, in hostile manner, invade or attempt the defeating of the sayd Plantations, or the hurt of the sayd Company and inhabitants; and vpon just causes, to invade and destroy the native Indians or other enemyes of the sayd Collony. Neverthelesse, our will and pleasure is and wee doe hereby declare to the rest of oure Collonies in New-England, that itt shall not bee lawefull ffor this our sayd Collony of Rhode-Island and Providence Plantations, in America, in New-England, to invade the natives inhabiting within the boundes and limitts of theire sayd Collonies without the knowledge and consent of the sayd other Collonies. And itt is hereby declared, that itt shall not bee lawfull to or ffor the rest of the Colonies to invade or molest the native Indians, or any other inhabitants, inhabiting within the bounds and lymitts hereafter mentioned (they having subjected themselves vnto vs, and being by vs taken into our speciall protection), without the knowledge and consent of the Governour and Company of our Collony of Rhode-Island and Providence Plantations. Alsoe our will and pleasure is, and wee doe hereby declare unto all Christian Kings, Princes and States, that if any person, which shall hereafter bee of the sayd Company or Plantations, or any other, by apoyntment of the sayd Governour and Company for the tyme beinge, shall at any tyme or tymes hereafter, rob or spoyle, by sea or land, or do any hurt, unlawfull hostillity to any of the subjects of vs, oure heires or successours, or any of the subjects of any Prince or State, beinge then in league with vs, oure heires, or successours, vpon complaint of such injury done to any such Prince or State, or theire subjects, wee, our heires and successours, will make open proclamation within any parts of oure realme of England, ffitt ffor that purpose, that the person or persons committing any such robbery or spoyle shall, within the tyme lymitted by such proclamation, make full restitution or satisfaction of all such injuries, done or committed, soe as the sayd Prince, or others soe complaineinge, may bee fully satisfyed and contented; and if the sayd person or persons whoe shall committ any such robbery or spoyle shall not make satysfaction, accordingly, within such tyme, soe to bee lymitted, that then wee, oure heires and successours, will putt such person or persons out of oure allegiance and protection; and that then itt shall and may bee lawefull and ffree ffor all Princes or others to prosecute, with hostillity, such offenders, and every of them, theire and every of theire procurers, ayders, abettors and counsellors, in that behalfe; Provided alsoe, and oure expresse will and pleasure is, and wee doe, by these presents, ffor vs, our heirs and successours, ordeyne and apoynt, that these presents shall not, in any manner, hinder any of oure lovinge subjects, whatsoever, ffrom vseing and exercising the trade of ffishing vpon the coast of New-England, in America; butt that they, and every or any of them, shall have ffull and ffree power and liberty to continue and vse the trade of ffishing vpon the sayd coast, in any of the seas thereunto adjoyninge, or any armes of the seas, or salt water, rivers and creeks, where they have been accustomed to ffish; and to build and to sett upon the waste land, belonginge to the sayd Collony and Plantations, such wharfes, stages and worke-houses as shall be necessary for the salting, drying and keepeing of theire ffish, to be taken or gotten upon that coast. And ffurther, for the encouragement of the inhabitants of our sayd Collony of Providence Plantations to sett vpon the businesse of takeing whales, itt shall bee lawefull ffor them, or any of them, having struck whale, dubertus, or other greate ffish, itt or them, to pursue unto any parte of that coaste, and into any bay, river, cove, creeke or shoare, belonging thereto, and itt or them, vpon the sayd coaste, or in the sayd bay, river, cove, creeke or shoare, belonging thereto, to kill and order for the best advantage, without molestation, they makeing noe wilfull waste or spoyle, any thinge in these presents conteyned, or any other matter or thing, to the contrary notwithstanding. And further alsoe, wee are gratiously pleased, and doe hereby declare, that if any of the inhabitants of oure sayd Collony doe sett upon the plantinge of vineyards (the soyle and clymate both seemeing naturally to concurr to the production of wynes), or bee industrious in the discovery of ffishing banks, in or about the sayd Collony, wee will, ffrom tyme to tyme, give and allow all due and fitting encouragement therein, as to others in cases of lyke nature. And further, of oure more ample grace, certayne knowledge, and meere motion, wee have given and graunted, and by these presents, ffor vs, oure heires and successours, doe give and graunt vnto the sayd Governour and Company of the English Collony of Rhode-Island and Providence Plantations, in the Narragansett Bay, in New-England in America, and to every inhabitant there, and to every person and persons trading thither, and to every such person or persons as are or shall bee ffree of the sayd Collony, full power and authority, from tyme to tyme, and att all tymes hereafter, to take, shipp, transport and carry away, out of any of our realmes and dominions, for and towards the plantation and defence of the sayd Collony, such and soe many of oure loveing subjects and strangers as shall or will willingly accompany them in and to their sayd Collony and Plantation; except such person or persons as are or shall be therein restrained by vs, oure heires and successours, or any law or statute of this realme: and also to shipp and transport all and all manner of goods, chattels, merchandizes, and other things whatsoever, that are or shall bee vsefull or necessary ffor the sayd Plantations, and defence thereof, and vsually transported, and nott prohibited by any lawe or statute of this our realme; yielding and paying vnto vs, our heires and successours, such the duties, customes and subsidies, as are or ought to bee payd or payable for the same. And ffurther, our will and pleasure is, and wee doe, ffor us, our heires and successours, ordeyn, declare and graunt, vnto the sayd Governour and Company, and their successours, that all and every the subjects of vs, our heires and successours, which are already planted and settled within our sayd Collony of Providence Plantations, or which shall hereafter goe to inhabit within the sayd Collony, and all and every of theire children, which have byn borne there, or which shall happen hereafter to bee borne there, or on the sea, goeing thither, or retourneing from thence, shall have and enjoye all libertyes and immunityes of ffree and naturall subjects within any the dominions of vs, our heires or successours, to all intents, constructions and purposes, whatsoever, as if they, and every of them, were borne within the realme of England. And ffurther, know ye, that wee, of our more abundant grace, certain knowledge and meere motion, have given, graunted and confirmed, and, by these presents, for vs, our heires and successours, doe give, graunt and confirme, vnto the sayd Governour and Company, and theire successours, all that parte of our dominiones in New-England, in America, conteyneing the Nahantick and Nanhyganset Bay, and countryes and partes adjacent, bounded on the west,

or westerly, to the middle or channel of a river there, commonly called
and known by the name of Pawcatuck, alias Pawcawtuck river, and soe
along the sayd river, as the greater or middle streame thereof reacheth or
lyes vpp into the north countrye, northward, unto the head thereof, and from
thence, by a streight lyne drawn due north, vntill itt meets with the south
lyne of the Massachusetts Collonie; and on the north, or northerly, by the
aforesayd south or southerly lyne of the Massachusettes Collony or Plantation, and extending towards the east, or eastwardly, three English miles to
the east and north-east of the most eastern and north-eastern parts of the
aforesayd Narragansett Bay, as the sayd bay lyeth or extendeth itself from
the ocean on the south, or southwardly, vnto the mouth of the river which
runneth towards the towne of Providence, and from thence along the eastwardly side or banke of the sayd river (higher called by the name of
Seacunck river), vp to the ffalls called Patuckett ffalls, being the most west-
wardly lyne of Plymouth Collony, and soe from the sayd ffalls, in a streight
lyne, due north, untill itt meete with the aforesayd line of the Massachusetts
Collony; and bounded on the south by the ocean: and, in particular, the
lands belonging to the townes of Providence, Pawtuxet, Warwicke, Misqua-
mmacok, alias Pawcatuck, and the rest vpon the maine land in the tract
aforesayd, together with Rhode-Island, Blocke-Island, and all the rest of
the islands and banks in the Narragansett Bay, and bordering vpon the coast
of the tract aforesayd (Ffisher's Island only excepted), together with all firme
lands, soyles, grounds, havens, ports, rivers, waters, ffishings, mines royall,
and all other mynes, mineralls, precious stones, quarries, woods, wood-
grounds, rocks, slates, and all the singular other commodities, jurisdictions,
royalties, priviledges, franchises, preheminences and hereditaments, whatsoever, within the sayd tract, bounds, landes, and islands, aforesayd, or to
them or any of them belonging, or in any wise appertaining: to have and to
hold the same, vnto the sayd Governour and Company, and their successours, forever, vpon trust, for the vse and benefitt of themselves and their
associates, ffreemen of the sayd Collony, their heires and assignes, to be
holden of vs, our heires and successours, as of the Mannor of East-
Greenwich, in our county of Kent, in free and comon soccage, and not in
capite, nor by knight service; yeilding and paying therefor, to vs, our heires
and successours, only the ffith part of all the oare of gold and silver which,
from tyme to tyme, and att all tymes hereafter, shall bee there gotten, had or
obtained, in lieu and satisfaction of all services, duties, ffynes, forfeitures,
made or to be made, claimes and demands, whatsoever, to bee to vs, our
heires or successours, therefor or thereout rendered, made or paid; any
graunt, or clause in a late graunt, to the Governour and Company of
Connecticutt Colony, in America, to the contrary thereof in any wise notwithstanding; the aforesayd Pawcatuck river haveing byn yielded, after much
debate, for the fixed and certain boundes betweene these our sayd Colonies,
by the agents thereof; whoe have alsoe agreed, that the sayd Pawcatuck river

shall bee alsoe called alias Norrogansett or Narrogansett river; and, to prevent future disputes, that otherwise might arise thereby, forever hereafter shall bee construed, deemed and taken to bee the Narragansett river in our late graunt to Connecticutt Colony mentioned as the easterly bounds of that Colony. And further, our will and pleasure is, that in all matters of publique controversy which may fall out betweene our Colony of Providence Plantations and the rest of our Colonies in New-England, itt shall and may bee lawfull to and for the Governour and Company of the sayd Colony of Providence Plantations to make their appeales therein to vs, our heirs and successours, for redresse in such cases, within this our realme of England: and that itt shall bee lawfull to and for the inhabitants of the sayd Colony of Providence Plantations, without let or molestation, to passe and repasse with freedome, into and thorough the rest of the English Collonies, vpon their lawfull and civill occasions, and to converse, and hold commerce and trade, with such of the inhabitants of our other English Collonies as shall bee willing to admitt them thereunto, they behaveing themselves peaceably among them; any act, clause or sentence, in any of the sayd Collonies provided, or that shall bee provided, to the contrary in anywise notwith-standing. And lastly, wee doe, for vs, our heires and successours, ordeyne and graunt vnto the sayd Governor and Company, and their successours, and by these presents, that these our letters patent shall be firme, good, effectuall and available in all things in the lawe, to all intents, constructions and purposes whatsoever, according to our true intent and meaning hereinbefore declared; and shall bee construed, reputed and adjudged in all cases most favorably on the behalfe, and for the benefitt and behoofe, of the sayd Governor and Company, and their successours; although express mention of the true yearly value or certainty of the premises, or any of them, or of any other gifts or graunts by vs, or by any of our progenitors or predecessors, heretofore made to the sayd Governor and Company of the English Colony of Rhode-Island and Providence Plantations, in the Narragansett Bay, New England, in America, in these presents is not made, or any statute, act, ordinance, provision, proclamation or restriction, heretofore had, made, en-acted, ordeyned or provided, or any other matter, cause or thing whatsoever, to the contrary thereof in anywise notwithstanding. In witnes whereof, wee have caused these our letters to bee made patent. Witnes our Selfe att Westminster, the eighth day of July, in the ffifteenth yeare of our reigne.

By the King: Howard

FUNDAMENTAL CONSTITUTIONS OF CAROLINA, 1669

Commentary

To the student of constitutional history, the document known as the Fundamental Constitutions of Carolina of 1669 is of particular interest because it was drafted by John Locke. In this document we have the rare example of the Platonic ideal in operation with a frame of government actually drawn up by one of the greatest names in political philosophy. Unfortunately, as has all too often been true, Plato become Solon has produced a fundamental law which (however attractive it may be to the speculative theorist) proved wholly unworkable as a practical Charter of government. It is, indeed, amazing that a mind as acute as Locke's should have produced so clumsy a document, with its reliance upon outmoded feudal conceptions and Graustarkian layers of nobility, with its palatines, signiories, baronies, manors, court-leets, landgraves, and caziques. Certainly, the elaborate structure, based on institutions which had even become anachronisms in the Old World, was completely out of place in a Colony like Carolina, which could scarcely be settled as a feudal kingdom in miniature. The Locke document was never put into full operation and remains of note solely because of the man who drafted it.

Since Locke was, however, so influential in the history of ideas, and above all in the development of the Whig theories of government, it is not surprising that the Carolina Constitutions contain several important provisions protecting individual rights. Best known of these is the provision in Article 109 that "No person whatsoever shall disturb, molest or persecute another for his speculative opinions in religion, or his way of worship." This is an early version of the right to freedom of conscience similar to that in the Rhode Island Charter (*supra* p. 96). In addition, Article 111 contains an express guarantee of trial by jury (though modified in Article 69 by requiring only a majority verdict) and Article 4 contains an early version of the prohibition against double jeopardy. To have these stated as basic rights by the political theorist who, more than any other, influenced American Constitution-makers was of great significance to the development of the federal Bill of Rights.

Fundamental Constitutions of Carolina, 1669*

Our sovereign lord the King having, out of his royal grace and bounty, granted unto us the province of Carolina, with all the royalties, properties, jurisdictions, and privileges of a county palatine, as large and ample as the

*Poore, *The Federal and State Constitutions, Colonial Charters and Other Organic Laws of the United States*, Vol. 2, pp. 1397–1408.

county palatine of Durham, with other great privileges; for the better settlement of the government of the said place, and establishing the interest of the lords proprietors with equality and without confusion; and that the government of this province may be made most agreeable to the monarchy under which we live and of which this province is a part; and that we may avoid erecting a numerous democracy, we, the lords and proprietors of the province aforesaid, have agreed to this following form of government, to be perpetually established amongst us, unto which we do oblige ourselves, our heirs and successors, in the most binding ways that can be devised.

One: The eldest of the lords proprietors shall be palatine; and, upon the decease of the palatine, the eldest of the seven surviving proprietors shall always succeed him.

Two: There shall be seven other chief offices erected, viz: the admirals, chamberlains, chancellors, constables, chief justices, high stewards, and treasurers; which places shall be enjoyed by none but the lords proprietors, to be assigned at first by lot; and, upon the vacancy of any one of the seven great offices, by death or otherwise, the eldest proprietor shall have his choice of the said place.

Three: The whole province shall be divided into counties; each county shall consist of eight signiories, eight baronies, and four precincts; each precinct shall consist of six colonies.

Four: Each signiory, barony, and colony shall consist of twelve thousand acres; the eight signiories being the share of the eight proprietors, and the eight baronies of the nobility; both which shares, being each of them one-fifth of the whole, are to be perpetually annexed, the one to the proprietors, the other to the hereditary nobility, leaving the colonies, being three-fifths, amongst the people; so that in setting out and planting the lands, the balance of the government may be preserved.

Five: At any time before the year one thousand seven hundred and one, any of the lords proprietors shall have power to relinquish, alienate, and dispose to any other person his proprietorship, and all the signiories, powers, and interest thereunto belonging, wholly and entirely together, and not otherwise. But after the year one thousand seven hundred, those who are then lords proprietors shall not have power to alienate or make over their proprietorship, with the signiories and privileges thereunto belonging, or any part thereof, to any person whatsoever, otherwise than in section eighteen; but it shall all descend unto their heirs male, and for want of heirs male, it shall all descend on that landgrave or cazique of Carolina who is descended of the next heirs female of the proprietor; and, for want of such heirs, it shall descend on the next heir general; and, for want of such heirs, the remaining seven proprietors shall, upon the vacancy, choose a landgrave to succeed the deceased proprietors, who, being chosen by the majority of the seven surviving proprietors, he and his heirs, successively shall be proprietors, as fully to all intents and purposes as any of the rest.

Six: That the number of eight proprietors may be constantly kept, if, upon the vacancy of any proprietorship, the seven surviving proprietors shall not choose a landgrave to be a proprietor before the second biennial parliament after the vacancy, then the next biennial parliament but one, after such vacancy, shall have power to choose any landgrave to be a proprietor.

Seven: Whosoever, after the year one thousand seven hundred, either by inheritance or choice, shall succeed any proprietor in his proprietorship, and signories thereunto belonging, shall be obliged to take the name and arms of that proprietor whom he succeeds; which from thenceforth shall be the name and arms of his family and their posterity.

Eight: Whatsoever landgrave or cazique shall any way come to be a proprietor, shall take the signiories annexed to the said proprietorship; but his former dignity, with the baronies annexed, shall devolve into the hands of the lords proprietors.

Nine: There shall be just as many landgraves as there are counties, and twice as many caziques, and no more. These shall be the hereditary nobility of the province, and by right of their dignity be members of parliament. Each landgrave shall have four baronies, and each cazique two baronies, hereditarily and unalterably annexed to and settled upon the said dignity.

Ten: The first landgraves and caziques of the twelve first counties to be planted shall be nominated thus, that is to say: of the twelve landgraves, the lords proprietors shall each of them, separately for himself, nominate and choose one; and the remaining four landgraves of the first twelve shall be nominated and chosen by the palatine's court. In like manner, of the twenty-four first caziques, each proprietor for himself shall nominate and choose two, and the remaining eight shall be nominated and chosen by the palatine's court; and when the twelve first counties shall be planted, the lords proprietors shall again in the same manner nominate and choose twelve more landgraves and twenty-four more caziques, for the next twelve counties to be planted; that is to say, two-thirds of each number by the single nomination of each proprietor for himself, and the remaining third by the joint election of the palatine's court, and so proceed in the same manner till the whole province of Carolina be set out and planted, according to the proportions in these fundamental constitutions.

Eleven: Any landgrave or cazique, at any time before the year one thousand seven hundred and one, shall have power to alienate, sell, or make over, to any other person, his dignity, with the baronies thereunto belonging, all entirely together. But after the year one thousand seven hundred, no landgrave or cazique shall have power to alienate, sell, make over, or let the hereditary baronies of his dignity, or any part thereof, otherwise than as in section eighteen; but they shall all entirely, with the dignity thereunto belonging, descend unto his heirs male; and for want of heirs male, all entirely and undivided to the next heir general; and for want of such heirs, shall devolve into the hands of the lords proprietors.

Twelve: That the due number of landgraves and caziques may be always kept up, if, upon the devolution of any landgraveship or caziqueship, the palatine's court shall not settle the devolved dignity, with the baronies thereunto annexed, before the second biennial parliament after such devolution, the next biennial parliament but one after such devolution shall have power to make any one landgrave or cazique in the room of him who dying without heirs, his dignity and baronies devolved.

Thirteen: No one person shall have more than one dignity, with the signiories or baronies thereunto belonging. But whensoever it shall happen that any one who is already proprietor, landgrave, or cazique shall have any of these dignities descend to him by inheritance, it shall be at his choice to keep which of the dignities, with the lands annexed, he shall like best; but shall leave the other, with the lands annexed, to be enjoyed by him who, not being his heir apparent and certain successor to his present dignity, is next of blood.

Fourteen: Whosoever, by right of inheritance, shall come to be landgrave or cazique, shall take the name and arms of his predecessor in that dignity, to be from thenceforth the name and arms of his family and their posterity.

Fifteen: Since the dignity of proprietor, landgrave, or cazique cannot be divided, and the signiories or baronies thereunto annexed must forever all entirely descend with and accompany that dignity, whensoever, for want of heirs male, it shall descend on the issue female, the eldest daughter and her heirs shall be preferred, and in the inheritance of those dignities, and in the signiories or baronies annexed, there shall be no coheirs.

Sixteen: In every signiory, barony, and manor, the respective lord shall have power, in his own name, to hold court-leet there, for trying of all causes, both civil and criminal; but where it shall concern any person being no inhabitant, vassal, or leet-man of the said signiory, barony, or manor, he, upon paying down of forty shillings to the lords proprietors' use, shall have an appeal from the signiory or barony court to the county court, and from the manor court to the precinct court.

Seventeen: Every manor shall consist of not less than three thousand acres, and not above twelve thousand acres, in one entire piece and colony, but any three thousand acres or more in one piece, and the possession of one man, shall not be a manor, unless it be constituted a manor by the grant of the palatine's court.

Eighteen: The lords of signiories and baronies shall have power only of granting estates not exceeding three lives, or twenty-one years, in two-thirds of said signiories or baronies, and the remaining third shall be always demesne.

Nineteen: Any lord of a manor may alienate, sell, or dispose to any other person and his heirs forever, his manor, all entirely together, with all the privileges and leet-men thereunto belonging, so far forth as any colony lands; but no grant of any part thereof, either in fee, or for any longer term than three lives, or one-and-twenty years, shall stand good against the next heir.

Twenty: No manor, for want of issue male, shall be divided amongst coheirs; but the manor, if there be but one, shall all entirely descend to the eldest daughter and her heirs. If there be more minors than one, the eldest daughter first shall have her choice, the second next, and so on, beginning again at the eldest, until all the manors be taken up; that so the privileges which belong to manors being indivisible, the lands of the manors, to which they are annexed, may be kept entire and the manor not lose those privileges which, upon parcelling out to several owners, must necessarily cease.

Twenty-one: Every lord of a manor, within his own manor, shall have all the rights, powers, jurisdictions, and privileges which a landgrave or cazique hath in his baronies.

Twenty-two: In every signiory, barony, and manor, all the leet-men shall be under the jurisdiction of the respective lords of the said signiory, barony, or manor, without appeal from him. Nor shall any leet-man or leet-woman have liberty to go off from the land of their particular lord and live anywhere else, without license obtained from their said lord, under hand and seal.

Twenty-three: All the children of leet-men shall be leet-men, and so to all generations.

Twenty-four: No man shall be capable of having a court-leet or leet-men but a proprietor, landgrave, cazique, or lord of a manor.

Twenty-five: Whoever shall voluntarily enter himself a leet-man in the registry of the county court, shall be a leet-man.

Twenty-six: Whoever is lord of leet-men, shall, upon the marriage of a leet-man or leet-woman of his, give them ten acres of land for their lives; they paying to him therefor not more than one-eighth part of all the yearly produce and growth of the said ten acres.

Twenty-seven: No landgrave or cazique shall be tried for any criminal cause in any but the chief justice's court, and that by a jury of his peers.

Twenty-eight: There shall be eight supreme courts. The first called the palatine's court, consisting of the palatine and the other seven proprietors. The other seven courts of the other seven great officers, shall consist each of them of a proprietor, and six councillors added to him. Under each of these latter seven courts shall be a college of twelve assistants. The twelve assistants of the several colleges shall be chosen, two out of the landgraves, caziques, or eldest sons of the proprietors, by the palatine's court; two out of the landgraves by the landgraves' chamber; two out of the caziques by the caziques' chamber; four more of the twelve shall be chosen by the commons' chamber, out of such as have been or are members of parliament, sheriffs, or justices of the county court, or the younger sons of proprietors, or the eldest sons of landgraves or caziques; the two others shall be chosen by the palatine's court, out of the same sort of persons out of which the commons' chamber is to choose.

Twenty-nine: Out of these colleges shall be chosen at first, by the palatine's court, six councillors, to be joined with each proprietor in his court; of which six one shall be of those who were chosen into any of the colleges by the palatine's court, out of the landgraves, caziques, or eldest sons of proprietors; one out of those who were chosen by the landgraves' chamber; one out of those who were chosen by the caziques' chamber; two out of those who were chosen by the commons' chamber; and one out of those who were chosen by the palatine's court, out of the proprietors' younger sons, or eldest sons of landgraves, caziques, or commons, qualified as aforesaid.

Thirty: When it shall happen that any councillor dies, and thereby there is a vacancy, the grand council shall have power to remove any councillor that is willing to be removed out of any of the proprietors' courts, to fill up the vacancy; provided they take a man of the same degree and choice the other was of, whose place is to be filled up. But if no councillor consent to be removed, or upon such remove, the last remaining vacant place, in any of the proprietors' courts, shall be filled up by the choice of the grand council, who shall have power to remove out of any of the colleges any assistant, who is of the same degree and choice that that councillor was of into whose vacant place he is to succeed. The grand council also have power to remove any assistant, that is willing, out of one college into another, provided he be of the same degree and choice. But the last remaining vacant place in any college shall be filled up by the same choice, and out of the same degree of persons the assistant was of who is dead or removed. No place shall be vacant in any college longer than the next session of parliament.

Thirty-one: No man, being a member of the grand council, or of any of the seven colleges, shall be turned out but for misdemeanor, of which the grand council shall be judge; and the vacancy of the person so put out shall be filled, not by the election of the grand council, but by those who first chose him, and out of the same degree he was of who is expelled. But it is not hereby to be understood that the grand council hath any power to turn out any one of the lords proprietors or their deputies, the lords proprietors having in themselves an inherent original right.

Thirty-two: All elections in the parliament, in the several chambers of the parliament, and in the grand council, shall be passed by balloting.

Thirty-three: The palatine's court shall consist of the palatine and seven proprietors, wherein nothing shall be acted without the presence and consent of the palatine or his deputy, and three other of the proprietors or their deputies. This court shall have power to call parliaments, to pardon all offences, to make elections of all officers in the proprietor's dispose, and to nominate and appoint port towns; and also shall have power by their order to the treasurer to dispose of all public treasure, excepting money granted by the parliament, and by them directed to some particular public use; and also shall have a negative upon all acts, orders, votes, and judgments of the grand council and the parliament, except only as in sections six and twelve; and shall have all the powers granted to the lords proprietors, by their patent from our sovereign lord the King, except in such things as are limited by these fundamental constitutions.

Thirty-four: The palatine himself, when he in person shall be either in the army or any of the proprietors' courts, shall then have the power of general, or of that proprietor in whose court he is then present, and the proprietor, in whose court the palatine then presides, shall, during his presence there, be but as one of the council.

Thirty-five: The chancellor's court, consisting of one of the proprietors, and his six councillors, who shall be called vice-chancellors, shall have the custody of the seal of the palatine, under which charters of lands, or otherwise, commissions and grants of the palatine's court shall pass. And it shall not be lawful to put the seal of the palatinate to any writing which is not signed by the palatine or his deputy and three other proprietors or their deputies. To this court also belong all state matters, despatches, and treaties with the neighbor Indians. To this court also belong all invasions of the law, of liberty of conscience, and all invasions of the public peace, upon pretence of religion, as also the license of printing. The twelve assistants belonging to this court shall be called recorders.

Thirty-six: Whatever passes under the seal of the palatinate, shall be registered in that proprietor's court to which the matter therein contained belongs.

Thirty-seven: The chancellor or his deputy shall be always speaker in parliament, and president of the grand council, and, in his and his deputy's absence, one of the vice-chancellors.

Thirty-eight: The chief justice's court, consisting of one of the proprietors and his six councillors, who shall be called justices of the bench, shall judge all appeals in cases both civil and criminal, except all such cases as shall be under the jurisdiction and cognizance of any other of the proprietor's courts, which shall be tried in those courts respectively. The government and regulation of registries of writings and contracts shall belong to the jurisdiction of this court. The twelve assistants of this court shall be called masters.

Thirty-nine: The constable's court, consisting of one of the proprietors and his six councillors, who shall be called marshals, shall order and determine of all military affairs by land, and all land-forces, arms, ammunition, artillery, garrisons, forts, &c., and whatever belongs unto war. His twelve assistants shall be called lieutenant-generals.

Forty: In time of actual war the constable, while he is in the army, shall be general of the army, and the six councillors, or such of them as the palatine's court shall for that time or service appoint, shall be the immediate great officers under him, and the lieutenant-generals next to them.

Forty-one: The admiral's court, consisting of one of the proprietors and his six councillors, called consuls, shall have the care and inspection over all ports, moles, and navigable rivers, so far as the tide flows, and also all the public shipping of Carolina, and stores thereunto belonging, and all maritime affairs. This court also shall have the power of the court of admiralty; and shall have power to constitute judges in port-towns to try cases belonging to law-merchant, as shall be most convenient for trade. The twelve assistants belonging to this court shall be called proconsuls.

Forty-two: In time of actual war, the admiral, whilst he is at sea, shall command in chief, and his six councillors, or such of them as the palatine's court shall for that time or service appoint, shall be the immediate great officers under him, and the proconsuls next to them.

Forty-three: The treasurer's court, consisting of a proprietor and his six councillors, called under-treasurers, shall take care of all matters that concern the public revenue and treasury. The twelve assistants shall be called auditors.

Forty-four: The high steward's court, consisting of a proprietor and his six councillors, called comptrollers, shall have the care of all foreign and domestic trade, manufactures, public buildings, work-houses, highways, passages by water above the flood of the tide, drains, sewers, and banks against inundation, bridges, posts, carriers, fairs, markets, corruption or infection of the common air or water, and all things in order to the public commerce and health; also setting out and surveying of lands; and also setting out and appointing places for towns to be built on in the precincts, and the prescribing and determining the figure and bigness of the said towns, according to such models as the said court shall order; contrary or differing from which models it shall not be lawful for any one to build in any town. This court shall have power also to make any public building, or any new highway, or enlarge any old highway, upon any man's land whatsoever; as also to make cuts, channels, banks, locks, and bridges, for making rivers navigable, or for draining fens, or any other public use. The damage the owner of such lands (on or through which any such public things shall be made) shall receive thereby shall be valued, and satisfaction made by such ways as the grand council shall appoint. The twelve assistants belonging to this court shall be called surveyors.

Forty-five: The chamberlain's court, consisting of a proprietor and six councillors, called vice-chamberlains, shall have the care of all ceremonies, precedency, heraldry, reception of public messengers, pedigrees, the registry of all births, burials, and marriages, legitimation, and all cases concerning matrimony, or arising from it; and shall also have power to regulate all fashions, habits, badges, games, and sports. To this court it shall also belong to convocate the grand council. The twelve assistants belonging to this court shall be called provosts.

Forty-six: All causes belonging to or under the jurisdiction of any of the proprietors' courts, shall in them respectively be tried, and ultimately determined, without any further appeal.

Forty-seven: The proprietors' courts shall have a power to mitigate all fines and suspend all execution in criminal causes, either before or after sentence, in any of the other inferior courts respectively.

Forty-eight: In all debates, hearings, or trials, in any of the proprietors' courts, the twelve assistants belonging to the said courts, respectively, shall have liberty to be present, but shall not interpose, unless their opinions be required, nor have any vote at all; but their business shall be, by the direction of the respective courts, to prepare such business as shall be committed to them; as also to bear such offices, and despatch such affairs, either where the court is kept or elsewhere, as the court shall think fit.

Forty-nine: In all the proprietors' courts, the proprietor, and any three of his councillors, shall make a quorum: Provided, always, That for the better despatch of business, it shall be in the power of the palatine's court to direct what sort of causes shall be heard and determined by a quorum of any three.

Fifty: The grand council shall consist of the palatine and seven proprietors, and the forty-two councillors of the several proprietors' courts, who shall have power to determine any controversy that may arise between any of the proprietors' courts, about their respective jurisdictions, or between the members of the same court, about their manner and methods of proceedings; to make peace and war, leagues, treaties, &c., with any of the neighbor Indians; to issue out their general orders to the constable's and admiral's courts, for the raising, disposing, or disbanding the forces, by land or by sea.

Fifty-one: The grand council shall prepare all matters to be proposed in parliament. Nor shall any matter whatsoever be proposed in parliament, but what has first passed the grand council; which, after having been read three several days in the parliament, shall by majority of votes be passed or rejected.

Fifty-two: The grand council shall always be judges of all causes and appeals that concern the palatine, or any of the lords proprietors, or any councillor of any proprietor's court, in any cause, which should otherwise have been tried in the court of which the said councillor is judge himself.

Fifty-three: The grand council, by their warrants to the treasurer's court, shall dispose of all the money given by the parliament, and by them directed to any particular public use.

Fifty-four: The quorum of the grand council shall be thirteen, whereof a proprietor or his deputy shall be always one.

Fifty-five: The grand council shall meet the first Tuesday in every month, and as much oftener as either they shall think fit, or they shall be convocated by the chamberlain's court.

Fifty-six: The palatine, or any of the lords proprietors, shall have power, under hand and seal, to be registered in the grand council, to make a deputy, who shall have the same power to all intents and purposes as he himself who deputes him; except in confirming acts of parliament, as in section seventy-six, and except also in nominating and choosing landgraves and caziques, as in section ten. All such deputations shall cease and determine at the end of four years, and at any time shall be revocable at the pleasure of the deputator.

Fifty-seven: No deputy of any proprietor shall have any power whilst the deputator is in any part of Carolina, except the proprietor whose deputy he is be a minor.

Fifty-eight: During the minority of any proprietor, his guardian shall have power to constitute and appoint his deputy.

Fifty-nine: The eldest of the lords proprietors, who shall be personally in Carolina, shall of course be the palatine's deputy, and if no proprietor be in Carolina, he shall choose his deputy out of the heirs apparent of any of the proprietors, if any such be there; and if there be no heir apparent of any of the lords proprietors above one-and-twenty years old in Carolina, then he shall choose for deputy any one of the landgraves of the grand council; till he have by deputation under hand and seal chosen any one of the forementioned heirs apparent or landgraves to be his deputy, the eldest man of the landgraves, and, for want of a landgrave, the eldest man of the caziques, who shall be personally in Carolina, shall of course be his deputy.

Sixty: Each proprietor's deputy shall be always one of his six councillors, respectively; and in case any of the proprietors hath not, in his absence out of Carolina, a deputy, commissioned under his hand and seal, the eldest nobleman of his court shall of course be his deputy.

Sixty-one: In every county there shall be a court, consisting of a sheriff, and four justices of the county, for every precinct one. The sheriff shall be an inhabitant of the county, and have at least five hundred acres of freehold within the said county; and the justices shall be inhabitants, and have each of them five hundred acres apiece freehold within the precinct for which they serve respectively. These five shall be chosen from time to time and commissioned by the palatine's court.

Sixty-two: For any personal causes exceeding the value of two hundred pounds sterling, or in title of land, or in any criminal cause, either party upon paying twenty pounds sterling to the lords proprietors' use, shall have liberty of appeal from the county court unto the respective proprietor's court.

Sixty-three: In every precinct there shall be a court, consisting of a steward and four justices of the precinct, being inhabitants and having three hundred acres of freehold within the said precinct, who shall judge all criminal causes; except for treason, murder, and any other offences punishable with death, and except all criminal causes of the nobility; and shall judge also all civil causes whatsoever; and in all personal actions not exceeding fifty pounds sterling, without appeal; but where the cause shall exceed that value, or concern a title of land, and in all criminal causes, there either party, upon paying five pounds sterling to the lords proprietors' use, shall have liberty of appeal to the county court.

Sixty-four: No cause shall be twice tried in any one court, upon any reason or pretence whatsoever.

Sixty-five: For treason, murder, and all other offences punishable with death, there shall be a commission, twice a year at least, granted unto one or more members of the grand council or colleges; who shall come as itinerant judges to the several counties, and with the sheriff and four justices shall hold assizes to judge all such causes; but, upon paying of fifty pounds sterling to the lords proprietors' use, there shall be liberty of appeal to the respective proprietor's court.

Sixty-six: The grand jury at the several assizes shall, upon their oaths, and under their hands and seals, deliver in to their itinerant judges a presentment of such grievances, misdemeanors, exigences, or defects, which they think necessary for the public good of the country; which presentments shall, by the itinerant judges, at the end of their circuit, be delivered in to the grand council at their next sitting. And whatsoever therein concerns the execution of laws already made, the several proprietors' courts, in the matters belonging to each of them, respectively, shall take cognizance of it, and give such order about it as shall be effectual for the due execution of the laws. But whatever concerns the making of any new law, shall be referred to the several respective courts to which that matter belongs, and be by them prepared and brought to the grand council.

Sixty-seven: For terms, there shall be quarterly such a certain number of days, not exceeding one-and-twenty at any one time, as the several respective courts shall appoint. The time for the beginning of the term, in the precinct court, shall be the first Monday in January, April, July, and October; in the county court, the first Monday in February, May, August, and November; and in the proprietors' courts the first Monday in March, June, September, and December.

Sixty-eight: In the precinct court no man shall be a juryman under fifty acres of freehold. In the county court, or at the assizes, no man shall be a grand-juryman under three hundred acres of freehold; and no man shall be a petty-juryman under two hunddred acres of freehold. In the proprietors' courts no man shall be a juryman under five hundred acres of freehold.

Sixty-nine: Every jury shall consist to twelve men; and it shall not be necessary they should all agree, but the verdict shall be according to the consent of the majority.

Seventy: It shall be a base and vile thing to plead for money or reward; nor shall any one (except he be a near kinsman, not farther off than cousin-german to the party concerned) be permitted to plead another man's cause, till, before the judge in open court, he hath taken an oath that he doth not plead for money or reward, nor hath nor will receive, nor directly nor indirectly bargained with the party whose cause he is going to plead, for money or any other reward for pleading his cause.

Seventy-one: There shall be a parliament, consisting of the proprietors or their deputies, the landgraves, and caziques, and one freeholder out of every precinct, to be chosen by the freeholders of the said precinct, respectively. They shall sit all together in one room, and have every member one vote.

Seventy-two: No man shall be chosen a member of parliament who has less than five hundred acres of freehold within the precinct for which he is chosen; nor shall any have a vote in choosing the said member that hath less than fifty acres of freehold within the said precinct.

Seventy-three: A new parliament shall be assembled the first Monday of the month of November every second year, and shall meet and sit in the town they last sat in, without any summons, unless by the palatine's court they be summoned to meet at any other place. And if there shall be any occasion of a parliament in these intervals, it shall be in the power of the palatine's court to assemble them in forty days notice, and at such time and place as the said court shall think fit; and the palatine's court shall have power to dissolve the said parliament when they shall think fit.

Seventy-four: At the opening of every parliament, the first thing that shall be done shall be the reading of these fundamental constitutions, which the palatine and proprietors, and the rest of the members then present, shall subscribe. Nor shall any person whatsoever sit or vote in the parliament till he hath that session subscribed these fundamental constitutions, in a book kept for that purpose by the clerk of the parliament.

Seventy-five: In order to the due election of members for the biennial parliament, it shall be lawful for the freeholders of the respective precincts to meet the first Tuesday in September every two years, in the same town or place that they last met in, to choose parliament men; and there choose those members that are to sit the next November following, unless the steward of the precinct shall, by sufficient notice thirty days before, appoint some other place for their meeting in order to the election.

Seventy-six: No act or order of parliament shall be of any force, unless it be ratified in open parliament, during the same session, by the palatine or his deputy, and three more of the lords proprietors or their deputies; and then not to continue longer in force but until the next biennial parliament, unless in the mean time it be ratified under the hands and seals of the palatine himself, and three more of the lords proprietors themselves, and by their order published at the next biennial parliament.

Seventy-seven: Any proprietor or his deputy may enter his protestation against any act of the parliament, before the palatine or his deputy's consent be given as aforesaid, if he shall conceive the said act to be contrary to this establishment, or any of these fundamental constitutions of the government. And in such case, after full and free debate, the several estates shall retire into four several chambers; the palatine and proprietors into one; the landgraves into another; the caziques into another; and those chosen by the precincts into a fourth; and if the major part of any of the four estates shall vote that the law is not agreeable to this establishment, and these fundamental constitutions of the government, then it shall pass no farther, but be as if it had never been proposed.

Seventy-eight: The quorum of the parliament shall be one-half of those who are members and capable of sitting in the house that present session of parliament. The quorum of each of the chambers of parliament shall be one-half of the members of that chamber.

Seventy-nine: To avoid multiplicity of laws, which by degrees always change the right foundations of the original government, all acts of parliament whatsoever, in whatsoever form passed or enacted, shall, at the end of a hundred years after their enacting, respectively cease and determine of themselves, and without any repeal become null and void, as if no such acts or laws had ever been made.

Eighty: Since multiplicity of comments, as well as of laws, have great inconveniences, and serve only to obscure and perplex, all manner of comments and expositions on any part of these fundamental constitutions, or on any part of the common or statute laws of Carolina, are absolutely prohibited.

Eighty-one: There shall be a registry in every precinct, wherein shall be enrolled all deeds, leases, judgments, mortgages, and other conveyances, which may concern any of the lands within the said precinct; and all such conveyances not so entered and registered shall not be of force against any person or party to the said contract or conveyance.

Eighty-two: No man shall be register of any precinct who hath not at least three hundred acres of freehold within the said precinct.

Eighty-three: The freeholders of every precinct shall nominate three men; out of which three the chief justice's court shall choose and commission one to be register of the said precinct, whilst he shall well behave himself.

Eighty-four: There shall be a registry in every signiory, barony, and colony, wherein shall be recorded all the births, marriages, and deaths that shall happen within the respective signiories, baronies, and colonies.

Eighty-five: No man shall be register of a colony that hath not above fifty acres of freehold within the said colony.

Eighty-six: The time of every one's age, that is born in Carolina, shall be reckoned from the day that his birth is entered in the registry, and not before.

Eighty-seven: No marriage shall be lawful, whatever contract and ceremony they have used, till both the parties mutually own it before the register of the place where they were married, and he register it, with the names of the father and mother of each party.

Eighty-eight: No man shall administer to the goods, or have a right to them, or enter upon the estate of any person deceased, till his death be registered in the respective registry.

Eighty-nine: He that doth not enter in the respective registry the birth or death of any person that is born or dies in his house or ground, shall pay to the said register one shilling per week for each such neglect, reckoning from the time of each birth or death, respectively, to the time of entering it in the register.

Ninety: In like manner, the births, marriages, and deaths of the lords proprietors, landgraves, and caziques shall be registered in the chamberlain's court.

Ninety-one: There shall be in every colony one constable, to be chosen annually, by the freeholders of the colony; his estate shall be above a hundred acres of freehold within the said colony, and such subordinate officers appointed for his assistance as the county court shall find requisite, and shall be established by the said county court. The election of the subordinate annual officers shall be also in the freeholders of the colony.

Ninety-two: All towns incorporate shall be governed by a mayor, twelve aldermen, and twenty-four of the common council. The said common council shall be chosen by the present householders of the said town; the aldermen shall be chosen out of the common council; and the mayor out of the aldermen, by the palatine's court.

Ninety-three: It being of great consequence to the plantation that port-towns should be built and preserved; therefore, whosoever shall lade or unlade any commodity at any other place than a port-town, shall forfeit to the lords proprietors, for each ton so laden or unladen, the sum of ten pounds sterling; except only such goods as the palatine's court shall license to be laden or unladen elsewhere.

Ninety-four: The first port-town upon every river shall be in a colony, and be a port-town forever.

Ninety-five: No man shall be permitted to be a freeman of Carolina, or to have any estate or habitation within it, that doth not acknowledge a God; and that God is publicly and solemnly to be worshipped.

Ninety-six: [As the country comes to be sufficiently planted and distributed into fit divisions, it shall belong to the parliament to take care for the building of churches, and the public maintenance of divines, to be employed in the exercise of religion, according to the Church of England; which being the only true and orthodox, and the national religion of all the King's dominions, is so also of Carolina; and, therefore, it alone shall be allowed to receive public maintenance, by grant of parliament.]

Ninety-seven: But since the natives of that place, who will be concerned in our plantation, are utterly strangers to Christianity, whose idolatry, ignorance, or mistake gives us no right to expel or use them ill; and those who remove from other parts to plant there will unavoidably be of different opinions concerning matters of religion, the liberty whereof they will expect to have allowed them, and it will not be reasonable for us, on this account, to keep them out, that civil peace may be maintained amidst diversity of opinions, and our agreement and compact with all men may be duly and faithfully observed; the violation whereof, upon what pretence soever, cannot be without great offence to Almighty God, and great scandal to the true religion which we profess; and also that Jews, heathens, and other dissenters from the purity of Christian religion may not be scared and kept at a distance from it, but, by having an opportunity of acquainting themselves with the truth and reasonableness of its doctrines, and the peaceableness and inoffensiveness of its professors, may, by good usage and persuasion, and all those convincing methods of gentleness and meekness, suitable to the rules and design of the gospel, be won ever to embrace and unfeignedly receive the truth; therefore, any seven or more persons agreeing in any religion, shall constitute a church or profession, to which they shall give some name, to distinguish it from others.

Ninety-eight: The terms of admittance and communion with any church or profession shall be written in a book, and therein be subscribed by all the members of the said church or profession; which book shall be kept by the public register of the precinct wherein they reside.

Ninety-nine: The time of every one's subscription and admittance shall be dated in the said book or religious record.

One hundred: In the terms of communion of every church or profession, these following shall be three; without which no agreement or assembly of men, upon pretence of religion, shall be accounted a church or profession within these rules:

> Ist. That there is a God.
> II. That God is publicly to be worshipped.
> III. That it is lawful and the duty of every man, being thereunto called by those that govern, to bear witness to truth; and that every church or profession shall, in their terms of communion, set down the external way whereby they witness a truth as in the presence of God, whether it be by laying hands on or kissing the bible, as in the Church of England, or by holding up the hand, or any other sensible way.

One hundred and one: No person above seventeen years of age shall have any benefit or protection of the law, or be capable of any place of profit or honor, who is not a member of some church or profession, having his name recorded in some one, and but one religious record at once.

One hundred and two: No person of any other church or profession shall disturb or molest any religious assembly.

One hundred and three: No person whatsoever shall speak anything in their religious assembly irreverently or seditiously of the government or governors, or of state matters.

One hundred and four: Any person subscribing the terms of communion, in the record of the said church or profession, before the precinct register, and any five members of the said church or profession, shall be thereby made a member of the said church or profession.

One hundred and five: Any person striking out his own name out of any religious record, or his name being struck out by any officer thereunto authorized by each church or profession respectively, shall cease to be a member of that church or profession.

One hundred and six: No man shall use any reproachful, reviling, or abusive language against any religion of any church or profession; that being the certain way of disturbing the peace, and of hindering the conversion of any to the truth, by engaging them in quarrels and animosities, to the hatred of the professors and that profession which otherwise they might be brought to assent to.

One hundred and seven: Since charity obliges us to wish well to the souls of all men, and religion ought to alter nothing in any man's civil estate or right, it shall be lawful for slaves, as well as others, to enter themselves, and be of what church or profession any of them shall think best, and, therefore, be as fully members as any freeman. But yet no slave shall hereby be exempted from that civil dominion his master hath over him, but be in all things in the same state and condition he was in before.

One hundred and eight: Assemblies, upon what pretence soever of religion, not observing and performing the above said rules, shall not be esteemed as churches, but unlawful meetings, and be punished as other riots.

One hundred and nine: No person whatsoever shall disturb, molest, or persecute another for his speculative opinions in religion, or his way of worship.

One hundred and ten: Every freeman of Carolina shall have absolute power and authority over his negro slaves, of what opinion or religion soever.

One hundred and eleven: No cause, whether civil or criminal, of any freeman, shall be tried in any court of judicature, without a jury of his peers.

One hundred and twelve: No person whatever shall hold or claim any land in Carolina by purchase or gift, or otherwise, from the natives, or any other whatsoever, but merely from and under the lords proprietors, upon pain of forfeiture of all his estate, movable or immovable, and perpetual banishment.

One hundred and thirteen: Whosoever shall possess any freehold in Carolina, upon what title or grant soever, shall, at the farthest, from and after the year one thousand six hundred and eighty-nine, pay yearly unto the lords proprietors, for each acre of land, English measure, as much fine silver as is at this present time in one English penny, or the value thereof, to be as a chief rent and acknowledgment to the lords proprietors, their heirs and successors, forever. And it shall be lawful for the palatine's court, by their officers, at any time to take a new survey of any man's land, not to oust him of any part of his possession, but that by such a survey the just number of acres he possesseth may be known, and the rent thereon due may be paid by him.

One hundred and fourteen: All wrecks, mines, minerals, quarries of gems, and precious stones, with pearl-fishing, whale-fishing, and one-half of all ambergris, by whomsoever found, shall wholly belong to the lords proprietors.

One hundred and fifteen: All revenues and profits belonging to the lords proprietors in common shall be divided into ten parts, whereof the palatine shall have three, and each proprietor one; but if the palatine shall govern by a deputy, the deputy shall have one of those three-tenths, and the palatine the other two-tenths.

One hundred and sixteen: All inhabitants and freemen of Carolina above seventeen years of age, and under sixty, shall be bound to bear arms and serve as soldiers, whenever the grand council shall find it necessary.

One hundred and seventeen: A true copy of these fundamental constitutions shall be kept in a great book by the register of every precinct, to be subscribed before the said register. Nor shall any person, of what degree or condition soever, above seventeen years old, have any estate or possession in Carolina, or protection or benefit of the law there, who hath not, before a precinct register, subscribed these fundamental constitutions in this form:

> I, A. B., do promise to bear faith and true allegiance to our sovereign lord King Charles II, his heirs and successors; and will be true and faithful to the palatine and lords proprietors of Carolina, their heirs and successors; and with my utmost power will defend them, and maintain the government according to this establishment in these fundamental constitutions.

One hundred and eighteen: Whatsoever alien shall, in this form, before any precinct register, subscribe these fundamental constitutions, shall be thereby naturalized.

One hundred and nineteen: In the same manner shall every person, at his admittance into any office, subscribe these fundamental constitutions.

One hundred and twenty: These fundamental constitutions, in number a hundred and twenty, and every part thereof, shall be and remain the sacred and unalterable form and rule of government of Carolina forever. Witness our hands and seals, the first day of March, sixteen hundred and sixty-nine.

CONCESSIONS AND AGREEMENTS OF
WEST NEW JERSEY, 1677

Commentary

The next significant step in the Colonial development of guarantees of personal liberty occurred in New Jersey, which was set up as a Proprietary Colony in 1664. To attract settlers, the Proprietors (Lord John Berkeley and Sir George Carteret) issued the Concession and Agreement of February, 1664, which provided for freedom of religion in terms similar to those in the Rhode Island Charter, and self-government through an elected legislature. In 1674 Berkeley sold his interest to Edward Byllynge and other Quakers. New Jersey was then divided between Carteret and the Quakers, with the latter occupying the unoccupied western half.

In 1677, the Quaker Proprietors issued what has been termed one of the more remarkable documents in American history: "The Concessions and Agreements of the Proprietors, Freeholders, and Inhabitants of the Province of West New Jersey." Chapters XIII-XXIII of this document was described in a subtitle as "The Charter or Fundamental Laws of West New Jersey, Agreed Upon."

The basic goal of the Concessions was stated by the Proprietors in a 1676 letter: "There we lay a foundation for after ages to understand their liberty as men and christians, that they may not be brought in bondage, but by their own consent; for we put the power in the people." They meant Chapters XIII-XXIII to serve as "the common law or fundamental rights and privileges . . . agreed upon . . . to be the foundation of the government." More than that, this fundamental law "is not to be altered by the Legislative authority" and the legislature is "to make such laws as agree with, and maintain the said fundamentals, and to make no laws that in the least contradict, differ or vary from the said fundamentals, under what pretence or allegation soever." Here we are very close to the seminal notion of a binding written Constitution and the doctrine of unconstitutional legislation.

Among the rights guaranteed by the 1677 Concessions were religious liberty (in terms even broader than those in the Rhode Island Charter from which it is derived), trial by jury, fair public trials, and freedom from imprisonment for debt. In addition, provision was made for wide dissemination of the Concessions, with the order that they "be writ in fair tables, in every common hall of justice within this Province" and be read four times a year to the people.

The West New Jersey Concessions marks an important step in the development which culminated in the federal Bill of Rights. It is not certain whether William Penn or Edward Byllynge was the primary author of the liberal guarantees. As was the case with the Massachusetts Body of Liberties, the West New Jersey Concessions extended the liberties belonging by right to its settlers beyond the limits recognized in the England of the day. And they did what English law had not yet done in their attempt to give specific content to the rights of the King's subjects. This was, indeed, to be the great American contribution to political science—the protection of individual rights through their specification in a written organic law, binding upon the possessors of governmental power for the time being.

Concessions and Agreements of West New Jersey, 1677*

*The Charter or Fundamental Laws, of
West New Jersey, Agreed Upon*

Chapter XIII

That these following concessions are the Common Law, or Fundamental Rights, of the Province of West New Jersey.

That the common law or fundamental rights and privileges of West New Jersey, are individually agreed upon by the Proprietors and freeholders thereof, to be the foundation of the government, which is not to be altered by the Legislative authority, or free Assembly hereafter mentioned and constituted, but that the said Legislative authority is constituted according to these fundamentals, to make such laws as agree with, and maintain the said fundamentals, and to make no laws that in the least contradict, differ or vary from the said fundamentals, under what pretence or alligation soever.

Chapter XIV

But if it so happen that any person or persons of the said General Assembly, shall therein designedly, willfully, and maliciously, move or excite any to move, any matter or thing whatsoever, that contradicts or any ways subverts, any fundamentals of the said laws in the Constitution of the government of this Province, it being proved by seven honest and reputable persons, he or they shall be proceeded against as traitors to the said government.

Chapter XV

That these Concessions, law or great charter of fundamentals, be recorded in a fair table, in the Assembly House, and that they be read at the beginning and dissolving of every general free Assembly: And it is further agreed and ordained, that the said Concessions, common law, or great charter of fundamentals, be writ in fair tables, in every common hall of justice within this Province, and that they be read in solemn manner four times every year, in the presence of the people, by the chief magistrates of those places.

*A. Leaming and J. Spicer, *The Grants, Concessions, and Original Constitutions of the Province of New Jersey,* 2nd ed., (1881), pp. 393–98.

Chapter XVI

That no men, nor number of men upon earth, hath power or authority to rule over men's consciences in religious matters, therefore it is consented, agreed and ordained, that no person or persons whatsoever within the said Province, at any time or times hereafter, shall be any ways upon any pretence whatsoever, called in question, or in the least punished or hurt, either in person, estate, or priviledge, for the sake of his opinion, judgment, faith or worship towards God in matters of religion. But that all and every such person, and persons, may from time to time, and at all times, freely and fully have, and enjoy his and their judgements, and the exercises of their consciences in matters of religious worship throughout all the said Province.

Chapter XVII

That no Proprietor, freeholder or inhabitant of the said Province of West New Jersey, shall be deprived or condemned of life, limb, liberty, estate, property or any ways hurt in his or their privileges, freedoms or franchises, upon any account whatsoever, without a due tryal, and judgment passed by twelve good and lawful men of his neighbourhood first had: And that in all causes to be tryed, and in all tryals, the person or persons, arraigned may except against any of the said neighbourhood, without any reason rendered, (not exceeding thirty five) and in case of any valid reason alleged, against every person nominated for that service.

Chapter XVIII

And that no Proprietor, freeholder, freedenison, or inhabitant in the said Province, shall be attached, arrested, or imprisoned, for or by reason of any debt, duty, or thing whatsoever (cases felonious, criminal and treasonable excepted) before he or she have personal summon or summons, left at his or her last dwelling place, if in the said Province, by some legal authorized officer, constituted and appointed for that purpose, to appear in some court of judicature for the said Province, with a full and plain account of the cause or thing in demand, as also the name or names of the person or persons at whose suit, and the court where he is to appear, and that he hath at least fourteen days time to appear and answer the said suit, if he or she live or inhabit within forty miles English of the said court, and if at a further distance, to have for every twenty miles, two days time more, for his and their appearance, and so proportionably for a larger distance of place.

That upon the recording of the summons, and non-appearance of such person and persons, a writ or attachment shall or may be issued out to arrest, or attach the person or persons of such defaulters, to cause his or their appearance in such court, returnable at a day certain, to answer the penalty or penalties, in such suit or suits; and if he or they shall be condemned by legal tryal and judgment, the penalty or penalties shall be paid and satisfied out of his or their real or personal estate so condemned, or cause the person or persons so condemned, to lie in execution till satisfaction of the debt and damages be made. Provided always, if such person or persons so condemned, shall pay and deliver such estate, goods, and chattles which he or any other person hath for his or their use, and shall solemnly declare and aver, that he or they have not any further estate, goods or chattles wheresoever, to satisfy the person or persons, (at whose suit, he or they are condemned) their respective judgments, and shall also bring and produce three other persons as compurgators, who are well known and of honest reputation, and approved of by the commissioners of that division, where they dwell or inhabit, which shall in such open court, likewise solemnly declare and aver, that they believe in their consciences, such person and persons so condemned, have not werewith further to pay the said condemnation or condemnations, he or they shall be thence forthwith discharged from their said imprisonment, any law or custom to the contrary thereof, heretofore in the said Province, notwithstanding. And upon such summons and default of appearance, recorded as aforesaid, and such person and persons not appearing within forty days after, it shall and may be lawful for such court of judicature to proceed to tryal, of twelve lawful men to judgment, against such defaulters, and issue forth execution against his or their estate, real and personal, to satisfy such penalty or penalties, to such debt and damages so recorded, as far as it shall or may extend.

Chapter XIX

That there shall be in every court, three justices or commissioners, who shall sit with the twelve men of the neighbourhood, with them to hear all causes, and to assist the said twelve men of the neighbourhood in case of law; and that they the said justices shall pronounce such judgment as they shall receive from, and be directed by the said twelve men, in whom only the judgment resides, and not otherwise.

And in case of their neglect and refusal, that then one of the twelve, by consent of the rest, pronounce their own judgment as the justices should have done.

And if any judgment shall be past, in any case civil or criminal, by any other person or persons, or any other way, then according to this agreement and appointment, it shall be held null and void, and such person or persons so presuming to give judgment, shall be severely fin'd, and upon complaint made to the General Assembly, by them be declared incapable of any office or trust within this Province.

Chapter XX

That in all matters and causes, civil and criminal, proof is to be made by the solemn and plain averment, of at least two honest and reputable persons; and in case that any person or persons shall bear false witness, and bring in his or their evidence, contrary to the truth of the matter as shall be made plainly to appear, that then every such person or persons, shall in civil causes, suffer the penalty which would be due to the person or persons he or they bear witness against. And in case any witness or witnesses, on the behalf of any person or persons, indicted in a criminal cause, shall be found to have born false witness for fear, gain, malice or favour, and thereby hinder the due execution of the law, and deprive the suffering person or persons of their due satisfaction, that then and in all other cases of false evidence, such person or persons, shall be first severly fined, and next that he or they shall forever be disabled from being admitted in evidence, or into any publick office, employment, or service within this Province.

Chapter XXI

That all and every person and persons whatsoever, who shall prosecute or prefer any indictment or information against others for any personal injuries, or matter criminal, or shall prosecute for any other criminal cause, (treason, murther, and felony, only excepted) shall and may be master of his own process, and have full power to forgive and remit the person or persons offending against him or herself only, as well before as after judgment, and condemnation, and pardon and remit the sentence, fine and punishment of the person or persons offending, be it personal or other whatsoever.

Chapter XXII

That the tryals of all causes, civil and criminal, shall be heard and decided by the virdict or judgment of twelve honest men of the neighbourhood, only to be summoned and presented by the sheriff of that division, or propriety where the fact or trespass is committed; and that no person or persons shall be compelled to fee any attorney or counciller to plead his cause, but that all persons have free liberty to plead his own cause, if he please: And that no person nor persons imprisoned upon any account whatsoever within this Province, shall be obliged to pay any fees to the officer or officers of the said prison, either when committed or discharged.

Chapter XXIII

That in all publick courts of justice for tryals of causes, civil or criminal, any person or persons, inhabitants of the said Province may freely come into, and attend the said courts, and hear and be present, at all or any such tryals as shall be there had or passed, that justice may not be done in a corner nor in any covert manner, being intended and resolved, by the help of the Lord, and by these our Concessions and Fundamentals, that all and every person and persons inhabiting the said Province, shall, as far as in us lies, be free from oppression and slavery.

PENNSYLVANIA FRAME OF GOVERNMENT, 1682

Commentary

In many ways, the most influential of the Colonial documents protecting individual rights were the Pennsylvania Frame of Government of 1682 and Charter of Privileges of 1701. Those two basic documents were intimately connected with the personality of William Penn and the persecutions he and his fellow Quakers had suffered in Stuart England. Penn received his Charter for Pennsylvania in 1681 and sought to erect there a government in line with his political and religious conceptions (as stated for example, in *England's Present Interest Considered*, extracts of which follow this Commentary). As Proprietor, Penn could draw up the fundamental law for what he termed "such a holy experiment." In drafting the Frame of Government of 1682, he sought (in his own words) to leave himself and later Governors "no power of doing mischief, that the will of one man may not hinder the good of a whole country."

The Frame of Government was a step closer to the modern Constitution than the earlier documents already discussed. It was based on the essential division between the powers of government and the rights of the individual upon which present-day Constitutions turn. The first part of the Penn document—the Frame of Government, strictly speaking—was essentially a Charter of government setting up the machinery of government and the powers vested in the different officials and institutions (providing in this respect for the first time the fully representative type of government that has come to characterize the American polity). The second part, titled the "Laws Agreed upon in England," was really what we should term a Bill of Rights, containing provisions protecting the essential rights of Pennsylvanians. Equally important was the fact that the Frame included another essential element of the modern Constitution, an amending clause (section XXIII)—the first in any written Constitution.

The Frame of Government starts with a Preface which sets forth Penn's theory of government. Most interesting to us is the statement at such an early date of the concept of the rule of law: "Any government is free to the people under it (whatever be the frame) where the laws rule and the people are a party to those laws." The purpose of the Frame is stated to be to secure the people from the abuse of power and to keep the proper balance between liberty and obedience—itself a good summary of the purpose of any Constitution.

The Frame itself declares that it is a "charter of liberties." That it deserves such a characterization is clear when we consider the second part, the "Laws Agreed upon in England," which (like the modern Bill of Rights) is based upon the concept of a government limited in its powers by the rights possessed by the governed. Here Penn was influenced directly by his own

130

experience as a persecuted Quaker. Thus, the Frame provided expressly for religious freedom; any person professing a belief in "one Almighty and eternal God" was guaranteed freedom of belief and worship (section XXXV). Though somewhat more restrictive than the already discussed Rhode Island and West New Jersey provision in the matter, the Penn guarantee also marked a significant break with the tradition of no toleration that still prevailed in England and most of Europe.

The most important guarantees of the Penn document (at least in their influence on later Bills of Rights) have to do with judicial procedure. They reflect the burdens under which the Quakers themselves had suffered so often in English courts, including Penn himself in his famous prosecution in 1670 for preaching a prohibited sermon to a Quaker meeting. (Extracts from the record of the trial follow, since they bear directly upon the guarantees later included in the Frame of Government.) Out of that prosecution had come the Court of Common Pleas decision in *Bushell's Case*—one of the landmarks of Anglo-American liberty, since it settled the jury's right to decide according to their own conscience, regardless of any contrary direction of the court. His own experience led Penn to provide for a broad right of trial by jury in all trials with the jury to "have the final judgment" (section VIII), as well as for public trials (section V).

In addition, other basic rights in judicial proceedings were guaranteed. At a time when an accused did not have the right to testify in English courts, all persons were given the right freely to appear and personally plead their own cause, or to plead through their friends (section VI) (an implied right of counsel). The right of bail is guaranteed (section XI) in terms that anticipate the language of most present-day state Constitutions (the language of the Eighth Amendment is somewhat different). Court proceedings and records were to be "in English and in an ordinary and plain character" (section VII); court fees were to be moderate and fixed by a public schedule (section IX); fines were also to be moderate and could not reach the defendant's means of livelihood (section XVIII); prisons were to "be free, as to fees, food and lodging" (section X).

Most of the rights guaranteed by Penn's Frame have become fundamental in the American system. In his political philosophy Penn was a Quaker-Whig, though the Frame itself may have been influenced (if not written in part) by Penn's republican friend Algernon Sydney. It speaks well both of the man and the philosophy that Penn, vested with all the legal rights of Proprietor, could voluntarily limit his own powers by a document so forward looking, seven years before the English Bill of Rights, at a time when the monarchy appeared more absolute than it had been since before the Long Parliament. But Penn knew that without liberal provisions for individual rights, his Colony would find it hard to attract settlers. As he put it in a 1700 letter, "What is the right of the English subject at home should be allowed here, since more and not less seems the Reasons . . . to plant this wilderness."

Pennsylvania Frame of Government, 1682*

The frame of the government of the province of Pensilvania, in America: together with certain laws agreed upon in England, by the Governor and divers freemen of the aforesaid province. To be further explained and confirmed there, by the first provincial Council, that shall be held, if they see meet.

Preface

When the great and wise God had made the world, of all his creatures, it pleased him to chuse man his Deputy to rule it: and to fit him for so great a charge and trust, he did not only qualify him with skill and power, but with integrity to use them justly. This native goodness was equally his honour and his happiness; and whilst he stood here, all went well; there was no need of coercive or compulsive means; the precept of divine love and truth, in his bosom, was the guide and keeper of his innocency. But lust prevailing against duty, made a lamentable breach upon it; and the law, that before had no power over him, took place upon him, and his disobedient posterity, that such as would not live comfortable to the holy law within, should fall under the reproof and correction of the just law without, in a judicial administration.

This the Apostle teaches in divers of his epistles: "The law (says he) was added because of transgression:" In another place, "Knowing that the law was not made for the righteous man; but for the disobedient and ungodly, for sinners, for unholy and prophane, for murderers, for whoremongers, for them that defile themselves with mankind, and for man-stealers, for lyers, for perjured persons," &c., but this is not all, he opens and carries the matter of government a little further: "Let every soul be subject to the higher powers; for there is no power but of God. The powers that be are ordained of God: whosoever therefore resisteth the power, resisteth the ordinance of God. For rulers are not a terror to good works, but to evil: wilt thou then not be afraid of the power? do that which is good, and thou shalt have praise of the same." "He is the minister of God to thee for good." "Wherefore ye must needs be subject, not only for wrath, but for conscience sake."

This settles the divine right of government beyond exception, and that for two ends: first, to terrify evil doers: secondly, to cherish those that do well; which gives government a life beyond corruption, and makes it as durable in the world, as good men shall be. So that government seems to me a part of religion itself, a thing sacred in its institution and end. For, if it does not directly remove the cause, it crushes the effects of evil, and is as such, (though a lower, yet) an emanation of the same Divine Power, that is both author and object of pure religion; the difference lying here, that the one is

*Thorpe, *The Federal and State Constitutions, Colonial Charters, and other Organic Laws*, Vol. 5, pp. 3052–63.

more free and mental, the other more corporal and compulsive in its operations: but that is only to evil doers; government itself being otherwise as capable of kindness, goodness and charity, as a more private society. They weakly err, that think there is no other use of government, than correction, which is the coarsest part of it: daily experience tells us, that the care and regulation of many other affairs, more soft, and daily necessary, make up much of the greatest part of government; and which must have followed the peopling of the world, had Adam never fell, and will continue among men, on earth, under the highest attainments they may arrive at, by the coming of the blessed Second Adam, the Lord from heaven. Thus much of government in general, as to its rise and end.

For particular frames and models, it will become me to say little; and comparatively I will say nothing. My reasons are:

First: That the age is too nice and difficult for it; there being nothing the wits of men are more busy and divided upon. It is true, they seem to agree to the end, to wit, happiness; but, in the means, they differ, as to divine, so to this human felicity; and the cause is much the same, not always want of light and knowledge, but want of using them rightly. Men side with their passions against their reason, and their sinister interests have so strong a bias upon their minds, that they lean to them against the good of the things they know.

Secondly: I do not find a model in the world, that time, place, and some singular emergences have not necessarily altered; nor is it easy to frame a civil government, that shall serve all places alike.

Thirdly: I know what is said by the several admirers of monarchy, aristocracy and democracy, which are the rule of one, a few, and many, and are the three common ideas of government, when men discourse on the subject. But I chuse to solve the controversy with this small distinction, and it belongs to all three: Any government is free to the people under it (whatever be the frame) where the laws rule, and the people are a party to those laws, and more than this is tyranny, oligarchy, or confusion.

But, lastly, when all is said, there is hardly one frame of government in the world so ill designed by its first founders, that, in good hands, would not do well enough; and story tells us, the best, in ill ones, can do nothing that is great or good; witness the Jewish and Roman states. Governments, like clocks, go from the motion men give them; and as governments are made and moved by men, so by them they are ruined too. Wherefore governments rather depend upon men, than men upon governments. Let men be good, and the government cannot be bad; if it be ill, they will cure it. But, if men be bad, let the government be never so good, they will endeavor to warp and spoil it to their turn.

I know some say, let us have good laws, and no matter for the men that execute them: but let them consider, that though good laws do well, good men do better: for good laws may want good men, and be abolished or evaded [invaded in Franklin's print] by ill men; but good men will never want good laws, nor suffer ill ones. It is true, good laws have some awe upon ill ministers, but that is where they have not power to escape or abolish them, and the people are generally wise and good: but a loose and depraved people (which is the question) love laws and an administration like themselves. That, therefore, which makes a good constitution, must keep it, viz: men of wisdom and virtue, qualities, that because they descend not with worldly inheritances, must be carefully propagated by a virtuous education of youth; for which after ages will owe more to the care and prudence of founders, and the successive magistracy, than to their parents, for their private patrimonies.

These considerations of the weight of government, and the nice and various opinions about it, made it uneasy to me to think of publishing the ensuing frame and conditional laws, forseeing both the censures, they will meet with, from men of differing humours and engagements, and the occasion they may give of discourse beyond my design.

But, next to the power of necessity, (which is a solicitor, that will take no denial) this induced me to a compliance, that we have (with reverence to God, and good conscience to men) to the best of our skill, contrived and composed the frame and laws of this government, to the great end of all government, viz: To support power in reverence with the people, and to secure the people from the abuse of power; that they may be free by their just obedience, and the magistrates honourable, for their just administration: for liberty without obedience is confusion, and obedience without liberty is slavery. To carry this evenness is partly owing to the constitution, and partly to the magistracy: where either of these fail, government will be subject to convulsions; but where both are wanting, it must be totally subverted; then where both meet, the government is like to endure. Which I humbly pray and hope God will please to make the lot of this of Pensilvania. Amen.

William Penn

The Frame, &c.—April 25, 1682

To all Persons, to whom these presents may come. Whereas, king Charles the Second, by his letters patents, under the great seal of England, bearing date the fourth day of March in the Thirty and Third Year of the King, for divers considerations therein mentioned, hath been graciously pleased to give and grant unto me William Penn, by the name of William Penn, Esquire, son and heir of Sir William Penn, deceased, and to my heirs and assigns forever, all that tract of land, or Province, called Pensilvania, in America, with divers great powers, pre-eminences, royalties, jurisdictions, and authorities, necessary for the well-being and government thereof: Now know ye, that for the well-being and government of the said province, and for the encouragement of all the freemen and planters that may be therein concerned, in pursuance of the powers aforementioned, I, the said William Penn, have declared, granted, and confirmed, and by these presents, for me, my heirs and assigns, do declare, grant, and confirm unto all the freemen, planters and adventurers of, in and to the said province, these liberties, franchises, and properties, to be held, enjoyed and kept by the freemen, planters, and inhabitants of the said province of Pensilvania for ever.

I. That the government of this province shall, according to the powers of the patent, consist of the Governor and freemen of the said province, in form of a provincial Council and General Assembly, by whom all laws shall be made, officers chosen, and public affairs transacted, as is hereafter respectively declared, that is to say—

II. That the freemen of the said province shall, on the twentieth day of the twelfth month, which shall be in this present year one thousand six hundred eighty and two, meet and assemble in some fit place, of which timely notice shall be before hand given by the Governor or his Deputy; and then, and there, shall chuse out of themselves seventy-two persons of most note for their wisdom, virtue and ability, who shall meet, on the tenth day of the first month next ensuing, and always be called, and act as, the provincial Council of the said province.

III. That, at the first choice of such provincial Council, one-third part of the said provincial Council shall be chosen to serve for three years, then next ensuing; one-third part, for two years then next ensuing; and one-third part, for one year then next ensuing such election, and no longer; and that the said third part shall go out accordingly: and on the twentieth day of the twelfth month, as aforesaid, yearly for ever afterwards, the freemen of the said province shall, in like manner, meet and assemble together, and then chuse twenty-four persons, being one-third of the said number, to serve in provincial Council for three years: it being intended, that one-third part of the whole provincial Council (always consisting, and to consist, of seventy-two persons, as aforesaid) falling off yearly, it shall be yearly supplied by such new yearly elections, as aforesaid; and that no one person shall continue therein longer than three years: and, in case any member shall decease before the last election during his time, that then at the next election ensuing his decease, another shall be chosen to supply his place, for the remaining time, he was to have served, and no longer.

IV. That, after the first seven years, every one of the said third parts, that goeth yearly off, shall be uncapable of being chosen again for one whole year following: that so all may be fitted for government, and have experience of the care and burden of it.

V. That the provincial Council, in all cases and matters of moment, as their arguing upon bills to be passed into laws, erecting courts of justice, giving judgment upon criminals impeached, and choice of officers, in such manner as is hereinafter mentioned, not less than two-thirds of the whole provincial Council shall make a *quorum*, and that the consent and approbation of two-thirds of such *quorum* shall be had in all such cases and matters of mement. And moreover that, in all cases and matters of lesser moment, twenty-four Members of the said provincial Council shall make a *quorum*, the majority of which twenty-four shall, and may, always determine in such cases and causes of lesser moment.

VI. That, in this provincial Council, the Governor or his Deputy, shall or may, always preside, and have a treble voice; and the said provincial Council shall always continue, and sit upon its own adjournments and committees.

VII. That the Governor and provincial Council shall prepare and propose to the General Assembly, hereafter mentioned, all bills, which they shall, at any time, think fit to be passed into laws, within the said province; which bills shall be published and affixed to the most noted places, in the inhabited parts thereof, thirty days before the meeting of the General Assembly, in order to the passing them into laws or rejecting of them, as the General Assembly shall see meet.

VIII. That the Governor and provincial Council shall take care, that all laws, statutes and ordinances, which shall at any time be made within the said province, be duly and diligently executed.

IX. That the Governor and provincial Council shall, at all times, have the care of the peace and safety of the province, and that nothing be by any person attempted to the subversion of this frame of government.

X. That the Governor and provincial Council shall, at all times, settle and order the situation of all cities, ports, and market towns in every county, modelling therein all public buildings, streets, and market places, and shall appoint all necessary roads, and high-ways in the province.

XI. That the Governor and provincial Council shall, at all times, have power to inspect the management of the public treasury, and punish those who shall convert any part thereof to any other use, than what hath been agreed upon by the Governor, provincial Council, and General Assembly.

XII. That the Governor and provincial Council, shall erect and order all public schools, and encourage and reward the authors of useful sciences and laudable inventions in the said province.

XIII. That, for the better management of the powers and trust aforesaid, the provincial Council shall, from time to time, divide itself into four distinct and proper committees, for the more easy administration of the affairs of the Province, which divides the seventy-two into four eighteens, every one of which eighteens shall consist of six out of each of the three orders, or yearly elections, each of which shall have a distinct portion of business, as fol-loweth: *First*, a committee of plantations, to situate and settle cities, ports, and market towns, and high-ways, and to hear and decide all suits and controversies relating to plantations. *Secondly*, a committee of justice and safety, to secure the peace of the Province, and punish the mal-administration of those who subvert justice to the prejudice of the public, or private, interest. *Thirdly*, a committee of trade and treasury, who shall regulate all trade and commerce, according to law, encourage manufacture and country growth, and defray the public charge of the Province. And, *Fourthly,* a committee of manners, education, and arts, that all wicked and scandalous living may be prevented, and that youth may be successively trained up in virtue and useful knowledge and arts: the *quorum* of each of which committees being six, that is, two out of each of the three orders, or yearly elections, as aforesaid, make a constant and standing Council of twenty-four, which will have the power of the provincial Council, being the quorum of it, in all cases not excepted in the fifth article; and in the said committees, and standing Council of the Province, the Governor, or his Deputy, shall, or may preside, as aforesaid; and in the absence of the Governor, or his Deputy, if no one is by either of them appointed, the said committees or Council shall appoint a President for that time, and not otherwise; and what shall be resolved at such committees, shall be reported to the said Council of the province, and shall be by them resolved and confirmed before the same shall be put in execution; and that these respective committees shall not sit at one and the same time, except in cases of necessity.

XIV. And, to the end that all laws prepared by the Governor and provincial Council aforesaid, may yet have the more full concurrence of the freemen of the province, it is declared, granted and confirmed, that, at the time and place or places, for the choice of a provincial Council, as aforesaid, the said freemen shall yearly chuse Members to serve in a General Assembly, as their representatives, not exceeding two hundred persons, who shall yearly meet on the twentieth day of the second month, which shall be in the year one thousand six hundred eighty and three following, in the capital town, or city, of the said province, where, during eight days, the several Members may freely confer with one another; and, if any of them see meet, with a committee of the provincial Council (consisting of three out of each of the four committees aforesaid, being twelve in all) which shall be, at that time, purposely appointed to receive from any of them proposals, for the alterations or amendment of any of the said proposed and promulgated bills: and on the ninth day from their so meeting, the said General Assembly, after reading over the proposed bills by the Clerk of the provincial Council, and the occasions and motives for them being opened by the Governor or his Deputy, shall give their affirmative or negative, which to them seemeth best, in such manner as hereinafter is expressed. But not less than two-thirds shall make a *quorum* in the passing of laws, and choice of such officers as are by them to be chosen.

XV. That the laws so prepared and proposed, as aforesaid, that are assented to by the General Assembly, shall be enrolled as laws of the Province, with this stile: By the Governor, with the assent and approbation of the freemen in provincial Council and General Assembly.

XVI. That, for the establishment of the government and laws of this province, and to the end there may be an universal satisfaction in the laying of the fundamentals thereof: the General Assembly shall, or may, for the first year, consist of all the freemen of and in the said province; and ever after it shall be yearly chosen, as aforesaid; which number of two hundred shall be enlarged as the country shall increase in people, so as it do not exceed five hundred, at any time; the appointment and proportioning of which, as also the laying and methodizing of the choice of the provincial Council and General Assembly, in future times, most equally to the divisions of the hundreds and counties, which the country shall hereafter be divided into, shall be in the power of the provincial Council to propose, and the General Assembly to resolve.

XVII. That the Governor and the provincial Council shall erect, from time to time, standing courts of justice, in such places and number as they shall judge convenient for the good government of the said province. And that the provincial Council shall, on the thirteenth day of the first month, yearly, elect and present to the Governor, or his Deputy, a double number of persons, to serve for Judges, Treasurers, Masters of Rolls, within the said province, for the year next ensuing; and the freemen of the said province, in the county courts, when they shall be erected, and till then, in the General Assembly, shall, on the three and twentieth day of the second month, yearly, elect and present to the Governor, or his Deputy, a double number of persons, to serve for Sheriffs, Justices of the Peace, and Coroners, for the year next ensuing; out of which respective elections and presentments, the Governor or his Deputy shall nominate and commissionate the proper number for each office, the third day after the said presentments, or else the first named in such presentment, for each office, shall stand and serve for that office the year ensuing.

XVIII. But forasmuch as the present condition of the province requires some immediate settlement, and admits not of so quick a revolution of officers; and to the end the said Province may, with all convenient speed, be well ordered and settled, I, William Penn, do therefore think fit to nominate and appoint such persons for Judges, Treasurers, Masters of the Rolls, Sheriffs, Justices of the Peace, and Coroners, as are most fitly qualified for those employments; to whom I shall make and grant commissions for the said offices, respectively, to hold to them, to whom the same shall be granted, for so long time as every such person shall well behave himself in the office, or place, to him respectively granted, and no longer. And upon the decease or displacing of any of the said officers, the succeeding officer, or officers, shall be chosen, as aforesaid.

XIX. That the General Assembly shall continue so long as may be needful to impeach criminals, fit to be there impeached, to pass bills into laws, that they shall think fit to pass into laws, and till such time as the Governor and provincial Council shall declare that they have nothing further to propose unto them, for their assent and approbation: and that declaration shall be a dismiss to the General Assembly for that time; which General

Assembly shall be, notwithstanding, capable of assembling together upon the summons of the provincial Council, at any time during that year, if the said provincial Council shall see occasion for their so assembling.

XX. That all the elections of members, or representatives of the people, to serve in provincial Council and General Assembly, and all questions to be determined by both, or either of them, that relate to passing of bills into laws, to the choice of officers, to impeachments by the General Assembly, and judgment of criminals upon such impeachments by the provincial Council, and to all other cases by them respectively judged of importance, shall be resolved and determined by the ballot; and unless on sudden and indispensible occasions, no business in provincial Council, or its respective committees, shall be finally determined the same day that it is moved.

XXI. That at all times when, and so often as it shall happen that the Governor shall or may be an infant, under the age of one and twenty years, and no guardians or commissioners are appointed in writing, by the father of the said infant, or that such guardians or commissioners, shall be deceased; that during such minority, the provincial Council shall, from time to time, as they shall see meet, constitute and appoint guardians or commissioners, not exceeding three; one of which three shall preside as deputy and chief guardian, during such minority, and shall have and execute, with the consent of the other two, all the power of a Governor, in all the public affairs and concerns of the said province.

XXII. That, as often as any day of the month, mentioned in any article of this charter, shall fall upon the first day of the week, commonly called the Lord's Day, the business appointed for that day shall be deferred till the next day, unless in case of emergency.

XXIII. That no act, law, or ordinance whatsoever, shall at any time hereafter, be made or done by the Governor of this province, his heirs or assigns, or by the freemen in the provincial Council, or the General Assembly, to alter, change, or diminish the form, or effect, of this charter, or any part, or clause thereof, without the consent of the Governor, his heirs, or assigns, and six parts of seven of the said freemen in provincial Council and General Assembly.

XXIV. And lastly, that I, the said William Penn, for myself, my heirs and assigns, have solemnly declared, granted and confirmed, and do hereby solemnly declare, grant and confirm, that neither I, my heirs, nor assigns, shall procure or do any thing or things, whereby the liberties, in this charter contained and expressed, shall be infringed or broken; and if any thing be procured by any person or persons contrary to these premises, it shall be held of no force or effect. In witness whereof, I, the said William Penn, have unto this present character of liberties set my hand and broad seal, this five and twentieth day of the second month, vulgarly called April, in the year of our Lord one thousand six hundred and eighty-two.

William Penn

Laws Agreed Upon in England, &c.

I. That the charter of liberties, declared, granted and confirmed the five and twentieth day of the second month, called April, 1682, before divers witnesses, by William Penn, Governor and chief Proprietor of Pensilvania, to all the freemen and planters of the said province, is hereby declared and approved, and shall be for ever held for fundamental in the government thereof, according to the limitations mentioned in the said charter.

II. That every inhabitant in the said province, that is or shall be, a purchaser of one hundred acres of land, or upwards, his heirs and assigns, and every person who shall have paid his passage, and taken up one hundred acres of land, at one penny an acre, and have cultivated ten acres thereof, and every person, that hath been a servant, or bonds-man, and is free by his service, that shall have taken up his fifty acres of land, and cultivated twenty thereof, and every inhabitant, artificer, or other resident in the said province, that pays scot and lot to the government; shall be deemed and accounted a freeman of the said province: and every such person shall, and may, be capable of electing, or being elected, representatives of the people, in provincial Council, or General Assembly, in the said province.

III. That all elections of members, or representatives of the people and freemen of the province of Pensilvania, to serve in provincial Council, or General Assembly, to be held within the said province, shall be free and voluntary: and that the elector, that shall receive any reward or gift, in meat, drink, monies, or otherwise, shall forfeit his right to elect; and such person as shall directly or indirectly give, promise, or bestow any such reward as aforesaid, to be elected, shall forfeit his election, and be thereby incapable to serve as aforesaid: and the provincial Council and General Assembly shall be the sole judges of the regularity, or irregularity of the elections of their own respective Members.

IV. That no money or goods shall be raised upon, or paid by, any of the people of this province by way of public tax, custom or contribution, but by a law, for that purpose made; and whoever shall levy, collect, or pay any money or goods contrary thereunto, shall be held a public enemy to the province and a betrayer of the liberties of the people thereof.

V. That all courts shall be open, and justice shall neither be sold, denied nor delayed.

VI. That, in all courts all persons of all persuasions may freely appear in their own way, and according to their own manner, and there personally plead their own cause themselves; or, if unable, by their friends: and the first process shall be the exhibition of the complaint in court, fourteen days before the trial; and that the party, complained against, may be fitted for the same, he or she shall be summoned, no less than ten days before, and a copy of the complaint delivered him or her, at his or her dwelling house. But before the complaint of any person be received, he shall solemnly declare in court, that he believes, in his conscience, his cause is just.

VII. That all pleadings, processes and records in courts, shall be short, and in English, and in an ordinary and plain character, that they may be understood, and justice speedily administered.

VIII. That all trials shall be by twelve men, and as near as may be, peers or equals, and of the neighborhood, and men without just exception; in cases of life, there shall be first twenty-four returned by the sheriffs, for a grand inquest, of whom twelve, at least, shall find the complaint to be true; and then the twelve men, or peers, to be likewise returned by the sheriff, shall have the final judgment. But reasonable challenges shall be always admitted against the said twelve men, or any of them.

IX. That all fees in all cases shall be moderate, and settled by the provincial Council, and General Assembly, and be hung up in a table in every respective court; and whosoever shall be convicted of taking more, shall pay twofold, and be dismissed his employment; one moiety of which shall go to the party wronged.

X. That all prisons shall be work-houses, for felons, vagrants, and loose and idle persons; whereof one shall be in every county.

XI. That all prisoners shall be bailable by sufficient sureties, unless for capital offences, where the proof is evident, or the presumption great.

XII. That all persons wrongfully imprisoned, or prosecuted at law, shall have double damages against the informer, or prosecutor.

XIII. That all prisons shall be free, as to fees, food and lodging.

XIV. That all lands and goods shall be liable to pay debts, except where there is legal issue, and then all the goods, and one-third of the land only.

XV. That all wills, in writing, attested by two witnesses, shall be of the same force as to lands, as other conveyances, being legally proved within forty days, either within or without the said province.

XVI. That seven years quiet possession shall give an unquestionable right, except in cases of infants, lunatics, married women, or persons beyond the seas.

XVII. That all briberies and extortion whatsoever shall be severely punished.

XVIII. That all fines shall be moderate, and saving men's contenements, merchandize, or wainage.

XIX. That all marriages (not forbidden by the law of God, as to nearness of blood and affinity by marriage) shall be encouraged; but the parents, or guardians, shall be first consulted, and the marriage shall be published before it be solemnized; and it shall be solemnized by taking one another as husband and wife, before credible witnesses; and a certificate of the whole, under the hands of parties and witnesses, shall be brought to the proper register of that county, and shall be registered in his office.

XX. And, to prevent frauds and vexatious suits within the said province, that all charters, gifts, grants, and conveyances of and (except leases for a year or under) and all bills, bonds, and specialties above five pounds, and not under three months, made in the said province, shall be enrolled, or registered in the public enrolment office of the said province, within the space of two months next after the making thereof, else to be void in law, and all deeds, grants, and conveyances of land (except as aforesaid) within the said province, and made out of the said province, shall be enrolled or registered, as aforesaid, within six months next after the making thereof, and settling and constituting an enrolment office or registry within the said province, else to be void in law against all persons whatsoever.

XXI. That all defacers or corrupters of charters, gifts, grants, bonds, bills, wills, contracts, and conveyances, or that shall deface or falsify any enrolment, registry or record, within this province, shall make double satisfaction for the same; half whereof shall go to the party wronged, and they shall be dismissed of all places of trust, and be publicly disgraced as false men.

XXII. That there shall be a register for births, marriages, burials, wills, and letters of administration, distinct from the other registry.

XXIII. That there shall be a register for all servants, where their names, time, wages, and days of payment shall be registered.

XXIV. That all lands and goods of felons shall be liable, to make satisfaction to the party wronged twice the value; and for want of lands or goods, the felons shall be bondmen to work in the common prison, or work-house, or otherwise, till the party injured be satisfied.

XXV. That the estates of capital offenders, as traitors and murderers, shall go, one-third to the next of kin to the sufferer, and the remainder to the next of kin to the criminal.

XXVI. That all witnesses, coming, or called, to testify their knowledge in or to any matter or thing, in any court, or before any lawful authority, within the said province, shall there give or deliver in their evidence, or testimony, by solemnly promising to speak the truth, the whole truth, and nothing but the truth, to the matter, or thing in question. And in case any person so called to evidence, shall be convicted of wilful falsehood, such person shall suffer and undergo such damage or penalty, as the person, or persons, against whom he or she bore false witness, did, or should, undergo; and shall also make satisfaction to the party wronged, and be publicly exposed as a false witness, never to be credited in any court, or before any Magistrate, in the said province.

XXVII. And, to the end that all officers chosen to serve within this province, may, with more care and diligence, answer the trust reposed in them, it is agreed, that no such person shall enjoy more than one public office at one time.

XXVIII. That all children, within this province, of the age of twelve years, shall be taught some useful trade or skill, to the end none may be idle, but the poor may work to live, and the rich, if they become poor, may not want.

XXIX. That servants be not kept longer than their time, and such as are careful, be both justly and kindly used in their service, and put in fitting equipage at the expiration thereof, according to custom.

XXX. That all scandalous and malicious reporters, backbiters, defamers and spreaders of false news, whether against Magistrates, or private persons, shall be accordingly severely punished, as enemies to the peace and concord of this province.

XXXI. That for the encouragement of the planters and traders in this province, who are incorporated into a society, the patent granted to them by William Penn, Governor of the said province, is hereby ratified and confirmed.

XXXII. *   *   *

XXXIII. That all factors or correspondents in the said province, wronging their employers, shall make satisfaction, and one-third over, to their said employers: and in case of the death of any such factor or correspondent, the committee of trade shall take care to secure so much of the deceased party's estate as belongs to his said respective employers.

XXXIV. That all Treasurers, Judges, Masters of the Rolls, Sheriffs, Justices of the Peace, and other officers and persons whatsoever, relating to courts, or trials of causes, or any other service in the government; and all Members elected to serve in provincial Council and General Assembly, and all that have right to elect such Members, shall be such as possess faith in Jesus Christ, and that are not convicted of ill fame, or unsober and dishonest conversation, and that are of one and twenty years of age, at least; and that all such so qualified, shall be capable of the said several employments and privileges, as aforesaid.

XXXV. That all persons living in this province, who confess and acknowledge the one Almighty and eternal God, to be the Creator, Upholder and Ruler of the world; and that hold themselves obliged in conscience to live peaceably and justly in civil society, shall, in no ways, be molested or prejudiced for their religious persuasion, or practice, in matters of faith and worship, nor shall they be compelled, at any time, to frequent or maintain any religious worship, place or ministry whatever.

XXXVI. That, according to the good example of the primitive Christians, and the case of the creation, every first day of the week, called the Lord's day, people shall abstain from their common daily labour, that they may the better dispose themselves to worship God according to their understandings.

XXXVII. That as a careless and corrupt administration of justice draws the wrath of God upon magistrates, so the wildness and looseness of the people provoke the indignation of God against a country: therefore, that all such offences against God, as swearing, cursing, lying, prophane talking, drunkenness, drinking of healths, obscene words, incest, sodomy, rapes, whoredom, fornication, and other uncleanness (not to be repeated) all treasons, misprisions, murders, duels, felony, seditions, maims, forcible entries, and other violences, to the persons and estates of the inhabitants within this province; all prizes, stage-plays, cards, dice, May-games, gamesters, masques, revels, bull-baitings, cock-fightings, bear-baitings, and the like, which excite the people to rudeness, cruelty, looseness, and irreligion, shall be respectively discouraged, and severely punished, according to the appointment of the Governor and freemen in provincial Council and General Assembly; as also all proceedings contrary to these laws, that are not here made expressly penal.

XXXVIII. That a copy of these laws shall be hung up in the provincial Council, and in public courts of justice: and that they shall be read yearly at the opening of every provincial Council and General Assembly, and court of justice; and their assent shall be testified, by their standing up after the reading thereof.

XXXIX. That there shall be, at no time, any alteration of any of these laws, without the consent of the Governor, his heirs, or assigns, and six parts of seven of the freemen, met in provincial Council and General Assembly.

XL. That all other matters and things not herein provided for, which shall, and may, concern the public justice, peace or safety of the said province; and the raising and imposing taxes, customs, duties, or other charges whatsoever, shall be, and are, hereby referred to the order, prudence and determination of the Governor and freemen, in provincial Council and General Assembly, to be held, from time to time, in the said province.

Signed and sealed by the Governor and freemen aforesaid, the fifth day of the third month, called May, one thousand six hundred and eighty-two.

The People's Ancient and Just Liberties Asserted, in the Trial of William Penn and William Mead, 1670*

*At the Sessions held at the Old Bailey, in London,
the 1st, 3d, 4th, and 5th of September, 1670,
against the most arbitrary procedure of that Court*

If ever it were time to speak, or write, it is now; so many strange occurrences requiring both.

How much thou art concerned in this ensuing trial, (where not only the prisoners, but the fundamental Laws of England, have been most arbitrarily arraigned) read, and thou mayest plainly judge.

Liberty of conscience is counted a pretence for rebellion; and religious assemblies, routs and riots; and the defenders of both are by them reputed factious and disaffected.

*The Select Works of William Penn, 4th ed., (1825), Vol. 1, pp. 179–96.

Magna charta is magna far—with the recorder of London; and to demand right, an affront to the court.

Will and power are their great charter; but to call for England's, is a crime, incurring the penalty of the baledock and nasty hole; nay, the menace of a gag, and iron shackles too.

The jury (though proper judges of law and fact) they would have overruled in both: as if their verdict signified no more, than to echo back the illegal charge of the bench. And because their courage and honesty did more than hold pace with the threat and abuse of those who sat as judges (after two days and two nights restraint for a verdict) in the end they were fined and imprisoned for giving it.

Oh! what monstrous and illegal proceedings are these! Who reasonably can call his coat his own, when property is made subservient to the will and interest of his judges? Or, who can truly esteem himself a free man, when all pleas for liberty are esteemed sedition, and the laws that give and maintain them, so many insignificant pieces of formality.

And what do they less than plainly tell us so, who at will and pleasure break open our locks, rob our houses, raze our foundations, imprison our persons, and finally deny us justice to our relief? As if they then acted most like Christian men, when they were most barbarous, in ruining such as are really so; and that no sacrifice could be so acceptable to God, as the destruction of those that most fear him.

In short, that the conscientious should only be obnoxious, and the just demand of our religious liberty the reason why we should be denied our civil freedom (as if to be a Christian and an Englishman were inconsistent); and that so much solicitude and deep contrivance should be employed only to ensnare and ruin so many ten thousand conscientious families (so eminently industrious, serviceable, and exemplary; whilst murders can so easily obtain pardon, rapes be remitted, public uncleanness pass unpunished, and all manner of levity, prodigality, excess, profaneness, and atheism, universally connived at, if not in some respect manifestly encouraged) cannot but be detestibly abhorrent to every serious and honest mind.

Yet that this lamentable state is true, and the present project in hand, let London's recorder, and Canterbury's chaplain, be heard.

The first, in his public panegyrick upon the Spanish Inquisition, 'highly admiring the prudence of the Romish church in the erection of it, as an excellent way to prevent schism.' Which unhappy expression at once passeth sentence, both against our fundamental laws, and Protestant reformation.

The second, in his printed mercenary discourse against toleration, asserting for a main principle, 'That it would be less injurious to the government to dispense with profane and loose persons, than to allow a toleration to religious dissenters.'—It were to overdo the business to say any more, where there is so much said already.

And therefore to conclude, we cannot chuse but admonish all, as well persecutors to relinquish their heady, partial, and inhuman persecutions (as what will certainly issue in disgrace here, and inevitable condign punishment hereafter); as those who yet dare express their moderation (however out of fashion, or made the brand of fanaticism) not to be huffed, or menaced out of that excellent temper, to make their parts and persons subject to the base humours and sinister designs of the biggest mortal upon earth; but reverence and obey the eternal just God, before whose great tribunal all must render their accounts, and where he will recompense to every person according to his works.

The Trial

As there can be no observation, where there is no action; so it is impossible there shall be a judicious intelligence without due observation.

And since there can be nothing more reasonable than a right information, especially of public acts; and well knowing how industrious some will be to misrepresent this trial, to the disadvantage of the cause and prisoners; it was thought requisite, in defence of both, and for the satisfaction of the people, to make it more public. Nor can there by any business wherein the people of England are more concerned, than in that which relates to their civil and religious liberties, questioned in the persons before named at the Old Bailey, the first, third, fourth and fifth of September 1670.

There being present on the bench, as justices,

Sam. Starling, mayor.
John Howell, recorder.
Tho. Bludworth, alderm.
William Peak, alderm.
Richard Ford, alderm.

John Robinson, alderm.
Joseph Shelden, alderm.
Richard Brown,
John Smith,   } sheriffs.
James Edwards,   }

The citizens of London that were summoned for jurors, appearing, were impanelled; viz.

Cle. Call over the jury.

Cry. Oyes, Thomas Veer, Ed. Bushel, John Hammond, Charles Milson, Gregory Walklet, John Brightman, Will. Plumstead, Henry Henley, James Damask, Henry Michel, Will. Lever, John Baily.

The form of the Oath

You shall well and truly try, and true deliverance make betwixt our sovereign lord the king, and the prisoners at the bar, according to your evidence. So help you God.

The Indictment

That William Penn, gent. and William Mead, late of London, linen draper, with divers other persons to the jurors unknown, to the number of three hundred, the 15th day of August, in the 22d year of the king, about eleven of the clock in the forenoon of the same day, with force and arms, &c. in the parish of St. Bennet Gracechurch, in Bridge-ward, London, in the street called Gracechurch-street, unlawfully and tumultuously did assemble and congregate themselves together, to the disturbance of the peace of the said lord the king: and the aforesaid William Penn and William Mead, together with other persons to the jurors aforesaid unknown, then and there so assembled and congregated together; the aforesaid William Penn, by agreement between him and William Mead before made, and by abetment of the aforesaid William Mead, then and there, in the open street, did take upon himself to preach and speak, and then and there did preach and speak, unto the aforesaid William Mead, and other persons there in the street aforesaid, being assembled and congregated together; by reason whereof a great concourse and tumult of people in the street aforesaid, then and there, a long time did remain and continue, in contempt of the said lord the king, and of his law; to the great disturbance of his peace, to the great terror and disturbance of many of his liege people and subjects, to the ill example of all others in the like case offenders, and against the peace of the said lord the king, his crown and dignity.

What say you William Penn, and William Mead? Are you guilty, as you stand indicted, in manner and form as aforesaid, or not guilty?

Penn. It is impossible that we should be able to remember the indictment *verbatim,* and therefore we desire a copy of it, as is customary on the like occasions.

Rec. You must first plead to the indictment, before you can have a copy of it.

Penn. I am unacquainted with the formality of the law, and therefore before I shall answer directly, I request two things of the court. First, That no advantage may be taken against me, nor I deprived of any benefit, which I might otherwise have received. Secondly, That you will promise me a fair hearing, and liberty of making my defence.

Court. No advantage shall be taken against you: you shall have liberty; you shall be heard.

Penn. Then I plead not guilty, in manner and form.

Cle. What sayest thou, William Mead? Art thou guilty in manner and form, as thou standest indicted, or not guilty?

Mead. I shall desire the same liberty as is promised to William Penn.

Court. You shall have it.

Mead. Then I plead not guilty, in manner and form.

The Court adjourned until the afternoon

Cry. Oyes, &c.

Cle. Bring William Penn and William Mead to the bar.

Observ. The said prisoners were brought, but were set aside, and other business prosecuted. Where we cannot chuse but observe, that it was the constant and unkind practice of the court to the prisoners, to make them wait upon the trials of felons and murderers, thereby designing, in all probability, both to affront and tire them. After five hours attendance, the court broke up, and adjourned to the third instant.

The third of September 1670, the Court sat

Cry. Oyes, &c.

Mayor. Sirrah, Who bid you put off their hats? Put on their hats again.

Obser. Whereupon one of the officers putting the prisoners hats upon their heads (pursuant to the order of the court) brought them to the bar.

Record. Do you know where you are?

Penn. Yes.

Rec. Do you know it is the king's court?

Penn. I know it to be a court, and I suppose it to be the king's court.

Rec. Do you know there is respect due to the court?

Penn. Yes.

Rec. Why do you not pay it then?

Penn. I do so.

Rec. Why do you not put off your hat then?

Penn. Because I do not believe that to be any respect.

Rec. Well, the court sets forty marks a-piece upon your heads, as a fine, for your contempt of the court.

Penn. I desire it may be observed, that we came into the court with our hats off (that is, taken off) and if they have been put on since, it was by order from the bench; and therefore not we, but the bench, should be fined.

Mead. I have a question to ask the recorder: Am I fined also?

Rec. Yes.

Mead. I desire the jury, and all people, to take notice of this injustice of the recorder, who spake not to me to pull off my hat, and yet hath he put a fine upon my head. O! fear the Lord, and dread his power, and yield to the guidance of his Holy Spirit; for he is not far from every one of you.

The Jury sworn again

Obser. J. Robinson, lieutenant of the Tower, disingenuously objected against Edward Bushel, as if he had not kissed the book, and therefore would have him sworn again; though indeed it was on purpose to have made use of his tenderness of conscience, in avoiding reiterated oaths, to have put him by his being a juryman, apprehending him to be a person not fit to answer their arbitrary ends.

The clerk read the indictment as aforesaid.

Cle. Call James Cook into the court, give him his oath.

Cle. James Cook, lay your hand upon the book; 'The evidence you shall give to the court, betwixt our sovereign the king, and the prisoners at the bar, shall be the truth, and the whole truth, and nothing but the truth. So help you God,' &c.

Cook. I was sent for from the Exchange, to go and disperse a meeting in Gracious-street, where I saw Mr. Penn speaking to the people, but I could not hear what he said, because of the noise. I endeavoured to make way to take him, but I could not get to him for the croud of people. Upon which Captain Mead came to me, about the kennel of the street, and desired me to let him go on; for when he had done, he would bring Mr. Penn to me.

Court. What number do you think might be there?

Cook. About three or four hundred people.

Court. Call Richard Read, give him his oath.

Read being sworn, was asked, What do you know concerning the prisoners at the bar?

Read. My lord, I went to Gracious-street, where I found a great croud of people, and I heard Mr. Penn preach to them; and I saw Captain Mead speaking to Lieutenant Cook, but what he said I could not tell.

Mead. What did William Penn say?

Read. There was such a great noise, that I could not tell what he said.

Mead. Jury, observe this evidence; he saith, he heard him preach; and yet saith, he doth not know what he said.

Jury, take notice, he swears now a clean contrary thing to what he swore before the mayor, when we were committed: for now he swears that he saw me in Gracious-street, and yet swore before the mayor, when I was committed, that he did not see me there. I appeal to the mayor himself if this be not true? (But no answer was given.)

Court. What number do you think might ber there?

Read. About four or five hundred.

Penn. I desire to know of him what day it was?

Read. The 14th day of August.

Penn. Did he speak to me, or let me know he was there? For I am very sure I never saw him.

Cle. Crier, call —— —— into the court.

Court. Give him his oath.

———— My lord, I saw a great number of people, and Mr. Penn I suppose was speaking. I saw him make a motion with his hands, and heard some noise, but could not understand what he said. But for Captain Mead, I did not see him there.

Rec. What say you, Mr. Mead? Were you there?

Mead. It is a maxim in your own law, *nemo tenetur accusare seipsum;* which if it be not true Latin, I am sure that it is true English, 'that no man is bound to accuse himself.' And why dost thou offer to ensnare me with such a question? Doth not this shew thy malice? Is this like unto a judge, that ought to be counsel for the prisoner at the bar?

Rec. Sir, hold your tongue; I did not go about to ensnare you.

Penn. I desire we may come more close to the point, and that silence be commanded in the court.

Cry. Oyes! All manner of persons keep silence, upon pain of imprisonment.—Silence in the court.

Penn. We confess ourselves to be so far from recanting, or declining to vindicate the assembling of ourselves, to preach, pray, or worship the eternal, holy, just God, that we declare to all the world, that we do believe it to be our indispensable duty to meet incessantly upon so good an account; nor shall all the powers upon earth be able to divert us from reverencing and adoring our God, who made us.

Brown. You are not here for worshipping God, but for breaking the law. You do yourselves a great deal of wrong in going on in that discourse.

Penn. I affirm I have broken no law, nor am I guilty of the indictment that is laid to my charge. And to the end the bench, the jury, and myself, with those that hear us, may have a more direct understanding of this procedure, I desire you would let me know by what law it is you prosecute me, and upon what law you ground my indictment.

Rec. Upon the common law.

Penn. Where is that common law?

Rec. You must not think that I am able to run up so many years, and over so many adjudged cases, which we call common law, to answer your curiosity.

Penn. This answer I am sure is very short of my question; for if it be common, it should not be so hard to produce.

Rec. Sir, will you plead to your indictment?

Penn. Shall I plead to an indictment that hath no foundation in law? If it contain that law you say I have broken, why should you decline to produce that law, since it will be impossible for the jury to determine, or agree to bring in the verdict, who have not the law produced, by which they should measure the truth of this indictment, and the guilt, or contrary, of my fact.

Rec. You are saucy, fellow. Speak to the indictment.

Penn. I say it is my place to speak to matter of law. I am arraigned a prisoner; my liberty, which is next to life itself, is now concerned. You are many mouths and ears against me; and if I must not be allowed to make the best of my case, it is hard. I say again, unless you shew me, and the people, the law you ground your indictment upon, I shall take it for granted your proceedings are merely arbitrary.

Obser. At this time several upon the bench urged hard upon the prisoner to bear him down.

Rec. The question is, Whether you are guilty of this indictment?

Penn. The question is not whether I am guilty of this indictment, but whether this indictment be legal. It is too general and imperfect an answer, to say it is the common law, unless we both knew where, and what it is. For where there is no law, there is no transgression; and that law which is not in being, is so far from being common, that it is no law at all.

Rec. You are an impertinent fellow. Will you teach the court what law is? It is *lex non scripta;* that which may have studied thirty or forty years to know; and would you have me tell you in a moment?

Penn. Certainly, if the common law be so hard to be understood, it is far from being very common. But if the Lord Coke, in his 'Institutes,' be of any consideration, he tells us, 'That common law is common right; and that common right is the great charter privileges, confirmed 9 Hen.3.29. 25 Edw.1.1. 2Edw. 3.8.' Coke Inst. 2, p. 56.

Rec. Sir, you are a troublesome fellow, and it is not for the honour of the court to suffer you to go on.

Penn. I have asked but one question, and you have not answered me; though the rights and privileges of every Englishman be concerned in it.

Rec. If I should suffer you to ask questions till to-morrow morning, you would be never the wiser.

Penn. That is according as the answers are.

Rec. Sir, we must not stand to hear you talk all night.

Penn. I design no affront to the court, but to be heard in my just plea. And I must plainly tell you, that if you will deny me the Oyer of that law, which you suggest I have broken, you do at once deny me an acknowledged right, and evidence to the whole world your resolution to sacrifice the privileges of Englishmen to your sinister and arbitrary designs.

Rec. Take him away. My lord, if you take not some course with this pestilent fellow, to stop his mouth, we shall not be able to do any thing to-night.

Mayor. Take him away, take him away; turn him into the bale-dock.

Penn. These are but so many vain exclamations. Is this justice, or true judgment? Must I therefore be taken away because I plead for the fundamental laws of England? However, this I leave upon your consciences, who are of the jury, (and my sole judges) that if these ancient fundamental laws, which relate to liberty and property, (and are not limited to particular persuasions in matters of religion) must not be indispensably maintained and observed, 'who can say he hath a right to the coat upon his back?' Certainly our liberties are openly to be invaded; our wives to be ravished; our children slaved; our families ruined; and our estates led away in triumph, by every sturdy beggar, and malicious informer, as their trophies, but our (pretended) forfeits for conscience sake. The Lord of heaven and earth will be judge between us in this matter.

Rec. Be silent there.

Penn. I am not to be silent in a case wherein I am so much concerned; and not only myself, but many ten thousand families besides.

*　　　*　　　*

Obser. The prisoners were put out of the court, into the bale-dock, and the charge given to the jury in their absence. At which W. P. with a very raised voice, (it being a considerable distance from the bench) spake.

Penn. I appeal to the jury, who are my judges, and this great assembly, whether the proceedings of the court are not most arbitrary, and void of all law, in offering to give the jury their charge in the absence of the prisoners. I say, it is directly opposite to, and destructive of, the undoubted right of every English prisoner, as Coke, in the 2 Inst.29. on the chapter of Magna Charta, speaks.

*   *   *

Obser. The jury were commanded up to agree upon their verdict, the prisoners remaining in the stinking hole. After an hour and a half's time, eight came down agreed, but four remained above; the court sent an officer for them, and they accordingly came down. The bench used many unworthy threats to the four that dissented; and the recorder, addressing himself to Bushel, said, Sir, you are the cause of this disturbance, and manifestly shew yourself an abettor of faction; I shall set a mark upon you, Sir.

J. Robinson. Mr. Bushel, I have known you near these fourteen years; you have thrust yourself upon this jury, because you think there is some service for you. I tell you, you deserve to be indicted more than any man that hath been brought to the bar this day.

Bushel. No, Sir John; there were threescore before me; and I would willingly have got off, but could not.

Bludw. I said, when I saw Mr. Bushel, what I see is come to pass: for I knew he would never yield. Mr. Bushel, we know what you are.

Mayor. Sirrah, you are an impudent fellow; I will put a mark upon you.

Obser. They used much menacing language, and behaved themselves very imperiously to the jury, as persons not more void of justice, than sober eduction. After this barbarous usage, they sent them to consider of bringing in their verdict; and after some considerable time they returned to the court. Silence was called for, and the jury called by their names.

Cle. Are you agreed upon your verdict?

Jury. Yes.

Cle. Who shall speak for you?

Jury. Our foreman.

Cle. Look upon the prisoners at the bar: how say you? Is William Penn guilty of the matter whereof he stands indicted in manner and form, or not guilty?

Foreman. Guilty of speaking in Gracious-street.

Court. Is that all?

Foreman. That is all I have in commission.

Rec. You had as good say nothing.

Mayor. Was it not an unlawful assembly? You mean he was speaking to a tumult of people there?

Foreman. My lord, this was all I had in commission.

Obser. Here some of the jury seemed to buckle to the questions of the court; upon which Bushel, Hammond, and some others, opposed themselves, and said, 'They allowed of no such word, as an unlawful assembly, in their verdict.' At which the recorder, mayor, Robinson, and Bludworth, took great occasion to vilify them with most opprobrious language; and this verdict not serving their turns, the recorder expressed himself thus:

Rec. The law of England will not allow you to depart, till you have given in your verdict.

Jury. We have given in our verdict, and we can give in no other.

Rec. Gentlemen, you have not given in your verdict, and you had as good say nothing. Therefore go and consider it once more, than we may make an end of this troublesome business.

Jury. We desire we may have pen, ink, and paper.

Obser. The court adjourns for half an hour; which being expired, the court returns, and the jury not long after.

The prisoners were brought to the bar, and the jurors names called over.

Cle. Are you agreed of your verdict?

Jury. Yes.

Cle. Who shall speak for you?

Jury. Our foreman.

Cle. Whay say you? Look upon the prisoners: Is William Penn guilty in manner and form, as he stands indicted, or not guilty?

Foreman. Here is our verdict (holding forth a piece of paper to the clerk of the peace, which follows):

We the jurors, hereafter named, do find William Penn to be guilty of speaking or preaching to an assembly, met together in Gracious-street, the 14th of August last 1670; and that William Mead is not guilty of the said indictment.

Foreman,	Thomas Veer,	Charles Milson,
	Edward Bushel,	Gregory Walklet,
	John Hammond,	John Bailey,
	Henry Henly,	William Lever,
	Henry Michel,	James Damask,
	John Brightman,	William Plumstead.

Obser. This both mayor and recorder resented at so high a rate, that they exceeded the bounds of all reason and civility.

Mayor. What! will you be led by such a silly fellow as Bushel! an impudent canting fellow? I warrant you, you shall come no more upon juries in haste: you are a foreman indeed! (addressing himself to the foreman) I thought you had understood your place better.

Rec. Gentlemen, you shall not be dismissed, till we have a verdict that the court will accept; and you shall be locked up, without meat, drink, fire and tobacco. You shall not think thus to abuse the court; we will have a verdict, by the help of God, or you shall starve for it.

Penn. My jury, who are my judges, ought not to be thus menaced. Their verdict should be free, and not compelled. The bench ought to wait upon them, but not forestall them. I do desire that justice may be done me, and that the arbitrary resolves of the bench may not be made the measure of my jury's verdict.

Rec. Stop that prating fellow's mouth, or put him out of the court.

Mayor. You have heard that he preached; that he gathered a company of tumultuous people; and that they do not only disobey the martial power, but the civil also.

Penn. It is a great mistake; we did not make the tumult, but they that interrupted us. The jury cannot be so ignorant, as to think that we met there with a design to disturb the civil peace; since, 1st, we were by force of arms kept out of our lawful house, and met as near it in the street as the soldiers would give us leave: and, 2dly, because it was no new thing, nor with the circumstances expressed in the indictment, but what was usual and customary with us. It is very well known, that we are a peaceable people, and cannot offer violence to any man.

Obser. The court being ready to break up, and willing to huddle the prisoners to their jail, and the jury to their chamber, Penn spake as follows:

Penn. The agreement of twelve men is a verdict in law; and such a one being given by the jury, 'I require the clerk of the peace to record it, as he will answer it at his peril.' And if the jury bring in another verdict contrary to this, I affirm they are perjured men in law. [And looking upon the jury, said] 'You are Englishmen; mind your privilege, give not away your right.'

Bushel. Nor will we ever do it.

Obser. One of the jurymen pleaded indisposition of body, and therefore desired to be dismissed.

Mayor. You are as strong as any of them. Starve then, and hold your principles.

Rec. Gentlemen, you must be content with your hard fate; let your patience overcome it; for the court is resolved to have a verdict, and that before you can be dismissed.

Jury. We are agreed, we are agreed, we are agreed.

Obser. The court swore several persons to keep the jury all night, without meat, drink, fire, or any other accommodation. They had not so much as a chamber-pot, though desired.

Cry. Oyes, &c.

Obser. The court adjourned till seven of the clock next morning (being the fourth instant, vulgarly called Sunday); at which time the prisoners were brought to the bar, the court sat, and the jury called in, to bring in their verdict.

Cry. Oyes, &c.—Silence in the court, upon pain of imprisonment.

The jury's names called over.

Cle. Are you agreed upon your verdict?

Jury. Yes.

Cle. Who shall speak for you?

Jury. Our foreman.

Cle. What say you? Look upon the prisoners at the bar: Is William Penn guilty of the matter whereof he stands indicted, in manner and form as aforesaid, or not guilty?

Foreman. William Penn is guilty of speaking in Gracious-street.

Mayor. To an unlawful assembly?

Bushel. No, my lord, we give no other verdict than what we gave last night: we have no other verdict to give.

Mayor. You are a factious fellow; I'll take a course with you.

Bludw. I knew Mr. Bushel would not yield.

Bushel. Sir Thomas, I have done according to my conscience.

Mayor. That conscience of yours would cut my throat.

Bushel. No, my lord, it never shall.

Mayor. But I will cut yours as soon as I can.

Rec. He has inspired the jury; he has the spirit of divination; methinks I feel him. I will have a positive verdict, or you shall starve for it.

Penn. I desire to ask the recorder one question: Do you allow of the verdict given of William Mead?

Rec. It cannot be a verdict, because you are indicted for a conspiracy; and one being found not guilty, and not the other, it could not be a verdict.

Penn. If not guilty be not a verdict, then you make of the jury, and magna charta, but a mere nose of wax.

Mead. How! Is not guilty no verdict?

Rec. No, it is no verdict.

Penn. I affirm, that the consent of a jury is a verdict in law. And if William Mead be not guilty, it consequently follows, that I am clear; since you have indicted us of a conspiracy, and I could not possibly conspire alone.

Obser. There were many passages that could not be taken, which passed between the jury and the court. The jury went up again, having received a fresh charge from the bench, if possible to extort an unjust verdict.

Cry. Oyes, &c.—Silence in the court.

Court. Call over the jury.—[Which was done.]

Cle. What say you? Is William Penn guilty of the matter whereof he stands indicted in manner and form aforesaid, or not guilty?

Foreman. Guilty of speaking in Gracious-street.

Rec. What is this to the purpose? I say I will have a verdict. [And speaking to E. Bushel said] You are a factious fellow; I will set a mark upon you. And whilst I have any thing to do in the city, I will have an eye upon you.

Mayor. Have you no more wit, than to be led by such a pitiful fellow? I will cut his nose.

Penn. It is intolerable that my jury should be thus menaced! Is this according to the fundamental law? Are not they my proper judges by the great charter of England? What hope is there of ever having justice done, when juries are threatened, and their verdicts rejected? I am concerned to speak, and grieved to see such arbitrary proceedings. Did not the lieutenant of the Tower render one of them worse than a felon? And do you not plainly seem to condemn such for factious fellows, who answer not your ends? Unhappy are those juries, who are threatened to be fined, and starved and ruined, if they give not in their verdicts contrary to their consciences.

Rec. My lord, you must take a course with that same fellow.

Mayor. Stop his mouth. Jailer, bring fetters, and stake him to the ground.

Penn. Do your pleasure; I matter not your fetters.

Rec. Till now I never understood the reason of the policy and prudence of the Spaniards in suffering the Inquisition among them. And certainly it will never be well with us, till something like the Spanish inquisition be in England.

Obser. The jury being required to go together, to find another verdict, and stedfastly refusing it (saying, they could give no other verdict than what was already given) the recorder in great passion was running off the bench, with these words in his mouth, 'I protest I will sit here no longer to hear these things.' At which the mayor calling, 'Stay, stay,' he returned and directed himself unto the jury, and spake as followeth:

Rec. Gentlemen, we shall not be at this pass always with you. You will find the next sessions of parliament there will be a law made, that those that will not conform, shall not have the protection of the law. Mr. Lee, draw up another verdict, that they may bring it in special.

Lee. I cannot tell how to do it.

Jury. We ought not to be returned; having all agreed, and set our hands to the verdict.

Rec. Your verdict is nothing; you play upon the court. I say, you shall go together, and bring in another verdict, or you shall starve; and I will have you carted about the city, as in Edward the Third's time.

Foreman. We have given in our verdict, and all agreed to it. And if we give in another, it will be a force upon us to save our lives.

Mayor. Take them up.

Officer. My lord, they will not go up.

Obser. The mayor spoke to the sheriff, and he came off his seat, and said:

Sher. Come, gentlemen, you must go up; you see I am commanded to make you go.

Obser. Upon which the jury went up; and several were sworn to keep them without any accommodation, as aforesaid, till they brought in their verdict.

Cry. Oyes, &c. The court adjourns till to-morrow morning, at seven of the clock.

Obser. The prisoners were remanded to Newgate, where they remained till next morning, and then were brought into the court; which being sat, they proceeded as followeth:

Cry. Oyes, &c. Silence in the court, upon pain of imprisonment.

Clerk. Set William Penn and William Mead to the bar. Gentlemen of the jury, answer to your names; Thomas Veer, Edward Bushel, John Hammond, Henry Henley, Henry Michel, John Brightman, Charles Milson, Gregory Walklet, John Bailey, William Lever, James Damask, William Plumstead; are you all agreed of your verdict?

Jury. Yes.

Clerk. Who shall speak for you?

Jury. Our foreman.

Clerk. Look upon the prisoners: What say you? Is William Penn guilty of the matter whereof he stands indicted, in manner and form, &c. or not guilty?

Foreman. You have there read in writing already our verdict, and our hands subscribed.

Obser. The clerk had the paper, but was stopped by the recorder from reading of it; and he commanded to ask for a positive verdict.

Foreman. If you will not accept of it, I desire to have it back again.

Court. That paper was no verdict; and there shall be no advantage taken against you by it.

Clerk. How say you? Is William Penn guilty, &c. or not guilty?

Foreman. Not guilty.

Clerk. How say you? Is William Mead guilty, &c. or not guilty?

Foreman. Not guilty.

Clerk. Then hearken to your verdict. You say that William Penn is not guilty in manner and form, as he stands indicted: you say that William Mead is not guilty in manner and form, as he stands indicted; and so you say all.

Jury. Yes, we do so.

Obser. The bench being unsatisfied with the verdict, commanded that every person should distinctly answer to their names, and give in their verdict; which they unanimously did, in saying, Not guilty, to the great satisfaction of the assembly.

Rec. I am sorry, gentlemen, you have followed your own judgments and opinions, rather than the good and wholesome advice which was given you. God keep my life out of your hands: but for this the court fines you forty marks a man, and imprisonment till paid. [At which Penn stepped up towards the bench, and said]

Penn. I demand my liberty, being freed by the jury.

Mayor. No! you are in for your fines.

Penn. Fines! for what?

Mayor. For contempt of the court.

Penn. I ask, if it be according to the fundamental laws of England, that any Englishman should be fined, or amerced, but by the judgment of his peers or jury? Since it expressly contradicts the fourteenth and twenty-ninth chapter of the great charter of England, which says, 'No freeman ought to be amerced, but by the oath of good and lawful men of the vicinage.'

Rec. Take him away, take him away, take him out of the court.

Penn. I can never urge the fundamental laws of England, but you cry, Take him away, take him away. But it is no wonder, since the Spanish inquisition hath so great a place in the recorder's heart. God Almighty, who is just, will judge you for all these things.

Obser. They haled the prisoners to the bale-dock, and from thence sent them to Newgate, for non-payment of the fines; and so were their jury.

England's Present Interest Considered, 1675*

Chapter 1

Of English Rights

There is no government in the world, but it must either stand upon will and power, or condition and contract: the one rules by men, the other by laws. And above all kingdoms under heaven, it is England's felicity to have her consitution so impartially just and free, that there cannot well be any thing more remote from arbitrariness, or more zealous of preserving the laws, by which its rights are maintained.

These laws are either fundamental, and so immutable; or more superficial and temporary, and consequently alterable.

By superficial laws, we understand such acts, laws, or statutes as are suited to present occurrences, and emergencies of states; and which may as well be abrogated, as they were first made, for the good of the kingdom: for instance, those statutes that relate to victuals, clothes, times and places of trade, &c. which have ever stood, whilst the reason of them was in force; but when that benefit, which did once redound, fell by fresh accidents, they ended according to that old maxim, *Cessante ratione legis, cessat lex.*

By fundamental laws, I do not only understand such as immediately spring from *synteresis* (that eternal principle of truth and sapience, more or less disseminated through mankind,) which are as the corner-stones of human structure, the basis of reasonable societies, without which all would run into heaps and confusion; to wit, *Honeste vivere, alterum non laedere, jus suum cuiq; tribuere*, that is, 'To live honestly, not to hurt another, and to give every one their right,' (excellent principles, and common to all nations) though that itself were sufficient to our present purpose; but those rights and privileges which I call English, and which are the proper birth-right of Englishmen, and may be reduced to these three:

I. An ownership, and undisturbed possession: that what they have is rightly theirs, and no body's else.

II. A voting of every law that is made, whereby that ownership or propriety may be maintained.

III. An influence upon, and a real share in, that judicatory power that must apply every such law; which is the ancient, necessary, and laudable use

*The Select Works of William Penn, Vol. 2, pp. 272–86.

of juries: if not found among the Britons, to be sure practised by the Saxons, and continued through the Normans to this very day.

That these have been the ancient and undoubted rights of Englishmen, as three great roots, under whose spacious branches the English people have been wont to shelter themselves against the storms of arbitrary government, I shall endeavour to prove.

*   *   *

Here are the three fundamentals comprehended, and expressed to have been the rights and privileges of Englishmen.

I. Ownership, consisting of liberty, and property. In that it supposes Englishmen to be free, there is liberty: next, that they have freeholds, there is property.

II. That they have the voting of their own laws: for that was an ancient free custom, as I have already proved, and all such customs are expressly confirmed by this great charter: besides, the people helped to make it.

III. An influence upon, and a real share in, the judicatory power, in the execution and application thereof.

This is a substantial part, thrice provided for in those sixteen lines of the great charter before rehearsed: '1. That no amercement shall be assessed, but by oath of good and honest men of the vicinage. 2. Nor shall we not pass upon him, nor condemn him, but by lawful judgment of his peers. 3. Or by the law of the land:' which is synonymous, or a saying of equal signification, with lawful judgment of peers: for law of the land, and lawful judgment of peers, are the *proprium quarto modo*, or essential qualities, of these chapters of our great charter; being communicable *omni soli et semper*, to all and every clause thereof alike.

Chief justice Coke well observes, in his Second Institutes, that *per legem terrae*, or by the law of the land, imports no more than a trial by process, and writ originally at common law; which cannot be without the lawful judgment of equals, or a common jury: therefore *per legale judicium parium*, by the lawful judgment of peers, and *per legem terrae*, by the law of the land, plainly signify the same privilege to the people. So that it is the judgment of the freemen of England, which gives the cast, and turns the scale, in English justice.

These being so evidently proved by long use, and several laws, to have been the first principles, or fundamentals, of the English free government, I take leave to propose this question: May the free people of England be justly disseised of all, or any, of these fundamentals, without their consent collectively?

Answer: With submission, I conceive, not; for which I shall produce, first, my reasons, then authorities.

I. Through the British, Saxon, and Norman times, the people of this island have been reputed and called freemen by kings, parliaments, records, and histories: and as a son supposes a father, so freemen suppose freedom. This qualification imports an absolute right: such a right as none has right to disseise or dispossess an Englishman of: therefore an unalterable fundamental part of the government.

II. It can never be thought that they entrusted any representatives with these capital privileges, farther than to use their best skill to secure and maintain them. They never so delegated or impowered any men, that *de jure*, they could deprive them of that qualification: and *à facto ad jus, non valet argumentum:* for the question is not, what may be done? but, what ought to be done? Overseers and stewards are impowered not to alienate, but preserve and improve, other men's inheritances. No owners deliver their ship and goods into any man's hands to give them away, or run upon a rock; neither do they consign their affairs to agents or factors without limitations. All trusts suppose such a fundamental right in them that give them, and for whom the trusts are, as is altogether indissolvable by the trustees. The trust is, the liberty and property of the people; the limitation is, that it should not be invaded, but inviolably preserved, according to the law of the land.

III. If *salus populi* be *suprema lex*, the safety of the people the highest law, (as say several of our ancient famous lawyers and law-books;) then, since the aforesaid rights are as the sinews that hold together this free body politic, it follows, they are at least a part of the supreme law, and therefore ought to be a rule and limit to all subsequent legislation.

IV. The estate goes before the steward; the foundation before the house; people before their representatives; and the Creator before the creature. The steward lives by preserving the estate; the house stands by reason of its foundation; the representative depends upon the people, as the creature subsists by the power of its Creator.

Every representative may be called, the creature of the people, because the people make them, and to them they owe their being. Here is no transessentiating, or transubstantiating of being, from people to a representative; no more than there is an absolute transferring of a title in a letter of attorney.

The very term representative is enough to the contrary; wherefore as the house cannot stand without its foundation, nor the creature subsist without its Creator, so there can be no representative without a people, nor that people free, (which all along is intended, as inherent to, and inseparable from, the English people) without freedom; nor can there be any freedom without something be fundamental.

In short, I would fain know of any man how the branches can cut up the root of the tree that bears them? How any representative, that has not only a mere trust to preserve fundamentals, the people's inheritance, but that is a representative that makes laws, by virtue of this fundamental law, viz. that the people have a power in legislation, (the 2d principle proved by me) can have a right to remove or destroy that fundamental? The fundamental makes the people free; this free people makes a representative: can this creature unqualify its creator? What spring ever rose higher than its head? The representative is at best but a true copy, an exemplification; the free people are the original, not cancellable by a transcript: and if that fundamental which gives to the people a power of legislation, be not nullable by that representative, because it makes them what they are; much less can that representative disseise men of their liberty and property, the first great fundamental, that is, parent of this other; and which entitles to a share in making laws for the preserving of the first inviolable.

Nor is the third fundamental other than the necessary production of the two first, to intercept arbitrary designs, and make power legal: for where the people have not a share in judgment, that is, in the application, as well as making of the law, the other two are imperfect; open to daily invasion, should it be our infelicity ever to have a violent prince. For as property is every day exposed, where those that have it are destitute of power to hedge it about by law-making; so those that have both, if they have not a share in the application of the law, how easily is that hedge broken down.

And indeed, as it is a most just and necessary, as well as ancient and honourable custom, so it is the prince's interest: for still the people are concerned in the inconveniences with him, and he is freed from the temptation of doing arbitrary things, and their importunities, that might else have some pretence for such addresses, as well as from the mischiefs that might ensue such actions.

*   *   *

NEW YORK CHARTER OF LIBERTYES
AND PRIVILEDGES, 1683

Commentary

The Colonial antecedents of the federal Bill of Rights were essentially of three types: 1) guarantees contained in Charters granted by the Crown; 2) guarantees contained in instruments issued by Colonial Proprietors; and 3) guarantees contained in enactments of the colonists themselves. The best known example of the third type was the Massachusetts Body of Liberties (*supra* p. 71). It is not generally known, however, that a comparable document was passed by the New York General Assembly in 1683, which guaranteed substantial personal rights to the inhabitants of that Colony.

The New York Charter was a direct result of the successful struggle for self-government which had agitated the Colony from the beginning of English rule. New York had become the Duke of York's own Colony and the future James II was scarcely the ruler to look favorably upon popular government. General assemblies, wrote the Duke to Governor Andros in 1676, "would be of dangerous consequence, nothing being more knowne than the aptness of such bodyes to assume to themselves many priviledges wch prove destructive to . . . the peace of ye governmt." Still, even the Duke recognized, in another letter to the New York Governor, that "ye people there seems desirous of [general assemblies] in imitacon of their neighbor Colonies."

In the end, the Duke gave in to the popular desire for a representative assembly for the same reason which had led English rulers (notably his father, Charles I, in 1640) to summon Parliaments, namely, the need for funds. New York was permitted to elect a General Assembly in 1683 on the condition that it vote the funds needed to govern the Colony. As had happened so frequently in English history, the legislature called to supply funds used the occasion to redress grievances. The very first law passed by the first General Assembly of New York was the Charter of Libertyes and Priviledges.

The 1683 Charter stated that it was enacted for "The better Establishing the Government of this province of New Yorke and that Justice and Right may be Equally done to all persons within the same" (a very early statement of the notion of equality before the law). Among the substantive provisions were paraphrases of section 39 of Magna Carta, providing that no freeman should be deprived of "his ffreehold of Libertye or ffree Customes . . . But by the Lawfull Judgment of his peers and by the Law of this province," and that no one should be injured in his person or property "without being brought to Answere by due Course of Law." The latter phrase is another version in the transition between the original language of Magna Carta and the Due Process Clause.

Among other important rights guaranteed by the New York Charter were the right to trial by jury (except in contempt cases), the right to a grand jury (perhaps the earliest version of the right included in the Fifth Amendment), and an absolute right to bail except in treason and felony cases (bearing in mind that felony cases were capital cases at the time). In addition, the Third Amendment was anticipated in the prohibition against the quartering of soldiers and sailors in private homes in peace time, and there was an express prohibition against "proceeding by Marshall Law against any of his Majestyes Subjects" except those in the military—a principle that the United States Supreme Court has had to read into the federal Constitution in a series of cases from *Ex parte Milligan,* 4 Wall. 2 (U.S. 1866) to *Reid* v. *Covert,* 354 U.S. 1 (1957).

The Duke of York was, of course, not the man to acquiesce in a document like the Charter of Libertyes; he vetoed that instrument in 1684. Two years later, having become James II, King of England, he issued a new commission empowering the Governor and Council to make laws and directing the Governor "to Declare Our Will and pleasure that ye said Bill or charter of Franchises bee forthwith repealed and disallowed." The New York colonists, however, continued undaunted in their devotion to the 1683 Charter. When, after the expulsion of James II from the throne, they again received the right of self-government, one of the first things the new General Assembly (which met in April, 1691,) did, was to enact "An Act declareing what are the Rights and Priviledges of their Majesties Subjects inhabiting within their Province of New York." That law repeated almost verbatim the rights guaranteed in the 1683 Charter (the one significant change was the inclusion in the 1691 act of a guarantee of liberty of conscience for Christians except for "persons of the Romish religion").

New York Charter of Libertyes and Priviledges, 1683*

The Charter of Libertyes and priviledges granted by his Royall
Highnesse to the Inhabitants of New Yorke and its Dependencyes.

For The better Establishing the Government of this province of New Yorke and that Justice and Right may be Equally done to all persons within the same.

Bee It Enacted by the Governour Councell and Representatives now in Generall Assembly mett and assembled and by the authority of the same.

That The Supreme Legislative Authority under his Majesty and Royall Highnesse James Duke of Yorke Albany &c Lord proprietor of the said province shall forever be and reside in a Governour, Councell, and the people mett in Generall Assembly.

That The Exercise of the Cheife Magistracy and Administracon of the Government over the said province shall bee in the said Governour assisted

Colonial Laws of New York (1894), Vol. 1, pp. 111–16.

by a Councell with whose advice and Consent or with at least four of them he is to rule and Governe the same according to the Lawes thereof.

That in Case the Governour shall dye or be absent out of the province and that there be noe person within the said province Comissionated by his Royal Highnesse his heires or Successours to be Governour or Comander in Cheife there That then the Councell for the time being or Soe many of them as are in the Said province doe take upon them the Administracon of the Governour and the Execucon of the Lawes thereof and powers and authorityes belonging to the Governour and Councell the first in nominacon in which Councell is to preside untill the said Governour shall returne and arrive in the said province againe, or the pleasure of his Royall Highnesse his heires or Successours Shall be further knowne.

That According to the usage Custome and practice of the Realme of England a sessions of a Generall Assembly be held in this province once in three yeares at least.

That Every ffreeholder within this province and ffreeman in any Corporacon Shall have his free Choise and Vote in the Electing of the Representatives without any manner of constraint or Imposicon. And that in all Eleccons the Majority of Voices shall carry itt and by freeholders is understood every one who is Soe understood according to the Lawes of England.

That the persons to be Elected to sitt as representatives in the Generall Assembly from time to time for the severall Cittyes townes Countyes Shires or Divisions of this province and all places within the same shall be according to the proporcon and number hereafter Expressed that is to say for the City and County of New Yorke four, for the County of Suffolke two, for Queens County two, for Kings County two, for the County of Richmond two for the County of West Chester two.

For the County of Ulster two for the County of Albany two and for Schenectade within the said County one for Dukes County two, for the County of Cornwall two and as many more as his Royall Highnesse shall think fitt to Establish.

That All persons Chosen and Assembled in manner aforesaid or the Major part of them shall be deemed and accounted the Representatives of this province which said Representatives together with the Governour and his Councell Shall forever be the Supreame and only Legislative power under his Royall Highnesse of the said province.

That The said Representatives may appoint their owne Times of meeting dureing their sessions and may adjourne their house from time to time to such time as to them shall seeme meet and convenient.

That The said Representatives are the sole Judges of the Qualificacons of their owne members, and likewise of all undue Eleccons and may from time to time purge their house as they shall see occasion dureing the said sessions.

That noe member of the general Assembly or their servants dureing the time of their Sessions and whilest they shall be goeing to and returning from the said Assembly shall be arrested sued imprisoned or any wayes molested or troubled nor be compelled to make answere to any suite, Bill, plaint, Declaracon or otherwise, (Cases of High Treason and felony only Excepted) provided the number of the said servants shall not Exceed three.

That All bills agreed upon by the said Representatives or the Major part of them shall be presented unto the Governour and his Councell for their Approbacon and Consent All and Every which Said Bills soe approved of Consented to by the Governour and his Councell shall be Esteemed and accounted the Lawes of the province, Which said Lawes shall continue and remaine of force untill they shall be repealed by the authority aforesaid that is to say the Governour Councell and Representatives in General Assembly by and with the Approbacon of his Royal Highnesse or Expire by their owne Limittacons.

That In all Cases of death or removall of any of the said Representatives The Governour shall issue out Sumons by Writt to the Respective Townes Cittyes Shires Countryes or Divisions for which he or they soe removed or deceased were Chosen willing and requireing the ffreeholders of the Same to Elect others in their place and stead.

That Noe freeman shall be taken and imprisoned or be disseized of his ffreehold or Libertye or ffree Customes or be outlawed or Exiled or any other wayes destroyed nor shall be passed upon adjudged or condemned But by the Lawfull Judgment of his peers and by the Law of this province. Justice nor Right shall be neither sold denyed or deferred to any man within this province.

That Noe aid, Tax, Tallage, Assessment, Custome, Loane, Benevolence or Imposicon whatsoever shall be layed assessed imposed or levyed on any of his Majestyes Subjects within this province or their Estates upon any manner of Colour or pretence but by the act and Consent of the Governour Councell and Representatives of the people in Generall Assembly mett and Assembled.

That Noe man of what Estate or Condicon soever shall be putt out of his Lands or Tenements, nor taken, nor imprisoned, nor disherited, nor banished nor any wayes distroyed without being brought to Answere by due Course of Law.

That A ffreeman Shall not be amerced for a small fault, but after the manner of his fault and for a great fault after the Greatnesse thereof Saveing to him his freehold, And a husbandman saveing to him his Wainage and a merchant likewise saveing to him his merchandize And none of the said Amerciaments shall be assessed but by the oath of twelve honest and Lawfull men of the Vicinage provided the faults and misdemeanours be not in Contempt of Courts of Judicature.

All Tryalls shall be by the verdict of twelve men, and as neer as may be peers or Equalls And of the neighbourhood and in the County Shire or Division where the fact Shall arise or grow Whether the Same be by

Indictment Infermacon Declaracon or otherwise against the person Offender or Defendant.

That In all Cases Capitall or Criminall there shall be a grand Inquest who shall first present the offence and then twelve men of the neighbourhood to try the Offender who after his plea to the Indictment shall be allowed his reasonable Challenges.

That In all Cases whatsoever Bayle by sufficient Suretyes Shall be allowed and taken unlesse for treason or felony plainly and specially Expressed and menconed in the Warrant of Committment provided Always that nothing herein contained shall Extend to discharge out of prison upon bayle any person taken in Execucon for debts or otherwise legally sentenced by the Judgment of any of the Courts of Record within the province.

That Noe ffreeman shall be compelled to receive any Marriners or Souldiers into his house and there suffer them to Sojourne, against their willes provided Always it be not in time of Actuall Warr within this province.

That Noe Comissions for proceeding by Marshall Law against any of his Majestyes Subjects within this province shall issue forth to any person or persons whatsoever Least by Colour of them any of his Majestyes Subjects bee destroyed or putt to death Except all such officers persons and Soldiers in pay throughout the Government.

That from hence forward Noe Lands Within this province shall be Esteemed or accounted a Chattle or personall Estate but an Estate of Inheritance according to the Custome and practice of his Majesties Realme of England.

That Noe Court or Courts within this province have or at any time hereafter Shall have any Jurisdiccon power or authority to grant out any Execucon or other writt whereby any mans Land may be sold or any other way disposed off without the owners Consent provided Always That the issues or meane proffitts of any mans Lands shall or may be Extended by Execucon or otherwise to satisfye just debts Any thing to the Contrary hereof in any wise Notwithstanding.

That Noe Estate of a feme Covert shall be sold or conveyed But by Deed acknowledged by her in Some Court of Record the Woman being secretly Examined if She doth it freely without threats or Compulsion of her husband.

That All Wills in writeing attested by two Credible Witnesses shall be of the same force to convey Lands as other Conveyances being registered in the Secretaryes Office within forty dayes after the testators death.

That A Widdow after the death of her husband shall have her Dower And shall and may tarry in the Cheife house of her husband forty dayes after the death of her husband within which forty dayes her Dower shall be assigned her And for her Dower shall be assigned unto her the third part of all the Lands of her husband dureing Coverture, Except shee were Endowed of Lesse before Marriage.

That All Lands and Heritages within this province and Dependencyes shall be free from all fines and Lycences upon Alienacons, and from all Herriotts Ward Shipps Liveryes primer Seizins yeare day and Wast Escheats and forfeitures upon the death of parents and Ancestors naturall unaturall casuall or Judiciall, and that forever; Cases of High treason only Excepted.

That Noe person or persons which professe ffaith in God by Jesus Christ Shall at any time be any wayes molested punished disquieted or called in Question for any Difference in opinion or Matter of Religious Concernment, who doe not actually disturb the Civill peace of the province, But that all and Every such person or persons may from time to time and at all times freely have and fully enjoy his or their Judgments or Consciencyes in matters of Religion throughout all the province, they behaveing themselves peaceably and quietly and not useing this Liberty to Lycentiousnesse nor to the civill Injury or outward disturbance of others provided Always that this liberty or any thing contained therein to the Contrary shall never be Construed or improved to make void the Settlement of any publique Minister on Long Island Whether Such Settlement be by two thirds of the voices in any Towne thereon which shall alwayes include the Minor part Or by Subscripcons of perticuler Inhabitants in Said Townes provided they are the two thirds thereon Butt that all such agreements Covenants and Subscripcons that are there already made and had Or that hereafter shall bee in this Manner Consented to agreed and Subcribed shall at all time and times hereafter be firme and Stable And in Confirmacon hereof It is Enacted by the Governour Councell and Representatives; That all Such Sumes of money soe agreed on Consented to or Subscribed as aforesaid for maintenance of said publick Ministers by the two thirds of any Towne on Long Island Shall alwayes include the Minor part who shall be regulated thereby And also Such Subscripcons and agreements as are before menconed are and Shall be alwayes ratified performed and paid, And if any Towne on said Island in their publick Capacity of agreement with any Such minister or any perticuler persons by their private Subscripcons as aforesaid Shall make default deny or withdraw from Such payment Soe Covenanted to agreed upon and Subscribed That in Such Case upon Complaint of any Collector appointed and Chosen by two thirds of Such Towne upon Long Island unto any Justice of that County Upon his hearing the Same he is here by authorized impowered and required to issue out his warrant unto the Constable or his Deputy or any other person appointed for the Collection of Said Rates or agreement to Levy upon the goods and Chattles of the Said Delinquent or Defaulter all such Sumes of money Soe convenanted and agreed to be paid by distresse with Costs and Charges without any further Suite in Law Any Lawe Custome or usage to the Contrary in any wise Notwithstanding.

Provided Always the said sume or sumes be under forty shillings otherwise to be recovered as the Law directs.

And whereas All the Respective Christian Churches now in practice within the City of New Yorke and the other places of this province doe appeare to be priviledged Churches and have beene Soe Established and Confirmed by the former authority of this Government bee it hereby Enacted by this Generall Assembly and by the authority thereof That all the Said Respective Christian Churches be hereby Confirmed therein And that they and Every of them Shall from henceforth forever be held and reputed as priviledged Churches and Enjoy all their former freedomes of their Religion in Divine Worshipp and Church Discipline And that all former Contracts made and agreed upon for the maintenances of the severall ministers of the Said Churches shall stand and continue in full force and virtue And that all Contracts for the future to be made Shall bee of the same power And all persons that are unwilling to performe their part of the said Contract Shall be Constrained thereunto by a warrant from any Justice of the peace provided it be under forty Shillings Or otherwise as this Law directs provided allsoe that all Christian Churches that Shall hereafter come and settle within this province shall have the Same priviledges.

PENNSYLVANIA CHARTER OF PRIVILEGES, 1701

Commentary

According to Channing's now-classic *History of the United States,* the Pennsylvania Charter of Privileges of 1701 was "the most famous of all colonial constitutions." It was the second great Charter of liberties which we associate with the name of William Penn. As already seen (*supra* p. 130), Penn had promulgated the 1682 Frame of Government as the organic law of his new Colony. He had not, however, intended the Frame to have anything like the inexorable effect of the fabled laws of the Medes and Persians. On the contrary, he well recognized that no Constitution could survive for long without changes, and (as stressed in our discussion of the Frame) that document provided expressly for an amending process. "Friends," said Penn in an oft-quoted statement, "if in the Constitution by charter there be anything that jars, alter it."

When Penn himself returned to his Colony in 1699, he found an increasing desire for political changes. Penn settled much of the controversy and, after some months discussion, the Frame of Government of 1682 was repealed by the necessary six-sevenths vote and the Charter of Privileges of 1701 promulgated in its place. It dealt with the principal popular discontent by providing for a unicameral legislature, excluding the council (which beginning in 1700 was appointed by the Proprietor) from direct participation in legislation.

As had been the case in 1682, one of Penn's principal concerns was to protect the liberties of the colonists, and it is as a fundamental law safeguarding individual rights that the Charter of Privileges is of importance. This time freedom of religion stands first in the rights protected (a position it was to retain in the First Amendment), "Because no People can be truly happy, though under the greatest Enjoyment of Civil Liberties, if abridged of the Freedom of their Consciences." The right to religious freedom is stated in the broadest terms in Article I for all who "acknowledge *One* almighty God"—they are to have freedom of belief and worship and are not to be compelled to attend any established services (repeating, in this respect, the Frame of Government's guarantee). In addition, all professed Christians are to be capable of holding any office (a significant step forward for the time even though it excluded Jews, Deists, and atheists from office). So fundamental was freedom of religion in the Penn scheme that, though provision was again made for amending the Charter (Article VIII) it was expressly provided that attempts to amend Article I would be invalid.

Of the individual rights guaranteed by the Charter of Privileges, three deserve particular mention. Under Article IV, no person was to answer regarding property "but in ordinary Course of Justice" (another version of

Magna Carta's section 39, which moves another step in the direction of the Due Process Clause). Article VIII mitigates the harsh rule of English law by prohibiting forfeiture to the government in cases of suicide. Most forward looking was the provision in Article V that "all criminals shall have the same Privileges of Witnesses and Council as their Prosecutors." The right to call witnesses was not possessed by all defendants in England until a year after the Pennsylvania Charter was issued. An even greater forward step was the express provision for the right of counsel. English law did not fully guarantee that right until the nineteenth century; nor did any other Colony in such absolute terms before the Revolution itself. The Pennsylvania Charter was the first to anticipate the Sixth Amendment provision in the matter—and that almost a century before the federal Bill of Rights itself was adopted.

The Charter of Privileges was the last great Colonial instrument to lay the foundation for the Revolutionary and post-Revolutionary constitutional protection of individual rights. The 1701 Charter continued in force until it was replaced by the Pennsylvania Constitution of 1776 (*infra* p. 262). The Liberty Bell itself (which was to ring out the news of American Independence) was originally cast for the celebration of the fiftieth anniversary of the Charter of Privileges.

Pennsylvania Charter of Privileges, 1701*

William Penn, Proprietary and Governor of the Province of Pensilvania and Territories thereunto belonging, To all to whom these Presents shall come, sendeth Greeting. Whereas King Charles the Second, by His Letters Patents, under the Great Seal of England, bearing Date the Fourth Day of March, in the Year One Thousand Six Hundred and Eighty-one, was graciously pleased to give and grant unto me, and my Heirs and Assigns for ever, this Province of Pensilvania, with divers great Powers and Jurisdictions for the well Government thereof.

And whereas the King's dearest Brother, James Duke of York and Albany, &c. by his Deeds of Feoffment, under his Hand and Seal duly perfected, bearing Date the Twenty-Fourth Day of August, One Thousand Six Hundred Eighty and Two, did grant unto me, my Heirs and Assigns, all that Tract of Land, now called the Territories of Pensilvania, together with Powers and Jurisdictions for the good Government thereof.

And Whereas for the Encouragement of all the Freemen and Planters, that might be concerned in the said Province and Territories, and for the good Government thereof, I the said William Penn, in the Year One Thousand Six Hundred Eighty and Three, for me, my Heirs and Assigns, did grant and confirm unto all the Freemen, Planters and Adventurers therein,

*Thorpe, *The Federal and State Constitutions, Colonial Charters, and Other Organic Laws*, Vol. 5, pp. 3076–81.

divers Liberties, Franchises and Properties, as by the said Grant, entituled, The Frame of the Government of the Province of Pensilvania, and Territories thereunto belonging, in America, may appear; which Charter or Frame being found in some Parts of it, not so suitable to the present Circumstances of the Inhabitants, was in the Third Month, in the Year One Thousand Seven Hundred, delivered up to me, by Six Parts of Seven of the Freemen of this Province and Territories, in General Assembly met, Provision being made in the said Charter, for that End and Purpose.

And Whereas I was then pleased to promise, That I would restore the said Charter to them again, with necessary Alterations, or in lieu thereof, give them another, better adapted to answer the present Circumstances and Conditions of the said Inhabitants; which they have now, by their Representatives in General Assembly met at Philadelphia, requested me to grant.

Know ye therefore, That for the further Well-being and good Government of the said Province, and Territories; and in Pursuance of the Rights and Powers before-mentioned, I the said William Penn do declare, grant and confirm, unto all the Freemen, Planters and Adventurers, and other Inhabitants of this Province and Territories, these following Liberties, Franchises and Privileges, so far as in me lieth, to be held, enjoyed and kept, by the Freemen, Planters and Adventurers, and other Inhabitants of and in the said Province and Territories thereunto annexed, for ever.

I

Because no People can be truly happy, though under the greatest Enjoyment of Civil Liberties, if abridged of the Freedom of their Consciences, as to their Religious Profession and Worship: And Almighty God being the only Lord of Conscience, Father of Lights and Spirits; and the Author as well as Object of all divine Knowledge, Faith and Worship, who only doth enlighten the Minds, and persuade and convince the Understandings of People, I do hereby grant and declare, That no Person or Persons, inhabiting in this Province or Territories, who shall confess and acknowledge One almighty God, the Creator, Upholder and Ruler of the World; and profess him or themselves obliged to live quietly under the Civil Government, shall be in any Case molested or prejudiced, in his or their Person or Estate, because of his or their conscientious Persuasion or Practice, nor be compelled to frequent or maintain any religious Worship, Place or Ministry, contrary to his or their Mind, or to do or suffer any other Act or Thing, contrary to their religious Persuasion.

And that all Persons who also profess to believe in Jesus Christ, the Saviour of the World, shall be capable (notwithstanding their other Persuasions and Practices in Point of Conscience and Religion) to serve this Government in any Capacity, both legislatively and executively, he or they solemnly promising, when lawfully required, Allegiance to the King as Sovereign, and Fidelity to the Proprietary and Governor, and taking the

Attests as now established by the Law made at New-Castle, in the Year One Thousand and Seven Hundred, entitled, An Act directing the Attests of several Officers and Ministers, as now amended and confirmed this present Assembly.

II

For the well governing of this Province and Territories, there shall be an Assembly yearly chosen, by the Freemen thereof, to consist of Four Persons out of each County, of most Note for Virtue, Wisdom and Ability, (or of a greater number at any Time, as the Governor and Assembly shall agree) upon the First Day of October for ever; and shall sit on the Fourteenth Day of the same Month, at Philadelphia, unless the Governor and Council for the Time being, shall see Cause to appoint another Place within the said Province or Territories: Which Assembly shall have Power to chuse a Speaker and other their Officers; and shall be Judges of the Qualifications and Elections of their own Members; sit upon their own Adjournments; appoint Committees; prepare Bills in order to pass into Laws; impeach Criminals, and redress Grievances; and shall have all other Powers and Privileges of an Assembly, according to the Rights of the free-born Subjects of England, and as is usual in any of the King's Plantations in America.

And if any County or Counties, shall refuse or neglect to chuse their respective Representatives as aforesaid, or if chosen, do not meet to serve in Assembly, those who are so chosen and met, shall have the full Power of an Assembly, in as ample Manner as if all the Representatives had been chosen and met, provided they are not less than Two Thirds of the whole Number that ought to meet.

And that the Qualifications of Electors and Elected, and all other Matters and Things relating to Elections of Representatives to serve in Assemblies, though not herein particularly expressed, shall be and remain as by a Law of this Government, made at New-Castle in the Year One Thousand Seven Hundred, entitled, An Act to ascertain the Number of Members of Assembly, and to regulate the Elections.

III

That the Freemen in each respective County, at the Time and Place of Meeting for Electing their Representatives to serve in Assembly may as often as there shall be Occasion, chuse a double Number of Person to present to the Governor for Sheriffs and Coroners to serve for Three Years, if so long they behave themselves well; out of which respective Elections and Presentments, the Governor shall nominate and commissionate one for each of the said Offices, the Third Day after such Presentment, or else the First named in such Presentment, for each Office as aforesaid, shall stand and serve in that Office for the Time before respectively limited; and in Case of Death or Default, such Vacancies shall be supplied by the Governor, to serve to the End of the said Term.

Provided always, That if the said Freemen shall at any Time neglect or decline to chuse a Person or Persons for either or both the aforesaid Offices, then and in such Case, the Persons that are or shall be in the respective Offices of Sheriffs or Coroners, at the Time of Election, shall remain therein, until they shall be removed by another Election as aforesaid.

And that the Justices of the respective Counties shall or may nominate and present to the Governor Three Persons, to serve for Clerk of the Peace for the said County, when there is a Vacancy, one of which the Governor shall commissionate within Ten Days after such Presentment, or else the First nominated shall serve in the said Office during good Behavior.

IV

That the Laws of this Government shall be in this Stile, viz. By the Governor, with the Consent and Approbation of the Freemen in General Assembly met; and shall be, after Confirmation by the Governor, forthwith recorded in the Rolls Office, and kept at Philadelphia, unless the Governor and Assembly shall agree to appoint another Place.

V

That all Criminals shall have the same Privileges of Witnesses and Council as their Prosecutors.

VI

That no Person or Persons shall or may, at any Time hereafter, be obliged to answer any Complaint, Matter or Thing whatsoever, relating to Property, before the Governor and Council, or in any other Place, but in ordinary Course of Justice, unless Appeals thereunto shall be hereafter by Law appointed.

VII

That no Person within this Government, shall be licensed by the Governor to keep an Ordinary, Tavern or House of Publick Entertainment, but such who are first recommended to him, under the Hands of the Justices of the respective Counties, signed in open Court; which Justices are and shall be hereby impowered, to suppress and forbid any Person, keeping such Publick-House as aforesaid, upon their Misbehaviour, on such Penalties as the Law doth or shall direct; and to recommend others from time to time, as they shall see Occasion.

VIII

If any person, through Temptation or Melancholy, shall destroy himself; his Estate, real and personal, shall notwithstanding descend to his Wife and Children, or Relations, as if he had died a natural Death; and if any Person shall be destroyed or killed by Casualty or Accident, there shall be no Forfeiture to the Governor by reason thereof.

And no Act, Law or Ordinance whatsoever, shall at any Time hereafter, be made or done, to alter, change or diminish the Form or Effect of this Charter, or of any Part or Clause therein, contrary to the true Intent and Meaning thereof, without the Consent of the Governor for the Time being, and Six Parts of Seven of the Assembly met.

But because the Happiness of Mankind depends so much upon the Enjoying of Liberty of their Consciences as aforesaid, I do hereby solemnly declare, promise and grant, for me, my Heirs and Assigns, That the First Article of this Charter relating to Liberty of Conscience, and every Part and Clause therein, according to the true Intent and Meaning thereof, shall be kept and remain, without any Alteration, inviolably for ever.

And lastly, I the said William Penn, Proprietary and Governor of the Province of Pensilvania, and Territories thereunto belonging, for myself, my Heirs and Assigns, have solemnly declared, granted and confirmed, and do hereby solemnly declare, grant and confirm, That neither I, my Heirs or Assigns, shall procure or do any Thing or Things whereby the Liberties in this Charter contained and expressed, nor any Part thereof, shall be infringed or broken: And if any thing shall be procured or done, by any Person or Persons, contrary to these Presents, it shall be held of no Force or Effect.

In witness whereof, I the said William Penn, at Philadelphia in Pensilvania, have unto this present Charter of Liberties, set my Hand and broad Seal, this Twenty-Eighth Day of October, in the Year of Our Lord One Thousand Seven Hundred and One, being the Thirteenth Year of the Reign of King William the Third, over England, Scotland, France and Ireland, &c. and the Twenty-First Year of my Government.

And notwithstanding the Closure and Test of this present Charter as aforesaid, I think fit to add this following Proviso thereunto, as Part of the same, That is to say, That notwithstanding any Clause or Clauses in the above-mentioned Charter, obliging the Province and Territories to join together in Legislation, I am content, and do hereby declare, that if the Representatives of the Province and Territories shall not hereafter agree to join together in Legislation, and that the same shall be signified unto me, or my Deputy, in open Assembly, or otherwise from under the Hands and Seals of the Representatives, for the Time being, of the Province and Territories, or the major Part of either of them, at any Time within Three Years from the Date hereof, that in such Case, the Inhabitants of each of the Three Counties of this Province, shall not have less than Eight Persons to represent them in Assembly, for the Province; and the Inhabitants of the Town of Philadelphia (when the said Town is incorporated) Two Persons to represent them in Assembly; and the Inhabitants of each County in the Territories, shall have as many Persons to represent them in a distinct Assembly for the Territories, as shall be by them requested as aforesaid.

Notwitstanding which Separation of the Province and Territories, in Respect of Legislation, I do hereby promise, grant and declare, That the Inhabitants of both Province and Territories, shall separately enjoy all other Liberties, Privileges and Benefits, granted jointly to them in this Charter, any Law, Usage or Custom of this Government heretofore made and practised, or any Law made and passed by this General Assembly, to the Contrary hereof, notwithstanding.

William Penn

This Charter of Privileges being distinctly read in Assembly; and the whole and every Part thereof, being approved of and agreed to, by us, we do thankfully receive the same from our Proprietary and Governor, at Philadelphia, this Twenty-Eighth Day of October, One Thousand Seven Hundred and One. Signed on Behalf, and by Order of the Assembly,

per Joseph Growdon, Speaker

Edward Shippen,	*Griffith Owen,*
Phineas Pemberton,	*Caleb Pusey,*
Samuel Carpenter,	*Thomas Story,*

Proprietary and Governor's Council

PART THREE
REVOLUTIONARY DECLARATIONS
AND CONSTITUTIONS

REVOLUTIONARY DECLARATIONS
AND CONSTITUTIONS

Commentary

Writing in 1764, Thomas Hutchinson (then Lieutenant Governor of Massachusetts) stated that the colonists had "thought themselves at full liberty . . . to establish such sort of government as they thought proper, and to form a new state as full to all intents and purposes as if they had been in a state of nature, and were making their first entrance into civil society."

Without a doubt, this Hutchinson comment overstates the case with regard to the colonists' freedom in creating their own governmental institutions. But the colonists had, by the end of the Colonial period, gone far toward creating the constitutional polity which is the great American contribution to political science. The Colonial period had seen the development of the conception of a fundamental law to define and limit government and its powers. That conception flowed naturally from the establishment of the first colonies under Charters granted by the Crown. The next step was the realization that the colonists themselves could provide their own fundamental laws—a step first taken in the Fundamental Orders of Connecticut, 1639. In the Massachusetts Body of Liberties, 1641, protection for individual rights was made a vital part of the organic enactment. By the time we get to the Pennsylvania Frame of Government, 1682, we have moved far in the direction of the modern Constitution and Bill of Rights.

The Colonial Charters and enactments were far more explicit than the comparable documents in English history in providing protection for specific individual rights. By the end of the Colonial period, many of the rights guaranteed in the Federal Bill of Rights were already expressly safeguarded in Charters and enactments. These include (following the order of the Federal Bill of Rights): freedom of religion (though only insofar as the right to free exercise was concerned—first guaranteed in broad terms in the Rhode Island Charter); freedom of speech and petition at public meetings (guaranteed in the Massachusetts Body of Liberties); the right not to have soldiers quartered in private homes (secured in the New York Charter of Libertyes); the right to a grand jury indictment (also first guaranteed in the New York enactment); the right against double jeopardy (first secured in the Massachusetts Body of Liberties); the right to due process (contained, in varying language derived from Magna Carta, in most of the Colonial fundamental documents starting with the Maryland Act for the Liberties of the People); the right not to have private property taken without just compensation (guaranteed in the Massachusetts Body of Liberties); the right to a public trial (contained in the West New Jersey Concessions); the right to witnesses and counsel (guaranteed in modern terms in the Pennsylvania Charter of Privileges); the right to trial by jury (guaranteed in virtually all the Colonial instruments after the Massachusetts Body of Liberties); the right to bail (first secured in the Massachusetts Body of Liberties); and the right against cruel and unusual punishments (also first provided for in the Massachusetts enactment).

This was certainly an impressive list of guarantees—especially when we remember that, with the exception of those contained in the Pennsylvania Charter of Privileges they were all contained in instruments drawn up before the English Bill of Rights. In fact, compared to Colonial documents like the Massachusetts Body of Liberties, the English Bill of Rights itself seems almost a primitive document, so far as the rights secured by it are concerned.

Most important of all, both the English Bill of Rights and the Colonial documents discussed did not really have the status of Constitutions, since they were subject to alteration or repeal by the discretion of the legislature. Even the Colonial Charters could be changed at will by the Crown or Parliament. To be sure, as the Colonial period came toward its end, a sharp conflict developed between the colonies and the mother country on the latter point. "In Britain," wrote Governor Bernard of Massachusetts in 1765, "the American Governments are considered as Corporations empowered to make by-Laws, existing only during the Pleasure of Parliament . . . In America they claim. . . to be perfect States, no otherwise dependent upon Great Britain than by having the same King."

The constitutional development during the Revolutionary period may be summarized as a movement from the British to the American conception. In strict law, of course, the British view was correct; while they remained colonies, the American governments were (to quote Lord Mansfield again) "all on the same footing as our great corporations in London." The Revolution itself, nevertheless, ensured the triumph of the American conception. This was done by replacing the governments set up under Colonial Charters and other organic documents with governments established under Constitutions adopted by the people of the colonies themselves.

The need to establish new governments to fill the vacuum caused by elimination of the royal governments led the Americans to follow the procedure first outlined in Vane's *Healing Question* (*supra* p. 30)—to elect constitutional conventions to draw up Constitutions establishing governments in the different states. But the newly independent states realized that it was not enough to draft new organic instruments to set up governments and delegate to them the powers needed to govern effectively. Colonial history had taught them that equally important was the provision of limitations upon governmental authority and protection for individual rights and liberties.

The Colonial right to self-government had constantly been subjected to challenge by the royal Governors. During the century-long friction between the Governors and the legislative assemblies, the appeal to fundamental

law—whether in the Charters or the principles of the British Constitution—
became a major weapon of the colonists. But they could readily see how
much weaker their claims were when they were based upon unwritten
principles than they would have been had they been articulated in a written
higher law which men had to live by. It was consequently logical for them to
develop the slogan "a government of laws and not of men." By the time of
the Revolution, Americans firmly believed that government should be operated only by men whose status, duties, and powers were firmly fixed in
specific fundamental laws. As a colonist wrote in 1771, though "we are all
rogues, there must be Law, and all we want is to be governed by Law, and
not by the Will of Officers, which to us is perfectly despotick and arbitrary."

The first state Constitutions were a direct result of the belief just discussed. The colonists had become sorely aware of the lack of higher laws
which were legally, as well as morally, beyond the reach of those who
exercised governmental power. When the time came, they sought to correct
the deficiency with binding written directions. They did so by providing Bills
of Rights as essential parts of the new state Constitutions.

The Revolutionary period thus saw the fruition of the Colonial development already discussed. Now specific guarantees of fundamental personal
rights were expressly included in written Constitutions vested with the status
of supreme law, and binding as such upon those exercising governmental
power. These were, however, to be the culmination of the Revolutionary
period. Before then, the notion of fundamental rights itself had to be further
developed in the course of the conflict that arose between the colonies and
the mother country.

Commentary

For an instrument such as the federal Bill of Rights to have practical meaning, it must be capable of enforcement in the courts. Such enforcement means that the courts will nullify any governmental act that conflicts with the rights guaranteed in the constitutional document. For that to happen, the doctrine of a Constitution as supreme law of the land must first be developed —together with its corollary that any governmental act contrary to the Constitution is unconstitutional and void. Before Americans could safely commit their freedoms to Bills of Rights, they needed the assurance that the rights safeguarded by those documents would be given effect by the courts even against legislation that conflicted with them.

Despite the fact that England did not have a written Constitution, the doctrine of unconstitutionality (based upon the notion of a body of higher law to which government was subject) was articulated by English jurists as a means of curbing the pretensions of both the Crown and Parliament. The best known example was the decision of Lord Coke in *Dr. Bonham's Case* (1610). In it—perhaps the most famous case decided by him—Coke seized the occasion to declare that the law was above the Parliament as well as above the King. Dr. Bonham had practiced medicine without a certificate from the Royal College of Physicians. The College Censors committed him to prison, and he sued for false imprisonment. The college set forth in defense its statute of incorporation, which authorized it to regulate all physicians and punish with fine and imprisonment practitioners not admitted by it. The statute in question, however, gave the college one half of all the fines imposed. This, said Coke, made the college not only judges, but also parties, in cases coming before them, and it is an established maxim of the common law that no man may be judge in his own cause.

But what of the statute, which appeared to give the college the power to judge Dr. Bonham? Coke's answer was that even the Parliament could not confer a power so contrary to common right and reason. In his words, "it appears in our books, that in many cases, the common law will controul Acts of Parliament, and sometimes adjudge them to be utterly void: for when an Act of Parliament is against common right and reason, or repugnant, or impossible to be performed, the common law will controul it, and adjudge such Act to be void."

Modern scholars have debated over the exact meaning of these words. To the men of the formative era of American constitutional history, on the other hand, such meaning was clear. The Chief Justice of Common Pleas was stating as a rule of positive law that there was a fundamental law which limited Crown and Parliament indifferently. Had not my Lord Coke concluded that when an Act of Parliament is contrary to such fundamental law, it must be adjudged void? Did not this mean that when the British government acted toward the colonies in a manner contrary to common right and reason, its decrees were of no legal force?

From Westminster Hall, where the judgment in *Dr. Bonham's Case* was delivered in 1610, to the Council Chamber of the Boston Town House a century and a half later was not really so far as it seemed. "That council chamber," wrote John Adams (whose famous 1817 account is given *infra* p. 192), "was as respectable an apartment as the House of Commons or the House of Lords in Great Britain. . . . In this chamber, round a great fire, were seated five Judges, with Lieutenant-Governor Hutchinson at their head, as Chief Justice, all arrayed in their new, fresh, rich robes of scarlet English broadcloth; in their large cambric bands, and immense judicial wigs." For it was in this chamber that, in February, 1761, James Otis delivered his landmark attack against general writs of assistance.

The Otis argument in *Lechmere's Case* has been characterized as the opening gun of the controversy leading to the Revolution. In it, Otis with "a torrent of impetuous eloquence . . . hurried away every thing before him." He argued the cause, Otis declared, "with the greater pleasure . . . as it is in opposition to a kind of power, the exercise of which, in former periods of English history, cost one King of England his head and another his throne." If Patrick Henry came close to treason in his famous speech of 1765, he at least had an excellent model in this Otis speech.

To demonstrate the illegality of the writs of assistance, Otis went straight back to Coke. As Horace Gray (later a Justice of the Supreme Court) put it in an 1865 comment, "His main reliance was the well-known statement of Lord Coke in *Dr. Bonham's Case.*" This may be seen clearly from John Adams' summary of the Otis argument: "As to acts of Parliament. An act against the Constitution is void: an Act against natural Equity is void: and if an Act of Parliament should be made in the very words of the petition, it would be void. The . . . Courts must pass such Acts into disuse."

The Otis oration, exclaimed Adams, "breathed into this nation the breath of life," and, "Then and there the child Independence was born." To which we may add that then and there American constitutional law was born. For Otis, in Justice Gray's words, "denied that [Parliament] was the final arbiter of the justice and constitutionality of its own acts; and . . . contended that the validity of statutes must be judged by the courts of justice; and thus foreshadowed the principle of American constitutional law, that it is the duty of the judiciary to declare unconstitutional statutes void."

Of course, the Coke concept of higher fundamental law gave way in Britain itself to the principle of Parliamentary supremacy. Starting with the Otis argument, however, the dictum in *Dr. Bonham's Case* was put to new use on the western side of the Atlantic. Otis had stated the doctrine (ultimately to take over the field in the American system) that an act contrary to the Constitution was void and the courts should refuse to enforce it. Only two years later, in a jury trial in the Hanover County Courthouse in Virginia, Patrick Henry went further and called into question the right of the Privy Council in London to disallow the so-called Two-penny Act passed by the Virginia Assembly in 1758. Henry also relied on the notion of unconstitutionality, stating (in the words of a contemporary observer) "That the act of 1758 . . . could not, consistently with what he called the original compact between the King and the people . . . be annulled."

The Otis-Henry doctrine was a necessary foundation both for the legal theory underlying the Revolution and the Constitutions and Bills of Rights which it produced. The claim that Britain was acting in an unconstitutional manner with regard to the colonies led naturally to the provision in written Constitutions of the basic rights which government might not infringe.

Lechmere's Case, 1761*

John Adams' Minutes of the Argument

Writs of Assistance

Gridley: The Constables distraining for Rates. More inconsistent with English Rights and Liberties than Writts of assistance. And Necessity authorizes both.

Thatcher: I have searched, in all the ancient Repertories of Precedents, in Fitzherberts Natura Brevium, and in the Register (Q. what the Register is) and have found no such Writt of assistance as this Petition prays. I have found two Writts of assistance in the Register but they are very different from the Writt pray'd for.

In a Book, intituled the Modern Practice of the Court of Exchequer there is indeed one such Writt, and but one.

By the Act of Parliament any other private Person may as well as a Custom House Officer take an officer, a sherriff, or Constable &c. and go into any shop, store &c. and seize: any Person authorized by such a Writt, under the seal of the Court of Exchequer, may. Not Custom House officers only. Strange.

Only a temporary Thing.

The most material Question is, whether the Practice of the Exchequer, will warrant this Court in granting the same.

The Act impowers all the officers of the Revenue to enter and seize in the Plantations, as well as in England. 7. & 8. Wm. 3, c. 22, § 6. gives the same as 13. & 14. of C[harles] gives in England. The Ground of Mr. Gridleys argument is this, that this Court has the Power of the Court of Exchequer. But This Court has renounced the Chancery Jurisdiction, which the Ex-

*L. K. Wroth and H. B. Zobel, eds., *Legal Papers of John Adams* (1965), Vol. 2, pp. 123–30.

chequer has in Cases where either Party is the Kings Debtor. Q. into that Case.

In England all Informations of uncust[om]ed or prohibited Importations, are in the Exchequer. So that the Custom House officers are the officers of that Court. Under the Eye and Direction of the Barons.

The Writ of Assistance is not returnable. If such seisure were brot before your Honours, youd often find a wanton Exercise of their Power.

At home, the officers seise at their Peril even with Probable Cause.

Otis: This Writ is against the fundamental Principles of Law. The Priviledge of House. A Man, who is quiet, is as secure in his House, as a Prince in his Castle, not with standing all his Debts, and civil Prossesses of any kind.—But

For flagrant Crimes, and in Cases of great public Necessity, the Priviledge may be [encroached?] on. For Felonies an officer may break upon Prossess, and oath—i.e. by a Special Warrant to search such an House, sworn to be suspected, and good Grounds of suspicion appearing.

Make oath coram Ld. Treasurer, or Exchequer, in England or a Magistrate here, and get a special Warrant, for the public good, to infringe the Priviledge of House.

General Warrant to search for Felonies, Hawk. Pleas Crown. Every petty officer from the highest to the lowest. And if some of em are (*comm[issioned]*, *others*) uncom[missioned] others are uncomm[issioned]. Gov[ernor and?] Justices used to issue such perpetual Edicts. (Q. with what particular Reference?)

But one Precedent, and that in the Reign of C. 2, when Star Chamber Powers, and all Powers but lawful and useful Powers were pushd to Extremity.

The Authority of this Modern Practice of the Court of Exchequer. It has an Imprimatur. But what may not have? It may be owing to some ignorant Clerk of the Exchequer.

But all Precedents and this among the Rest are under the Control of the Principles of Law. Ld. Talbot. Better to observe the known Principles of Law than any one Precedent, tho in the House of Lords.

As to Acts of Parliament. An Act against the Constitution is void: an Act against natural Equity is void: and if an Act of Parliament should be made, in the very Words of this Petition, it would be void. The executive Courts must pass such Acts into disuse. 8. Rep. 118. from Viner. Reason of the Common Law to control an Act of Parliament. Iron Manufacture. Noble Lord's Proposal, that we should send our Horses to England to be shod.

If an officer will justify under a Writ he must return it. 12th. Mod. 396. Perpetual Writ.

Stat. C. 2. We have all as good Right to inform as Custom House officers. And any Man may have a general, irreturnable (Writ) Commission to break Houses.

By 12. of C. on oath before Ld. Treasurer, Barons of Exchequer, or Chief Magistrate to break with an officer. 14th. C. to issue a Warrant requiring sherriff &c. to assist the officers to search for Goods not enterd, or prohibited. 7 & 8th. W. & M. gives officers in Plantation same Powers with officers in England.

Continuance of Writts and Prossesses proves no more, nor so much as I grant a special Writ of assistance on special oath, for special Purpose.

Pew indorsd Warrant to Ware. Justice Walley searchd House. Law Prov. Bill in Chancery. This Court confind their Chancery Power to Revenue, &c.

Gridley: By the 7. & 8. of Wm. c. 22. § 6th. This authority, of breaking and Entring ships, Warehouses Cellars &c. given to the Customs House officers in England by the statutes of the 12th. and 14th. of Charl. 2d. is extended to the Custom House officers in the Plantations: and by the statute of the 6th. of Anne, Writts of assistance are continued, in Company with all other legal Prossesses for 6 months after the Demise of the Crown.—Now What this Writ of assistance is, we can know only by Books of Precedents. And We have producd, in a Book intituld the modern Practice of the Court of Exchequer, a form of such a Writ of assistance to the officers of the Customs. The Book has the Imprimatur of Wright, C.J. of the King's Bench which is as great a sanction as any Books of Precedents ever have, altho Books of Reports are usually approvd by all the Judges. And I take Brown the Author of this Book to have been a very good Collector of Precedents. I have two Volumes of Precedents of his Collection, which I look upon as good as any, except Coke and Rastal.

And the Power given in this Writ is no greater Infringement of our Liberty, than the Method of collecting Taxes in this Province.

Every Body knows that the subject has the Priviledge of House only against his fellow subjects, not vs. the King either in matters of Crime or fine.

*   *   *

John Adams' "Abstract of the Argument," 1761*

On the second Tuesday of the Court's sitting, appointed by the rule of the Court for argument of special matters, came on the dispute on the petition of Mr. Cockle and others on the one side, and the Inhabitants of Boston on the other, concerning Writs of Assistance. Mr. Gridley appeared for the former, Mr. Otis for the latter. Mr. Thacher was joined with him at the desire of the Court.

Mr. Gridley: I appear on the behalf of Mr. Cockle and others, who pray "that as they cannot fully exercise their Offices in such a manner as his

Legal Papers of John Adams, pp. 134–44. This Abstract was apparently written by Adams in the Spring of 1761.

Majesty's Service and their Laws in such cases require, unless your Honors who are vested with the power of a Court of Exchequer for this Province will please to grant them Writs of Assistance. They therefore pray that they and their Deputies may be aided in the Execution of their Offices by Writs of Assistance under the Seal of this Court and in legal form, and according to the Usage of his Majesty's Court of Exchequer in Great Britain."

May it please your Honors, it is certain it has been the practice of the Court of Exchequer in England, and of this Court in this Province, to grant Writs of Assistance to Custom House Officers. Such Writs are mentioned in several Acts of Parliament, in several Books of Reports; and in a Book called the Modern Practice of the Court of Exchequer, We have a Precedent, a form of a Writ, called a Writ of Assistance for Custom house Officers, of which the following a few years past to Mr. Paxton under the Seal of this Court, and tested by the late Chief Justice Sewall is a literal Translation.

The first Question therefore for your Honors to determine is, whether this practice of the Court of Exchequer in England (which it is certain, has taken place heretofore, how long or short a time soever it continued) is legal or illegal. And the second is, whether the practice of the Exchequer (admitting it to be legal) can warrant this Court in the same practice.

In answer to the first, I cannot indeed find the Original of this Writ of Assistance. It may be of very antient, to which I am inclined, or it may be of modern date. This however is certain, that the Stat. of the 14th. Char. 2nd. has established this Writ almost in the words of the Writ itself. "And it shall be lawful to and for any person or persons authorised by Writ of Assistance under the seal of his Majesty's Court of Exchequer to take a Constable, Headborough, or other public Officer, inhabiting near unto the place, and in the day time to enter and go into any house, Shop, Cellar, Warehouse, room, or any other place, and in case of Resistance, to break open doors, Chests, Trunks and other Package, and there to seize any kind of Goods or Merchandize whatever prohibited, and to put the same into his Majesty's Warehouse in the Port where Seisure is made."

By this act and that of 12 Char. 2nd. all the powers in the Writ of Assistance mentioned are given, and it is expressly said, the persons shall be authorised by Writs of Assistance under the seal of the Exchequer. Now the Books in which we should expect to find these Writs, and all that relates to them are Books of Precedents, and Reports in the Exchequer, which are extremely scarce in this Country; we have one, and but one that treats of Exchequer matters, and that is called the "Modern practice of the Court of Exchequer," and in this Book we find one Writ of Assistance, translated above. Books of Reports have commonly the Sanction of all the Judges, but books of Precedents never have more than that of the Chief Justice. Now this Book has the Imprimatur of Wright, who was Chief Justice of the King's Bench, and it was wrote by Brown, whom I esteem the best Collector of

Precedents; I have Two Volumes of them by him, which I esteem the best except Rastall and Coke. But we have a further proof of the legality of these Writs, and of the settled practice at home of allowing them; because by the Stat. 6th Anne which continues all Processes and Writs after the Demise of the Crown, Writs of Assistance are continued among the Rest.

It being clear therefore that the Court of Exchequer at home has a power by Law of granting these Writs, I think there can be but little doubt, whether this Court as a Court of Exchequer for this Province has this power. By the Statute of the 7th. & 8th. W. 3d., it is enacted "that all the Officers for collecting and managing his Majesty's Revenue, and inspecting the Plantation Trade in any of the said Plantations, shall have the same powers &c. as are provided for the Officers of the Revenue in England; also to enter Houses, or Warehouses, to search for and seize any such Goods, and that the like Assistance shall be given to the said Officers as is the Custom in England."

Now what is the Assistance which the Officers of the Revenue are to have here, which is like that they have in England. Writs of Assistance under the Seal of his Majesty's Court of Exchequer at home will not run here. They must therefore be under the Seal of this Court. For by the law of this Province 2 W. 3d. Ch. 3 "there shall be a Superior Court &c. over the whole Province &c. who shall have cognizance of all pleas &c. and generally of all other matters, as fully and [amply] to all intents and purposes as the Courts of King's Bench, Common Pleas and Exchequer within his Majesty's Kingdom of England have or ought to have."

It is true the common privileges of Englishmen are taken away in this Case, but even their privileges are not so in cases of Crime and fine. 'Tis the necessity of the Case and the benefit of the Revenue that justifies this Writ. Is not the Revenue the sole support of Fleets and Armies abroad, and Ministers at home? without which the Nation could neither be preserved from the Invasions of her foes, nor the Tumults of her own Subjects. Is not this I say infinitely more important, than the imprisonment of Thieves, or even Murderers? yet in these Cases 'tis agreed Houses may be broke open.

In fine the power now under consideration is the same with that given by the Law of this Province to Treasurers towards Collectors, and to them towards the subject. A Collector may when he pleases distrain my goods and Chattels, and in want of them arrest my person, and throw me instantly into Goal. What! shall my property be wrested from me!—shall my Liberty be destroyed by a Collector, for a debt, unadjudged, without the common Indulgence and Lenity of the Law? So it is established, and the necessity of having public taxes effectually and speedily collected is of infinitely greater moment to the whole, than the Liberty of any Individual.

*   *   *

Otis: May it please your Honours,

I was desired by one of the court to look into the books, and consider the question now before the court, concerning Writs of Assistance. I have accordingly considered it, and now appear not only in obedience to your order, but also in behalf of the inhabitants of this town, who have presented another petition, and out of regard to the liberties of the subject. And I take this opportunity to declare, that whether under a fee or not, (for in such a cause as this I despise a fee) I will to my dying day oppose, with all the powers and faculties God has given me, all such instruments of slavery on the one hand, and villainy on the other, as this writ of assistance is. It appears to me (may it please your honours) the worst instrument of arbitrary power, the most destructive of English liberty, and the fundamental principles of the constitution, that ever was found in an English law-book. I must therefore beg your honours patience and attention to the whole range of an argument, that may perhaps appear uncommon in many things, as well as points of learning, that are more remote and unusual, that the whole tendency of my design may the more easily be perceived, the conclusions better descend, and the force of them better felt.

I shall not think much of my pains in this cause as I engaged in it from principle. I was sollicited to engage on the other side. I was sollicited to argue this cause as Advocate-General, and because I would not, I have been charged with a desertion of my office; to this charge I can give a very sufficient answer, I renounced that office, and I argue this cause from the same principle; and I argue it with the greater pleasure as it is in favour of British liberty, at a time, when we hear the greatest monarch upon earth declaring from his throne, that he glories in the name of Briton, and that the privileges of his people are dearer to him than the most valuable prerogatives of his crown. And as it is in opposition to a kind of power, the exercise of which in former periods of English history, cost one King of England his head and another his throne. I have taken more pains in this cause, than I ever will take again: Although my engaging in this and another popular cause has raised much resentment; but I think I can sincerely declare, that I cheerfully submit myself to every odious name for conscience sake; and from my soul I despise all those whose guilt, malice or folly has made my foes. Let the consequences be what they will, I am determined to proceed. The only principles of public conduct that are worthy a gentleman, or a man are, to sacrifice estate, ease, health and applause, and even life itself to the sacred calls of his country. These manly sentiments in private life make the good citizen, in public life, the patriot and the hero.—I do not say, when brought to the test, I shall be invincible; I pray God I may never be brought to the melancholy trial; but if ever I should, it would be then known, how far I can reduce to practice principles I know founded in truth.—In the mean time I will proceed to the subject of the writ. In the first, may it please your Honours, I will admit, that writs of one kind, may be legal, that is, special writs, directed to special officers, and to search certain houses, &c. especially set forth in the writ, may be granted by the Court of Exchequer at home, upon oath made before the Lord Treasurer by the person, who asks, that he suspects such goods to be concealed in those very places he desires to search. The Act of 14th Car. II. which Mr. Gridley mentions proves this. And in this light the writ appears like a warrant from a justice of peace to search for stolen goods. Your Honours will find in the old book, concerning the office of a justice of peace, precedents of general warrants to search suspected houses. But in more modern books you will find only special warrants to search such and such houses specially named, in which the complainant has before sworn he suspects his goods are concealed; and you will find it adjudged that special warrants only are legal. In the same manner I rely on it, that the writ prayed for in this petition being general is illegal. It is a power that places the liberty of every man in the hands of every petty officer. I say I admit that special writs of assistance to search special houses, may be granted to certain persons on oath; but I deny that the writ now prayed for can be granted, for I beg leave to make some observations on the writ itself before I proceed to other Acts of Parliament.

In the first place the writ is universal, being directed "to all and singular justices, sheriffs, constables and all other officers and subjects, &c." So that in short it is directed to every subject in the king's dominions; every one with this writ may be a tyrant: If this commission is legal, a tyrant may, in a legal manner also, controul, imprison or murder any one within the realm.

In the next place, it is perpetual; there's no return, a man is accountable to no person for his doings, every man may reign secure in his petty tyranny, and spread terror and desolation around him, until the trump of the arch angel shall excite different emotions in his soul.

In the third place, a person with this writ, in the day time may enter all houses, shops, &c. at will, and command all to assist.

Fourth, by this not only deputies, &c. but even their menial servants are allowed to lord it over us—What is this but to have the curse of Canaan with a witness on us, to be the servant of servants, the most despicable of God's creation. Now one of the most essential branches of English liberty, is the freedom of one's house. A man's house is his castle; and while he is quiet, he is as well guarded as a prince in his castle. This writ, if it should be declared legal, would totally annihilate this privilege. Custom house officers may enter our houses when they please—we are commanded to permit their entry— their menial servants may enter—may break locks, bars and every thing in their way—and whether they break through malice or revenge, no man, no court can inquire—bare suspicion without oath is sufficient. This wanton exercise of this power is no chimerical suggestion of a heated Brain—I will mention some facts. Mr. Pew had one of these writs, and when Mr. Ware succeeded him, he endorsed this writ over to Mr. Ware, so that these writs are negotiable from one officer to another, and so your Honours have no opportunity of judging the persons to whom this vast power is delegated. Another instance is this. Mr. Justice Wally had called this same Mr. Ware before him by a constable, to answer for a breach of the Sabbath day acts, or that of profane swearing. As soon as he had done, Mr. Ware asked him if he had done, he replied, yes. Well then, says he, I will shew you a little of my power—I command you to permit me to search your house for unaccustomed goods; and went on to search his house from the garret to the cellar, and then served the constable in the same manner. But to shew another absurdity in this writ, if it should be established, I insist upon it every person by 14th of Car. II. has this power as well as Custom-house officers; the words are, "it shall be lawful for any person or persons authorized, &c." What a scene does this open! Every man prompted by revenge, ill humour or wantonness to inspect the inside of his neighbour's house, may get a writ of assistance; others will ask it from self defence; one arbitrary exertion will provoke another, until society will be involved in tumult and in blood. Again these writs are not returned. Writs in their nature are temporary things; when the purposes for which they are issued are answered, they exist no more; but these monsters in the law live forever, no one can be called to account. Thus reason and the constitution are both against this writ. Let us see what authority there is for it. No more than one instance can be found of it in all our law books, and that was in the zenith of arbitrary power, viz. In the reign of Car. II. when Star-chamber powers were pushed in extremity by some ignorant clerk of the Exchequer. But had this writ been in any book whatever it would have been illegal. All precedents are under the controul of the principles of the law. Lord Talbot says, it is better to observe these than any precedents though in the House of Lords, the last resort of the subject. No Acts of Parliament can establish such a writ; Though it should be made in the very words of the petition it would be void, "An act against the constitution is void." Vid. Viner. But these prove no more than what I before observed, that special writs may be granted on oath and probable suspicion. The Act of 7th and 8th of William III. that the officers of the plantations shall have the same powers, &c. is confined to this sense, that an officer should show probable grounds, should take his oath on it, should do this before a magistrate, and that such magistrate, if he thinks proper should issue a special warrant to a constable to search the places. That of 6th of Anne can prove no more.

It is the business of this court to demolish this monster of oppression, and to tear into rags this remnant of Starchamber tyranny—&c.

The court suspended the absolute determination of this matter. I have omitted many authorities; also many fine touches in the order of reasoning, and numberless Rhetorical and popular flourishes.

John Adams to William Tudor, 1817*

Mar. 29, 1817

Is your daughter, Mrs. Stuart, who I am credibly informed is one of the most accomplished of ladies, a painter? Are you acquainted with Miss Lydia Smith, who, I am also credibly informed, is one of the most accomplished ladies, and a painter? Do you know Mr. Sargent? Do you correspond with your old companion in arms, Colonel John Trumbull? Do you think Fisher will be an historical painter?

Whenever you shall find a painter, male or female, I pray you to suggest a scene and a subject for the pencil.

The scene is the Council Chamber in the old Town House in Boston. The date is in the month of February, 1761, nine years before you entered my office in Cole Lane. As this was five years before you entered college, you must have been in the second form of master Lovell's school.

That council chamber was as respectable an apartment as the House of Commons or the House of Lords in Great Britain, in proportion, or that in the State House in Philadelphia, in which the declaration of independence was signed, in 1776. In this chamber, round a great fire, were seated five Judges, with Lieutenant-Governor Hutchinson at their head, as Chief Justice, all arrayed in their new, fresh, rich robes of scarlet English broadcloth; in their large cambric bands, and immense judicial wigs. In this chamber were seated at a long table all the barristers at law of Boston, and of the neighboring county of Middlesex, in gowns, bands, and tie wigs. They were not seated on ivory chairs, but their dress was more solemn and more pompous than that of the Roman Senate, when the Gauls broke in upon them.

In a corner of the room must be placed as a spectator and an auditor, wit, sense, imagination, genius, pathos, reason, prudence, eloquence, learning, and immense reading, hanging by the shoulders on two crutches, covered with a great cloth coat, in the person of Mr. Pratt, who had been solicited on both sides, but would engage on neither, being, as Chief Justice of New York, about to leave Boston forever. Two portraits, at more than full length, of King Charles the Second and of King James the Second, in splendid golden frames, were hung up on the most conspicuous sides of the apartment. If my young eyes or old memory have not deceived me, these were as fine pictures as I ever saw; the colors of the royal ermines and long flowing robes were the most glowing, the figures the most noble and graceful, the features the most distinct and characteristic, far superior to those of the King and Queen of France in the Senate chamber of Congress—these were

*C. F. Adams, ed., *The Works of John Adams* (1856), Vol. 10, pp. 244–49.

192

worthy of the pencils of Rubens and Vandyke. There was no painter in England capable of them at that time. They had been sent over without frames in Governor Pownall's time, but he was no admirer of Charles or James. The pictures were stowed away in a garret, among rubbish, till Governor Bernard came, who had them cleaned, superbly framed, and placed in council for the admiration and imitation of all men—no doubt with the advice and concurrence of Hutchinson and all his nebula of stars and satellites.

One circumstance more. Samuel Quincy and John Adams had been admitted barristers at that term. John was the youngest; he should be painted looking like a short thick archbishop of Canterbury, seated at the table with a pen in his hand, lost in admiration, now and then minuting those poor notes which your pupil, Judge Minot, has printed in his history, with some interpolations. . . .

You have now the stage and the scenery; next follows a narration of the subject. I rather think that we lawyers ought to call it a brief of the cause.

When the British ministry received from General Amherst his despatches, announcing the conquest of Montreal, and the consequent annihilation of the French government in America, in 1759, they immediately conceived the design, and took the resolution, of conquering the English colonies, and subjecting them to the unlimited authority of Parliament. With this view and intention they sent orders and instructions to the collector of the customs in Boston, Mr. Charles Paxton, to apply to the civil authority for writs of assistance, to enable the custom-house officers, tidewaiters, landwaiters, and all, to command all sheriffs and constables, &c., to attend and aid them in breaking open houses, stores, shops, cellars, ships, bales, trunks, chests, casks, packages of all sorts, to search for goods, wares, and merchandises, which had been imported against the prohibitions or without paying the taxes imposed by certain acts of Parliament, called the acts of trade; that is, by certain parliamentary statutes, which had been procured to be passed from time to time for a century before, by a combination of selfish intrigues between West India planters and North American royal governors. These acts never had been executed as revenue laws, and there never had been a time, when they would have been or could have been obeyed as such.

Mr. Paxton, no doubt consulting with Governor Bernard, Lieutenant-Governor Hutchinson, and all the principal crown officers, thought it not prudent to commence his operations in Boston. For obvious reasons, he instructed his deputy collector in Salem, Mr. Cockle, to apply by petition to the Superior Court, in November, 1760, then sitting in that town, for writs of assistance. Stephen Sewall was then Chief Justice of that Court, an able man, an uncorrupted American, and a sincere friend of liberty, civil and religious. He expressed great doubts of the legality of such a writ, and of the authority of the Court to grant it. Not one of his brother judges uttered a word in favor of it; but as it was an application on the part of the crown, it must be heard and determined. After consultation, the Court ordered the question to be argued at the next February term in Boston, namely in 1761.

In the mean time Chief Justice Sewall died, and Lieutenant-Governor Hutchinson was appointed Chief Justice of that Court in his stead. Every observing and thinking man knew that this appointment was made for the direct purpose of deciding this question in favor of the crown, and all others in which it should be interested. An alarm was spread far and wide. Merchants of Salem and Boston applied to Mr. Pratt, who refused, and to Mr. Otis and Mr. Thacher, who accepted, to defend them against the terrible menacing monster, the writ of assistance. Great fees were offered, but Otis, and, I believe, Thacher, would accept of none. "In such a cause," said Otis, "I despise all fees."

I have given you a sketch of the stage, and the scenery, and the brief of the cause, or, if you like the phrase better, the tragedy, comedy, or farce.

Now for the actors and performers. Mr. Gridley argued with his characteristic learning, ingenuity, and dignity, and said every thing that could be said in favor of Cockle's petition; all depending, however, on the "if the Parliament of Great Britain is the sovereign legislature of all the British empire." Mr. Thacher followed him on the other side, and argued with the softness of manners, the ingenuity and cool reasoning, which were remarkable in his amiable character.

But Otis was a flame of fire!—with a promptitude of classical allusions, a depth of research, a rapid summary of historical events and dates, a profusion of legal authorities, a prophetic glance of his eye into futurity, and a torrent of impetuous eloquence, he hurried away every thing before him. American independence was then and there born; the seeds of patriots and heroes were then and there sown, to defend the vigorous youth, the *non sine Diis animosus infans.* Every man of a crowded audience appeared to me to go away, as I did, ready to take arms against writs of assistance. Then and there was the first scene of the first act of opposition to the arbitrary claims of Great Britain. Then and there the child Independence was born. In fifteen years, namely in 1776, he grew up to manhood, and declared himself free.

*   *   *

The minutes of Mr. Otis's argument are no better a representation of it than the gleam of a glow-worm to the meridian blaze of the sun. I fear I shall make you repent bringing out the old gentleman. *Ridendo dicere verum quid vetat?*

DECLARATION OF RIGHTS AND GRIEVANCES, 1765

Commentary

As already indicated (*supra* p. 18–19), the reaction of the colonists to the Stamp Act crisis was influenced by the authority of Lord Coke—both in arguing the invalidity of acts of Parliament which restricted Colonial rights and in preparing a Declaration of Rights and Grievances declaring the rights of Americans. It was, indeed, in the controversy over the Stamp Act that Coke's influence had its most important American results. We have seen (*supra* p. 183) that John Adams attributed the honor of starting the nation on the road to independence to Otis. In 1776, on the other hand, he had stated that the "author of the first Virginia Resolutions against the stamp act . . . will have the glory with posterity, of beginning . . . this great Revolution."

On May 29, 1765, Patrick Henry sprang to the fore in the Virginia House of Burgesses, while that assembly was considering the newly enacted Stamp Act. It was known that Mr. Henry was not really learned in the law (he had, indeed, been admitted to the bar after six weeks' study of only Coke and the Virginia Statutes). Yet he had read in *Coke upon Littleton* that an act of Parliament against the Magna Carta, or common right, or reason was void. And it was on the flyleaf of his old copy of that book that the unlearned young lawyer wrote out a set of resolutions protesting against the Stamp Act. It was these resolutions which Henry presented to the Virginia assembly, together with the "treasonable" speech with which his name has forever remained associated. Young Thomas Jefferson, who witnessed the scene, later recalled how "torrents of sublime eloquence from Mr. Henry . . . prevailed" to secure passage of most of the resolutions.

Throughout the colonies, the Stamp Act was opposed on the same ground that Otis had urged in *Lechmere's Case.* John Adams used the Otis argument in presenting a petition "that the Stamp Act was null because unconstitutional" to the Governor and Council of Massachusetts, and a committee of the legislative assembly of that Colony resolved that business should be done without stamps. The "prevailing reason" given for their resolve, as well as the action of the people in following it, according to Thomas Hutchinson, then Lieutenant Governor of Massachusetts, was "that the Act of Parliament is against Magna Carta and the natural rights of Englishmen, and therefore according to Lord Coke null and void."

Even the judges appointed by the royal Governors were not prepared to deny this principle. Justice William Cushing, a member of the highest Massachusetts bench, in a letter, dated "In a hurry Feby. 7, 1766," to Lieutenant Governor Hutchinson (who was then also Chief Justice of Massachusetts), wrote, "Its true It is said an Act of Parliament against natural Equity is

195

void." That being the case, "If we admit evidence unstamped . . . Q. if it can be said we do wrong." Later, his opinion more settled, Cushing could write to John Adams, "I can tell the grand jury the nullity of Acts of Parliament."

The Virginia judges went even further, for a court in that Colony actually ruled, in February, 1766, that the Stamp Act was void. The judges "unanimously declared it to be their opinion," we are told in a contemporary account, "that the said act did not bind, affect, or concern the inhabitants of this colony inasmuch as they conceive the same to be unconstitutional."

Men whose education had been, in large part, based upon Coke quite naturally gave a legal turn to their disaffection with the Stamp Act. "Our friends to liberty," wrote Thomas Hutchinson during the heat of the Stamp Act controversy, "take the advantage of a maxim they find in Lord Coke that an Act of Parliament against Magna Carta or the peculiar rights of Englishmen is ipso facto void." This, Hutchinson went on, is what "seems to have determined a great part of the colony to oppose the execution of the act with force."

When the time came for the colonists to present a united front in opposition to the Stamp Act by convening the Stamp Act Congress, that body followed Coke's example when he had been a leader of the 1628 Parliament. The Stamp Act Congress drew up a Declaration of Rights and Grievances. This famous document (probably drafted by John Dickinson) starts by affirming the allegiance of the colonists to the Crown and their "due subordination" to Parliament. Moderate though its tone was, however, it asserted the basic Colonial theory that the colonists were entitled to all the rights of Englishmen. It went on to question the constitutionality of the Stamp Act, declaring that such a statute was "unreasonable and inconsistent with the principles and spirit of the British constitution." In addition, it stated flatly that trial by jury was a fundamental right of every colonist and that the colonists had the right to petition the King or Parliament.

The Declaration of Rights of the Stamp Act Congress is an assertion by the colonies acting through a Congress (to which nine colonies had sent delegates) of the fundamental concept of constitutionality without which neither Constitutions nor Bills of Rights would have been possible. The doctrine of *Dr. Bonham's Case* (heresy though it was in English law) had crossed the Atlantic there to be used as the foundation for the constitutional edifice which Americans have erected.

Declaration of Rights and Grievances, 1765*

The members of this Congress, sincerely devoted with the warmest sentiments of affection and duty to His Majesty's person and Government,

*S. E. Morison, ed., *Sources and Documents Illustrating the American Revolution* (1965), pp. 32–34.

inviolably attached to the present happy establishment of the Protestant succession, and with minds deeply impressed by a sense of the present and impending misfortunes of the British colonies on this continent; having considered as maturely as time will permit the circumstances of the said colonies, esteem it our indispensible duty to make the following declarations of our humble opinion respecting the most essential rights and liberties of the colonists, and of the grievances under which they labour, by reason of several late Acts of Parliament.

I. That His Majesty's subjects in these Colonies owe the same allegiance to the Crown of Great Britain that is owing from his subjects born within the realm, and all due subordination to that august body the Parliament of Great Britain.

II. That His Majesty's liege subjects in these colonies are intitled to all the inherent rights and liberties of his natural born subjects within the kingdom of Great Britain.

III. That it is inseparably essential to the freedom of a people, and the undoubted right of Englishmen, that no taxes be imposed on them but with their own consent, given personally or by their representatives.

IV. That the people of these colonies are not, and from their local circumstances cannot be, represented in the House of Commons in Great Britain.

V. That the only representatives of the people of these colonies are persons chosen therein by themselves, and that no taxes ever have been, or can be constitutionally imposed on them, but by their respective legislatures.

VI. That all supplies to the Crown being free gifts of the people, it is unreasonable and inconsistent with the principles and spirit of the British Constitution, for the people of Great Britain to grant to His Majesty the property of the colonists.

VII. That trial by jury is the inherent and invaluable right of every British subject in these colonies.

VIII. That the late Act of Parliament, entitled *An Act for granting and applying certain stamp duties, and other duties, in the British colonies and plantations in America, etc.*, by imposing taxes on the inhabitants of these colonies; and the said Act, and several other Acts, by extending the jurisdiction of the courts of Admiralty beyond its ancient limits, have a manifest tendency to subvert the rights and liberties of the colonists.

IX. That the duties imposed by several late Acts of Parliament, from the peculiar circumstances of these colonies, will be extremely burthensome and grievous; and from the scarcity of specie, the payment of them absolutely impracticable.

X. That as the profits of the trade of these colonies ultimately center in Great Britain, to pay for the manufactures which they are obliged to take from thence, they eventually contribute very largely to all supplies granted there to the Crown.

XI. That the restrictions imposed by several late Acts of Parliament on the trade of these colonies will render them unable to purchase the manufactures of Great Britain.

XII. That the increase, prosperity, and happiness of these colonies depend on the full and free enjoyments of their rights and liberties, and an intercourse with Great Britain mutually affectionate and advantageous.

XIII. That it is the right of the British subjects in these colonies to petition the King or either House of Parliament.

Lastly, That it is the indispensible duty of these colonies to the best of sovereigns, to the mother country, and to themselves, to endeavour by a loyal and dutiful address to His Majesty, and humble applications to both Houses of Parliament, to procure the repeal of the Act for granting and applying certain stamp duties, of all clauses of any other Acts of Parliament, whereby the jurisdiction of the Admiralty is extended as aforesaid, and of the other late Acts for the restriction of American commerce.

THE RIGHTS OF THE COLONISTS AND A LIST OF
INFRINGEMENTS AND VIOLATIONS OF RIGHTS, 1772

Commentary

As the conflict between the colonies and the mother country grew in intensity during the next decade, the focus of resistance centered in Massachusetts, with Samuel Adams and his Sons of Liberty playing a dominant role in radicalizing that Colony. In 1772, the new Governor of Massachusetts, Thomas Hutchinson, announced that his salary and those of Massachusetts judges would thenceforth be paid by the Crown. This was bitterly opposed by the colonists, for it would render the officials concerned free from local control. At Boston Town Meeting, the Governor was questioned about the matter and replied in a letter that said, in effect, that it was none of the colonists' business. Adams then moved that a Committee of Correspondence be appointed "to state the Rights of the Colonists and of this Province in particular, as men, as Christians, and as subjects; and to communicate the same to the several towns in this Province, and to the World." The Committee prepared a report in two parts: the first the Rights of the Colonists, the second a List of Infringements and Violations of Rights. Sam Adams himself played the major role in the draft of this document.

The Boston document is noteworthy as an indication of the rights considered fundamental by the colonists on the eve of the Revolution, stated both in affimative form (in the Rights of the Colonists) and in negative form (in the List of Infringements). Among the rights stated as fundamental are ones which have recurred in earlier Colonial documents: freedom of conscience; the right to "all the natural essential, inherent and inseperable Rights Liberties and Privileges of Subjects born in Great Britain"; the right not to have troops quartered without consent; "their inestimable right to tryals by *Juries.*"

Even more significant is the assertion of rights not previously provided for in Colonial Charters, enactments, and Declarations. Foremost among these is the right against unreasonable searches and seizures that was to ripen into the Fourth Amendment. This was apparently the first legislative assertion of the right and is explained by the abuses suffered by the colonists from writs of assistance and general warrants, under which "Officers . . . break thro' the sacred rights of the *Domicil*, ransack men's houses, destroy their securities, carry off their property, and . . . commit the most horred murders." In addition, the right of the colonists to Life, Liberty, and Property is declared in ringing terms. This was, of course, the Lockean trilogy later to be protected by perhaps the most important provision of the Bill of Rights—the Due Process Clause of the Fifth Amendment. Also stated was a right to be free from the attempts "which have been made and are now making to establish an American Espiscopate." Here we have for the first time an assertion of a right to be free of a particular established Church. This was to develop into the general prohibition against an establishment of religion in the First Amendment.

The Rights of the Colonists and a List of Infringements and Violations of Rights, 1772*

The Committee appointed by the Town the second Instant "to State the Rights of the Colonists and of this Province in particular, as Men, as Christians, and as Subjects; to communicate and publish the same to the several Towns in this Province and to the World as the sense of this Town with the Infringements and Violations thereof that have been, or from Time to Time may be made. Also requesting of each Town a free Communication of their Sentiments Reported—

First, a State of the Rights of the Colonists and of this Province in particular.

Secondly, A List of the Infringements, and Violations of those Rights.

Thirdly, A Letter of Correspondence with the other Towns.

1. *Natural Rights of the Colonists as Men*—

Among the Natural Rights of the Colonists are these First. a Right to Life; Secondly to Liberty; thirdly to Property; together with the Right to support and defend them in the best manner they can. Those are evident Branches of, rather than deductions from the Duty of Self Preservation, commonly called the first Law of Nature—

All Men have a Right to remain in a State of Nature as long as they please: And in case of intollerable Oppression, Civil or Religious, to leave the Society they belong to, and enter into another.

When Men enter into Society, it is by voluntary consent; and they have a right to demand and insist upon the performance of such conditions, And previous limitations as form an equitable original compact.

Every natural Right not expressly given up or from the nature of a Social Compact necessarily ceded remains.

All positive and civil laws, should conform as far as possible, to the Law of natural reason and equity.

As neither reason requires, nor religeon permits the contrary, every Man living in or out of a state of civil society, has a right peaceably and quietly to worship God according to the dictates of his conscience.

"Just and true liberty, equal and impartial liberty" in matters spiritual and temporal, is a thing that all Men are clearly entitled to, by the eternal and immutable laws Of God and nature, as well as by the law of Nations, & all well grounded municipal laws, which must have their foundation in the former.

*H. A. Cushing, ed., *The Writings of Samuel Adams* (1906), Vol. 2, pp. 350–69.

In regard to Religeon, mutual tolleration in the different professions there-of, is what all good and candid minds in all ages have ever practiced; and both by precept and example inculcated on mankind: And it is now general-ly agreed among christians that this spirit of toleration in the fullest extent consistent with the being of civil society "is the chief characteristical mark of the true church" & In so much that Mr. Lock has asserted, and proved beyond the possibility of contradiction on any solid ground, that such toler-ation ought to be extended to all whose doctrines are now subversive of society. The only Sects which he thinks ought to be, and which by all wise laws are excluded from such toleration, are those who teach Doctrines subversive of the Civil Government under which they live. The Roman Catholicks or Papists are excluded by reason of such Doctrines as these "that Princes excommunicated may be deposed, and those they call Hereticks may be destroyed without mercy; besides their recognizing the Pope in so absolute a manner, in subversion of Government, by introducing as far as possible into the states, under whose protection they enjoy life, liberty and property, that solecism in politicks, Imperium in imperio leading directly to the worst anarchy and confusion, civil discord, war and blood shed—

The natural liberty of Men by entring into society is abridg'd or re-strained so far only as is necessary for the Great end of Society the best good of the whole—

In the state of nature, every man is under God, Judge and sole Judge, of his own rights and the injuries done him: By entering into society, he agrees to an Arbiter or indifferent Judge between him and his neighbours; but he no more renounces his original right, than by taking a cause out of the ordinary course of law, and leaving the decision to Referees or indifferent Arbitra-tions. In the last case he must pay the Referees for time and trouble; he should be also willing to pay his Just quota for the support of government, the law and constitution; the end of which is to furnish indifferent and impartial Judges in all cases that may happen, whether civil ecclesiastical, marine or military.

"The natural liberty of man is to be free from any superior power on earth, and not to be under the will or legislative authority of man; but only to have the law of nature for his rule."

In the state of nature men may as the Patriarchs did, employ hired servants for the defence of their lives, liberty and property: and they should pay them reasonable wages. Government was instituted for the purposes of common defence; and those who hold the reins of government have an equitable natural right to an honourable support from the same principle "that the labourer is worthy of his hire" but then the same community which they serve, ought to be assessors of their pay: Governors have no right to seek what they please; by this, instead of being content with the station assigned them, that of honourable servants of the society, they would soon become Absolute masters, Despots, and Tyrants. Hence as a private man has a right to say, what wages he will give in his private affairs, so has a Community to determine what they will give and grant of their Substance, for the Administration of publick affairs. And in both cases more are ready generally to offer their Service at the proposed and stipulated price, than are able and willing to perform their duty.

In short it is the greatest absurdity to suppose it in the power of one or any number of men at the entering into society, to renounce their essential natural rights, or the means of preserving those rights when the great end of civil government from the very nature of its institution is for the support, protection and defence of those very rights: the principal of which as is before observed, are life liberty and property. If men through fear, fraud or mistake, should in terms renounce and give up any essential natural right, the eternal law of reason and the great end of society, would absolutely vacate such renunciation; the right to freedom being the gift of God Almighty, it is not in the power of Man to alienate this gift, and voluntarily become a slave—

2. *The Rights of the Colonists as Christians*—

These may be best understood by reading—and carefully studying the institutes of the great Lawgiver and head of the Christian Church: which are to be found closely written and promulgated in the New Testament—

By the Act of the British Parliament commonly called the Toleration Act, every subject in England Except Papists &c was restored to, and re-established in, his natural right to worship God according to the dictates of his own conscience. And by the Charter of this Province it is granted ordained and established (that it is declared as an original right) that there shall be liberty of conscience allowed in the worship of God, to all christians except Papists, inhabiting or which shall inhabit or be resident within said Province or Territory. Magna Charta itself is in substance but a constrained Declaration, or proclamation, and promulgation in the name of King, Lord, and Commons of the sense the latter had of their original inherent, indefeazible natural Rights, as also those of free Citizens equally perdurable with the other. That great author that great jurist, and even that Court writer Mr. Justice Blackstone holds that this recognition was justly obtained of King John sword in hand: and peradventure it must be one day sword in hand again rescued and preserved from total destruction and oblivion.

3. *The Rights of the Colonists as Subjects*—

A Common Wealth or state is a body politick or civil society of men, united together to promote their mutual safety and prosperity, by means of their union.

The absolute Rights of Englishmen, and all freemen in or out of Civil society, are principally, personal security personal liberty and private property.

All Persons born in the British American Colonies are by the laws of God and nature, and by the Common law of England, exclusive of all charters from the Crown, well Entitled, and by the Acts of the British Parliament are declared to be entitled to all the natural essential, inherent & inseperable Rights Liberties and Privileges of Subjects born in Great Britain, or within the Realm. Among those Rights are the following; which no men or body of men consistently with their own rights as men and citizens or members of society, can for themselves give up, or take away from others.

First, "The first fundamental positive law of all Commonwealths or States, is the establishing the legislative power; as the first fundamental natural law also, which is to govern even the legislative power itself, is the preservation of the Society."

Secondly, The Legislative has no right to absolute arbitrary power over the lives and fortunes of the people: Nor can mortals assume a prerogative, not only too high for men, but for Angels; and therefore reserved for the exercise of the Deity alone.

"The Legislative cannot Justly assume to itself a power to rule by extempore arbitrary decrees; but it is bound to see that Justice is dispensed, and that the rights of the subjects be decided, by promulgated, standing and known laws, and authorized independent Judges;" that is independent as far as possible of Prince or People. "There shall be one rule of Justice for rich and poor; for the favorite in Court, and the Countryman at the Plough."

Thirdly, The supreme power cannot Justly take from any man, any part of his property without his consent, in person or by his Representative.

These are some of the first principles of natural law & Justice, and the great Barriers of all free states, and of the British Constitution in particular. It is utterly irreconcileable to these principles, and to many other fundamental maxims of the common law, common sense and reason, that a British house of commons, should have a right, at pleasure, to give and grant the property of the Colonists. That these Colonists are well entitled to all the essential rights, liberties and privileges of men and freemen, born in Britain, is manifest, not only from the Colony charter, in general, but acts of the British Parliament. The statute of the 13th of George 2. c. 7. naturalizes even foreigners after seven years residence. The words of the Massachusetts Charter are these, "And further our will and pleasure is, and we do hereby for us, our heirs and successors, grant establish and ordain, that all and every of the subjects of us, our heirs and successors, which shall go to and inhabit within our said province or territory and every of their children which shall happen to be born there, or on the seas in going thither, or returning from thence shall have and enjoy, all liberties and immunities of free and natural subjects within any of the dominions of us, our heirs and successors, to all intents constructions & purposes whatsoever as if they and every of them were born within this our Realm of England." Now what liberty can there be, where property is taken away without consent? Can it be said with any colour of truth and Justice, that this Continent of three thousand miles in length, and of a breadth as yet unexplored, in which however, its supposed, there are five millions of people, has the least voice, vote or influence in the decisions of the British Parliament? Have they, all together, any more right or power to return a single number to that house of commons, who have not inadvertently, but deliberately assumed a power to dispose of their lives, Liberties and properties, then to choose. an Emperor of China! Had the Colonists a right to return members to the british parliament, it would only be hurtfull; as from their local situation and circumstances it is impossible they should be ever truly and properly represented there. The inhabitants of this country in all probability in a few years will be more numerous, than those of Great Britain and Ireland together; yet it is absurdly expected by the promoters of the present measures, that these, with their posterity to all generations, should be easy while their property, shall be disposed of by a house of commons at three thousand miles distant from them; and who cannot be supposed to have the least care or concern for their real interest: Who have not only no natural care for their interest, but must be in effect bribed against it; as every burden they lay on the colonists is so much saved or gained to themselves. Hitherto many of the Colonists have been free from Quit Rents; but if the breath of a british house of commons can originate an act for taking away all our money, our lands will go next or be subject to rack rents from haughty and relentless landlords who will ride at ease, while we are trodden in the dirt. The Colonists have been branded with the odious names of traitors and rebels, only for complaining of their grievances; How long such treatment will, or ought to be born is submitted.

A List of Infringements & Violations of Rights

We cannot help thinking, that an enumeration of some of the most open infringments of our rights, will by every candid Person be Judged sufficient to Justify whatever measures have been already taken, or may be thought proper to be taken, in order to obtain a redress of the Grievances under which we labour. Among many others we Humbly conceive, that the following will not fail to excite the attention of all who consider themselves interested in the happiness and freedom of mankind in general, and of this continent and province in particular.

1. The British Parliament have assumed the power of legislation for the Colonists in all cases whatsoever, without obtaining the consent of the Inhabitants, which is ever essentially necessary to the right establishment of such a legislative.

2. They have exerted that assumed power, in raising a Revenue in the Colonies without their consent; thereby depriving them of that right which every man has to keep his own earnings in his own hands until he shall in person, or by his Representative, think fit to part with the whole or any portion of it. This infringement is the most extraordinary, when we consider the laudable care which the British House of Commons have taken to reserve intirely and absolutely to themselves the powers of giving and

granting moneys. They not only insist on originating every money bill in their own house, but will not even allow the House of Lords to make an amendment in these bills. So tenacious are they of this privilege, so jealous of any infringement of the sole & absolute right the people have to dispose of their own money. And what renders this infringement the more grievous is, that what of our earnings still remains in our own hands is in a great measure deprived of its value, so long as the British Parliament continue to claim and exercise this power of taxing us; for we cannot Justly call that our property which others may, when they please take away from us against our will.

In this respect we are treated with less decency and regard than the Romans shewed even to the Provinces which They had conquered. They only determined upon the sum which each should furnish, and left every Province to raise it in the manner most easy and convenient to themselves.

3. A number of new Officers, unknown in the Charter of this Province, have been appointed to superintend this Revenue, whereas by our Charter the Great & General Court or Assembly of this Province has the sole right of appointing all civil officers, excepting only such officers, the election and constitution of whom is in said charter expressly excepted; among whom these Officers are not included.

4. These Officers are by their Commission invested with powers altogether unconstitutional, and entirely destructive to that security which we have a right to enjoy; and to the last degree dangerous, not only to our property; but to our lives: For the Commissioners of his Majestys customs in America, or any three of them, are by their Commission impowered, "by writing under their hands and seales to constitute and appoint inferior Officers in all and singular the Port within the limits of their commissions" Each of these petty officers so made is intrusted with power more absolute and arbitrary than ought to be lodged in the hands of any man or body of men whatsoever; for in the commission aforementioned, his Majesty gives & grants unto his said Commissioners, or any three of them, and to all and every the Collectors Deputy Collectors, Ministers, Servants, and all other Officers serving and attending in all and every the Ports and other places within the limits of their Commission, full power and authority from time to time, at their and any of their wills and pleasures, as well By Night as by day to enter and go on board any Ship, Boat, or other Vessel, riding lying or being within, or coming into any Port, Harbour, Creek or Haven, within the limits of their commission; and also in the day time to go into any house, shop, cellar, or any other place where any goods wares or merchandizes lie concealed, or are suspected to lie concealed, whereof the customs & other duties, have not been, or shall not be. duly paid and truly satisfied, answered or paid unto the Collectors, Deputy Collectors, Ministers, Servants, and other Officers respectively, or otherwise agreed for; and the said house, shop, warehouse, cellar, and other place to search and survey, and all and every the boxes, trunks, chests and packs then and there found to break open.

Thus our houses and even our bed chambers, are exposed to be ransacked, our boxes chests & trunks broke open ravaged and plundered by wretches, whom no prudent man would venture to employ even as menial servants; whenever they are pleased to say they suspect there are in the house wares &c for which the dutys have not been paid. Flagrant instances of the wanton exercise of this power, have frequently happened in this and other sea port Towns. By this we are cut off from that domestick security which renders the lives of the most unhappy in some measure agreable. Those Officers may under colour of law and the cloak of a general warrant. break thro' the sacred rights of the Domicil, ransack mens houses, destroy their securities, carry off their property, and with little danger to themselves commit the most horred murders.

And we complain of it as a further grievance, that notwithstanding by the Charter of this Province, the Governor and the Great and General Court or Assembly of this Province or Territory, for the time being shall have full power and authority, from time to time, to make, ordain and establish all manner of wholesome and reasonable laws, orders, statutes, and ordinances, directions and instructions, and that if the same shall not within the term of three years after presenting the same to his Majesty in privy council be disallowed, they shall be and continue in full force and effect, untill the same shall be repealed by the Great and General Assembly of this Province: Yet the Parliament of Great Britain have rendered or attempted to render, null and void a law of this Province made and passed in the Reign of his late Majesty George the first, intitled "An Act stating the Fees of the Customhouse Officers within this Province" and by meer dint of power, in violation of the Charter aforesaid, established other and exorbitant fees, for the same Officers; any law of the Province to the contrary notwithstanding.

5. Fleets and Armies have been introduced to support these unconstitutional Officers in collecting and managing this unconstitutional Revenue; and troops have been quarter'd in this Metropolis for that purpose. Introducing and quartering standing Armies in a free Country in times of peace without the consent of the people either by themselves or by their Representatives, is, and always has been deemed a violation of their rights as freemen; and of the Charter or Compact made between the King of Great Britain, and the People of this Province, whereby all the rights of British Subjects are confirmed to us.

6. The Revenue arising from this tax unconstitutionally laid, and committed to the management of persons arbitrarily appointed and supported by an armed force quartered in a free City, has been in part applyed to the most destructive purposes. It is absolutely necessary in a mixt government like that of this Province, that a due proportion or balance of power should be established among the several branches of legislative. Our Ancestors received from King William & Queen Mary a Charter by which it was understood by both parties in the contract, that such a proportion or balance

was fixed; and therefore every thing which renders any one branch of the Legislative more independent of the other two than it was originally designed, is an alteration of the constitution as settled by the Charter; and as it has been untill the establishment of this Revenue, the constant practise of the General Assembly to provide for the support of Government, so it is an essential part of our constitution, as it is a necessary means of preserving an equilibrium, without which we cannot continue a free state.

In particular it has always been held, that the dependence of the Governor of this Province upon the General Assembly for his support, was necessary for the preservation of this equilibrium; nevertheless his Majesty has been pleased to apply fifteen hundred pounds sterling annually out of the American revenue, for the support of the Governor of this Province independent of the Assembly, whereby the ancient connection between him and this people is weakened, the confidence in the Governor lessened and the equilibrium destroyed, and the constitution essentially altered.

And we look upon it highly probable from the best intelligence we have been able to obtain, that not only our Governor and Lieuvetenant Governor, but the Judges of the Superior Court of Judicature, as also the Kings Attorney and Solicitor General are to receive their support from this Grievous tribute. This will if accomplished compleat our slavery. For if taxes are raised from us by the Parliament of Great Britain without our consent, and the men on whose opinions and decisions our properties liberties and lives, in a great measure depend, receive their support from the Revenues arising from these taxes, we cannot, when we think on the depravity of mankind, avoid looking with horror on the danger to which we are exposed? The British Parliament have shewn their wisdom in making the Judges there as independent as possible both on the Prince and People, both for place and support: But our Judges hold their Commissions only during pleasure; the granting them salaries out of this Revenue is rendering them independent on the Crown for their support. The King upon his first accession to the Throne, for giving the last hand to the independency of the Judges in England, not only upon himself but his Successors by recommending and consenting to an act of Parliament, by which the Judges are continued in office, notwithstanding the demise of a King, which vacates all other Commissions, was applauded by the whole Nation. How alarming must it then be to the Inhabitants of this Province, to find so wide a difference made between the Subjects in Britain and America, as the rendering the Judges here altogether dependent on the Crown for their support.

7. We find ourselves greatly oppressed by Instructions sent to our Governor from the Court of Great Britain, whereby the first branch of our legislature is made merely a ministerial engine. And the Province has already felt such effects from these Instructions, as We think Justly intitle us to say that they threaten an entire destruction of our liberties, and must soon, if not checked, render every branch of our Government a useless burthen upon

the people. We shall point out some of the alarming effects of these Instructions which have already taken place.

In consequence of Instructions, the Governor has called and adjourned our General Assemblies to a place highly inconvenient to the Members and grately disadvantageous to the interest of the Province, even against his own declared intention—

In consequence of Instructions, the Assembly has been prorogued from time to time, when the important concerns of the Province required their Meeting—

In obedience to Instructions, the General Assembly was Anno 1768 dissolved by Governor Bernard, because they would not consent to rescind the resolution of a former house, and thereby sacrifise the rights of their constituents.

By an Instruction, the honourable his Majesty Council are forbid to meet and transact matters of publick concern as a Council of advice to the Governor, unless called by the Governor; and if they should from a zealous regard to the interest of the Province so meet at any time, the Governor is ordered to negative them at the next Election of Councellors. And although by the Charter of this Province the Great & General Court have full power and authority to impose taxes upon the estates and persons of all and every the proprietors and inhabitants of this Province, yet the Governor has been forbidden to give his consent to act imposing a tax for the necessary support of government, unless such persons as were pointed out In the said instruction, were exempted from paying their Just proportion of said tax—

His Excellency has also pleaded Instructions for giving up the provincial fortress, Castle William into the hands of troops, over whom he had declared he had no controul (and that at a time when they were menaceing the Slaughter of the Inhabitants of the Town, and our Streets were stained with the blood which they had barbariously shed) Thus our Governor, appointed and paid from Great Britain with money forced from us, is made an instrument of totally preventing or at least of rendering [futile], every attempt of the other two branches of the Legislative in favor of a distressed and wronged people: And least the complaints naturally occasioned by such oppression should excite compassion in the Royal breast, and induce his Majesty seriously to set about relieving us from the cruel bondage and insult which we his loyal Subjects have so long suffered, the Governor is forbidden to consent to the payment of an Agent to represent our grievances at the Court of Great Britain, unless he the Governor consent to his election, and we very well know what the man must be to whose appointment a Governor in such circumstances will consent—

While we are mentioning the infringement of the rights of this Colony in particular by means of Instructions, we cannot help calling to remembrance the late unexampled suspension of the legislative of a Sister Colony, New York by force of an Instruction, untill they should comply with an Arbitrary

Act of the British Parliament for quartering troops, designed by military execution, to enforce the raising of a tribute.

8. The extending the power of the Courts of Vice Admirality to so enormous a degree as deprives the people in the Colonies in a great measure of their inestimable right to tryals by Juries: which has ever been Justly considered as the grand Bulwark and security of English property.

This alone is sufficient to rouse our jealousy: And we are again obliged to take notice of the remarkable contrast, which the British Parliament has been pleased to exhibit between the Subjects in Great Britain & the Colonies. In the same Statute, by which they give up to the decision of one dependent interested Judge of Admirality the estates and properties of the Colonists, they expressly guard the estates & properties of the people of Great Britain; for all forfeitures & penalties inflicted by the Statute of George the Third, or any other Act of Parliament relative to the trade of the Colonies, may be sued for in any Court of Admiralty in the Colonies; but all penalties and forfeitures which shall be incurred in Great Britain, may be sued for in any of his Majestys Courts of Record in Westminster or in the Court of Exchequer in Scotland, respectively. Thus our Birth Rights are taken from us; and that too with every mark of indignity, insult and contempt. We may be harrassed and dragged from one part of the Continent to the other (which some of our Brethren here and in the Country Towns already have been) and finally be deprived of our whole property, by the arbitrary determination of one biassed, capricious Judge of the Admirality.

9. The restraining us from erecting Stilling Mills for manufacturing our Iron the natural produce of this Country, Is an infringement of that right with which God and nature have invested us, to make use of our skill and industry in procuring the necessaries and conveniences of life. And we look upon the restraint laid upon the manufacture and transportation of Hatts to be altogether unreasonable and grievous. Although by the Charter all Havens Rivers, Ports, Waters, &c. are expressly granted the Inhabitants of the Province and their Successors, to their only proper use and behoof forever, yet the British Parliament passed an Act, whereby they restrain us from carrying our Wool, the produce of our own farms, even over a ferry; whereby the Inhabitants have often been put to the expence of carrying a Bag of Wool near an hundred miles by land, when passing over a River or Water of one quarter of a mile, of which the Province are the absolute Proprietors, would have prevented all that trouble.

10. The Act passed in the last Session of the British Parliament, intitled, *An Act for the better preserving his Majestys Dock Yards, Magizines, Ships, Ammunition and Stores,* is, as we apprehend a violent infringement of our Rights. By this Act any one of us may be taken from his Family, and carried to any part of Great Britain, there to be tried whenever it shall be pretended that he has been concerned in burning or otherwise destroying any Boat or Vessel, or any Materials for building &c. any Naval or Victualling Store &c.

belonging to his Majesty. For by this Act all Persons in the Realm, or in any of the places thereto belonging (under which denomination we know the Colonies are meant to be included) may be indicted and tryed either in any County or Shire within this Realm, in like manner and form as if the offence had been committed in said County, as his Majesty and his Successors may deem Most expedient. Thus we are not only deprived of our grand right to tryal by our Peers in the Vicinity, but any Person suspected, or pretended to be suspected, may be hurried to Great Britain, to take his tryal in any County the King or his Successors shall please to direct; where, innocent or guilty he is in great danger of being condemned; and whether condemned or acquitted he will probably be ruined by the expense attending the tryal, and his long absence from his Family and business; and we have the strongest reason to apprehend that we shall soon experience the fatal effects of this Act, as about the year 1769 the British Parliament passed Resolves for taking up a number of Persons in the Colonies and carrying them to Great Britain for tryal, pretending that they were authorised so to do, by a Statute passed in the Reign of Henry the Eighth, in which they say the Colonies were included, although the Act was passed long before any Colonies were settled, or even in contemplation.

11. As our Ancestors came over to this Country that they might not only enjoy their civil but their religeous rights, and particularly desired to be free from the Prelates, who in those times cruilly persecuted all who differed in sentiment from the established Church; we cannot see without concern the various attempts, which have been made and are now making, to establish an American Episcopate. Our Episcopal Brethren of the Colonies do enjoy, and rightfully ought ever to enjoy, the free exercise of their religeon, we cannot help fearing that they who are are so warmly contending for such an establishment, have views altogether inconsistent with the universal and peaceful enjoyment of our christian privileges: And doing or attempting to do any thing which has even the remotest tendency to endanger this enjoyment, is Justly looked upon a great grievance, and also an infringement of our Rights, which is not barely to exercise, but peaceably & securely to enjoy, that liberty wherewith Christ has made us free.

And we are further of Opinion, that no power on Earth can justly give either temporal or spiritual Jurisdiction within this Province, except the Great & General Court. We think therefore that every design for establishing the Jurisdiction of a Bishop in this Province, is a design both against our Civil and Religeous rights: And we are well informed, that the more candid and Judicious of our Brethren of the Church of England in this and the other Colonies, both Clergy and Laity, conceive of the establishing an American Episcopate both unnecessary and unreasonable.

12. Another Grievance under which we labour is the frequent alteration of the bounds of the Colonies by decisions before the King and Council, explanatory of former grants and Charters. This not only subjects Men to

live under a constitution to which they have not consented, which in itself is a great Grievance; but moreover under color, that the right of Soil is affected by such declarations, some Governors, or Ministers, or both in conjunction, have pretended to Grant in consequence of a Mandamus many thousands of Acres of Lands appropriated near a Century past; and rendered valuable by the labors of the present Cultivators and their Ancestors. There are very notable instances of Setlers, who having first purchased the Soil of the Natives, have at considerable expence obtained confermation of title from this Province; and on being transferred to the Jurisdiction of the Province of New Hampshire have been put to the trouble and cost of a new Grant or confermation from thence; and after all this there has been a third declaration of Royal Will, that they should thence forth be considered as pertaining To the Province of New York. The troubles, expences and dangers which hundreds have been put to on such occasions, cannot here be recited; but so much may be said, that they have been most cruelly harrassed, and even threatned with a military force, to dragoon them into a compliance, with the most unreasonable demands.

REPLY OF THE TOWN OF TRURO, 1773

Commentary

The Boston Town Meeting sent the preceding statement on the Rights of the Colonists and a List of Infringments and Violations of Rights, together with a Letter of Correspondence to the other towns of Massachusetts. The Letter, dated November 20, 1772, stated that the Boston meeting had "briefly Recapitulated the sense we have of our invaluable Rights, as Men, as Christians, and as Subjects; and wherein we conceive those Rights to have been violated, which we are desirous may be laid before your Town, that the subject may be weighed as its importance requires and the collected wisdom of the whole People be obtained. A free communication of your sentiments to this Town, of our common danger, is earnestly solicited and will be gratefully received."

As Samuel Adams and his colleagues had intended, Boston soon received letters of support from many of the Massachusetts towns. The letter from the Town of Truro which follows is one of these letters. It is important in showing that the notion of fundamental rights, upon which the Boston statement was based, was widely supported. When we think of the development of political thought at the time, we tend to confine ourselves to centers like Boston and Philadelphia. We forget that the basic concept upon which later Bills of Rights were to be constructed was spreading in the hinterland as well. The little town of Truro could solemnly vote endorsement of the Adams inventory, agreeing "that our Rights as Men, as Christians, and as Subjects are therein well stated." It was because of the support of towns like Truro that the movement to assert the colonists' rights could spread. Ultimately, it was such popular recognition that led to the movement to add a Bill of Rights to the Constitution of the new nation.

Reply of the Town of Truro, 1773*

At a Meeting of the Freeholders and Other Inhabitants of the Town of Truro legally Assembled by Adjournment on Monday the 24th day of January 1773. The Committee Chosen at a former Meeting, to take into consideration a Letter communicated by the Selectmen from the Town of Boston, with a Pamphlet enclosed and prepare an Answer; reported the following—

To the Committee of Correspondence of the Town of Boston
Gentlemen:

*Original in private collection.

In your obliging Letter of the 20th of Nov. you desire a free communication of our Sentiments of our common danger: having dully considered your said Letter and the Pamphlet enclosed, we are of opinion that our Rights as Men, as Christians, and as Subjects are therein well stated: and that in many instances those Rights are violated and infringed. And that the intolerable Grievances we at present labour under and which are daily encroaching upon us, threatens the final ruin of our happy and Glorious Constitution: which to prevent we will readily concur with our brethren in every part of the Province, in all Legal and Constitutional Measures to recover our lost rights and Liberties and in defense of those we still enjoy:

We return our Sincere and Hearty Thanks to the Town of Boston for their vigilance and care of our Public Rights and Liberties. And may the all Wise Governour of the Universe Direct us all in such measures as will obtain a redress of all our Grievances and fix our Just Rights and Liberties on a Solid and Lasting Foundation, which is the fervent Prayer, of Gentlemen your Sincere friends in the common cause of our Country. By order and in behalf of the Town.

Town Clerk

At a Meeting of the Freeholders and other Inhabitants of the Town of Truro legally Assembled by Adjournment on Monday ye 24th day of January 1773. Voted that the foregoing letter be transmitted to the Committee of Correspondence of the Town of Boston and Signed by the Town Clerk in behalf of the Town.

DECLARATION AND RESOLVES OF THE FIRST CONTINENTAL CONGRESS, 1774

Commentary

The relations between the colonies and Britain deteriorated rapidly the next two years. The American position had been acutely stated by Benjamin Franklin during his questioning in 1766 by a committee of the House of Commons. He was asked whether, if the Stamp Act were repealed, it would induce the American assemblies to acknowledge the right of Parliament to tax them and to erase their resolutions against the Stamp Act. "No, never," was his reply. His questioner went on, "Is there no means of obliging them to erase those resolutions?" "None that I know of," answered the good Doctor, "they will never do it unless compelled by force of arms."

Within less than a decade, of course, there came precisely that attempt through British arms to compel the Americans to renounce their claims. Once both sides became publicly committed to their constitutional positions, the situation really became that stated by George III in 1774: "The die is cast. The colonists must either triumph or submit."

When the Coercive Acts made open rebellion in America all but inevitable, the colonists once again resorted to a Congress at which a common front could be presented. The First Continental Congress (composed of delegates from all the colonies except Georgia) met early in September, 1774. It was widely felt that the Congress should (as the letter of Samuel Adams that follows put it) "agree in one general Bill of Rights." To give effect to this view, the Congress set up a committee to state the rights of the Colonies, as well as the instances in which they had been infringed. The Declaration and Resolves prepared by this committee was adopted on October 14, 1774.

Though the official title of this document is Declaration and Resolves, the title page of a printing in New York in 1774, calls it "The Bill of Rights." This indicates that the popular conception at the time was, in accordance with the Adams view, that the document was an American equivalent of the Bill of Rights of 1689. This was apparently the first specific use of the term in connection with an American document.

In its Declaration, the Continental Congress expressed the prevailing conception on the rights possessed by Americans and it did so with substantial agreement. The Journal of the Congress tells us that eight of the resolutions were adopted without dissent, *nemine contradicente* (abbreviated to N.C.D. in the final text), while only two encountered opposition. The Declaration, following the theory upon which the colonists' legal case was based, relies upon the basic doctrine of constitutionality, declaring that British acts in violation of the colonists' rights are "unconstitutional," "illegal," "against law," and "infringements".

The 1774 Declaration, like the Boston document of two years earlier, starts by asserting the right to life, liberty, and property, as well as the claim "to all the rights, liberties, and immunities" of Englishmen. In addition, the right to trial by jury is reaffirmed—and more particularly the right to be tried by a jury "of the vicinage" (perhaps the first express anticipation of the Sixth Amendment guarantee of the right to be tried by a jury "of the . . . district wherein the crime shall have been committed"). Also declared is the right not to have soldiers quartered and the right "peacably to assemble, consider of their grievances, and petition the king." Both the British Bill of Rights and the Declaration of the Stamp Act Congress had asserted a right to petition the Crown. The 1774 Declaration brings us a step closer to the language of the First Amendment by coupling the right to petition with the right to assemble.

The Declaration and Resolves of the First Continental Congress was the direct precursor of the Declarations of Rights contained in the Revolutionary State Constitutions, starting with the Virginia Declaration of Rights of 1776. (*infra* p. 234). In the 1774 Declaration, the American is emerging from his Colonial status, for the rights declared are based upon more than the principles of the English Constitution and Colonial Charters and compacts. In declaring that the rights of the colonists are natural rights, the Declaration and Resolves anticipates the more famous statement in the Declaration of Independence and prepares the way for the elevation of the rights involved to the constitutional plane.

Declaration and Resolves of the First Continental Congress, 1774*

Whereas, since the close of the last war, the British parliament, claiming a power of right to bind the people of America, by statute in all cases whatsoever, hath in some acts expressly imposed taxes on them, and in others, under various pretences, but in fact for the purpose of raising a revenue, hath imposed rates and duties payable in these colonies, established a board of commissioners, with unconstitutional powers, and extended the jurisdiction of courts of Admiralty, not only for collecting the said duties, but for the trial of causes merely arising within the body of a county.

And whereas, in consequence of other statutes, judges, who before held only estates at will in their offices, have been made dependant on the Crown alone for their salaries, and standing armies kept in times of peace:

And it has lately been resolved in Parliament, that by force of a statute, made in the thirty-fifth year of the reign of king Henry the eighth, colonists may be transported to England, and tried there upon accusations for treasons, and misprisions, or concealments of treasons committed in the colonies;

*W. C. Ford, ed., *Journals of the Continental Congress, 1774-1789* (1904), Vol. I, pp. 63-74.

and by a late statute, such trials have been directed in cases therein mentioned.

And whereas, in the last session of parliament, three statutes were made; "one, intituled "An act to discontinue, in such manner and for such time as are therein mentioned, the landing and discharging, lading, or shipping of goods, wares & merchandise, at the town, and within the harbour of Boston, in the province of Massachusetts-bay, in North-America;" another, intituled "An act for the better regulating the government of the province of the Massachusetts-bay in New-England;" and another, intituled "An act for the impartial administration of justice, in the cases of persons questioned for any act done by them in the execution of the law, or for the suppression of riots and tumults, in the province of the Massachusetts-bay, in New-England." And another statute was then made, "for making more effectual provision for the government of the province of Quebec, &c." All which statutes are impolitic, unjust, and cruel, as well as unconstitutional, and most dangerous and destructive of American rights.

And whereas, Assemblies have been frequently dissolved, contrary to the rights of the people, when they attempted to deliberate on grievances; and their dutiful, humble, loyal, & reasonable petitions to the crown for redress, have been repeatedly treated with contempt, by his majesty's ministers of state:

The good people of the several Colonies of New-hampshire, Massachusetts-bay, Rhode-island and Providence plantations, Connecticut, New-York, New-Jersey, Pennsylvania, Newcastle, Kent and Sussex on Delaware, Maryland, Virginia, North Carolina, and South Carolina, justly alarmed at these arbitrary proceedings of parliament and administration, have severally elected, constituted, and appointed deputies to meet and sit in general congress, in the city of Philadelphia, in order to obtain such establishment, as that their religion, laws, and liberties may not be subverted:

Whereupon the deputies so appointed being now assembled, in a full and free representation of these Colonies, taking into their most serious consideration, the best means of attaining the ends aforesaid, do, in the first place, as Englishmen, their ancestors in like cases have usually done, for asserting and vindicating their rights and liberties, declare,

That the inhabitants of the English Colonies in North America, by the immutable laws of nature, the principles of the English constitution, and the several charters or compacts, have the following Rights:

Resolved, N. C. D. 1. That they are entitled to life, liberty, & property, and they have never ceded to any sovereign power whatever, a right to dispose of either without their consent.

Resolved, N. C. D. 2. That our ancestors, who first settled these colonies, were at the time of their emigration from the mother country, entitled to all the rights, liberties, and immunities of free and natural-born subjects, within the realm of England.

Resolved, N. C. D. 3. That by such emigration they by no means forfeited, surrendered, or lost any of those rights, but that they were, and their descendants now are, entitled to the exercise and enjoyment of all such of them, as their local and other circumstances enable them to exercise and enjoy.

Resolved, 4. That the foundation of English liberty, and of all free government, is a right in the people to participate in their legislative council: and as the English colonists are not represented, and from their local and other circumstances, cannot properly be represented in the British parliament, they are entitled to a free and exclusive power of legislation in their several provincial legislatures, where their right of representation can alone be preserved, in all cases of taxation and internal polity, subject only to the negative of their sovereign, in such manner as has been heretofore used and accustomed. But, from the necessity of the case, and a regard to the mutual interest of both countries, we cheerfully consent to the operation of such acts of the British parliament, as are bona fide, restrained to the regulation of our external commerce, for the purpose of securing the commercial advantages of the whole empire to the mother country, and the commercial benefits of its respective members; excluding every idea of taxation, internal or external, for raising a revenue on the subjects in America, without their consent.

Resolved, N. C. D. 5. That the respective colonies are entitled to the common law of England, and more especially to the great and inestimable privilege of being tried by their peers of the vicinage, according to the course of that law.

Resolved, 6. That they are entitled to the benefit of such of the English statutes as existed at the time of their colonization; and which they have, by experience, respectively found to be applicable to their several local and other circumstances.

Resolved, N. C. D. 7. That these, his majesty's colonies, are likewise entitled to all the immunities and privileges granted & confirmed to them by royal charters, or secured by their several codes of provincial laws.

Resolved, N. C. D. 8. That they have a right peaceably to assemble, consider of their grievances, and petition the King; and that all prosecutions, prohibitory proclamations, and commitments for the same, are illegal.

Resolved, N. C. D. 9. That the keeping a Standing army in these colonies, in times of peace, without the consent of the legislature of that colony, in which such army is kept, is against law.

Resolved, N. C. D. 10. It is indispensably necessary to good government, and rendered essential by the English constitution, that the constituent branches of the legislature be independent of each other; that, therefore, the exercise of legislative power in several colonies, by a council appointed, during pleasure, by the crown, is unconstitutional, dangerous, and destructive to the freedom of American legislation.

All and each of which the aforesaid deputies, in behalf of themselves and their constituents, do claim, demand, and insist on, as their indubitable rights and liberties; which cannot be legally taken from them, altered or abridged by any power whatever, without their own consent, by their representatives in their several provincial legislatures.

In the course of our inquiry, we find many infringements and violations of the foregoing rights, which, from an ardent desire, that harmony and mutual intercourse of affection and interest may be restored, we pass over for the present, and proceed to state such acts and measures as have been adopted since the last war, which demonstrate a system formed to enslave America.

Resolved, N. C. D. That the following acts of Parliament are infringements and violations of the rights of the colonists; and that the repeal of them is essentially necessary in order to restore harmony between Great-Britain and the American colonies, viz:

The several acts of 4 Geo. 3. ch. 15, & ch. 34.—5 Geo. 3. ch. 25.—6 Geo. 3. ch. 52.—7 Geo. 3. ch. 41, & ch. 46.—8 Geo. 3. ch. 22, which impose duties for the purpose of raising a revenue in America, extend the powers of the admiralty courts beyond their ancient limits, deprive the American subject of trial by jury, authorize the judges' certificate to indemnify the prosecutor from damages, that he might otherwise be liable to, requiring oppressive security from a claimant of ships and goods seized, before he shall be allowed to defend his property, and are subversive of American rights.

Also the 12 Geo. 3. ch. 24, entitled "An act for the better securing his Majesty's dock-yards, magazines, ships, ammunition, and stores," which declares a new offence in America, and deprives the American subject of a constitutional trial by a jury of the vicinage, by authorizing the trial of any person, charged with the committing any offence described in the said act, out of the realm, to be indicted and tried for the same in any shire or county within the realm.

Also the three acts passed in the last session of parliament, for stopping the port and blocking up the harbour of Boston, for altering the charter & government of the Massachusetts-bay, and that which is entituled "An act for the better administration of Justice," &c.

Also the act passed in the same session for establishing the Roman Catholick Religion in the province of Quebec, abolishing the equitable system of English laws, and erecting a tyranny there, to the great danger, from so total a dissimilarity of Religion, law, and government of the neighbouring British colonies, by the assistance of whose blood and treasure the said country was conquered from France.

Also the act passed in the same session for the better providing suitable quarters for officers and soldiers in his Majesty's service in North-America.

Also, that the keeping a standing army in several of these colonies, in time of peace, without the consent of the legislature of that colony in which such army is kept, is against law.

To these grievous acts and measures, Americans cannot submit, but in hopes that their fellow subjects in Great-Britain will, on a revision of them, restore us to that state in which both countries found happiness and prosperity, we have for the present only resolved to pursue the following peaceable measures:

Resolved, unanimously, That from and after the first day of December next, there be no importation into British America, from Great Britain or Ireland of any goods, wares or merchandize whatsoever, or from any other place of any such goods, wares or merchandize.[1]

1. To enter into a non-importation, non-consumption, and non-exportation agreement or association.

2. To prepare an address to the people of Great-Britain and a memorial to the inhabitants of British America, &

3. To prepare a loyal address to his Majesty; agreeable to Resolutions already entered into.

Samuel Adams to Richard Henry Lee, 1774*

I have lately been favour'd with three Letters from you, and must beg you to attribute my omitting to make a due Acknowledgment till this Time, to a Multiplicity of Affairs to which I have been oblig'd to give my constant Attention.

The unrighteous and oppressive Act of the British Parliament for shutting up this Harbour, although executed with a Rigour beyond the Intent even of the Framers of it, has hitherto faild, and I believe will continue to fail of the Effect which the Enemies of America flatter'd themselves it would have. The Inhabitants still wear chearful countenances. Far from being in the least Degree intimidated they are resolved to undergo the greatest Hardships, rather than Submit in any Instance to the Tyrannical Act. They are daily encouraged to persevere, by the Intelligence which they receive from their Brethren not of this Province only, but of every other Colony, that they are consider'd as suffering in the common Cause; and the Resolution of all, to support them in the Conflict. Lord North had no Expectation that we should be thus Sustained; on the Contrary he trusted that Boston would be left by all her Friends to Struggle and fall alone. He has therefore made no Preparation for the Effects of an Union. From the Information I have had from Intelligent Persons in England, I verily believe the Design was to seize some Persons here, and send them Home; but the Steadiness and Prudence of the People, and the unexpected Union of the Colonies, evidenc'd by liberal Contributions for our Support, have disconcerted them; and they are at a loss how to proceed further. Four Regiments are now encamp'd on our

---

[1] This paragraph was struck out.

* *The Writings of Samuel Adams*, Vol. 3, pp. 136–39.

Common, and more are expected; but I trust the People will, by a circumspect Behavior, prevent their taking occasion to Act. The Port Bill, is follow'd by two other Acts of the British Parliament; the one for regulating the Government of this Province, or rather totally to destroy our free Constitution and substitute an absolute Government in its Stead; the other for the more impartial Administration of Justice or as some term it for the screening from Punishment any Soldier who shall Murder an American for asserting his Right. A Submission to these Acts will doubtless be requir'd and expected; but whether General Gage will find it an easy thing to force the People to submit to so great and fundamental a Change of Government, is a Question I think, worthy his Consideration—Will the People of America consider these measures, as Attacks on the Constitution of an Individual Province in which the rest are not interested; or will they view the model of Government prepar'd for us as a Sistem for the whole Continent. Will they, as unconcern'd Spectators, look upon it to be design'd only to top off the exuberant Branches of Democracy in the Constitution of this Province? Or, as part of a plan to reduce them all to Slavery? These are Questions, in my Opinion of Importance, which I trust will be thoroughly weighed in a general Congress.—May God inspire that intended Body with Wisdom and Fortitude, and unite and Prosper their Councils!

The People of this Province are thoroughly Sensible of the Necessity of breaking off all Commercial Connection with the Country, whose political Councils direct to Measures to enslave them. They however the Body of the Nation, are being kept in profound Ignorance of the Nature of the Dispute between Britain and the Colonies; and taught to believe that we are a perfidious & rebellious People.

It is with Reluctance that they come into any Resolutions, which must distress those who are not the objects of their Resentment but they are urg'd to it from Motives of Self-preservation, and therefore are signing an agreement in the several Towns, not to consume any British Goods which shall be imported after the last of August next; and that they may not be impos'd upon, they are to require an Oath of those from whom they shall hereafter purchase such Goods. It is the Virtue of the Yeomanry that we are chiefly to depend upon. Our Friends in Maryland talk of withholding the Exportation of Tobacco; this was first hinted to us by the Gentlemen of the late House of Burgesses of Virginia who had been called together after the Dissolution of your Assembly—This would be a Measure greatly interesting to the Mother Country.

Should America hold up her own Importance to the Body of the Nation and at the same Time agree in one general Bill of Rights, the Dispute might be settled on the Principles of Equity and Harmony restored between Britain and the Colonies.

I am with great Regard
Your Friend & Fellow Countryman

ADDRESS TO THE INHABITANTS OF QUEBEC, 1774

Commentary

The last of the Resolutions of the First Continental Congress of 1774 stated that the Congress would prepare addresses and memorials to the people of Britain, the inhabitants of British America, and the King. Among these was an Address to the Inhabitants of Quebec, approved on October 26, 1774. It contains another exposition of the fundamental rights of the colonists, as they were understood by a representative assembly chosen from all the colonies. This statement is of great importance both for its more detailed statement of the right to jury trial and its assertion of two rights not mentioned in the other Colonial documents already discussed. The first was plainly recognized by both English and Colonial law and was to find specific expression in American Constitutions—the right to personal liberty vindicated by the Great Writ of Habeas Corpus (apparently first expressly recognized in the colonies in a 1692 Massachusetts statute modeled upon the English Habeas Corpus Act). The second was the first declaration by an official assembly of the right to freedom of the press which (starting with the Virginia Declaration of Rights, 1776, *infra* p. 234) was to be an essential part of American Bills of Rights.

Address to the Inhabitants of Quebec, 1774*

We, the Delegates of the Colonies of New-Hampshire, Massachusetts-Bay, Rhode-Island and Providence Plantations, Connecticut, New-York, New-Jersey, Pennsylvania, the Counties of Newcastle Kent and Sussex on Delaware, Maryland, Virginia, North-Carolina and South-Carolina, deputed by the inhabitants of the said Colonies, to represent them in a General Congress at Philadelphia, in the province of Pennsylvania, to consult together concerning the best methods to obtain redress of our afflicting grievances, having accordingly assembled, and taken into our most serious consideration the state of public affairs on this continent, have thought proper to address your province, as a member therein deeply interested.

When the fortune of war, after a gallant and glorious resistance, had incorporated you with the body of English subjects, we rejoiced in the truly valuable addition, both on our own and your account; expecting, as courage and generosity are naturally united, our brave enemies would become our hearty friends, and that the Divine Being would bless to you the dispensations of his over-ruling providence, by securing to you and your latest posterity the inestimable advantages of a free English constitution of government, which it is the privilege of all English subjects to enjoy.

*Journals of the Continental Congress, 1774–1789, Vol. 1, pp. 105–13.

These hopes were confirmed by the King's proclamation, issued in the year 1763, plighting the public faith for your full enjoyment of those advantages.

Little did we imagine that any succeeding Ministers would so audaciously and cruelly abuse the royal authority, as to with-hold from you the fruition of the irrevocable rights, to which you were thus justly entitled.

But since we have lived to see the unexpected time, when Ministers of this flagitious temper, have dared to violate the most sacred compacts and obligations, and as you, educated under another form of goverment, have artfully been kept from discovering the unspeakable worth of that form you are now undoubtedly entitled to, we esteem it our duty, for the weighty reasons herein after mentioned, to explain to you some of its most important branches.

"In every human society," says the celebrated Marquis Beccaria, "there is an effort, continually tending to confer on one part the heighth of power and happiness, and to reduce the other to the extreme of weakness and misery. The intent of good laws is to oppose this effort, and to diffuse their influence universally and equally."

Rulers stimulated by this pernicious "effort," and subjects animated by the just "intent of opposing good laws against it," have occasioned that vast variety of events, that fill the histories of so many nations. All these histories demonstrate the truth of this simple position, that to live by the will of one man, or sett of men, is the production of misery to all men.

On the solid foundation of this principle, Englishmen reared up the fabrick of their constitution with such a strength, as for ages to defy time, tyranny, treachery, internal and foreign wars: And, as an illustrious author of your nation, hereafter mentioned, observes,—"They gave the people of their Colonies, the form of their own government, and this government carrying prosperity along with it, they have grown great nations in the forests they were sent to inhabit."

In this form, the first grand right, is that of the people having a share in their own government by their representatives chosen by themselves, and, in consequence, of being ruled by laws, which they themselves approve, not by edicts of men over whom they have no controul. This is a bulwark surrounding and defending their property, which by their honest cares and labours they have acquired, so that no portions of it can legally be taken from them, but with their own full and free consent, when they in their judgment deem it just and necessary to give them for public service, and precisely direct the easiest, cheapest, and most equal methods, in which they shall be collected.

The influence of this right extends still farther. If money is wanted by Rulers, who have in any manner oppressed the people, they may retain it, until their grievances are redressed; and thus peaceably procure relief, without trusting to despised petitions, or disturbing the public tranquillity.

The **next great** right is that of trial by jury. This provides, that neither life, liberty nor property, can be taken from the possessor, until twelve of his unexceptionable countrymen and peers of his vicinage, who from that neighbourhood may reasonably be supposed to be acquainted with his character, and the characters of the witnesses, upon a fair trial, and full enquiry, face to face, in open Court, before as many of the people as chuse to attend, shall pass their sentence upon oath against him; a sentence that cannot injure him, without injuring their own reputation, and probably their interest also: as the question may turn on points, that, in some degree, concern the general welfare; and if it does not, their verdict may form a precedent, that, on a similar trial of their own, may militate against themselves.

Another right relates merely to the liberty of the person. If a subject is seized and imprisoned, tho' by order of Government, he may, by virtue of this right, immediately obtain a writ, termed a Habeas Corpus, from a Judge, whose sworn duty it is to grant it, and thereupon procure any illegal restraint to be quickly enquired into and redressed.

A fourth right, is that of holding lands by the tenure of easy rents, and not by rigorous and oppressive services, frequently forcing the possessors from their families and their business, to perform what ought to be done, in all well regulated states, by men hired for the purpose.

The last right we shall mention, regards the freedom of the press. The importance of this consists, besides the advancement of truth, science, morality, and arts in general, in its diffusion of liberal sentiments on the administration of Government, its ready communication of thoughts between subjects, and its consequential promotion of union among them, whereby oppressive officers are shamed or intimidated, into more honourable and just modes of conducting affairs.

These are the invaluable rights, that form a considerable part of our mild system of government; that, sending its equitable energy through all ranks and classes of men, defends the poor from the rich, the weak from the powerful, the industrious from the rapacious, the peaceable from the violent, the tenants from the lords, and all from their superiors.

These are the rights, without which a people cannot be free and happy, and under the protecting and encouraging influence of which, these colonies have hitherto so amazingly flourished and increased. These are the rights, a profligate Ministry are now striving, by force of arms, to ravish from us, and which we are, with one mind, resolved never to resign but with our lives.

These are the rights you are entitled to and ought at this moment in perfection, to exercise. And what is offered to you by the late Act of Parliament in their place? Liberty of conscience in your religion? No. God gave it to you; and the temporal powers with which you have been and are connected, firmly stipulated for your enjoyment of it. If laws, divine and human, could secure it against the despotic caprices of wicked men, it was secured before. Are the French laws in civil cases restored? It seems so. But observe the cautious kindness of the Ministers, who pretend to be your benefactors. The words of the statute are—that those "laws shall be the rule, until they shall be varied or altered by any ordinances of the Governor and Council." Is the "certainty and lenity of the criminal law of England, and its benefits and advantages," commended in the said statute, and said to "have been sensibly felt by you," secured to you and your descendants? No. They too are subjected to arbitrary "alterations" by the Governor and Council; and a power is expressly reserved of appointing "such courts of criminal, civil, and ecclesiastical jurisdiction, as shall be thought proper." Such is the precarious tenure of mere will, by which you hold your lives and religion. The Crown and its Ministers are impowered, as far as they could be by Parliament, to establish even the Inquisition itself among you. Have you an Assembly composed of worthy men, elected by yourselves, and in whom you can confide, to make laws for you, to watch over your welfare, and to direct in what quantity, and in what manner, your money shall be taken from you? No. The power of making laws for you is lodged in the governor and council, all of them dependent upon, and removeable at, the pleasure of a Minister. Besides, another late statute, made without your consent, has subjected you to the impositions of Excise, the horror of all free states; thus wresting your property from you by the most odious of taxes, and laying open to insolent tax-gatherers, houses, the scenes of domestic peace and comfort, and called the castles of English subjects in the books of their law. And in the very act for altering your government, and intended to flatter you, you are not authorized to "assess, levy, or apply any rates and taxes, but for the inferior purposes of making roads, and erecting and repairing public buildings, or for other local conveniences, within your respective towns and districts." Why this degrading distinction? Ought not the property, honestly acquired by Canadians, to be held as sacred as that of Englishmen? Have not Canadians sense enough to attend to any other public affairs, than gathering stones from one place, and piling them up in another? Unhappy people! who are not only injured, but insulted. Nay more!—With such a superlative contempt of your understanding and spirit, has an insolent Ministry presumed to think of you, our respectable fellow-subjects, according to the information we have received, as firmly to perswade themselves that your gratitude, for the injuries and insults they have recently offered to you, will engage you to take up arms, and render yourselves the ridicule and detestation of the world, by becoming tools, in their hands, to assist them in taking that freedom from us, which they have treacherously denied to you; the unavoidable consequence of which attempt, if successful, would be the extinction of all hopes of you or your posterity being ever restored to freedom: For idiocy itself cannot believe, that, when their drudgery is performed, they will treat you with less cruelty than they have us, who are of the same blood with themselves.

What would your countryman, the immortal Montesquieu, have said to such a plan of domination, as has been framed for you? Hear his words, with an intenseness of thought suited to the importance of the subject.—"In a free state, every man, who is supposed a free agent, ought to be concerned in his own government: Therefore the legislative should reside in the whole body of the people, or their representatives."—"The political liberty of the subject is a tranquillity of mind, arising from the opinion each person has of his safety. In order to have this liberty, it is requisite the government be so constituted, as that one man need not be afraid of another. When the power of making laws, and the power of executing them, are united in the same person, or in the same body of Magistrates, there can be no liberty; because apprehensions may arise, lest the same Monarch or Senate, should enact tyrannical laws, to execute them in a tyrannical manner."

"The power of judging should be exercised by persons taken from the body of the people, at certain times of the year, and pursuant to a form and manner prescribed by law. There is no liberty, if the power of judging be not separated from the legislative and executive powers."

"Military men belong to a profession, which may be useful, but is often dangerous."—"The enjoyment of liberty, and even its support and preservation, consists in every man's being allowed to speak his thoughts, and lay open his sentiments."

Apply these decisive maxims, sanctified by the authority of a name which all Europe reveres, to your own state. You have a Governor, it may be urged, vested with the executive powers, or the powers of administration: In him, and in your Council, is lodged the power of making laws. You have Judges, who are to decide every cause affecting your lives, liberty or property. Here is, indeed, an appearance of the several powers being separated and distributed into different hands, for checks one upon another, the only effectual mode ever invented by the wit of men, to promote their freedom and prosperity. But scorning to be illuded by a tinsel'd outside, and exerting the natural sagacity of Frenchmen, examine the specious device, and you will find it, to use an expression of holy writ, "a whited sepulchre," for burying your lives, liberty and property.

Your Judges, and your Legislative Council, as it is called, are dependant on your Governor, and he is dependant on the servant of the Crown, in Great-Britain. The legislative, executive and judging powers are all moved by the nods of a Minister. Privileges and immunities last no longer than his smiles. When he frowns, their feeble forms dissolve. Such a treacherous ingenuity has been exerted in drawing up the code lately offered you, that every sentence, beginning with a benevolent pretension, concludes with a destructive power; and the substance of the whole, divested of its smooth words, is—that the Crown and its Ministers shall be as absolute throughout your extended province, as the despots of Asia or Africa. What can protect your property from taxing edicts, and the rapacity of necessitous and cruel masters? your persons from Letters de Cachet, goals, dungeons, and oppressive services? your lives and general liberty from arbitrary and unfeeling rulers? We defy you, casting your view upon every side, to discover a **single** circumstance, promising from any quarter the faintest hope of liberty to you or your posterity but from an entire adoption into the union of these Colonies.

What advice would the truly great man before-mentioned, that advocate of freedom and humanity, give you, was he now living, and knew that we, your numerous and powerful neighbours, animated by a just love of our invaded rights, and united by the indissoluble bands of affection and interest, called upon you, by every obligation of regard for yourselves and your children, as we now do, to join us in our righteous contest, to make common cause with us therein, and take a noble chance for emerging from a humiliating subjection under Governors, Intendants, and Military Tyrants, into the firm rank and condition of English freemen, whose custom it is, derived from their ancestors, to make those tremble, who dare to think of making them miserable?

Would not this be the purport of his address? "Seize the opportunity presented to you by Providence itself. You have been conquered into liberty, if you act as you ought. This work is not of man. You are a small people, compared to those who with open arms invite you into a fellowship. A moment's reflection should convince you which will be most for your interest and happiness, to have all the rest of North-America your unalterable friends, or your inveterate enemies. The injuries of Boston have roused and associated every colony, from Nova-Scotia to Georgia. Your province is the only link wanting, to compleat the bright and strong chain of union. Nature has joined your country to theirs. Do you join your political interests. For their own sakes, they never will desert or betray you. Be assured, that the happiness of a people inevitably depends on their liberty, and their spirit to assert it. The value and extent of the advantages tendered to you are immense. Heaven grant you may not discover them to be blessings after they have bid you an eternal adieu."

We are too well acquainted with the liberality of sentiment distinguishing your nation, to imagine, that difference of religion will prejudice you against a hearty amity with us. You know, that the transcendant nature of freedom elevates those, who unite in her cause, above all such low-minded infirmities. The Swiss Cantons furnish a memorable proof of this truth. Their union is composed of Roman Catholic and Protestant States, living in the utmost concord and peace with one another, and thereby enabled, ever since they bravely vindicated their freedom, to defy and defeat every tyrant that has invaded them.

Should there be any among you, as there generally are in all societies, who prefer the favours of Ministers, and their own private interests, to the welfare of their country, the temper of such selfish persons will render them incredibly active in opposing all public-spirited measures, from an expectation of being well rewarded for their sordid industry, by their superiors; but we doubt not you will be upon your guard against such men, and not sacrifice the liberty and happiness of the whole Canadian people and their posterity, to gratify the avarice and ambition of individuals.

We do not ask you, by this address, to commence acts of hostility against the government of our common Sovereign. We only invite you to consult your own glory and welfare, and not to suffer yourselves to be inveigled or intimidated by infamous ministers so far, as to become the instruments of their cruelty and despotism, but to unite with us in one social compact, formed on the generous principles of equal liberty, and cemented by such an exchange of beneficial and endearing offices as to render it perpetual. In order to complete this highly desirable union, we submit it to your consideration, whether it may not be expedient for you to meet together in your several towns and districts, and elect Deputies, who afterwards meeting in a provincial Congress, may chuse Delegates, to represent your province in the continental Congress to be held at Philadelphia on the tenth day of May, 1775.

In this present Congress, beginning on the fifth of the last month, and continued to this day, it has been, with universal pleasure and an unanimous vote, resolved, That we should consider the violation of your rights, by the act for altering the government of your province, as a violation of our own, and that you should be invited to accede to our confederation, which has no other objects than the perfect security of the natural and civil rights of all the constituent members, according to their respective circumstances, and the preservation of a happy and lasting connection with Great-Britain, on the salutary and constitutional principles herein before mentioned. For effecting these purposes, we have addressed an humble and loyal petition to his Majesty, praying relief of our and your grievances; and have associated to stop all importations from Great-Britain and Ireland, after the first day of December, and all exportations to those Kingdoms and the West-Indies, after the tenth day of next September, unless the said grievances are redressed.

That Almighty God may incline your minds to approve our equitable and necessary measures, to add yourselves to us, to put your fate, whenever you suffer injuries which you are determined to oppose, not on the small influence of your single province, but on the consolidated powers of North-America, and may grant to our joint exertions an event as happy as our cause is just, is the fervent prayer of us, your sincere and affectionate friends and fellow-subjects.

By order of the Congress,

Henry Middleton, President

RESOLUTION OF THE SECOND
CONTINENTAL CONGRESS, 1776

Commentary

"The blessings of society," wrote John Adams in 1776, "depend entirely on the constitutions of government." Hence, it was only natural that the men of the Revolution should turn to Constitution-making when once the conflict with Britain reached the stage where independence was the only real alternative to submission. Full separation from the mother country made necessary a new governmental structure in the colonies, which were thenceforth to be free States absolved from allegiance to the British Crown.

While British Governors were being driven from power or fleeing in the face of popular feeling, civil government had to be carried on; a new legal basis had to be provided for that which had been forcibly dissolved. The problem confronting the colonists is shown by the experience of New Hampshire, the first Colony to draw up its own system of independent self-government. At the beginning of 1776, the Congress of that Colony declared:

> The sudden and abrupt departure of . . . our late Governor and several of the Council, leaving us destitute of Legislation; and no Executive Courts being open to punish criminal offenders, whereby the lives and properties of the honest people of the Colony, are liable to the machinations and evil designs of wicked men: Therefore, for the preservation of peace and good order, and for the security of the lives and properties of the inhabitants of this Colony, we conceive ourselves reduced to the necessity of establishing a form of Government.

The establishment of governments to meet the vacuum caused by the elimination of the royal governments was treated at first as only a temporary expedient—intended, in the words of the New Hampshire Congress, "to continue during the present unhappy and unnatural contest." It was soon seen, however, that something more formal and abiding was necessary. "Each colony," John Adams wrote in March, 1776, "should establish its own government and then a league should be formed between them all." Two months later, the Second Continental Congress adopted a resolution calling for the full exercise of local government and the suppression of all royal authority and urging the various colonies to set up governments of their own. Adams termed this "the most important Resolution that ever was taken in America." Though Adams sometimes overdid his use of superlatives, this characterization was not too wide of the mark.

Effect was given to the congressional resolution of May, 1776, by the drawing up of Constitutions establishing the new governments which had been called for. By the end of the Revolution, written Constitutions had been adopted in all the states. Eleven of these were wholly new documents, while two of them, (those of Connecticut and Rhode Island) were essentially the old royal charters with minor modifications.

Most important of all, the May 1776 Resolution and the state Constitutions drafted to give effect to it enabled individual rights to be placed for the first time upon a firm constitutional foundation. No longer were those rights contained in Charters or Concessions (granted as a matter of grace and revocable at will by the grantor), legislative enactments subject to alteration or repeal at the discretion of the legislature, or Declarations and Resolutions without binding legal effect. Thenceforth the fundamental rights of Americans could be guaranteed in written Constitutions, vested with the status of supreme law, and enforceable as such against the American successors of both the Crown and Parliament.

Resolution of the Second Continental Congress, 1776*

[Friday, May 10, 1776]
The Congress then resumed the consideration of the report from the committee of the whole, which being read was agreed to as follows:

Resolved, That it be recommended to the respective assemblies and conventions of the United Colonies, where no government sufficient to the exigencies of their affairs have been hitherto established, to adopt such government as shall, in the opinion of the representatives of the people, best conduce to the happiness and safety of their constituents in particular, and America in general.

Resolved, That a committee of three be appointed to prepare a preamble to the foregoing resolution:

The members chosen, Mr. J[ohn] Adams, Mr. [Edward] Rutledge, and Mr. R[ichard] H[enry] Lee.

*   *   *

[Wednesday, May 15, 1776]
The Congress took into consideration the draught of the preamble brought in by the committee, which was agreed to as follows:

Whereas his Britannic Majesty, in conjunction with the lords and commons of Great Britain, has, by a late act of Parliament, excluded the inhabitants of these United Colonies from the protection of his crown; And whereas, no answer, whatever, to the humble petitions of the colonies for redress of grievances and reconciliation with Great Britain, has been or is likely to be given; but, the whole force of that kingdom, aided by foreign mercenaries, is to be exerted for the destruction of the good people of these colonies; And whereas, it appears absolutely irreconcileable to reason and good Conscience, for the people of these colonies now to take the oaths and affirmations necessary for the support of any government under the crown of Great Britain, and it is necessary that the exercise of every kind of authority under the said crown should be totally suppressed, and all the powers of government exerted, under the authority of the people of the colonies, for the preservation of internal peace, virtue, and good order, as well as for the defence of their lives, liberties, and properties, against the hostile invasions and cruel depredations of their enemies; therefore, resolved, &c.

Ordered, That the said preamble, with the resolution passed the 10th instant, be published.

*   *   *

VIRGINIA DECLARATION OF RIGHTS, 1776

Commentary

The Virginia Declaration of Rights of 1776 is the first true Bill of Rights in the modern American sense, since it is the first protection for the rights of the individual to be contained in a Constitution adopted by the people acting through an elected convention. The Virginia Convention of 1776 was the fifth and last of the Virginia Colonial Conventions which had originally been convened in 1774 to fill the governmental gap caused by Lord Dunmore's dissolution of the House of Burgesses. On May 15, 1776, the Convention adopted the famous Resolutions for Proposing Independence drafted by Edmund Pendleton, the Convention President. The first of these Resolutions instructed the Virginia delegates in the Continental Congress to propose a Declaration of Independence (the first formal proposal of the official Declaration that came less than two months later). The second Resolution provided "that a committee be appointed to prepare a Declaration of Rights, and such a plan of government as will be most likely to maintain peace and order in this colony and secure substantial and equal liberty to the people."

The committee named on May 15 to prepare a Declaration of Rights and a Constitution, in accordance with Pendleton's second Resolution, consisted of 28 members. As soon as they took their seats in the Convention, James Madison (on May 16) and George Mason (on May 18) were added to the committee. The additions were of crucial importance, since it was Mason who drafted virtually the entire Virginia Declaration of Rights and Madison who was the draftsman of the federal Bill of Rights. The work of the 1776 Virginia Convention was thus crucial in the history of the federal Bill of Rights, both as the first constitutional instrument upon which the federal Bill of Rights was modelled and as the training-ground of the man who was later to become known as the father of both the federal Constitution and its Bill of Rights. In his brief *Autobiography,* Madison states that he was "initiated into the political career" by his work in the 1776 Convention. "Being young," he did not participate in the debates, though he did suggest a key amendment in the guarantee of religious freedom.

On May 27, Archibald Cary, the Chairman of the Committee to Prepare a Constitution, reported that the "committee had accordingly prepared a Declaration of Rights, which he read in his place." It was discussed by the Convention on June 3-5; on June 11, several amendments were made to it; and on June 12, it passed the Convention on its third reading, *nem. con.* The body of the Constitution itself (providing for the new state government) was adopted on June 29, prefaced by a lengthy preamble written by Thomas Jefferson, which sets forth the grievances of the colonists against George III, in language essentially similar to the more famous list of charges in the Declaration of Independence.

The *Journal* of the Virginia Convention (like most documents of the kind at the time) consists only of unrevealing formal entries and it is necessary to resort to sources outside its pages to find the facts with regard to adoption of the 1776 Declaration of Rights. Of these, the most important is the summary contained in Edmund Randolph's *Essay,* written years after the event. Randolph (who had been the youngest delegate to the Convention) tells us that, though "many projects of a bill of rights" were presented to the drafting committee, "that proposed by George Mason swallowed up all the rest." Madison also confirms that "This important and meritorious instrument was drawn by George Mason." Added to this is the fact that there is a copy of the first draft of the Virginia Declaration of Rights in Mason's handwriting which states that it was "by G.M."

If we compare the Mason first draft with the Declaration as adopted, (*infra* p. 234) we find that the two are virtually identical. Mason at the end of his copy of the first draft, states that "it received few alterations or additions in the Virginia Convention," saying that only "Two more articles were added, viz., the 10th and 14th in the adopted bill—not of fundamental nature." In actuality, Mason understates the significance of the changes made. Article 10, which was added, contains the direct antecedent of the Fourth Amendment and the change in Article 16 suggested by Madison (as described in the extract from his *Autobiography* which follows) contains the term "free exercise of religion," (first used in the Maryland Toleration Act, (*supra* p. 88)—thus anticipating Madison's use of the term in the First Amendment. Yet, even with this said, it remains true that the Declaration was virtually all Mason's work. Randolph's statement to the contrary with regard to Articles 15 and 16 was based upon his mistaken recollection 30 years later. The extent of Mason's contribution is even clearer when we compare it with the provisions protecting personal rights in Jefferson's suggested Constitution (*infra* p. 243).

That an almost uneducated planter with little legal training, could draw up a document like the Virginia Declaration of Rights must remain a constant source of wonder. According to the 1855 account by Hugh Grigsby, "when Mason sat down in his room in the Raleigh Tavern to write that paper, it is probable that no copy of the reply to Sir Robert Filmer or of the Essay on Government by Algernon Sydney and Locke . . . was within his reach. The diction, the design, the thoughts are all his own." He goes on to say that "Mason was a planter, untutored in the schools, whose life . . . had been spent in a thinly settled colony."

In a letter written to Richard Henry Lee, on the very day when he took his seat in the Convention, Mason declared, "We are now going upon the most important of all subjects — government!" In settling the constitutional frame of government, he and his colleagues were at one in their agreement on the necessity for a Declaration of Rights as an integral part of the new Constitution. The Declaration could be drawn up by one man and adopted with so few changes because, by 1776, a consensus had developed among Americans on the fundamental rights which the law should protect. In giving specific content to those rights, Mason was more the codifier than the transforming innovator.

The Virginia Declaration completely omits the references to English law and Colonial Charters and grants upon which the earlier American documents contained in this volume had been based. Instead (like the Declaration and Resolves of the First Continental Congress) it asserts the law of nature as the source of individual rights and it does so in language remarkably similar to that which Jefferson was shortly to use in the Declaration of Independence. As in the 1774 Declaration, the trilogy of life, liberty, and property is stated as the basic end to be protected.

Of the 16 articles in the Virginia Declaration, nine state fundamental general principles of a free republic (of these perhaps the most consequential was the statement in Article 5 of the separation of powers as a rule of positive law—apparently the first such statement in an organic instrument). The remaining seven articles safeguard specific individual rights. Among them, we find repeated from prior documents the right against excessive bail and fines and cruel and unusual punishment (this time using the very language of the English Bill of Rights that was to become the Eighth Amendment); that to trial by jury in both civil and criminal cases (anticipating the Sixth and Seventh Amendments in this regard); the right not to be deprived of liberty "except by the law of the land or the judgment of his peers" (still another version of section 39 of Magna Carta on the way to the Due Process Clause of the Fifth Amendment); and the right to freedom of conscience (containing, as already seen, the term "free exercise" which Madison was to use again in the First Amendment). Of special significance is Article 8, which anticipates so directly the rights guaranteed in the Sixth Amendment: that to a speedy trial by a jury of the vicinage, to be informed of the cause and nature of the accusation, and to be confronted with the accuser and witnesses. But Mason did not rest content with writing a compendium of the rights recognized in earlier documents. He also included other fundamental rights: that not to be compelled to give evidence against oneself (the first constitutional statement of what was to become the privilege against self-incrimination of the Fifth Amendment); and that against general warrants (the first constitutional assertion of the right protected by the Fourth Amendment, anticipating the language of the latter on the particularity to be required in warrants). Most important of all was the guarantee of freedom of the press (apparently the first enactment, constitutional or statutory, to protect freedom of the press and thus the direct precursor of the freedom guaranteed in the First Amendment).

All in all, Mason's accomplishment in the Virginia Declaration was a landmark in the development that was to culminate in the federal Bill of Rights. As already stated, the Mason Declaration was the first document that may truly be called an American Bill of Rights. Mason and his colleagues recognized this, for they consistently referred to the document in the Convention debates as the *Bill of Rights*—just as Randolph was to do in his *Essay* of 30 years later. Technically, of course, the term "Bill" was inaccurate (as it is, indeed, in the case of the federal Bill of Rights). Unlike the English Bill of Rights, neither the Virginia Declaration nor the federal Bill of Rights had ever been bills which were enacted as statutes. Both were adopted as constitutional enactments which are superior to all bills and statutes.

In his *Essay,* Randolph appropriately terms the Virginia Declaration the cornerstone of the constitutional system. He states the two objects of the document in terms that serve equally well for all similar organic enactments: "one, that the legislature should not in their acts violate any of those canons; the other, that in all the revolutions of time, of human opinion, and of government, a perpetual standard should be erected."

Virginia Declaration of Rights, 1776*

A Declaration of Rights made by the Representatives of the good people of Virginia, assembled in full and free Convention; which rights do pertain to them and their posterity, as the basis and foundation of Government.

1. That all men are by nature equally free and independent, and have certain inherent rights, of which, when they enter into a state of society, they cannot, by any compact, deprive or divest their posterity; namely, the enjoyment of life and liberty, with the means of acquiring and possessing property, and persuing and obtaining happiness and safety.

2. That all power is vested in, and consequently derived from, the People; that magistrates are their trustees and servants, and at all times amenable to them.

3. That Government is, or ought to be, instituted for the common benefit, protection, and security of the people, nation, or community; of all the various modes and forms of Government that is best which is capable of producing the greatest degree of happiness and safety, and is most effectually secured against the danger of mal-administration; and that, whenever any Government shall be found inadequate or contrary to these purposes, a majority of the community hath an indubitable, unalienable, and indefeasible right, to reform, alter, or abolish it, in such manner as shall be judged most conducive to the publick weal.

4. That no man, or set of men, are entitled to exclusive or separate emoluments and privileges from the community, but in consideration of publick services; which, not being descendible, neither ought the offices of Magistrate, Legislator, or Judge, to be hereditary.

*P. Force, ed., *American Archives*, Fourth Series (1846), Vol. 6, p. 1561.

5. That the Legislative and Executive powers of the State should be separate and distinct from the Judicative; and, that the members of the two first may be restrained from oppression, by feeling and participating the burdens of the people, they should, at fixed periods, be reduced to a private station, return into that body from which they were originally taken, and the vacancies be supplied by frequent, certain, and regular elections, in which all, or any part of the former members, to be again eligible, or ineligible, as the law shall direct.

6. That elections of members to serve as Representatives of the people, in Assembly, ought to be free; and that all men, having sufficient evidence of permanent common interest with, and attachment to, the community, have the right of suffrage, and cannot be taxed or deprived of their property for publick uses without their own consent or that of their Representative so elected, nor bound by any law to which they have not, in like manner, assented, for the publick good.

7. That all power of suspending laws, or the execution of laws, by any authority, without consent of the Representatives of the people, is injurious to their rights, and ought not to be exercised.

8. That in all capital or criminal prosecutions a man hath a right to demand the cause and nature of his accusation, to be confronted with the accusers and witnesses, to call for evidence in his favour, and to a speedy trial by an impartial jury of his vicinage, without whose unanimous consent he cannot be found guilty, nor can he be compelled to give evidence against himself; that no man be deprived of his liberty except by the law of the land, or the judgment of his peers.

9. That excessive bail ought not to be required, nor excessive fines imposed, nor cruel and unusual punishments inflicted.

10. That general warrants, whereby any officer or messenger may be commanded to search suspected places without evidence of a fact committed, or to seize any person or persons not named, or whose offence is not particularly described and supported by evidence, are grievous and oppressive, and ought not to be granted.

11. That in controversies respecting property, and in suits between man and man, the ancient trial by Jury is preferable to any other, and ought to be held sacred.

12. That the freedom of the Press is one of the greatest bulwarks of liberty, and can never be restrained but by despotick Governments.

13. That a well-regulated Militia, composed of the body of the people, trained to arms, is the proper, natural, and safe defence of a free State; that Standing Armies, in time of peace, should be avoided as dangerous to liberty; and that, in all cases, the military should be under strict subordination to, and governed by, the civil power.

14. That the people have a right to uniform Government; and, therefore, that no Government separate from, or independent of, the Government of Virginia, ought to be erected or established within the limits thereof.

15. That no free Government, or the blessing of liberty, can be preserved to any people but by a firm adherence to justice, moderation, temperance, frugality, and virtue, and by frequent recurrence to fundamental principles.

16. That Religion, or the duty which we owe to our Creator, and the manner of discharging it, can be directed only by reason and conviction, not by force or violence; and, therefore, all men are equally entitled to the free exercise of religion, according to the dictates of conscience; and that it is the mutual duty of all to practise Christian forbearance, love, and charity, towards each other.

Journal of the Virginia Convention, 1776*

May 15, 1776

Resolved, unanimously, That the Delegates appointed to represent this Colony in General Congress be instructed to propose to that respectable body to declare the United Colonies free and independent States, absolved from all allegiance to, or dependance upon, the Crown or Parliament of Great Britain; and that they give the assent of this Colony to such declaration, and to whatever measures may be thought proper and necessary by the Congress for forming foreign alliances, and a Confederation of the Colonies, at such time and in the manner as to them shall seem best: Provided, That the power of forming Government for, and the regulations of the internal concerns of each Colony, be left to the respective Colonial Legislatures.

Resolved, unanimously, That a Committee be appointed to prepare a Declaration of Rights, and such a plan of Government as will be most likely to maintain peace and order in this Colony, and secure substantial and equal liberty to the people.

And a Committee was appointed of the following gentlemen: Mr. Archibald Cary, Mr. Meriwether Smith, Mr. Mercer, Mr. Henry Lee, Mr. Treasurer, Mr. Henry, Mr. Dundridge, Mr. Edmund Randolph, Mr. Gilmer, Mr. Bland, Mr. Digges, Mr. Carrington, Mr. Thomas Ludwell Lee, Mr. Cabell, Mr. Jones, Mr. Blair, Mr. Fleming, Mr. Tazewell, Mr. Richard Cary, Mr. Bullitt, Mr. Watts, Mr. Banister, Mr. Page, Mr. Starke, Mr. David Mason, Mr. Adams, Mr. Read, and Mr. Thomas Lewis.

*   *   *

May 16, 1776

Ordered, That Mr. Madison, Mr. Rutherford, and Mr. Watkins, be added to the Committee appointed to prepare a Declaration of Rights, and such a

*American Archives, pp. 1523–68.

plan of Government as will be most likely to maintain peace and order in this Colony, and secure substantial and equal liberty to the people.

*   *   *

May 18, 1776

Ordered, That Mr. George Mason be added to the Committee of Privileges and Elections, and to the Committee of Propositions and Grievances, and to the Committee appointed to prepare a Declaration of Rights, and such a form of Government as will be most likely to maintain peace and order in this Colony, and secure substantial and equal liberty to the people.

*   *   *

May 27, 1776

Mr. Cary, from the Committee appointed to prepare a Declaration of Rights, and such a plan of Government as will be most likely to maintain peace and order in this Colony, and secure substantial and equal liberty to the people, reported, that the Committee had accordingly prepared a Declaration of Rights; which he read in his place, and afterwards delivered in at the Clerk's table, where the same was again read, and ordered to be committed to a Committee of the whole Convention.

The following Declaration was reported to the Convention by the Committee appointed to prepare the same, and referred to the consideration of a Committee of the whole Convention; and, in the mean time, is ordered to be printed for the perusal of the Members:

A Declaration of Rights, made by the Representatives of the good people of Virginia, assembled in full and free Convention, which rights do pertain to us and our posterity, as the basis and foundation of Government.

1. That all men are born equally free and independent, and have certain inherent natural rights, of which they cannot, by any compact, deprive or divest their posterity; among which are the enjoyment of life and liberty, with the means of acquiring and possessing property, and pursuing and obtaining happiness and safety.

2. That all power is vested in, and consequently derived from, the People; that magistrates are their trustees and servants, and at all times amenable to them.

3. That Government is, or ought to be, instituted for the common benefit, protection, and security of the people, nation, or community. Of all the various modes and forms of Government, that is best which is capable of producing the greatest degree of happiness and safety, and is most effectually secured against the danger of mal-administration; and also whenever any

Government shall be found inadequate or contrary to these purposes, a majority of the community hath an indubitable, amenable, and indefeasible right to reform, alter, or abolish it, in such manner as shall be judged most conducive to the publick weal.

4. That no man, or set of men, are entitled to exclusive or separate emoluments or privileges from the community, but in consideration of publick services; which, not being descendible or hereditary, the idea of a man being born a Magistrate, a Legislator, or a Judge, is unnatural and absurd.

5. That the Legislative and Executive powers of the State should be separate and distinct from the Judicative; and that the members of the two first may be restrained from oppression, by feeling and participating the burdens of the people, they should, at fixed periods, be reduced to a private station, return into that body from which they were originally taken, and the vacancies be supplied by frequent, certain, and regular elections.

6. That elections of members to serve as Representatives of the people in Assembly, ought to be free; and that all men, having sufficient evidence of permanent common interest with, and attachment to the community, have the right of suffrage.

7. That no part of a man's property can be taken from him, or applied to publick uses, without his own consent, or that of his legal representatives; nor are the people bound by any laws but such as they have in like manner assented to for their common good.

8. That all power of suspending laws, or the execution of laws, by any authority, without the consent of the Representatives of the people, is injurious to their rights, and ought not to be exercised.

9. That laws having retrospect to crimes, and punishing offences committed before the existence of such laws, are generally oppressive, and ought to be avoided.

10. That in all capital or criminal prosecutions a man hath a right to demand the cause and nature of his accusation, to be confronted with the accusers or witnesses, to call for evidence in his favour, and a speedy trial by an impartial jury of his vicinage, without whose unanimous consent he cannot be found guilty, nor can he be compelled to give evidence against himself; that no man be deprived of his liberty except by the law of the land, or the judgment of his peers.

11. That excessive bail ought not to be required, nor excessive fines imposed, nor cruel and unusual punishments inflicted.

12. That warrants unsupported by evidence, whereby any officer or messenger may be commanded or required to search suspected places, or to seize any person or persons, his or their property, not particularly described, are grievous and oppressive, and ought not to be granted.

13. That in controversies respecting property, and in suits between man and man, the ancient trial by Jury is preferable to any other, and ought to be held sacred.

14. That the freedom of the Press is one of the great bulwarks of liberty, and can never be restrained but by despotick Governments.

15. That a well-regulated Militia, composed of the body of the people, trained to arms, is the proper, natural, and safe defence of a free State; that Standing Armies, in time of peace, should be avoided, as dangerous to liberty; and that, in all cases, the military should be under strict subordination to and governed by the civil power.

16. That the people have a right to uniform Government, and therefore, that no Government separate from, or independent of, the Government of Virginia, ought, of right, to be erected or established within the limits thereof.

17. That no free Government, or the blessings of liberty, can be preserved to any people but by a firm adherence to justice, moderation, temperance, frugality, and virtue, and by frequent recurrence to fundamental principles.

18. That Religion, or the duty we owe to our Creator, and the manner of discharging it, can be directed only by reason and conviction, not by force or violence; and therefore that all men should enjoy the fullest toleration in the exercise of religion, according to the dictates of conscience, unpunished and unrestrained by the magistrate, unless, under colour of religion, any man disturb the peace, the happiness, or safety of society. And that it is the mutual duty of all to practise Christian forbearance, love, and charity towards each other.

*   *   *

May 29, 1776

The Convention then, according to the Order of the Day, resolved itself into a Committee on the Declaration of Rights, and after some time spent therein, Mr. President resumed the chair, and Mr. Cary reported, that the Committee had, according to order, had under their consideration the said Declaration, but not having time to go through the same, had directed him to move for leave to sit again.

Resolved, That this Convention will, to-morrow, again resolve itself into a Committee on the said Declaration.

*   *   *

May 30, 1776

The Orders of the Day, for the Convention to resolve itself into a Committee on the Declaration of Rights, and on the state of the Colony, being read, Ordered, That the same be put off till to-morrow.

*   *   *

June 1, 1776

The Orders of the Day, for the Convention to resolve itself into a Committee on the state of the Colony, on the Declaration of Rights, and on the Ordinance for augmenting the Ninth Regiment of Regular forces, providing for the better defence of the frontiers of this Colony, and for raising four Troops of Horse, being read,
Ordered, That the same be put off till to-morrow.

*   *   *

June 3, 1776

The Convention then, according to the Order of the Day, resolved itself into a Committee on the Declaration of Rights; and after some time spent therein, Mr. President resumed the chair, and Mr. Cary reported, that the Committee had, recording to order, had under their consideration the Declaration of Rights, and had made some progress therein, but not having time to go through the same, had directed him to move for leave to sit again.
Resolved, That this Convention will to-morrow again resolve itself into the said Committee.

*   *   *

June 4, 1776

The Convention then, according to the Order of the Day, resolved itself into a Committee on the Declaration of Rights; and after some time spent therein, Mr. President resumed the chair, and Mr. Cary reported that the Committee had, recording to order, had under their consideration the Declaration of Rights, and had made a further progress therein, but not having time to go through the same, had directed him to move for leave to sit again.
Resolved, That this Convention will to-morrow again resolve itself into the said Committee.

*   *   *

June 5, 1776

The Convention then, according to the Order of the Day, resolved itself into a Committee on the Declaration of Rights; and after some time spent therein, Mr. President resumed the chair, and Mr. Cary reported, that the Committee had, according to order, had under their consideration the Declaration of Rights, and had made a further progress therein, but not having time to go through the same, had directed him to move for leave to sit again.
Resolved, That this Convention will, to-morrow, again resolve itself into the said Committee.

*   *   *

June 10, 1776

The Convention then, according to the Order of the Day, resolved itself into a Committee on the Declaration of Rights; and after some time spent therein, Mr. President resumed the chair, and Mr. Blair reported that the Committee had, according to order, had under their consideration the Declaration of Rights, and had gone through the same, and made several amendments thereto, which he read in his place, and afterwards delivered in at the Clerk's table.

Ordered, That the consideration of the said Amendments be put off till to-morrow.

*   *   *

June 11, 1776

The Convention then proceeded to the consideration of the Amendments reported to the Declaration of Rights; and having gone through the same, and agreed thereto.

Ordered, That the said Declaration of Rights with the Amendments, be fairly transcribed, and read a third time.

*   *   *

June 12, 1776

The Declaration of Rights having been fairly transcribed, was read a third time, and passed, as follows, *nem. con.:*

A Declaration of Rights made by the Representatives of the good people of Virginia, assembled in full and free Convention; which rights do pertain to them and their posterity, as the basis and foundation of Government. [the Declaration text follows].

*   *   *

June 29, 1776

The Plan of Government for this Colony was read a third time.
Resolved, unanimously, That the said Plan of Government do pass.

*   *   *

Original Draft of the Virginia Declaration of Rights, 1776*

By George Mason

A Declaration of Rights made by the Representatives of the good people of Virginia, assembled in full and free convention, which rights do pertain to them and their posterity, as the basis and foundation of government.

*K. M. Rowland, *The Life of George Mason* (1892), Vol. 1, pp. 433–36.

1. That all men are created equally free and independent, and have certain inherent natural rights, of which they cannot, by any compact, deprive or divest their posterity; among which are the enjoyment of life and liberty, with the means of acquiring and possessing property, and pursuing and obtaining happiness and safety.

2. That all power is by God and Nature vested in, and consequently derived from, the people; that magistrates are their trustees and servants, and at all times amenable to them.

3. That government is, or ought to be, instituted for the common benefit, protection, and security of the people, nation, or community. Of all the various modes and forms of government, that is best which is capable of producing the greatest degree of happiness and safety, and is most effectually secured against the danger of mal-administration; and that whenever any government shall be found inadequate or contrary to these purposes, a majority of the community hath an indubitable, unalienable, and indefeasible right to reform, alter, or abolish it, in such manner as shall be judged most conducive to the public weal.

4. That no man, or set of men, are entitled to exclusive or separate emoluments or privileges from the community, but in consideration of public services; which not being descendible, neither ought the offices of magistrate, legislator, or judge to be hereditary.

5. That the legislative and executive powers of the State should be separate and distinct from the judicial; and that the members of the two first may be restrained from oppression by feeling and participating the burthens of the people, they should, at fixed periods, be reduced to a private station, and return into that body from which they were originally taken, and the vacancies be supplied by frequent, certain, and regular elections.

6. That elections of members to serve as representatives of the people in the legislature ought to be free, and that all men, having sufficient evidence of permanent, common interest with and attachment to the community, have the right of suffrage, and cannot be taxed, or deprived of their property for public uses, without their own consent, or that of their representatives so elected, nor bound by any law to which they have not, in like manner, assented for the common good.

7. That all power of suspending laws, or the execution of laws, by any authority, without consent of the representatives of the people, is injurious to their rights, and ought not to be exercised.

8. That in all capital or criminal prosecutions, a man hath a right to demand the cause and nature of his accusation, to be confronted with the accusers and witnesses, to call for evidence in his favor, and to a speedy trial by an impartial jury of his vicinage, without whose unanimous consent he cannot be found guilty, nor can he be compelled to give evidence against himself; and that no man be deprived of his liberty, except by the law of the land or the judgment of his peers.

9. That excessive bail ought not to be required, nor excessive fines imposed, nor cruel and unusual punishments inflicted.

10. That in controversies respecting property, and in suits between man and man, the ancient trial by jury is preferable to any other, and to be held sacred.

11. That the freedom of the press is one of the great bulwarks of liberty, and can never be restrained but by despotic governments.

12. That a well regulated militia, composed of the body of the people, trained to arms, is the proper, natural, and safe defence of a free State; that standing armies in time of peace should be avoided, as dangerous to liberty; and that in all cases, the military should be under strict subordination to, and governed by, the civil power.

13. That no free government, or the blessing of liberty, can be preserved to any people but by a firm adherence to justice, moderation, temperance, frugality, and virtue, and by frequent recurrence to fundamental principles.

14. That religion, or the duty which we owe to our Creator, and the manner of discharging it, can be directed only by reason and conviction, not by force or violence; and, therefore, that all men should enjoy the fullest toleration in the exercise of religion, according to the dictates of conscience, unpunished and unrestrained by the magistrate, unless, under color of religion, any man disturb the peace, the happiness, or the safety of society. And that it is the mutual duty of all to practise Christian forbearance, love, and charity towards each other.

(Two more articles were added, viz., the 10th and 14th in the adopted bill—not of fundamental nature.)

This Declaration of Rights was the first in America; it received few alterations or additions in the Virginia Convention (some of them not for the better), and was afterwards closely imitated by the other United States.

[This paper in all its parts is in the handwriting of George Mason—a memorandum is prefixed: "Virginia Declaration of Rights in 1776. Copy of first Draught by G. M." The note at the foot is also in George Mason's hand.]

Thomas Jefferson's Draft Virginia Constitution, 1776*

*   *   *

III. Judiciary
The Judiciary powers shall be exercised
First by County courts and other inferior jurisdictions:
Secondly by a General court & a High court of Chancery:
Thirdly by a Court of Appeals.

*J. P. Boyd, ed., *The Papers of Thomas Jefferson* (1950), Vol. 1, pp. 361–64.

The judges of the County courts and other inferior jurisdictions shall be appointed by the Administrator, subject to the negative of the privy council. they shall not be fewer than [five] in number. their jurisdiction shall be defined from time to time by the legislature: and they shall be removeable for misbehavior by the court of Appeals.

The Judges of the General court and of the High court of Chancery shall be appointed by the Administrator and Privy council. if kept united they shall be [5] in number, if separate, there shall be [5] for the General court & [3] for the High court of Chancery. the appointment shall be made from the faculty of the law, and of such persons of that faculty as shall have actually exercised the same at the bar of some court or courts of record within this colony for [seven] years. they shall hold their commissions during good behavior, for breach of which they shall be removeable by the court of Appeals. their jurisdiction shall be defined from time to time by the Legislature.

The Court of Appeals shall consist of not less than [7] nor more than [11] members, to be appointed by the house of Representatives: they shall hold their offices during good behavior, for breach of which they shall be removeable by an act of the legislature only, their jurisdiction shall be to determine finally all causes removed before them from the General court or High court of Chancery on suggestion of error: to remove judges of the General court or High court of Chancery, or of the County courts or other inferior jurisdictions for misbehavior: [to try impeachments against high offenders lodged before them by the house of representatives for such crimes as shall hereafter be precisely defined by the Legislature, and for the punishment of which the said legislature shall have previously prescribed certain and determinate pains.] in this court the judges of the General court and High court of Chancery shall have session and deliberative voice, but no suffrage.

All facts in causes, whether of Chancery, Common, Ecclesiastical, or Marine law, shall be tried by a jury upon evidence given viva voce, in open court: but there witnesses are out of the colony or unable to attend through sickness or other invincible necessity, their depositions may be submitted to the credit of the jury.

All Fines and Amercements shall be assessed, & Terms of imprisonment for Contempts & Misdemeanors shall be fixed by the verdict of a jury.

All Process Original & Judicial shall run in the name of the court from which it issues.

Two thirds of the members of the General court, High court of Chancery, or Court of Appeals shall be a Quorum to proceed to business.

IV. Rights Private and Public

Unappropriated or Forfeited lands shall be appropriated by the Administrator with the consent of the Privy council.

Every person of full age neither owning nor having owned [50] acres of land, shall be entitled to an appropriation of [50] acres or to so much as shall make up what he owns or has owned [50] acres in full and absolute dominion, and no other person shall be capable of taking an appropriation.

Lands heretofore holden (in fee) of the crown in feesimple, and those hereafter to be appropriated shall be holden in full and absolute dominion, of no superior whatever.

No lands shall be appropriated until purchased of the Indian native proprietors; nor shall any purchases be made of them but on behalf of the public, by authority of acts of the General assembly to be passed for every purchase specially.

The territories contained within the charters erecting the colonies of Maryland Pennsylvania, North and South Carolina, are hereby ceded, released, & for ever confirmed to the people of those colonies respectively, with all the rights of property, jurisdiction and government and all other rights whatsoever which might at any time heretofore have been claimed by this colony. the Western and Northern extent of this country shall in all other respects stand as fixed by the charter of   until by act of the Legislature one or more territories shall be laid off Westward of the Alleghaney mountains for new colonies, which colonies shall be established on the same fundamental laws contained in this instrument, and shall be free and independant of this colony and of all the world.

Descents shall go according to the laws of Gavelkind, save only that females shall have equal rights with males.

No person hereafter coming into this country shall be held within the same in slavery under any pretext whatever.

All persons who by their own oath or affirmation, or by other testimony shall give satisfactory proof to any court of record in this colony that they purpose to reside in the same [7] years at the least and who shall subscribe the fundamental laws, shall be considered as residents and entitled to all the rights of persons natural born.

All persons shall have full and free liberty of religious opinion; nor shall any be compelled to frequent or maintain any religious institution.

No freeman shall be debarred the use of arms [within his own lands or tenements]

There shall be no standing army but in time of actual war.

Printing presses shall be free, except so far as by commission of private injury cause may be given of private action.

All Forfeitures heretofore going to the king, shall go to the state; save only such as the legislature may hereafter abolish.

The royal claim to Wrecks, waifs, strays, treasure-trove, royal mines, royal fish, royal birds, are declared to have been usurpations on common right.

No Salaries or Perquisites shall be given to any officer but by some future act of the legislature. no salaries shall be given to the Administrator, members of the Legislative houses, judges of the court of Appeals, judges of the County courts, or other inferior jurisdictions, Privy counsellors, or Delegates to the American Congress: but the reasonable expences of the Administrator, members of the house of representatives, judges of the court of Appeals, Privy counsellors, & Delegates, for subsistence while acting in the duties of their office, may be borne by the public, if the Legislature shall so direct.

(The Qualifications of all officers not otherwise hereby directed, shall be an oath of fidelity to the state, and the having given no bribe to obtain their office) No person shall be capable of acting in any office, Civil, Military [or Ecclesiastical] who shall have given any bribe to obtain such office, or who shall not previously take an oath of fidelity to the state.

None of these fundamental laws and principles of government shall be repealed or altered, but by the personal consent of the people on summons to meet in their respective counties on one and the same day by an act of Legislature to be passed for every special occasion: and if in such county meetings the people of two thirds of the counties shall give their suffrage for any particular alteration or repeal referred to them by the said act, the same shall be accordingly repealed or altered, and such repeal or alteration shall take it's place among these fundamentals & stand on the same footing with them, in lieu of the article repealed or altered.

The laws heretofore in force in this colony shall remain (still) in force, except so far as they are altered by the foregoing fundamental laws, or so far as they may be hereafter altered by acts of the Legislature.

Edmund Randolph's Essay*

*   *   *

As soon as the convention had pronounced the vote of independence, the formation of a constitution or frame of government followed of course. For with the royal authority, the existing organs of police and the laws ceased, and the tranquillity of society was floating upon the will of popular committees, and the virtue of the people.

To this work, then unprecedented in America, talents were requisite of a higher order, than those, which could foment a revolution. Patriotism, firmness and a just foresight of the dangers to be encountered, were sufficient to dissolve an empire. But the deepest research which had then been made here into the theory of government, seemed too short for those scenes, which the new order of things was to unfold, and for those evils, which human passions, with new opportunities and solicitations must beget.

Mr. Jefferson, who was in congress, urged a youthful friend in the conven-

*E. Randolph, "Essay on the Revolutionary History of Virginia," *Virginia Magazine of History and Biography,* Vol. 44, (1936), pp. 43–47. According to Vol. 43 *id.* at 115–16, this essay was written after Randolph's retirement from office, near the end of his life—sometime between 1809 and 1813.

tion, to oppose a permanent constitution, until the people should elect deputies for the special purpose. He denied the power of the body elected (as he conceived them to be agents for the management of the war) to exceed some temporary regimen. The member alluded to, communicated the ideas of Mr. Jefferson to some of the leaders in the house, Edmund Pendleton, Patrick Henry, and George Mason. These gentlemen saw no distinction between the conceded power to declare independence, and its necessary consequence, the fencing of society by the institution of government. Nor were they sure, that to be backward in this act of sovereignty might not imply a distrust, whether the rule had been wrested from the king. The attempt to postpone the formation of a constitution, until a commission of greater latitude, and one more specific should be given by the people, was a task too hardy for an inexperienced young man.

A very large committee was nominated to prepare the proper instruments, and many projects of a bill of rights and constitution, discovered the ardor for political notice, rather than a ripeness in political wisdom. That proposed by George Mason swallowed up all the rest, by fixing the grounds and plan, which after great discussion and correction, were finally ratified.

The celebrated notes on Virginia have since become the vehicle of the former objections of its author made *in limine*.

"When the enemey shall be expelled from our bowels, when peace shall be established, and leisure given us for intrenching within good forms the rights for which we have bled, let no man be found indolent enough to decline a little more trouble for placing them beyond the reach of question, if anything more may be requisite to produce a conviction of the expediency of calling a convention at a proper season, to fix our form of government," etc. "The ordinary legislature may alter the constitution itself." There are indeed defects in it of magnitude; and there is no doubt, a power resident in the people to change it, as they please. If Mr. Jefferson's observations have contributed to some degree of restlessness under it, they ought if just to be adverted to. They have been disarmed of the possibility of mischief, by the solemn recognitions, in our courts of the validity of the constitution. It would be useless to revive a discussion, which has been thus put to sleep; though it may be yet asked, whether the confirmation of the people by their acquiescence for so many years, be no argument against the unhinging of such various authorities, which have been exercised under it, and possibly of some rights, which have been derived from it? Is it nothing, that independence was established, with as little premonition to the people, as the constitution was; and that the constitution, considered only as temporary, until a more legitimate one shall be adopted (which is the extent of his demand) can no more be revoked by the legislature, which is the creature of it, appointed to execute it, than the trustees of power can transcend their instructions? But happily, practical utility will always exterminate questions, too refined for public safety.

It has been often doubted too, whether a written constitution has any superiority over one unwritten. This is a point of comparison between the English constitution, and that of Virginia. An unwritten constitution can, upon the appearance of a defect, be amended, without agitating the people. A written one is a standing ark, to which first principles can be brought on to a test. Whatever merit is due to either opinion, it should not be forgotten, that the spirit of a people will in construction frequently bend words seemingly inflexible, and derange the organization of power. This has happened in Virginia, where the line of partition between the legislative and judicial department has been so remote from vulgar apprehension, or plausible necessity has driven such consideration before it.

The bill of rights and the constitution are monuments which deserve the attention of every republican, as containing some things which we may wish to be retrenched, and others, which cannot be too much admired.

The declaration in the first article in the bill of rights, that all men are by nature equally free and independent, was opposed by Robert Carter Nicholas, as being the forerunner of pretext or civil convulsion. It was answered, perhaps with too great an indifference to futurity, and not without inconsistency, that with arms in our hands, asserting the general rights of man, we ought not to be too nice and too much restricted in the delineation of them; but that slaves not being constituent members of our society could never pretend to any benefit from such a maxim.

The second article, derives all power from the people, and declares magistrates to be always amenable to them.

The third article affirms the supremacy of a majority in a community.

The fourth explodes an inheritance in office.

The fifth separates the legislative, executive and judicial functions, and reduces the members of the two former at fixed periods, to private stations.

One part of the sixth provides for the freedom of elections, and another confers the right of suffrage on all having sufficient evidence of a permanent common interest with, and of attachment to the community. But it did not intend to leave this right to the will of the legislature according to capricious views of expediency.

It reserved a more specific provision for the constitution. The seventh against the suspension of laws by any other authority than that of the representatives of the people was suggested by an arbitrary practice of the king of England before the revolution in 1688.

The eight reenacts in substance, modes for defence, for accused persons, similar to those under the English law.

The ninth against excessive bail and excessive fines, was also borrowed from England with additional reprobation of cruel and unusual punishments.

The tenth against general warrants was dictated by the remembrance of the seisure of Wilkes's paper under a warrant from a Secretary of State.

The eleventh preserving the trial by jury was not considered as a mandate to legislatures without the possibility of exception.

The twelfth, securing the freedom of the press, and the thirteenth, preferring militia to standing armies were the fruits of genuine democracy and historical experience.

The fourteenth prohibiting the erection of a government within the limits of Virginia proceeded partly from local circumstances; when the charter boundaries of Virginia, were abridged by royal *fiats* in favor of Lord Baltimore and Lord Fairfax, much to the discontent of the people: and partly from recent commotions in the west.

The fifteenth, recommending an adherence and frequent recurrence to fundamental principles, and the sixteenth, unfettering the exercise of religion were proposed by Mr. Henry. The latter, coming from a gentleman, who was supposed to be a dissenter, caused an appeal to him, whether it was designed as a prelude to an attack on the established church, and he disclaimed such an object.

An article prohibiting bills of attainder was defeated by Henry, who with a terrifying picture of some towering public offender, against whom ordinary laws would be impotent, saved that dread power from being expressly proscribed.

In the formation of this bill of rights two objects were contemplated: one, that the legislature should not in their acts violate any of those cannons; the other, that in all the revolutions of time, of human opinion, and of government, a perpetual standard should be erected, around which the people might rally, and by a notorious record be forever admonished to be watchful, firm and virtuous.

The corner stone being thus laid, a constitution, delegating portions of power to different organs under certain modifications was of course to be raised upon it.

*   *   *

James Madison's Autobiography*

*   *   *

In 1775, he was elected a member of the Comee for the County, living at the time with his father (who was chairman of it) and had a part in the County proceedings belonging to the period. The spirit of the epoch may be seen in the address to P. H. on his expedition having for its object the military stores in Williamsburg, rifled by Gov. Dunmore.

He was restrained from entering into the military service by the unsettled state of his health and the discourageing feebleness of his constitution of

---

*D. Adair, ed., "James Madison's Autobiography," *William and Mary Quarterly,* Third Ser., Vol. 2, (1945), p. 199. According to *id.* at 193, it will probably never be possible to date the *Autobiography* exactly. According to Irving Brant, *ibid.,* the *Autobiography* was probably written after August 1833.

which he was fully admonished by his experience during the exercises and movements of a minute Company which he had joined.

In the spring of 1776 he was initiated into the political career by a County election to the convention, which formed the original Constitution of the State with the Declaration of Rights prefixed to it; and which on the 16th day of May unanimously instructed her deputies in Congress to propose the final separation from G. Britain, as declared by that Body on the 4th of July following. Being young & in the midst of distinguished and experienced members of the Convention he did not enter into its debates; tho' he occasionally suggested amendments; the most material of which was a change of the terms in which the freedom of Conscience was expressed in the proposed Declaration of Rights. This important and meritorious instrument was drawn by Geo. Mason, who had inadvertently adopted the word toleration in the article on that subject. The change suggested and accepted, substituted a phraseology which—declared the freedom of conscience to be a natural and absolute right.

*   *   *

DECLARATION OF INDEPENDENCE, 1776

Commentary

It is difficult to say anything about the Declaration of Independence without being trite. Certainly it was a crucial step in the development that led to the federal Bill of Rights. Without Independence, there was no legal authority to draw up Constitutions and Bills of Rights free of any grant of authority from London. Nor could any instrument drafted by Americans be given anything more than subordinate constitutional status. Once Independence was formally declared, the legal picture became a different one. The newly independent States could follow the method proposed by Sir Henry Vane (*supra* p. 30) and call Conventions to form Constitutions to take the place of the Colonial instruments under which they had been governed. Virginia (as already seen) was the first to adopt a written Constitution and Declaration of Rights (and that even before the formal declaring of Independence). The other states were soon to follow suit. Seven states and Vermont (not recognized as a State by Congress until 1791) adopted Constitutions which included Bills of Rights. Four other states enacted Constitutions which did not contain separate Bills of Rights, though they did (as we shall see) contain provisions in their texts safeguarding individual rights.

The Declaration of Independence itself was not drawn up as a Declaration of Rights. Instead, it sought to justify the American action by listing the misdeeds from which the Colonies had suffered. But it does contain a list of the basic rights that had been invaded by the Crown. These are stated in a manner similar to that in previous Declarations of the Continental Congress, and include the right against quartering of troops, trial by jury, and the right to local trials. Also, stated for the first time is the fundamental right to an independent judiciary not "dependent on his will alone, for the tenure of their offices, and . . . their salaries." That right, recognized in Britain since the expulsion of James II, had been overridden by the prerogative in the colonies. It did not prove necessary to include it in the federal Bill of Rights, since it was to serve as the basis of Article III of the Federal Constitution itself.

Declaration of Independence, 1776*

*The Unanimous Declaration of the
Thirteen United States of America*

When, in the course of human events, it becomes necessary for one people to dissolve the political bands which have connected them with another, and

United States Statutes at Large (1845), Vol. 1, pp. 1–4.

to assume, among the powers of the earth, the separate and equal station to which the laws of nature and of nature's God entitle them, a decent respect to the opinions of mankind requires that they should declare the causes which impel them to the separation.

We hold these truths to be self-evident: that all men are created equal; that they are endowed, by their Creator, with certain unalienable rights; that among these are life, liberty, and the pursuit of happiness. That to secure these rights, governments are instituted among men, deriving their just powers from the consent of the governed; that whenever any form of government becomes destructive of these ends, it is the right of the people to alter or to abolish it, and to institute a new government, laying its foundation on such principles, and organizing its powers in such form, as to them shall seem most likely to effect their safety and happiness. Prudence, indeed, will dictate, that governments long established, should not be changed for light and transient causes; and accordingly all experience hath shown, that mankind are more disposed to suffer, while evils are sufferable, than to right themselves by abolishing the forms to which they are accustomed. But when a long train of abuses and usurpations, pursuing invariably the same object, evinces a design to reduce them under absolute despotism, it is their right, it is their duty, to throw off such government, and to provide new guards for their future security. Such has been the patient sufferance of these colonies; and such is now the necessity which constrains them to alter their former systems of government. The history of the present King of Great Britain is a history of repeated injuries and usurpations, all having in direct object the establishment of an absolute tyranny over these states. To prove this, let facts be submitted to a candid world.

He has refused his assent to laws the most wholesome and necessary for the public good.

He has forbidden his governors to pass laws of immediate and pressing importance, unless suspended in their operation till his assent should be obtained; and when so suspended, he has utterly neglected to attend to them.

He has refused to pass other laws for the accommodation of large districts of people, unless those people would relinquish the right of representation in the legislature; a right inestimable to them, and formidable to tyrants only. He has called together legislative bodies at places unusual, uncomfortable, and distant from the depository of their public records, for the sole purpose of fatiguing them into compliance with his measures.

He has dissolved representative houses repeatedly, for opposing, with manly firmness, his invasions on the rights of the people.

He has refused for a long time, after such dissolutions, to cause others to be elected; whereby the legislative powers, incapable of annihilation, have returned to the people at large for their exercise; the state remaining, in the mean time, exposed to all the dangers of invasions from without, and convulsions within.

He has endeavored to prevent the population of these States; for that purpose obstructing the laws for naturalization of foreigners; refusing to pass others to encourage their migrations hither, and raising the conditions of new appropriations of lands.

He has obstructed the administration of justice, by refusing his assent to laws for establishing judiciary powers.

He has made judges dependent on his will alone, for the tenure of their offices, and the amount and payment of their salaries.

He has erected a multitude of new offices, and sent hither swarms of officers, to harass our people, and eat out their substance.

He has kept among us, in times of peace, standing armies, without the consent of our legislatures.

He has affected to render the military independent of, and superior to the civil power.

He has combined with others to subject us to a jurisdiction foreign to our constitution, and unacknowledged by our laws; giving his assent to their acts of pretended legislation:

For quartering large bodies of armed troops among us;

For protecting them, by a mock trial, from punishment for any murders which they should commit on the inhabitants of these States;

For cutting off our trade with all parts of the world;

For imposing taxes on us without our consent;

For depriving us, in many cases, of the benefits of trial by jury;

For transporting us beyond seas to be tried for pretended offences;

For abolishing the free system of English laws in a neighbouring province, establishing therein an arbitrary government, and enlarging its boundaries, so as to render it at once an example and fit instrument for introducing the same absolute rule into these colonies;

For taking away our charters, abolishing our most valuable laws, and altering fundamentally the forms of our governments;

For suspending our own legislatures, and declaring themselves invested with power to legislate for us in all cases whatsoever.

He has abdicated government here, by declaring us out of his protection, and waging war against us.

He has plundered our seas, ravaged our coasts, burnt our towns, and destroyed the lives of our people.

He is at this time transporting large armies of foreign mercenaries to complete the works of death, desolation, and tyranny, already begun with circumstances of cruelty and perfidy, scarcely paralleled in the most barbarous ages, and totally unworthy the head of a civilized nation.

He has constrained our fellow-citizens, taken captive on the high seas, to bear arms against their country, to become the executioners of their friends and brethren, or to fall themselves by their hands.

He has excited domestic insurrections amongst us, and has endeavoured to bring on the inhabitants of our frontiers the merciless Indian savages, whose known rule of warfare is an undistinguished destruction of all ages, sexes, and conditions.

In every state of these oppressions we have petitioned for redress in the most humble terms. Our repeated petitions have been answered only by repeated injury. A prince, whose character is thus marked by every act which may define a tyrant, is unfit to be the ruler of a free people.

Nor have we been wanting in attentions to our British brethren. We have warned them, from time to time, of attempts by their legislature to extend an unwarrantable jurisdiction over us. We have reminded them of the circumstances of our emigration and settlement here. We have appealed to their native justice and magnanimity, and we have conjured them by the ties of our common kindred to disavow these usurpations, which would inevitably interrupt our connexions and correspondence. They too have been deaf to the voice of justice and of consanguinity. We must, therefore, acquiesce in the necessity which denounces our separation, and hold them, as we hold the rest of mankind, enemies in war, in peace friends.

We, therefore, the representatives of the United States of America, in General Congress assembled, appealing to the Supreme Judge of the world for the rectitude of our intentions, do, in the name, and by authority of the good people of these colonies, solemnly publish and declare, That these United Colonies are, and of right ought to be, free and independent States; that they are absolved from all allegiance, to the British crown, and that all political connexion between them and the state of Great Britain is, and ought to be, totally dissolved; and that, as free and independent States, they have full power to levy war, conclude peace, contract alliances, establish commerce, and to do all other acts and things which independent States may of right do. And for the support of this Declaration, with a firm reliance on the protection of Divine Providence, we mutually pledge to each other our lives, our fortunes, and our sacred honour.

John Hancock

New Hampshire—*Josiah Bartlett, William Whipple, Matthew Thornton.*

Massachusetts Bay—*Samuel Adams, John Adams, Robert Treat Paine, Elbridge Gerry.*

Rhode Island, &c.—*Stephen Hopkins, William Ellery.*

Connecticut—*Roger Sherman, Samuel Huntington, William Williams, Oliver Wolcott.*

New York—*William Floyd, Philip Livingston, Francis Lewis, Lewis Morris.*

New Jersey—*Richard Stockton, John Witherspoon, Francis Hopkinson, John Hart, Abraham Clark.*

Pennsylvania—*Robert Morris, Benjamin Rush, Benjamin Franklin, John Morton, George Clymer, James Smith, George Taylor, James Wilson, George Ross.*

Delaware—*Caesar Rodney, George Read, Thomas M'Kean.*

Maryland—*Samuel Chase, William Paca, Thomas Stone, Charles Carroll of Carrollton.*

Virginia—*George Wythe, Richard Henry Lee, Thomas Jefferson, Benjamin Harrison, Thomas Nelson, Jun., Francis Lightfoot Lee, Carter Braxton.*

North Carolina—*William Hooper, Joseph Hewes, John Penn.*

South Carolina—*Edward Rutledge, Thomas Hayward, Jun., Thomas Lynch, Jun., Arthur Middleton.*

Georgia—*Button Gwinnett, Lyman Hall, George Walton.*

NEW JERSEY CONSTITUTION, 1776

Commentary

The Virginia Declaration of Rights (*supra* p. 234) set the example for eight of the 12 states which framed new Constitutions during the Revolutionary period. Like Virginia, they adopted fundamental laws which included specific Bills of Rights. The other four states did not preface their new Constitutions with separate Bills of Rights. Instead, they adopted Constitutions which contained provisions protecting individual rights in the text of the Constitution itself. This was, of course, to be the method followed in the drafting of the federal Constitution, which does contain specific guarantees of individual rights in various provisions, though it did not have any separate Bill of Rights in its original text.

The first state to enact a Revolutionary Constitution without a Bill of Rights was New Jersey. Its Convention promulgated a new Constitution a few days after the Virginia Convention adjourned. Among the protections for individual rights included in the text of the New Jersey Constitution are trial by jury, which "shall remain confirmed as a part of the law . . . without repeal, forever" (Article XXII). In addition, there is an express provision that criminal defendants "shall be admitted to the same privileges of witnesses and counsel, as their prosecutors" (Article XVI). This provision is taken verbatim from the Pennsylvania Charter of Privileges, 1701 (*supra* p. 170), and is apparently the first recognition of the right to counsel in a modern American Constitution.

Even more important are the New Jersey Constitution's provisions for freedom of religion, which recognize, again apparently for the first time, that that basic right has a two-fold aspect (as was to be recognized ultimately in the First Amendment's division into an Establishment Clause and a Free Exercise Clause). Article XVIII guarantees the right of the individual to worship "in a manner agreeable to the dictates of his own conscience." Article XIX provides, "That there shall be no establishment of any one religious sect." This is the first prohibition against an established Church in an American constitutional provision (almost a decade before Jefferson's famous Bill for Establishing Religious Freedom was enacted in Virginia). Well might Ezra Stiles say that the New Jersey provisions on religion were even superior to those in the Virginia Declaration of Rights, writing in his *Literary Diary* that, "The Constitution of New Jersey surpasses it in the Catholic Establishment of Universal, equal religious, protestant Liberty."

New Jersey Constitution, 1776*

Whereas all the constitutional authority ever possessed by the kings of Great Britain over these colonies, or their other dominions, was, by compact,

---

*Poore, *The Federal and State Constitutions, Colonial Charters and Other Organic Laws of the United States* (1878), Vol. 2, pp. 1310–14.

derived from the people, and held of them, for the common interest of the whole society; allegiance and protection are, in the nature of things, reciprocal ties, each equally depending upon the other, and liable to be dissolved by the others being refused or withdrawn. And whereas George the Third, king of Great Britain, has refused protection to the good people of these colonies; and, by assenting to sundry acts of the British parliament, attempted to subject them to the absolute dominion of that body; and has also made war upon them, in the most cruel and unnatural manner, for no other cause, than asserting their just rights—all civil authority under him is necessarily at an end, and a dissolution of government in each colony has consequently taken place.

And whereas, in the present deplorable situation of these colonies, exposed to the fury of a cruel and relentless enemy, some form of government is absolutely necessary, not only for the preservation of good order, but also the more effectually to unite the people, and enable them to exert their whole force in their own necessary defence: and as the honorable the continental congress, the supreme council of the American colonies, has advised such of the colonies as have not yet gone into measures, to adopt for themselves, respectively, such government as shall best conduce to their own happiness and safety, and the well-being of America in general: We, the representatives of the colony of New Jersey, having been elected by all the counties, in the freest manner, and in congress assembled, have, after mature deliberations, agreed upon a set of charter rights and the form of a Constitution, in manner following, viz.

I. That the government of this Province shall be vested in a Governor, Legislative Council, and General Assembly.

II. That the Legislative Council, and General Assembly, shall be chosen, for the first time, on the second Tuesday in August next; the members whereof shall be the same in number and qualifications as are herein after mentioned; and shall be and remain vested with all the powers and authority to be held by any future Legislative Council and Assembly of this Colony, until the second Tuesday in October, which shall be in the year of our Lord one thousand seven hundred and seventy-seven.

III. That on the second Tuesday in October yearly, and every year forever (with the privilege of adjourning from day to day as occasion may require) the counties shall severally choose one person, to be a member of the Legislative Council of this Colony, who shall be, and have been, for one whole year next before the election, an inhabitant and freeholder in the county in which he is chosen, and worth at least one thousand pounds proclamation money, of real and personal estate, within the same county; that, at the same time, each county shall also choose three members of Assembly; provided that no person shall be entitled to a seat in the said Assembly unless he be, and have been, for one whole year next before the election, an inhabitant of the county he is to represent, and worth five hundred pounds proclamation money, in real and personal estate, in the same county: that on the second Tuesday next after the day of election, the Council and Assembly shall separately meet; and that the consent of both Houses shall be necessary to every law; provided, that seven shall be a quorum of the Council, for doing business, and that no law shall pass, unless there be a majority of all the Representatives of each body personally present, and agreeing thereto. Provided always, that if a majority of the representatives of this Province, in Council and General Assembly convened, shall, at any time or times hereafter, judge it equitable and proper, to add to or diminish the number or proportion of the members of Assembly for any county or counties in this Colony, then, and in such case, the same may, on the principles of more equal representation, be lawfully done; anything in this Charter to the contrary notwithstanding: so that the whole number of Representatives in Assembly shall not, at any time, be less than thirty-nine.

IV. That all inhabitants of this Colony, of full age, who are worth fifty pounds proclamation money, clear estate in the same, and have resided within the county in which they claim a vote for twelve months immediately preceding the election, shall be entitled to vote for Representatives in Council and Assembly; and also for all other public officers, that shall be elected by the people of the county at large.

V. That the Assembly, when met, shall have power to choose a Speaker, and other their officers; to be judges of the qualifications and elections of their own members; sit upon their own adjournments; prepare bills, to be passed into laws; and to empower their Speaker to convene them, whenever any extraordinary occurrence shall render it necessary.

VI. That the Council shall also have power to prepare bills to pass into laws, and have other like powers as the Assembly, and in all respects be a free and independent branch of the Legislature of this Colony; save only, that they shall not prepare or alter any money bill—which shall be the privilege of the Assembly; that the Council shall, from time to time, be convened by the Governor or Vice-President, but must be convened, at all times, when the Assembly sits; for which purpose the Speaker of the House of Assembly shall always, immediately after an adjournment, give notice to the Governor, or Vice-President, of the time and place to which the House is adjourned.

VII. That the Council and Assembly jointly, at their first meeting after each annual election, shall, by a majority of votes, elect some fit person within the Colony, to be Governor for one year, who shall be constant President of the Council, and have a casting vote in their proceedings; and that the Council themselves shall choose a Vice-President who shall act as such in the absence of the Governor.

VIII. That the Governor, or, in his absence, the Vice-President of the Council, shall have the supreme executive power, be Chancellor of the Colony, and act as captain-general and commander in chief of all the militia, and other military force in this Colony; and that any three or more of the Council shall, at all times, be a privy-council, to consult them; and that the Governor be ordinary or surrogate-general.

IX. That the Governor and Council, (seven whereof shall be a quorum) be the Court of Appeals, in the last resort, in all clauses of law, as heretofore; and that they possess the power of granting pardons to criminals, after condemnation, in all cases of treason, felony, or other offences.

X. That captains, and all other inferior officers of the militia, shall be chosen by the companies, in the respective counties; but field and general officers, by the Council and Assembly.

XI. That the Council and Assembly shall have power to make the Great Seal of this Colony, which shall be kept by the Governor, or, in his absence, by the Vice-President of the Council, to be used by them as occasion may require: and it shall be called, The Great Seal of the Colony of New Jersey.

XII. That the Judges of the Supreme Court shall continue in office for seven years: the Judges of the Inferior Court of Common Pleas in the several counties, Justices of the Peace, Clerks of the Supreme Court, Clerks of the Inferior Court of Common Pleas and Quarter Sessions, the Attorney-General, and Provincial Secretary, shall continue in office for five years: and the provincial Treasurer shall continue in office for one year; and that they shall be severally appointed by the Council and Assembly, in manner aforesaid, and commissioned by the Governor, or, in his absence, the Vice-President of the Council. Provided always, that the said officers, severally, shall be capable of being re-appointed, at the end of the terms severally before limited; and that any of the said officers shall be liable to be dismissed, when adjudged guilty of misbehaviour, by the Council, on an impeachment of the Assembly.

XIII. That the inhabitants of each county, qualified to vote as aforesaid, shall at the time and place of electing their Representatives, annually elect one Sheriff, and one or more Coroners; and that they may re-elect the same person to such offices, until he shall have served three years, but no longer; after which, three years must elapse before the same person is capable of being elected again. When the election is certified to the Governor, or Vice-President, under the hands of six freeholders of the county for which they were elected, they shall be immediately commissioned to serve in their respective offices.

XIV. That the townships, at their annual town meetings for electing other officers, shall choose constables for the districts respectively; and also three or more judicious freeholders of good character, to hear and finally determine all appeals, relative to unjust assessments, in cases of public taxation; which commissioners of appeal shall, for that purpose, sit at some suitable time or times, to be by them appointed, and made known to the people by advertisements.

XV. That the laws of the Colony shall begin in the following style, viz. "Be it enacted by the Council and General Assembly of this Colony, and it is hereby enacted by authority of the same:" that all commissions, granted by the Governor or Vice-President, shall run thus—"The Colony of New-Jersey to A. B. &c. greeting:" and that all writs shall likewise run in the name of the

Colony: and that all indictments shall conclude in the following manner, viz. "Against the peace of this Colony, the government and dignity of the same."

XVI. That all criminals shall be admitted to the same privileges of witnesses and counsel, as their prosecutors are or shall be entitled to.

XVII. That the estates of such persons as shall destroy their own lives, shall not, for that offence, be forfeited; but shall descend in the same manner, as they would have done, had such persons died in the natural way; nor shall any article, which may occasion accidentally the death of any one, be henceforth deemed a deodand, or in anywise forfeited, on account of such misfortune.

XVIII. That no person shall ever, within this Colony, be deprived of the inestimable privilege of worshipping Almighty God in a manner agreeable to the dictates of his own conscience; nor, under any pretence whatever, be compelled to attend any place of worship, contrary to his own faith and judgment; nor shall any person, within this Colony, ever be obliged to pay tithes, taxes, or any other rates, for the purpose of building or repairing any other church or churches, place or places of worship, or for the maintenance of any minister or ministry, contrary to what he believes to be right, or has deliberately or voluntarily engaged himself to perform.

XIX. That there shall be no establishment of any one religious sect in this Province, in preference to another; and that no Protestant inhabitant of this Colony shall be denied the enjoyment of any civil right, merely on account of his religious principles; but that all persons, professing a belief in the faith of any Protestant sect, who shall demean themselves peaceably under the government, as hereby established, shall be capable of being elected into any office of profit or trust, or being a member of either branch of the Legislature, and shall fully and freely enjoy every privilege and immunity, enjoyed by others their fellow subjects.

XX. That the legislative department of this government may, as much as possible, be preserved from all suspicion of corruption, none of the Judges of the Supreme or other Courts, Sheriffs, or any other person or persons possessed of any post of profit under the government, other than Justices of the Peace, shall be entitled to a seat in the Assembly: but that, on his being elected, and taking his seat, his office or post shall be considered as vacant.

XXI. That all the laws of this Province, contained in the edition lately published by Mr. Allinson, shall be and remain in full force, until altered by the Legislature of this Colony (such only excepted, as are incompatible with this Charter) and shall be, according as heretofore, regarded in all respects, by all civil officers, and others, the good people of this Province.

XXII. That the common law of England, as well as so much of the statute law, as have been heretofore practised in this Colony, shall still remain in force, until they shall be altered by a future law of the Legislature; such parts only excepted, as are repugnant to the rights and privileges contained in this Charter; and that the inestimable right of trial by jury shall remain confirmed as a part of the law of this Colony, without repeal, forever.

XXIII. That every person, who shall be elected as aforesaid to be a member of the Legislative Council, or House of Assembly, shall, previous to his taking his seat in Council or Assembly, take the following oath or affirmation, viz:

> I, A. B., do solemnly declare, that, as a member of the Legislative Council, [or Assembly, as the case may be,] of the Colony of New-Jersey, I will not assent to any law, vote or proceeding, which shall appear to me injurious to the public welfare of said Colony, nor that shall annul or repeal that part of the third section in the Charter of this Colony, which establishes, that the elections of members of the Legislative Council and Assembly shall be annual; nor that part of the twenty-second section in said Charter, respecting the trial by jury, nor that shall annul, repeal or alter any part or parts of the eighteenth or nineteenth sections of the same.

And any person or persons, who shall be elected as aforesaid, is hereby empowered to administer to the said members the said oath or affirmation.

Provided always, and it is the true intent and meaning of this Congress, that if a reconciliation between Great-Britain and these Colonies should take place, and the latter be taken again under the protection and government of the crown of Britain, this Charter shall be null and void—otherwise to remain firm and inviolable.

In Provincial Congress, New Jersey,
Burlington, July 2, 1776
By order of Congress
Samuel Tucker, Pres.
William Paterson, Secretary

PENNSYLVANIA DECLARATION OF RIGHTS, 1776

Commentary

The first state to follow the example of Virginia (*supra* p. 234) was Pennsylvania. That state's Constitutional Convention met in July, 1776 and completed its work the next month. By then, the Virginia Declaration of Rights had been widely distributed. Samuel Adams, writing Richard Henry Lee from Philadelphia on July 15, sent thanks for a copy of "the Form of Govern't agreed upon by your Countrymen. I have not yet had time to peruse it, but dare say it will be a Feast to our little Circle." There is no doubt then that the Pennsylvania Constitution-makers had the Virginia Declaration before them as they wrote, and that they were strongly influenced by the Virginia example. The Pennsylvania Constitution, like the Virginia one, is prefaced by a Declaration of Rights which is similar in many respects to the Virginia model. Indeed, according to a 1779 statement by John Adams in his *Diary,* "The [Pennsylvania] Bill of Rights is taken almost verbatim from that of Virginia."

The Adams statement is somewhat unfair, though it is repeated by virtually all commentators. There is no doubt that the Pennsylvania Declaration was modelled upon the Virginia one. It is virtually a duplicate of the earlier Declaration in its statement of the natural rights of men (Article I) and criminal procedure (Article VIII), repeating the right to know the accusation, to confront witnesses, to call evidence, to a speedy public trial by jury, and the privilege against self-incrimination. But even here the Pennsylvania document adds the fundamental rights to counsel (the first provision for that right in a Bill of Rights). In addition, Article X deals with the right against searches and seizures in language somewhat different from that in the Virginia Declaration.

There are also provisions in the Pennsylvania Declaration that are new in organic documents. Article XIII declares the right of the people to bear arms (in language that anticipates the Second Amendment). The provision on religious freedom (Article II) is somewhat broader than that in the Virginia Declaration, moving in the direction of the future Establishment Clause, and forbidding religious tests, as well as exempting conscientious objectors from military service (Article VIII). There is also an express recognition of the right of the people to assemble and petition for redress of grievances (Article XVI) that was later to be included in the First Amendment.

Most important of all is Article XII of the Pennsylvania Declaration. For the first time in any constitutional enactment, it guarantees freedom of speech, as well as freedom of the press (being the direct precurser of perhaps the most significant guarantee of the federal Bill of Rights). Certainly the

262

inclusion of the freedom of speech in the list of fundamental rights guaranteed was a seminal step in the development that led to the federal Bill of Rights. We unfortunately do not know how freedom of speech came to be added to the Pennsylvania Declaration, but it is more than mere coincidence that (as John Adams tells us) Thomas Paine was one of the four principal makers of the Pennsylvania Constitution.

Two further points should be noted about the Pennsylvania Declaration of Rights. The first is that it did not cover the field so far as constitutional protection for individual rights was concerned. The body of the Constitution (entitled the Frame of Government, following the Penn 1683 precedent) adopted by the 1776 Pennsylvania Convention also contained provisions guaranteeing personal liberties—notably the right to trial by jury "as heretofore" (section 25), that to bail and against excessive fines (section 29), and virtual elimination of imprisonment for debt (section 28), and most religious tests (section 10). In addition, there was an interesting attempt to place fundamental liberties above even the amending process. Section 46 of the Constitution provided: "The declaration of rights is hereby declared to be a part of the constitution of this commonwealth, and ought never to be violated on any pretence whatever."

Pennsylvania Declaration of Rights, 1776*

Whereas all government ought to be instituted and supported for the security and protection of the community as such, and to enable the individuals who compose it to enjoy their natural rights, and the other blessings which the Author of existence has bestowed upon man; and whenever these great ends of government are not obtained, the people have a right, by common consent to change it, and take such measures as to them may appear necessary to promote their safety and happiness. And whereas the inhabitants of this commonwealth have in consideration of protection only, heretofore acknowledged allegiance to the king of Great Britain; and the said king has not only withdrawn that protection, but commenced, and still continues to carry on, with unabated vengeance, a most cruel and unjust war against them, employing therein, not only the troops of Great Britain, but foreign mercenaries, savages and slaves, for the avowed purpose of reducing them to a total and abject submission to the despotic domination of the British parliament, with many other acts of tyranny, (more fully set forth in the declaration of Congress) whereby all allegiance and fealty to the said king and his successors, are dissolved and at an end, and all power and authority derived from him ceased in these colonies. And whereas it is absolutely necessary for the welfare and safety of the inhabitants of said colonies, that they be

*Thorpe, *The Federal and State Constitutions, Colonial Charters, and Other Organic Laws* (1909), Vol. 5, pp. 3081–92.

henceforth free and independent States, and that just, permanent, and proper forms of government exist in every part of them, derived from and founded on the authority of the people only, agreeable to the directions of the honourable American Congress. We, the representatives of the freemen of Pennsylvania, in general convention met, for the express purpose of framing such a government, confessing the goodness of the great Governor of the universe (who alone knows to what degree of earthly happiness mankind may attain, by perfecting the arts of government) in permitting the people of this State, by common consent, and without violence, deliberately to form for themselves such just rules as they shall think best, for governing their future society; and being fully convinced, that it is our indispensable duty to establish such original principles of government, as will best promote the general happiness of the people of this State, and their posterity, and provide for future improvements, without partiality for, or prejudice against any particular class, sect, or denomination of men whatever, do, by virtue of the authority vested in use by our constituents, ordain, declare, and establish, the following Declaration of Rights and Frame of Government, to be the Constitution of this commonwealth, and to remain in force therein for ever, unaltered, except in such articles as shall hereafter on experience be found to require improvement, and which shall by the same authority of the people, fairly delegated as this frame of government directs, be amended or improved for the more effectual obtaining and securing the great end and design of all government, herein before mentioned.

A Declaration of the Rights of the Inhabitants of the Commonwealth, or State of Pennsylvania

I. That all men are born equally free and independent, and have certain natural, inherent and inalienable rights, amongst which are, the enjoying and defending life and liberty, acquiring, possessing and protecting property, and pursuing and obtaining happiness and safety.

II. That all men have a natural and unalienable right to worship Almighty God according to the dictates of their own consciences and understanding: And that no man ought or of right can be compelled to attend any religious worship, or erect or support any place of worship, or maintain any ministry, contrary to, or against, his own free will and consent: Nor can any man, who acknowledges the being of a God, be justly deprived or abridged of any civil right as a citizen, on account of his religious sentiments or peculiar mode of religious worship: And that no authority can or ought to be vested in, or assumed by any power whatever, that shall in any case interfere with, or in any manner controul, the right of conscience in the free exercise of religious worship.

III. That the people of this State have the sole, exclusive and inherent right of governing and regulating the internal police of the same.

IV. That all power being originally inherent in, and consequently derived from, the people; therefore all officers of government, whether legislative or executive, are their trustees and servants, and at all times accountable to them.

V. That government is, or ought to be, instituted for the common benefit, protection and security of the people, nation or community; and not for the particular emolument or advantage of any single man, family, or sett of men, who are a part only of that community; And that the community hath an indubitable, unalienable and indefeasible right to reform, alter, or abolish government in such manner as shall be by that community judged most conducive to the public weal.

VI. That those who are employed in the legislative and executive business of the State, may be restrained from oppression, the people have a right, at such periods as they may think proper, to reduce their public officers to a private station, and supply the vacancies by certain and regular elections.

VII. That all elections ought to be free; and that all free men having a sufficient evident common interest with, and attachment to the community, have a right to elect officers, or to be elected into office.

VIII. That every member of society hath a right to be protected in the enjoyment of life, liberty and property, and therefore is bound to contribute his proportion towards the expence of that protection, and yield his personal service when necessary, or an equivalent thereto: But no part of a man's property can be justly taken from him, or applied to public uses, without his own consent, or that of his legal representatives: Nor can any man who is conscientiously scrupulous of bearing arms, be justly compelled thereto, if he will pay such equivalent, nor are the people bound by any laws, but such as they have in like manner assented to, for their common good.

IX. That in all prosecutions for criminal offences, a man hath a right to be heard by himself and his council, to demand the cause and nature of his accusation, to be confronted with the witnesses, to call for evidence in his favour, and a speedy public trial, by an impartial jury of the country, without the unanimous consent of which jury he cannot be found guilty; nor can he be compelled to give evidence against himself; nor can any man be justly deprived of his liberty except by the laws of the land, or the judgment, of his peers.

X. That the people have a right to hold themselves, their houses, papers, and possessions free from search and seizure, and therefore warrants without oaths or affirmations first made, affording a sufficient foundation for them, and whereby any officer or messenger may be commanded or required to search suspected places, or to seize any person or persons, his or their property, not particularly described, are contrary to that right, and ought not to be granted.

XI. That in controversies respecting property, and in suits between man and man, the parties have a right to trial by jury, which ought to be held sacred.

XII. That the people have a right to freedom of speech, and of writing, and publishing their sentiments: therefore the freedom of the press ought not to be restrained.

XIII. That the people have a right to bear arms for the defence of themselves and the state; and as standing armies in the time of peace are dangerous to liberty, they ought not to be kept up; And that the military should be kept under strict subordination to, and governed by, the civil power.

XIV. That a frequent recurrence to fundamental principles, and a firm adherence to justice, moderation, temperance, industry, and frugality are absolutely necessary to preserve the blessings of liberty, and keep a government free: The people ought therefore to pay particular attention to these points in the choice of officers and representatives, and have a right to exact a due and constant regard to them, from their legislatures and magistrates, in the making and executing such laws as are necessary for the good government of the state.

XV. That all men have a natural inherent right to emigrate from one state to another that will receive them, or to form a new state in vacant countries, or in such countries as they can purchase, whenever they think that thereby they may promote their own happiness.

XVI. That the people have a right to assemble together, to consult for their common good, to instruct their representatives, and to apply to the legislature for redress of grievances, by address, petition, or remonstrance.

Plan or Frame of Government for Commonwealth or State of Pennsylvania

Section 1. The commonwealth or state of Pennsylvania shall be governed hereafter by an assembly of the representatives of the freemen of the same, and a president and council, in manner and form following—

Sect. 2. The supreme legislative power shall be vested in a house of representatives of the freemen of the commonwealth or state of Pennsylvania.

Sect. 3. The supreme executive power shall be vested in a president and council.

Sect. 4. Courts of justice shall be established in the city of Philadelphia, and in every county of this state.

Sect. 5. The freemen of this commonwealth and their sons shall be trained and armed for its defence under such regulations, restrictions, and exceptions as the general assembly shall by law direct, preserving always to the people the right of choosing their colonels and all commissioned officers under that rank, in such manner and as often as by the said laws shall be directed.

Sect. 6. Every freemen of the full age of twenty-one years, having resided in this state for the space of one whole year next before the day of election for representatives, and paid public taxes during that time, shall enjoy the right of an elector: Provided always, that sons of freeholders of the age of twenty-one years shall be intitled to vote although they have not paid taxes.

Sect. 7. The house of representatives of the freemen of this commonwealth shall consist of persons most noted for wisdom and virtue, to be chosen by the freemen of every city and county of this commonwealth respectively. And no person shall be elected unless he has resided in the city or county for which he shall be chosen two years immediately before the said election; nor shall any member, while he continues such, hold any other office, except in the militia.

Sect. 8. No person shall be capable of being elected a member to serve in the house of representatives of the freemen of this commonwealth more than four years in seven.

Sect. 9. The members of the house of representatives shall be chosen annually by ballot, by the freemen of the commonwealth, on the second Tuesday in October forever, (except this present year.) and shall meet on the fourth Monday of the same month, and shall be stiled, The general assembly of the representatives of the freemen of Pennsylvania, and shall have power to choose their speaker, the treasurer of the state, and their other officers; sit on their own adjournments; prepare bills and enact them into laws; judge of the elections and qualifications of their own members; they may expel a member, but not a second time for the same cause; they may administer oaths or affirmations on examination of witnesses; redress grievances; impeach state criminals; grant charters of incorporation; constitute towns, boroughs, cities, and counties; and shall have all other powers necessary for the legislature of a free state or commonwealth: But they shall have no power to add to, alter, abolish, or infringe any part of this constitution.

Sect. 10. A quorum of the house of representatives shall consist of two-thirds of the whole number of members elected; and having met and chosen their speaker, shall each of them before they proceed to business take and subscribe, as well the oath or affirmation of fidelity and allegiance hereinafter directed, as the following oath or affirmation, viz:

> I ——— do swear (or affirm) that as a member of this assembly, I will not propose or assent to any bill, vote, or resolution, which shall appear to me injurious to the people; nor do or consent to any act or thing whatever, that shall have a tendency to lessen or abridge their rights and privileges, as declared in the constitution of this state; but will in all things conduct myself as a faithful honest representative and guardian of the people, according to the best of my judgment and abilities.

And each member, before he takes his seat, shall make and subscribe the following declaration, viz:

> I do believe in one God, the creator and governor of the universe, the rewarder of the good and the punisher of the wicked. And I do acknowledge the Scriptures of the Old and New Testament to be given by Divine inspiration.

And no further or other religious test shall ever hereafter be required of **any** civil officer or magistrate in this State.

Sect. 11. Delegates to represent this state in congress shall be chosen by ballot by the future general assembly at their first meeting, and annually forever afterwards, as long as such representation shall be necessary. Any delegate may be superseded at any time, by the general assembly appointing another in his stead. No man shall sit in congress longer than two years successively, nor be capable of re-election for three years afterwards: and no person who holds any office in the gift of the congress shall hereafter be elected to represent this commonwealth in congress.

Sect. 12. If any city or cities, county or counties shall neglect or refuse to elect and send representatives to the general assembly, two-thirds of the members from the cities or counties that do elect and send representatives, provided they be a majority of the cities and counties of the whole state, when met, shall have all the powers of the general assembly, as fully and amply as if the whole were present.

Sect. 13. The doors of the house in which the representatives of the freemen of this state shall sit in general assembly, shall be and remain open for the admission of all persons who behave decently, except only when the welfare of this state may require the doors to be shut.

Sect. 14. The votes and proceedings of the general assembly shall be printed weekly during their sitting, with the yeas and nays, on any question, vote or resolution, where any two members require it, except when the vote is taken by ballot; and when the yeas and nays are so taken every member shall have a right to insert the reasons of his vote upon the minutes, if he desires it.

Sect. 15. To the end that laws before they are enacted may be more maturely considered, and the inconvenience of hasty determinations as much as possible prevented, all bills of public nature shall be printed for the consideration of the people, before they are read in general assembly the last time for debate and amendment; and, except on occasions of sudden necessity, shall not be passed into laws until the next session of assembly; and for the more perfect satisfaction of the public, the reasons and motives for making such laws shall be fully and clearly expressed in the preambles.

Sect. 16. The stile of the laws of this commonwealth shall be, "Be it enacted, and it is hereby enacted by the representatives of the freemen of the commonwealth of Pennsylvania in general assembly met, and by the authority of the same." And the general assembly shall affix their seal to every bill, as soon as it is enacted into a law, which seal shall be kept by the assembly, and shall be called, The seal of the laws of Pennsylvania, and shall not be used for any other purpose.

Sect. 17. The city of Philadelphia and each county of this commonwealth respectively, shall on the first Tuesday of November in this present year, and on the second Tuesday of October annually for the two next succeeding years, viz. the year one thousand seven hundred and seventy-seven, and the year one thousand seven hundred and seventy-eight, choose six persons to represent them in general assembly. But as representation in proportion to the number of taxable inhabitants is the only principle which can at all times secure liberty, and make the voice of a majority of the people the law of the land; therefore the general assembly shall cause complete lists of the taxable inhabitants in the city and each county in the commonwealth respectively, to be taken and returned to them, on or before the last meeting of the assembly elected in the year one thousand seven hundred and seventy-eight, who shall appoint a representation to each, in proportion to the number of taxables in such returns; which representation shall continue for the next seven years afterwards at the end of which, a new return of the taxable inhabitants shall be made, and a representation agreeable thereto appointed by the said assembly, and so on septennially forever. The wages of the representatives in general assembly, and all other state charges shall be paid out of the state treasury.

Sect. 18. In order that the freemen of this commonwealth may enjoy the benefit of election as equally as may be until the representation shall commence, as directed in the foregoing section, each county at its own choice may be divided into districts, hold elections therein, and elect their representatives in the county, and their other elective officers, as shall be hereafter regulated by the general assembly of this state. And no inhabitant of this state shall have more than one annual vote at the general election for representatives in assembly.

Sect. 19. For the present the supreme executive council of this state shall consist of twelve persons chosen in the following manner: The freemen of the city of Philadelphia, and of the counties of Philadelphia, Chester, and Bucks, respectively, shall choose by ballot one person for the city, and one for each county aforesaid, to serve for three years and no longer, at the time and place for electing representatives in general assembly. The freemen of the counties of Lancaster, York, Cumberland, and Berks, shall, in like manner elect one person for each county respectively, to serve as counsellors for two years and no longer. And the counties of Northampton, Bedford, Northumberland and Westmoreland, respectively, shall, in like manner, elect one person for each county, to serve as counsellors for one year, and no longer. And at the expiration of the time for which each counsellor was chosen to serve, the freemen of the city of Philadelphia, and of the several counties in this state, respectively, shall elect one person to serve as counsellor for three years and no longer; and so on every third year forever. By this mode of election and continual rotation, more men will be trained to public business, there will in every subsequent year be found in the council a number of persons acquainted with the proceedings of the foregoing years, whereby the business will be more consistently conducted, and moreover the danger of establishing an inconvenient aristocracy will be effectually prevented. All vacancies in the council that may happen by death, resignation, or otherwise, shall be filled at the next general election for representatives in general assembly, unless a particular election for that purpose shall be sooner appointed by the president and council. No member of the general assembly or delegate in congress, shall be chosen a member of the council. The president and vice-president shall be chosen annually by the joint ballot of the general assembly and council, of the member of the council. Any person having served as a counsellor for three successive years, shall be incapable of holding that office for four years afterwards. Every member of the council shall be a justice of the peace for the whole commonwealth, by virtue of his office.

In case new additional counties shall hereafter be erected in this state, such county or counties shall elect a counsellor, and such county or counties shall be annexed to the next neighbouring counties, and shall take rotation with such counties.

The council shall meet annually, at the same time and place with the general assembly.

The treasurer of the state, trustees of the loan office, naval officers, collectors of customs or excise, judge of the admirality, attornies general, sheriffs, and prothonotaries, shall not be capable of a seat in the general assembly, executive council, or continental congress.

Sec. 20. The president, and in his absence the vice-president, with the council, five of whom shall be a quorum, shall have power to appoint and commissionate judges, naval officers, judge of the admiralty, attorney general and all other officers, civil and military, except such as are chosen by the general assembly or the people, agreeable to this frame of government, and the laws that may be made hereafter; and shall supply every vacancy in any office, occasioned by death, resignation, removal or disqualification, until the office can be filled in the time and manner directed by law or this constitution. They are to correspond with other states, and transact business with the officers of government, civil and military; and to prepare such business as may appear to them necessary to lay before the general assembly. They shall sit as judges, to hear and determine on impeachments, taking to their assistance for advice only, the justices of the supreme court. And shall have power to grant pardons, and remit fines, in all cases whatsoever, except in cases of impeachment; and in cases of treason and murder, shall have power to grant reprieves, but not to pardon, until the end of the next sessions of assembly; but there shall be no remission or mitigation of punishments on impeachments, except by act of the legislature; they are also to take care that the laws be faithfully executed; they are to expedite the execution of such measures as may be resolved upon by the general assembly; and they may draw upon the treasury for such sums as shall be appropriated by the house: They may also lay embargoes, or prohibit the exportation of any commodity, for any time, not exceeding thirty days, in the recess of the house only: They may grant such licences, as shall be directed by law, and shall have power to call together the general assembly when necessary, before the day to which they shall stand adjourned. The president shall be commander in chief of the forces of the state, but shall not command in person, except advised thereto by the council, and then only so long as they shall approve thereof. The president and council shall have a secretary, and keep fair books of their proceedings, wherein any counsellor may enter his dissent, with his reasons in support of it.

Sect. 21. All commissions shall be in the name, and by the authority of the freemen of the commonwealth of Pennsylvania, sealed with the state seal, signed by the president or vice-president, and attested by the secretary; which seal shall be kept by the council.

Sect. 22. Every officer of state, whether judicial or executive, shall be liable to be impeached by the general assembly, either when in office, or after his resignation or removal for mal-administrations. All impeachments shall be before the president or vice-president and council, who shall hear and determine the same.

Sect. 23. The judges of the supreme court of judicature shall have fixed salaries, be commissioned for seven years only, though capable of re-appointment at the end of that term, but removable for misbehaviour at any time by the general assembly; they shall not be allowed to sit as members in the continental congress, executive council, or general assembly, nor to hold any other office civil or military, nor to take or receive fees or perquisites of any kind.

Sect. 24. The supreme court, and the several courts of common pleas of this commonwealth, shall, besides the powers usually exercised by such courts, have the powers of a court of chancery, so far as relates to the perpetuating testimony, obtaining evidence from places not within this state, and the care of the persons and estates of those who are *non compotes mentis,* and such other powers as may be found necessary by future general assemblies, not inconsistent with this constitution.

Sect. 25. Trials shall be by jury as heretofore: And it is recommended to the legislature of this state, to provide by law against every corruption or partiality in the choice, return, or appointment of juries.

Sect. 26. Courts of sessions, common pleas, and orphans courts shall be held quarterly in each city and county; and the legislature shall have power to establish all such other courts as they may judge for the good of the inhabitants of the state. All courts shall be open, and justice shall be impartially administered without corruption or unnecessary delay: All their officers shall be paid an adequate but moderate compensation for their services: And if any officer shall take greater or other fees than the law allows him, either directly or indirectly, it shall ever after disqualify him from holding any office in this state.

Sect. 27. All prosecutions shall commence in the name and by the authority of the freemen of the commonwealth of Pennsylvania; and all indictments shall conclude with these words, "Against the peace and dignity of the same." The style of all process hereafter in this state shall be, The commonwealth of Pennsylvania.

Sect. 28. The person of a debtor, where there is not a strong presumption of fraud, shall not be continued in prison, after delivering up, *bona fide*, all his estate real and personal, for the use of his creditors, in such manner as shall be hereafter regulated by law. All prisoners shall be bailable by sufficient sureties, unless for captial offences, when the proof is evident, or presumption great.

Sect. 29. Excessive bail shall not be exacted for bailable offences: And all fines shall be moderate.

Sect. 30. Justices of the peace shall be elected by the freeholders of each city and county respectively, that is to say, two or more persons may be chosen for each ward, township, or district, as the law shall hereafter direct: And their names shall be returned to the president in council, who shall commissionate one or more of them for each ward, township, or district so returning, for seven years, removable for misconduct by the general assembly. But if any city or county, ward, township, or district in this commonwealth, shall hereafter incline to change the manner of appointing their justices of the peace as settled in this article, the general assembly may make laws to regulate the same, agreeable to the desire of a majority of the freeholders of the city or county, ward, township, or district so applying. No justice of the peace shall sit in the general assembly unless he first resigns his commission; nor shall he be allowed to take any fees, nor any salary or allowance, except such as the future legislature may grant.

Sect. 31. Sheriffs and coroners shall be elected annually in each city and county, by the freemen; that is to say, two persons for each office, one of whom for each, is to be commissioned by the president in council. No person shall continue in the office of sheriff more than three successive years, or be capable of being again elected during four years afterwards. The election shall be held at the same time and place appointed for the election of representatives: And the commissioners and assessors, and other officers chosen by the people, shall also be then and there elected, as has been usual heretofore, until altered or otherwise regulated by the future legislature of this state.

Sect. 32. All elections, whether by the people or in general assembly, shall be by ballot, free and voluntary: And any elector, who shall receive any gift or reward for his vote, in meat, drink, monies, or otherwise, shall forfeit his right to elect for that time, and suffer such other penalties as future laws shall direct. And any person who shall directly or indirectly give, promise, or bestow any such rewards to be elected, shall be thereby rendered incapable to serve for the ensuing year.

Sect. 33. All fees, licence money, fines and forfeitures heretofore granted, or paid to the governor, or his deputies for the support of government, shall hereafter be paid into the public treasury, unless altered or abolished by the future legislature.

Sect. 34. A register's office for the probate of wills and granting letters of administration, and an office for the recording of deeds, shall be kept in each city and county: The officers to be appointed by the general assembly, removable at their pleasure, and to be commissioned by the president in council.

Sect. 35. The printing presses shall be free to every person who undertakes to examine the proceedings of the legislature, or any part of government.

Sect. 36. As every freeman to preserve his independence, (if without a sufficient estate) ought to have some profession, calling, trade or farm, whereby he may honestly subsist, there can be no necessity for, nor use in establishing offices of profit, the usual effects of which are dependence and servility unbecoming freemen, in the possessors and expectants; faction, contention, corruption, and disorder among the people. But if any man is called into public service, to the prejudice of his private affairs, he has a right to a reasonable compensation: And whenever an office, through increase of fees or otherwise, becomes so profitable as to occasion many to apply for it, the profits ought to be lessened by the legislature.

Sect. 37. The future legislature of this state, shall regulate intails in such a manner as to prevent perpetuities.

Sect. 38. The penal laws as heretofore used shall be reformed by the legislature of this state, as soon as may be, and punishments made in some cases less sanguinary, and in general more proportionate to the crimes.

Sect. 39. To deter more effectually from the commission of crimes, by continued visible punishments of long duration, and to make sanguinary punishments less necessary; houses ought to be provided for punishing by hard labour, those who shall be convicted of crimes not capital; wherein the criminals shall be imployed for the benefit of the public, or for reparation of injuries done to private persons: And all persons at proper times shall be admitted to see the prisoners at their labour.

Sect. 40. Every officer, whether judicial, executive or military, in authority under this commonwealth, shall take the following oath or affirmation of allegiance, and general oath of office before he enters on the execution of his office.

The Oath or Affirmation of Allegiance

> I——do swear (or affirm) that I will be true and faithful to the commonwealth of Pennsylvania: And that I will not directly or indirectly do any act or thing prejudicial or injurious to the constitution or government thereof, as established by the convention.

The Oath or Affirmation of Office

> I——do swear (or affirm) that I will faithfully execute the office of——for the——of——and will do equal right and justice to all men, to the best of my judgment and abilities, according to law.

Sect. 41. No public tax, custom or contribution shall be imposed upon, or paid by the people of this state, except by a law for that purpose: And before any law be made for raising it, the purpose for which any tax is to be raised ought to appear clearly to the legislature to be of more service to the community than the money would be, if not collected; which being well observed, taxes can never be burthens.

Sect. 42. Every foreigner of good character who comes to settle in this state, having first taken an oath or affirmation of allegiance to the same, may purchase, or by other just means acquire, hold, and transfer land or other real estate; and after one year's residence, shall be deemed a free denizen thereof, and entitled to all the rights of a natural born subject of this state, except that he shall not be capable of being elected a representative until after two years residence.

Sect. 43. The inhabitants of this state shall have liberty to fowl and hunt in seasonable times on the lands they hold, and on all other lands therein not inclosed; and in like manner to fish in all boatable waters, and others not private property.

Sect. 44. A school or schools shall be established in each county by the legislature, for the convenient instruction of youth, with such salaries to the masters paid by the public, as may enable them to instruct youth at low prices: And all useful learning shall be duly encouraged and promoted in one or more universities.

Sect. 45. Laws for the encouragement of virtue, and prevention of vice and immorality, shall be made and constantly kept in force, and provision shall be made for their due execution: And all religious societies or bodies of men heretofore united or incorporated for the advancement of religion or learning, or for other pious and charitable purposes, shall be encouraged and protected in the enjoyment of the privileges, immunities and estates which they were accustomed to enjoy, or could of right have enjoyed, under the laws and former constitution of this state.

Sect. 46. The declaration of rights is hereby declared to be a part of the constitution of this commonwealth, and ought never to be violated on any pretence whatever.

Sect. 47. In order that the freedom of the commonwealth may be preserved inviolate forever, there shall be chosen by ballot by the freemen in each city and county respectively, on the second Tuesday in October, in the year one thousand seven hundred and eighty-three, and on the second Tuesday in October, in every seventh year thereafter, two persons in each city and county of this state, to be called the Council of Censors; who shall meet together on the second Monday of November next ensuing their election; the majority of whom shall be a quorum in every case, except as to calling a convention, in which two-thirds of the whole number elected shall agree: And whose duty it shall be to enquire whether the constitution has been preserved inviolate in every part; and whether the legislative and executive branches of government have performed their duty as guardians of the people, or assumed to themselves, or exercised other or greater powers than they are intitled to by the constitution: They are also to enquire whether the public taxes have been justly laid and collected in all parts of this commonwealth, in what manner the public monies have been disposed of, and whether the laws have been duly executed. For these purposes they shall have power to send for persons, papers, and records; they shall have authority to pass public censures, to order impeachments, and to recommend to the legislature the repealing such laws as appear to them to have been enacted contrary to the principles of the constitution. These powers they shall continue to have, for and during the space of one year from the day of their election and no longer: The said council of censors shall also have power to call a convention, to meet within two years after their sitting, if there appear to them an absolute necessity of amending any article of the constitution which may be defective, explaining such as may be thought not clearly expressed, and of adding such as are necessary for the preservation of the rights and happiness of the people: But the articles to be amended, and the amendments proposed, and such articles as are proposed to be added or abolished, shall be promulgated at least six months before the day appointed for the election of such convention, for the previous consideration of the people, that they may have an opportunity of instructing their delegates on the subject.

Passed in Convention the 28th day of September, 1776, and signed by their order.

Benj. Franklin, Prest.

DELAWARE DECLARATION OF RIGHTS, 1776

Commentary

The next state to adopt a Bill of Rights as part of its Constitution was Delaware which acted through a Convention which met on August 27, 1776. The Convention adopted a Declaration of Rights on September 11 and a Constitution on September 20. The Delaware Declaration was plainly drafted with the Pennsylvania and Virginia Declarations of Rights as examples. In addition, the Delaware delegates had available the draft of the Declaration of Rights prepared in August by a committee in the adjoining State of Maryland (though the Maryland Declaration was not formally adopted until almost two months after the Delaware document). According to a September 17, 1776 letter of George Read (Chairman of the committee which drew up the Delaware Declaration), "the Declaration of Rights . . . has been completed somedays past but there being nothing particularly in it—I did not think it an object of much curiosity, it is made out of the Pensilvania & Maryland Draughts."

The Delaware Declaration was, as Read states, based upon the prior work of the Pennsylvania and Virginia Conventions, as well as the Maryland draft to which reference has been made. Among the fundamental rights protected by the earlier documents which are guaranteed in the Delaware Declaration are the rights of petition, to protection for life, liberty, and property, trial by jury, to be informed of the accusation and confrontation, counsel, speedy trial, those against self-incrimination, excessive bail and fines, cruel and unusual punishments, and searches and seizures under general warrants, as well as freedom of the press.

But the Delaware Declaration also was the first constitutional document to contain a prohibition against quartering of soldiers, as well as against retrospective legislation. (Though a proposal for a similar prohibition had been considered by the Virginia Convention, it had been defeated largely because of the opposition of Patrick Henry, who, as Edmund Randolph tells us, [*supra* p. 249] drew "a terrifying picture of some towering public offender, against whom ordinary laws would be impotent.") The Delaware provision in section 11 was the antecedent of the Ex Post Facto Clauses of Article I, sections 9 and 10 of the federal Constitution as well as of similar prohibitions in later state Bills of Rights.

Delaware Declaration of Rights, 1776*

A Declaration of Rights and Fundamental Rules of the Delaware State, formerly stiled, The Government of the counties of New-Castle, Kent and Sussex, upon Delaware.

*Laws of the State of Delaware, 1700–1797 (1797), Vol. 1, appendix, pp. 79–81.

Section 1. That all government of right originates from the people, is founded in compact only, and instituted solely for the good of the whole.

Sect. 2. That all men have a natural and unalienable right to worship Almighty God according to the dictates of their own consciences and under-standings; and that no man ought or of right can be compelled to attend any religious worship or maintain any ministry contrary to or against his own free will and consent, and that no authority can or ought to be vested in, or assumed by any power whatever that shall in any case interfere with, or in any manner controul the right of conscience in the free exercise of religious worship.

Sect. 3. That all persons professing the Christian religion ought forever to enjoy equal rights and privileges in this state, unless under colour of religion, any man distrub the peace, the happiness or safety of society.

Sect. 4. That people of this state have the sole exclusive and inherent right of governing and regulating the internal police of the same.

Sect. 5. That persons intrusted with the Legislative and Executive Powers are the Trustees and Servants of the public, and as such accountable for their conduct; wherefore whenever the ends of government are perverted, and public liberty manifestly endangered by the Legislative singly, or a treacherous combination of both, the people may, and of right ought to establish a new, or reform the old government.

Sect. 6. That the right in the people to participate in the Legislature, is the foundation of liberty and of all free government, and for this end all elections ought to be free and frequent, and every freeman, having sufficient evidence of a permanent common interest with, and attachment to the community, hath a right of suffrage.

Sect. 7. That no power of suspending laws, or the execution of laws, ought to be exercised unless by the Legislature.

Sect. 8. That for redress of grievances, and for amending and strengthening of the laws, the Legislature ought to be frequently convened.

Sect. 9. That every man hath a right to petition the Legislature for the redress of grievances in a peaceable and orderly manner.

Sect. 10. That every member of society hath a right to be protected in the enjoyment of life, liberty and property, and therefore is bound to contribute his proportion towards the expense of that protection, and yield his personal service when necessary, or an equivalent thereto; but no part of a man's property can be justly taken from him or applied to public uses without his own consent or that of his legal Representatives: Nor can any man that is conscientiously scrupulous of bearing arms in any case be justly compelled thereto if he will pay such equivalent.

Sect. 11. That retrospective laws, punishing offences committed before the existence of such laws, are oppressive and unjust, and ought not to be made.

Sect. 12. That every freeman for every injury done him in his goods, lands or person, by any other person, ought to have remedy by the course of the law of the land and ought to have justice and right for the injury done to him freely without sale, fully without any denial, and speedily without delay, according to the law of the land.

Sect. 13. That trial by jury of facts where they arise is one of the greatest securities of the lives, liberties and estates of the people.

Sect. 14. That in all prosecutions for criminal offences, every man hath a right to be informed of the accusation against him, to be allowed counsel, to be confronted with the accusers or witnesses, to examine evidence on oath in his favour, and to a speedy trial by an impartial jury, without whose unanimous consent he ought not to be found guilty.

Sect. 15. That no man in the Courts of Common Law ought to be compelled to give evidence against himself.

Sect. 16. That excessive bail ought not to be required, nor excessive fines imposed, nor cruel or unusual punishments inflicted.

Sect. 17. That all warrants without oath to search suspected places, or to seize any person or his property, are grievous and oppressive; and all general warrants to search suspected places, or to apprehend all persons suspected, without naming or describing the place or any person in special, are illegal and ought not to be granted.

Sect. 18. That a well regulated militia is the proper, natural and safe defence of a free government.

Sect. 19. That standing armies are dangerous to liberty, and ought not to be raised or kept up without the consent of the Legislature.

Sect. 20. That in all cases and at all times the military ought to be under strict subordination to and governed by the civil power.

Sect. 21. That no soldier ought to be quartered in any house in time of peace without the consent of the owner; and in time of war in such manner only as the Legislature shall direct.

Sect. 22. That the independency and uprightness of judges are essential to the impartial administration of justice, and a great security to the rights and liberties of the people.

Sect. 23. That the liberty of the press ought to be inviolably preserved.

MARYLAND DECLARATION OF RIGHTS, 1776

Commentary

As already stated, the Maryland Declaration of Rights was actually drafted in August, 1776, though it was not approved by the Maryland Convention until November 3, 1776. The Maryland Declaration was drafted by a seven-man committee appointed on motion of Samuel Chase (later a controversial Supreme Court Justice), which included Chase himself, and five other prominent lawyers among its members. The committee reported a draft on August 10. It was debated extensively in October. The delegates indicated that they well understood (in the words of one of them) that "establishing a Bill of Rights" was a matter "of the utmost importance to the good people of this State, and their posterity." When the debate on the new Declaration went slowly, the delegates agreed to remain in session "while that business is transacting, every evening till eight o'clock," and the Declaration was finally approved in a Sunday session, on November 3.

The Maryland Declaration of Rights was much more detailed than its predecessors, containing 42 articles. Most of them repeat provisions contained in earlier state Declarations (though usually with variations in language), including guarantees of trial by jury, freedom of speech (though confined only to legislative proceedings), the right of petition, that against cruel and unusual punishment, ex post facto laws (containing the first constitutional use of the term—the original draft of this provision, Article XV, antedated and probably influenced the Delaware prohibition, *supra* p. 276), the right to accusation and indictment or charge, counsel, confrontation, witnesses, and to a speedy trial, protection of life, liberty, and property (not to be deprived of same "but by the judgment of his peers, or by the law of the land"), that against excessive bail and fines, searches on oathless warrants or general warrants, and quartering of soldiers, as well as freedom of conscience and freedom of the press.

The most significant innovation made in the Maryland Declaration was the inclusion of an express prohibition against bills of attainder (Article XVI). This was apparently the first such constitutional prohibition and was the forerunner of the Bill of Attainder Clauses of Article I, sections 9 and 10 of the federal Constitution. The Maryland provision was most liberal for its time. Bills of attainder were principal weapons against the Tories during the Revolutionary period and the Maryland Convention deserves all the more credit for outlawing them when it did, rather than postpone it to a time when (as Charles Carroll of Carrollton wrote) "there is greater certainty than we have at present, of possessing a country & People to govern."

Maryland Declaration of Rights, 1776*

A Declaration of Rights, and the Constitution and Form of Government agreed to by the Delegates of Maryland, in free and full Convention assembled.

The parliament of Great Britain, by a declaratory act, having assumed a right to make laws to bind the Colonies in all cases whatsoever, and, in pursuance of such claim, endeavoured, by force of arms, to subjugate the United Colonies to an unconditional submission to their will and power, and having at length constrained them to declare themselves independent States, and to assume government under the authority of the people;—Therefore we, the Delegates of Maryland, in free and full Convention assembled, taking into our most serious consideration the best means of establishing a good Constitution in this State, for the sure foundation and more permanent security thereof, declare,

I. That all government of right originates from the people, is founded in compact only, and instituted solely for the good of the whole.

II. That the people of this State ought to have the sole and exclusive right of regulating the internal government and police thereof.

III. That the inhabitants of Maryland are entitled to the common law of England, and the trial by jury, according to the course of that law, and to the benefit of such of the English statutes, as existed at the time of their first emigration, and which, by experience, have been found applicable to their local and other circumstances, and of such others as have been since made in England, or Great Britain, and have been introduced, used and practised by the courts of law or equity; and also to acts of Assembly, in force on the first of June seventeen hundred and seventy-four, except such as may have since expired, or have been or may be altered by acts of Convention, or this Declaration of Rights—subject, nevertheless, to the revision of, and amendment or repeal by, the Legislature of this State: and the inhabitants of Maryland are also entitled to all property, derived to them, from or under the Charter, granted by his Majesty Charles I. to Caecilius Calvert, Baron of Baltimore.

IV. That all persons invested with the legislative or executive powers of government are the trustees of the public, and, as such, accountable for their conduct; wherefore, whenever the ends of government are perverted, and public liberty manifestly endangered, and all other means of redress are ineffectual, the people may, and of right ought, to reform the old or establish a new government. The doctrine of non-resistance, against arbitrary power and oppression, is absurd, slavish, and destructive of the good and happiness of mankind.

*Thorpe, *The Federal and State Constitutions, Colonial Charters, and Other Organic Laws*, Vol. 3, pp. 1686–91.

V. That the right in the people to participate in the Legislature is the best security of liberty, and the foundation of all free government; for this purpose, elections ought to be free and frequent, and every man, having property in, a common interest with, and an attachment to the community, ought to have a right of suffrage.

VI. That the legislative, executive and judicial powers of government, ought to be forever separate and distinct from each other.

VII. That no power of suspending laws, or the execution of laws, unless by or derived from the Legislature, ought to be exercised or allowed.

VIII. That freedom of speech and debates, or proceedings in the Legislature, ought not to be impeached in any other court or judicature.

IX. That a place for the meeting of the Legislature ought to be fixed, the most convenient to the members thereof, and to the depository of public records; and the Legislature ought not to be convened or held at any other place, but from evident necessity.

X. That, for redress of grievances, and for amending, strengthening and preserving the laws, the Legislature ought to be frequently convened.

XI. That every man hath a right to petition the Legislature, for the redress of grievances, in a peaceable and orderly manner.

XII. That no aid, charge, tax, fee, or fees, ought to be set, rated, or levied, under any pretence, without consent of the Legislature.

XIII. That the levying taxes by the poll is grievous and oppressive, and ought to be abolished; that paupers ought not to be assessed for the support of government; but every other person in the State ought to contribute his proportion of public taxes, for the support of government, according to his actual worth, in real or personal property, within the State; yet fines, duties, or taxes, may properly and justly be imposed or laid, with a political view, for the good government and benefit of the community.

XIV. That sanguinary laws ought to be avoided, as far as is consistent with the safety of the State: and no law, to inflict cruel and unusual pains and penalties, ought to be made in any case, or at any time hereafter.

XV. That retrospective laws, punishing facts committed before the existence of such laws, and by them only declared criminal, are oppressive, unjust, and incompatible with liberty; wherefore no *ex post facto* law ought to be made.

XVI. That no law, to attaint particular persons of treason or felony, ought to be made in any case, or at any time hereafter.

XVII. That every freeman, for any injury done him in his person or property, ought to have remedy, by the course of the law of the land, and ought to have justice and right freely without sale, fully without any denial, and speedily without delay, according to the law of the land.

XVIII. That the trial of facts where they arise, is one of the greatest securities of the lives, liberties and estates of the people.

XIX. That, in all criminal prosecutions, every man hath a right to be informed of the accusation against him; to have a copy of the indictment or charge in due time (if required) to prepare for his defence; to be allowed counsel; to be confronted with the witnesses against him; to have process for his witnesses; to examine the witnesses, for and against him, on oath; and to a speedy trial by an impartial jury, without whose unanimous consent he ought not to be found guilty.

XX. That no man ought to be compelled to give evidence against himself, in a common court of law, or in any other court, but in such cases as have been usually practised in this State, or may hereafter be directed by the Legislature.

XXI. That no freeman ought to be taken, or imprisoned, or disseized of his freehold, liberties, or privileges, or outlawed, or exiled, or in any manner destroyed, or deprived of his life, liberty, or property, but by the judgment of his peers, or by the law of the land.

XXII. That excessive bail ought not be be required, nor excessive fines imposed, nor cruel or unusual punishments inflicted; by the courts of law.

XXIII. That all warrants, without oath or affirmation, to search suspected places, or to seize any person or property, are grievous and oppressive; and all general warrants—to search suspected places, or to apprehend suspected persons, without naming or describing the place, or the person in special— are illegal, and ought not to be granted.

XXIV. That there ought to be no forfeiture of any part of the estate of any person, for any crime except murder, or treason against the State, and then only on conviction and attainder.

XXV. That a well-regulated militia is the proper and natural defence of a free government.

XXVI. That standing armies are dangerous to liberty, and ought not to be raised or kept up, without consent of the Legislature.

XXVII. That in all cases, and at all times, the military ought to be under strict subordination to and control of the civil power.

XXVIII. That no soldier ought to be quartered in any house, in time of peace, without the consent of the owner; and in time of war, in such manner only, as the Legislature shall direct.

XXIX. That no person, except regular soldiers, mariners, and marines in the service of this State, or militia when in actual service, ought in any case to be subject to or punishable by martial law.

XXX. That the independency and uprightness of Judges are essential to the impartial administration of justice, and a great security to the rights and liberties of the people; wherefore the Chancellor and Judges ought to hold commissions during good behaviour; and the said Chancellor and Judges shall be removed for misbehaviour, on conviction in a court of law, and may be removed by the Governor, upon the address of the General Assembly; Provided, That two-thirds of all the members of each House concur in such address. That salaries, liberal, but not profuse, ought to be secured to the Chancellor and the Judges, during the continuance of their commissions, in such manner, and at such times, as the Legislature shall hereafter direct, upon consideration of the circumstances of this State. No Chancellor or Judge ought to hold any other office, civil or military, or receive fees or perquisites of any kind.

XXXI. That a long continuance, in the first executive departments of power or trust, is dangerous to liberty; a rotation, therefore, in those departments, is one of the best securities of permanent freedom.

XXXII. That no person ought to hold, at the same time, more than one office of profit, nor ought any person, in public trust, to receive any present from any foreign prince or state, or from the United States, or any of them, without the approbation of this State.

XXXIII. That, as it is the duty of every man to worship God in such manner as he thinks most acceptable to him; all persons, professing the Christian religion, are equally entitled to protection in their religious liberty; wherefore no person ought by any law to be molested in his person or estate on account of his religious persuasion or profession, or for his religious practice; unless, under colour of religion, any man shall disturb the good order, peace or safety of the State, or shall infringe the laws of morality, or injure others, in their natural, civil, or religious rights; nor ought any person to be compelled to frequent or maintain, or contribute, unless on contract, to maintain any particular place of worship, or any particular ministry: yet the Legislature may, in their discretion, lay a general and equal tax, for the support of the Christian religion; leaving to each individual the power of appointing the payment over of the money, collected from him, to the support of any particular place of worship or minister, or for the benefit of the poor of his own denomination, or the poor in general of any particular county: but the churches, chapels, glebes, and all other property now belonging to the church of England, ought to remain to the the church of England forever. And all acts of Assembly, lately passed, for collecting monies for building or repairing particular churches or chapels of ease, shall continue in force, and be executed, unless the Legislature shall, by act, supersede or repeal the same: but no county court shall assess any quantity of tobacco, or sum of money, hereafter, on the application of any vestry-men or church-wardens; and every encumbent of the church of England, who hath remained in his parish, and performed his duty, shall be entitled to receive the provision and support established by the act, entitled "An act for the support of the clergy of the church of England, in this Province," till the November court of this present year, to be held for the county in which his parish shall lie, or partly lie, or for such time as he hath remained in his parish, and performed his duty.

XXXIV. That every gift, sale, or devise of lands, to any minister, public teacher, or preacher of the gospel, as such, or to any religious sect, order or denomination, or to or for the support, use or benefit of, or in trust for, any minister, public teacher, or preacher of the gospel, as such, or any religious sect, order or denomination—and every gift or sale of goods, or chattels, to go in succession, or to take place after the death of the seller or donor, or to or for such support, use or benefit—and also every devise of goods or chattels to or for the support, use or benefit of any minister, public teacher, or preacher of the gospel, as such, or any religious sect, order, or denomination, without the leave of the Legislature, shall be void; except always any sale, gift, lease or devise of any quantity of land, not exceeding two acres, for a church, meeting, or other house of worship, and for a burying-ground, which shall be improved, enjoyed or used only for such purpose—or such sale, gift, lease, or devise, shall be void.

XXXV. That no other test or qualification ought to be required, on admission to any office of trust or profit, then such oath of support and fidelity to this State, and such oath of office, as shall be directed by this Convention, or the Legislature of this State, and a declaration of a belief in the Christian religion:

XXXVI. That the manner of administering an oath to any person, ought to be such, as those of the religious persuasion, profession, or denomination, of which such person is one, generally esteem the most effectual confirmation, by the attestation of the Divine Being. And that the people called Quakers, those called Dunkers, and those called Menonists, holding it unlawful to take an oath on any occasion, ought to be allowed to make their solemn affirmation, in the manner that Quakers have been heretofore allowed to affirm; and to be of the same avail as an oath, in all such cases, as the affirmation of Quakers hath been allowed and accepted within this State, instead of an oath. And further, on such affirmation, warrants to search for stolen goods, or for the apprehension or commitment of offenders, ought to be granted, or security for the peace awarded, and Quakers, Dunkers or Menonists ought also, on their solemn affirmation as aforesaid, to be admitted as witnesses, in all criminal cases not capital.

XXXVII. That the city of Annapolis ought to have all its rights, privileges and benefits, agreeable to its Charter, and the acts of Assembly confirming and regulating the same, subject nevertheless to such alteration as may be made by this Convention, or any future Legislature.

XXXVIII. That the liberty of the press ought to be inviolably preserved.

XXXIX. That monopolies are odious, contrary to the spirit of a free government, and the principles of commerce; and ought not to be suffered.

XL. That no title of nobility, or hereditary honours, ought to be granted in this State.

XLI. That the subsisting resolves of this and the several Conventions held for this Colony, ought to be in force as laws, unless altered by this Convention, or the Legislature of this State.

XLII. That this Declaration of Rights, or the Form of Government, to be established by this Convention, or any part or either of them, ought not to be altered, changed or abolished, by the Legislature of this State, but in such manner as this Convention shall prescribe and direct.

This Declaration of Rights was assented to, and passed, in Convention of the Delegates of the freemen of Maryland, begun and held at Annapolis, the 14th day of August, A. D. 1776.

By order of the Convention.

Mat. Tilghman, President

NORTH CAROLINA DECLARATION OF RIGHTS, 1776

Commentary

Soon after the Maryland Constitutional Convention adjourned, a similar body convened in North Carolina. The day after it first met, on November 13, 1776, the North Carolina delegates selected a committee of 18 to prepare a Declaration of Rights and Constitution. On December 12, the committee reported a Declaration of Rights and it was adopted on December 17. The North Carolina Declaration was plainly modelled upon those already enacted in Virginia, Pennsylvania, Delaware, and Maryland. The North Carolina Declaration contains a compendium of most of the fundamental rights which had come to be recognized by American Constitution-makers: trial by jury, right to accusation and confrontation, privilege against self-incrimination, right against excessive bail or fines, cruel and unusual punishment and general warrants, that not to be deprived of life, liberty, or property "but by the law of the land," freedom of the press, right to bear arms, freedom of conscience, and prohibition of ex post facto laws. Though it is said by commentators that nothing new was added by the North Carolina Declaration, that is not entirely true, Article VIII contains an implied guarantee of the right to an indictment (apparently the first such provision in a state Constitution and, as such, the direct precursor of the guarantee in the Fifth Amendment).

North Carolina Declaration of Rights, 1776*

I. That all political power is vested in and derived from the people only.

II. That the people of this State ought to have the sole and exclusive right of regulating the interal government and police thereof.

III. That no man or set of men are entitled to exclusive or separate emoluments or privileges from the community, but in consideration of public services.

IV. That the legislative, executive, and supreme judicial powers of government, ought to be forever separate and distinct from each other.

V. That all powers of suspending laws, or the execution of laws, by any authority, without consent of the Representatives of the people, is injurious to their rights, and ought not to be exercised.

VI. That elections of members, to serve as Representatives in General Assembly, ought to be free.

*Poore, *The Federal and State Constitutions, Colonial Charters and Other Organic Laws of the United States*, Vol. 2, pp. 1409–11.

VII. That, in all criminal prosecutions, every man has a right to be informed of the accusation against him, and to confront the accusers and witnesses with other testimony, and shall not be compelled to give evidence against himself.

VIII. That no freeman shall be put to answer any criminal charge, but by indictment, presentment, or impeachment.

IX. That no freeman shall be convicted of any crime, but by the unanimous verdict of a jury of good and lawful men, in open court, as heretofore used.

X. That excessive bail should not be required, nor excessive fines imposed, nor cruel or unusual punishments inflicted.

XI. That general warrants—whereby an officer or messenger may be commanded to search suspected places, without evidence of the fact committed, or to seize any person or persons, not named, whose offences are not particularly described, and supported by evidence—are dangerous to liberty, and ought not to be granted.

XII. That no freeman ought to be taken, imprisoned, or disseized of his freehold, liberties or privileges, or outlawed, or exiled, or in any manner destroyed, or deprived of his life, liberty, or property, but by the law of the land.

XIII. That every freeman, restrained of his liberty, is entitled to a remedy, to inquire into the lawfulness thereof, and to remove the same, if unlawful; and that such remedy ought not to be denied or delayed.

XIV. That in all controversies at law, respecting property, the ancient mode of trial, by jury, is one of the best securities of the rights of the people, and ought to remain sacred and inviolable.

XV. That the freedom of the press is one of the great bulwarks of liberty, and therefore ought never to be restrained.

XVI. That the people of this State ought not to be taxed, or made subject to the payment of any impost or duty, without the consent of themselves, or their Representatives in General Assembly, freely given.

XVII. That the people have a right to bear arms, for the defence of the State; and as standing armies, in time of peace, are dangerous to liberty, they ought not to be kept up; and that the military should be kept under strict subordination to, and governed by the civil power.

XVIII. That the people have a right to assemble together, to consult for their common good, to instruct their Representatives, and to apply to the Legislature, for redress of grievances.

XIX. That all men have a natural and unalienable right to worship Almighty God according to the dictates of their own consciences.

XX. That for redress of grievances, and for amending and strengthening the laws, elections ought to be often held.

XXI. That a frequent recurrence to fundamental principles is absolutely necessary, to preserve the blessings of liberty.

XXII. That no hereditary emoluments, privileges or honors ought to be granted or conferred in this State.

XXIII. That perpetuities and monopolies are contrary to the genius of a free State, and ought not to be allowed.

XXIV. That retrospective laws, punishing facts committed before the existence of such laws, and by them only declared criminal, are oppressive, unjust, and incompatible with liberty; wherefore no *ex post facto* law ought to be made.

XXV. The property of the soil, in a free government, being one of the essential rights of the collective body of the people, it is necessary, in order to avoid future disputes, that the limits of the State should be ascertained with precision: and as the former temporary line between North and South Carolina, was confirmed, and extended by Commissioners, appointed by the Legislatures of the two States, agreeable to the order of the late King George II. in Council, that line, and that only, should be esteemed the southern boundary of this State—that is to say, beginning on the sea side, at a cedar stake, at or near the mouth of Little River (being the southern extremity of Brunswic county,) and running from thence a northwest course, through the boundary house, which stands in thirty-three degrees fifty-six minutes, to thirty-five degrees north latitude; and from thence a west course so far as is mentioned in the Charter of King Charles II. to the late Proprietors of Carolina. Therefore all the territory, seas, waters, and harbours, with their appurtenances, lying between the line above described, and the southern line of the State of Virginia, which begins on the sea shore, in thirty-six degrees thirty minutes, north latitude, and from thence runs west, agreeable to the said Charter of King Charles, are the right and property of the people of this State, to be held by them in sovereignty; any partial line, without the consent of the Legislature of this State, at any time thereafter directed, or laid out, in anywise notwithstanding: Provided always, That this Declaration of Rights shall not prejudice any nation or nations of Indians, from enjoying such hunting-grounds as may have been, or hereafter shall be, secured to them by any former or future Legislature of this State: And provided also, That it shall not be construed so as to prevent the establishment of one or more governments westward of this State, by consent of the Legislature: And provided further, That nothing herein contained shall affect the titles or possessions of individuals holding or claiming under the laws heretofore in force, or grants heretofore made by the late King George II. or his predecessors, or the late lords proprietors, or any of them.

CONNECTICUT DECLARATION OF RIGHTS, 1776

Commentary

Connecticut and Rhode Island did not frame new Constitutions in response to the May, 1776, congressional resolution recommending the establishment of independent state governments. They merely enacted the continuation of their Colonial Charters as the fundamental laws of those states. The Connecticut enactment to that effect contains a brief Declaration of Rights, containing three guarantees. The first is another version of section 39 of Magna Carta. The second is a forerunner of the Privileges and Immunities Clause of Article IV of the federal Constitution. The third is a guarantee of the right to bail. The fact that this is the shortest of the Revolutionary Bills of Rights is to be explained by the fact that it was not drawn up in connection with the framing of a new Constitution. Brief though it was, it does deserve a place in the catalogue of Bills of Rights of the period. There were thus nine state Bills of Rights during the Revolutionary period—not eight (as virtually all commentators tell us).

Connecticut Declaration of Rights, 1776*

*An Act containing an Abstract and Declaration of the Rights
and Privileges of the People of this State,
and securing the same.*

The People of this State, being by the Providence of God, free and independent, have the sole and exclusive Right of governing themselves as a free, sovereign, and independent State; and having from their Ancestors derived a free and excellent Constitution of Government whereby the Legislature depends on the free and annual Election of the People, they have the best Security for the Preservation of their civil and religious Rights and Liberties. And forasmuch as the free Fruition of such Liberties and Privileges as Humanity, Civility and Christianity call for, as is due to every Man in his Place and Proportion, without Impeachment and Infringement, hath ever been, and will be the Tranquility and Stability of Churches and Commonwealths; and the Denial thereof, the Disturbance, if not the Ruin of both.

1. Be it enacted and declared by the Governor, and Council, and House of Representatives, in General Court assembled, That the ancient Form of Civil Government, contained in the Charter from Charles the Second, King

*Poore, *The Federal and State Constitutions, Colonial Charters and Other Organic Laws of the United States*, Vol. 1, pp. 257–58.

of England, and adopted by the People of this State, shall be and remain the Civil Constitution of this State, under the sole authority of the People thereof, independent of any King or Prince whatever. And that this Republic is, and shall forever be and remain, a free, sovereign and independent State, by the Name of the State of Connecticut.

2. And be it further enacted and declared, That no Man's Life shall be taken away: No Man's Honor or good Name shall be stained: No Man's Person shall be arrested, restrained, banished, dismembered, nor any Ways punished: No Man shall be deprived of his Wife or Children: No Man's Goods or Estate shall be taken away from him, nor any Ways indamaged under the Colour of Law, or Countenance of Authority; unless clearly warranted by the Laws of this State.

3. That all the free Inhabitants of this or any other of the United States of America, and Foreigners in Amity with this State, shall enjoy the same justice and Law within this State, which is general for the State, in all Cases proper for the Cognizance of the Civil Authority and Court of Judicature within the same, and that without Partiality or Delay.

4. And that no Man's Person shall be restrained, or imprisoned, by any authority whatsoever, before the Law hath sentenced him thereunto, if he can and will give sufficient Security, Bail, or Mainprize for his Appearance and good Behaviour in the mean Time, unless it be for Capital Crimes, Contempt in open Court, or in such Cases wherein some express Law doth allow of, or order the same.

GEORGIA CONSTITUTION, 1777

Commentary

When the people of Georgia met in Convention on October, 1776, in accordance with the May resolution of the Continental Congress, to frame a Constitution setting up an independent state government, they followed the example of New Jersey (*supra* p. 256) in not prefacing the new organic instrument with any Declaration of Rights. As is true of the New Jersey Constitution, however, the Georgia Constitution adopted early in 1777 contains guarantees for individual liberties, of the type normally found in Bills of Rights, in the body of its text. Included among these guarantees were the rights to be tried in the county where the crime was committed (Article XXXIX), to free exercise of religion (Article LVI), against excessive fines and bail (Article LIX), to habeas corpus (Article LX), and to freedom of the press and trial by jury (Article LXI). In addition, Article I provides for the separation of powers in terms that anticipate the famous statement in the Massachusetts Declaration of Rights.

The Georgia provisions contribute nothing new to the history of Bills of Rights; all of them are contained in earlier state Constitutions. But they lend emphasis to the fact that Americans of the Revolutionary era did agree on an irreducible minimum of rights which should be protected by fundamental law. With or without a Bill of Rights, these were the rights that should be guaranteed in any organic instrument.

Georgia Constitution, 1777*

Whereas the conduct of the legislature of Great Britain for many years past has been so oppressive on the people of America that of late years they have plainly declared and asserted a right to raise taxes upon the people of America, and to make laws to bind them in all cases whatsoever, without their consent; which conduct, being repugnant to the common rights of mankind, hath obliged the Americans, as freemen, to oppose such oppressive measures, and to assert the rights and privileges they are entitled to by the laws of nature and reason: and accordingly it hath been done by the general consent of all the people of the States of New Hampshire, Massachusetts Bay, Rhode Island, Connecticut, New York, New Jersey, Pennsylvania, the counties of New Castle, Kent, and Sussex on Delaware, Maryland, Virginia, North Carolina, South Carolina, and Georgia, given by their representatives met together in general Congress, in the city of Philadelphia;

*Thorpe, *The Federal and State Constitutions, Colonial Charters, and Other Organic Laws,* Vol. 2, pp. 777–85.

And whereas it hath been recommended by the said Congress, on the fifteenth of May last, to the respective assemblies and conventions of the United States, where no government, sufficient to the exigencies of their affairs, hath been hitherto established, to adopt such government as may, in the opinion of the representatives of the people, best conduce to the happiness and safety of their constituents in particular and America in general;

And whereas the independence of the United States of America has been also declared, on the fourth day of July, one thousand seven hundred and seventy-six, by the said honorable Congress, and all political connection between them and the Crown of Great Britain is in consequence thereof dissolved:

We, therefore, the representatives of the people, from whom all power originates, and for whose benefit all government is intended, by virtue of the power delegated to us, do ordain and declare, and it is hereby ordained and declared, that the following rules and regulations be adopted for the future government of this State:

Article I. The legislative, executive, and judiciary departments shall be separate and distinct, so that neither exercise the powers properly belonging to the other.

Art. II. The legislature of this State shall be composed of the representatives of the people, as is hereinafter pointed out; and the representatives shall be elected yearly, and every year, on the first Tuesday in December; and the representatives so elected shall meet the first Tuesday in January following, at Savannah, or any other place or places where the house of assembly for the time being shall direct.

On the first day of the meeting of the representatives so chosen, they shall proceed to the choice of a governor, who shall be styled "honorable;" and of an executive council, by ballot out of their own body, viz: two from each county, except those counties which are not yet entitled to send ten members. One of each county shall always attend, where the governor resides, by monthly rotation, unless the members of each county agree for a longer or shorter period. This is not intended to exclude either member attending. The remaining number of representatives shall be called the house of assembly; and the majority of the members of the said house shall have power to proceed on business.

Art. III. It shall be an unalterable rule that the house of assembly shall expire and be at an end, yearly and every year, on the day preceding the day of election mentioned in the foregoing rule.

Art. IV. The representation shall be divided in the following manner: ten members from each county, as is hereinafter directed, except the county of Liberty, which contains three parishes, and that shall be allowed fourteen.

The ceded lands north of Ogechee shall be one county, and known by the name of Wilkes.

The parish of Saint Paul shall be another county, and known by the name of Richmond.

The parish of Saint George shall be another county, and known by the name of Burke.

The parish of Saint Matthew, and the upper part of Saint Philip, above Canouchee, shall be another county, and known by the name of Effingham.

The parish of Christ Church, and the lower part of Saint Philip, below Canouchee, shall be another county, and known by the name of Chatham.

The parishes of Saint John, Saint Andrew, and Saint James shall be another county, and known by the name of Liberty.

The parishes of Saint David and Saint Patrick shall be another county, and known by the name of Glynn.

The parishes of Saint Thomas and Saint Mary shall be another county, and known by the name of Camden.

The port and town of Savannah shall be allowed four members to represent their trade.

The port and town of Sunbury shall be allowed two members to represent their trade.

Art. V. The two counties of Glynn and Camden shall have one representative each, and also they, and all other counties that may hereafter be laid out by the house of assembly, shall be under the following regulations, viz: at their first institution each county shall have one member, provided the inhabitants of the said county shall have ten electors; and if thirty, they shall have two; if forty, three; if fifty, four; if eighty, six; if a hundred and upward, ten; at which time two executive councillors shall be chosen from them, as is directed for the other counties.

Art. VI. The representatives shall be chosen out of the residents in each county, who shall have resided at least twelve months in this State, and three months in the county where they shall be elected; except the freeholders of the counties of Glynn and Camden, who are in a state of alarm, and who shall have the liberty of choosing one member each, as specified in the articles of this constitution, in any other county, until they have residents sufficient to qualify them for more; and they shall be of the Protestent religion, and of the age of twenty-one years, and shall be possessed in their own right of two hundred and fifty acres of land, or some property to the amount of two hundred and fifty pounds.

Art. VII. The house of assembly shall have power to make such laws and regulations as may be conducive to the good order and well-being of the State; provided such laws and regulations be not repugnant to the true intent and meaning of any rule or regulation contained in this constitution.

The house of assembly shall also have power to repeal all laws and ordinances they find injurious to the people; and the house shall choose its own speaker, appoint its own officers, settle its own rules of proceeding, and direct writs of election for supplying intermediate vacancies, and shall have power of adjournment to any time or times within the year.

Art. VIII. All laws and ordinances shall be three times read, and each reading shall be on different and separate days, except in cases of great necessity and danger; and all laws and ordinances shall be sent to the executive council after the second reading, for their perusal and advice.

Art. IX. All male white inhabitants, of the age of twenty-one years, and possessed in his own right of ten pounds value, and liable to pay tax in this State, or being of any mechanic trade, and shall have been resident six months in this State, shall have a right to vote at all elections for representatives, or any other officers, herein agreed to be chosen by the people at large; and every person having a right to vote at any election shall vote by ballot personally.

Art. X. No officer whatever shall serve any process, or give any other hinderances to any person entitled to vote, either in going to the place of election, or during the time of the said election, or on their returning home from such election; nor shall any military officer, or soldier, appear at any election in a military character, to the intent that all elections may be free and open.

Art. XI. No person shall be entitled to more than one vote, which shall be given in the county where such person resides, except as before excepted; nor shall any person who holds any title of nobility be entitled to a vote, or be capable of serving as a representative, or hold any post of honor, profit, or trust in this State, whilst such person claims his title of nobility; but if the person shall give up such distinction, in the manner as may be directed by any future legislation, then, and in such case, he shall be entitled to a vote, and represent, as before directed, and enjoy all the other benefits of a free citizen.

Art. XII. Every person absenting himself from an election, and shall neglect to give in his or their ballot at such election, shall be subject to a penalty not exceeding five pounds; the mode of recovery, and also the appropriation thereof, to be pointed out and directed by act of the legislature : Provided, nevertheless, That a reasonable excuse shall be admitted.

Art. XIII. The manner of electing representatives shall be by ballot, and shall be taken by two or more justices of the peace in each county, who shall provide a convenient box for receiving the said ballots: and, on closing the poll, the ballots shall be compared in public with the list of votes that have been taken, and the majority immediately declared; a certificate of the same being given to the persons elected, and also a certificate returned to the house of representatives.

Art. XIV. Every person entitled to vote shall take the following oath or affirmation, if required, viz:

> I, A B, do voluntarily and solemnly swear (or affirm, as the case may be) that I do owe true allegiance to this State, and will support the constitution thereof; so help me God.

Art. XV. Any five of the representatives elected, as before directed, being met, shall have power to administer the following oath to each other; and they, or any other member, being so sworn, shall, in the house, administer the oath to all other members that attend, in order to qualify them to take their seats, viz:

> I, A B, do solemnly swear that I will bear true allegiance to the State of Georgia, and will truly perform the trusts reposed in me; and that I will execute the same to the best of my knowledge, for the benefit of this State, and the support of the constitution thereof, and that I have obtained my election without fraud or bribe whatever; so help me God.

Art. XVI. The continental delegates shall be appointed annually by ballot, and shall have a right to sit, debate, and vote in the house of assembly, and be deemed a part thereof, subject, however, to the regulations contained in the twelfth article of the Confederation of the United States.

Art. XVII. No person bearing any post of profit under this State, or any person bearing any military commission under this or any other State or States, except officers of the militia, shall be elected a representative. And if any representative shall be appointed to any place of profit or military commission, which he shall accept, his seat shall immediately become vacant, and he shall be incapable of reelection whilst holding such office.

By this article it is not to be understood that the office of a justice of the peace is a post of profit.

Art. XVIII. No person shall hold more than one office of profit under this State at one and the same time.

Art. XIX. The governor shall, with the advice of the executive council, exercise the executive powers of government, according to the laws of this State and the constitution thereof, save only in the case of pardons and remission of fines, which he shall in no instance grant; but he may reprieve a criminal, or suspend a fine, until the meeting of the assembly, who may determine therein as they shall judge fit.

Art. XX. The governor, with the advice of the executive council, shall have power to call the house of assembly together, upon any emergency, before the time which they stand adjourned to.

Art. XXI. The governor, with the advice of the executive council, shall fill up all intermediate vacancies that shall happen in offices till the next general election; and all commissions, civil and military, shall be issued by the governor, under his hand and the great seal of the State.

Art. XXII. The governor may preside in the executive council at all times, except when they are taking into consideration and perusing the laws and ordinances offered to them by the house of assembly.

Art. XXIII. The governor shall be chosen annually by ballot, and shall not be eligible to the said office for more than one year out of three, nor shall he hold any military commission under any other State or States.

The governor shall reside at such place as the house of assembly for the time being shall appoint.

Art. XXIV. The governor's oath:

> I, A B, elected governor of the State of Georgia, by the representatives thereof, do solemnly promise and swear that I will, during the term of my appointment, to the best of my skill and judgment, execute the said office faithfully and conscientiously, according to law, without favor, affection, or partiality; that I will, to the utmost of my power, support, maintain, and defend the State of Georgia, and the constitution of the same; and use my utmost endeavors to protect the people thereof in the secure enjoyment of all their rights, franchises, and privileges; and that the laws and ordinances of the State be duly observed, and that law and justice in mercy be executed in all judgments. And I do further solemnly promise and swear that I will peaceably and quietly resign the government to which I have been elected at the period to which my continuance in the said office is limited by the constitution. And, lastly, I do also solemnly swear that I have not accepted of the government whereunto I am elected contrary to the articles of this constitution; so help me God.

This oath to be administered to him by the speaker of the assembly.

The same oath to be administered by the speaker to the president of the council.

No person shall be eligible to the office of governor who has not resided three years in this State.

Art. XXV. The executive council shall meet the day after their election, and proceed to the choice of a president out of their own body; they shall have power to appoint their own officers and settle their own rules of proceedings.

The council shall always vote by counties, and not individually.

Art. XXVI. Every councillor, being present, shall have power of entering his protest against any measures in council he has not consented to, provided he does it in three days.

Art. XXVII. During the sitting of the assembly the whole of the executive council shall attend, unless prevented by sickness, or some other urgent necessity; and, in that case, a majority of the council shall make a board to examine the laws and ordinances sent them by the house of assembly; and all laws and ordinances sent to the council shall be returned in five days after, with their remarks hereon.

Art. XXVIII. A committee from the council, sent with any proposed amendments to any law or ordinance, shall deliver their reasons for such proposed amendments, sitting and covered; the whole house at that time, except the speaker, uncovered.

Art. XXIX. The president of the executive council, in the absence or sickness of the governor, shall exercise all the powers of the governor.

Art. XXX. When any affair that requires secrecy shall be laid before the governor and the executive council, it shall be the duty of the governor, and he is hereby obliged, to administer the following oath, viz:

I, A B, do solemnly swear that any business that shall be at this time communicated to the council I will not, in any manner whatever, either by speaking, writing, or otherwise, reveal the same to any person whatever, until leave given by the council, or when called upon by the house of assembly; and all this I swear without any reservation whatever; so help me God.

And the same oath shall be administered to the secretary and other officers necessary to carry the business into execution.

Art. XXXI. The executive power shall exist till renewed as pointed out by the rules of this constitution.

Art. XXXII. In all transactions between the legislative and executive bodies the same shall be communicated by message, to be delivered from the legislative body to the governor or executive council by a committee, and from the governor to the house of assembly by the secretary of the council, and from the executive council by a committee of the said council.

Art. XXXIII. The governor for the time being shall be captain-general and commander-in-chief over all the militia, and other military and naval forces belonging to this State.

Art. XXXIV. All militia commissions shall specify that the person commissioned shall continue during good behavior.

Art. XXXV. Every county in this State that has, or hereafter may have, two hundred and fifty men, and upwards, liable to bear arms, shall be formed into a battalion; and when they become too numerous for one battalion, they shall be formed into more, by bill of the legislature; and those counties that have a less number than two hundred and fifty shall be formed into independent companies.

Art. XXXVI. There shall be established in each county a court, to be called a superior court, to be held twice in each year.

On the first Tuesday in March, in the county of Chatham.

The second Tuesday in March, in the county of Effingham.

The third Tuesday in March, in the county of Burke.

The fourth Tuesday in March, in the county of Richmond.

The next Tuesday, in the county of Wilkes.

And Tuesday fortnight, in the county of Liberty.

The next Tuesday, in the county of Glynn.

The next Tuesday, in the county of Camden.

The like courts to commence in October and continue as above.

Art. XXXVII. All causes and matters of dispute, between any parties residing in the same county, to be tried within the county.

Art. XXXVIII. All matters in dispute between contending parties residing in different counties shall be tried in the county where the defendant resides, except in cases of real estate, which shall be tried in the county where such real estate lies.

Art. XXXIX. All matters of breach of the peace, felony, murder, and treason against the State to be tried in the county where the same was committed. All matters of dispute, both civil and criminal, in any county where there is not a sufficient number of inhabitants to form a court, shall be tried in the next adjacent county where a court is held.

Art. XL. All causes, of what nature soever, shall be tried in the supreme court, except as hereafter mentioned; which court shall consist of the chief-justice, and three or more of the justices residing in the county. In case of the absence of the chief-justice, the senior justice on the bench shall act as chief-justice, with the clerk of the county, attorney for the State, sheriff, coroner, constable, and the jurors; and in case of the absence of any of the aforementioned officers, the justices to appoint others in their room *pro tempore.* And if any plaintiff or defendant in civil causes shall be dissatisfied with the determination of the jury, then, and in that case, they shall be at liberty, within three days, to enter an appeal from that verdict, and demand a new trial by a special jury, to be nominated as follows, viz: each party, plaintiff and defendant, shall choose six, six more names shall be taken indifferently out of a box provided for that purpose, the whole eighteen to be summoned, and their names to be put together into the box, and the first twelve that are drawn out, being present, shall be the special jury to try the cause, and from which there shall be no appeal.

Art. XLI. The jury shall be judges of law, as well as of fact, and shall not be allowed to bring in a special verdict; but if all or any of the jury have any doubts concerning points of law, they shall apply to the bench, who shall each of them in rotation give their opinion.

Art. XLII. The jury shall be sworn to bring in a verdict according to law, and the opinion they entertain of the evidence; provided it be not repugnant to the rules and regulations contained in this constitution.

Art. XLII. The special jury shall be sworn to bring in a verdict according to law, and the opinion they entertain of the evidence; provided it be not repugnant to justice, equity, and conscience, and the rules and regulations contained in this constitution, of which they shall judge.

Art. XLIV. Captures, both by sea and land, to be tried in the county where such shall be carried in; a special court to be called by the chief-justice, or in his absence by the then senior justice in the said county, upon application of the captors or claimants, which cause shall be determined within the space of ten days. The mode of proceeding and appeal shall be the same as in the superior courts, unless, after the second trial, an appeal is made to the Continental Congress; and the distance of time between the first and second trial shall not exceed fourteen days; and all maritime causes to be tried in like manner.

Art. XLV. No grand jury shall consist of less than eighteen, and twelve may find a bill.

Art. XLVI. That the court of conscience be continued as heretofore practiced, and that the jurisdiction thereof be extended to try causes not amounting to more than ten pounds.

Art. XLVII. All executions exceeding five pounds, except in the case of a court-merchant, shall be stayed until the first Monday in March; provided security be given for debt and costs.

Art. XLVIII. All the costs attending any action in the superior court shall not exceed the sum of three pounds, and that no cause be allowed to depend in the superior court longer than two terms.

Art. XLIX. Every officer of the State shall be liable to be called to account by the house of assembly.

Art. L. Every county shall keep the public records belonging to the same, and authenticated copies of the several records now in the possession of this State shall be made out and deposited in that county to which they belong.

Art. LI. Estates shall not be entailed; and when a person dies intestate, his or her estate shall be divided equally among their children; the widow shall have a child's share, or her dower, at her option; all other intestates' estates to be divided according to the act of distribution, made in the reign of Charles the Second, unless otherwise altered by any future act of the legislature.

Art. LII. A register of probates shall be appointed by the legislature in every county, for proving wills and granting letters of administration.

Art. LIII. All civil officers in each county shall be annually elected on the day of the general election, except justices of the peace and registers of probates, who shall be appointed by the house of assembly.

Art. LIV. Schools shall be erected in each county, and supported at the general expense of the State, as the legislature shall hereafter point out.

Art. LV. A court-house and jail shall be erected at the public expense in each county, where the present convention or the future legislature shall point out and direct.

Art. LVI. All persons whatever shall have the free exercise of their religion; provided it be not repugnant to the peace and safety of the State; and shall not, unless by consent, support any teacher or teachers except those of their own profession.

Art. LVII. The great seal of this State shall have the following device: on one side a scroll, whereon shall be engraved, "The Constitution of the State of Georgia;" and the motto, *"Pro bono publico."* On the other side, an elegant house, and other buildings, fields of corn, and meadows covered with sheep and cattle; a river running through the same, with a ship under full sail, and the motto, *"Deus nobis haec otia fecit."*

Art. LVIII. No person shall be allowed to plead in the courts of law in this State, except those who are authorized so to do by the house of assembly; and if any person so authorized shall be found guilty of malpractice before the house of assembly, they shall have power to suspend them. This is not intended to exclude any person from that inherent privilege of every freeman, the liberty to plead his own cause.

Art. LIX. Excessive fines shall not be levied, nor excessive bail demanded.

Art. LX. The principles of the *habeas-corpus* act shall be a part of this constitution.

Art. LXI. Freedom of the press and trial by jury to remain inviolate forever.

Art. LXII. No clergyman of any denomination shall be allowed a seat in the legislature.

Art. LXIII. No alteration shall be made in this constitution without petitions from a majority of the counties, and the petitions from each county to be signed by a majority of voters in each county within this State; at which time the assembly shall order a convention to be called for that purpose, specifying the alterations to be made, according to the petitions preferred to the assembly by the majority of the counties as aforesaid.

Done at Savannah, in convention, the fifth day of February, in the year of our Lord one thousand seven hundred and seventy-seven, and in the first year of the Independence of the United States of America.

NEW YORK CONSTITUTION, 1777

Commentary

New York, like most of the other states, began work on a Constitution soon after the congressional resolution of May, 1776 (*supra* p. 229), urging the establishment of state governments. The New York Convention first met on July 10, 1776. It was not able to finish its work (being continually inter-rupted by the actual military operations in the area) until April, 1777, when the Constitution was adopted, with only one dissenting vote. The new organic document was drafted by John Jay, and it follows the precedent of New Jersey and Georgia (*supra* pp. 256, 291), rather than that of Virginia, since it contains no separate Bill of Rights. The body of the New York Constitution does, however, contain guarantees for individual rights of the type included in Bills of Rights of the day. These include a guarantee against deprivation of rights and privileges, "unless by the law of the land, or the judgment of his peers" (Article XIII—still another version of section 39 of Magna Carta); right of counsel (Article XXXIV); free-exercise of religion (Article XXXVIII); trial by jury and prohibition of bills of attainder (Arti-cle XLI). None of these provisions are new; they are included in most of the organic provisions safeguarding personal liberties of the Revolutionary period.

New York Constitution, 1777*

Whereas the many tyrannical and oppressive usurpations of the King and Parliament of Great Britain on the rights and liberties of the people of the American colonies had reduced them to the necessity of introducing a government by congresses and committees, as temporary expedients, and to exist no longer than the grievances of the people should remain without redress; And whereas the congress of the colony of New York did, on the thirty-first day of May now last past, resolve as follows, viz:

Whereas the present government of this colony, by congress and commit-tees, was instituted while the former government, under the Crown of Great Britain, existed in full force, and was established for the sole purpose of opposing the usurpation of the British Parliament, and was intended to expire on a reconciliation with Great Britain, which it was then apprehended would soon take place, but is now considered as remote and uncertain;

And whereas many and great inconveniences attend the said mode of government by congress and committees, as of necessity, in many instances,

*Thorpe, *The Federal and State Constitutions, Colonial Charters, and Other Organic Laws,* Vol. 5, pp. 2623–38.

legislative, judicial, and executive powers have been vested therein, especially since the dissolution of the former government by the abdication of the
late governor and the exclusion of this colony from the protection of the King
of Great Britain;

And whereas the Continental Congress did resolve as followeth, to wit:
[text of May, 1776 Resolution, *supra* p. 229, follows]

And whereas doubts have arisen whether this congress are invested with
sufficient power and authority to deliberate and determine on so important a
subject as the necessity of erecting and constituting a new form of government and internal police, to the exclusion of all foreign jurisdiction, dominion, and control whatever; and whereas it appertains of right solely to the
people of this colony to determine the said doubts: Therefore,

Resolved, That it be recommended to the electors in the several counties
in this colony, by election, in the manner and form prescribed for the
election of the present congress, either to authorize (in addition to the
powers vested in this congress) their present deputies, or others in the stead
of their present deputies, or either of them, to take into consideration the
necessity and propriety of instituting such new government as in and by the
said resolution of the Continental Congress is described and recommended;
and if the majority of the counties, by their deputies in provincial congress,
shall be of opinion that such new government ought to be instituted and
established, then to institute and establish such a government as they shall
deem best calculated to secure the rights, liberties, and happiness of the good
people of this colony; and to continue in force until a future peace with
Great Britain shall render the same unnecessary; and

Resolved, That the said elections in the several counties ought to be had
on such day, and at such place or places, as by the committee of each county
respectively shall be determined. And it is recommended to the said committees to fix such early days for the said elections as that all the deputies to be
elected have sufficient time to repair to the city of New York by the second
Monday in July next; on which day all the said deputies ought punctually to
give their attendance.

And whereas the object of the aforegoing resolutions is of the utmost
importance to the good people of this colony:

Resolved, That it be, and it is hereby, earnestly recommended to the
committees, freeholders, and other electors in the different counties in this
colony diligently to carry the same into execution."

And whereas the good people of the said colony, in pursuance of the said
resolution, and reposing special trust and confidence in the members of this
convention, have appointed, authorized, and empowered them for the purposes, and in the manner, and with the powers in and by the said resolve
specified, declared, and mentioned.

And whereas the Delegates of the United American States, in general
Congress convened, did, on the fourth day of July now last past, solemnly

publish and declare, in the words following, viz: [text of Declaration of Independence, *supra* p. 251, follows]

And whereas this convention, having taken this declaration into their most serious consideration, did, on the ninth day of July last past, unanimously resolve that the reasons assigned by the Continental Congress for declaring the united colonies free and independent States are cogent and conclusive; and that while we lament the cruel necessity which has rendered that measure unavoidable, we approve the same, and will, at the risk of our lives and fortunes, join with the other colonies in supporting it.

By virtue of which several acts, declarations, and proceedings mentioned and contained in the afore-cited resolves or resolutions of the general Congress of the United American States, and of the congresses or conventions of this State, all power whatever therein hath reverted to the people thereof, and this convention hath by their suffrages and free choice been appointed, and among other things authorized to institute and establish such a government as they shall deem best calculated to secure the rights and liberties of the good people of this State, most conducive of the happiness and safety of their constituents in particular, and of America in general.

I. This convention, therefore, in the name and by the authority of the good people of this State, doth ordain, determine, and declare that no authority shall, on any pretence whatever, be exercised over the people or members of this State but such as shall be derived from and granted by them.

II. This convention doth further, in the name and by the authority of the good people of this State, ordain, determine, and declare that the supreme legislative power within this State shall be vested in two separate and distinct bodies of men; the one to be called the assembly of the State of New York, the other to be called the senate of the State of New York; who together shall form the legislature, and meet once at least in every year for the despatch of business.

III. And whereas laws inconsistent with the spirit of this constitution, or with the public good, may be hastily and unadvisedly passed: Be it ordained, that the governor for the time being, the chancellor, and the judges of the supreme court, or any two of them, together with the governor, shall be, and hereby are, constituted a council to revise all bills about to be passed into laws by the legislature; and for that purpose shall assemble themselves from time to time, when the legislature shall be convened; for which, nevertheless, they shall not receive any salary or consideration, under any pretence whatever. And that all bills which have passed the senate and assembly shall, before they become laws, be presented to the said council for their revisal and consideration; and if, upon such revision and consideration, it should appear improper to the said council, or a majority of them, that the said bill should become a law of this State, that they return the same, together with their objections thereto in writing, to the senate or house of assembly (in which soever the same shall have originated) who shall enter the objection sent down by the council at large in their minutes, and proceed to reconsider the said bill. But if, after such reconsideration, two-thirds of the said senate or house of assembly shall, notwithstanding the said objections, agree to pass the same, it shall, together with the objections, be sent to the other branch of the legislature, where it shall also be reconsidered, and, if approved by two-thirds of the members present, shall be a law.

And in order to prevent any unnecessary delays, be it further ordained, that if any bill shall not be returned by the council within ten days after it shall have been presented, the same shall be a law, unless the legislature shall, by their adjournment, render a return of the said bill within ten days impracticable; in which case the bill shall be returned on the first day of the meeting of the legislature after the expiration of the said ten days.

IV. That the assembly shall consist of at least seventy members, to be annually chosen in the several counties, in the proportions following, viz:

For the city and county of New York, nine.

The city and county of Albany, ten.

The county of Dutchess, seven.

The county of Westchester, six.

The county of Ulster, six.

The county of Suffolk, five.

The county of Queens, four.

The county of Orange, four.

The county of Kings, two.

The county of Richmond, two.

Tryon County, six.

Charlotte County, four.

Cumberland County, three.

Gloucester County, two.

V. That as soon after the expiration of seven years (subsequent to the termination of the present war) as may be a census of the electors and inhabitants in this State be taken, under the direction of the legislature. And if, on such census, it shall appear that the number of representatives in assembly from the said counties is not justly proportioned to the number of electors in the said counties respectively, that the legislature do adjust and apportion the same by that rule. And further, that once in every seven years, after the taking of the said first census, a just account of the electors resident in each county shall be taken, and if it shall thereupon appear that the number of electors in any county shall have increased or diminished one or more seventieth parts of the whole number of electors, which, on the said first census, shall be found in this State, the number of representatives for such county shall be increased or diminished accordingly, that is to say, one representative for every seventieth part as aforesaid.

VI. And whereas an opinion hath long prevailed among divers of the good people of this State that voting at elections by ballot would tend more to preserve the liberty and equal freedom of the people than voting *viva voce:* To the end, therefore, that a fair experiment be made, which of those two methods of voting is to be preferred—

Be it ordained, That as soon as may be after the termination of the present war between the United States of America and Great Britain, an act or acts be passed by the legislature of this State for causing all elections thereafter to be held in this State for senators and representatives in assembly to be by ballot, and directing the manner in which the same shall be conducted. And whereas it is possible that, after all the care of the legislature in framing the said act or acts, certain inconveniences and mischiefs, unforseen at this day, may be found to attend the said mode of electing by ballot:

It is further ordained, That if, after a full and fair experiment shall be made of voting by ballot aforesaid, the same shall be found less conducive to the safety or interest of the State than the method of voting *viva voce,* it shall be lawful and constitutional for the legislature to abolish the same, provided two-thirds of the members present in each house, respectively, shall concur therein. And further, that, during the continuance of the present war, and until the legislature of this State shall provide for the election of senators and representatives in assembly by ballot, the said election shall be made *viva voce.*

VII. That every male inhabitant of full age, who shall have personally resided within one of the counties of this State for six months immediately preceding the day of election, shall, at such election, be entitled to vote for representatives of the said county in assembly; if, during the time aforesaid, he shall have been a freeholder, possessing a freehold of the value of twenty pounds, within the said county, or have rented a tenement therein of the yearly value of forty shillings, and been rated and actually paid taxes to this State: Provided always, That every person who now is a freeman of the city of Albany, or who was made a freeman of the city of New York on or before the fourteenth day of October, in the year of our Lord one thousand seven hundred and seventy-five, and shall be actually and usually resident in the said cities, respectively, shall be entitled to vote for representatives in assembly within his said place of residence.

VIII. That every elector, before he is admitted to vote, shall, if required by the returning-officer or either of the inspectors, take an oath, or, if of the people called Quakers, an affirmation, of allegiance to the State.

IX. That the assembly, thus constituted, shall choose their own speaker, be judges of their own members, and enjoy the same privileges, and proceed in doing business in like manner as the assemblies of the colony of New York of right formerly did; and that a majority of the said members shall, from time to time, constitute a house, to proceed upon business.

X. And this convention doth further, in the name and by the authority of the good people of this State, ordain, determine, and declare, that the senate of the State of New York shall consist of twenty-four freeholders to be chosen out of the body of the freeholders; and that they be chosen by the freeholders of this State, possessed of freeholds of the value of one hundred pounds, over and above all debts charged thereon.

XI. That the members of the senate be elected for four years; and, immediately after the first election, they be divided by lot into four classes, six in each class, and numbered one, two, three, and four; that the seats of the members of the first class shall be vacated at the expiration of the first year, the second class the second year, and so on continually; to the end that the fourth part of the senate, as nearly as possible, may be annually chosen.

XII. That the election of senators shall be after this manner: That so much of this State as is now parcelled into counties be divided into four great districts; the southern district to comprehend the city and county of New York, Suffolk, Westchester, Kings, Queens, and Richmond Counties; the middle district to comprehend the counties of Dutchess, Ulster, and Orange; the western district, the city and county of Albany, and Tyron County; and the eastern district, the counties of Charlotte, Cumberland, and Gloucester. That the senators shall be elected by the freeholders of the said districts, qualified as aforesaid, in the proportions following, to wit: in the southern district, nine; in the middle district, six; in the western district, six; and in the eastern district, three. And be it ordained, that a census shall be taken, as soon as may be after the expiration of seven years from the termination of the present war, under the direction of the legislature; and if, on such census, it shall appear that the number of senators is not justly proportioned to the several districts, that the legislature adjust the proportion, as near as may be, to the number of freeholders, qualified as aforesaid, in each district. That when the number of electors, within any of the said districts, shall have increased one twenty-fourth part of the whole number of electors, which, by the said census, shall be found to be in this State, an additional senator shall be chosen by the electors of such district. That a majority of the number of senators to be chosen aforesaid shall be necessary to constitute a senate sufficient to proceed upon business; and that the senate shall, in like manner with the assembly, be the judges of its own members. And be it ordained, that it shall be in the power of the future legislatures of this State, for the convenience and advantage of the good people thereof, to divide the same into such further and other counties and districts as shall to them appear necessary.

XIII. And this convention doth further, in the name and by the authority of the good people of this State, ordain, determine, and declare, that no member of this State shall be disfranchised, or deprived of any the rights or privileges secured to the subjects of this State by this constitution, unless by the law of the land, or the judgment of his peers.

XIV. That neither the assembly or the senate shall have the power to adjourn themselves, for any longer time than two days, without the mutual consent of both.

XV. That whenever the assembly and senate disagree, a conference shall be held, in the preference of both, and be managed by committees, to be by them respectively chosen by ballot. That the doors, both of the senate and assembly, shall at all times be kept open to all persons, except when the welfare of the State shall require their debates to be kept secret. And the journals of all their proceedings shall be kept in the manner heretofore accustomed by the general assembly of the colony of New York; and except such parts as they shall, as aforesaid, respectively determine not to make public be from day to day (if the business of the legislature will permit) published.

XVI. It is nevertheless provided, that the number of senators shall never exceed one hundred, nor the number of the assembly three hundred; but that whenever the number of senators shall amount to one hundred, or of the assembly to three hundred, then and in such case the legislature shall, from time to time thereafter, by laws for that purpose, apportion and distribute the said one hundred senators and three hundred representatives among the great districts and counties of this State, in proportion to the number of their respective electors; so that the representation of the good people of this State, both in the senate and assembly, shall forever remain proportionate and adequate.

XVII. And this convention doth further, in the name and by the authority of the good people of this State, ordain, determine, and declare that the supreme executive power and authority of this State shall be vested in a governor; and that statedly, once in every three years, and as often as the seat of government shall become vacant, a wise and descreet freeholder of this State shall be, by ballot, elected governor, by the freeholders of this State, qualified, as before described, to elect senators; which elections shall be always held at the times and places of choosing representatives in assembly for each respective county; and that the person who hath the greatest number of votes within the said State shall be governor thereof.

XVIII. That the governor shall continue in office three years, and shall, by virtue of his office, be general and commander-in-chief of all the militia, and admiral of the navy of this State; that he shall have power to convene the assembly and senate on extraordinary occasions; to prorogue them from time to time, provided such prorogations shall not exceed sixty days in the space of any one year; and, at his discretion, to grant reprieves and pardons to persons convicted of crimes, other than treason or murder, in which he may suspend the execution of the sentence, until it shall be reported to the legislature at their subsequent meeting; and they shall either pardon or direct the execution of the criminal, or grant a further reprieve.

XIX. That it shall be the duty of the governor to inform the legislature, at every session, of the condition of the State, so far as may respect his department; to recommend such matters to their consideration as shall appear to him to concern its good government, welfare, and prosperity; to correspond with the Continental Congress, and other States; to transact all necessary business with the officers of government, civil and military; to take care that the laws are faithfully executed to the best of his ability; and to expedite all such measures as may be resolved upon by the legislature.

XX. That a lieutenant-governor shall, at every election of a governor, and as often as the lieutenant-governor shall die, resign, or be removed from office, be elected in the same manner with the governor, to continue in office until the next election of a governor; and such lieutenant-governor shall, by virtue of his office, be president of the senate, and, upon an equal division, have a casting voice in their decisions, but not vote on any other occasion. And in case of the impeachment of the governor, or his removal from office, death, resignation, or absence from the State, the lieutenant-governor shall exercise all the power and authority appertaining to the office of governor until another be chosen, or the governor absent or impeached shall return or be acquitted: Provided, That where the governor shall, with the consent of the legislature, be out of the State, in time of war, at the head of a military force thereof, he shall still continue in his command of all the military force of this State both by sea and land.

XXI. That whenever the government shall be administered by the lieutenant-governor, or he shall be unable to attend as president of the senate, the senators shall have power to elect one of their own members to the office of president of the senate, which he shall exercise *pro hac vice*. And if, during such vacancy of the office of governor, the lieutenant-governor shall be impeached, displaced, resign, die, or be absent from the State, the president of the senate shall, in like manner as the lieutenant-governor, administer the government, until others shall be elected by the suffrage of the people, at the succeeding election.

XXII. And this convention doth further, in the name and by the authority of the good people of this State, ordain, determine, and declare, that the treasurer of this State shall be appointed by act of the legislature, to originate with the assembly: Provided, that he shall not be elected out of either branch of the legislature.

XXIII. That all officers, other than those who, by this constitution, are directed to be otherwise appointed, shall be appointed in the manner following, to wit: The assembly shall, once in every year, openly nominate and appoint one of the senators from each great district, which senators shall form a council for the appointment of the said officers, of which the governor for the time being, or the lieutenant-governor, or the president of the senate, when they shall respectively administer the government, shall be president and have a casting voice, but no other vote; and with the advice and consent of the said council, shall appoint all the said officers; and that a majority of the said council be a quorum. And further, the said senators shall not be eligible to the said council for two years successively.

XXIV. That all military officers be appointed during pleasure; that all commissioned officers, civil and military, be commissioned by the governor; and that the chancellor, the judges of the supreme court, and first judge of the county court in every county, hold their offices during good behavior or until they shall have respectively attained the age of sixty years.

XXV. That the chancellor and judges of the supreme court shall not, at the same time, hold any other office, excepting that of Delegate to the general Congress, upon special occasions; and that the first judges of the county courts, in the several counties, shall not, at the same time, hold any other office, excepting that of Senator or Delegate to the general Congress. But if the chancellor, or either of the said judges, be elected or appointed to any other office, excepting as is before excepted, it shall be at his option in which to serve.

XXVI. That sheriffs and coroners be annually appointed; and that no person shall be capable of holding either of the said offices more than four years successively; nor the sheriff of holding any other office at the same time.

XXVII. And be it further ordained, That the register and clerks in chancery be appointed by the chancellor; the clerks of the supreme court, by the judges of the said court; the clerk of the court of probate, by the judge of the said court; and the register and marshal of the court of admiralty, by the judge of the admiralty. The said marshal, registers, and clerks to continue in office during the pleasure of those by whom they are appointed as aforesaid.

And that all attorneys, solicitors, and counsellors at law hereafter to be appointed, be appointed by the court, and licensed by the first judge of the court in which they shall respectively plead or practise, and be regulated by the rules and orders of the said courts.

XXVIII. And be it further ordained, That where, by this convention, the duration of any office shall not be ascertained, such office shall be construed to be held during the pleasure of the council of appointment: Provided, That new commissions shall be issued to judges of the county courts (other than to the first judge) and to justices of the peace, once at the least in every three years.

XXIX. That town clerks, supervisors, assessors, constables, and collectors, and all other officers, heretofore eligible by the people, shall always continue to be so eligible, in the manner directed by the present or future acts of the legislature.

That loan officers, county treasurers, and clerks of the supervisors, continue to be appointed in the manner directed by the present or future acts of the legislature.

XXX. That Delegates to represent this State in the general Congress of the United States of America be annually appointed as follows, to wit: The senate and assembly shall each openly nominate as many persons as shall be equal to the whole number of Delegates to be appointed; after which nomination they shall meet together, and those persons named in both lists shall be Delegates; and out of those persons whose names are not on both lists, one-half shall be chosen by the joint ballot of the senators and members of assembly so met together as aforesaid.

XXXI. That the style of all laws shall be as follows, to wit: "Be it enacted by the people of the State of New York, represented in senate and assembly"; and that all writs and other proceedings shall run in the name of "The people of the State of New York," and be tested in the name of the chancellor, or chief judge of the court from whence they shall issue.

XXXII. And this convention doth further, in the name and by the authority of the good people of this State, ordain, determine, and declare, that a court shall be instituted for the trial of impeachments, and the correction of errors, under the regulations which shall be established by the legislature; and to consist of the president of the senate, for the time being, and the senators, chancellor, and judges of the supreme court, or the major part of them; except that when an impeachment shall be prosecuted against the chancellor, or either of the judges of the supreme court, the person so impeached shall be suspended from exercising his office until his acquittal; and, in like manner, when an appeal from a decree in equity shall be heard, the chancellor shall inform the court of the reasons of his decree, but shall not have a voice in the final sentence. And if the cause to be determined shall be brought up by writ of error, on a question of law, on a judgment in the supreme court, the judges of that court shall assign the reasons of such their judgment, but shall not have a voice for its affirmance or reversal.

XXXIII. That the power of impeaching all officers of the State, formal and corrupt conduct in their respective offices, be vested in the representatives of the people in assembly; but that it shall always be necessary that two third parts of the members present shall consent to and agree in such impeachment. That previous to the trial of every impeachment, the members of the said court shall respectively be sworn truly and impartially to try and determine the charge in question, according to evidence; and that no judgment of the said court shall be valid unless it be assented to by two third parts of the members then present; nor shall it extend farther than to removal from office, and disqualification to hold or enjoy any place of honor, trust, or profit under this State. But the party so convicted shall be, nevertheless, liable and subject to indictment, trial, judgment, and punishment, according to the laws of the land.

XXXIV. And it is further ordained That in every trial on impeachment, or indictment for crimes or misdemeanors, the party impeached or indicted shall be allowed counsel, as in civil actions.

XXXV. And this convention doth further, in the name and by the authority of the good people of this State, ordain, determine, and declare that such parts of the common law of England, and of the statute law of England and Great Britain, and of the acts of the legislature of the colony of New York, as together did form the law of the said colony on the 19th day of April, in the year of our Lord one thousand seven hundred and seventy-five, shall be and continue the law of this State, subject to such alterations and provisions as the legislature of this State shall, from time to time, make concerning the same. That such of the said acts, as are temporary, shall expire at the times limited for their duration, respectively. That all such parts of the said common law, and all such of the said statutes and acts aforesaid, or parts thereof, as may be construed to establish or maintain any particular denomination of Christians or their ministers, or concern the allegiance heretofore yielded to, and the supremacy, sovereignty, government, or prerogatives claimed or exercised by, the King of Great Britain and his predecessors, over the colony of New York and its inhabitants, or are repugnant to this constitution, be, and they hereby are, abrogated and rejected. And this convention doth further ordain, that the resolves or resolutions of the congresses of the colony of New York, and of the convention of the State of New York, now in force, and not repugnant to the government established by this constitution, shall be considered as making part of the laws of this State; subject, nevertheless, to such alterations and provisions as the legislature of this State may, from time to time, make concerning the same.

XXXVI. And be it further ordained, That all grants of lands within this State, made by the King of Great Britain, or persons acting under his authority, after the fourteenth day of October, one thousand seven hundred and seventy-five, shall be null and void; but that nothing in this constitution contained shall be construed to affect any grants of land within this State, made by the authority of the said King or his predecessors, or to annul any charters to bodies-politic by him or them, or any of them, made prior to that day. And that none of the said charters shall be adjudged to be void by reason of any non-user or misuser of any of their respective rights or privileges between the nineteenth day of April, in the year of our Lord one thousand seven hundred and seventy-five and the publication of this constitution. And further, that all such of the officers described in the said charters respectively as, by the terms of the said charters, were to be appointed by the governor of the colony of New York, with or without the advice and consent of the council of the said King, in the said colony, shall henceforth be appointed by the council established by this constitution for the appointment of officers in this State, until otherwise directed by the legislature.

XXXVII. And whereas it is of great importance to the safety of this State that peace and amity with the Indians within the same be at all times supported and maintained; and whereas the frauds too often practised towards the said Indians, in contracts made for their lands, have, in divers instances, been productive of dangerous discontents and animosities: Be it ordained, that no purchases or contracts for the sale of lands, made since the fourteenth day of October, in the year of our Lord one thousand seven hundred and seventy-five, or which may hereafter be made with or of the said Indians, within the limits of this State, shall be binding on the said Indians, or deemed valid, unless made under the authority and with the consent of the legislature of this State.

XXXVIII. And whereas we are required, by the benevolent principles of rational liberty, not only to expel civil tyranny, but also to guard against that spiritual oppression and intolerance wherewith the bigotry and ambition of weak and wicked priests and princes have scourged mankind, this convention doth further, in the name and by the authority of the good people of this State, ordain, determine, and declare, that the free exercise and enjoyment of religious profession and worship, without discrimination or preference, shall forever hereafter be allowed, within this State, to all mankind: Provided, That the liberty of conscience, hereby granted, shall not be so construed as to excuse acts of licentiousness, or justify practices inconsistent with the peace or safety of this State.

XXXIX. And whereas the ministers of the gospel are, by their profession, dedicated to the service of God and the care of souls, and ought not to be diverted from the great duties of their function; therefore, no minister of the gospel, or priest of any denomination whatsoever, shall, at any time hereafter, under any pretence or description whatever, be eligible to, or capable of holding, any civil or military office or place within this State.

XL. And whereas it is of the utmost importance to the safety of every State that it should always be in a condition of defence; and it is the duty of every man who enjoys the protection of society to be prepared and willing to defend it; this convention therefore, in the name and by the authority of the good people of this State, doth ordain, determine, and declare that the militia of this State, at all times hereafter, as well in peace as in war, shall be armed and disciplined, and in readiness for service. That all such of the inhabitants of this State being of the people called Quakers as, from scruples of conscience, may be averse to the bearing of arms, be therefrom excused by the legislature; and do pay to the State such sums of money, in lieu of their personal service, as the same may, in the judgment of the legislature, be worth. And that a proper magazine of warlike stores, proportionate to the number of inhabitants, be, forever hereafter, at the expense of this State, and by acts of the legislature, established, maintained, and continued in every county in this State.

XLI. And this convention doth further ordain, determine, and declare, in the name and by the authority of the good people of this State, that trial by jury, in all cases in which it hath heretofore been used in the colony of New York, shall be established and remain inviolate forever. And that no acts of attainder shall be passed by the legislature of this State for crimes, other than those committed before the termination of the present war; and that such acts shall not work a corruption of blood. And further, that the legislature of this State shall, at no time hereafter, institute any new court or courts, but such as shall proceed according to the course of the common law.

XLII. And this convention doth further, in the name and by the authority of the good people of this State, ordain, determine, and declare that it shall be in the discretion of the legislature to naturalize all such persons, and in such manner, as they shall think proper: Provided, All such of the persons so to be by them naturalized, as being born in parts beyond sea, and out of the United States of America, shall come to settle in and become subjects of this State, shall take an oath of allegiance to this State, and abjure and renounce all allegiance and subjection to all and every foreign king, prince, potentate, and State in all matters, ecclesiastical as well as civil.

Leonard Gansevoort,
President pro tempore

THOMAS PAINE ON A BILL OF RIGHTS, 1777

Commentary

The following article is of interest, as it gives the views of Thomas Paine, just at the time when the Revolutionary Bills of Rights were being drafted. It was called forth by a letter critical of the 1776 Pennsylvania Constitution, which Paine stoutly defended and which he had helped to draft. Paine's article is an indication of the evolving American conception of Bills of Rights. Paine asserts the view which was to prevail that a Bill of Rights "should be a plain positive declaration of the rights *themselves* rather than of the great principles of natural liberty." A comparison of the federal Bill of Rights with the French Declaration of the Rights of Man will demonstrate how right Paine was on this essential point—at least in 1777. Paine is also correct in his rejection of the notion that even a Bill of Rights is unalterable, as well as in his recognition of the doctrine of unconstitutionality of laws not consistent with a Bill of Rights.

Thomas Paine on a Bill of Rights, 1777*

Candid and Critical Remarks on a Letter Signed Ludlow

Every subject for discussion may be treated two several ways, generally or particularly. In a general review exactness is not expected; but when a writer undertakes to examine and lay down the parts of his subject separately and systematically, the greatest possible degree of exactness is necessary, and a failure in this part would be fatal to him.

The writer of the letter in question has attempted the latter, and in the course of his reasonings, says, "the present Constitution is deficient in point of perspecuity and method." I am not considering whether he is writing for or against the Constitution, but how far he appears to be master of "perspecuity and method" himself; as, by that only, we can judge of his abilities to reform the errors of others.

Many pieces, by being distributed into parts of 1, 2, 3, etc. have much the appearance of order to the eye, but unless the matter be first justly arranged in the mind of the author, and transmitted in the same order into writing, his numbers 1, 2, 3 etc. will make no impression on the understanding of the reader; and this gentleman, whom I shall be very candid with, will, I fear, stand convicted on the same charge he has brought against the Constitution.

*P. S. Foner, ed., *The Complete Works of Thomas Paine* (1945), pp. 273–77.

He sets out with giving, first, a sort of general description of "a Free Government." Secondly, a particular description of the parts thereof; each of which he has endeavored to illustrate by a simile; consequently, the same correspondence must exist between the similies as between the parts which they are supposed to represent: but if there be a want of harmony, the fault is, that either the similes are unnatural, the parts defective, or both. Thirdly, he proposes to "apply those principles (which ought rather to be called description) to the Bill of Rights, Constitution and Laws of Pennsylvania," against, he means, or for the purpose of detecting their imperfections.

"Every Free Government," he says, "should consist of three parts, viz. 1st, A Bill of Rights. 2dly, A Constitution. 3dly Laws."

Remark: As freedom depends as much on the Execution as on the Constitution, I conceive there to be something wanting to make the description complete.

I. The Bill of Rights should contain the great principles of natural and civil liberty. It should be to a community what the eternal laws and obligations of morality are to the conscience. It should be unalterable by any human power.

Remark: "The Bill of Rights should contain the great principles of natural and civil liberty." This is a huge metaphysical expression, and I conceive an erroneous one. This gentleman frequently confounds rights with principles, and uses them synonymously. I conceive a Bill of Rights should be a plain positive declaration of the rights themselves: and, instead of saying it should "contain the great principles of natural and civil liberty," that it should retain such natural rights as are either consistent with, or absolutely necessary toward our happiness in a state of civil government; for were all the great natural rights, or principles, as this writer calls them, to be admitted, it would be impossible that any government could be formed thereon, and instead of being a Bill of Rights fitted to a state of civil government, it would be a Bill of Rights fitted to man in a state of nature without any government at all. It would be an Indian Bill of Rights.

If a Bill of Rights, as this writer says, is to contain both natural and civil rights, then I cannot see how his following expression can be admitted, viz. "that it shall be unalterable by any human power." If we will have a Bill of Rights to be unalterable, it must be confined to natural rights only, for it is impossible to say what improvements may be made on civil ones; and as a matter of opinion for myself, I think it would be best so to do, and to comprehend all civil rights in that part which we call the Constitution; because, that is the part in which we are supposed to emerge from a state of nature, and erect ourselves into civil community for the mutual good and support of each other.

But here a matter arises, which this gentleman, in his description of a Bill of Rights, ought particularly to have attended to, but has wholly omitted, viz. What are natural rights and what are civil ones? I answer, A natural right is an animal right; and the power to act it, is supposed, either fully or in part, to be mechanically contained within ourselves as individuals. Civil rights are derived from the assistance or agency of other persons: they form a sort of common stock, which, by the consent of all, may be occasionally used for the benefit of any. They are substituted in the room of some natural rights, either defective in power or dangerous in practice, and are contrived to fit the members of the community with greater ease to themselves and safety to others, than what the natural ones could the individual in a state of nature: for instance, a man has a natural right to redress himself whenever he is injured, but the full exercise of this, as a natural right, would be dangerous to society, because it admits him a judge in his own cause; on the other hand, he may not be able, and must either submit to the injury or expose himself to greater: Therefore, the civil right of redressing himself by an appeal to public justice, which is the substitute, makes him stronger than the natural one, and less dangerous. Either party likewise, has a natural right to plead his own cause; this right is consistent with safety, therefore it is retained; but the parties may not be able, nay, they may be dumb, therefore the civil right of pleading by proxy, that is, by a council, is an appendage to the natural right and the trial by jury, is perfectly a civil right common to both parties.

I come now to the simile which this gentleman uses to illustrate his Bill of Rights by: "It should be," says he, "to a community what the eternal laws and obligations of morality are to the conscience." How "rights" which always imply inherent liberty can be compared with the laws of conscience, which always imply inherent restraint, I cannot conceive; they do not of their own natures admit of comparison. But this gentleman has unfortunately applied his comparison to the wrong part, for if a Bill of Rights be binding and restraining in the manner he expresses it, it is so not on the "community," because it is to them a prerogative, but on the Legislative and Executive powers, that they invade it not.

II. "A Constitution," says our author, "is the executive part of the Bill of Rights. It should contain the division and distribution of the power of the people. The modes and forms of making laws, of executing justice, and of transacting business: Also the limitation of power, as to time and jurisdiction. It is to a community what modes of worship are in religion. It should be unalterable by the legislature, and should be changed only by a representation of the people, chosen for that purpose." The last period is fully admitted.

Remark: How the "Constitution" can be called the "Executive part of the Bill of Rights," I am quite at a loss to conceive. The Constitution must be considered as a dead letter till put into execution by some external object; it has not the power of action in itself, therefore cannot be regarded as the executive of any thing. It should contain, says he, "the division and distribution of the power of the people," the modes and forms "of transacting business": These expressions are obscure. The Constitution does not "contain the division and distribution of the power of the people," but describes the portions of power with which the people invest the legislative and executive bodies, and the portions which they retain for themselves. His description, as I conceive, is partly unjust and partly perplexed; and the simile, by which he means to illustrate it, wholly unnatural. A Constitution, says he, "is to a community what modes of worship are in religion." I think it is a great deal more; a man may be religiously happy without modes, but he cannot be civilly happy without a Constitution. But taking this gentleman on his own plan it will follow, that, if a constitution "contains the divisions and distributions of the power of the people," then must "modes of worship" contain the division and distribution of the power of religion. Again, if the Constitution be the "executive part of the Bill of Rights," then must "modes of worship be the executive part of the eternal laws and obligations of morality."

The fault of this gentleman is, that he writes straight forward without regard to consistency.

III. "Laws are the executive part of a constitution. They cease to be binding whenever they transgress the principles of Liberty, as laid down in the Constitution and Bill of Rights. They are to a community what the practice of morality is in religion."

Remark: There is the same confusion of ideas in this description as in the former two. Laws should be made consistent with and agreeable to the Constitution and the Bill of Rights. They naturally cease to be binding when they oppose them, and when they vary from them, must be amended, and this is all that can be said. But to suppose "Laws executive" is a false conception: And how is it possible to compare "Laws" which are in themselves motionless and have no capacity of action, with the practice of morality, which not only implies motion, but the power of continuing it, and even of generating it, is, to me, and, I believe, to all others, incomprehensible. But to take this gentleman again on his own grounds; if the "laws" be, as he says, "the executive part of the Constitution," then must "the practice of morality" be the "executive part of modes of worship," which no man, not even the writer of it, can give his consent to.

Having laid down these three paragraphs, he proceeds to "apply them," but what he means by applying them I cannot conceive, as all that follows might as well stand without them as with them.

Whatever faults or defects the Constitution has, and no doubt it has some (for I suppose nothing is perfect, nor ever will), it ought to be every man's wish to have them pointed out, and every man's duty to have them amended; but I see no use can arise from this loose unconnected way of writing, but the propagation of further errors.

Several very scurrilous pieces under different signatures have appeared in the papers on both sides the question. In Dunlap's paper of the 18th of March is a piece signed *"Common Sense"* which is the only one that is mine since the dispute first began. The design of that piece is to keep men in temper with each other, and to show the impropriety of having our minds taken up about a form of government (which we can reconsider at any time) till we knew whether we should have one of our own forming or of the enemy's. And, as a man ought to be ashamed to publish any thing which he is ashamed to own, I have therefore put a signature to this by which I shall be known; and have likewise left my real name with the Printer, which he is welcome to give to any one that requires it.

Common Sense

VERMONT DECLARATION OF RIGHTS, 1777

Commentary

The Vermont Constitution of 1777 was the first by a state which had not been a separate Colony before Independence. Though Vermont was not officially admitted as a state until 1791, it set up its own government early in 1777. Later that year, on July 2, a Convention met to draw up a Constitution. On July 8, both the Constitution and the Declaration of Rights by which it is prefaced were adopted. The speed of the Convention is explained by the fact that they received word that Ticonderoga was being evacuated and most of the delegates wanted to get home as soon as possible. The Declaration repeats the Pennsylvania guarantees of freedom of conscience (though slightly diluted), the right to life, liberty, and property, conscientious objection, criminal procedure, the right against searches and seizures, trial by jury in civil cases, freedom of speech and press, right to bear arms, and the right of assembly and petition. All of these provisions are virtually verbatim repetitions of the relevant Pennsylvania articles. At the beginning of the Vermont Declaration, however, there was a new provision—that part of Article I which outlaws slavery and indentured servitude. There was, of course, to be no comparable provision in the federal Constitution until the ratification of the Thirteenth Amendment. In addition, the Vermont Declaration contains in Article II an express requirement that, where private property is taken for public use, "the owner ought to receive an equivalent in money." This is the forerunner of the just compensation requirement of the Fifth Amendment and is the first constitutional provision containing any such requirement (though there had been a provision on the matter in the Massachusetts Body of Liberties, 1641, *supra* p. 71).

Vermont Declaration of Rights, 1777*

Whereas, all government ought to be instituted and supported, for the security and protection of the community, as such, and to enable the individuals who compose it, to enjoy their natural rights, and the other blessings which the Author of existence has bestowed upon man; and whenever those great ends of government are not obtained, the people have a right, by common consent, to change it, and take such measures as to them may appear necessary to promote their safety and happiness.

And whereas, the inhabitants of this State have (in consideration of protection only) heretofore acknowledged allegiance to the King of Great

*Thorpe, *The Federal and State Constitutions, Colonial Charters, and Other Organic Laws,* Vol. 6, pp. 3737–41.

Britain, and the said King has not only withdrawn that protection, but commenced, and still continues to carry on, with unabated vengeance, a most cruel and unjust war against them; employing therein, not only the troops of Great Britain, but foreign mercenaries, savages and slaves, for the avowed purpose of reducing them to a total and abject submission to the despotic domination of the British parliament, with many other acts of tyranny, (more fully set forth in the declaration of Congress) whereby all allegiance and fealty to the said King and his successors, are dissolved and at an end: and all power and authority derived from him, ceased in the American Colonies.

And whereas, the territory which now comprehends the State of Vermont, did antecedently, of right, belong to the government of New-Hampshire: and the former Governor thereof, viz. his Excellency Benning Wentworth, Esq., granted many charters of lands and corporations, within this State, to the present inhabitants and others. And whereas, the late Lieutenant Governor Colden, of New-York, with others, did, in violation of the tenth command, covet those very lands; and by a false representation made to the court of Great Britain, (in the year 1764, that for the convenience of trade and administration of justice, the inhabitants were desirous of being annexed to that government,) obtained jurisdiction of those very identical lands ex-parte; which ever was, and is, disagreeable to the inhabitants. And whereas, the legislature of New-York, ever have, and still continue to disown the good people of this State, in their landed property, which will appear in the complaints hereafter inserted, and in the 36th section of their present consti-tution, in which is established the grants of land made by that government.

They have refused to make regrants of our lands to the original proprie-tors and occupants, unless at the exorbitant rate of 2300 dollars fees for each township; and did enhance the quit-rent, three fold, and demanded an immediate delivery of the title derived before, from New-Hampshire.

The judges of their supreme court have made a solemn declaration, that the charters, conveyances, &c. of the lands included in the before described premises, were utterly null and void, on which said title was founded: in consequence of which declaration, writs of possession have been by them issued, and the sheriff of the county of Albany sent, at the head of six or seven hundred men, to enforce the execution thereof.

They have passed an act, annexing a penalty thereto, of thirty pounds fine and six months imprisonment, on any person who should refuse assisting the sheriff, after being requested, for the purpose of executing writs of posses-sion.

The Governors, Dunmore, Tryon and Colden, have made re-grants of several tracts of land, included in the premises, to certain favorite land jobbers in the government of New-York, in direct violation of his Britannic majesty's express prohibition, in the year 1767.

They have issued proclamations, wherein they have offered large sums of money, for the purpose of apprehending those very persons who have dared boldly, and publicly, to appear in defence of their just rights.

They did pass twelve acts of outlawry, on the 9th day of March, A. D. 1774, impowering the respective judges of their supreme court, to award execution of death against those inhabitants in said district, that they should judge to be offenders, without trial.

They have, and still continue, an unjust claim to those lands, which greatly retards emigration into, and the settlement of, this State.

They have hired foreign troops, emigrants from Scotland, at two different times, and armed them, to drive us out of possession.

They have sent the savages on our frontiers, to distress us.

They have proceeded to erect the counties of Cumberland and Glocester, and establish courts of justice there, after they were discountenanced by the authority of Great Britain.

The free convention of the State of New-York, at Harlem, in the year 1776, unanimously voted, "That all quit-rents, formerly due to the King of Great Britain, are now due and owing to this Convention, or such future government as shall be hereafter established in this State."

In the several stages of the aforesaid oppressions, we have petitioned his Britannic majesty, in the most humble manner, for redress, and have, at very great expense, received several reports in our favor; and, in other instances, wherein we have petitioned the late legislative authority of New-York, those petitions have been treated with neglect.

And whereas, the local situation of this State, from New-York, at the extreme part, is upward of four hundred and fifty miles from the seat of that government, which renders it extreme difficult to continue under the jurisdiction of said State.

Therefore, it is absolutely necessary, for the welfare and safety of the inhabitants of this State, that it should be, henceforth, a free and independent State; and that a just, permanent, and proper form of government, should exist in it, derived from, and founded on, the authority of the people only, agreeable to the direction of the honorable American Congress.

We the representatives of the freemen of Vermont, in General Convention met, for the express purpose of forming such a government,—confessing the goodness of the Great Governor of the universe, (who alone, knows to what degree of earthly happiness, mankind may attain, by perfecting the arts of government,) in permitting the people of this State, by common consent, and without violence, deliberately to form for themselves, such just rules as they shall think best for governing their future society; and being fully convinced that it is our indispensable duty, to establish such original principles of government, as will best promote the general happiness of the people of this State, and their posterity, and provide for future improvements, without partiality for, or prejudice against, any particular class, sect, or denomination of men whatever,—do, by virtue of authority vested in us, by our constituents ordain, declare, and establish, the following declaration of rights, and frame of government, to be the Constitution of this Commonwealth, and to remain in force therein, forever, unaltered, except in such articles, as shall, hereafter, on experience, be found to require improvement, and which shall, by the same authority of the people, fairly delegated, as this frame of government directs, be amended or improved, for the more effectual obtaining and securing the great end and design of all government, herein before mentioned.

Chapter I
A Declaration of the Rights of the Inhabitants of the State of Vermont

I. That all men are born equally free and independent, and have certain natural, inherent and unalienable rights, amongst which are the enjoying and defending life and liberty; acquiring, possessing and protecting property, and pursuing and obtaining happiness and safety. Therefore, no male person, born in this country, or brought from over sea, ought to be holden by law, to serve any person, as a servant, slave or apprentice, after he arrives to the age of twenty-one years, nor female, in like manner, after she arrives to the age of eighteen years, unless they are bound by their own consent, after they arrive to such age, or bound by law, for the payment of debts, damages, fines, costs, or the like.

II. That private property ought to be subservient to public uses, when necessity requires it; nevertheless, whenever any particular man's property is taken for the use of the public, the owner ought to receive an equivalent in money.

III. That all men have a natural and unalienable right to worship Almighty God, according to the dictates of their own consciences and understanding, regulated by the word of God; and that no man ought, or of right can be compelled to attend any religious worship, or erect, or support any place of worship, or maintain any minister, contrary to the dictates of his conscience; nor can any man who professes the protestant religion, be justly deprived or abridged of any civil right, as a citizen, on account of his religious sentiment, or peculiar mode of religious worship, and that no authority can, or ought to be vested in, or assumed by, any power whatsoever, that shall, in any case, interfere with, or in any manner controul, the rights of conscience, in the free exercise of religious worship: nevertheless, every sect or denomination of people ought to observe the Sabbath, or the Lord's day, and keep up, and support, some sort of religious worship, which to them shall seem most agreeable to the revealed will of God.

IV. That the people of this State have the sole, exclusive and inherent right of governing and regulating the internal police of the same.

V. That all power being originally inherent in, and consequently, derived from, the people; therefore, all officers of government, whether legislative or executive, are their trustees and servants, and at all times accountable to them.

VI. That government is, or ought to be, instituted for the common benefit, protection, and security of the people, nation or community; and not for the particular emolument or advantage of any single man, family or set of men, who are a part only of that community; and that the community hath an indubitable, unalienable and indefeasible right to reform, alter, or abolish, government, in such manner as shall be, by that community, judged most conducive to the public weal.

VII. That those who are employed in the legislative and executive business of the State, may be restrained from oppression, the people have a right, at such periods as they may think proper, to reduce their public officers to a private station, and supply the vacancies by certain and regular elections.

VIII. That all elections ought to be free; and that all freemen, having a sufficient, evident, common interest with, and attachment to, the community, have a right to elect officers, or be elected into office.

IX. That every member of society hath a right to be protected in the enjoyment of life, liberty and property, and therefore, is bound to contribute his proportion towards the expense of that protection, and yield his personal service, when necessary, or an equivalent thereto; but no part of a man's property can be justly taken from him, or applied to public uses, without his own consent, or that of his legal representatives; nor can any man who is conscientiously scrupulous of bearing arms, be justly compelled thereto, if he will pay such equivalent; nor are the people bound by any law, but such as they have, in like manner, assented to, for their common good.

X. That, in all prosecutions for criminal offences, a man hath a right to be heard, by himself and his counsel—to demand the cause and nature of his accusation—to be confronted with the witnesses—to call for evidence in his favor, and a speedy public trial, by an impartial jury of the country; without the unanimous consent of which jury, he cannot be found guilty; nor can be be compelled to give evidence against himself; nor can any man be justly deprived of his liberty, except by the laws of the land or the judgment of his peers.

XI. That the people have a right to hold themselves, their houses, papers and possessions free from search or seizure; and therefore warrants, without oaths or affirmations first made, affording a sufficient foundation for them, and whereby any officer or messenger may be commanded or required to search suspected places, or to seize any person or persons, his, her or their property, nor particularly described, are contrary to that right, and ought not to be granted.

XII. That no warrant or writ to attach the person or estate, of any freeholder within this State, shall be issued in civil action, without the person or persons, who may request such warrant or attachment, first make oath, or affirm, before the authority who may be requested to issue the same, that he, or they, are in danger of losing his, her or their debts.

XIII. That, in controversies respecting property, and in suits between man and man, the parties have a right to a trial by jury; which ought to be held sacred.

XIV. That the people have a right to freedom of speech, and of writing and publishing their sentiments; therefore, the freedom of the press ought not be restrained.

XV. That the people have a right to bear arms for the defence of themselves and the State; and, as standing armies, in the time of peace, are dangerous to liberty, they ought not to be kept up; and that the military should be kept under strict subordination to, and governed by, the civil power.

XVI. That frequent recurrence to fundamental principles, and a firm adherence to justice, moderation, temperance, industry and frugality, are absolutely necessary to preserve the blessings of liberty, and keep government free. The people ought, therefore, to pay particular attention to these points, in the choice of officers and representatives, and have a right to exact a due and constant regard to them, from their legislators and magistrates, in the making and executing such laws as are necessary for the good government of the State.

XVII. That all people have a natural and inherent right to emigrate from one State to another, that will receive them; or to form a new State in vacant countries, or in such countries as they can purchase, whenever they think that thereby they can promote their own happiness.

XVIII. That the people have a right to assemble together, to consult for their common good—to instruct their representatives, and to apply to the legislature for redress of grievances, by address, petition or remonstrance.

XIX. That no person shall be liable to be transported out of this State for trial, for any offence committed within this State.

SOUTH CAROLINA CONSTITUTION, 1778

Commentary

Even before the May, 1776, resolution of the Continental Congress urging the establishment of independent state governments, the Provincial Congress of South Carolina had framed a Constitution. That document adopted March 26, 1776, was, however, intended only as a temporary provision of government and a more permanent Constitution was framed by the General Assembly in March, 1778. The 1778 Constitution does not contain any separate Bill of Rights. Instead, like the New Jersey, Georgia, and New York Constitutions (*supra* pp. 256, 291, 301), it contains provisions guaranteeing individual rights in the body of its text. Among the rights thus guaranteed are those to freedom of conscience (Article XXXVIII—through express provision is made for an established religion, a backward step that is fortunately not duplicated in any other Revolutionary Constitution), against disproportionate punishments (Article XL), not to be deprived of life, liberty, or property "but by the judgment of his peers, or by the law of the land" (Article XLI), and freedom of the press (Article XLIII). Compared to the other state Constitutions, the South Carolina protections are rudimentary, if not skeletal. Most of the protections which Americans had come to deem fundamental are omitted from the South Carolina text.

South Carolina Constitution, 1778*

An act for establishing the Constitution of the State of South Carolina

Whereas the constitution or form of government agreed to and resolved upon by the freemen of this country, met in congress, the twenty-sixth day of March, one thousand seven hundred and seventy-six, was temporary only, and suited to the situation of their public affairs at that period, looking forward to an accommodation with Great Britain, an event then desired; and whereas the United Colonies of America have been since constituted independent States, and the political connection heretofore subsisting between them and Great Britain entirely dissolved by the declaration of the honorable the Continental Congress, dated the fourth day of July, one thousand seven hundred and seventy-six, for the many great and weighty reasons therein particularly set forth: It therefore becomes absolutely necessary to frame a constitution suitable to that great event.

*Poore, *The Federal and State Constitutions, Colonial Charters and Other Organic Laws of the United States*, Vol. 2, pp. 1620–27.

Be it therefore constituted and enacted, by his excellency Rawlins Lowndes, esq., president and commander-in-chief in and over the State of South Carolina, by the honorable the legislative council and general assembly, and by the authority of the same:

That the following articles, agreed upon by the freemen of this State, now met in general assembly, be deemed and held the constitution and form of government of the said State, unless altered by the legislative authority thereof, which constitution or form of government shall immediately take place and be in force from the passing of this act, excepting such parts as are hereafter mentioned and specified.

I. That the style of this country be hereafter the State of South Carolina.

II. That the legislative authority be vested in a general assembly, to consist of two distinct bodies, a senate and house of representatives, but that the legislature of this State, as established by the constitution or form of government passed the twenty-sixth of March, one thousand seven hundred and seventy-six, shall continue and be in full force until the twenty-ninth day of November ensuing.

III. That as soon as may be after the first meeting of the senate and house of representatives, and at every first meeting of the senate and house of representatives thereafter, to be elected by virtue of this constitution, they shall jointly in the house of representatives choose by ballot from among themselves or from the people at large a governor and commander-in-chief, a lieutenant-governor, both to continue for two years, and a privy council, all of the Protestant religion, and till such choice shall be made the former president or governor and commander-in-chief, and vice-president or lieutenant-governor, as the case may be, and privy council, shall continue to act as such.

IV. That a member of the senate or house of representatives, being chosen and acting as governor and commander-in-chief or lieutenant-governor, shall vacate his seat, and another person shall be elected in his room.

V. That every person who shall be elected governor and commander-in-chief of the State, or lieutenant-governor, or a member of the privy council, shall be qualified as followeth: that is to say, the governor and lieutenant-governor shall have been residents in this State for ten years, and the members of the privy council five years, preceding their said election, and shall have in this State a settled plantation of free-hold in their and each of their own right of the value of at least ten thousand pounds currency, clear of debt, and on being elected they shall respectively take an oath of qualification in the house of representatives.

VI. That no future governor and commander-in-chief who shall serve for two years shall be eligible to serve in the said office after the expiration of the said term until the full end and term of four years.

VII. That no person in this State shall hold the office of governor thereof, or lieutenant-governor, and any other office or commission, civil or military, (except in the militia,) either in this or any other State, or under the authority of the Continental Congress, at one and the same time.

VIII. That in case of the impeachment of the governor and commander-in-chief, or his removal from office, death, resignation, or absence from the State, the lieutenant-governor shall succeed to his office, and the privy council shall choose out of their own body a lieutenant-governor of the State. And in case of the impeachment of the lieutenant-governor, or his removal from office, death, resignation, or absence from the State, one of the privy council, to be chosen by themselves, shall succeed to his office until a nomination to those offices respectively, by the senate and house of representatives, for the remainder of the time for which the officer so impeached, removed from office, dying, resigning, or being absent was appointed.

IX. That the privy council shall consist of the lieutenant-governor for the time being, and eight other members, five of whom shall be a quorum, to be chosen as before directed; four to serve for two years, and four for one year, and at the expiration of one year four others shall be chosen in the room of the last four, to serve for two years, and all future members of the privy council shall thenceforward be elected to serve two years, whereby there will be a new election every year for half the privy council, and a constant rotation established; but no member of the privy council who shall serve for two years shall be eligible to serve therein after the expiration of the said term until the full end and term of four years: Provided always, That no officer of the army or navy in the service of the continent or this State, nor judge of any of the courts of law, shall be eligible, nor shall the father, son, or brother to the governor for the time being be elected in the privy council during his administration. A member of the senate and house of representatives being chosen of the privy council, shall not thereby lose his seat in the senate or house of representatives, unless he be elected lieutenant-governor, in which case he shall, and another person shall be chosen in his stead. The privy council is to advise the governor and commander-in-chief when required, but he shall not be bound to consult them unless directed by law. If a member of the privy council shall die or depart this State during the recess of the general assembly, the privy council shall choose another to act in his room, until a nomination by the senate and house of representatives shall take place. The clerk of the privy council shall keep a regular journal of all their proceedings, in which shall be entered the yeas and nays on every question, and the opinion, with the reasons at large, of any member who desires it; which journal shall be laid before the legislature when required by either house.

X. That in case of the absence from the seat of government or sickness of the governor and lieutenant-governor, any one of the privy council may be empowered by the governor, under his hand and seal, to act in his room, but such appointment shall not vacate his seat in the senate, house of representatives, or privy council.

XI. That the executive authority be vested in the governor and commander-in-chief, in manner herein mentioned.

XII. That each parish and district throughout this State shall on the last Monday in November next and the day following, and on the same days of every succeeding year thereafter, elect by ballot one member of the senate, except the district of Saint Philip and Saint Michael's parishes, Charleston, which shall elect two members: and except also the district between Broad and Saluda Rivers, in three divisions, viz: the Lower district, the Little River district, and the Upper or Spartan district, each of which said divisions shall elect one member; and except the parishes of Saint Matthew and Orange, which shall elect one member; and also except the parishes of Prince George and All Saints, which shall elect one member; and the election of senators for such parishes, respectively, shall, until otherwise altered by the legislature, be at the parish of Prince George for the said parish and the parish of All Saints, and at the parish of Saint Matthew for that parish and the parish of Orange; to meet on the first Monday in January then next, at the seat of government, unless the casualties of war or contagious disorders should render it unsafe to meet there, in which case the governor and commander-in-chief for the time being may, by proclamation, with the advice and consent of the privy council, appoint a more secure and convenient place of meeting; and to continue for two years from the said last Monday in November; and that no person shall be eligible to a seat in the said senate unless he be of the Protestant religion, and hath attained the age of thirty years, and hath been a resident in this State at least five years. Not less than thirteen members shall be a quorum to do business, but the president or any three members may adjourn from day to day. No person who resides in the parish or district for which he is elected shall take his seat in the senate, unless he possess a settled estate and freehold in his own right in the said parish or district of the value of two thousand pounds currency at least, clear of debt; and no non-resident shall be eligible to a seat in the said senate unless he is owner of a settled estate and freehold in his own right, in the parish or district where he is elected, of the value of seven thousand pounds currency at least, also clear of debt.

XIII. That on the last Monday in November next and the day following, and on the same days of every second year thereafter, members of the house of representatives shall be chosen, to meet on the first Monday in January then next, at the seat of government unless the casualties of war or contagious disorders should render it unsafe to meet there, in which case the governor and commander-in-chief for the time being may, by proclamation, with the advice and consent of the privy council, appoint a more secure and convenient place of meeting, and to continue for two years from the said last Monday in November. Each parish and district within this State shall send members to the general assembly in the following proportions; that is to say, the parish of Saint Philip and Saint Michael's, Charleston, thirty members;

the parish of Christ Church, six members; the parish of Saint John's, in Berkely County, six members; the parish of Saint Andrew, six members; the parish of Saint George, Dorchester, six members; the parish of Saint James, Goose Creek, six members; the parish of Saint Thomas and Saint Dennis, six members; the parish of Saint Paul, six members; the parish of Saint Bartholomew, six members; the parish of Saint Helena, six members; the parish of Saint James, Santee, six members; the parish of Prince George, Winyaw, four members; the parish of All Saints, two members; the parish of Prince Frederick, six members; the parish of Saint John, in Colleton County, six members; the parish of Saint Peter, six members; the parish of Prince William, six members; the parish of Saint Stephen, six members; the district to the eastward of Wateree River, ten members; the district of Ninety-six, ten members; the district of Saxe Gotha, six members; the district between Broad and Saluda Rivers, in three divisions, viz: the lower district, four members; the Little River district, four members; the Upper or Spartan district, four members; the district between Broad and Catawba Rivers, ten members; the district called the New Acquisition, ten members; the parish of Saint Matthew, three members; the parish of Orange, three members; the parish of Saint David, six members; the district between the Savannah River and the North Fork of Edisto, six members. And the election of the said members shall be conducted as near as may be agreeable to the directions of the present or any future election act or acts, and where there are no churches or church-wardens in a district or parish, the house of representatives, at some convenient time before their expiration, shall appoint places of election and persons to receive votes and make returns. The qualification of electors shall be that every free white man, and no other person, who adknowledges the being of a God, and believes in a future state of rewards and punishments, and who has attained to the age of one and twenty years, and hath been a resident and an inhabitant in this State for the space of one whole year before the day appointed for the election he offers to give his vote at, and hath a freehold at least of fifty acres of land, or a town lot, and hath been legally seized and possessed of the same at least six months previous to such election, or hath paid a tax the preceding year, or was taxable the present year, at least six months previous to the said election, in a sum equal to the tax on fifty acres of land, to the support of this government, shall be deemed a person qualified to vote for, and shall be capable of electing, a representative or representatives to serve as a member or members in the senate and house of representatives, for the parish or district where he actually is a resident, or in any other parish or district in this State where he hath the like freehold. Electors shall take an oath or affirmation of qualification, if required by the returning officer. No person shall be eligible to sit in the house of representatives unless he be of the Protestant religion, and hath been a resident in this State for three years previous to his election. The qualification of the elected, if residents in the parish or district for which they shall be returned, shall be the same as mentioned in the election act, and construed to mean clear of debt. But no non-resident shall be eligible to a seat in the house of representatives unless he is owner of a settled estate and freehold in his own right of the value of three thousand and five hundred pounds currency at least, clear of debt, in the parish or district for which he is elected.

XIV. That if any parish or district neglects or refuses to elect members, or if the members chosen do not meet in general assembly, those who do meet shall have the powers of the general assembly. Not less than sixty-nine members shall make a house of representatives to do business, but the speaker or any seven members may adjourn from day to day.

XV. That at the expiration of seven years after the passing of this constitution, and at the end of every fourteen years thereafter, the representation of the whole State shall be proportioned in the most equal and just manner according to the particular and comparative strength and taxable property of the different parts of the same, regard being always had to the number of white inhabitants and such taxable property.

XVI. That all money bills for the support of government shall originate in the house of representatives, and shall not be altered or amended by the senate, but may be rejected by them, and that no money be drawn out of the public treasury but by the legislative authority of the State. All other bills and ordinances may take rise in the senate or house of representatives, and be altered, amended, or rejected by either. Acts and ordinances having passed the general assembly shall have the great seal affixed to them by a joint committee of both houses, who shall wait upon the governor to receive and return the seal, and shall then be signed by the president of the senate and speaker of the house of representatives, in the senate-house, and shall thenceforth have all the force and validity of a law, and be lodged in the secretary's office. And the senate and house of representatives, respectively, shall enjoy all other privileges which have at any time been claimed or exercised by the commons house of assembly.

XVII. That neither the senate nor house of representatives shall have power to adjourn themselves for any longer time than three days, without the mutual consent of both. The governor and commander-in-chief shall have no power to adjourn, prorogue, or dissolve them, but may, if necessary, by and with the advice and consent of the privy council, convene them before the time to which they shall stand adjourned. And where a bill hath been rejected by either house, it shall not be brought in again that session, without leave of the house, and a notice of six days being previously given.

XVIII. That the senate and house of representatives shall each choose their respective officers by ballot, without control, and that during a recess the president of the senate and speaker of the house of representatives shall issue writs for filling up vacancies occasioned by death in their respective houses, giving at least three weeks and not more than thirty-five days' previous notice of the time appointed for the election.

XIX. That if any parish or district shall neglect to elect a member or members on the day of election, or in case any person chosen a member of either house shall refuse to qualify and take his seat as such, or die, or depart the State, the senate or house of representatives, as the case may be, shall appoint proper days for electing a member or members in such cases respectively.

XX. That if any member of the senate or house of representatives shall accept any place of emolument, or any commission, (except in the militia or commission of the peace, and except as is excepted in the tenth article,) he shall vacate his seat, and there shall thereupon be a new election: but he shall not be disqualified from serving upon being reelected, unless he is appointed secretary of the State, a commissioner of the treasury, an officer of the customs, register of mesne conveyances, a clerk of either of the courts of justice, sheriff, powder-reviewer, clerk of the senate, house of representatives, or privy council, surveyor-general, or commissary of military stores, which officers are hereby declared disqualified from being members either of the senate or house of representatives.

XXI. And whereas the ministers of the gospel are by their profession dedicated to the service of God and the cure of souls, and ought not to be diverted from the great duties of their function, therefore no minister of the gospel or public preacher of any religious persuasion, while he continues in the exercise of his pastoral function, and for two years after, shall be eligible either as governor, lieutenant-governor, a member of the senate, house of representatives, or privy council in this State.

XXII. That the delegates to represent this State in the Congress of the United States be chosen annually by the senate and house of representatives jointly, by ballot, in the house of representatives, and nothing contained in this constitution shall be construed to extend to vacate the seat of any member who is or may be a delegate from this State to Congress as such.

XXIII. That the form of impeaching all officers of the State for mal and corrupt conduct in their respective offices, not amenable to any other jurisdiction, be vested in the house of representatives. But that it shall always be necessary that two-third parts of the members present do consent to and agree in such impeachment. That the senators and such of the judges of this State as are not members of the house of representatives, be a court for the trial of impeachments, under such regulations as the legislature shall establish, and that previous to the trial of every impeachment, the members of the said court shall respectively be sworn truly and impartially to try and determine the charge in question according to evidence, and no judgment of the said court, except judgment of acquittal, shall be valid, unless it shall be assented to by two-third parts of the members then present, and on every trial, as well on impeachments as others, the party accused shall be allowed counsel.

XXIV. That the lieutenant-governor of the State and a majority of the privy council for the time being shall, until otherwise altered by the legislature, exercise the powers of a court of chancery, and there shall be ordinaries appointed in the several districts of this State, to be chosen by the senate and house of representatives jointly by ballot, in the house of representatives, who shall, within their respective districts, exercise the powers heretofore exercised by the ordinary, and until such appointment is made the present ordinary in Charleston shall continue to exercise that office as heretofore.

XXV. That the jurisdiction of the court of admiralty be confined to maritime causes.

XXVI. That justices of the peace shall be nominated by the senate and house of representatives jointly, and commissioned by the governor and commander-in-chief during pleasure. They shall be entitled to receive the fees heretofore established by law; and not acting in the magistracy, they shall not be entitled to the privileges allowed them by law.

XXVII. That all other judicial officers shall be chosen by ballot, jointly by the senate and house of representatives, and, except the judges of the court of chancery, commissioned by the governor and commander-in-chief during good behavior, but shall be removed on address of the senate and house of representatives.

XXVIII. That the sheriffs, qualified as by law directed, shall be chosen in like manner by the senate and house of representatives, when the governor, lieutenant-governor, and privy council are chosen, and commissioned by the governor and commander-in-chief, for two years, and shall give security as required by law, before they enter on the execution of their office. No sheriff who shall have served for two years shall be eligible to serve in the said office after the expiration of the said term, until the full end and term of four years, but shall continue in office until such choice be made; nor shall any person be eligible as sheriff in any district unless he shall have resided therein for two years previous to the election.

XXIX. That two commissioners of the treasury, the secretary of the State, the register of mesne conveyances in each district, attorney-general, sur-veyer-general, powder-receiver, collectors and comptrollers of the customs and waiters, be chosen in like manner by the senate and house of representatives jointly, by ballot, in the house of representatives, and commissioned by the governor and commander-in-chief, for two years; that none of the said officers, respectively, who shall have served for four years, shall be eligible to serve in the said offices after the expiration of the said term, until the full end and term of four years, but shall continue in office until a new choice be made: Provided, That nothing herein contained shall extend to the several persons appointed to the above offices respectively, under the late constitu-tion; and that the present and all future commissioners of the treasury, and powder-receivers, shall each give bond with approved security agreeable to law.

XXX. That all the officers in the army and navy of this State, of and above the rank of captain, shall be chosen by the senate and house of representatives jointly, by ballot in the house of representatives, and commissioned by the governor and commander-in-chief, and that all other officers in the army and navy of this State shall be commissioned by the governor and commander-in-chief.

XXXI. That in case of vacancy in any of the offices above directed to be filled by the senate and house of representatives, the governor and commander-in-chief, with the advice and consent of the privy council, may appoint others in their stead, until there shall be an election by the senate and house of representatives to fill those vacancies respectively.

XXXII. That the governor and commander-in-chief, with the advice and consent of the privy council, may appoint during pleasure, until otherwise directed by law, all other necessary officers, except such as are now by law directed to be otherwise chosen.

XXXIII. That the governor and commander-in-chief shall have no power to commence war, or conclude peace, or enter into any final treaty without the consent of the senate and house of representatives.

XXXIV. That the resolutions of the late congress of this State, and all laws now of force here, (and not hereby altered,) shall so continue until altered or repealed by the legislature of this State, unless where they are temporary, in which case they shall expire at the times respectively limited for their duration.

XXXV. That the governor and commander-in-chief for the time being, by and with the advice and consent of the privy council, may lay embargoes or prohibit the exportation of any commodity, for any time not exceeding thirty days, in the recess of the general assembly.

XXXVI. That all persons who shall be chosen and appointed to any office or to any place of trust, civil or military, before entering upon the execution of office, shall take the following oath: "I, A. B., do acknowledge the State of South Carolina to be a free, sovereign, and independent State, and that the people thereof owe no allegiance or obedience to George the Third, King of Great Britain, and I do renounce, refuse, and abjure any allegiance or obedience to him. And I do swear [or affirm, as the case may be] that I will, to the utmost of my power, support, maintain, and defend the said State against the said King George the Third, and his heirs and successors, and his or their abettors, assistants, and adherents, and will serve the said State, in the office of——, with fidelity and honor, and according to the best of my skill and understanding: So help me God."

XXXVII. That adequate yearly salaries be allowed to the public officers of this State, and be fixed by law.

XXXVIII. That all persons and religious societies who acknowledge that there is one God, and a future state of rewards and punishments, and that God is publicly to be worshipped, shall be freely tolerated. The Christian Protestant religion shall be deemed, and is hereby constituted and declared to be, the established religion of this State. That all denominations of

Christian Protestants in this State, demeaning themselves peaceably and faithfully, shall enjoy equal religious and civil privileges. To accomplish this desirable purpose without injury to the religious property of those societies of Christians which are by law already incorporated for the purpose of religious worship, and to put it fully into the power of every other society of Christian Protestants, either already formed or hereafter to be formed, to obtain the like incorporation, it is hereby constituted, appointed, and declared that the respective societies of the Church of England that are already formed in this State for the purpose of religious worship shall still continue incorporate and hold the religious property now in their possession. And that whenever fifteen or more male persons, not under twenty-one years of age, professing the Christian Protestant religion, and agreeing to unite themselves in a society for the purposes of religious worship, they shall, (on complying with the terms hereinafter mentioned,) be, and be constituted, a church, and be esteemed and regarded in law as of the established religion of the State, and on a petition to the legislature shall be entitled to be incorporated and to enjoy equal privileges. That every society of Christians so formed shall give themselves a name or denomination by which they shall be called and known in law, and all that associate with them for the purposes of worship shall be esteemed as belonging to the society so called. But that previous to the establishment and incorporation of the respective societies of every denomination as aforesaid, and in order to entitle them thereto, each society so petitioning shall have agreed to and subscribed in a book the following five articles, without which no agreement or union of men upon pretence of religion shall entitle them to be incorporated and esteemed as a church of the established religion of this State:

> 1st. That there is one eternal God, and a future state of rewards and punishments.
> 2d. That God is publicly to be worshipped.
> 3d. That the Christian religion is the true religion.
> 4th. That the holy scriptures of the Old and New Testaments are of divine inspiration, and are the rule of faith and practice.
> 5th. That it is lawful and the duty of every man being thereunto called by those that govern, to bear witness to the truth.

And that every inhabitant of this State, when called to make an appeal to God as a witness to truth, shall be permitted to do it in that way which is most agreeable to the dictates of his own conscience. And that the people of this State may forever enjoy the right of electing their own pastors or clergy, and at the same time that the State may have sufficient security for the due discharge of the pastoral office, by those who shall be admitted to be clergymen, no person shall officiate as minister of any established cnurch who shall not have been chosen by a majority of the society to which he shall minister, or by persons appointed by the said majority, to choose and procure a minister for them; nor until the minister so chosen and appointed shall have made and subscribed to the following declaration, over and above the aforesaid five articles, viz: "That he is determined by God's grace out of the holy scriptures, to instruct the people committed to his charge, and to teach nothing as required of necessity to eternal salvation but that which he shall be persuaded may be concluded and proved from the scripture; that he will use both public and private admonitions, as well to the sick as to the whole within his care, as need shall require and occasion shall be given, and that he will be diligent in prayers, and in reading of the holy scriptures, and in such studies as help to the knowledge of the same; that he will be diligent to frame and fashion his own self and his family according to the doctrine of Christ, and to make both himself and them, as much as in him lieth, wholesome examples and patterns to the flock of Christ; that he will maintain and set forwards, as much as he can, quietness, peace, and love among all people, and especially among those that are or shall be committed to his charge. No person shall disturb or molest any religious assembly; nor shall use any reproachful, reviling, or abusive language against any church, that being the certain way of disturbing the peace, and of hindering the conversion of any to the truth, by engaging them in quarrels and animosities, to the hatred of the professors, and that profession which otherwise they might be brought to assent to. No person whatsoever shall speak anything in their religious assembly irreverently or seditiously of the government of this State. No person shall, by law, be obliged to pay towards the maintenance and support of a religious worship that he does not freely join in, or has not voluntarily engaged to support. But the churches, chapels, parsonages, glebes, and all other property now belonging to any societies of the Church of England, or any other religious societies, shall remain and be secured to them forever. The poor shall be supported, and elections managed in the accustomed manner, until laws shall be provided to adjust those matters in the most equitable way.

XXXIX. That the whole State shall, as soon as proper laws can be passed for these purposes, be divided into districts and counties, and county courts established.

XL. That the penal laws, as heretofore used, shall be reformed, and punishments made in some cases less sanguinary, and in general more proportionate to the crime.

XLI. That no freeman of this State be taken or imprisoned, or disseized of his freehold, liberties, or privileges, or outlawed, exiled, or in any manner destroyed or deprived of his life, liberty, or property, but by the judgment of his peers or by the law of the land.

XLII. That the military be subordinate to the civil power of the State.

XLIII. That the liberty of the press be inviolably preserved.

XLIV. That no part of this constitution shall be altered without notice being previously given of ninety days, nor shall any part of the same be changed without the consent of a majority of the members of the senate and house of representatives.

XLV. That the senate and house of representatives shall not proceed to the election of a governor or lieutenant-governor, until there be a majority of both houses present.

In the council-chamber, the 19th day of March, 1778.

Assented to.

Rawlins Lowndes

Hugh Rutledge,
Speaker of the Legislative Council.
Thomas Bee,
Speaker of the General Assembly.

MASSACHUSETTS DECLARATION OF RIGHTS, 1780

Commentary

Massachusetts had, of course, been the leader in the conflict which led to Independence. But it was one of the last states to give effect to the congressional resolution of May, 1776, calling for the setting up of new governments by adopting a new Constitution to replace its royal Charter. The first Massachusetts Constitution was not adopted until 1780. Government until then was carried on by the General Court (as the Massachusetts legislature was called) acting without a Governor. In 1778, the legislature itself drew up a Constitution, but it was rejected by the people by an overwhelming majority. Among the main reasons for the rejection was the absence of any Bill of Rights in the proposed Constitution. The provisions in that document protecting trial by jury and freedom of religion (using the term "free exercise") were not deemed sufficient to protect personal rights. The feeling of the people in this respect was amply demonstrated in the Declarations on the 1778 Constitution by different towns. The best known of these was the Declaration prepared by a convention at Ipswich, Essex County, which also published a pamphlet explaining their position known as the "Essex Result." (Extracts of these follow to illustrate the popular feeling in favor of a Bill of Rights.) The Essex theory (which was to play an important part in the Massachusetts Convention which ratified the federal Constitution) was that the Bill of Rights was an essential prerequisite for "ratification of any constitution." A Bill of Rights was "the equivalent every man receives, as a consideration for the rights he has surrendered."

In response to the popular demand, a Constitutional Convention was chosen in 1779. At its very first session, on September 2, the delegates voted, "That there be a Declaration of Rights prepared previous to the framing a new Constitution of Government." The next day the Convention formally "Resolved, that the Convention will prepare a Declaration of Rights of the People of the Massachusetts Bay." The vote on the resolution was 250 to 1. A committee of 30 members was chosen to prepare a draft Declaration. It delegated its task to a subcommittee (composed of James Bowdoin, John Adams, and Samuel Adams), which drew up the original draft of both the Declaration of Rights and the Constitution itself. John Adams himself was the principal author of both documents and was, in later life, extremely proud of his accomplishment. As far as the Declaration of Rights is concerned, Adams stated in 1812 that "the Declaration of Rights was drawn by me, who was appointed alone by the Grand Committee to draw it up."

Both the Adams draft and the Declaration of Rights as adopted by the Convention are contained in the materials following this Commentary. Com-

337

parison between them shows that Adams' role in the Massachusetts Declaration was almost as important as that of George Mason in the Virginia Declaration.

The Adams draft was accepted by the Convention with relatively few modifications. To the constitutional historian, the most important of these was the inclusion of perhaps the most famous provision of the Massachusetts Declaration, Article XXX, with its celebrated statement of the separation of powers, "to the end it may be a government of laws and not of men." This was substituted during the Convention debate for the skeleton version contained in Adams' draft—but the Convention Journal does not unfortunately tell us who drafted the substitute or what debate it provoked.

To contemporaries, the most noted change made by the Convention was Article III (substituted for the Adams version), which turned out to be the most controversial provision of the Declaration. It was a backward measure, since its effect was to place the Congregational Church in a favored position, despite the statement at its end that "no subordination of any one sect or denomination to another shall ever be established by law". Otherwise, the draft prepared by Adams was adopted with little change. The most important revisions were the elimination from the draft of Article XVII of "a right to the freedom of speaking" and the addition to Article X that reasonable compensation must be paid for takings of property for a public use—the second constitutional forerunner of the Fifth Amendment. The just compensation requirement (derived from a provision in the Body of Liberties, 1641 [*supra* p. 71]) is, like the rest of the Massachusetts Declaration, marked throughout by the pedantic archaisms of Adams' style, notably in his use of the word "subject" to designate those whose rights are protected.

The Massachusetts Declaration is a compendium of the earlier state Declarations of Rights. Among the rights protected in terms similar to those in prior Declarations are that of criminal accusation, against self-incrimination, to confrontation and counsel, not to be deprived of "life, liberty, or estate, but by the judgment of his peers, or the law of the land," trial by jury, against unreasonable searches and seizures (the language here moves much closer to that in the Fourth Amendment, containing all the essential elements of the later provision), freedom of the press, right to bear arms, freedom of speech (but only in the legislature), right against ex post facto laws, excessive bail or fines, cruel or unusual punishment, quartering of soldiers and bills of attainder.

There are also provisions which do not appear in earlier constitutional documents. The one which commentators have most noted was the statement of the separation of powers. Also worthy of mention is Article IV (an early statement of the principle to be articulated in the Tenth Amendment that the powers not delegated to the nation are reserved to the states), the requirement of just compensation in Article X, and the strong provisions in Article

XXIX for judicial tenure during good behavior and fixed salaries (which has its counterpart in Article III of the federal Constitution).

The Massachusetts Declaration of Rights is a summary of the fundamental rights of Americans at the end of the Revolutionary period. It gains particular significance from the fact that Massachusetts was to be the first state to act on the notion that a Bill of Rights was to be recommended as part of ratification of the federal Constitution (*infra* p. 674). The Massachusetts Declaration of Rights was a precedent for the amendments recommended by the 1788 Massachusetts Ratifying Convention.

Massachusetts Declaration of Rights, 1780*

A Constitution or Frame of Government, Agreed upon by the Delegates of the People of the State of Massachusetts-Bay,—In Convention,—Began and held at Cambridge, on the First of September, 1779, and continued by Adjournments to the Second of March, 1780.

Preamble

The end of the institution, maintenance and administration of government, is to secure the existence of the body-politic; to protect it; and to furnish the individuals who compose it, with the power of enjoying, in safety and tranquillity, their natural rights, and the blessings of life; And whenever these great objects are not obtained, the people have a right to alter the government, and to take measures necessary for their safety, prosperity and happiness.

The body-politic is formed by a voluntary association of individuals: It is a social compact, by which the whole people covenants with each citizen, and each citizen with the whole people, that all shall be governed by certain laws for the common good. It is the duty of the people, therefore, in framing a Constitution of Government, to provide for an equitable mode of making laws, as well as for an impartial interpretation, and a faithful execution of them; that every man may, at all times, find his security in them.

We, therefore, the people of Massachusetts, acknowledging, with grateful hearts, the goodness of the Great Legislator of the Universe, in affording us, in the course of His providence, an opportunity, deliberately and peaceably, without fraud, violence or surprise, of entering into an original, explicit, and solemn compact with each other; and of forming a new Constitution of Civil Government, for ourselves and posterity; and devoutly imploring His direc-

*Journal of the Convention for Framing a Constitution of Government for the State of Massachusetts Bay, 1779–1780 (1832), pp. 222–27.

tion in so interesting a design, Do agree upon, ordain and establish, the following Declaration of Rights, and Frame of Government, as the Constitution of the Commonwealth of Massachusetts.

Part the First
A Declaration of the Rights of the Inhabitants of the Commonwealth of Massachusetts

I. All men are born free and equal, and have certain natural, essential, and unalienable rights; among which may be reckoned the right of enjoying and defending their lives and liberties; that of acquiring, possessing, and protecting property; in fine, that of seeking and obtaining their safety and happiness.

II. It is the right as well as the duty of all men in society, publicly, and at stated seasons, to worship the Supreme Being, the great creator and preserver of the universe. And no subject shall be hurt, molested, or restrained, in his person, liberty, or estate, for worshipping God in the manner and season most agreeable to the dictates of his own conscience; or for his religious profession or sentiments; provided he doth not disturb the public peace, or obstruct others in their religious worship.

III. As the happiness of a people, and the good order and preservation of civil government, essentially depend upon piety, religion and morality; and as these cannot be generally diffused through a community, but by the institution of the public worship of God, and of public instructions in piety, religion and morality: Therefore, to promote their happiness and to secure the good order and preservation of their government, the people of this Commonwealth have a right to invest their legislature with power to authorize and require, and the legislature shall, from time to time, authorize and require, the several towns, parishes, precincts, and other bodies-politic, or religious societies, to make suitable provision, at their own expense, for the institution of the public worship of God, and for the support and maintenance of public protestant teachers of piety, religion and morality, in all cases where such provision shall not be made voluntarily.

And the people of this Commonwealth have also a right to, and do, invest their legislature with authority to enjoin upon all the subjects an attendance upon the instructions of the public teachers aforesaid, at stated times and seasons, if there be any on whose instructions they can conscientiously and conveniently attend.

Provided notwithstanding, that the several towns, parishes, precincts, and other bodies-politic, or religious societies, shall, at all times, have the exclusive right of electing their public teachers, and of contracting with them for their support and maintenance.

And all monies paid by the subject to the support of public worship, and of the public teachers aforesaid, shall, if he require it, be uniformly applied to the support of the public teacher or teachers of his own religious sect or denomination, provided there be any on whose instructions he attends: otherwise it may be paid towards the support of the teacher or teachers of the parish or precinct in which the said monies are raised.

And every denomination of christians, demeaning themselves peaceably, and as good subjects of the Commonwealth, shall be equally under the protection of the law; And no subordination of any one sect or denomination to another shall ever be established by law.

IV. The people of this Commonwealth have the sole and exclusive right of governing themselves as a free, sovereign, and independent state; and do, and forever hereafter shall, exercise and enjoy every power, jurisdiction, and right, which is not, or may not hereafter, be by them expressly delegated to the United States of America, in Congress assembled.

V. All power residing originally in the people, and being derived from them, the several magistrates and officers of government, vested with authority, whether legislative, executive, or judicial, are their substitutes and agents, and are at all times accountable to them.

VI. No man, nor corporation, or association of men, have any other title to obtain advantages, or particular and exclusive privileges, distinct from those of the community, than what arises from the consideration of services rendered to the public; and this title being in nature neither hereditary, nor transmissible to children, or descendants, or relations by blood, the idea of a man born a magistrate, lawgiver, or judge, is absurd and unnatural.

VII. Government is instituted for the common good; for the protection, safety, prosperity and happiness of the people; and not for the profit, honor, or private interest of any one man, family, or class of men: Therefore the people alone have an incontestible, unalienable, and indefeasible right to institute government; and to reform, alter, or totally change the same, when their protection, safety, prosperity and happiness require it.

VIII. In order to prevent those, who are vested with authority, from becoming oppressors, the people have a right, at such periods and in such manner as they shall establish by their frame of government, to cause their public officers to return to private life; and to fill up vacant places by certain and regular elections and appointments.

IX. All elections ought to be free; and all the inhabitants of this Commonwealth, having such qualifications as they shall establish by their frame of government, have an equal right to elect officers, and to be elected, for public employments.

X. Each individual of the society has a right to be protected by it in the enjoyment of his life, liberty and property, according to standing laws. He is obliged, consequently, to contribute his share to the expense of this protection; to give his personal service, or an equivalent, when necessary: But no part of the property of any individual, can, with justice, be taken from him, or applied to public uses without his own consent, or that of the representative body of the people: In fine, the people of this Commonwealth are not controlable by any other laws, than those to which their constitutional representative body have given their consent. And whenever the public exigencies require, that the property of any individual should be appropriated to public uses, he shall receive a reasonable compensation therefor.

XI. Every subject of the Commonwealth ought to find a certain remedy, by having recourse to the laws, for all injuries or wrongs which he may receive in his person, property, or character. He ought to obtain right and justice freely, and without being obliged to purchase it; completely, and without any denial; promptly, and without delay; conformably to the laws.

XII. No subject shall be held to answer for any crime or offence, until the same is fully and plainly, substantially and formally, described to him; or be compelled to accuse, or furnish evidence against himself. And every subject shall have a right to produce all proofs, that may be favorable to him; to meet the witnesses against him face to face, and to be fully heard in his defence by himself, or his council, at his election. And no subject shall be arrested, imprisoned, despoiled, or deprived of his property, immunities, or privileges, put out of the protection of the law, exiled, or deprived of his life, liberty, or estate; but by the judgment of his peers, or the law of the land.

And the legislature shall not make any law, that shall subject any person to a capital or infamous punishment, excepting for the government of the army and navy, without trial by jury.

XIII. In criminal prosecutions, the verification of facts in the vicinity where they happen, is one of the greatest securities of the life, liberty, and property of the citizen.

XIV. Every subject has a right to be secure from all unreasonable searches, and seizures of his person, his houses, his papers, and all his possessions. All warrants, therefore, are contrary to this right, if the cause or foundation of them be not previously supported by oath or affirmation; and if the order in the warrant to a civil officer, to make search in suspected places, or to arrest one or more suspected persons, or to seize their property, be not accompanied with a special designation of the persons or objects of search, arrest, or seizure: and no warrant ought to be issued but in cases, and with the formalities, prescribed by the laws.

XV. In all controversies concerning property, and in all suits between two or more persons, except in cases in which it has heretofore been otherways used and practised, the parties have a right to a trial by jury; and this method of procedure shall be held sacred, unless, in causes arising on the high-seas, and such as relate to mariners wages, the legislature shall hereafter find it necessary to alter it.

XVI. The liberty of the press is essential to the security of freedom in a state: it ought not, therefore, to be restrained in this Commonwealth.

XVII. The people have a right to keep and to bear arms for the common defence. And as in time of peace armies are dangerous to liberty, they ought not to be maintained without the consent of the legislature; and the military power shall always be held in an exact subordination to the civil authority, and be governed by it.

XVIII. A Frequent recurrence to the fundamental principles of the constitution, and a constant adherence to those of piety, justice, moderation, temperance, industry, and frugality, are absolutely necessary to preserve the advantages of liberty, and to maintain a free government: The people ought, consequently, to have a particular attention to all those principles, in the choice of their officers and representatives: And they have a right to require of their law-givers and magistrates, an exact and constant observance of them, in the formation and execution of the laws necessary for the good administration of the Commonwealth.

XIX. The people have a right, in an orderly and peaceable manner, to assemble to consult upon the common good; give instructions to their representatives; and to request of the legislative body, by the way of addresses, petitions, or remonstrances, redress of the wrongs done them, and of the grievances they suffer.

XX. The power of suspending the laws, or the execution of the laws, ought never to be exercised but by the legislature, or by authority derived from it, to be exercised in such particular cases only as the legislature shall expressly provide for.

XXI. The freedom of deliberation, speech and debate, in either house of the legislature, is so essential to the rights of the people, that it cannot be the foundation of any accusation or prosecution, action or complaint, in any other court or place whatsoever.

XXII. The legislature ought frequently to assemble for the redress of grievances, for correcting, strengthening, and confirming the laws, and for making new laws, as the common good may require.

XXIII. No subsidy, charge, tax, impost, or duties, ought to be established, fixed, laid, or levied, under any pretext whatsoever, without the consent of the people, or their representatives in the legislature.

XXIV. Laws made to punish for actions done before the existence of such laws, and which have not been declared crimes by preceding laws, are unjust, oppressive, and inconsistent with the fundamental principles of a free government.

XXV. No subject ought, in any case, or in any time, to be declared guilty of treason or felony by the legislature.

XXVI. No magistrate or court of law shall demand excessive bail or sureties, impose excessive fines, or inflict cruel or unusual punishments.

XXVII. In time of peace no soldier ought to be quartered in any house without the consent of the owner; and in time of war such quarters ought not to be made but by the civil magistrate, in a manner ordained by the legislature.

XXVIII. No person can in any case be subjected to law-martial, or to any penalties or pains, by virtue of that law, except those employed in the army or navy, and except the militia in actual service, but by authority of the legislature.

XXIX. It is essential to the preservation of the rights of every individual, his life, liberty, property and character, that there be an impartial interpretation of the laws, and administration of justice. It is the right of every citizen to be tried by judges as free, impartial and independent as the lot of humanity will admit. It is therefore not only the best policy, but for the security of the rights of the people, and of every citizen, that the judges of the supreme judicial court should hold their offices as long as they behave themselves well; and that they should have honorable salaries ascertained and established by standing laws.

XXX. In the government of this Commonwealth, the legislative department shall never exercise the executive and judicial powers, or either of them: The executive shall never exercise the legislative and judicial powers, or either of them: The judicial shall never exercise the legislative and executive powers, or either of them: to the end it may be a government of laws and not of men.

Essex Result, 1778*

Result of the Convention of Delegates holden at Ipswich in the County of Essex, who were deputed to take into consideration the Constitution and form of Government proposed by the Convention of the State of Massachusetts-Bay.

In Convention of Delegates from the several towns of Lynn, Salem, Danvers, Wenham, Manchester, Gloucester, Ipswich, Newbury-Port, Salisbury, Methuen, Boxford, & Topsfield, holden by adjournment at Ipswich, on the twenty-ninth day of April, one thousand seven hundred & seventy-eight. Peter Coffin Esq; in the Chair.

The Constitution and form of Government framed by the Convention of this State, was read paragraph by paragraph, and after debate, the following votes were passed.

1. That the present situation of this State renders it best, that the framing of a Constitution therefor, should be postponed 'till the public affairs are in a more peaceable and settled condition.

2. That a bill of rights, clearly ascertaining and defining the rights of conscience, and that security of person and property, which every member in the State hath a right to expect from the supreme power thereof, ought to be settled and established, previous to the ratification of any constitution for the State.

3. That the executive power in any State, ought not to have any share or voice in the legislative power in framing the laws, and therefore, that the second article of the Constitution is liable to exception.

*T. Parsons, Jr., *Memoir of Theophilus Parsons* (1859), pp. 359–402.

4. That any man who is chosen Governor, ought to be properly qualified in point of property—that the qualification therefor, mentioned in the third article of the Constitution, is not sufficient—nor is the same qualification directed to be ascertained on fixed principles, as it ought to be, on account of the fluctuation of the nominal value of money, and of property.

5. That in every free Republican Government, where the legislative power is rested in an house or houses of representatives, all the members of the State ought to be equally represented.

6. That the mode of representation proposed in the sixth article of the constitution, is not so equal a representation as can reasonably be devised.

7. That therefore the mode of representation in said sixth article is exceptionable.

8. That the representation proposed in said article is also exceptionable, as it will produce an unwieldy assembly.

9. That the mode of election of Senators pointed out in the Constitution is exceptionable.

10. That the rights of conscience, and the security of person and property each member of the State is entitled to, are not ascertained and defined in the Constitution, with a precision sufficient to limit the legislative power—and therefore, that the thirteenth article of the constitution is exceptionable.

11. That the fifteenth article is exceptionable, because the numbers that constitute a quorum in the House of Representatives and Senate, are too small.

12. That the seventeenth article of the constitution is exceptionable, because the supreme executive officer is not vested with proper authority—and because an independence between the executive and legislative body is not preserved.

13. That the nineteenth article is exceptionable, because a due independence is not kept up between the supreme legislative, judicial, and executive powers, nor between any two of them.

14. That the twentieth article is exceptionable, because the supreme executive officer hath a voice, and must be present in that Court, which alone hath authority to try impeachments.

15. That the twenty second article is exceptionable, because the supreme executive power is not preserved distinct from, and independent of, the supreme legislative power.

16. That the twenty third article is exceptionable, because the power of granting pardons is not solely vested in the supreme executive power of the State.

17. That the twenty eighth article is exceptionable, because the delegates for the Continental Congress may be elected by the House of Representatives, when all the Senators may vote against the election of those who are delegated.

18. That the thirty fourth article is exceptionable, because the rights of

conscience are not therein clearly defined and ascertained; and further, because the free exercise and enjoyment of religious worship is there said to be allowed to all the protestants in the State, when in fact, that free exercise and enjoyment is the natural and uncontroulable right of every member of the State.

A committee was then appointed to attempt the ascertaining of the true principles of government, applicable to the territory of the Massachusetts-Bay; to state the non-conformity of the constitution proposed by the Convention of this State to those principles, and to delineate the general outlines of a constitution conformable thereto; and to report the same to this Body.

This Convention was then adjourned to the twelfth day of May next, to be holden at Ipswich.

The Convention met pursuant to adjournment, and their committee presented the following report.

The committee appointed by this Convention at their last adjournment, have proceeded upon the service assigned them. With diffidence have they undertaken the several parts of their duty, and the manner in which they have executed them, they submit to the candor of this Body. When they considered of what vast consequence, the forming of a Constitution is to the members of this State, the length of time that is necessary to canvass and digest any proposed plan of government, before the establishment of it, and the consummate coolness, and solemn deliberation which should attend, not only those gentlemen who have, reposed in them, the important trust of delineating the several lines in which the various powers of government are to move, but also all those, who are to form an opinion of the execution of that trust, your committee must be excused when they express a surprise and regret, that so short a time is allowed the freemen inhabiting the territory of the Massachusetts-Bay, to revise and comprehend the form of government proposed to them by the convention of this State, to compare it with those principles on which every free government ought to be founded, and to ascertain it's conformity or non-conformity thereto. All this is necessary to be done, before a true opinion of it's merit or demerit can be formed. This opinion is to be certified within a time which, in our apprehension, is much too short for this purpose, and to be certified by a people who, during that time, have had and will have their minds perplexed and oppressed with a variety of public cares. The committee also beg leave to observe, that the constitution proposed for public approbation, was formed by gentlemen, who, at the same time, had a large share in conducting an important war, and who were employed in carrying into execution almost all the various powers of government.

The committee however proceeded in attempting the task assigned them, and the success of that attempt is now reported.

The reason and understanding of mankind, as well as the experience of all ages, confirm the truth of this proposition, that the benefits resulting to individuals from a free government, conduce much more to their happiness, than the retaining of all their natural rights in a state of nature. These benefits are greater or less, as the form of government, and the mode of exercising the supreme power of the State, are more or less conformable to those principles of equal impartial liberty, which is the property of all men from their birth as the gift of their Creator, compared with the manners and genius of the people, their occupations, customs, modes of thinking, situation, extent of country, and numbers. If the constitution and form of government are wholly repugnant to those principles, wretched are the subjects of that State. They have surrendered a portion of their natural rights, the enjoyment of which was in some degree a blessing, and the consequence is, they find themselves stripped of the remainder. As an anodyne to compose the spirits of these slaves, and to lull them into a passively obedient state, they are told, that tyranny is preferable to no government at all; a proposition which is to be doubted, unless considered under some limitation. Surely a state of nature is more excellent than that, in which men are meanly submissive to the haughty will of an imperious tyrant, whose savage passions are not bounded by the laws of reason, religion, honor, or a regard to his subjects, and the point to which all his movements center, is the gratification of a brutal appetite. As in a state of nature much happiness cannot be enjoyed by individuals, so it has been conformable to the inclinations of almost all men, to enter into a political society so constituted, as to remove the inconveniences they were obliged to submit to in their former state, and, at the same time, to retain all those natural rights, the enjoyment of which would be consistent with the nature of a free government, and the necessary subordination to the supreme power of the state.

To determine what form of government, in any given case, will produce the greatest possible happiness to the subject, is an arduous task, not to be compassed perhaps by any human powers. Some of the greatest geniuses and most learned philosophers of all ages, impelled by their sollicitude to promote the happiness of mankind, have nobly dared to attempt it: and their labours have crowned them with immortality. A Solon, a Lycurgus of Greece, a Numa of Rome are remembered with honor, when the wide extended empires of succeeding tyrants, are hardly important enough to be faintly sketched out on the map, while their superb thrones have long since crumbled into dust. The man who alone undertakes to form a constitution, ought to be an unimpassioned being; one enlightened mind; biassed neither by the lust of power, the allurements of pleasure, nor the glitter of wealth; perfectly acquainted with all the alienable and unalienable rights of mankind; possessed of this grand truth, that all men are born equally free, and that no man ought to surrender any part of his natural rights, without receiving the greatest possible equivalent; and influenced by the impartial principles of rectitude and justice, without partiality for, or prejudice against the interest or professions of any individuals or class of men. He ought also to be master of the histories of all the empires and states which are now existing, and all those which have figured in antiquity, and thereby able to collect and blend their respective excellencies, and avoid those defects which experience hath pointed out. Rousseau, a learned foreigner, a citizen of Geneva, sensible of the importance and difficulty of the subject, thought it impossible for any body of people, to form a free and equal constitution for themselves, in which, every individual should have equal justice done him, and be permitted to enjoy a share of power in the state, equal to what should be enjoyed by any other. Each individual, said he, will struggle, not only to retain all his own natural rights, but to acquire a controul over those of others. Fraud, circumvention, and an union of interest of some classes of people, combined with an inattention to the rights of posterity, will prevail over the principles of equity, justice, and good policy. The Genevans, perhaps the most virtuous republicans now existing, thought like Rousseau. They called the celebrated Calvin to their assistance. He came, and, by their gratitude, have they embalmed his memory.

The freemen inhabiting the territory of the Massachusetts-Bay are now forming a political society for themselves. Perhaps their situation is more favorable in some respects, for erecting a free government, than any other people were ever favored with. That attachment to old forms, which usually embarrasses, has not place amongst them. They have the history and experience of all States before them. Mankind have been toiling through ages for their information; and the philosophers and learned men of antiquity have trimmed their midnight lamps, to transmit to them instruction. We live also in an age, when the principles of political liberty, and the foundation of governments, have been freely canvassed, and fairly settled. Yet some difficulties we have to encounter. Not content with removing our attachment to the old government, perhaps we have contracted a prejudice against some part of it without foundation. The idea of liberty has been held up in so dazzling colours, that some of us may not be willing to submit to that subordination necessary in the freest States. Perhaps we may say further, that we do not consider ourselves united as brothers, with an united interest, but have fancied a clashing of interests amongst the various classes of men, and have acquired a thirst of power, and a wish of domination, over some of the community. We are contending for freedom—Let us all be equally free—It is possible, and it is just. Our interests when candidly considered are one. Let us have a constitution founded, not upon party or prejudice—not one for to-day or to-morrow—but for posterity. Let Esto perpetua be it's motto. If it is founded in good policy; it will be founded in justice and honesty. Let all ambitious and interested views be discarded, and let regard be had only to the good of the whole, in which the situation and rights of posterity must be considered: and let equal justice be done to all the members of the community; and we thereby imitate our common father, who at our births, dispersed his favors, not only with a liberal, but with an equal hand.

Was it asked, what is the best form of government for the people of the Massachusetts-Bay? we confess it would be a question of infinite importance: and the man who could truly answer it, would merit a statue of gold to his memory, and his fame would be recorded in the annals of late posterity, with unrivalled lustre. The question, however, must be answered, and let it have the best answer we can possibly give it. Was a man to mention a despotic government, his life would be a just forfeit to the resentments of an affronted people. Was he to hint monarchy, he would deservedly be hissed off the stage, and consigned to infamy. A republican form is the only one consonant to the feelings of the generous and brave Americans. Let us now attend to those principles, upon which all republican governments, who boast any degree of political liberty, are founded, and which must enter into the spirit of a free republican constitution. For all republics are not free.

All men are born equally free. The rights they possess at their births are equal, and of the same kind. Some of those rights are alienable, and may be parted with for an equivalent. Others are unalienable and inherent, and of that importance, that no equivalent can be received in exchange. Sometimes we shall mention the surrendering of a power to controul our natural rights, which perhaps is speaking with more precision, than when we use the expression of parting with natural rights—but the same thing is intended. Those rights which are unalienable, and of that importance, are called the rights of conscience. We have duties, for the discharge of which we are accountable to our Creator and benefactor, which no human power can cancel. What those duties are, is determinable by right reason, which may be, and is called, a well informed conscience. What this conscience dictates as our duty, is so; and that power which assumes a controul over it, is an usurper; for no consent can be pleaded to justify the controul, as any consent in this case is void. The alienation of some rights, in themselves alienable, may be also void, if the bargain is of that nature, that no equivalent can be received. Thus, if a man surrender all his alienable rights, without reserving a controul over the supreme power, or a right to resume in certain cases, the surrender is void, for he becomes a slave; and a slave can receive no equivalent. Common equity would set aside this bargain.

When men form themselves into society, and erect a body politic or State, they are to be considered as one moral whole, which is in possession of the supreme power of the State. This supreme power is composed of the powers of each individual collected together, and voluntarily parted with by him. No individual, in this case, parts with his unalienable rights, the supreme power therefore cannot controul them. Each individual also surrenders the power of controuling his natural alienable rights, only when the good of the whole requires it. The supreme power therefore can do nothing but what is for the good of the whole; and when it goes beyond this line, it is a power usurped. If the individual receives an equivalent for the right of controul he has parted with, the surrender of that right is valid; if he receives no equivalent, the surrender is void, and the supreme power as it respects him is an usurper. If the supreme power is so directed and executed that he does not enjoy political liberty, it is an illegal power, and he is not bound to obey. Political liberty is by some defined, a liberty of doing whatever is not prohibited by law. The definition is erroneous. A tyrant may govern by laws. The republics of Venice and Holland govern by laws, yet those republics have degenerated into insupportable tyrannies. Let it be thus defined; political liberty is the right every man in the state has, to do whatever is not prohibited by laws, to which he has given his consent. This definition is in unison with the feelings of a free people. But to return—If a fundamental principle on which each individual enters into society is, that he shall be bound by no laws but those to which he has consented, he cannot be considered as consenting to any law enacted by a minority: for he parts with the power of controuling his natural rights, only when the good of the whole requires it; and of this there can be but one absolute judge in the State. If the minority can assume the right of judging, there may then be two judges; for however large the minority may be, there must be another body still larger, who have the same claim, if not a better, to the right of absolute determination. If therefore the supreme power should be so modelled and exerted, that a law may be enacted by a minority, the inforcing of that law upon an individual who is opposed to it, is an act of tyranny. Further, as every individual, in entering into the society, parted with a power of controuling his natural rights equal to that parted with by any other, or in other words, as all the members of the society contributed an equal portion of their natural rights, towards the forming of the supreme power, so every member ought to receive equal benefit from, have equal influence in forming, and retain an equal controul over, the supreme power.

It has been observed, that each individual parts with the power of controuling his natural alienable rights, only when the good of the whole requires it; he therefore has remaining, after entering into political society, all his unalienable natural rights, and a part also of his alienable natural rights, provided the good of the whole does not require the sacrifice of them. Over the class of unalienable rights the supreme power hath no controul, and they ought to be clearly defined and ascertained in a Bill of Rights, previous to the ratification of any constitution. The bill of rights should also contain the equivalent every man receives, as a consideration for the rights he has surrendered. This equivalent consists principally in the security of his person and property, and is also unassailable by the supreme power: for if the equivalent is taken back, those natural rights which were parted with to purchase it, return to the original proprietor, as nothing is more true, than that allegiance and protection are reciprocal.

The committee also proceeded to consider upon what principles, and in what manner, the supreme power of the state thus composed of the powers of the several individuals thereof, may be formed, modelled, and exerted in a republic, so that every member of the state may enjoy political liberty. This is called by some, the ascertaining of the political law of the state. Let it now be called the forming of a constitution.

The reason why the supreme governor of the world is a rightful and just governor, and entitled to the allegiance of the universe is, because he is infinitely good, wise, and powerful. His goodness prompts him to the best measures, his wisdom qualifies him to discern them and his power to effect them. In a state likewise, the supreme power is best disposed of, when it is so modelled and balanced, and rested in such hands, that it has the greatest share of goodness, wisdom, and power which is consistent with the lot of humanity.

That state, (other things being equal) which has reposed the supreme power in the hands of one or a small number of persons, is the most powerful state. An union, expedition, secrecy and dispatch are to be found only here. Where power is to be executed by a large number, there will not probably be either of the requisites just mentioned. Many men have various opinions: and each one will be tenacious of his own, as he thinks it preferable to any other; for when he thinks otherwise, it will cease to be his opinion. From this diversity of opinions results disunion; from disunion, a want of expedition and dispatch. And the larger the number to whom a secret is entrusted, the greater is the probability of it's disclosure. This inconvenience more fully strikes us when we consider that want of secrecy may prevent the successful execution of any measures, however excellently formed and digested.

But from a single person, or a very small number, we are not to expect that political honesty, and upright regard to the interest of the body of the people, and the civil rights of each individual, which are essential to a good and free constitution. For these qualities we are to go to the body of the people. The voice of the people is said to be the voice of God. No man will be so hardy and presumptuous, as to affirm the truth of that proposition in it's fullest extent. But if this is considered as the intent of it, that the people have always a disposition to promote their own happiness, and that when they have time to be informed, and the necessary means of information given them, they will be able to determine upon the necessary measures therefor, no man, of a tolerable acquaintance with mankind, will deny the truth of it. The inconvenience and difficulty in forming any free permanent constitution are, that such is the lot of humanity, the bulk of the people, whose happiness is principally to be consulted in forming a constitution, and in legislation, (as they include the majority) are so situated in life, and such are their laudable occupations, that they cannot have time for, nor the means of furnishing themselves with proper information, but must be indebted to some of their fellow subjects for the communication. Happy is the man, and blessings will attend his memory, who shall improve his leisure, and those abilities which heaven has indulged him with, in communicating that true information, and impartial knowledge, to his fellow subjects, which will insure their happiness. But the artful demagogue, who to gratify his ambition or avarice, shall, with the gloss of false patriotism, mislead his countrymen, and meanly snatch from them the golden glorious opportunity of forming a system of political and civil liberty, fraught with blessings for themselves, and remote posterity, what language can paint his demerit? The execrations of ages will be a punishment inadequate; and his name, though ever blackening as it rolls down the stream of time, will not catch its proper hue.

Yet, when we are forming a Constitution, by deductions that follow from established principles, (which is the only good method of forming one for futurity,) we are to look further than to the bulk of the people, for the greatest wisdom, firmness, consistency, and perseverance. These qualities will most probably be found amongst men of education and fortune. From such men we are to expect genius cultivated by reading, and all the various advantages and assistances, which art, and a liberal education aided by wealth, can furnish. From these result learning, a thorough knowledge of the interests of their country, when considered abstractedly, when compared with the neighbouring States, and when with those more remote, and an acquaintance with it's produce and manufacture, and it's exports and imports. All these are necessary to be known, in order to determine what is the true interest of any state; and without that interest is ascertained, impossible will it be to discover, whether a variety of certain laws may be beneficial or hurtful. From gentlemen whose private affairs compel them to take care of their own household, and deprive them of leisure, these qualifications are not to be generally expected, whatever class of men they are enrolled in.

Let all these respective excellencies be united. Let the supreme power be so disposed and ballanced, that the laws may have in view the interest of the whole; let them be wisely and consistently framed for that end, and firmly adhered to; and let them be executed with vigour and dispatch.

*   *   *

The following principles now seem to be established.

1. That the supreme power is limited, and cannot controul the unalienable rights of mankind, nor resume the equivalent (that is, the security of person and property) which each individual receives, as a consideration for the alienable rights he parted with in entering into political society.

2. That these unalienable rights, and this equivalent, are to be clearly defined and ascertained in a Bill of Rights, previous to the ratification of any constitution.

3. That the supreme power should be so formed and modelled, as to exert the greatest possible power, wisdom, and goodness.

4. That the legislative, judicial, and executive powers, are to be lodged in different hands, that each branch is to be independent, and further, to be so ballanced, and be able to exert such checks upon the others, as will preserve it from a dependence on, or an union with them.

5. That government can exert the greatest power when it's supreme authority is vested in the hands of one or a few.

6. That the laws will be made with the greatest wisdom, and best intentions, when men of all the several classes in the state concur in the enacting of them.

7. That a government which is so constituted, that it cannot afford a degree of political liberty nearly equal to all it's members, is not founded upon principles of freedom and justice, and where any member enjoys no degree of political liberty, the government, so far as it respects him, is a tyranny, for he is controuled by laws to which he has never consented.

8. That the legislative power of a state hath no authority to controul the natural rights of any of it's members, unless the good of the whole requires it.

9. That a majority of the state is the only judge when the general good does require it.

10. That where the legislative power of the state is so formed, that a law may be enacted by the minority, each member of the state does not enjoy political liberty. And

11. That in a free government, a law affecting the person and property of it's members, is not valid, unless it has the consent of a majority of the members, which majority should include those, who hold a major part of the property in the state.

*   *   *

The committee have now compleated the general out lines of a constitution, which they suppose may be conformable to the principles of a free republican government—They have not attempted the description of the less important parts of a constitution, as they naturally and obviously are determinable by attention to those principles—Neither do they exhibit these general out lines, as the only ones which can be consonant to the natural rights of mankind, to the fundamental terms of the original social contract, and to the principles of political justice; for they do not assume to themselves infallibility. To compleat the task assigned them by this body, this constitution is held up in a general view, to convince us of the practicability of enjoying a free republican government, in which our natural rights are attended to, in which the original social contract is observed, and in which political justice governs; and also to justify us in our objections to the constitution proposed by the convention of this state, which we have taken the liberty to say is, in our apprehension, in some degree deficient in those respects.

To balance a large society on republican or general laws, is a work of so great difficulty, that no human genius, however comprehensive, is perhaps able, by the mere dint of reason and reflection, to effect it. The penetrating and dispassionate judgments of many must unite in this work: experience must guide their labour: time must bring it to perfection: and the feeling of inconveniencies must correct the mistakes which they will probably fall into, in their first trials and experiments.

The plan which the preceeding observations were intended to exhibit in a general view, is now compleated. The principles of a free republican form of government have been attempted, some reasons in support of them have been mentioned, the out lines of a constitution have been delineated in conformity to them, and the objections to the form of government proposed by the general convention have been stated.

This was at least the task enjoined upon the committee, and whether it has been successfully executed, they presume not to determine. They aimed at modelling the three branches of the supreme power in such a manner, that the government might act with the greatest vigour and wisdom, and with the best intentions—They aimed that each of those branches should retain a check upon the others, sufficient to preserve it's independence—They aimed that no member of the state should be controuled by any law, or be deprived of his property, against his consent—They aimed that all the members of the state should enjoy political liberty, and that their civil liberties should have equal care taken of them—and in fine, that they should be a free and an happy people—The committee are sensible, that the spirit of a free republican constitution, or the moving power which should give it action, ought to be political virtue, patriotism, and a just regard to the natural rights of mankind. This spirit, if wanting, can be obtained only from that Being, who infused the breath of Life into our first parent.

The committee have only further to report, that the inhabitants of the several towns who deputed delegates for this convention, be seriously advised, and solemnly exhorted, as they value the political freedom and happiness of themselves and of their posterity, to convene all the freemen of their several towns in town meeting, for this purpose regularly notified, and that they do unanimously vote their disapprobation of the constitution and form of government, framed by the convention of this state; that a regular return of the same be made to the secretary's office, that it may there remain a grateful monument to our posterity of that consistent, impartial and persevering attachment to political, religious, and civil liberty, which actuated their fathers, and in defence of which, they bravely fought, chearfully bled, and gloriously died.

The above report being read was accepted.

Attest,   *Peter Coffin, Chairman*

Massachusetts Convention Journal, 1779*

[Thursday, Sept. 2]

Resolved, That it is the opinion of this Convention, that they have sufficient authority from the People of the Massachusetts Bay to proceed to the framing a new Constitution of Government, to be laid before them agreeably to their instructions.

On a motion, made and seconded,

Voted, That the Convention proceed, at the adjournment, to the consideration of a Declaration of Rights.

On a motion made and seconded,

Voted, That the Convention be adjourned to 3 o'clock, P.M.

The Convention was adjourned accordingly.

Three o'clock, P.M. Met according to adjournment.

The Convention, agreeably to their vote in the forenoon, entered upon the consideration of a Declaration of Rights.

On a motion, made and seconded,

Voted, That there be a Declaration of Rights prepared, previous to the framing a new Constitution of Government.

A motion was then made and seconded, that a Committee be appointed for that purpose.

After a very general and extensive debate, on a motion,

Voted, That the further consideration of the Declaration of Rights be postponed to the morning.

*   *   *

[Friday, Sept. 3]

Met according to adjournment.

On a motion, made and seconded,

Ordered, that the bell be rung a quarter of an hour before the time to which this Convention shall from time to time be adjourned.

A motion was then made and seconded, that those gentlemen of the Clergy, who have seats in this Convention, be requested to open the Convention with Prayer, every morning, in rotation, which passed in the affirmative.

On a motion, made and seconded,

Voted, That there be a reconsideration of the vote passed yesterday, viz: "that there be a Declaration of Rights prepared previous to the framing a Constitution of Government."

Resolved, That the Convention will prepare a Declaration of Rights of the People of the Massachusetts Bay.

*Journal of the Convention for Framing a Constitution of Government for the State of Massachusetts Bay, 1779–1780, pp. 22–151.

Upon this Question, the whole number present as returned by the Monitors, were 251, of which, 250 were for the affirmative.

A motion was then made and seconded, as follows, viz.

Resolved, that this Convention will proceed to the framing a new Constitution of Government. After some debate thereon, a motion was made and seconded, that a Committee be appointed to prepare a Declaration of Rights, previous to the framing a new Constitution.

*   *   *

Three o'clock, P.M. The Convention met according to adjournment, and resumed the consideration of the motion made in the forenoon, viz. "That a Committee be appointed to prepare a Declaration of Rights, previous to the framing a new Constitution." After some further debates thereon, it passed in the negative.

The question was then put upon the motion made in the forenoon, viz.

Resolved, That this Convention will proceed to the framing a new Constitution of Government, which passed in the affirmative.

Upon a motion made by the Hon'ble Gen. Hancock, it was

Voted, That a time be assigned for the Convention to proceed to the choice of a Committee to prepare a Declaration of Rights, and Frame of a Constitution.

*   *   *

Voted, That a Committee of five persons be appointed, for the purpose of ascertaining the manner in which the Committee to be hereafter appointed to prepare a new Constitution of Government and Declaration of Rights, shall be chosen, the number of which it shall consist, and the number for each county.

The Convention then proceeded to the choice of a Committee for that purpose, and the following gentlemen were chosen, viz:

Nathaniel Gorham, Esq.
The Hon. Mr. Pickering,
The Hon. Col. Goodman,
John Lowell, Esq. and
Major Washburn.

The Committee last appointed were desired to withdraw and proceed on the business for which they were chosen, and report as soon as may be

*   *   *

The Committee appointed this afternoon for the purpose of ascertaining the manner, in which the Committee, to be hereafter appointed to prepare a Frame of a Constitution and Declaration of Rights, shall be chosen, the number of which the same shall consist, and the number for each County, made Report as follows:

"The Committee appointed *"ut supra,"* report as their opinion, That the Committee consist of thirty one, to be proportioned as follows:

For the County of Suffolk,	3
Essex,	3
Middlesex,	3
Worcester,	3
Hampshire,	3
Bristol,	2
York,	2
Plymouth,	2
Berkshire,	2
Barnstable,	1
Cumberland,	1
Lincoln,	1
Nantucket, and	
Dukes County,	1
	—
	27
At large,	4
	—
	31

And that the Members of each County have liberty to nominate the Members for their respective Counties, after having chosen them by ballot, at a meeting of the Members [of] the County for that purpose; and that the four to be chosen at large, be chosen by ballot." Which Report having been read was accepted.

On a motion, made and seconded,

Voted, That the first member of the senior town in each County shall determine the time when the members for their respective Counties shall meet, for the purposes mentioned in the preceding Report, and that the members make Report of their several nominations to-morrow morning.

The Convention then adjourned to to-morrow morning at eight o'clock.

[Saturday, Sept. 4]

The Convention met according to adjournment.

*   *   *

The Committee for preparing a nomination list of Candidates for the several Counties, for the choice of the Convention, on a Committee for preparing a Declaration of Rights, and the Form of a Constitution, to be laid before them at the adjournment to be had for that purpose, reported the following list, having been chosen by ballot of the Delegates from the several Counties, viz:

For the County of Suffolk
The Hon. James Bowdoin, Esq.
The Hon. John Adams, Esq.
John Lowell, Esq.

For the County of Essex
Theophilus Parsons, Esq.
Mr. Jonathan Jackson.
Mr. Samuel Phillips, jr.

For the County of Middlesex
The Hon. James Sullivan, Esq.
Nathl. Gorham, Esq.
The Hon. Eleazer Brooks, Esq.

For the County of Hampshire
The Hon. Noah Goodman, Esq.
Major Hezekiah Smith.
Mr. John Billing.

For the County of Plymouth
John Cotton, Esq.
Rev. Mr. Gad Hitchcock.

For the County of Barnstable
Enoch Hallett, Esq.

For the County of Bristol
The Hon. R. Treat Paine, Esq.
The Rev. Mr. Samuel West.

For the County of York
The Hon. Benjamin Chadbourn, Esq.
The Hon. David Sewall, Esq.

For the County of Worcester
The Hon. Jedediah Foster, Esq.
Joseph Dorr, Esq.
Israel Nichols, Esq.

For the County of Berkshire
James Harris, Esq.
Capt. William Walker.

On a motion made, the Convention resumed a free conversation, begun yesterday, on the general principles of a Declaration of Rights, and a Form or Constitution of Government.

The Committee not having reported any persons as candidates for the choice of the Convention on the Committee aforesai , for the Counties of Cumberland and Lincoln.

On a motion, made and seconded,

Voted, That the name of Mr. Samuel Small, be added to the nomination list for the County of Cumberland.

On a motion, made and seconded,

Voted, That the name of Mr. Benjamin Brainard, be added to the nomination list, for the County of Lincoln.

There being no Delegates in Convention from the County of Nantucket or Dukes County, no candidate was returned by the Committee, or added by the Convention to the nomination list, for said Counties.

12 o'clock: the Order of the Day being called for,

On a motion, made and seconded,

Voted, That a nomination list be opened on the Secretary's table, in order to the choice of four gentlemen at large, to complete the Committee for framing a Declaration of Rights, and Form of a Constitution, to be laid before the Convention.

On a motion, made and seconded,

Voted, That the names of the gentlemen on the nomination list, for the several counties, be put up singly, in order, to the Committee aforesaid. Which being done, the following gentlemen were unanimously chosen, viz:

For the County of Suffolk
The Hon. James Bowdoin, Esq.
The Hon. John Adams, Esq.
John Lowell, Esq.

For the County of Essex
Theophilus Parsons, Esq.
Mr. Jonathan Jackson.
Mr. Samuel Phillips, jr.

For the County of Middlesex
The Hon. James Sullivan, Esq.
Nathaniel Gorham, Esq.
The Hon. Eleazer Brooks, Esq.

For the County of Hampshire
The Hon. Noah Goodman, Esq.
Major Hezekiah Smith.
Mr. John Billing.

For the County of Plymouth
John Cotton, Esq.
Rev. Mr. Gad Hitchcock.

For the County of Barnstable
Enoch Hallet, Esq.

For the County of Bristol
The Hon. Robert Treat Paine, Esq.
The Rev. Mr. Samuel West.

For the County of York
The Hon. Benjamin Chadbourn, Esq.
The Hon. David Sewall, Esq.

For Dukes County and Nantucket

For the County of Worcester
The Hon. Jedediah Foster, Esq.
Joseph Dorr, Esq.
Israel Nichols, Esq.

For the County of Cumberland
Mr. Samuel Small.

For the County of Lincoln
Mr. Benjamin Brainard.

For the County of Berkshire
James Harris, Esq.
Capt. William Walker.

*   *   *

The Convention being desired to withdraw, and bring in their votes for four gentlemen at large, to complete the Committee for framing a Declaration of Rights and a Constitution of Government,

On a motion, made and seconded,

Voted, That the six Monitors be a Committee to receive, count and sort the votes.

On a motion, made and seconded,

Voted, That if more than four gentlemen shall have the majority of votes, the gentlemen, who have [the] greatest number shall be declared duly elected.

The Committee proceeded accordingly, and reported that they had attended that service, and that the number of votes were 237, and that 119 made a vote; and that there were for

The Hon. Samuel Adams, Esq.	209
The Hon. John Pickering, Esq.	156
Caleb Strong, Esq.	203

Those Gentlemen were accordingly chosen.

On a motion, made and seconded,

Voted, That the choice of one gentleman to complete the Committee be postponed to the afternoon, and that the Convention now adjourn to that time. The Convention adjourned accordingly.

Three o'clock, P. M. The Convention met according to adjournment.

The Committee were directed, agreeably to the order of the day, to receive and sort the votes for one gentleman to complete the Committee for framing a Constitution of Government and a Declaration of Rights.

The Committee proceeded accordingly, and reported that there was no choice.

They were then directed to proceed again.

The Committee aforesaid having received and sorted the votes, reported, that on counting the same, it appeared that the number of voters were 198, that 100 made a vote, and that the Hon. William Cushing, Esq. had 135 votes. That gentleman was accordingly declared duly elected.

[Tuesday, Sept. 7]

*   *   *

The Committee appointed to prepare a Declaration of Rights and the Form of a Constitution, to be laid before the Convention, at the adjournment, having retired to determine the time and place of their meeting to transact the important business assigned them, returned and acquainted the Convention, that they had determined to meet at the New Court House, in Boston, on Monday next, 3 o'clock, P. M. for the purpose aforesaid.

*   *   *

The Committee appointed to prepare a draught of a Declaration of Rights and Form of Government made report of the same, which, being read a motion was made and seconded, that a printed Copy of the Declaration of Rights be distributed among the members to-morrow morning.

*   *   *

[Thursday, Sept. 28]

On advice of the President, Mr. S. Adams, and several other gentlemen, the various alterations, which were made by the Convention in the Report of the Committee, as finally agreed to, were respectively minuted on the printed Copy, and the numerous votes for the several amendments, and for transposing, accepting or rejecting words, propositions, paragraphs, articles, sections, &c. generally omitted.

[Friday, Sept. 29]

Three o'clock, P. M. Met according to adjournment.

The Convention went into the consideration of the Declaration of Rights, and directed the same to be read; previous to the reading of which, a motion was made and seconded,

That 12 o'clock to-morrow be assigned for the consideration of the question, whether the Convention shall adjourn from this place.

Which, being put, passed in the affirmative. The Declaration of Rights was then read, and on a motion, made and seconded, the same was voted to be taken up by propositions.

The preamble and the 1st. article, after sundry amendments, being accepted,

On a motion, made and seconded,

Voted, to adjourn to 9 o'clock, to-morrow morning.

[Saturday, Sept. 30]

Met according to adjournment.

The Rev. Mr. Chaplin prayed.

The Convention resumed the consideration of the Declaration of Rights.

The 2d article, after debates and amendments, being accepted, the order of the day was called for.

*   *   *

Three o'clock, P. M. Met according to adjournment.

The Convention resumed the consideration of the Declaration of Rights.

The 3d article being read, on a motion made and seconded,

Voted, That the same be put by propositions. The two first of which were accordingly put and accepted. When the subsequent propositions relating to the support of religious worship and instruction were taken up and largely debated.

A motion was then made and seconded, that the further consideration of this article be postponed to the adjournment.

On a motion, made and seconded,

Voted, to adjourn to Monday morning, 9 o'clock.

[Monday, Nov. 1]

Met according to adjournment.

The Rev. Mr. West prayed.

The 3d. article aforesaid being read and debated,

On a motion, the debates were suspended, in order to the distribution of the remaining sheets of the Report of the Committee among the members present, and to the having a fuller House for the consideration of so important an article.

After which, a motion was made and seconded, to assign 10 o'clock to-morrow morning, for further debates on this article.

Which being put, passed in the affirmative.

The 4th, 5th, 6th, 7th, 8th, and 9th articles were then severally considered and accepted, after some amendments in the 4th, 8th and 9th, (as will appear by reference being had to the amended copy of the report.)

The Convention then adjourned to 3 o'clock, P. M.

Three o'clock, P. M. Met according to adjournment.

The Convention proceeded in the consideration of the Declaration of Rights.

The 10th, 11th, 13th, 14th, and 15th articles were taken up and passed, with some other amendments on the 10th, and 15th, (see the Copy aforesaid.)

The 12th, on a motion, made and seconded, was committed for amendment to the Hon. Judge Sergeant, the Hon. Mr. Paine, and Mr. Parsons.

The 16th, on a motion made and seconded, was committed to the same gentlemen, with the addition of the Hon. Judge Sewall.

The 17th, after large debate, was, on a motion made and seconded, committed to the Hon. Timothy Danielson, and Walter Spooner, Esqrs. and Caleb Strong, Esq. for amendments.

The Convention then adjourned to to-morrow morning, 9 o'clock.

[Tuesday, Nov. 2]

Met according to adjournment.

The Committee on the 12th article reported two several amendments, viz. a substitution of the word "or," instead of the words "he cannot," and after the word "confession," the insertion of the words "or other conviction agreeable to law." The former of which, being put, was unanimously accepted; the latter was largely debated, and several alterations proposed, when, on a motion made and seconded, the article was recommitted, and the Hon. Mr. Pickering added to the Committee.

Ten o'clock, A. M. The order of the day being called for, the Convention went into the consideration of the 3d article; which, being largely debated, the further consideration of the same was postponed to 3 o'clock, P. M.

On a motion made and seconded,

Voted, to adjourn to said time.

Three o'clock, P. M. Met according to adjournment.

Resumed the debates on the 3d article, which being very extensive, on a motion made and seconded,

Voted, That the rule of the Convention, which prescribes "that no member shall speak more than twice to a question without leave being first obtained," be suspended during the debates on this article. A free and general debate then ensued, when, on a motion made and seconded,

Voted, to postpone the further consideration of the article to the adjournment. . . .

The Convention then adjourned to to-morrow morning, 9 o'clock.

[Wednesday, Nov. 3]

Met according to adjournment.

The Convention resumed the consideration of the 3d article, and after long debate thereon, the same was postponed to the afternoon.

*   *   *

Three o'clock, P. M. Met according to adjournment.

The 3d article being resumed and largely debated, it was moved and seconded, "that a Committee be appointed to consider of the proposed amendments of the said article as offered for the consideration of the Convention, and report thereon," which, being put, passed in the affirmative.

The Convention then made choice of the following gentlemen for that purpose, viz:

> The Rev. Mr. Alden.
> The Hon. Mr. Danielson.
> Theop. Parsons, Esq.
> The Hon. Samuel Adams, Esq.
> The Hon. Mr. Paine.
> The Rev. Mr. Sanford, and
> Caleb Strong, Esq.

Then adjourned to Friday morning, 9 o'clock.

[Friday, Nov. 5]

Met according to adjournment.

The Rev. Mr. Thatcher prayed.

On a motion, made and seconded,

Voted, That the several proposals for amendments on the 3d article be delivered to the Committee on the same.

The Committee on the 17th article in the Declaration of Rights reported the following as a substitute therefor, viz: "The liberty of the Press being essential to the security of freedom in a State, it therefore ought not to be restrained in this Commonwealth." Which, being put, was accepted, and ordered to be inserted in lieu of 17th article accordingly.

The Committees on the 12th and 16th articles, not being ready to report, the Convention went into the consideration of 18th article, (the subject military power,) and after considerable debate, and expunging the word "standing" before the word "armies," accepted the same;—also the 19th and 20th articles, without amendment. The 21st was after some debate suspended to the afternoon, and the 22d accepted. Then adjourned to 3 o'clock.

Three o'clock, P. M. Met according to adjournment.

The 21st art. was resumed and debated, when the same was suspended by the consideration of the 23d, 24th, 25th, 26th, 27th, 28th, and 29th, which (after the substitution of the word "Subject," instead of "Man," and obliterating the words "any act of," before the word "Legislature,") were severally accepted, as also the 30th, after inserting the words "of the Supreme Jucicial Court."

On a motion, made and seconded,

Voted, That the Convention will sit to-morrow till 3 o'clock, and then adjourn to Monday morning.

The Convention then adjourned [to] to-morrow morning, 9 o'clock.

[Saturday, Nov. 6]

Met according to adjournment.

The Rev. Mr. Hewins prayed.

The Committee on the 3d article of the Declaration of Rights reported a new draught of the whole, which being read, on a motion made and seconded,

Voted, That the further consideration of the same be assigned to Wednesday morning, 11 o'clock.

The Convention then resumed the consideration of the 21st article in the said Declaration, when a motion was made and seconded, for expunging the last clause, beginning at the words "and there shall be;" which, being put, passed in the affirmative.

On a motion made and seconded,

The 30th article was voted to be reconsidered, so as to lay open for debate in its first state, by expunging the words inserted yesterday.

When, after long debate, it was moved and seconded, that the sense of the Convention be taken upon the word "Judges" in said article, in order to which a question was moved and seconded, viz. "whether it be the sense of this Convention that the Judges of the Supreme Judicial Court of this Commonwealth, ought to be appointed to hold their offices during good behavior;" which, being put, passed in the affirmative, by 78 out of 113.

*　　　*　　　*

[Monday, Nov. 8]

*　　　*　　　*

Three o'clock. Met according to adjournment.

The 30th article in the Declaration of Rights was then further considered and debated.

It was then moved and seconded, that a Question be put, whether it is the opinion of this Convention that the Judges of the Courts of Common Pleas in this Commonwealth ought to be appointed to hold their offices during good behaviour, which was accordingly put, and passed in the negative, by 57 out of 119.

On a motion, made and seconded,

Voted, That the consideration of Justices of the Peace be postponed, until they come to be considered in their order in the Frame of Government.

It was then moved and seconded, that the words "of the Supreme Judicial Court," be inserted between the word "Judges," and "should," in the 30th article, which, being put, passed in the affirmative. The article was then put as amended and was accepted.

The 31st article was then taken up and debated, when the further consideration of it was suspended by a motion, made and seconded, to adjourn.

[Tuesday Nov. 9]

Met according to adjournment.

The Rev. Mr. Shute prayed.

On a motion, made and seconded, that some provision be made relative to the appointment of Jurors, the consideration of the same was referred to the Committee on the 16th article.

*   *   *

[Wednesday, Nov. 10]

Three o'clock, P. M. Met according to adjournment.

The Report of the Committee on the 3d article being resumed, the same was very largely debated, particularly the last paragraph.

Several motions were made, which were respectively debated, as additions to be made to the words, "Christians of all denominations," viz. "whose avowed principles are not inconsistent with the peace and safety of Society,"—"except such whose principles are repugnant to the Constitution,"—"being Protestants,"—"except Papists," &c. When a motion was made and seconded, that the 3d article in the Declaration of Rights, with all the amendments, be expunged;—which, being put, passed in the negative. It was then moved, and seconded, that the report be taken up by propositions;—which, being put, passed in the affirmative. The Report was accordingly taken up and debated, by propositions.

On which, several amendments were proposed and debated, some of which were accepted.

The whole Report with the amendments was then put, and accepted;—and the same ordered to be inserted as the 3d article in the Declaration of Rights, instead of that in the printed report of the General Committee, as follows, viz.

Art 3d. "As the happiness of a People, and the good order and preservation of Civil Government, essentially depend upon piety, religion and morality, and as these cannot be generally diffused through a community, but by the institution of the publick worship of God, and of publick instructions in piety, religion and morality; therefore, to promote their happiness, and to secure the good order and preservation of their Government, the People of this Commonwealth have a right to invest their Legislature with power to authorize and require, and their Legislature shall, from time to time, authorize and require, the several towns, parishes, precincts, or other bodies politic, or religious societies, to make suitable provision, at their own expense, for the institution of the publick worship of God, and for the support and maintenance of publick Protestant Teachers of piety, religion and morality, in all cases where such provision shall not be made voluntarily."

"And the People of this Commonwealth have also a right to, and do, invest their Legislature with authority to enjoin upon all the subjects an attendance upon the instructions of the public teachers aforesaid, at stated times and seasons, if there be any on whose instructions they can conscientiously and conveniently attend."

"Provided, notwithstanding, that the several towns, parishes, precincts, or other bodies politic, and religious societies, shall at all times have the exclusive right of electing their public teachers, and of contracting with them for their support and maintenance."

"And all monies paid by the subject to the support of public worship, and of the public teachers aforesaid, shall, if he require it, be uniformly applied to the support of the public teacher or teachers of his own religious sect or denomination, provided there be any, on whose instructions he attends, otherwise it may be paid towards the support of the teacher or teachers of the parish or precinct in which the said monies are raised."

"And Christians of all denominations, demeaning themselves peaceably, and as good subjects of the Commonwealth, shall be equally under the protection of the laws, and no subordination of any one sect or denomination to another shall ever be established by law."

The Convention then adjourned to to-morrow morning, 9 o'clock.

*   *   *

The Declaration of Rights was then resumed, and the several articles in the same having been acted upon, except the 12th and 16th, which were committed, and the Committees not ready to report, and the 31st. The last article, viz. the 31st, was read and debated.

It was then moved, and seconded, that the words "separate from and," be expunged, which was superseded by a motion made, and seconded, that the whole article be expunged, and that the following words be substituted, by which the article aforesaid, and the 2d paragraph in the preamble of the 2d chapter, formerly voted to be considered together, may be consolidated, and the sense of both expressed, viz:

"In the Government of this Commonwealth, the Legislative shall never exercise the Executive and Judicial powers, or either of them. The Executive shall never exercise the Legislative and Judicial powers or either of them. The Judicial shall never exercise the Legislative and Executive powers or either of them, to the end that it may be a government of laws and not of men." Which, being put, passed in the affirmative.

The Committee on the 12th and 16th article, not being ready to report, and two gentlemen, who were on that Committee absent, it was moved, and seconded, that the said Committee be now filled up. Which, being put, passed in the affirmative.

A nomination being called for, the following gentlemen, viz: Mr. Lowell, and the Hon. Judge Sullivan, were appointed.

*   *   *

[Tuesday, Nov. 17]

Met according to adjournment.

The Rev. Mr. Howard was introduced, and prayed with the Convention.

The Committee on the 12th article in the Declaration of Rights made report, that the 12th and 14th articles be incorporated. (I) Which, being debated, on a motion, made and seconded,

Voted, That the report be recommitted for amendment.

It was moved, and seconded, that Mr. Lowell be added to the Committee. Which, being put, passed in the affirmative.

It was moved, and seconded, that Judge Cushing be added to the Committee. Which, being put, passed in the affirmative.

*   *   *

The Committee on the 12th article made report of the following addition to the report brought in this morning, viz: "Provided." It was then moved, and seconded, that the word "And" be substituted in lieu of the word "Provided." Which, being put, passed in the affirmative.

It was then moved, and seconded, that the words "excepting for the government of the army and navy," be added. Which, being put, passed in the affirmative.

The report of the Committee was then read as amended, and

On motion, made and seconded, it was

Voted, To accept the same, and that it stand in the Declaration of Rights in lieu of the 12th and 14th articles in the report of the General Committee, as follows, viz. "No subject shall be held to answer for any crime or offence until the same is fully and plainly, substantially and formally, described to him, or be compelled to accuse or furnish evidence against himself, and every subject shall have a right to produce all proofs that may be favourable to him, to meet the witnesses against him face to face, and to be fully heard in his defence by himself or his Council, at his election; and no subject shall be arrested, imprisoned, despoiled, or deprived of his property, immunities, or privileges, put out of the protection of the law, exiled or deprived of his life, liberty or estate, but by the judgment of his peers, or the law of the land. And the Legislature shall not make any law, that shall subject any person to a capital or infamous punishment, excepting for the government of the army and navy, without trial by Jury."

*   *   *

Massachusetts Declaration of Rights Committee Draft, 1779*

The Report of a Constitution, or Form of Government, for the Commonwealth of Massachusetts;—Agreed upon by the Committee—to be laid before the Convention of Delegates, assembled at Cambridge, on the first day of September, A. D. 1779; and continued by Adjournment to the twenty-eighth day of October following.

To the Honorable the Convention of Delegates from the several Towns in the State of Massachusetts, appointed for the forming a new Constitution of Government for the said State.

Gentlemen,

Your Committee, in pursuance of your instructions, have prepared the Draught of a new Constitution of Government for this State; and now make report of it: which is respectfully laid before you, in the following pages, for your consideration and correction.

In the name of the Committee,

James Bowdoin, Chairman

*Constitution or Form of Government for the
Commonwealth of Massachusetts*

Preamble

The end of the institution, maintenance and administration of government, is to secure the existence of the body politic; to protect it, and to furnish the individuals who compose it, with the power of enjoying, in safety and tranquillity, their natural rights, and the blessings of life: And whenever these great objects are not obtained, the people have a right to alter the government, and to take measures necessary for their safety, happiness and prosperity.

The body politic is formed by a voluntary association of individuals: It is a social compact, by which the whole people covenants with each citizen, and each citizen with the whole people, that all shall be governed by certain laws for the common good. It is the duty of the people, therefore, in framing a Constitution of Government, to provide for an equitable mode of making laws, as well as for an impartial interpretation, and a faithful execution of them, that every man may, at all times, find his security in them.

We, therefore, the Delegates of the People of Massachusetts, in General Convention assembled, for the express and sole purpose of framing a Constitution or Form of Government, to be laid before our Constituents, according to their instructions, acknowledging, with grateful hearts, the goodness of the Great Legislator of the Universe, in affording to this people, in the course of

Journal of the Convention for Framing a Constitution of Government for the State of Massachusetts Bay, 1779–1780, p. 191–97.

His Providence, an opportunity of entering into an original, explicit, and solemn compact with each other, deliberately and peaceably, without fraud, violence, or surprise; and of forming a new Constitution of Civil Government, for themselves and their posterity; and devoutly imploring His direction in a design so interesting to them and their posterity,—Do, by virtue of the authority vested in us, by our constituents, agree upon the following Declaration of Rights, and Frame of Government, as the Constitution of the Commonwealth of Massachusetts.

Chapter I
A Declaration of the Rights of the Inhabitants of the Commonwealth of Massachusetts

I. All men are born equally free and independent, and have certain natural, essential, and unalienable rights: among which may be reckoned the right of enjoying and defending their lives and liberties; that of acquiring, possessing, and protecting their property; in fine, that of seeking and obtaining their safety and happiness.

II. It is the duty of all men in society, publicly, and at stated seasons, to worship the Supreme Being, the great creator and preserver of the universe. And no subject shall be hurt, molested, or restrained, in his person, liberty or estate, for worshiping God in the manner most agreeable to the dictates of his own conscience; or for his religious profession or sentiments; provided he doth not disturb the public peace, or obstruct others in their religious worship.

III. Good morals being necessary to the preservation of civil society: and the knowledge and belief of the being of God, His providential government of the world, and of a future state of rewards and punishment, being the only true foundation of morality, the legislature hath therefore a right, and ought, to provide at the expense of the subject, if necessary, a suitable support for the public worship of God, and of the teachers of religion and morals; and to enjoin upon all the subjects an attendance upon their instructions, at stated times and seasons: Provided there be any such teacher, on whose ministry they can conscientiously and conveniently attend.

All monies, paid by the subject to the support of public worship, and of the instructors in religion and morals, shall, if he requires it, be uniformly applied to the support of the teacher or teachers of his own religious denomination, if there be such whose ministry he attends upon: otherwise it may be paid to the teacher or teachers of the parish or precinct where he usually resides.

IV. The people of this Commonwealth have the sole and exclusive right of governing themselves, as a free, sovereign, and independent state; and do, and forever hereafter shall, exercise and enjoy every power, jurisdiction, and right, which are not, or may not hereafter, be by them expressly delegated to the United States of America, in Congress assembled.

V. All power residing originally in the people, and being derived from them, the several magistrates and officers of government, vested with authority, whether legislative, executive or judicial, are their substitutes and agents, and are at all times accountable to them.

VI. No man, nor corporation or association of men, have any other title to obtain advantages, or particular and exclusive privileges, distinct from those of the community, than what arises from the consideration of services rendered to the public; and this title being in nature neither hereditary, nor transmissible to children, or descendants, or relations by blood, the idea of a man born a magistrate, law-giver, or judge, is absurd and unnatural.

VII. Government is instituted for the common good; for the protection, safety, prosperity and happiness of the people; and not for the profit, honor, or private interest of any one man, family, or class of men: Therefore the people alone have an incontestible, unalienable, and indefeasible right to institute government; and to reform, alter, or totally change the same, when their protection, safety, prosperity and happiness require it.

VIII. In order to prevent those who are vested with authority from becoming oppressors, the people have a right, at such periods and in such manner as may be delineated in their frame of government, to cause their public officers to return to private life, and to fill up vacant places by certain and regular elections.

IX. All elections ought to be free; and all the male inhabitants of this Commonwealth, having sufficient qualifications, have an equal right to elect officers, and to be elected for public employments.

X. Each individual of the society has a right to be protected by it in the enjoyment of his life, liberty and property, according to standing laws. He is obliged, consequently, to contribute his share to the expense of this protection; to give his personal service, or an equivalent, when necessary: But no part of the property of any individual can, with justice, be taken from him, or applied to public uses, without his own consent, or that of the representative body of the people. In fine, the people of this Commonwealth are not controlable by any other laws, than those to which their constitutional representative body have given their consent.

XI. Every subject of the Commonwealth ought to find a certain remedy, by having recourse to the laws, for all injuries or wrongs which he may receive in his person, property or character: He ought to obtain right and justice freely, and without being obliged to purchase it; completely, and without any denial; promptly, and without delay; conformably to the laws.

XII. No subject shall be held to answer for any crime or offence, until the same is fully and plainly, substantially and formally, described to him. He cannot be compelled to accuse himself, or to furnish evidence against himself; and every subject shall have a right to be fully heard in his defence, by himself or his council, at his election; to meet the witnesses against him face to face; to produce all proofs that may be favourable to him; to require a speedy and public trial by an impartial jury of the country, without whose unanimous consent, or his own voluntary confession, he cannot finally be declared guilty, or sentenced to loss of life, liberty or property.

XIII. In criminal prosecutions, the verification of facts, in the vicinity where they happen, is one of the greatest securities of the life, liberty and property of the citizen.

XIV. No subject of the Commonwealth shall be arrested, imprisoned, despoiled, or deprived of his property, immunities or privileges, put out of the protection of the law, exiled, or deprived of his life, liberty or estate, but by the judgment of his peers or the law of the land.

XV. Every man has a right to be secure from all unreasonable searches and seizures of his person, his houses, his papers, and all his possessions. All warrants, therefore, are contrary to this right, if the cause or foundation of them be not previously supported by oath or affirmation; and if the order in the warrant to a civil officer, to make search in suspected places, or to arrest one or more suspected persons, or to seize their property, be not accompanied with a special designation of the persons or objects of search, arrest or seizure; and no warrant ought to be issued but in cases and with the formalities prescribed by the laws.

XVI. In all controversies concerning property, and in all suits between two or more persons, the parties have a right to a trial by a jury; and this method of procedure shall be held sacred; unless, in causes arising on the high-seas, and such as relate to mariners wages, the legislature shall hereafter find it necessary to alter it.

XVII. The people have a right to the freedom of speaking, writing and publishing their sentiments: The liberty of the press therefore ought not to be restrained.

XVIII. The people have a right to keep and to bear arms for the common defence. And as in time of peace standing armies are dangerous to liberty, they ought not to be maintained without the consent of the legislature; and the military power shall always be held in an exact subordination to the civil authority, and be governed by it.

XIX. A frequent recurrence to the fundamental principles of the constitution, and a constant adherence to those of piety, justice, moderation, temperance, industry and frugality, are absolutely necessary to preserve the advantages of liberty, and to maintain a free government: The people ought, consequently, to have a particular attention to all those principles in the choice of their officers and representatives: And they have a right to require of their law-givers and magistrates an exact and constant observance of them, in the formation and execution of the laws necessary for the good administration of the Commonwealth.

XX. The people have a right, in an orderly and peaceable manner, to assemble to consult upon the common good; give instructions to their representatives; and to request of the legislative body, by the way of addresses, petitions, or remonstrances, redress of the wrongs done them, and the grievances they suffer.

XXI. The power of suspending the laws, or the execution of the laws, ought never to be exercised but by the legislature, or by authority derived from it, to be exercised in such particular cases only as the legislature shall expressly provide for: And there shall be no suspension of any law for the private interest, advantage, or emolument, of any one man or class of men.

XXII. The freedom of deliberation, speech and debate, in either house of the legislature, is so essential to the rights of the people, that it cannot be the foundation of any accusation or prosecution, action or complaint, in any other court or place whatsoever.

XXIII. The legislature ought frequently to assemble for the redress of grievances, for correcting, strengthening and confirming the laws, and for making new laws as the common good may require.

XXIV. No subsidy, charge, tax, impost or duties ought to be established, fixed, laid, or levied, under any pretext whatsoever, without the consent of the people or their representatives in the legislature.

XXV. Laws made to punish for actions done before the existence of such laws, and which have not been declared crimes by preceding laws, are unjust, oppressive, and inconsistent with the fundamental principles of a free government.

XXVI. No man ought in any case, or in any time, to be declared guilty of treason or felony by any act of the legislature.

XXVII. No magistrate or court of law shall demand excessive bail, or sureties, impose excessive fines, or inflict cruel or unusual punishments.

XXVIII. In time of peace, no soldier ought to be quartered in any house without the consent of the owner; and in time of war, such quarters ought not to be made, but by the civil magistrate in a manner ordained by the legislature.

XXIX. No person can in any case be subjected to law martial, or to any penalties or pains, by virtue of that law, except those employed in the army or navy, and except the militia in actual service, but by authority of the legislature.

XXX. It is essential to the preservation of the rights of every individual, his life, liberty, property and character, that there be an impartial interpretation of the laws, and administration of justice. It is the right of every citizen to be tried by judges as free, impartial and independent as the lot of humanity will admit. It is therefore not only the best policy, but for the security of the rights of the people, and of every citizen, that the judges should hold their offices as long as they behave themselves well; and that they should have honorable salaries ascertained and established by standing laws.

XXXI. The judicial department of the State ought to be separate from, and independent of, the legislative and executive powers.

NEW HAMPSHIRE BILL OF RIGHTS, 1783

Commentary

New Hampshire had been the first state to set up its own independent government (*supra* p. 228); but it was the last of the states which adopted Bills of Rights during the Revolutionary period to act in that respect. The New Hampshire Congress had adopted a Constitution without any Bill of Rights in January, 1776. It was intended only as a temporary measure and was incomplete as a frame of government (making no provision, for example, for establishment of the judiciary). As it turned out, the 1776 Constitution remained the fundamental law of the state for over seven years. A new Constitution was proposed by a Convention which met in 1778, but it was rejected by the people. A second Convention met in 1781. Two drafts submitted by it (containing Declarations of Rights modelled upon that of Massachusetts) were also rejected. A third draft was finally approved in October, 1783 and went into effect the next year.

Few changes of substance were made in the proposed Declaration of Rights in the successive redrafts. The delegates did, however, change the title in the 1783 draft, calling Part I of the Constitution "The Bill of Rights," and that is the title it bears in the document finally approved. Hence the New Hampshire Bill of Rights has the honor of being the first American constitutional document formally to bear the title of Bill of Rights.

In content, the New Hampshire Bill of Rights is basically similar to the Massachusetts Declaration of Rights, even using that document's peculiar reference to "subjects" rather than "persons." It repeats the Massachusetts provisions on protection of life, liberty, and property, criminal procedure and unreasonable searches and seizures, jury trials in civil cases, freedom of the press, quartering of soldiers, freedom of speech (limited to the legislature), assembly and petition, excessive bail and fines, cruel and unusual punishment, as well as judicial independence and separation of powers. The one important Massachusetts provision not repeated was the bill of attainder prohibition.

In a few respects, there are important additions made by the New Hampshire document to the Massachusetts model. The New Hampshire provision on religion declares freedom of conscience to be "a natural and unalienable right" (not "the right as well as the duty" of the Massachusetts Declaration); it also forbids establishment by law of any one sect. Retrospective laws are expressly outlawed in both civil and criminal matters (earlier Declarations had prohibited only retroactive criminal laws, as was to be true of the Ex Post Facto Clauses of the federal Constitution as they have been interpreted by the Supreme Court). A progressive provision is also contained in Article XVIII of the New Hampshire document; though it did not lead to any

374

federal Bill of Rights provision, it was the forerunner of modern attempts at penal reform.

Perhaps the most important addition made by the New Hampshire Bill of Rights was its inclusion in Article XVI of an express prohibition against double jeopardy. This was the first provision in an American Bill of Rights elevating the common law rule against a second prosecution to the constitutional plane and was the immediate precursor of the Fifth Amendment prohibition.

New Hampshire Bill of Rights, 1783*

I. All men are born equally free and independent; therefore, all government of right originates from the people, is founded in consent, and instituted for the general good.

II. All men have certain natural, essential, and inherent rights; among which are—the enjoying and defending life and liberty—acquiring, possessing and protecting property—and in a word, of seeking and obtaining happiness.

III. When men enter into a state of society, they surrender up some of their natural rights to that society, in order to insure the protection of others; and, without such an equivalent, the surrender is void.

IV. Among the natural rights, some are in their very nature unalienable, because no equivalent can be given or received for them. Of this kind are the rights of conscience.

V. Every individual has a natural and unalienable right to worship God according to the dictates of his own conscience, and reason; and no subject shall be hurt, molested, or restrained in his person, liberty or estate for worshipping God, in the manner and season most agreeable to the dictates of his own conscience, or for his religious profession, sentiments or persuasion; provided he doth not disturb the public peace, or disturb others, in their religious worship.

VI. As morality and piety, rightly grounded on evangelical principles, will give the best and greatest security to government, and will lay in the hearts of men the strongest obligations to due subjection: and as the knowledge of these, is most likely to be propagated through a society by the institution of the public worship of the Deity, and of public instruction in morality and religion; therefore, to promote those important purposes, the people of this state have a right to impower, and do hereby fully impower the legislature to authorize from time to time, the several towns, parishes, bodies-corporate, or religious societies within this state, to make adequate provision at their own

*Thorpe, *The Federal and State Constitutions, Colonial Charters, and Other Organic Laws*, Vol. 4, pp. 2453–57.

expence, for the support and maintenance of public protestant teachers of piety, religion and morality:

Provided notwithstanding, That the several towns, parishes, bodies-corporate, or religious societies, shall at all times have the exclusive right of electing their own public teachers, and of contracting with them for their support and maintenance. And no portion of any one particular religious sect or denomination, shall ever be compelled to pay towards the support of the teacher or teachers of another persuasion, sect or denomination.

And every denomination of christians demeaning themselves quietly, and as good subjects of the state, shall be equally under the protection of the law: and no subordination of any one sect or denomination to another, shall ever be established by law.

And nothing herein shall be understood to affect any former contracts made for the support of the ministry; but all such contracts shall remain, and be in the same state as if this constitution had not been made.

VII. The people of this state, have the sole and exclusive right of governing themselves as a free, sovereign, and independent state, and do, and forever hereafter shall, exercise and enjoy every power, jurisdiction and right pertaining thereto, which is not, or may not hereafter be by them expressly delegated to the United States of America in Congress assembled.

VIII. All power residing originally in, and being derived from the people, all the magistrates and officers of government, are their substitutes and agents, and at all times accountable to them.

IX. No office or place whatsoever in government, shall be hereditary—the abilities and integrity requisite in all, not being transmissible to posterity or relations.

X. Government being instituted for the common benefit, protection, and security of the whole community, and not for the private interest or emolument of any one man, family or class of men; therefore, whenever the ends of government are perverted, and public liberty manifestly endangered, and all other means of redress are ineffectual, the people may, and of right ought, to reform the old, or establish a new government. The doctrine of non-resistance against arbitrary power, and oppression, is absurd, slavish, and destructive of the good and happiness of mankind.

XI. All elections ought to be free, and every inhabitant of the state having the proper qualifications, has equal right to elect, and be elected into office.

XII. Every member of the community has a right to be protected by it in the enjoyment of his life, liberty and property; he is therefore bound to contribute his share in the expence of such protection, and to yield his personal service when necessary, or an equivalent. But no part of a man's property shall be taken from him, or applied to public uses, without his own consent, or that of the representative body of the people. Nor are the inhabitants of this state controllable by any other laws than those to which they or their representative body have given their consent.

XIII. No person who is conscientiously scrupulous about the lawfulness of bearing arms, shall be compelled thereto, provided he will pay an equivalent.

XIV. Every subject of this state is entitled to a certain remedy, by having recourse to the laws, for all injuries he may receive in his person, property or character, to obtain right and justice freely, without being obliged to purchase it; completely, and without any denial; promptly, and without delay, conformably to the laws.

XV. No subject shall be held to answer for any crime, or offence, until the same is fully and plainly, substantially and formally, described to him; or be compelled to accuse or furnish evidence against himself. And every subject shall have a right to produce all proofs that may be favorable to himself; to meet the witnesses against him face to face, and to be fully heard in his defence by himself, and counsel. And no subject shall be arrested, imprisoned, despoiled, or deprived of his property, immunities, or privileges, put out of the protection of the law, exiled or deprived of his life, liberty, or estate, but by the judgment of his peers or the law of the land.

XVI. No subject shall be liable to be tried, after an acquittal, for the same crime or offence. Nor shall the legislature make any law that shall subject any person to a capital punishment, excepting for the government of the army and navy, and the militia in actual service, without trial by jury.

XVII. In criminal prosecutions, the trial of facts in the vicinity where they happen, is so essential to the security of the life, liberty and estate of the citizen, that no crime or offence ought to be tried in any other county than that in which it is committed; except in cases of general insurrection in any particular county, when it shall appear to the Judges of the Superior Court, that an impartial trial cannot be had in the county where the offence may be committed, and upon their report, the assembly shall think proper to direct the trial in the nearest county in which an impartial trial can be obtained.

XVIII. All penalties ought to be proportioned to the nature of the offence. No wise legislature will affix the same punishment to the crimes of theft, forgery and the like, which they do to those of murder and treason; where the same undistinguishing severity is exerted against all offences; the people are led to forget the real distinction in the crimes themselves, and to commit the most flagrant with as little compunction as they do those of the lightest dye: For the same reason a multitude of sanguinary laws is both impolitic and unjust. The true design of all punishments being to reform, not to exterminate, mankind.

XIX. Every subject hath a right to be secure from all unreasonable searches and seizures of his person, his houses, his papers, and all his possessions. All warrants, therefore, are contrary to this right, if the cause or foundation of them be not previously supported by oath, or affirmation; and if the order in the warrant to a civil officer, to make search in suspected places, or to arrest one or more suspected persons, or to seize their property, be not accompanied with a special designation of the persons or objects of search, arrest, or seizure; and no warrant ought to be issued but in cases, and with the formalities prescribed by the laws.

XX. In all controversies concerning property, and in all suits between two or more persons, except in cases in which it has been heretofore otherwise used and practiced, the parties have a right to a trial by jury; and this method of procedure shall be held sacred, unless in causes arising on the high seas, and such as relate to mariners wages, the legislature shall think it necessary hereafter to alter it.

XXI. In order to reap the fullest advantage of the inestimable privilege of the trial by jury, great care ought to be taken that none but qualified persons should be appointed to serve; and such ought to be fully compensated for their travel, time and attendance.

XXII. The Liberty of the Press is essential to the security of freedom in a state; it ought, therefore, to be inviolably preserved.

XXIII. Retrospective laws are highly injurious, oppressive and unjust. No such laws, therefore, should be made, either for the decision of civil causes, or the punishment of offences.

XXIV. A well regulated militia is the proper, natural, and sure defence of a state.

XXV. Standing armies are dangerous to liberty, and ought not to be raised or kept up without the consent of the legislature.

XXVI. In all cases, and at all times, the military ought to be under strict subordination to, and governed by the civil power.

XXVII. No soldier in time of peace, shall be quartered in any house without the consent of the owner; and in time or war, such quarters ought not to be made but by the civil magistrate, in a manner ordained by the legislature.

XXVIII. No subsidy, charge, tax, impost or duty shall be established, fixed, laid, or levied, under any pretext whatsoever, without the consent of the people or their representatives in the legislature, or authority derived from that body.

XXIX. The power of suspending the laws, or the execution of them, ought never to be exercised but by the legislature, or by authority derived therefrom, to be exercised in such particular cases only as the legislature shall expressly provide for.

XXX. The freedom of deliberation, speech, and debate, in either house of the legislature, is so essential to the rights of the people, that it cannot be the foundation of any action, complaint, or prosecution, in any other court or place whatsoever.

XXXI. The legislature ought frequently to assemble for the redress of grievances, for correcting, strengthening and confirming the laws, and for making new ones, as the common good may require.

XXXII. The people have a right in an orderly and peaceable manner, to assemble and consult upon the common good, give instructions to their representatives; and to request of the legislative body, by way of petition or remonstrance, redress of the wrongs done them, and of the grievances they suffer.

XXXIII. No magistrate or court of law shall demand excessive bail or sureties, impose excessive fines, or inflict cruel or unusual punishments.

XXXIV. No person can in any case be subjected to law martial, or to any pains, or penalties, by virtue of that law, except those employed in the army or navy, and except the militia in actual service, but by authority of the legislature.

XXXV. It is essential to the preservation of the rights of every individual, his life, liberty, property and character, that there be an impartial interpretation of the laws, and administration of justice. It is the right of every citizen to be tried by judges as impartial as the lot of humanity will admit. It is therefore not only the best policy, but for the security of the rights of the people, that the judges of the supreme (or superior) judicial court should hold their offices so long as they behave well; and that they should have honorable salaries, ascertained and established by standing laws.

XXXVI. Economy being a most essential virtue in all states, especially in a young one; no pension shall be granted, but in consideration of actual services, and such pensions ought to be granted with great caution, by the legislature, and never for more than one year at a time.

XXXVII. In the government of this state, the three essential powers thereof, to wit, the legislative, executive and judicial, ought to be kept as separate from and independent of each other, as the nature of a free government will admit, or as is consistent with that chain of connection that binds the whole fabric of the constitution in one indissoluble bond of union and amity.

XXXVIII. A frequent recurrence to the fundamental principles of the Constitution, and a constant adherence to justice, moderation, temperance, industry, frugality, and all the social virtues, are indispensably necessary to preserve the blessings of liberty and good government; the people ought, therefore, to have a particular regard to all those principles in the choice of their officers and representatives: and they have a right to require of their law-givers and magistrates, an exact and constant observance of them in the formation and execution of the laws necessary for the good administration of government.

PART FOUR
CONFEDERATION AND JUDICIAL REVIEW

CONFEDERATION AND JUDICIAL REVIEW

Commentary

By the end of the Revolutionary period, the concept of a Bill of Rights had been fully developed in the American system. Eleven of the 13 states (and Vermont as well) had enacted Constitutions to fill in the political gap caused by the overthrow of British authority. These were true Constitutions in the modern American use of the term, in accordance with Justice Samuel Miller's classic definition: "A constitution in the American sense of the word is a written instrument by which the fundamental powers of the government are established, limited, and defined, and by which these powers are distributed among several departments, for their more sage and useful exercise, for the benefit of the body politic." The Constitutions drafted during the Revolution were the first organic instruments which may truly be termed Constitutions in this sense.

In the American conception, a Constitution both sets forth the frame of government and provides protection for fundamental rights. The latter is the province of a Bill of Rights. Eight of the Revolutionary Constitutions were prefaced by Bills of Rights, while four contained guarantees of many of the most important individual rights in the body of their texts. Included in these Revolutionary constitutional provisions were all of the rights that were to be protected in the federal Bill of Rights. By the time of the Treaty of Paris (1783) then, the American inventory of individual rights had been virtually completed and included in the different state Constitutions whether in separate Bills of Rights or the organic texts themselves.

That being the case, it is surprising that the first instrument of Union for the new nation was practically bare of provisions protecting individual rights. The Articles of Confederation contain only the provisions in Article IV guaranteeing "the free inhabitants of each of these States . . . all privileges and immunities of free citizens in the several states" (the forerunner of the Privileges and Immunities Clause of Article IV of the federal Constitution), free ingress and egress to and from the states for their citizens, as well as reciprocal privileges of trade and commerce. But the Articles are completely silent on the great rights of freedom of religion, freedom of expression, and all the other fundamental rights safeguarded in the different state Bills of Rights and Constitutions.

The lack of the Articles of Confederation in this respect is explained by the weakness of the government set up by the Articles, which made it unnecessary to provide protection against infringements upon personal rights by such government. The whole subject of individual rights was entirely within state competence. This was made categorically clear by Article II of the Articles, which provides, "Each State retains . . . every power, jurisdiction, and right, which is not by this confederation expressly delegated to the United States." This was, of course, the direct precursor of the Tenth Amendment, being closer to that Amendment than the comparable Massachusetts provision, (*supra* p. 339), and earlier than the latter, since the Articles were agreed to by Congress in 1777, though not approved by the states until 1781.

There was to be no demand for a national Bill of Rights until the weak government provided for by the Articles of Confederation was replaced by the Federal Government created by the Constitution of 1787. When the federal Constitution itself was written, the precedent of the Articles was followed, insofar as a Bill of Rights was concerned. This time, however, the lack of specific protection for personal liberties did not commend itself to the people in the states. The concentration of power in the new national government led to increasing agitation for express guarantees against infringements upon individual rights. The outcome was the federal Bill of Rights itself as an indispensable adjunct of the new fundamental law.

NORTHWEST ORDINANCE, 1787

Commentary

Although the Articles of Confederation did not contain any Bill of Rights or, indeed, any provisions guaranteeing fundamental rights, except for the minor exceptions mentioned (*supra* p. 383), it is not accurate to assume that the first Federal Government was wholly inactive in protecting personal liberties. While the Congress had no power in the matter within the several states, the same was not true of the vast territories which came within congressional jurisdiction upon the cession of state claims. The congressional attempt to provide for the government of those territories resulted in the Northwest Ordinance of 1787—perhaps the greatest achievement of the Confederation government. The Northwest Ordinance contained the first Bill of Rights enacted by the Federal Government.

The extracts which follow from the *Journal* of the Confederation Congress indicate that the inclusion of broad guarantees of individual rights came comparatively late in the legislative history of the Ordinance. The original plan of government for the Northwest Territory, prepared by Jefferson and introduced in 1784, contained no provisions securing personal liberties (though it did abolish slavery after 1800, anticipating the absolute abolition provided in the 1787 Ordinance). The Jefferson Ordinance was passed (minus its abolition provision) but never went into effect. An Ordinance of 1785 provided a surveying system for the Territory. In the meantime, congressional committees were continuing to consider plans for governing the Northwest. In September, 1786, for the first time, a provision was added dealing with personal rights, providing a guarantee of habeas corpus and trial by jury. The committee recommendation was embodied in a bill introduced in Congress on May 10, 1787. The text of this bill as it appears in the congressional *Journal* follows. From it we can see how sketchy was the provision protecting personal liberty in the first draft of the Ordinance. As the *Journal* shows, the proposed Ordinance did not receive its third reading.

In the meantime, a committee prepared a new draft Ordinance which was introduced on July 11. This draft (in the handwriting of Nathan Dane) marked a substantial step forward from the May 10 version, so far as personal liberties were concerned. This version was passed by Congress on July 13, substantially as it was recommended by the committee. There were two changes of importance made in the congressional debate. The first was the addition of the most famous provision of the Ordinance, that in Article VI prohibiting slavery. The other was the deletion of a phrase "extending *to all parts of the Confederacy* the fundamental principles of civil and religious liberty." It is unfortunate that we do not have the debates which led to the deletion, since we do not know the effect intended by the deleted phrase.

Could it have been intended to make the enactment a true federal Bill of Rights extending to all parts of the nation? If so, upon what constitutional theory could the provision have been based (bearing in mind the limited powers of the Confederation Congress)?

The Northwest Ordinance as enacted contains a virtual Bill of Rights "as articles of compact between the original States and the people," which shall "forever remain unalterable, unless by common consent." The rights protected are stated to be "the fundamental principles of civil and religious liberty." The Ordinance guarantees in this respect were plainly modelled upon the state Bills of Rights. Indeed, according to Nathan Dane in an 1830 letter, "The Ordinance of '87 was framed mainly from the laws of Massachusetts." As such the rights guaranteed by the Ordinance are the traditional ones covered in the Revolutionary Declarations of Rights: freedom of religion, habeas corpus, trial by jury, bail, moderate fines, prohibition of cruel and unusual punishments, deprivation of liberty or property "but by the judgement of his peers, or the law of the land," taking of property without "full compensation," as well as a new prohibition against laws that "interfere with or affect contracts" (the direct precursor of the Contract Clauses in Article I, section 10 of the federal Constitution). In addition, there is a guarantee of republican form of government which anticipates that in Article IV of the federal Constitution.

Northwest Ordinance Journals of Congress, 1786-1787

[Tuesday, Sept. 19, 1786]*

*   *   *

The Committee consisting of Mr. [William Samuel] Johnson, Mr. [Charles] Pinckney, Mr. [Melancton] Smith, Mr. [Nathan] Dane and Mr. [William] Henry appointed to prepare a plan of a temporary government for such districts or new States as shall be laid out by the United States upon the principles of the acts of cession from individual States and admitted into the confederacy, submit the following report to the consideration of Congress:

The United States in Congress assembled will appoint a governor, whose Commission shall continue in force for the term of three years unless sooner revoked by Congress.

There shall be appointed by Congress from time to time a Secretary whose Commission shall continue in force for two years unless sooner revoked by Congress. It shall be his duty to keep and preserve the Acts and laws passed by the general Assembly and public records of the district, and of the

*W. C. Ford, ed., *Journals of the Continental Congress, 1774–1789* (1904), Vol. 21, pp. 669–72.

proceedings of the governor in his executive department and transmit an Authentic copy thereof every three months to the Secretary of Congress.

There shall also be appointed a Court to consist of five Judges who shall have a common law and Chancery Jurisdiction and whose Commissions shall continue in force during good behaviour.

And to secure the rights of personal liberty and property to the inhabitants and other purchasers in the said districts it is hereby

Resolved, That the inhabitants of such districts shall always be entitled to the benefits of the Act of habeas Corpus and of the trial by Jury.

That the Judges shall agree on the Criminal Laws of some one State, in their Opinion the most perfect, which shall prevail in said district, until the Organization of the general Assembly, but afterwards the general Assembly shall have authority to alter them as they shall think fit.

That the real estates of resident proprietors dying intestate previous to the Organization of the general Assembly shall descend to the heirs of such proprietors Male and female in equal parts, that is to say, if a father dies intestate leaving a Son and two daughters the real estate shall be divided into three equal parts, and descend to each in such equal proportions; provided however, that such proprietors shall be at liberty to dispose of such lands by alienation by bargain and sale testamentary devise or otherwise as he shall think proper; but after the Organization of the general Assembly the estates of resident proprietors shall be subject to such disposition by alienation bargain and sale descent or otherwise as the said assembly shall direct.

The real estate of non resident proprietors shall be subject to such alienation while living and disposal by testamentary devise as they shall think fit; but the real estates of non resident proprietors dying intestate shall descend in the same manner as those of resident proprietors, previous to the organization of the general assembly until such district shall be admitted into the Confederacy.

The Governor for the time being shall be commander in chief of the Militia; and appoint and Commission all officers in the same below the rank of General Officers; all officers of that rank shall be appointed and Commissioned by Congress.

Previous to the Organization of the general Assembly the governor shall appoint such Magistrates and other Civil Officers in each County or township, as he shall find Necessary for the preservation of peace and good order in the same.

After the general Assembly shall be Organized, the number of Magistrates and other Civil Officers with their powers and duties and term of services shall be regulated and defined by the said Assembly. But all Magistrates and other Civil Officers not herein otherwise directed shall during the continuance of this temporary Government, be appointed by the Governor.

The Governor shall as soon as may be, proceed to lay out the land into Counties and Townships, subject however to such Alterations as may thereafter be made by the Legislature.

So soon as there shall be   free male Inhabitants of full age within the said district, upon giving due proof thereof to the Governor they shall receive authority, with time and place to elect representatives from their Counties or Townships as aforesaid to represent them in general assembly; provided that for every   free male Inhabitants there shall be one representative, and so on progressively with the number of free male Inhabitants shall the right of representation increase until the number of representatives amount to   after which the number and proportion of representatives shall be regulated by the Legislature; Provided that no person shall be eligible or qualified to act as a representative unless he shall be a Citizen of one of the United States, or have resided within such district three years and shall likewise hold in his own right in fee simple 200 acres of land within the same; provided also that a freehold or life estate in fifty acres of land if a Citizen of any of the United States and one years residence if a foreigner in addition shall be necessary to qualify a man as elector for the said representative.

The representatives thus elected shall serve for the term of one year; and in case of the death of a representative or his resignation or renunciation of Office the governor shall issue a writ to the County or Township for which he was a member to elect another in his stead to serve for the residue of the time.

The General Assembly shall consist of the Governor, a Legislative Council to consist of five members, any three of whom to be a quorum, to be appointed by the United States in Congress Assembled and to continue in Office during pleasure; and a house of representatives who shall have a Legislative authority complete in all cases for the good government of the district; provided that no act of the said general Assembly shall be construed to affect any lands the property of the United States; and provided further that the lands of the non-resident proprietors shall in no instance be taxed higher than the lands of residents.

All money bills shall Originate in the house of representatives, and all other bills indifferently either in the Council or house of representatives, and having been passed by a Majority in both houses shall be referred to the governor for his assent, after obtaining which they shall be complete and valid; but no bill, resolution, Ordinance or Legislative Act whatever shall be valid or of any force without his assent.

The Governor shall have power to convene or prorogue the general Assembly at their request, or when in his Opinion it shall be expedient.

The said Inhabitants or settlers shall be subject to pay a part of the federal debts contracted or to be contracted, and to bear a proportional part of the burthens of the Government to be apportioned on them by Congress according to the same common rule and measure by which apportionments thereof shall be made on the other States.

The annual salary of the Governor shall be   , of the Legislative Council   , of the Judges   , and of the Secretary   per annum.

The Governor, Judges, Legislative Council, Secretary and such other Officers as Congress shall at any time think proper to appoint in such district shall take an Oath of Office before   presented on the   day of   to the Secretary at War *Mutatis Mutandis.*

Whensoever any of the said States shall have of free inhabitants as many as are equal in number to the one thirteenth part of the Citizens of the Original States, to be computed from the last enumeration, such State shall be admitted by its delegates into the Congress of the United States on an equal footing with the said original States; provided the consent of so many States in Congress is first obtained as may at that time be competent to such admission.

[Thursday, May 10, 1787]*

An Ordinance for the [temporary] government of the ~~Western~~ Territory [of the USNW of the River Ohio, ~~until the same shall be divided into different States~~]

It is hereby ordained by the United States in Congress assembled, that there shall be appointed from time to time, a governor, whose commission shall continue in force for the term of three years, unless sooner revoked by Congress.

There shall be appointed by Congress, from time to time, a secretary, whose commission shall continue in force for four years, unless sooner revoked by Congress. It shall be his duty to keep and preserve the acts and laws passed by the general assembly, and public records ~~of the district,~~ and ~~of~~ the proceedings of the governor in his executive department, and transmit authentic copies of such acts and proceedings every six months, to the secretary of Congress.

There shall also be appointed a court, to consist of three judges, any two of whom shall form a court, who shall have a common law jurisdiction, whose commissions shall continue in force during good behaviour.

And to secure the rights of personal liberty and property to the inhabitants and others, purchasers in the said ~~district~~ [territory], it is hereby ordained, that the inhabitants ~~of such districts~~ [thereof] shall always be entitled to the benefits of the act of *habeas corpus,* and of the trial by jury.

The governor and judges, or a majority of them shall adopt and publish in the ~~districts~~ [territory afores], such laws of the original states, criminal and civil, as may be necessary, and best suited to the circumstances of the ~~district~~ [inhabitants], and report them to Congress from time to time, which [laws] shall ~~prevail~~ [be in force] in said ~~district~~ [territory], until the organization of

*Journals of the Continental Congress, Vol. 22, pp. 281–343. Reading the text with the lined type and omitting the bracketed portions gives the form in which the Ordinance stood after the debate of May 9. Reading the text with the bracketed portions and omitting the lined type gives the form, resulting from the debate of May 10 and July 9, in which it was recommitted on July 9, 1787.

the general assembly, unless disapproved of by Congress; but afterwards the general assembly shall have authority to alter them as they shall think fit; provided, however, that said assembly shall have no power to create perpetuities.

The governor for the time being shall be commander in chief of the militia, and appoint and commission all officers in the same, below the rank of general officers; all officers of that rank shall be appointed and commissioned by Congress.

Previous to the organization of the general assembly, the governor shall appoint such magistrates and other civil officers in each county or township, as he shall find necessary for the preservation of peace and good order in the same. After the general assembly shall be organized, the powers and duties of magistrates and other civil officers shall be regulated and defined by the said assembly; but all magistrates and other civil officers, not herein otherwise directed, shall during the continuance of this temporary government, be appointed by the governor.

The governor shall, as soon as may be, proceed to lay out the district [said territory], into counties and townships, subject however to such alterations, as may thereafter be made by the legislature, so soon as there shall be 5000 free male inhabitants, of full age, within the said district [territory], upon giving due proof thereof to the governor, they shall receive authority, with time and place, to elect representatives from their counties or townships as aforesaid, to represent them in general assembly; provided that for every 500 free male inhabitants there shall be one representative, and so on progressively with the number of free male inhabitants, shall the right of representation encrease, until the number of representatives amount to 25, after which the number and proportion of representatives shall be regulated by the legislature; provided that no person shall be eligible or qualified to act as a representative unless he shall be a citizen of one of the United States, or have resided within such district [territory] three years, and shall likewise hold in his own right, in fee simple, 200 acres of land within the same; provided also, that a freehold, or life estate in fifty acres of land in the said district, if a citizen of any of the United States, and two years residence if a foreigner, in addition, shall be necessary to qualify a man as elector for the said representative.

The representatives thus elected, shall serve for the term of two years, and in case of the death of a representative or removal from office, the governor shall issue a writ to the county or township for which he was a member to elect another in his stead, to serve for the residue of the time.

The general assembly shall consist of the governor, a legislative council, to consist of five members, to be appointed by the United States in Congress assembled, to continue in office during pleasure, any three of whom to be a quorum, and a house of representatives, who shall have a legislative authority complete in all cases for the good government of said district [territory]; provided that no act of the said general assembly shall be construed to affect any lands the property of the United States, and provided further, that the lands of non-resident proprietors shall in no instance be taxed higher than the lands of residents.

All bills shall originate indifferently either in the council or house of representatives, and having been passed by a majority in both houses, shall be referred to the governor for his assent, after obtaining which, they shall be complete and valid; but no bill or legislative act whatever, shall be valid or of any force without his assent.

The governor shall have power to convene, prorogue and dissolve the general assembly when in his opinion it shall be expedient.

The said inhabitants or settlers shall be subject to pay a part of the federal debts, contracted, or to be contracted, and to bear a proportional part of the burthens of the government, to be apportioned on them by Congress, according to the same common rule and measure by which apportionments thereof shall be made on the other states.

The governor, judges, legislative council, secretary and such other officers as Congress shall at any time think proper to appoint in such ~~district~~ [territory], shall take an oath or affirmation of fidelity [and of office]; the governor before the president of Congress, and all other officers before the governor; ~~[according to the form] prescribed on the 27th day of January, 1785, to the secretary at War, *mutatis mutandis*.~~

~~Whensoever any of the said states shall have of free inhabitants as many as are equal in number to the one thirteenth part of the citizens of the original states, to be computed from the last enumeration, such state shall be admitted by its delegates into the Congress of the United States, on an equal footing with the said original states; provided the consent of so many states in Congress is first obtained, as may at that time be competent to such admission.~~

Resolved, That the resolutions of the 23d of April, 1784, be, and the same are hereby annulled and repealed.

The order of the day was called by the State of Massachusetts, for the third reading of the Ordinance for a temporary government of the western territory, and being postponed.

* * *

[Wednesday, July 11, 1787]

Congress assembled present the seven states above mentioned.

The Comee. consisting of Mr [Edward] Carrington Mr [Nathan] Dane Mr R[ichard] H[enry] Lee Mr [John] Kean and Mr [Melancton] Smith to whom was referred the report of a comee touchg the temporary government of the western territory reported an Ordinance for the government of the territory of the United States North West of the river Ohio, which was read a first time.

An Ordinance for the Government of the territory of the United States North West of the river Ohio [1]

Be it ordained by the United States in Congress Assembled, that the said Territory, for the purposes of Temporary Government, be one district; subject, however, to be divided into two districts, as future circumstances may, in the opinion of Congress, make it expedient.

Be it ordained by the Authority aforesaid that the estates both of resident and non resident proprietors in said Territory dying intestate, shall descend to, and be distributed among their children and the descendents of a deceased child in equal parts; the descendents of a deceased child or grand child to take the share of their deceased parent in equal parts among them. And where there shall be no children or descendents then in equal parts to the next a kin in equal degree, ~~computing by the rules of the civil law,~~ and among Collaterals the children of a deceased brother or sister of the intestate, shall have in equal parts among them their deceased parent's share. Saving in all Cases to the widow of the intestate, her third part of the real estate for life, and where there shall be no children of the intestate, one third part of the personal estate; and this law relative to descents and dower shall remain in full force until altered by the Legislature of the district. And until the Governor and Judges shall adopt laws as herein after mentioned, estates in said Territory may be devised or bequeathed by wills in writing signed and sealed by him or her in whom the estate may be, (being of full age) and attested by three witnesses. And real estates may be conveyed by lease, or bargain and sale, signed, sealed, and delivered by the person being of full age, in whom the estate may be, and attested by two witnesses, provided such wills be duly proved, and such conveyances be acknowledged, or the execution thereof duly proved, and be recorded within one year after proper magistrates, Courts, and registries shall be appointed for that purpose. And personal property may be transferred by delivery. Saving, however, to the Inhabitants of Kaskaskias and post Vincents their laws and customs now in force among them relative to the descent and conveyance of property.

Be it ordained by the Authority aforesaid, that there shall be appointed from time to time by Congress, a Governor, whose commission shall continue in force for the term of three years, unless sooner revoked by Congress; he shall reside in the district and have a freehold estate therein, in one thousand acres of land, while in the exercise of his office.

There shall be appointed from time to time by Congress, a Secretary whose commission shall continue in force for four years, unless sooner revoked, he shall reside in the district, and have a freehold estate therein, in five hundred acres of land, while in the exercise of his office It shall be his duty to keep and preserve the Acts and laws passed by the legislature, and the public records of the district, and the proceedings of the Governor in his

---

[1] The words underlined in the text were struck out during the debate.

executive department; and transmit Authentic copies of such Acts and proceedings, every six months, to the Secretary of Congress. There shall also be appointed a Court to consist of three Judges, any two of whom to form a Court, who shall have a Common law Jurisdiction, and reside in the district and have each therein a freehold estate in five hundred acres of land, while in the exercise of their offices; and their commissions shall continue in force during good behaviour.

The Governor and Judges, or a majority of them, shall adopt and publish in the district, such laws of the original States, criminal and civil, as may be necessary, and best suited to the circumstances of the district, and report them to Congress, from time to time, which laws shall be in force in the district until the organization of the General Assembly therein, unless disapproved of by Congress; but afterwards the legislature shall have authority to alter them as they shall think fit.

The Governor for the time being, shall be commander in chief of the militia, appoint and commission all officers in the same, below the rank of General Officers; all officers above that rank shall be appointed and commissioned by Congress.

Previous to the organization of the General Assembly the Governor shall appoint such magistrates and other civil officers in each County or township, as he shall find necessary for the preservation of the peace and good order in the same. After the General Assembly shall be organised, the powers and duties of magistrates and other civil Officers shall be regulated and defined by the said Assembly; but all magistrates and other civil Officers, not herein otherwise directed, shall, during the continuance of this temporary Government, be appointed by the Governor.

For the prevention of crimes and Injuries the laws to be adopted or made shall have force in all parts of the district and for the execution of process criminal and civil the Governor shall make proper divisions thereof. And he shall proceed, from time to time, as circumstances may require to lay out the parts of the district in which the Indian titles shall have been extinguished into Counties and townships subject however to such alterations, as may thereafter be made by the Legislature.

So soon as there shall be 5000 free male Inhabitants, of full age, in the district upon giving proof thereof to the Governor, they shall receive authority, with time and place to elect representatives from their Counties or townships, to represent them in the General Assembly; provided that for every 500 free male Inhabitants there shall be one representative, and so on progressively with the number of free male Inhabitants, shall the right of representation increase, until the number of representatives shall amount to 25, after which the number and proportion of representatives shall be regulated by the legislature, provided that no person be eligible or qualified to Act as a representative unless he shall have been a Citizen of one of the United States three years and be resident in the district, or unless he shall have resided in the district three years, and in either Case shall likewise hold in his own right, in fee simple, 200 acres of land within the same, provided Also that a freehold of fifty acres of land in the district, having been a Citizen of one of the States and being resident in the district; or the like freehold and two years residence in the district shall be necessary to qualify a man as an elector of a representative.

The representatives thus elected shall serve for the term of two years, and in Case of the death of a representative, or removal from office, the Governor shall issue a writ to the County or township for which he was a member to elect another in his stead, to serve for the residue of the term.

The General Assembly, or legislature, shall consist of the Governor, legislative Council, and a House of representatives. The legislative Council shall consist of 5 members to continue in office 5 years, unless sooner removed by Congress, any three of whom to be a quorum and the members of the Council shall be nominated and appointed in the following manner to wit, as soon as representatives shall be elected the Governor shall appoint a time and place for them to meet together and when met they shall nominate ten persons residents in the district and each possessed of a freehold in 500 acres of land and return the names to Congress five of whom Congress shall appoint and commission to serve as aforesaid; and whenever a vacancy shall happen in the Council by death, or removal from office, the House of representatives shall nominate two persons qualified as aforesaid for each vacancy, and return their names to Congress, one of whom Congress shall appoint and commission for the residue of the term; and every five years, four months, at least, before the expiration of the time of service of the members of Council the said House shall nominate ten persons qualified as aforesaid, and return their names to Congress, five of whom Congress shall appoint and commission to serve as members of the Council five years unless sooner removed. And the Governor, legislative Council, and House of Representatives shall have authority to make laws in all Cases for the good government of the district not repugnant to the principles and articles in this ordinance established and declared. And all bills having passed by a majority in the House and by a majority in the Council, shall be referred to the Governor for his assent; but no bill or legislative Act whatever shall be of any force without his assent. The Governor shall have power to convene, prorogue and dissolve the General Assembly when in his opinion it shall be expedient.

The Governor, Judges, legislative Council, Secretary and Such other officers as Congress shall appoint in the district, shall take an oath or affirmation of fidelity, and of office, the Governor before the president of Congress, and all other officers before the Governor. As soon as a legislature shall be formed in the district the Council and House assembled in one room shall have authority by Joint ballot to elect a Delegate to Congress who shall have a seat in Congress with a right of debating but not of voting during this temporary Government.

And for extending to all parts of the Confederacy the fundamental principles of civil and religious liberty which form the basis whereon these republics, their laws and Constitutions are erected; to fix and establish those principles as the basis of all laws Constitutions and Governments, which forever hereafter shall be formed in the said Territory; to provide also for the establishment of States and permanent Government therein, and for their admission to a share in the federal Councils on an equal footing with the original States at as early periods as may be consistent with the General Interest,

It is hereby ordained and declared by the authority aforesaid that the following articles shall be considered as articles of compact between the original States and the people and States in the said Territory, and forever remain unalterable unless by Common Consent to wit,

Article the first. no person demeaning himself in a peaceable and orderly manner shall ever be molested on account of his mode of worship or religious sentiments in the said Territory.

Article the second. the Inhabitants of the said Territory shall always be entitled to the benefits of the writ of habeas corpus, and of the trial by Jury; of a proportional representation of the people in the legislature, and of Judicial proceedings according to the Course of the Common law; all persons shall be bailable unless for capital offences where the proof shall be evident, or the presumption great; all fines shall be moderate and no cruel or unusual punishments shall be inflicted. No man shall be deprived of his liberty or property but by the Judgment of his peers or the law of the land, and should the public exigencies make it necessary for the common preservation to take any persons property or to demand his particular services, full compensation shall be made therefor, and in the Just preservation of rights and property it is understood and declared, that no law ought ever to be made, or have force in the said Territory, that shall in any manner whatever interfere with, or effect private contracts or engagements, bona fide and without fraud previously formed.

Article the third. Institutions for the promotion of religion and morality, schools and the means of education shall forever be encouraged, and all persons while young shall be taught some useful Occupation. The utmost good lands shall always be observed towards the Indians; their lands and property shall never be taken from them without their consent; and in their property, rights, and liberty, they never shall be invaded or disturbed, unless in Just and lawful wars authorised by Congress; but laws founded in Justice and humanity shall, from time to time, be made, for preventing wrongs being done to them, and for preserving peace and friendship with them.

Article the fourth. The said Territory and the States which may be formed therein shall forever remain a part of this Confederacy of the United States of America subject to the articles of Confederation and to such alterations therein as shall be constitutionally made; and to all the acts and ordinances of the United States in Congress assembled conformable thereto. The Inhabitants and settlers in said Territory shall be subject to pay a part of the federal debts contracted or to be contracted, and a proportional part of the expences of Government, to be apportioned on them by Congress according to the same common rule and measure by which apportionments thereof shall be made on the other States; and the taxes for paying their proportion shall be laid and levied by the authority and direction of the legislatures of the district or districts or new States, as in the original States, within the time agreed upon by the United States in Congress assembled. The legislatures of those districts, or new States, shall never interfere with the primary disposal of the soil by the United States in Congress assembled, nor with any regulations Congress may find necessary for securing the title in such soil to the bona fide purchasers, no tax shall be imposed on lands the property of the United States, and in no Case shall non resident proprietors be taxed higher than residents. No laws shall ever be made in said Territory for creating perpetuities therein, and the navigable waters leading into the Mississippi and St. Lawrence, and the carrying places between the same shall be common high ways, and forever free, as well to the Inhabitants of the said Territory, as to the Citizens of the United States, and those of any other States, that may be admitted into the Confederacy without any tax, impost or duty therefor.

Article the fifth. There shall be formed in the said Territory not less than three nor more than five States and the boundaries of the States, as soon as Virginia shall alter her act of cession and authorise the same shall become fixed and established as follows to wit. the Western State in said territory shall be bounded by the Mississippi, the Ohio and Wabash rivers, a direct line drawn from the Wabash and post Vincents due North to the territorial line between the United States and Canada, and by said Territorial line to the lake of the Woods and Mississippi. The middle State shall be bounded by the said direct line the Wabash from post Vincents to the Ohio, by the Ohio, by a direct line drawn due North from the mouth of the Great Miami to said territorial line and by said territorial line. The Eastern State shall be bounded by the last mentioned direct line, the Ohio, Pennsylvania, and the said territorial line, provided however and it is further understood and declared that the boundaries of these three States shall be subject so far to be altered, that if Congress hereafter shall find it expedient they shall have authority to form one or two States in that part of the said territory which lies North of an East and West line drawn through the Southerly bend or extremity of lake Michigan; and whenever any of the said States shall have sixty thousand free Inhabitants therein, such State shall be admitted by its Delegates into the Congress of the United States, on an equal footing with the original States in all respects whatever, and shall be at liberty to form a permanent Constitution and State Government, provided the Constitution and Government so to be formed shall be republican and in conformity to the principles contained in these articles and so far as it can be consistent with the General Interest of the Confederacy such admission shall be allowed at an earlier period and when there may be a less number of free Inhabitants in the State than sixty thousand.

Be it ordained by the authority aforesaid that the resolutions of the 23d of April, 1784, be, and the same are hereby repealed and declared null and void.

Ordered: That to morrow be assigned for 2d reading.

*   *   *

[Friday, July 13, 1787]

Congress assembled present as yesterday

According to Order the Ordinance for the government of the territory of the United States North West of the river Ohio was read a third time and passed as follows

An Ordinance for the government of the territory of the United States North West of the river Ohio[2]

Be it ordained by the United States in Congress Assembled that the said territory for the purposes of temporary government be one district, subject however to be divided into two districts as future circumstances may in the Opinion of Congress make it expedient.

Be it ordained by the authority aforesaid, that the estates both of resident and non resident proprietors in the said territory dying intestate shall descend to and be distributed among their children and the descendants of a deceased child in equal parts; the descendants of a deceased child or grand child to take the share of their deceased parent in equal parts among them; and where there shall be no children or descendants then in equal parts to the next of kin in equal degree and among collaterals the children of a deceased brother or sister of the intestate shall have in equal parts among them their deceased parent's share and there shall in no case be a distinction between kindred of the whole and half blood; saving in all cases to the widow of the intestate her third part of the real estate for life, and one third part of the personal estate; and this law relative to descents and dower shall remain in full force until altered by the legislature of the district. And until the governor and judges shall adopt laws as hereinafter mentioned estates in the said territory may be devised or bequeathed by wills in writing signed and sealed by him or her in whom the estate may be, being of full age, and attested by three witnesses, and real estates may be conveyed by lease and release or bargain and sale signed, sealed and delivered by the person being

[2]The portions of the Ordinance underlined were added to the original report by amendment during the debate.

of full age in whom the estate may be and attested by two witnesses provided such wills be duly proved and such conveyances be acknowledged or the execution thereof duly proved and be recorded within one year after proper magistrates, courts and registers shall be appointed for that purpose and personal property may be transferred by delivery saving however to the french and canadian inhabitants and other settlers of the Kaskaskies, Saint Vincents and the neighbouring villages who have heretofore professed themselves citizens of Virginia, their laws and customs now in force among them relative to the descent and conveyance of property.

Be it ordained by the authority aforesaid that there shall be appointed from time to time by Congress a governor, whose commission shall continue in force for the term of three years, unless sooner revoked by Congress; he shall reside in the district and have a freehold estate therein, in one thousand acres of land while in the exercise of his office. There shall be appointed from time to time by Congress a secretary, whose commission shall continue in force for four years, unless sooner revoked; he shall reside in the district and have a freehold estate therein in five hundred acres of land while in the exercise of his office; It shall be his duty to keep and preserve the acts and laws passed by the legislature and the public records of the district and the proceedings of the governor in his executive department and transmit authentic copies of such acts and proceedings every six months to the Secretary of Congress. There shall also be appointed a court to consist of three judges any two of whom to form a court, who shall have a common law jurisdiction and reside in the district and have each therein a freehold estate in five hundred acres of land while in the exercise of their offices, and their commissions shall continue in force during good behaviour.

The governor, and judges or a majority of them shall adopt and publish in the district such laws of the original states criminal and civil as may be necessary and best suited to the circumstances of the district and report them to Congress from time to time, which laws shall be in force in the district until the organization of the general assembly therein, unless disapproved of by Congress; but afterwards the legislature shall have authority to alter them as they shall think fit.

The governor for the time being shall be Commander in chief of the militia, appoint and commission all officers in the same below the rank of general Officers; All general Officers shall be appointed and commissioned by Congress.

Previous to the Organization of the general Assembly the governor shall appoint such magistrates and other civil officers in each county or township, as he shall find necessary for the preservation of the peace and good order in the same. After the general Assembly shall be organized, the powers and duties of magistrates and other civil officers shall be regulated and defined by the said Assembly; but all magistrates and other civil officers, not herein otherwise directed shall during the continuance of this temporary government be appointed by the governor.

For the prevention of crimes and injuries the laws to be adopted or made shall have force in all parts of the district and for the execution of process criminal and civil, the governor shall make proper divisions thereof, and he shall proceed from time to time as circumstances may require to lay out the parts of the district in which the indian titles shall have been extinguished into counties and townships subject however to such alterations as may thereafter be made by the legislature.

So soon as there shall be five thousand free male inhabitants of full age in the district upon giving proof thereof to the governor, they shall receive authority with time and place to elect representatives from their counties or townships to represent them in the general assembly, provided that for every five hundred free male inhabitants there shall be one representative and so on progressively with the number of free male inhabitants shall the right of representation encrease until the number of representatives shall amount to twenty five after which the number and proportion of representatives shall be regulated by the legislature; provided that no person be eligible or qualified to act as a representative unless he shall have been a citizen of one of the United States three years and be a resident in the district or unless he shall have resided in the district three years and in either case shall likewise hold in his own right in fee simple two hundred acres of land within the same; provided also that a freehold in fifty acres of land in the district having been a citizen of one of the states and being resident in the district; or the like freehold and two years residence in the district shall be necessary to qualify a man as an elector of a representative.

The representatives thus elected shall serve for the term of two years and in case of the death of a representative or removal from office, the governor shall issue a writ to the county or township for which he was a member, to elect another in his stead to serve for the residue of the term.

The general assembly or legislature shall consist of the governor, legislative council and a house of representatives. The legislative council shall consist of five members to continue in Office five years unless sooner removed by Congress any three of whom to be a quorum and the members of the council shall be nominated and appointed in the following manner, to wit; As soon as representatives shall be elected, the governor shall appoint a time and place for them to meet together, and when met they shall nominate ten persons residents in the district and each possessed of a freehold in five hundred acres of Land and return their names to Congress; five of whom Congress shall appoint and commission to serve as aforesaid; and whenever a vacancy shall happen in the council by death or removal from office, the house of representatives shall nominate two persons qualified as aforesaid, for each vacancy, and return their names to Congress, one of whom Congress shall appoint and commission for the residue of the term, and every five years, four months at least before the expiration of the time of service of the Members of Council, the said house shall nominate ten persons qualified as aforesaid, and return their names to Congress, five of whom Congress shall appoint and commission to serve as Members of the council five years, unless sooner removed. And the Governor, legislative council, and house of representatives, shall have authority to make laws in all cases for the good government of the district, not repugnant to the principles and Articles in this Ordinance established and declared. And all bills having passed by a majority in the house, and by a majority in the council, shall be referred to the Governor for his assent; but no bill or legislative Act whatever, shall be of any force without his assent. The Governor shall have power to convene, prorogue and dissolve the General Assembly, when in his opinion it shall be expedient.

The Governor, Judges, legislative Council, Secretary, and such other Officers as Congress shall appoint in the district shall take an Oath or Affirmation of fidelity, and of Office, the Governor before the president of Congress, and all other Officers before the Governor. As soon as a legislature shall be formed in the district, the Council and house assembled in one room, shall have authority by joint ballot to elect a Delegate to Congress, who shall have a seat in Congress, with a right of debating, but not of voting, during this temporary Government.

And for extending the fundamental principles of civil and religious liberty, which form the basis whereon these republics, their laws and constitutions are erected; to fix and establish those principles as the basis of all laws, constitutions and governments, which forever hereafter shall be formed in the said territory; to provide also for the establishment of States and permanent government therein, and for their admission to a share in the federal Councils on an equal footing with the original States, at as early periods as may be consistent with the general interest,

It is hereby Ordained and declared by the authority aforesaid, That the following Articles shall be considered as Articles of compact between the Original States and the people and States in the said territory, and forever remain unalterable, unless by common consent, to wit,

Article the First. No person demeaning himself in a peaceable and orderly manner shall ever be molested on account of his mode of worship or religious sentiments in the said territory.

Article the Second. The Inhabitants of the said territory shall always be entitled to the benefits of the writ of habeas corpus, and of the trial by Jury; of a proportionate representation of the people in the legislature, and of judicial proceedings according to the course of the common law; all persons shall be bailable unless for capital offences, where the proof shall be evident, or the presumption great; all fines shall be moderate, and no cruel or unusual punishments shall be inflicted; no man shall be deprived of his liberty or property but by the judgment of his peers, or the law of the land; and should the public exigencies make it necessary for the common preservation to take any persons property, or to demand his particular services, full compensation shall be made for the same; and in the just preservation of rights and property it is understood and declared; that no law ought ever to be made, or have force in the said territory, that shall in any manner whatever interfere with, or affect private contracts or engagements, bona fide and without fraud previously formed.

Article the Third. Religion, Morality and knowledge being necessary to good government and the happiness of mankind, Schools and the means of education shall forever be encouraged. The utmost good faith shall always be observed towards the Indians, their lands and property shall never be taken from them without their consent; and in their property, rights and liberty, they never shall be invaded or disturbed, unless in just and lawful wars authorised by Congress; but laws founded in justice and humanity shall from time to time be made, for preventing wrongs being done to them, and for preserving peace and friendship with them.

Article the Fourth. The said territory, and the States which may be formed therein shall forever remain a part of this Confederacy of the United States of America, subject to the Articles of Confederation, and to such alterations therein as shall be constitutionally made; and to all the Acts and Ordinances of the United States in Congress Assembled, conformable thereto. The Inhabitants and Settlers in the said territory, shall be subject to pay a part of the federal debts contracted or to be contracted, and a proportional part of the expences of Government, to be apportioned on them by Congress, according to the same common rule and measure by which apportionments thereof shall be made on the other States; and the taxes for paying their proportion, shall be laid and levied by the authority and direction of the legislatures of the district or districts or new States, as in the original States, within the time agreed upon by the United States in Congress Assembled. The Legislatures of those districts, or new States, shall never interfere with the primary disposal of the Soil by the United States in Congress Assembled, nor with any regulations Congress may find necessary for securing the title in such soil to the bona fide purchasers. No tax shall be imposed on lands the property of the United States; and in no case shall non resident proprietors be taxed higher than residents. The navigable Waters leading into the Mississippi and St. Lawrence, and the carrying places between the same shall be common highways, and forever free, as well to the Inhabitants of the said territory, as to the Citizens of the United States, and those of any other States that may be admitted into the Confederacy, without any tax, impost or duty therefor.

Article the Fifth. There shall be formed in the said territory, not less than three nor more than five States, and the boundaries of the States, as soon as Virginia shall alter her act of cession and consent to the same, shall become fixed and established as follows, to wit: The Western State in the said territory, shall be bounded by the Mississippi, the Ohio and Wabash rivers; a direct line drawn from the Wabash and post Vincents due North to the territorial line between the United States and Canada, and by the said territorial line to the lake of the Woods and Mississippi. The middle State shall be bounded by the said direct line, the Wabash from post Vincents to the Ohio; by the Ohio, by direct line drawn due North from the mouth of the great Miami to the said territorial line, and by the said territorial line. The eastern State shall be bounded by the last mentioned direct line, the Ohio, Pennsylvania, and the said territorial line; provided however, and it is further understood and declared, that the boundaries of these three States, shall be subject so far to be altered, that if Congress shall hereafter find it expedient, they shall have authority to form one or two States in that part of the said territory which lies north of an east and west line drawn through the southerly bend or extreme of lake Michigan; and whenever any of the said States shall have sixty thousand free Inhabitants therein, such State shall be admitted by its Delegates into the Congress of the United States, on an equal footing with the original States, in all respects whatever; and shall be at liberty to form a permanent constitution and State government, provided the constitution and government so to be formed, shall be republican, and in conformity to the principles contained in these Articles; and so far as it can be consistent with the general interest of the Confederacy, such admission shall be allowed at an earlier period, and when there may be a less number of free Inhabitants in the State than sixty thousand.

Article the Sixth. There shall be neither Slavery nor involuntary Servitude in the said territory otherwise than in the punishment of crimes, whereof the party shall have been duly convicted; provided always that any person escaping into the same, from whom labor or service is lawfully claimed in any one of the original States, such fugitive may be lawfully reclaimed and conveyed to the person claiming his or her labor or service as aforesaid.

Be it Ordained by the Authority aforesaid, that the Resolutions of the 23d of April 1784 relative to the subject of this ordinance be, and the same are hereby repealed and declared null and void.

Done &c.

On passing the above Ordinance the yeas and nays being required by Mr [Abraham] Yates

Massachusetts			Virginia		
Mr Holten	ay	} ay	Mr Grayson	ay	} ay
Mr Dane	ay		Mr R H Lee	ay	
New York			Mr Carrington	ay	
Mr Smith	ay	} ay	North Carolina		
Mr Haring	ay		Mr Blount	ay	} ay
Mr Yates	no		Mr Hawkins	ay	
New Jersey			South Carolina		
Mr Clarke	ay	} ay	Mr Kean	ay	} ay
Mr Schurman	ay		Mr Huger	ay	
Delaware			Georgia		
Mr Kearny	ay	} ay	Mr Few	ay	} ay
Mr Mitchell	ay		Mr Pierce	ay	

So it was resolved in the affirmative.

When Madison introduced the amendments that became the federal Bill of Rights in the first session of the Congress set up by the Constitution, he could state (with reference to the rights guaranteed by the new organic provisions) "independent tribunals of justice will consider themselves in a peculiar manner the guardians of those rights." To the draftsman of the Bill of Rights, judicial review was already an implicit aspect of the constitutional structure. The guarantees for individual liberty which he was inserting into the Constitution would, he knew, be more than hortatory maxims of public morality, for they would be directly enforced by the courts, who would have the duty of declaring void all acts contrary to the new guarantees.

Judicial review was the inarticulate major premise upon which the movement to secure a federal Bill of Rights was ultimately based. As seen (*supra* p. 183) the doctrine of unconstitutionality was asserted by Americans even before the first written Constitutions in this country. The doctrine could, however, become a principle of positive law only after Independence, when written Constitutions were adopted as supreme laws in the different states. The notion of fundamental law itself had been appealed to as the source of Colonial rights during the pre-Independence stages of the conflict with the mother country. When the time came for the states to set up their own governments, they reduced the fundamental principles to written form in charters or government which would contain binding limitations, beyond the reach of those who exercised governmental power. Of what avail would such limitations be, however, if there were no legal machinery to enforce them? Even a Constitution is naught but empty words if it cannot be enforced by the courts.

The doctrine of judicial review (upon which the practical value of an organic document like the federal Bill of Rights really turns) was (as seen *supra* p. 183) put forward by James Otis and Patrick Henry even before the Revolution. But it first became a part of the living law during the decade before the federal Constitution. It was during that time that American courts first began to assert the power to rule on the constitutionality of legislative acts and to hold unconstitutional statutes void. By the time of the federal Convention of 1787 (and certainly by the time Madison drew up his draft of the Bill of Rights), it was generally assumed that the federal constitutional provisions which were being written would be enforced by the courts.

Cases in at least eight states between 1780 and 1787 involved direct assertions of the power of judicial review. Materials from the four most important of them follow. The principal difficulty in getting an adequate picture arises from the fact that there was no meaningful reporting of most cases in the modern sense at the time these cases were decided. Reported opinions (such as those which now abound in the *United States Reports*) were mainly skimpy or non-existent. That is why recourse has been had to other materials (such as arguments of counsel and articles) to present two of the cases concerned.

The first case which follows is the New Jersey case of *Holmes v. Walton* (1780). That case was unreported and perhaps the best account of what happened there is in the article by Austin Scott, from which extracts follow. Some recent commentators (notably Louis Boudin and W. W. Crosskey) have attacked the conclusion that *Holmes* v. *Walton* was a precedent for judicial review. It cannot be denied, however, that it was widely thought of as such at the time the federal Constitution and bill of Rights were adopted. As the Scott article points out, a 1785 message by Gouverneur Morris (then Governor of Pennsylvania) to the legislature of that state mentioned that "a law was once passed in New Jersey, which the judges pronounced unconstitutional, and therefore void." (Even Crosskey assumes that this refers to *Holmes* v. *Walton.*) In addition, there is the 1804 case cited by Scott, which states that in *Holmes* v. *Walton,* an "act upon solemn argument was adjudged to be unconstitutional and in that case inoperative." At the least, these indicate that contemporaries did regard *Holmes* v. *Walton* as a precedent for judicial review.

The second case which follows is the 1782 case of *Commonwealth* v. *Caton.* Since it was officially reported, we are about to give the case as it was reported in *Call's Virginia Reports.* In the *Caton* case, we have the first clear statement by American judges of the power to hold statutes unconstitutional (since we do not have the probably oral opinion delivered in *Holmes* v. *Walton*). Again more recent scholars (notably Crosskey) challenge *Caton* as a precedent for judicial review. One who reads the extracts which follow can have no such doubt, for the language of the Virginia judges is as clear as words can be. Of particular importance was the opinion of Judge Wythe, which must have had great influence because of Wythe's prestige as perhaps the leading American jurist of his day. (Wythe was the first holder of an American law professorship and among his students was John Marshall, who was to elevate the *Caton* principle to the federal constitutional plane in *Marbury* v. *Madison.*)

The third case which follows is the 1786 Rhode Island case of *Trevett* v. *Weeden.* That case, too, was unreported and our account is taken from a 1787 pamphlet published by James M. Varnum (better known as one of Washington's generals), who argued the case against the statute. Varnum's argument received wide dissemination and demonstrated the unconstitutionality of the legislative attempt to deprive Weeden of his right to trial by jury. That the judges agreed with him is shown by the following brief account in the *Providence Gazette* of October 7, 1786:

> The court adjourned to next morning, upon opening of which, Judge Howell, in a firm, sensible, and judicious speech, assigned the reasons which induced him to be of the opinion that the information was not

cognizable by the court—declared himself independent as a judge—the penal law to be repugnant and unconstitutional—and therefore gave it as his opinion that the court could not take cognizance of the information! Judge Devoe was of the same opinion. Judge Tillinghast took notice of the stricking repugnancy of the expressions of the act . . . and on that ground gave his judgment the same way. Judge Hazard voted against taking cognizance. The Chief Justice declared the judgment of the court without giving his own opinion.

The fourth case which follows is the 1787 North Carolina case of *Boyard* v. *Singleton,* and our extract is from the official report. It shows that the judges realized the full implications of what they were doing, in holding that a statute contrary to the trial by jury guarantee in the North Carolina Declaration of Rights "must of course . . . stand as abrogated and without any effect." No legislative "Act could by any means repeal or alter the Constitution" so long as the Constitution remains "standing in full force as the fundamental law of the land." Of particular significance is the fact that among the judges who decided *Boyard* v. *Singleton* was James Iredell, who was later appointed to the United States Supreme Court.

Holmes v. Walton: The New Jersey Precedent, 1779*

A Chapter in the History of Judicial Power and Unconstitutional Legislation

After the battle of Monmouth in June, 1778, the British commander made his way to Sandy Hook and thence to New York, where he established permanent headquarters, retaining, during the rest of the war, possession of Staten Island adjacent to New Jersey. On the 8th of October, 1778, the New Jersey legislature passed a law to prevent the increasing evil of intercourse with the enemy. This act made it "lawful for any person or persons whomsoever to seize and secure provisions, goods, wares and merchandize attempted to be carried or conveyed into or brought from within the lines or encampments or any place in the possession of the subjects or troops of the King of Great Britain." These goods and the persons in whose possession they might be found were to be taken before a justice of the peace of the county. The law required the justice, on the demand of either party, to grant a jury according to the law of February 11, 1775, which provided for a jury of six men, and further stipulated, "that in every cause where a jury of six men give a verdict as aforesaid there shall be no appeal allowed." The law of October, 1778, further provided that if the plaintiff should win the suit the proceeds from the sale of the goods were to be divided among the persons seizing them.

By virtue of this law, Elisha Walton, a major of militia, seized a quantity of goods in the possession of John Holmes and Solomon Ketcham, whom he

* A. Scott, *American Historical Review* (1899), Vol. IV, pp. 456–69.

charged with having brought them from within the lines of the enemy. The goods were of considerable value, there being between seven hundred and eight hundred yards of silk, between four hundred and five hundred yards of silk gauze, "mode," and many other articles, "such a quantity and such a quality as could not be purchased in all the stores of New Jersey." The case was tried before John Anderson, a justice of the peace of Monmouth County, on the 24th of May, 1779, with a jury of six men, who brought in a verdict in favor of Walton and judgment was given accordingly.

While the suit was pending, the defendants had already applied to the Supreme Court then in session at Burlington, and the Chief Justice, Robert Morris, issued a writ of certiorari to Anderson, returnable at the next session of the Supreme Court to be held at Hillsborough in Somerset County, the first Tuesday of September. Meantime Morris resigned his seat on the bench and on the 10th of June David Brearly was appointed Chief Justice. The court opened at Hillsborough on the 7th of September, and on the 9th it was orderd that the case of Holmes *vs.* Walton be argued on the   Thursday of the next term. Accordingly on Thursday, November 11, 1779, the case was argued before the Supreme Court sitting at Trenton. In offering his argument for the plaintiffs in certiorari, William Willcocks, their attorney, filed his reasons why the judgment of Justice Anderson should be reversed. The seventh reason reads as follows: "Because the jury sworn to try the above cause and on whose verdict judgment was entered, consisted of six men only, when by the Laws of the Land it should have consisted of twelve men." The same attorney, at the same trial, also filed separately "additional reasons," which read as follows:

> For that the said justice had not jurisdiction of the said cause or plaint but the same was *coram non judice.*
> For that the jury who tryed the said plaint before the said justice consisted of six men only contrary to law.
> For that the jury who tried the said plaint before the said justice consisted of six men only contrary to the constitution of New Jersey.
> For that the proceedings and trial in the said plaint in the court below, and the judgment thereon given were had and given contrary to the constitution, practices and laws of the land.

At the close of the argument, the record shows that "on the reasons filed a *curia advisare vult* is entered." Under date of the following Monday, November 15, the minutes state that "the court will further advise on the arguments had on this cause until the next term." In the succeeding term, April, 1780, the minute states, "The court not being ready to give judgment on the reasons filed and argued in this cause—Ordered, that a *curia advisare vult* until next term be entered; on motion of Mr. Elias Boudinot." In the minutes of the May term there is no record of the case. At the succeeding term, however, on Thursday, September 7, 1780, ten months after the case had been argued, judgment was given.

Before investigating the nature of the decision given and the probable cause of the delay in rendering it, it may be proper to inquire with what color of right the counsel could urge his plea against the constitutional validity of the statute of October 8, 1778, which allowed a six-man jury. Section XXII. of the constitution of New Jersey, adopted July 2, 1776, reads as follows: "That the common law of England, as well as so much of the statute law as have been heretofore practiced in this colony shall still remain in force, until they shall be altered by a future law of the legislature; such parts only excepted as are repugnant to the rights and privileges contained in this Charter; and that the inestimable right of trial by jury shall remain confirmed as a part of the law of this colony, without repeal forever." The final section of the same constitution prescribes as a part of the oath to be taken by each member of the legislature, that he will not assent to any law, vote, or proceeding to repeal or annul "that part of the twenty-second section respecting the trial by jury."

The assumption that the phrase "trial by jury" as thus used meant exactly twelve jurors must find its warrant farther back. In addition to immemorial custom, the "common law" of England, which may have been held to have had validity in this case, two documents may have been appealed to as fundamentally relevant and as constituting in New Jersey a part of the "law of the land:" the first, Chapter XXII. of the West Jersey "Concessions and Agreements" of 1676, "Not to be altered by the legislative authority," which begins thus, "That the trial of all causes, civil and criminal, shall be heard and decided by the verdict or judgment of twelve honest men of the neighborhood." The second was a formal declaration of the "Rights and Privileges" passed by the House of Representatives in East Jersey on March 13, 1699, and accepted by the governor and council, which asserted that "all trials shall be by the verdict of twelve men." Other acts of the assembly in each of the two Jersey provinces before their union in 1702, show that the right to a trial before a jury of twelve men was regarded as fundamental; notably the act of November, 1681, in West Jersey, and that of March, 1683, in East Jersey.

The foregoing details have been recited as inferentially the basis of the argument of the attorney for the plaintiffs and of the decision of the court rendered on September 7, 1780. On that day a full bench was present, David Brearly, the Chief Justice, with Isaac Smith and John Cleves Symmes, his associates. The minute of the court reads thus: "John Holmes and Solomon Ketcham *vs.* Elisha Walton, sur certiorari to John Anderson, Esq. . . . This cause having been argued several terms past and the court having taken time to consider the same, and being now ready to deliver their opinion gave the same seriatim for the plaintiffs in certiorari. And on motion of Boudinot for the plaintiffs, judgment is ordered for the plaintiffs, and that the judgment of the justice in the court below be reversed and the said plaintiffs be restored to all things, etc."

Persistent search has failed to discover the opinion of Chief Justice Brearly delivered in this case. It was probably an oral opinion and never written. Happily, however, there exists incontestable proof as to its import. On the afternoon of the 8th of December, 1780, in the House of Assembly, "a petition from sixty inhabitants of the county of Monmouth was presented and read, complaining that the justices of the Supreme Court have set aside some of the laws as unconstitutional, and made void the proceedings of the magistrates, though strictly agreeable to the said laws, to the encouragement of the disaffected and great loss to the loyal citizens of the state and praying redress."

A second unquestionable proof that the decision of Brearly nullified the laws allowing a jury of six men appears in the subsequent proceedings of the Holmes-Walton case, which dragged along for years. In July, 1781, in the course of the new trial before the justice ordered by the Supreme Court, Willcocks, counsel for Holmes, argues thus: "That the present cause being commenced and undetermined at the time of the late law authorizing a trial by twelve men [i.e., an act of December 22, 1780, to be referred to later] it is not comprehended by the late law, it not having in it any retrospective clause; and as a trial by six men is unconstitutional, there is no law existing by which this cause could be tried."

A message from Governor Livingston to the assembly on the 7th of June, 1782, is not without significance in the history of the recognition of this judicial function at this time and presumably in connection with this case. After stating that the chancellor (in that day, the governor) must seal a writ of replevin on the application of any citizen, Livingston continues, "But if an act of legislation can constitutionally be made, declaring that no person in whose possession any goods, wares or merchandise shall be seized and captured as effects illegally imported from the enemy, shall be entitled to such a writ . . . . if such an act, I say, should be passed it would probably encourage such seizures and give additional check to that most pernicious and detestable trade, the total suppression of which is one of the most important objects that can engage the attention of the legislature."

From the contemporary evidence cited above no doubt can remain that Brearly met the question of constitutionality squarely and on September 7, 1780, announced the principle of judicial guardianship of the organic law against attempted or inadvertent encroachment by the ordinary law.

*   *   *

The full significance within New Jersey of the decree of the court and the action of the legislature is acknowledged in the following words of Chief Justice Kirkpatrick in 1804, in his opinion in the case of State *vs.* Parkhurst: "This question" (viz. whether the court has power to control the operation of an act of the legislature upon the principle of its being contrary to the constitution) "was brought forward in the case of Holmes *vs.* Walton, arising on what was then called the seizure laws. There it had been enacted that the trial should be by a jury of six men; and it was objected that this was not a constitutional jury; and so it was held; and the act upon solemn argument was adjudged to be unconstitutional and in that case inoperative. And upon this decision the act, or at least that part of it which relates to the six-man jury, was repealed and a constitutional jury of twelve men substituted in its place. This then is not only a judicial decision but a decision recognized and acquiesced in by the legislative body of the State."

Was the case of Holmes *vs.* Walton of value beyond the borders of New Jersey? It made a deep impression in one important quarter at least. In 1785, Gouverneur Morris sent to the Pennsylvania legislature an address, whose object was to dissuade that body from passing a law to repeal the charter of the National Bank. In the course of that address he says: "A law was once passed in New Jersey, which the judges pronounced unconstitutional, and therefore void. Surely no good citizen can wish to see this point decided in the tribunals of Pennsylvania. Such power in judges is dangerous; but unless it somewhere exists, the time employed in framing a bill of rights and form of government was merely thrown away."

*   *   *

The following summary expresses in brief the reasons for the view of the present writer that the case of Holmes *vs.* Walton is of considerable importance in our constitutional history:

1. It seems to take precedence in point of time of all similar decisions. The question of constitutionality was raised before the Supreme Court of New Jersey on the 11th of November, 1779, and decided on the 7th of September, 1780.

2. The question of constitutionality was brought squarely before the court and was squarely decided. Other questions and other principles were apparently not involved in the decision.

3. The judgment was not given *ad captandum*. It was clearly announced after long and careful consideration and evidently with a complete and intelligent view of its immediate, and in some degree of its far-reaching importance in the state at least. The evidence warrants the conclusion that the New Jersey judges desired to fix the scope of this power. They would leave intact all those portions of the law which were not plainly void.

4. The decision does not recognize "necessity" or extra-constitutional legislative war-powers or the special plea of patriotic motives in construing the organic law.

5. It is a happy circumstance that the decision guards one of the oldest and most important of constitutional rights, that of trial by a real jury.

6. The decision, though meeting with some opposition, was ratified by a legislature fresh from the people.

7. It had its influence outside of New Jersey, being cited in the appeal by Gouverneur Morris to the Pennsylvania legislature five years after it was rendered. This appeal was published in Philadelphia, then the central city of

the Union, where Congress had had its sessions and where the Federal Convention two years later was to assemble.

8. It must have had a value in preparing for the special duty of formally proposing the principle, Brearly the chief-justice, who rendered the decision, Paterson the attorney-general, and Livingston the governor, the three Jersey-men who in the Federal Convention gave form and name and support to the "Jersey plan."

9. To the "New Jersey plan" is due the formal proposal and therefore, in large part, in due time and by due process, the final acceptance of this principle of judicial control in our legal system.

Commonwealth v. Caton, Virginia, 1782*

This case came before the court by adjournment from the General Court, and was as follows:

John Caton, Joshua Hopkins, and John Lamb were condemned for treason, by the General Court, under the Act of Assembly concerning that offence, passed in 1776, which takes from the executive the power of granting pardon in such cases. The House of Delegates by resolution of the 18th of June, 1782, granted them a pardon, and sent it to the Senate for concurrence; which they refused. The men, however, were not executed, but continued in jail under the sentence; and, in October, 1782, the Attorney-General moved in the General Court, that execution of the judgment might be awarded. The prisoners pleaded the pardon granted by the House of Delegates. The Attorney-General denied the validity of the pardon, as the Senate had not concurred in it: and the General Court adjourned the case, for novelty and difficulty, to the Court of Appeals.

The resolution of the House of Delegates was in the following words:

In the House of Delegates,
Tuesday the 18th of June, 1782

Resolved that James Lamb, Joshua Hopkins, and John Caton, who stand convicted and attainted of treason by judgment of the General Court, at their last session, and appear to be proper objects of mercy, be and are hereby declared to be pardoned for the said treason, and exempted from all pains and penalties for the same; provided they and each of them repair to the county of Augusta within—days from this time, and continue within the said county during their natural lives respectively. Ordered that Mr. Patrick Henry do carry the said resolution to the Senate and desire their concurrence.

The cause was argued in the Court of Appeals by Mr. Randolph, the Attorney-General, for the Commonwealth, and by Mr. Hardy and several other distinguished gentlemen for the prisoners.

*4 Call Virginia Reports, pp. 5–12.

For the Commonwealth it was contended, that the pardon was void, as the Senate had not concurred. That the clause in the Constitution might be read two ways, either of which would destroy the pardon. One was, to throw the words, "or the law shall otherwise particularly direct," into a parenthesis; which would confine the separate power of the Lower House to cases of impeachment only; and would leave those where the assembly had taken it from the executive to the direction of the laws made for the purpose. The other was, to take the whole sentence as it stands, and then the construction will, according to the obvious meaning of the Constitution, be that, although the House of Delegates must originate the resolution, the Senate must in all cases concur, or it will have no effect. For it would be absurd to suppose, that the same instrument which required the whole legislature to make a law, should authorize one branch to repeal it.

For the prisoners, it was contended, that the language of the Constitution embraced both sets of cases, as well those of impeachment, as those where the assembly should take the power of pardoning from the executive: and, in both, that the direction was express that the power of pardoning belonged to the House of Delegates. That the words of the Constitution, and not conjectures drawn from the supposed meaning of the framers of it, should give the rule. That the Act of Assembly was contrary to the plain declaration of the Constitution; and therefore void. That the prisoners were misguided and unfortunate men; and that the construction ought, in favor of life, to incline to the side of mercy.

The Attorney-General, in reply, insisted, that compassion for the prisoners could not enter into the case; and that the Act of Assembly pursued the spirit of the Constitution. But that, whether it did or not, the court were not authorized to declare it void.   *Cur. adv. vult.*

Wythe, J. : Among all the advantages which have arisen to mankind from the study of letters, and the universal diffusion of knowledge, there is none of more importance than the tendency they have had to produce discussions upon the respective rights of the sovereign and the subject; and upon the powers which the different branches of government may exercise. For, by this means, tyranny has been sapped, the departments kept within their own spheres, the citizens protected, and general liberty promoted. But this beneficial result attains to higher perfection, when those who hold the purse and the sword, differing as to the powers which each may exercise, the tribunals, who hold neither, are called upon to declare the law impartially between them. For thus the pretensions of each party are fairly examined, their respective powers ascertained, and the boundaries of authority peaceably established. Under these impressions, I approach the question which has been submitted to us; and although it was said the other day, by one of the judges, that, imitating that great and good man Lord Hale, he would sooner quit the Bench than determine it, I feel no alarm; but will meet the crisis as I ought; and, in the language of my oath of office, will decide it, according to the best of my skill and judgment.

I have heard of an English Chancellor who said, and it was nobly said, that it was his duty to protect the rights of the subject against the encroachments of the Crown, and that he would do it, at every hazard. But if it was his duty to protect a solitary individual against the rapacity of the sovereign, surely, it is equally mine, to protect one branch of the legislature, and, consequently, the whole community, against the usurpations of the other; and, whenever the proper occasion occurs, I shall feel the duty, and fearlessly perform it. Whenever traitors shall be fairly convicted, by the verdict of their peers, before the competent tribunal, if one branch of the legislature, without the concurrence of the other, shall attempt to rescue the offenders from the sentence of the law, I shall not hesitate, sitting in this place, to say to the General Court, *Fiat justitia, ruat coelum;* and, to the usurping branch of the legislature, you attempt worse than a vain thing; for although you cannot succeed, you set an example which may convulse society to its centre. Nay more, if the whole legislature, an event to be deprecated, should attempt to overleap the bounds prescribed to them by the people, I, in administering the public justice of the country, will meet the united powers at my seat in this tribunal; and, pointing to the Constitution, will say to them, here is the limit of your authority, and hither shall you go, but no further.

Waiving, however, longer discussion upon those subjects, and proceeding to the question immediately before us, the case presented is, that three men, convicted of treason against the State, and condemned by the General Court, have pleaded a pardon, by the House of Delegates, upon which that House insists, although the Senate refuses to concur; and the opinion of the court is asked, whether the General Court should award execution of the judgment, contrary to the allegation of the prisoners, that the House of Delegates alone have the power to pardon them, under that article of the Constitution which says, "But he (the Governor) shall, with the advice of the Council of State, have the power of granting reprieves or pardons, except where the prosecution shall have been carried on by the House of Delegates, or the law shall otherwise particularly direct; in which cases, no reprieve or pardon shall be granted, but by resolve of the House of Delegates."

Two questions are made,

1. Whether this court has jurisdiction in the case?

2. Whether the pardon is valid?

The first appears, to me, to admit of no doubt; for the Act constituting this court is express, that the court shall have jurisdiction "In such cases as shall be removed before them, by adjournment from the other courts before mentioned, when questions, in their opinion new and difficult, occur." Chan. Rev. 102: which emphatically embraces the case under consideration.

The sole inquiry therefore is, whether the pardon be valid?

If we consider the genius of our institutions, it is clear that the pretensions of the House of Delegates cannot be sustained. For, throughout the whole structure of the government, concurrence of the several branches of each department is required to give effect to its operations. Thus the Governor, with the advice of the Council of State, may grant pardons, commission officers, and embody the militia; but he can do neither without the assent of the council: the two branches of the legislature may pass laws, but a bill passed by one of them has no force: and the two houses of assembly may elect a judge; but an appointment, by one of them only, would be useless. This general requisition of union seems of itself to indicate that nothing was intended to be done, in any department, without it; and, accordingly, the fourth section of the Constitution declares, that "The legislature shall be formed of two distinct branches, who, together, shall be a complete legislature;" and the eighth, "that all laws shall originate in the House of Delegates, to be approved or rejected by the Senate." Thus requiring, in conformity to the regulations throughout the whole fabric of government, an union of the two branches, to constitute a legislature; and an union of sentiment in the united body, to give effect to their acts. And it is not to be believed, that, when this union was so steadfastly demanded, even in the smallest cases, it was meant to be dispensed with, in one of the first magnitude, and which might involve the vital interests of the community.

But if we advert to the motive for the regulation, the necessity for concurrence will be more apparent. For it is obvious, that the contests in England between the House of Commons and the Crown, relative to impeachments, gave rise to it, as the king generally pardoned the offender, and frustrated the prosecution. With this in view, the power of pardoning cases of that kind was taken from the executive here, and committed to other hands, in order that the evil complained of there might be removed. But the interpretation contended for by the House of Delegates, in effect, reverses the object. Thus the object was to put a check to prerogative in one department; the effect is to remove all check, and establish prerogative in another department. The object was to prevent disappointment, by one department, of the national will; the effect is to enable less than a department to defeat it. . . .

These arguments receive some illustration from the twentieth section of the Constitution, recognizing the power of the whole legislature, and not one branch, to abolish penalties and forfeitures: which is contravened by the other construction; for, if the House of Delegates can remit part of the penalty, they may the whole, as well the forfeiture of the goods, as the corporal suffering. An idea utterly inconsistent with the recognition of a power, in the whole legislature, to do it.

Every view of the subject, therefore, repels the construction of the House of Delegates; and, accordingly, the practice is said to have been against it, ever since the formation of the government: which seems to have been the understanding upon the present occasion; for the resolution provides that it shall be sent to the Senate for concurrence.

This mode of considering the subject obviates the objection made by the prisoners' counsel, relative to the constitutionality of the law concerning treason; for, according to the interpretation just discussed, there is nothing unconstitutional in it.

I am, therefore, of opinion, that the pardon pleaded by the prisoners is not valid; and that it ought to be so certified to the General Court.

Pendleton, President: . . . The question, upon the merits, is whether by the paper stated in the record as the resolution of the House of Delegates, these three unhappy men stand pardoned of the treason of which they are attainted in the General Court, or still remain subject to the execution of the judgment which passed against them upon their conviction? If the exclusive power of the House of Delegates on this occasion was to be admitted, it would be difficult to maintain that this resolution should operate as a pardon, since those who made it, by sending it to the Senate for their concurrence, appear to have suspended its operation until the concurrence of the Senate should be obtained, which not having happened, the force of it stands as yet suspended; or rather the Senate, by rejecting this, and the House of Delegates not passing another, their power remains unexercised, and the attainder retains its full force. But, as I do not make this the ground of my judgment, I shall pass to the two great points into which the question has been divided, whether, if the constitution of government and the Act declaring what shall be treason are at variance on this subject, which shall prevail and be the rule of judgment? And then, whether they do contravene each other? The constitution of other governments, in Europe or elsewhere, seem to throw little light upon this question, since we have a written record of that which the citizens of this State have adopted as their social compact; and beyond which we need not extend our researches. It has been very properly said, on all sides, that this Act, declaring the rights of the citizens, and forming their government, divided it into three great branches, the legislative, executive, and judiciary, assigning to each its proper powers, and directing that each shall be kept separate and distinct, must be considered as a rule obligatory upon every department, not to be departed from on any occasion. But how far this court, in whom the judiciary powers may in some sort be said to be concentrated, shall have power to declare the nullity of a law passed in its forms by the legislative power, without exercising the power of that branch, contrary to the plain terms of that constitution, is indeed a deep, important, and I will aed, a tremendous question, the decision of which might involve consequences to which gentlemen may not have extended their ideas. I am happy in being of opinion there is no occasion to consider it upon this occasion; and still more happy in the hope that the wisdom and prudence of the legislature will prevent the disagreeable necessity of ever deciding it, by suggesting the propriety of making the principles of the Constitution the great rule to direct the spirit of their laws.

It was argued by the counsel for the prisoners, that the interpretation, now to be made, ought, in favor of life, to incline to the side of mercy, and that compassion for the misguided and unfortunate ought to have some influence on our decision.

Mercy—divine attribute! Often necessary to the best, sometimes due to the worst, and from the infirmities of our nature always to be regarded, when circumstances will admit of it. But how, in public concerns, this is to be accomplished with just attention to the general welfare, has, in every age, been a *desideratum* with statesmen and legislators. For, in human associations, other considerations, as well as the dictates of mercy, must be attended to. Compassion for the individual must frequently yield to the safety of the community. Society proceeds upon that principle. Men surrender part of their natural rights to insure protection for the residue against domestic violence, and hostilities from abroad; which can only be effected by the due execution of wholesome laws calculated to maintain the rights of private citizens, and the integrity of the State. But how would this be promoted by letting loose, notorious offenders to burn, to rob, and to murder, or to aid a foreign foe in his unjust attempts upon the liberties of the country? Mercy, in such cases, to one, would be cruelty to the rest.

Aware of this, the makers of the Constitution, considering that although, in representative governments, the laws should be mild, they ought to be rigidly executed; and that, although a power to pardon, which had often been abused in England, should exist somewhere, it ought never to be exercised without proper cause, framed the clause now under consideration; which provides that the Governor, or Chief Magistrate, "shall not, under any pretence, exercise any power or prerogative by virtue of any law, statute, or custom of England; but he shall, with the advice of the Council of State, have the power of granting reprives and pardons:" not in all cases indiscriminately, but in such only as were least liable to abuse; the rest were confided to agents less exposed to temptation.

Thus the power was, in general, committed to the executive: but as to cases concerning the conduct of public officers, and those which policy might suggest to the legislature as proper to be taken from the Chief Magistrate and his council, it was thought a safer depository, beyond the reach of the various passions and motives which might influence a few individuals, would be found in the General Assembly; and therefore the clause excepts cases of impeachment, and those which the law might otherwise provide for. In these, the power of pardoning is reserved to the representatives of the people: but whether to one or both Houses is the important question. A question which should be decided according to the spirit, and not by the words of the Constitution.

The language of the clause is inaccurate, and admits of both the constructions mentioned by the Attorney-General, that is to say, 1. By throwing the words, "or the law shall otherwise particularly direct," into a parenthesis, to confine the power of pardoning, by resolution of the House of Delegates alone, to cases of impeachment only; and to leave those which the General Assembly might take from the executive, to the direction of the laws made for the purpose. 2. By taking the clause altogether, to make the representatives of the people the source of mercy, provided the consent of the Senate was obtained. Either view of the subject satisfies the present inquiry; but I prefer the first, as most congenial to the spirit, and not inconsistent with the letter, of the Constitution.

The treason law appears to have been framed upon this idea; and, in passing it, the legislature have, in my opinion, pursued, and not violated, the Constitution. Indeed, the House of Delegates appear to have understood it so themselves, as they sent the resolution to the Senate for their concurrence, which not having been obtained, the resolution is of no force, and the pardon falls to the ground.

Chancellor Blair and the rest of the judges were of opinion, that the court had power to declare any resolution or Act of the Legislature, or of either branch of it, to be unconstitutional and void; and that the resolution of the House of Delegates, in this case, was inoperative, as the Senate had not concurred in it. That this would be the consequence clearly if the words, "or the law shall otherwise particularly direct," were read in a parenthesis; for then the power of pardoning by the House of Delegates would be expressly confined to cases of impeachment by that House; and, if read without the parenthesis, then the only difference would be, that the assent of the two Houses would be necessary; for it would be absurd to suppose that it was intended by the Constitution that the Act of the whole Legislature should be repealed by the resolution of one branch of it, against the consent of the other.

The certificate to the General Court was as follows:

"The court proceeded, pursuant to an order of the court of Thursday last, to render their judgment on the adjourned question, from the General Court, in the case of John Caton, Joshua Hopkins, and James Lamb; whereupon it is ordered to be certified, to the said General Court, as the opinion of this court, that the pardon, by resolution of the House of Delegates, severally pleaded and produced in the said court, by the said John Caton, Joshua Hopkins, and James Lamb, as by the record of their case appears, is invalid."

N. B.—It is said, that this was the first case in the United States, where the question relative to the nullity of an unconstitutional law was ever discussed before a judicial tribunal: and the firmness of the judges (particularly of Mr. Wythe) was highly honorable to them, and will always be applauded, as having incidentally fixed a precedent, whereon a general practice, which the people of this country think essential to their rights and liberty, has been established.

Trevett v. Weeden, Rhode Island, 1786*

Upon the laft Monday of September, in the eleventh year of the Independence of the United States, in the city of Newport, and State of Rhode-Ifland, &c. was heard, before the Superior Court of Judicature, Court of Affize, and General Gaol-Delivery, a certain information, John Trevett againft John Weeden, for refufing to receive the paper bills of this State, in payment for meat fold in market, equivalent to filver or gold: And upon the day following the Court delivered the unanimous opinion of the Judges, that the information was not cognizable before them.

That this important decifion may be fully comprehended, it will be neceffary to recur to the acts of the General Affembly, which fuperinduced the trial. At the laft May feffion, an act was made for emitting the fum of one hundred thoufand pounds, lawful money, in bills, upon land fecurity, which fhould pafs in all kinds of bufinefs, and payments of former contracts, upon par with filver and gold, eftimating an ounce of coined filver at fix fhillings and eightpence. Another act was paffed in the June following, fubjecting every perfon who fhould refufe the bills in payment for articles offered for fale, or fhould make a diftinction in value between them and filver and gold, or who fhould in any manner attempt to depreciate them, to a penalty of one hundred pounds, lawful money; one moiety to the State, and the other moiety to the informer; to be recovered before either of the Courts of General Seffions of the Peace, or the Superior Court of Judicature, &c.

Experience foon evinced the inadequacy of this meafure to the objects of the Adminiftration: And at a feffion of the General Affembly, fpecially convened by his Excellency the Governor, upon the third Monday of the following Auguft, another act was paffed, in addition to and amendment of that laft mentioned, wherein it is provided, that the fine of one hundred pounds be varied; and that for the future the fine fhould not be less than six, nor exceed thirty pounds for the first offence. The mode of profecution and trial was alfo changed, agreeably to the following claufes, "that the complainant fhall apply to either of the Judges of the Superior Court of Judicature, &c. within this State, or to either of the Judges of the Inferior Court of Common Pleas within the county where fuch offence fhall be committed, and lodge his certain information, which fhall be iffued by the Judge in the following form," &c. It is then provided, that the perfon complained of come before a Court to be fpecially convened by the Judge, in three days; "that the faid Court, when fo convened, fhall proceed to the trial of faid offender, and they are hereby authorized fo to do, without any jury, by a majority of the Judges prefent, according to the laws of the land, and to make adjudica-

---

*J. M. Varnum, *The Case, Trevett v. Weeden* (1787), pp. 1–36.

tion and determination, and that three members be fufficient to conftitute a Court, and that the judgment of the Court, if againft the offender fo complained of, be forthwith complied with, or that he ftand committed to the county gaol, where the faid Court may be fitting, till fentence be performed, and that the faid judgment of faid Court fhall be final and conclufive, and from which there fhall be no appeal; and in faid procefs no effoin, protection, privilege or injunction, fhall be in anywife prayed, granted or allowed."

In confequence of a fuppofed violation of this act, John Trevett exhibited his complaint to the Hon. Paul Mumford, Efq; Chief Juftice of the Superior Court, at his chamber, who caufed a Special Court to be convened: But as the information was given during the term of the Court, it was referred into the term for confideration and final determination.

John Weeden, being demanded and prefent in Court, made the following anfwer: "That it appears by the act of the General Affembly, whereon faid information is founded; that the faid act hath expired, and hath no force: Alfo, for that by the faid act the matters of complaint are made triable before Special Courts, incontroulable by the Supreme Judiciary Court of the State: And alfo for that the Court is not, by faid act, authorized and empowered to impannel a jury to try the facts charged in the information; and fo the fame is unconftitutional and void."

This anfwer was enforced, by the author of thefe ftrictures, nearly in the following words:

I do not appear, may it pleafe the Honourable Court, upon the prefent occafion, fo much in the line of my profeffion, as in the character of a citizen, deeply interefted in the conftitutional laws of a free, fovereign, independent State. And, indeed, whenever the rights of all the citizens appear to be effentially connected with a controverted queftion, confcious of the dignity of man, we exercife our legal talents only as means conducive to the great end of political fociety, general happinefs. In this arduous, though pleafing purfuit, fhould my efforts appear too feeble to fupport the attempt, I fhall derive a confolation in reflecting, that the learned and honourable gentleman at my right is with me in the defence.

Well may a profound filence mark the attention of this numerous and refpectable affembly! Well may anxiety be difplayed in every countenance! Well may the dignity of the Bench condefcend to our folicitude for a moft candid and ferious attention, feeing that from the firft fettlement of this country until the prefent moment, a queftion of fuch magnitude as that upon which the judgment of the Court is now prayed, hath not been judicially agitated!

Happy am I, may it pleafe your Honours, in making my warmeft acknowledgments to the Court, for permitting the information and the plea to be confidered by them in their fupreme judiciary capacity! By this indulgent conceffion, we feel ourfelves at liberty to animadvert freely upon the illegality of the new-fangled jurifdictions erected by the General Affembly in the act more immediately in contemplation. The embarraffments naturally accompanying a plea to the jurifdiction, by removing the caufe from the Special Court into this Court, are totally removed; and, with them, the painful neceffity of confidering your Honours as individually compofing fo dangerous a tribunal. The idea of that neceffity is truly alarming, and we cannot do juftice to our own feelings, without expreffing a fervent wifh that it may hereafter be ever banifhed from the human breaft!

In difcuffing the feveral points ftated in the plea, we muft neceffarily call in queftion the validity of the legiflative act upon which the information is grounded. We fhall attempt moft clearly to evince, that it is contrary to the fundamental laws of the State, and therefore, as the civilians exprefs it, a mere nullity, and void, *ab initio*. We fhall treat, with decent firmnefs, upon the nature, limits and extent, of the legiflative powers; and deduce, from a variety of obfervations and authorities, that the Legiflature may err, do err; and that this act, if we confine ourfelves to the fubject matter of it, can only be confidered as an act of ufurpation; but having been enacted by Legiflators of whofe integrity and virtue we have the cleareft conviction, and of whofe good intentions we have not a doubt, it will be viewed as an hafty refolution, inconfiderately adopted, and fubject to legal reprehenfion.

*   *   *

May it pleafe your Honours,

As all the glory of the folar fyftem is reflected from yonder refulgent luminary, fo the irradiations of the inferior jurifdictions are derived from the refplendent controul of this *primum mobile* in the civil adminiftration. Under its genial influence, therefore, we beg liberty to confider the laft point fubmitted to the judgment of the Court, "that by the act of the Legiflature the Court is not authorized or empowered to impannel a jury for trying the facts complained of in the information."

The propofition cannot be controverted: The expreffions in the act, "that the majority of the Judges prefent fhall proceed to hear, &c. without any jury," do not require a comment.

Should it be objected that this claufe of the act only empowers the Judges to try the fact, when the parties will agree to wave the trial by jury, it will be fufficient to anfwer; that the General Affembly intended directly the contrary. It is well known by all prefent, that on one day this claufe was rejected, but on the day following (in confequence of a nocturnal *imperium in imperio,* or convention of part of the members) a motion was made for receding, and they did recede accordingly. The general tenor of the act was fo repugnant to the honeft feelings of the people, when excited by fober reflection, that the junto out of doors, and poffibly fome leading men within, were apprehenfive that convictions would not take place in the ufual mode of trial. They aimed therefore at a fummary procefs, flattering themfelves that the Judges, being elected by the Legiflators, would blindly fubmit to their fovereign will and pleafure. But, happy for the State, our Courts in general are not intimidated by the dread, nor influenced by the debauch of power!

This part of the fubject, and which is by far the moft important, will require a more ample difcuffion than the preceding. I muft therefore beg the attention of the Honourable Court to the following confiderations: That the trial by jury is a fundamental right, a part of our legal conftitution: That the Legiflature cannot deprive the citizens of this right: And that your Honours can, and we truft will, fo determine.

*   *   *

The fettlers in this country, from whom we are defcended, were Englifhmen: They gloried in their rights as fuch: But being perfecuted in matters of religion, over which no earthly tribunal can have the controul, they bravely determined to quit their native foil, to bid a final adieu to the alluring charms of their fituation, and commit their future exiftence to that Almighty Power, whofe authority they dared not to infringe, but in whofe protection they could fafely confide. They tempted the foaming billows, they braved, they conquered the boifterous Atlantic, and refted in an howling wildernefs, amidft the horrid caverns of the untamed beafts, and the more dangerous haunts of favage men! They retained their virtue, their religion, and their inviolable attachment to the conftitutional rights of their former country. They did not withdraw or wifh to withdraw themfelves from their allegiance to the Crown, but emigrated under a folemn affurance of receiving protection, fo far as their fituation might require, and other circumftances render practicable.

The laws of the realm, being the birthright of all the fubjects, followed thefe pious adventurers to their new habitations, where, increafing in numbers, amidft innumerable difficulties, they were formed into Colonies by royal Charters, in nature of folemn compacts, confirming and enlarging their privileges.

In the Charter granted to our forefathers, the following paragraph claims our particular attention: "That all and every the fubjects of us, our heirs and fucceffors, which are already planted and fettled within our faid Colony of Providence Plantations, which fhall hereafter go to inhabit within the faid Colony, and all and every of their children, which have been born there, or on the fea going thither, or returning from thence, fhall have and enjoy all liberties and immunities of free and natural fubjects, within any of the dominions of us, our heirs or fucceffors, to all intents, conftructions and purpofes whatfoever, as if they, and every of them, were born within the realm of England."

This conceffion was declaratory of, and fully confirmed to the people the Magna Charta, and other fundamental laws of England. And accordingly, in the very firft meeting of the General Affembly, after receiving the charter, in the year one thoufand fix hundred and fixty-three, they made and paffed an act, "declaring the rights and privileges of his Majefty's fubjects within this Colony," whereby it is enacted, "that no freeman fhall be taken or imprifoned, or be deprived of his freehold or liberty, or free cuftoms, or be outlawed, or exiled or otherwife deftroyed, nor fhall be paffed upon, judged or condemned, but by the lawful judgment of his peers, or by the laws of this Colony: And that no man, of what eftate or condition foever, fhall be put out of his lands and tenements, nor taken, nor imprifoned, nor difinherited, nor banifhed, nor any ways deftroyed, nor molefted, without for it being brought to anfwer by due courfe of law. And that all rights and privileges, granted to this Colony by his Majefty's Charter, be entirely kept and preferved to all his Majefty's fubjects, refiding in or belonging to the fame."

This act, may it pleafe the Honourable Court, was not creative of a new law, but declaratory of the rights of all the people, as derived through the Charter from their progenitors, time out of mind. It exhibited the moft valuable part of their political conftitution, and formed a facred ftipulation that it fhould never be violated. . . .

Have the citizens of this State ever entrufted their legiflators with the power of altering their conftitution? If they have, when and where was the folemn meeting of all the people for that purpofe? By what public inftrument have they declared it, or in what part of their conduct have they betrayed fuch extravagance and folly? For what have they contended through a long, painful and bloody war, but to fecure inviolate, and tranfmit unfullied to pofterity, the ineftimable privileges they received from their forefathers? Will they fuffer the glorious price of all their toils to be wrefted from them, and loft forever, by the men of their own creating? They who have fnatched their liberty from the jaws of the Britifh lion, amidft the thunders of contending nations, will they bafely furrender it to the Adminiftration of a year? As foon may the great Michael kick the beam, and Lucifer riot in the fpoils of angels!

Constitution! we have none: Who dares to fay that? None but a Britifh emiffary, or a traitor to his country. Are there any fuch amongft us? The language hath been heard, and God forbid that they fhould continue!

If we have not a conftitution, by what authority doth our General Affembly convene to make laws, and levy taxes? Their appointment by the freemen of the towns, excluding the idea of a pre-exifting focial compact, cannot feparately give them power to make laws compulfory upon the other towns. They could only meet, in that cafe, to form a focial compact between the people of the towns. But they do meet by the appointment of their refpective towns, at fuch times and places, and in fuch numbers, as they have been accuftomed to do from the beginning. When met, they make laws and levy taxes, and their conftituents obey thofe laws, and pay their taxes. Confequently they meet, deliberate and enact, in virtue of a conftitution, which, if they attempt to deftroy, or in any manner infringe, they violate the truft repofed in them, and fo their acts are not to be confidered as laws, or binding upon the people.

But as the Legiflative is the fupreme power in government, who is to judge whether they have violated the conftitutional rights of the people? I anfwer, their fupremacy (confifting in the power of making laws, agreeably to their appointment) is derived from the conftitution, is fubordinate to it, and therefore, whenever they attempt to enflave the people, and carry their attempts into execution, the people themfelves will judge, as the only refort in the laft ftages of oppreffion. But when they proceed no farther than merely to enact what they may call laws, and refer thofe to the Judiciary Courts for determination, then, (in difcharge of the great truft repofed in them, and to prevent the horrors of a civil war, as in the prefent cafe) the Judges can, and we truft your Honours will, decide upon them.

In defpotic countries, where the fovereign mandate iffues from the throne furrounded by fervile flatterers, fycophants and knaves, the Judge hath nothing more to do than execute. His office is altogether minifterial, being the paffive tool of that lawlefs domination by which he was appointed. Properly fpeaking, the judiciary power cannot exift where political freedom is banifhed from the adminiftration. For without a fyftem of laws, defining and protecting the rights of the people, there can be no fixed principles or rules of decifion. Hence it is, that wherever the diftinct powers of government are united in one head, whether that head confifts of one, or of many, the fubjects groan under perpetual fervitude.

I say of one or of many: For it is very immaterial by whom fcourges, chains and tortures, are inflicted, provided we muft fubmit to them. The ftudied and unheard of cruelties of a Dionyfius, who violated every right of humanity in his tyranny over the Syracufians during the fpace of thirty-eight years, were not more horrid and execrable than the united barbarities of the Council of Thirty, eftablifhed at Athens, who caufed more citizens to be murdered in eight months of peace than their enemies had deftroyed in a thirty years war!

Nor am I capable of diftinguifhing between an eftablifhed tyranny, and that government where the Legiflative makes the law, and dictates to the Judges their adjudication. For in that cafe, were they to enact tyrannical laws, they would be fure to have them executed in a tyrannical manner. The fervility of the Courts would render them totally fubfervient to the will of their mafters, and the people muft be inflaved, or fly to arms.

In civil as well as moral agency there is a freedom of the will neceffarily exerted in forming the judgment. Without the exercife of this, we cannot be faid to determine at all, but our actions are wholly paffive; and fo, in a moral fenfe, we could not be accountable, and in a civil point of view we fhould be deprived of all liberty.

Every being naturally endeavours its own prefervation; and the more conformably its actions are to its nature, the nearer it approaches to perfection: But when its actions are impelled by external force, it is deprived of the means both of prefervation and of perfection.

A nation may be confidered as a moral being, whofe health and ftrength confift in the due proportion, nice adjuftment and equal prefervation, of all its parts: And when one branch of the government fteps into the place of another, and ufurps its functions, the health and the ftrength of the nation are impaired: And fhould the evil be continued, fo as that the one be deftroyed by the other, the nation itfelf would be in danger of diffolution.

Have the Judges a power to repeal, to amend, to alter laws, or to make new laws? God forbid! In that cafe they would become Legiflators. Have the Legiflators power to direct the Judges how they fhall determine upon the laws already made? God forbid! In that cafe they would become Judges. The true diftinction lies in this, that the Legiflative have the incontroulable power of making laws not repugnant to the conftitution: The Judiciary have the fole power of judging of thofe laws, and are bound to execute them; but cannot admit any act of the Legiflative as law, which is against the conftitution.

The Judges are fworn "truly and impartially to execute the laws that now are or fhall hereafter be made, according to the beft or their fkill and underftanding." They are alfo fworn "to bear true allegiance and fidelity to this State of Rhode-Ifland and Providence Plantations, as a free, fovereign and independent State." But this became a State in order to fupport its fundamental, conftitutional laws, againft the encroachments of Great-Britain. The trial by jury, as hath been fully fhewn, is a fundamental, a conftitutional law; and therefore is binding upon the Judges by a double tie, the oath of allegiance, and the oath of office.

It is a rule in ethics, "that if two duties or obligations, both of which cannot be performed, urge us at the fame time, we muft omit the leffer, and embrace the greater."

Let the queftion then fairly be ftated. The General Affembly have made a law, and directed the Judges to execute it by a mode of trial repugnant to the conftitution. What are the Judges to refolve? Did the nature of their jurifdiction admit of fuch a mode of trial at the times of their appointment and taking the oath of office? Surely it did not. The act of Affembly then erects a new office, the exercife of which, other things equal, they may undertake, or refufe, at their own option. There is no duty, no obligation in the way. In refufing, they incur no penalty; nor can their fo doing work a forfeiture of their offices as Judges of the Supreme Judiciary Court. But when it is confidered that the exercife of this office would be acting contrary to their oath of allegiance, and the oath of office, they are bound to reject it, unlefs the General Affembly have power to abfolve them from thefe oaths, and compel them to accept of any appointment they may be pleafed to make.

I have heard fome gentlemen fpeak of the laws of the General Affembly. I know of no fuch laws, diftinct from the laws of the State. The idea is dangerous; it borders upon treafon! " 'tis rank—it fmells to heaven!"

Laws are made by the General Affembly under the powers they derive from the conftitution, but when made they become the laws of the land, and as fuch the Court is fworn to execute them. But if the General Affembly attempt to make laws contrary hereunto, the Court cannot receive them as laws; they cannot fubmit to them. If they fhould, let me fpeak it with reverence, they would incur the guilt of a double perjury!

The life, liberty and property of the citizens are fecured by the general law of the State. We will then fuppofe (as the very nature of the argument allows us to view the fubject in every poffible light) that the General Affembly fhold pafs an act directing that no citizen fhould leave his houfe, nor fuffer any of his family to move out of the fame, for the fpace of fix months, upon the pain of death. This would be contrary to the laws of nature. Suppofe they fhould enact that every parent fhould deftroy his firft-born child. This would be contrary to the laws of God. But, upon the common principles, the Court would be as much bound to execute thefe acts as any others. For if they can determine upon any act, that it is not law, and fo reject it, they muft neceffarily have the power of determining what acts are laws, and fo on the contrary. There is no middle line. The Legiflative hath power to go all lengths, or not to overleap the bounds of its appointment at all. So it is with the Judiciary; it muft reject all acts of the Legiflative that are contrary to the truft repofed in them by the people, or it muft adopt all.

But the Judges, and all others, are bound by the laws of nature in preference to any human laws, becaufe they were ordained by God himfelf anterior to any civil or political inftitutions. They are bound, in like manner, by the principles of the conftitution in preference to any acts of the General Affembly, becaufe they were ordained by the people anterior to and created the powers of the General Affembly.

This mode of reafoning will equally apply in law as in philofophy. For wherever there is a given force applied to put a body in motion, that motion will continue until the body is oppofed by an equal or a greater force. And the Judges being fworn to execute the fundamental laws, they muft continue to execute them until they fhall be controuled by laws of a fuperior nature. But that can never happen until all the people affemble for the purpofe of making a new conftitution. And indeed I very much doubt if the citizens of any one State have power to adopt fuch a kind of government, as to exclude the trial by jury, confiftently with the principles of the confederation.

It having been fhewn that this Court poffeffes all the powers in this State, that the Courts of King's Bench, Common Pleas, and Exchequer, poffefs in England, let us turn to the authorities, and obferve the adjudications of thofe Courts in fimilar cafes.

Judge Blackftone informs us, that "acts of Parliament that are impoffible to be performed; and if there arife out of them collaterally any abfurd confequences, manifeftly contradictory to common reafon, they are, with regard to thofe collateral confequences, void." The fame author having previoufly obferved, that "the Judges are the depofitory of the laws; the living oracles, who muft decide in all cafes of doubt, and who are bound by oath to decide according to the law of the land."

In Bacon's abridgment we read, "if a ftatute be againft common right or reafon, or repugnant, or impoffible to be performed, the common law fhall controul it, and adjudge it to be void."

Here permit me, may it pleafe your Honours, to apply the authority to the act, and fee how exactly it correfponds.

Is it confiftent with common right or reafon, that any man fhall be compelled to receive paper, when he hath contracted to receive filver? That for bread he fhall receive a ftone, or for fifh a ferpent? Is it confiftent with common right or reafon that he fhall receive the paper dollar for dollar with filver, when it is fully known that the difcount in general is from three to four for one, among thofe who receive the paper at all and that there are very many who totally refufe it? That he fhould be called from his bufinefs, and fubjected to a fine for his refufal, when there is not a man in the State, but upon principles of juftice to himfelf and family would have done the fame? Is it right or reafonable that for fuch refufal he fhould be called to trial in a fummary manner, in three days, and that no effoin, protection, privilege or injunction, fhall be in anywife prayed, granted or allowed? Suppofe him to be confined to his bed by ficknefs, is he to be paffed upon *exparte?* No man is to be injured by the act of God, or by the act of the law. Suppofe his witneffes are fick or abfent, and cannot be procured by the time, he is not allowed even to pray for an indulgence; or if he fhould pray ever fo fervently, he cannot be heard. Suppofe him to be fummoned to attend at two, or at all the counties at the fame time, upon different informations, he is ftill to be condemned unheard. Even fuppofe him to ftand in need of profeffional affiftance, but that he cannot obtain at the moment, the gentlement of the law being all neceffarily attending upon a fpecial feffion of the General Affembly, is he to be deprived of council?

"Repugnant, or impoffible to be performed." Is not the act repugnant when it authorizes the Judges to "proceed to trial without any jury, according to the laws of the land?" The laws of the land conftitute the jurors the triers of facts, and the Judges the triers of law only, according to the known maxim, "*ad queftionem juris refpondent judices, ad queftionem facti refpondent juratores.*" How is it poffible then that the Judges fhould try, without jury, and they are directed as well as authorized fo to do, "the faid Court fhall proceed," and at the fame time according to the laws of the land, when thofe laws direct "that no man, of what eftate and condition foever, fhall be molefted, without being, for it, brought to anfwer by due courfe of law, nor paffed upon nor condemned, but by the lawful judgment of his peers?" Can contraries exift, and be executed at the fame time? This act therefore is impoffible to be executed.

Here is a new office indeed! And were your Honours to fuffer the fpecial jurifdictions to attempt to carry the act into effect, what inconceivable mifchiefs would enfue? Is there a member of the Adminiftration, or any other, that will fell his beef, his pork, his corn, or his cheefe, fo as to enable the retailers and huxters to fell thofe articles again for paper, at the fame rate they could be afforded for filver or gold? There is not. What's the confequence? Every evil-minded perfon in the State is invited by law to turn informer (a moft defpicable office) and more than five hundred profecutions would take place in the courfe of a week! Horrid reflection! The idle, the profligate, the abandoned of every character, would appear in the group of profecutors or witneffes, urged and pufhed on by petty Conventions and defigning Juntos, till perjury would run down our ftreets like a ftream, and violence like a mighty river! The Judges themfelves might be tempted, by the perquifites of office, to encourage informations, until every man of induftry, of bufinefs, and of property, muft quit the State, retire from bufinefs, give up his property, or join in an oppofition of force! The temptation is great, and ferioufly alarming! For to fecure the Judges individually, and their perfonal influence, the very emitting act directs that they fhall receive all monies tendered and refufed for paft contracts, and at the expiration of three months depofite them in the General-Treafury. What room for fpeculation, what inducement to corruption, what incentives to depreciate the currency!

Oh! it is an abominable act! Yet fome there are, and, to our fhame be it fpoken, too many, who tend it, who nurfe it, who hug it to their bofom as a darling child. But let me tell them it is a fpurious offspring, conceived by an unlawful Convention, and brought forth by   at an unguarded hour! 'Tis a monfter! and, as the immortal Pope expreffes it upon another occafion,

> *It is a monfter of fo frightful mein,*
> *As to be hated, needs but to be feen,*
> *Yet feen too oft, familiar with her face,*
> *We firft endure, then pity, then embrace!*

Let us fee it therefore but once! Let us confign it, O ye Judges, to its fate! Death is in its conftitution, and die it muft!

But to return, for I muft confefs the digreffion is not particularly directed to the point more immediately in queftion:

We again read in Bacon's Abridgment, that "the power of conftruing a ftatute is in the Judges; for they have authority over all laws, more efpecially over ftatutes, to mould them according to reafon and convenience to the beft and trueft ufe."

Here the author refers to Hobart, Plowden, and Lord Coke, who fully juftify the doctrine he advances. They are upon the table, and will be produced, if your Honours require it; but we prefume it would be only trefpaffing upon your patience, too much exhaufted already, by a tedious difcuffion.

The fatisfaction you are pleafed to exprefs upon this head, enables us to purfue the fubject in another point of view. Perhaps there is not a civilized country on earth, where fo fmall a portion of natural liberty is given into the ftock of political fociety, as by the people of this State. There is a certain period in every year when the powers of government feem to expire; for the authority of the old officers ceafes with the appointment of the new, and thefe cannot act until they are commiffioned and fworn. The Legiflative of one Houfe being compofed of new members, or members newly elected twice in the year, feels and carries into effect the fentiments of the people, founded upon the extremes of liberty. The electors in the refpective towns have generally fome point to obtain; or, which is more unfriendly to public liberty, they are divided by parties, and fo the members elected become the advocates of local, interefted meafures, without comparing them with the more extenfive objects of the community. The feffions feldom exceed the limits of a week: New laws are propofed, acted upon and adopted, according to the firft or the preconcerted impreffions of paffion, without time for deliberation or reflection. The Upper Houfe, it is true, hath a negative upon the Houfe of Deputies; but they never perfift in exercifing it without endangering their next election. The appointment of the Judges, Juftices of the Peace, and other officers of government, being made by the members of both Houfes in a Grand Committee, is very often the refult of political arrangements; and more attention is paid to the carrying of certain points, than to the qualification of the candidates; fo that the people feel no great reftraint from this quarter.

What is there then, in the nature of our government, to prevent anarchy and confufion on the one hand, or tyranny and opprefion on the other? Before the revolution, the King, as Supreme Executive, formed the balance; but fince, the Executive Power hath become blended with the Legiflative, and we have not, like the other States in the union, adopted any fubftitute for this defect.

The moment therefore that this Court feels itfelf dependent upon the Legiflature, in the exercife of its judiciary powers, there will be an end of political liberty: For there is not an individual of mankind but wifhes, if poffible, to be exempt from the compacts that bind others. And there may be conjunctures in which the love of natural liberty will bid defiance to the reftraints of law, if the Legiflature are blindly guided by the general impulfe. Or fhould thefe attachments be more ftrongly fixed to the interefts of a few defigning men than to the public wifh, tyranny would fpring out of anarchy. In either cafe, the interpofition of the Judiciary may fave the conftitution, at leaft for a time; and, by averting the immediate evil, will give fcope for reflection, and fo prevent a diffolution of government.

It is extremely to be regretted, that this Court is not as independent in the tenure by which the Judges hold their commiffions, as they are in the exercife of their judicial proceedings. The frequent changes that arife from annual appointments may have an influence upon legal decifions, and fo deftroy that uniformity which is effentially requifite to the fecurity of individuals. But from thefe confiderations we have nothing to fear upon the prefent occafion: For the knowledge, the integrity, the firmnefs of the Bench, will rife fuperior to every obftacle; and the dignity of their determinations will difplay a luftre awful even to tyranny itfelf!

To this Honourable Court the warmeft thanks of the defendant, of this affembly, of every citizen, are due, for their folicitous attention to their unalienable rights! Their expectations, their joyous hopes, await your determination; and we all pray to heaven, that before to-morrow's fun fhall deck the weftern fky, our hopes may wanton in complete enjoyment!

> *Then ev'ry gen'rous breaft fhall glow with pureft flame*
> *Of gratitude; and fathers, anxious for the public good,*
> *Relate the glorious deed to their attentive fons,*
> *Who'll venerate the names of thofe immortal Five,*
> *Who nobly dar'd to fave our dying laws!*

May it pleafe your Honours,

I cannot further purfue the fubject, but muft come to a conclufion.

We have attempted to fhew, that the act, upon which the information is founded, hath expired: That by the act fpecial jurifdictions are erected, incontroulable by the Supreme Judiciary Court of the State: And that, by the act, this Court is not authorized or empowered to impannel a jury to try the facts contained in the information: That the trial by jury is a fundamental, a conftitutional right—ever claimed as fuch—ever ratified as fuch—ever held moft dear and facred: That the Legiflative derives all its authority from the conftitution—hath no power of making laws but in fubordination to it—cannot infringe or violate it: That therefore the act is unconftitutional and void: That this Court hath power to judge and determine what acts of the General Affembly are agreeable to the conftitution; and, on the contrary, that this Court is under the moft folemn obligations to execute the laws of the land, and therefore cannot, will not, confider this act as a law of the land.

Oh! ye Judges, what a godlike pleafure muft you now feel in having the power, the legal power, of ftopping the torrent of lawlefs fway, and fecuring to the people their ineftimable rights! Reft, ye venerable fhades of our pious anceftors! our inheritance is yet fecure! Be at peace, ye bleffed fpirits of our valiant countrymen, whofe blood hath juft ftreamed at our fides, to fave a finking land!

When the tear is fcarcely wiped from the virgin's eye, lamenting an affectionate father, a beloved brother, or a more tender friend! While the matron ftill mourns, and the widow bewails her only hope! While the fathers of their country, fuperior to the ills of flaughter, are completing the mighty fabric of our freedom and independence, fhall the decifion of a moment rob us of our birthright, and blaft forever our nobleft profpects? Forbid it, thou Great Legislator of the Universe! No:

> The ftars shall fade away,
> The fun himself grow dim with age,
> And nature fink in years;
> But thou (fair liberty) thou fhalt flourifh in immortal youth,
> Unhurt amidft the war of elements,
> The wreck of matter, and the crufh of worlds!

Den d. Bayard and Wife v. Singleton, North Carolina, 1787*

Ejectment: This action was brought for the recovery of a valuable house and lot, with a wharf and other appurtenances, situate in the town of Newbern.

The defendant pleaded Not guilty, under the common rule.

He held under a title derived from the State, by a deed, from a Superintendent Commissioner of confiscated estates.

At May Term, 1786, Nash, for the defendant, moved that the suit be dismissed, according to an Act of the last session, entitled an Act to secure and quiet in their possession all such persons, their heirs and assigns, who have purchased or may hereafter purchase lands and tenements, goods and chattels, which have been sold or may hereafter be sold by commissioners of forfeited estates, legally appointed for that purpose, 1785, 7, 553.

The Act requires the courts, in all cases where the defendant makes affidavit that he holds the disputed property under a sale from a commissioner of forfeited estates, to dismiss the suit on motion.

The defendant had filed an affidavit, setting forth that the property in dispute had been confiscated and sold by the commissioner of the district.

This brought on long arguments from the counsel on each side, on constitutional points.

The court made a few observations on our Constitution and system of government.

Ashe, J. observed, that at the time of our separation from Great Britain, we were thrown into a similar situation with a set of people shipwrecked and cast on a marooned island,—without laws, without magistrates, without government, or any legal authority—that being thus circumstanced, the people of this country, with a general union of sentiment, by their delegates, met in Congress, and formed that system or those fundamental principles comprised in the Constitution, dividing the powers of government into separate and distinct branches, to wit: the legislative, the judicial, and executive,

* *1 Martin North Carolina Reports,* pp. 42–44.

and assigning to each, several and distinct powers, and prescribing their several limits and boundaries: this he said without disclosing a single sentiment upon the cause of the proceeding, or the law introduced in support of it.   *Cur. adv. vult.*

At May Term, 1787, Nash's motion was resumed, and produced a very lengthy debate from the Bar.

Whereupon the court recommended to the parties to consent to a fair decision of the property in question, by a jury according to the common law of the land, and pointed out to the defendant the uncertainty that would always attend his title, if this cause should be dismissed without a trial; as upon a repeal of the present Act (which would probably happen sooner or later), suit might be again commenced against him for the same property, at the time when evidences, which at present were easy to be had, might be wanting. But this recommendation was without effect.

Another mode was proposed for putting the matter in controversy on a more constitutional footing for a decision, than that of the motion under the aforesaid Act. The court then, after every reasonable endeavor had been used in vain for avoiding a disagreeable difference between the legislature and the judicial powers of the State, at length with much apparent reluctance, but with great deliberation and firmness, gave their opinion separately, but unanimously, for overruling the aforementioned motion for the dismission of the said suits.

In the course of which the judges observed, that the obligation of their oaths, and the duty of their office required them, in that situation, to give their opinion on that important and momentous subject; and that notwithstanding the great reluctance they might feel against involving themselves in a dispute with the legislature of the State, yet no object of concern or respect could come in competition or authorize them to dispense with the duty they owed the public, in consequence of the trust they were invested with under the solemnity of their oaths.

That they therefore were bound to declare that they considered, that whatever disabilities the persons under whom the plaintiffs were said to derive their titles, might justly have incurred, against their maintaining or prosecuting any suits in the courts of this State; yet that such disabilities in their nature were merely personal, and not by any means capable of being transferred to the present plaintiffs, either by descent or purchase; and that these plaintiffs, being citizens of one of the United States, are citizens of this State, by the confederation of all the States; which is to be taken as a part of the law of the land, unrepealable by any Act of the General Assembly.

That by the Constitution every citizen had undoubtedly a right to a decision of his property by a trial by jury. For that if the legislature could take away this right, and require him to stand condemned in his property without a trial, it might with as much authority require his life to be taken way without a trial by jury, and that he should stand condemned to die, without the formality of any trial at all; that if the members of the General Assembly could do this, they might with equal authority, not only render themselves the legislators of the State for life, without any further election of the people, from thence transmit the dignity and authority of legislation down to their heirs male forever.

But that it was clear, that no Act they could pass, could by any means repeal or alter the Constitution, because, if they could do this, they would at the same instant of time destroy their own existence as a legislature, and dissolve the government thereby established. Consequently the Constitution (which the judicial power was bound to take notice of as much as of any other law whatever), standing in full force as the fundamental law of the land, notwithstanding the Act on which the present motion was grounded, the same Act must of course, in that instance, stand as abrogated and without any effect.

Nash's motion was overruled

And at this term the cause was tried.

*   *   *

PART FIVE
UNITED STATES CONSTITUTION

UNITED STATES CONSTITUTION

Commentary

By 1787, the stage was set for a federal Bill of Rights. By that date, most of the states had adopted Bills of Rights and their provisions provided a consensus of the fundamental rights which should be protected by American Constitutions (all of the important provisions of the federal Bill of Rights were, in fact, derived from the state Declarations of Rights). In addition, the decade before adoption of the federal Constitution had seen the assertion by courts in states in all parts of the country of the power of judicial review. Hence, those who drafted Bills of Rights knew they were drawing up guarantees which would be enforced by the courts even against the legislature. Despite the development in these respects, it is well known that the federal Constitution did not contain any Bill of Rights. How can we explain the framers' inaction in the matter?

The answer is to be found in the basic goal of the Philadelphia Convention. The Convention itself had been called to remedy the fundamental weaknesses of the pre-Constitution government. The Articles of Confederation had provided for a government without power to tax, to raise troops, to regulate commerce, or to execute or enforce its own laws or treaties. The sword and the purse—the two essentials of any effective polity—remained entirely outside the realm of national power. Well might Washington declare, in 1785, that "the confederation appears to me to be little more than a shadow without the substance; and congress a nugatory body, their ordinances being little attended to."

The men who came to Philadelphia in the sultry summer of 1787 had the overriding aim of making such alterations in the constitutional structure as would (in the words of the Confederation Congress calling the Convention) "render the Federal Constitution adequate to the exigencies of Government." That being the case, it is scarcely surprising that the delegates directed their energies almost entirely to that end. Virtually all of the drafting and discussion by the men who burned midnight candles in Philadelphia focused on giving the new Federal Government the powers that would be needed to govern effectively.

As the extracts from the proceedings of the Constitutional Convention which follow show, a motion was actually made on September 12 "to appoint a Committee to prepare a Bill of Rights." The stimulus for the motion was provided by George Mason during a debate on trial by jury. The author of the Virginia Declaration of Rights expressed the wish that "the plan had been prefaced with a Bill of Rights and would second a motion made for the purpose." The motion to set up a committee was made by

435

Elbridge Gerry, but it was defeated unanimously (the states voting as units). Interestingly, Mason had asserted that "with the aid of the State declarations, a bill might be prepared in a few hours"—bearing out the point we have emphasized on the existence of a contemporary consensus on the fundamental rights which should be protected by organic provisions.

It is difficult to say with any certainty why the Mason proposal for a Bill of Rights was so summarily rejected. Certainly the fact that it was made so close to the end of the Convention (which finally adjourned on September 17) influenced the delegates' almost cavalier action. Having sweltered for months over the difficult issues involved in the new Constitution during Philadelphia's hottest summer within memory, they naturally resented the bringing up of a vast new subject when they were almost at the end of their endeavors. On the merits, Roger Sherman (the one delegate to speak on the matter) stated the view that was later to be expressed to justify the omission of a Bill of Rights (notably in *The Federalist, [infra* p. 581] , that a federal Bill of Rights was unnecessary; the state Declarations of Rights were sufficient to protect the rights of their citizens, and the new Federal Government was not given any power to infringe upon the rights thus protected.

In addition to the general Mason proposal, other attempts were made at the framers' Convention to protect specific rights later to be included in the Bill of Rights, notably in a proposal by Charles Pinckney to guarantee liberty of the press and freedom from quartering of troops, as well as supremacy of civil over military power, and a motion by Pinckney and Gerry for a declaration "that the liberty of the Press should be inviolably observed," which was defeated after Sherman had repeated the argument that the guarantee was unnecessary, since the "power of Congress does not extend to the Press."

It should, however, be borne in mind that though the Constitution drafted in 1787 did not contain any Bill of Rights, it did (as Hamilton was to emphasize in *The Federalist, [infra* p. 579] contain provisions protecting individual liberties, which would normally be contained in a Bill of Rights. These include the guarantees of habeas corpus (the provision authorizing suspension of the writ has uniformly been interpreted as guaranteeing habeas corpus in the absence of suspension), trial by jury in criminal cases, the privileges and immunities of state citizens, and the prohibitions against bills of attainder, ex post facto laws, and religious tests. These guarantees would doubtless have been included in the federal Bill of Rights, had they not already been contained in the text of the Constitution.

After the relevant extracts from the Philadelphia Convention debates, there is printed the interesting letter from Jonas Phillips to the Convention. Though sent to a body without authority to do what Phillips requests, it is pertinent to one interested in guarantees of personal liberty. It indicates the need for protection of religious freedom of the type later included in the First Amendment. Phillips' approach is similar to the two-fold one followed in the First Amendment—a ban on establishment and a guarantee of free exercise.

After the Philadelphia Convention itself, a further attempt to secure a federal Bill of Rights was made in the Confederation Congress. Richard Henry Lee moved that that body amend the Constitution by adding to it a Bill of Rights, before it was submitted for ratification to the states. Madison's letter to Washington (*infra* p. 440) describes Lee's attempt and its reception. Congress rejected Lee's motion and instead adopted the resolution quoted by Madison, adopting the ratification procedure recommended by the Philadelphia Convention.

Federal Convention, 1787*

[Monday, Aug. 20]

Mr. Pinkney submitted to the House, in order to be referred to the Committee of detail, the following propositions—

"Each House shall be the Judge of its own privileges, and shall have authority to punish by imprisonment every person violating the same; or who, in the place where the Legislature may be sitting and during the time of its Session, shall threaten any of its members for any thing said or done in the House, or who shall assault any of them therefore—or who shall assault or arrest any witness or other person ordered to attend either of the Houses in his way going or returning; or who shall rescue any person arrested by their order."

"Each branch of the Legislature, as well as the Supreme Executive shall have authority to require the opinions of the supreme Judicial Court upon important questions of law, and upon solemn occasions"

"The privileges and benefit of the Writ of Habeas corpus shall be enjoyed in this Government in the most expeditious and ample manner; and shall not be suspended by the Legislature except upon the most urgent and pressing occasions, and for a limited time not exceeding   months."

"The liberty of the Press shall be inviolably preserved"

"No troops shall be kept up in time of peace, but by consent of the Legislature"

"The military shall always be subordinate to the Civil power, and no grants of money shall be made by the Legislature for supporting military Land forces, for more than one year at a time"

"No soldier shall be quartered in any House in time of peace without consent of the owner."

"No person holding the office of President of the U.S., a Judge of their Supreme Court, Secretary for the department of Foreign Affairs, of Finance, of Marine, of War, or of   , shall be capable of holding at the same time any other office of Trust or Emolument under the U.S. or an individual State."

*M. Farrand, *The Records of the Federal Convention of 1787* (1911), Vol. 2, pp. 340-618.

"No religious test or qualification shall ever be annexed to any oath of office under the authority of the U.S."

"The U.S. shall be for ever considered as one Body corporate and politic in law, and entitled to all the rights privileges, and immunities, which to Bodies corporate do or ought to appertain"

"The Legislature of the U.S. shall have the power of making the great Seal which shall be kept by the President of the U.S. or in his absence by the President of the Senate, to be used by them as the occasion may require.—It shall be called the great Seal of the U.S. and shall be affixed to all laws."

"All Commissions and writs shall run in the name of the U.S."

"The Jurisdiction of the supreme Court shall be extended to all controversies between the U.S. and an individual State, or the U.S. and the Citizens of an individual State"

These propositions were referred to the Committee of detail without debate or consideration of them, by the House.

*   *   *

[Wednesday, Sept. 12]

Mr. Williamson, observed to the House that no provision was yet made for juries in Civil cases and suggested the necessity of it.

Mr. Gorham. It is not possible to discriminate equity cases from those in which juries are proper. The Representatives of the people may be safely trusted in this matter.

Mr. Gerry urged the necessity of Juries to guard agst. corrupt Judges. He proposed that the Committee last appointed should be directed to provide a clause for securing the trial by Juries.

Col. Mason perceived the difficulty mentioned by Mr. Gorham. The jury cases cannot be specified. A general principle laid down on this and some other points would be sufficient. He wished the plan had been prefaced with a Bill of Rights, & would second a Motion if made for the purpose—It would give great quiet to the people; and with the aid of the State declarations, a bill might be prepared in a few hours.

Mr. Gerry concurred in the idea & moved for a Committee to prepare a Bill of Rights. Col. Mason 2ded the motion.

Mr. Sherman. was for securing the rights of the people where requisite. The State Declarations of Rights are not repealed by this Constitution; and being in force are sufficient—There are many cases where juries are proper which cannot be discriminated. The Legislature may be safely trusted.

Col. Mason. The Laws of the U.S. are to be paramount to State Bills of Rights. On the question for a Come to prepare a Bill of Rights.

N.H. no. Mas. abst. Ct no. N— J— no. Pa. no. Del— no. Md no. Va no. N— C. no. S— C— no— Geo— no. [Ayes—0; noes— 10; absent—1.]

*   *   *

[Friday, Sept. 14]

Mr. Pinkney & Mr. Gerry, moved to insert a declaration "that the liberty of the Press should be inviolably observed—"

Mr. Sherman—It is unnecessary—The power of Congress does not extend to the Press. On the question, (it passed in the negative)

N—H—no—Mas —ay—Ct no. N—J. no. Pa no. Del. no. Md. ay. Va. ay. N.C. no. S.C. ay. Geo—no. [Ayes—4; noes—7.]

Jonas Phillips to the President and Members of the Convention, 1787*

Sires

With leave and submission I address myself To those in whome there is wisdom understanding and knowledge. they are the honourable personages appointed and Made overseers of a part of the terrestrial globe of the Earth, Namely the 13 united states of america in Convention Assembled, the Lord preserve them amen—

I the subscriber being one of the people called Jews of the City of Philadelphia, a people scattered and despersed among all nations do behold with Concern that among the laws in the Constitution of Pennsylvania their is a Clause Sect. 10 to viz—I do believe in one God the Creature and governour of the universe the Rewarder of the good and the punisher of the wicked—and I do acknowledge the scriptures of the old and New testament to be given by a devine inspiration—to swear and believe that the new testament was given by devine inspiration is absolutly against the Religious principle of a Jew. and is against his Conscience to take any such oath—By the above law a Jew is deprived of holding any publick office or place of Government which is a Contridectory to the bill of Right Sect 2. viz

That all men have a natural and unalienable Right To worship almighty God according to the dectates of their own Conscience and understanding, and that no man aught or of Right can be Compelled to attend any Religious Worship or Erect or support any place of worship or Maintain any minister contrary to or against his own free will and Consent nor Can any man who acknowledges the being of a God be Justly deprived or abridged of any Civil Right as a Citizen on account of his Religious sentiments or peculiar mode of Religious Worship, and that no authority Can or aught to be vested in or assumed by any power what ever that shall in any Case interfere or in any manner Controul the Right of Conscience in the free Exercise of Religious Worship—

It is well known among all the Citizens of the 13 united States that the Jews have been true and faithful whigs, and during the late Contest with

*The Records of the Federal Convention of 1787, Vol. 3, pp. 78–79.

England they have been foremost in aiding and assisting the States with their lifes and fortunes, they have supported the Cause, have bravely faught and bleed for liberty which they Can not Enjoy—

Therefore if the honourable Convention shall in ther Wisdom think fit and alter the said oath and leave out the words to viz—and I do acknoweledge the scripture of the new testement to be given by devine inspiration then the Israeletes will think them self happy to live under a government where all Relegious societys are on an Eaquel footing—I solecet this favour for my self my Childreen and posterity and for the benefit of all the Isrealetes through the 13 united States of america

My prayers is unto the Lord. May the people of this States Rise up as a great and young lion, May they prevail against their Enemies, May the degrees of honour of his Excellencey the president of the Convention George Washington, be Extollet and Raise up. May Every one speak of his glorious Exploits. May God prolong his days among us in this land of Liberty—May he lead the armies against his Enemys as he has done hereuntofore—May God Extend peace unto the united States—May they get up to the highest Prosperetys—May God Extend peace to them and their seed after them so long as the Sun and moon Endureth—and may the almighty God of our father Abraham Isaac and Jacob endue this Noble Assembly with wisdom Judgement and unamity in their Councells, and may they have the Satisfaction to see that their present toil and labour for the wellfair of the united States may be approved of, Through all the world and perticular by the united States of america is the ardent prayer of Sires

Your Most devoted obed Servant
Jonas Phillips

Philadelphia 24th Ellul 5547 or Sepr 7th 1787

James Madison to George Washington, 1787*

Sept. 30, 1787

Dear Sir,

I found on my arrival here that certain ideas unfavorable to the Act of the Convention which had created difficulties in that body, had made their way into Congress. They were patronised chiefly by Mr. R. H. L[ee] and Mr. Dane of Massts. It was first urged that, as the new Constitution was more than an alteration of the Articles of Confederation under which Congress acted, and even subverted those Articles altogether, there was a constitutional impropriety in their taking any positive agency in the work. The answer given was that the Resolution of Congress in Feby. had recommended the

*G. Hunt, ed., *The Writings of James Madison* (1904), Vol. 5, pp. 4–8.

Convention as the best mean of obtaining a firm national Government; that, as the powers of the Convention were defined by their Commissions in nearly the same terms with the powers of Congress given by the Confederation on the subject of alterations, Congress were not more restrained from acceding to the new plan, than the Convention were from proposing it. If the plan was within the powers of the Convention it was within those of Congress; if beyond those powers, the same necessity which justified the Convention would justify Congress; and a failure of Congress to Concur in what was done would imply either that the Convention had done wrong in exceeding their powers, or that the Government proposed was in itself liable to insuperable objections; that such an inference would be the more natural, as Congress had never scrupled to recommend measures foreign to their constitutional functions, whenever the public good seemed to require it; and had in several instances, particularly in the establishment of the new Western Governments, exercised assumed powers of a very high & delicate nature, under motives infinitely less urgent than the present state of our affairs, if any faith were due to the representations made by Congress themselves, echoed by 12 States in the Union, and confirmed by the general voice of the people. An attempt was made in the next place by R. H. L. to amend the Act of the Convention before it should go forth from Congress. He proposed a bill of Rights,—provision for juries in civil cases, & several other things corresponding with the ideas of Colonel M[ason.] He was supported by Mr. M[elancthon] Smith of this state. It was contended that Congress had an undoubted right to insert amendments, and that it was their duty to make use of it in a case where the essential guards of liberty had been omitted. On the other side the right of Congress was not denied, but the inexpediency of exerting it was urged on the following grounds;—1. that every circumstance indicated that the introduction of Congress as a party to the reform was intended by the States merely as a matter of form and respect. 2. that it was evident, from the contradictory objections which had been expressed by the different members who had animadverted on the plan, that a discussion of its merits would consume much time, without producing agreement even among its adversaries. 3. that it was clearly the intention of the States that the plan to be proposed should be the act of the Convention, with the assent of Congress, which could not be the case, if alterations were made, the Convention being no longer in existence to adopt them. 4. that as the Act of the Convention, when altered would instantly become the mere act of Congress, and must be proposed by them as such, and of course be addressed to the Legislatures, not Conventions of the States, and require the ratification of thirteen instead of nine States, and as the unaltered act would go forth to the States directly from the Convention under the auspices of that Body,—Some States might ratify the one & some the other of the plans, and confusion & disappointment be the least evils that would ensue. These difficulties which at one time threatened a serious division in Congs. and popular alterations

with the yeas and nays on the Journals, were at length fortunately termi-
nated by the following Resolution: "Congress having recd. the Report of the
Convention lately assembled in Philada., Resold. unanimously that the said
Report, with the Resolutions & letter accompanying the same, be transmitted
to the several Legislatures, in order to be submitted to a Convention of
Delegates chosen in each State by the people thereof, in conformity to the
Resolves of the Convention made & provided in that case." Eleven States
were present, the absent ones, R. I. & Maryland. A more direct approbation
would have been of advantage in this & some other States, where stress will
be laid on the agency of Congress in the matter, and a handle be taken by
adversaries of any ambiguity on the subject. With regard to Virginia & some
other States, reserve on the part of Congress will do no injury. The circumstance of unanimity must be favourable every where.

The general voice of this City seems to espouse the new Constitution. It is
supposed nevertheless that the party in power is strongly opposed to it. The
country must finally decide, the sense of which is as yet wholly unknown. As
far as Boston & Connecticut have been heard from, the first impression
seems to be auspicious. I am waiting with anxiety for the echo from Virginia,
but with very faint hopes of its corresponding with my wishes.

With every sentiment of respect & esteem, & every wish for your health &
happiness, I am Dear Sir

Your Obedient, humble Servt.

P.S. A small packet of the size 2 Vol 8° addressed to you lately came to
my hands with books of my own from France. Genl. Pinkney has been so
good as to take charge of them. He set out yesterday for S. Carolina, &
means to call at Mount Vernon.

GEORGE MASON'S OBJECTIONS TO THE PROPOSED FEDERAL CONSTITUTION, 1787

Commentary

The movement to add a Bill of Rights to the federal Constitution received powerful impetus from the critical writings that appeared soon after the Philadelphia Convention's work. Both the Federalists (as the pro-Constitution party came to be called) and the Antifederalists (the popular name for those opposing the Constitution) flooded the public with articles, pamphlets, addresses, and letters explaining the advantages and defects of the new organic law. Much of the writing on the matter focussed upon the Bill of Rights issue. The Antifederalists strongly criticized the absence of a Bill of Rights, asserting that without one, the Constitution was inadequate to protect individual rights and liberties. The Federalists defensively sought to show that a Bill of Rights was unnecessary—though popular pressure on the matter later led them to concede the need for amendments protecting fundamental rights. The debate then shifted to the issue of previous versus subsequent amendments—to whether amendments should be adopted as a condition of ratification or whether ratification should be accompanied by recommendations for later amendments.

The materials that follow contain extracts from the leading Federalist and Antifederalist writings, which bear upon the Bill of Rights issue. They start with the *Objections to the Constitution* written by George Mason during the heat of the Philadelphia Constitution debate itself. Mason wrote his *Objections* on September 13 (or shortly thereafter) on the blank pages of his copy of the report of the "Committee on stile and arrangement," while the Convention rebuff to his attempt to preface the Constitution with a Bill of Rights was still fresh. Naturally, then, Mason starts his *Objections* by the assertion, "There is no declaration of rights," and, since federal laws are made supreme, "the declarations of rights, in the separate states, are no security." After going into other objections to the new system, he comes back to the Bill of Rights issue: "There is no declaration of any kind for preserving the liberty of the press, the trial by jury in civil cases, nor against the danger of standing armies in time of peace."

Mason's *Objections* gives every impression of being only the first reaction of the author before he had really had time to work out his criticisms in detail. Despite its unpolished nature, it was widely disseminated (in part by Mason himself, as his letter to Washington shows). The reputation of the author, particularly as the draftsman of the Virginia Declaration of Rights, ensured a broad popular response to his initial cry for a federal Bill of Rights.

The Federalists could scarcely leave Mason's attack unanswered. Extracts are given from two of the best-known replies to Mason, as well as Madison's letter to Washington on Mason's *Objections.* The two articles in answer to Mason were by leading lawyers, who were later to be appointed to the Supreme Court. The first is the *Answers to Mr. Mason's Objections* by James Iredell, who deals with the Mason objections *seriatim,* starting with the lack of a Bill of Rights. Iredell declares that a Bill of Rights is unnecessary in a system where the Constitution delegates only the powers enumerated in it, so that the government may not act beyond those powers: "to say that they shall exercise no other powers . . . would seem to me both nugatory and ridiculous. As well might a Judge when he condemns a man to be hanged, give a strong injunction to the Sheriff that he should not be beheaded."

The second reply to Mason which follows is from the letters of "A Landholder" published in a Connecticut newspaper by Oliver Ellsworth (later the third Chief Justice). Ellsworth devoted his letter of December 10, 1787, to answering Mason's *Objections.* In the American system, said Ellsworth, Bills of Rights "are insignificant since . . . all the power government now has is a grant from the people." The Constitution itself limits and defines powers and thus "becomes now to the legislator and magistrate, what originally a bill of rights was to the people." It is not necessary for the Constitution to contain any declaration to preserve liberty of the press, "Nor . . . liberty of conscience, or of matrimony, or of burial of the dead." Congress has no power to prohibit any of these and therefore no provision specifically protecting any of these is necessary.

Iredell and Ellsworth state what was the common Federalist answer to the demand for a Bill of Rights (later to be given classic form in *The Federalist,* [*infra* p. 581] —that a Bill of Rights was unnecessary, since the Constitution did not give the Federal Government any power over individual rights and liberties. As the debate went on, however, the Federalist answer became increasingly less persuasive. Even if, in technical law, the Federalists were correct, it did not quiet the popular apprehension. Even if a Bill of Rights was not necessary, legally speaking, it could certainly do no harm. At the least, it would provide additional assurance that the new government would not swallow up the liberties of the people. Thus, the debate on the Constitution led to increasing popular pressure for a Bill of Rights to be added to that instrument. Even the Federalists were to yield to the pressure and admit the need for some amendments to protect fundamental rights.

George Mason's Objections to the Proposed Federal Constitution, 1787*

There is no declaration of rights: and the laws of the general government being paramount to the laws and constitutions of the several states, the declarations of rights, in the separate states, are no security. Nor are the

*P. L. Ford, *Pamphlets on the Constitution of the United States* (1888), pp. 327–32.

people secured even in the enjoyment of the benefit of the common law, which stands here upon no other foundation than its having been adopted by the respective acts forming the constitutions of the several states.

In the House of Representatives there is not the substance, but the shadow only of representation; which can never produce proper information in the legislature, or inspire confidence in the people. The laws will, therefore, be generally made by men little concerned in, and unacquainted with their effects and consequences.

The Senate have the power of altering all money-bills, and of originating appropriations of money, and the salaries of the officers of their appointment, in conjunction with the President of the United States—although they are not the representatives of the people, or amenable to them. These, with their other great powers, (viz. their powers in the appointment of ambassadors, and all public officers, in making treaties, and in trying all impeachments) their influence upon, and connection with, the supreme executive from these causes, their duration of office, and their being a constant existing body, almost continually sitting, joined with their being one complete branch of the legislature, will destroy any balance in the government, and enable them to accomplish what usurpations they please, upon the rights and liberties of the people.

The judiciary of the United States is so constructed and extended, as to absorb and destroy the judiciaries of the several states; thereby rendering laws as tedious, intricate, and expensive, and justice as unattainable by a great part of the community, as in England; and enabling the rich to oppress and ruin the poor.

The President of the United States has no constitutional council (a thing unknown in any safe and regular government.) he will therefore be unsupported by proper information and advice; and will generally be directed by minions and favorites—or he will become a tool to the Senate—or a council of state will grow out of the principal officers of the great departments—the worst and most dangerous of all ingredients for such a council, in a free country; for they may be induced to join in any dangerous or oppressive measures, to shelter themselves, and prevent an inquiry into their own misconduct in office. Whereas, had a constitutional council been formed (as was proposed) of six members, viz., two from the eastern, two from the middle, and two from the southern states, to be appointed by vote of the states in the House of Representatives, with the same duration and rotation of office as the Senate, the executive would always have had safe and proper information and advice; the president of such a council might have acted as Vice-President of the United States, *pro tempore,* upon any vacancy or disability of the chief magistrate; and long continued sessions of the Senate, would in a great measure have been prevented. From this fatal defect of a constitutional council, has arisen the improper power of the Senate, in the appointment of the public officers, and the alarming dependence and connexion between that branch of the legislature and the supreme executive. Hence, also, sprung that unnecessary officer, the Vice-President, who, for want of other employment, is made President of the Senate; thereby dangerously blending the executive and legislative powers; besides always giving to some of the states an unnecessary and unjust pre-eminence over the others.

The President of the United States has the unrestrained power of granting pardon for treason; which may be sometimes exercised to screen from punishment those whom he had secretly instigated to commit the crime, and thereby prevent a discovery of his own guilt. By declaring all treaties supreme laws of the land, the executive and the Senate have, in many cases, an exclusive power of legislation, which might have been avoided, by proper distinctions with respect to treaties, and requiring the assent of the House of Representatives, where it could be done with safety.

By requiring only a majority to make all commercial and navigation laws, the five southern states (whose produce and circumstances are totally different from those of the eight northern and eastern states) will be ruined: for such rigid and premature regulations may be made, as will enable the merchants of the northern and eastern states not only to demand an exorbitant freight, but to monopolize the purchase of the commodities, at their own price, for many years, to the great injury of the landed interest, and the impoverishment of the people: and the danger is the greater, as the gain on one side will be in proportion to the loss on the other. Whereas, requiring two-thirds of the members present in both houses, would have produced mutual moderation, promoted the general interest, and removed an insuperable objection to the adoption of the government.

Under their own construction of the general clause at the end of the enumerated powers, the Congress may grant monopolies in trade and commerce, constitute new crimes, inflict unusual and severe punishments, and extend their power as far as they shall think proper; so that the state legislatures have no security for the powers now presumed to remain to them; or the people for their rights. There is no declaration of any kind for preserving the liberty of the press, the trial by jury in civil cases, nor against the danger of standing armies in time of peace.

The state legislatures are restrained from laying export duties on their own produce—the general legislature is restrained from prohibiting the further importation of slaves for twenty odd years, though such importations render the United States weaker, more vulnerable, and less capable of defence. Both the general legislature, and the state legislatures are expressly prohibited making *ex post facto* laws, though there never was, nor can be, a legislature, but must and will make such laws, when necessity and the public safety require them, which will hereafter be a breach of all the constitutions in the union, and afford precedents for other innovations.

This government will commence in a moderate aristocracy; it is at present impossible to foresee whether it will, in its operation, produce a monarchy, or a corrupt oppressive aristocracy; it will most probably vibrate some years between the two, and then terminate in the one or the other.

George Mason to George Washington, 1787*

Oct. 7, 1787

I take the Liberty to enclose you my Objections to the new Constitution of Government; which a little Moderation & Temper, in the latter End of the Convention, might have removed. I am however most decidedly of Opinion, that it ought to be submitted to a Convention chosen by the People, for that special Purpose; and shou'd any Attempt be made to prevent the calling such a Convention here, such a Measure shall have every Opposition in my Power to give it. You will readily observe, that my Objections are not numerous (the greater Part of the inclosed paper containing Reasonings upon the probable Effects of the exceptionable Parts) tho' in my mind, some of them are capital ones.

Madison to Washington, 1787†

Oct. 18, 1787

Dear Sir,—I have been this day honored with your favor of the 10th instant, under the same cover with which is a copy of Col. Mason's objections to the Work of the Convention. As he persists in the temper which produced his dissent it is no small satisfaction to find him reduced to such distress for a proper gloss on it; for no other consideration surely could have led him to dwell on an objection which he acknowledged to have been in some degree removed by the Convention themselves—on the paltry right of the Senate to propose alterations in money bills—on the appointment of the vice President President of the Senate instead of making the President of the Senate the vice President, which seemed to be the alternative—and on the possibility, that Congress may misconstrue their powers & betray their trust so far as to grant monopolies in trade &c—. If I do not forget too some of his other reasons were either not at all or very faintly urged at the time when alone they ought to have been urged, such as the power of the Senate in the case of treaties & of impeachments; and their duration in office. With respect to the latter point I recollect well that he more than once disclaimed opposition to it. My memory fails me also if he did not acquiesce in if not

---

*The Records of the Federal Convention of 1787, Vol. 3, p. 102.
†The Writings of James Madison, Vol. 5, pp. 11–15.

vote for, the term allowed for the further importation of slaves, and the prohibition of duties on exports by the States. What he means by the dangerous tendency of the Judiciary I am at some loss to comprehend. It was never intended, nor can it be supposed that in ordinary cases the inferior tribunals will not have final jurisdiction in order to prevent the evils of which he complains. The great mass of suits in every State lie between Citizen & Citizen, and relate to matters not of federal cognizance. Notwithstanding the stress laid on the necessity of a Council to the President I strongly suspect, tho' I was a friend to the thing, that if such an one as Col. Mason proposed, had been established, and the power of the Senate in appointments to offices transferred to it, that as great a clamour would have been heard from some quarters which in general echo his objections. What can he mean by saying that the Common law is not secured by the new Constitution, though it has been adopted by the State Constitutions. The common law is nothing more than the unwritten law, and is left by all constitutions equally liable to legislative alterations. I am not sure that any notice is particularly taken of it in the Constitutions of the States. If there is, nothing more is provided than a general declaration that it shall continue along with other branches of law to be in force till legally changed. The Constitution of Virga. drawn up by Col Mason himself, is absolutely silent on the subject. An ordinance passed during the same Session, declared the common law as heretofore & all Statutes of prior date to the 4 of James I to be still the law of the land, merely to obviate pretexts that the separation from G. Britain threw us into a State of nature, and abolished all civil rights and objections. Since the Revolution every State has made great inroads & with great propriety in many instances on this monarchical code. The "revisal of the laws" by a Comittee of wch. Col. Mason was a member, though not an acting one, abounds with such innovations. The abolition of the right of primogeniture, which I am sure Col. Mason does not disapprove, falls under this head. What could the Convention have done? If they had in general terms declared the Common law to be in force, they would have broken in upon the legal Code of every State in the most material points; they wd. have done more, they would have brought over from G. B. a thousand heterogeneous & antirepublican doctrines, and even the ecclesiastical Hierarchy itself, for that is a part of the Common law. If they had undertaken a discrimination, they would have formed a digest of laws, instead of a Constitution. This objection surely was not brought forward in the Convention, or it wd. have been placed in such a light that a repetition of it out of doors would scarcely have been hazarded. Were it allowed the weight which Col. M. may suppose it deserves, it would remain to be decided whether it be candid to arraign the Convention for omissions which were never suggested to them—or prudent to vindicate the dissent by reasons which either were not previously thought of, or must have been wilfully concealed. But I am running into a comment as prolix as it is out of place.

I find by a letter from the Chancellor (Mr. Pendleton) that he views the act of the Convention in its true light, and gives it his unequivocal approbation. His support will have great effect. The accounts we have here of some other respectable characters vary considerably. Much will depend on Mr. Henry, and I [am] glad to find by your letter that his favorable decision on the subject may yet be hoped for.—The Newspapers here begin to teem with vehement & violent calumniations of the proposed Govt. As they are chiefly borrowed from the Pensylvania papers, you see them of course. The reports however from different quarters continue to be rather flattering.

With the highest respect & sincerest attachment I remain Dear Sir, Yr. Obedt. & Affecte. Servt.

Answers to Mr. Mason's Objections to the New Constitution, 1788*

Recommended by the late Convention

I. Objection

"There is no declaration of rights, and the laws of the general government being paramount to the laws and constitutions of the several States, the declarations of rights in the separate States are no security. Nor are the people secured even in the enjoyment of the benefit of the common law, which stands here upon no other foundation than its having been adopted by the respective acts forming the Constitutions of the several States."

Answer

1. As to the want of a declaration of rights. The introduction of these in England, from which the idea was originally taken, was in consequence of usurpations of the Crown, contrary, as was conceived, to the principles of their government. But there no original constitution is to be found, and the only meaning of a declaration of rights in that country is, that in certain particulars specified, the Crown had no authority to act. Could this have been necessary had there been a constitution in being by which it could have been clearly discerned whether the Crown had such authority or not? Had the people, by a solemn instrument, delegated particular powers to the Crown at the formation of their government, surely the Crown, which in that case could claim under that instrument only, could not have contended for more power than was conveyed by it. So it is in regard to the new Constitution here: the future government which may be formed under that authority certainly cannot act beyond the warrant of that authority. As well might they attempt to impose a King upon America, as go one step in any other respect beyond the terms of their institution. The question then only is, whether

*Pamphlets on the Constitution of the United States, pp. 333–70.

more power will be vested in the future government than is necessary for the general purposes of the union. This may occasion a ground of dispute—but after expressly defining the powers that are to be exercised, to say that they shall exercise no other powers (either by a general or particular enumeration) would seem to me both nugatory and ridiculous. As well might a Judge when he condemns a man to be hanged, give strong injunctions to the Sheriff that he should not be beheaded. [1]

2. As to the common law, it is difficult to know what is meant by that part of the objection. So far as the people are now entitled to the benefit of the common law, they certainly will have a right to enjoy it under the new Constitution until altered by the general legislature, which even in this point has some cardinal limits assigned to it. What are most acts of Assembly but a deviation in some degree from the principles of the common law? The people are expressly secured (contrary to Mr. Mason's wishes) against *ex post facto* laws; so that the tenure of any property at any time held under the principles of the common law, cannot be altered by any future act of the general legislature. The principles of the common law, as they now apply, must surely always hereafter apply, except in those particulars in which express authority is given by this constitution; in no other particulars can the Congress have authority to change it, and I believe it cannot be shown that any one power of this kind given is unnecessarily given, or that the power would answer its proper purpose if the legislature was restricted from any innovations on the principles of the common law, which would not in all cases suit the vast variety of incidents that might arise out it.

*   *   *

VIII. Objection

"Under their own construction of the general clause at the end of the enumerated powers, the Congress may grant monopolies in trade and commerce, constitute new crimes, inflict unusual and severe punishment, and extend their power as far as they shall think proper; so that the State Legislatures have no security for the powers now presumed to remain to them: or the people for their rights. There is no declaration of any kind for preserving the liberty of the press, the trial by jury in civil causes, nor against the danger of standing armies in time of peace."

Answer

The general clause at the end of the enumerated power is as follows:

---

[1] It appears to me a very just remark of Mr. Wilson's, in his celebrated speech, that a bill of rights would have been dangerous, as implying that without such a reservation the Congress would have had authority in the cases enumerated, so that if any had been omitted (and who would undertake to recite all the State and individual rights not relinquished by the new Constitution?) they might have been considered at the mercy of the general legislature.

> To make all laws which shall be necessary and proper for carrying into execution the foregoing powers, and all other powers vested by this Constitution in the United States, or in any department or office thereof.

Those powers would be useless, except acts of legislation could be exercised upon them. It was not possible for the Convention, nor is it for any human body, to foresee and provide for all contingent cases that may arise. Such cases must therefore be left to be provided for by the general Legislature as they shall happen to come into existence. If Congress, under pretence of exercising the power delegated to them, should in fact, by the exercise of any other power, usurp upon the rights of the different Legislatures, or of any private citizens, the people will be exactly in the same situation as if there had been an express provision against such power in particular, and yet they had presumed to exercise it. It would be an act of tyranny, against which no parchment stipulations can guard; and the Convention surely can be only answerable for the propriety of the powers given, not for the future virtues of all with whom those powers may be intrusted. It does not therefore appear to me that there is any weight in this objection more than in others. But that I may give it every fair advantage, I will take notice of every particular injurious act of power which Mr. Mason points out as exercisable by the authority of Congress under this general clause.

The first mentioned is, "That the Congress may grant monopolies in trade and commerce." Upon examining the constitution I find it expressly provided, "That no preference shall be given to the ports of one State over those of another;" and that "citizens of each State shall be entitled to all privileges and immunities of citizens in the several States." These provisions appear to me to be calculated for the very purpose Mr. Mason wishes to secure. Can they be consistent with any monoply in trade and commerce?[2] I apprehend therefore, under this expression must be intended more than is expressed, and if I may conjecture from another publication of a gentleman of the same State and in the same party of opposition, I should suppose it arose from a jealousy of the eastern States very well known to be often expressed by some gentlemen of Virginia. They fear, that a majority of the States may establish regulations of commerce which will give great advantage to the carrying trade of America, and be a means of encouraging New England vessels rather than Old England. Be it so. No regulations can give such advantage to New England vessels, which will not be enjoyed by all

---

[2]One of the powers given to Congress is, "To promote the progress of science and useful arts, by securing for limited times to authors and inventors the exclusive right to their respective writings and discoveries." I am convinced Mr. Mason did not mean to refer to this clause. He is a gentleman of too much taste and knowledge himself to wish to have our government established upon such principles of barbarism as to be able to afford no encouragement to genius.

other American vessels and many States can build as well as New England, though not at present perhaps in equal proportion.[3] And what could conduce more to the preservation of the Union than allowing to every kind of industry in America a peculiar preference! Each State exerting itself in its own way, but the exertions of all contributing to the common security, and increasing the rising greatness of our country! Is it not the aim of every wise country to be as much the carriers of their own produce as they can be? And would not this be the means in our own of producing a new source of activity among the people, giving to our fellow-citizens what otherwise must be given to strangers, and laying the foundation of an independent trade among ourselves, and of gradually raising a navy in America which, however distant the prospect, ought certainly not to be out of our sight. There is no great probability however that our country is likely soon to enjoy so glorious an advantage. We must have treaties of commerce, because without them we cannot trade to other countries. We already have such with some nations; we have none with Great Britain, which can be imputed to no other cause but our not having a strong respectable government to bring that haughty nation to terms. And surely no man, who feels for the honor of his country, but must view our present degrading commerce with that country with the highest indignation, and the most ardent wish to extricate ourselves from so disgraceful a situation. This only can be done by a powerful government which can dictate conditions of advantage to ourselves, as an equivalent for advantages to them; and this could undoubtedly be easily done by such a government, without diminishing the value of any articles of our own produce; or if there was any diminution it would be too slight to be felt by any patriot in competition with the honor and interest of his country.

As to the constituting of new crimes, and inflicting unusual and severe punishment, certainly the cases enumerated wherein the Congress are empowered either to define offences, or prescribe punishments, are such as are proper for the exercise of such authority in the general Legislature of the Union. They only relate to "counterfeiting the securities and current coin of the United States," to "piracies and felonies committed on the high seas, and offences against the law of nations," and to "treason against the United States." These are offences immediately affecting the security, the honor or the interest of the United States at large, and of course must come within the sphere of the Legislative authority which is intrusted with their protection. Beyond these authorities, Congress can exercise no other power of this kind,

---

[3]Some might apprehend, that in this case as New England would at first have the greatest share of the carrying trade, the vessels of that country might demand an unreasonable freight. But no attempt could be more injurious to them as it would immediately set the Southern States to building, which they could easily do, and thus a temporary loss would be compensated with a lasting advantage to us; the very reverse would be the case witth them. Besides, that from that country alone there would probably be competititon enough for freight to keep it on reasonable terms.

except in the enacting of penalties to enforce their acts of legislation in the cases where express authority is delegated to them, and if they could not enforce such acts by the enacting of penalties those powers would be altogether useless, since a legislative regulation without some sanction would be an absurd thing indeed. The Congress having, for these reasons, a just right to authority in the above particulars, the question is, whether it is practicable and proper to prescribe limits to its exercise, for fear that they should inflict punishments unusual and severe. It may be observed, in the first place, that a declaration against "cruel and unusual punishments" formed part of an article in the Bill of Rights at the revolution in England in 1688. The prerogative of the Crown having been grossly abused in some preceding reigns, it was thought proper to notice every grievance they had endured, and those declarations went to an abuse of power in the Crown only, but were never intended to limit the authority of Parliament. Many of these articles of the Bill of Rights in England, without a due attention to the difference of the cases, were eagerly adopted when our constitutions were formed, the minds of men then being so warmed with their exertions in the cause of liberty as to lean too much perhaps towards a jealousy of power to repose a proper confidence in their own government. From these articles in the State constitutions many things were attempted to be transplanted into our new Constitution, which would either have been nugatory or improper. This is one of them. The expressions "unusual and severe" or "cruel and unusual" surely would have been too vague to have been of any consequence, since they admit of no clear and precise signification. If to guard against punishments being too severe, the Convention had enumerated a vast variety of cruel punishments, and prohibited the use of any of them, let the number have been ever so great, an inexhaustible fund must have been unmentioned, and if our government had been disposed to be cruel their invention would only have been put to a little more trouble. If to avoid this difficulty, they had determined, not negatively what punishments should not be exercised, but positively what punishments should, this must have led them into a labyrinth of detail which in the original constitution of a government would have appeared perfectly ridiculous, and not left a room for such changes, according to circumstances, as must be in the power of every Legislature that is rationally formed. Thus when we enter into particulars, we must be convinced that the proposition of such a restriction would have led to nothing useful, or to something dangerous, and therefore that its omission is not chargeable as a fault in the new Constitution. Let us also remember, that as those who are to make those laws must themselves be subject to them, their own interest and feelings will dictate to them not to make them unnecessarily severe; and that in the case of treason, which usually in every country exposes men most to the avarice and rapacity of government, care is taken that the innocent family of the offender shall not suffer for the treason of their relation. This is the crime with respect to which a jealousy is of the most importance, and accordingly it is defined with great plainness and accuracy, and the temptations to abusive prosecutions guarded against as much as possible. I now proceed to the three great cases: The liberty of the press, the trial by jury in civil cases, and a standing army in time of peace.

The liberty of the press is always a grand topic for declamation, but the future Congress will have no other authority over this than to secure to authors for a limited time an exclusive privilege of publishing their works. This authority has been long exercised in England, where the press is as free as among ourselves or in any country in the world; and surely such an encouragement to genius is no restraint on the liberty of the press, since men are allowed to publish what they please of their own, and so far as this may be deemed a restraint upon others it is certainly a reasonable one, and can be attended with no danger of copies not being sufficiently multiplied, because the interest of the proprietor will always induce him to publish a quantity fully equal to the demand. Besides, that such encouragement may give birth to many excellent writings which would otherwise have never appeared.[4] If the Congress should exercise any other power over the press than this, they will do it without any warrant from this constitution, and must answer for it as for any other act of tyranny.

In respect to the trial by jury in civil cases, it must be observed it is a mistake to suppose that such a trial takes place in all civil cases now. Even in the common law courts, such a trial is only had where facts are disputed between the parties, and there are even some facts triable by other methods. In the Chancery and Admiralty Courts, in many of the States, I am told they have no juries at all. The States in these particulars differ very much in their practice from each other. A general declaration therefore to preserve the trial by jury in all civil cases would only have produced confusion, so that the courts afterwards in a thousand instances would not have known how to have proceeded. If they had added, "as heretofore accustomed," that would not have answered the purpose, because there has been no uniform custom about it. If therefore the Convention had interfered, it must have been by entering into a detail highly unsuitable to a fundamental constitution of government; if they had pleased some States they must have displeased others by innovating upon the modes of administering justice perhaps endeared to them by habit, and agreeable to their settled conviction of propriety. As this was the case it appears to me it was infinitely better, rather than endanger everything by attempting too much, to leave this complicated business of detail to the regulation of the future Legislature, where it can be adjusted coolly and at ease, and upon full and exact information. There is no

[4]If this provision had not been made in the new constitution no author could have enjoyed such an advantage in all the United States, unless a similar law had constantly subsisted in each of the States separately.

danger of the trial by jury being rejected, when so justly a favorite of the whole people. The representatives of the people surely can have no interest in making themselves odious, for the mere pleasure of being hated, and when a member of the House of Representatives is only sure of being so for two years, but must continue a citizen all his life, his interest as a citizen, if he is a man of common sense, to say nothing of his being a man of common honesty, must ever be uppermost in his mind. We know the great influence of the monarchy in the British government, and upon what a different tenure the Commons there have their seats in Parliament from that prescribed to our representatives. We know also they have a large standing army. It is in the power of the Parliament, if they dare to exercise it, to abolish the trial by jury altogether. But woe be to the man who should dare to attempt it. It would undoubtedly produce an insurrection, that would hurl every tyrant to the ground who attempted to destroy that great and just favorite of the English nation. We certainly shall be always sure of this guard at least upon any such act of folly or insanity in our representatives. They soon would be taught the consequence of sporting with the feelings of a free people. But when it is evident that such an attempt cannot be rationally apprehended, we have no reason to anticipate unpleasant emotions of that nature. There is indeed little probability that any degree of tyranny which can be figured to the most discolored imagination as likely to arise out of our government, could find an interest in attacking the trial by jury in civil cases;—and in criminal ones, where no such difficulties intervene as in the other, and where there might be supposed temptations to violate the personal security of a citizen, it is sacredly preserved.

The subject of a standing army has been exhausted in so masterly a manner in two or three numbers of the Federalist (a work which I hope will soon be in every body's hands) that but for the sake of regularity in answering Mr. Mason's objections, I should not venture upon the same topic, and shall only presume to do so, with a reference for fuller satisfaction to that able performance. It is certainly one of the most delicate and proper cases for the consideration of a free people, and so far as a jealousy of this kind leads to any degree of caution not incompatible with the public safety, it is undoubtedly to be commended. Our jealousy of this danger has descended to us from our British ancestors; in that country they have a Monarch, whose power being limited, and at the same time his prerogatives very considerable, a constant jealousy of him is both natural and proper. The two last of the Stuarts having kept up a considerable body of standing forces in time of peace for the clear and almost avowed purpose of subduing the liberties of the people, it was made an article of the bill of rights at the revolution, "That the raising or keeping a standing army within the kingdom in time of peace, unless it be with the consent of Parliament, is against law;" but no attempt was made, or I dare say even thought of, to restrain the

Parliament from exercise of that right. An army has been kept on foot annually by authority of Parliament, and I believe ever since the revolution they have had some standing troops; disputes have frequently happened about the number, but I don't recollect any objection by the most zealous patriot, to the keeping up of any at all. At the same time, notwithstanding the above practice of an annual vote (arising from a very judicious caution), it is still in the power of Parliament to authorize the keeping up of any number of troops for an indefinite time, and to provide for their subsistence for any number of years. Considerations of prudence, not constitutional limits to their authority, alone restrain such an exercise of it—our Legislature however will be strongly guarded, though that of Great Britain is without any check at all. No appropriations of money for military services can continue longer than two years. Considering the extensive services the general government may have to provide for upon this vast continent, no forces with any serious prospect of success could be attempted to be raised for a shorter time. Its being done for so short a period, if there were any appearance of ill designs in the government, would afford time enough for the real friends of their country to sound an alarm, and when we know how easy it is to excite jealousy of any government, how difficult for the people to distinguish from their real friends, those factious men who in every country are ready to disturb its peace for personal gratifications of their own, and those desperate ones to whom every change is welcome, we shall have much more reason to fear that the government may be overawed by groundless discontents, than that it should be able, if contrary to every probability such a government could be supposed willing, to effect any designs for the destruction of their own liberties as well as those of their constituents; for surely we ought ever to remember, that there will not be a man in the government but who has been either mediately or immediately recently chosen by the people, and that for too limited a time to make any arbitrary designs consistent with common sense, when every two years a new body of representatives with all the energy of popular feelings will come, to carry the strong force of a severe national control into every department of government. To say nothing of the one-third to compose the Senate coming at the same time, warm with popular sentiments, from their respective assemblies. Men may be sure to suggest dangers from any thing, but it may truly be said that those who can seriously suggest the danger of a premeditated attack on the liberties of the people from such a government as this, could with ease assign reasons equally plausible for mistrusting the integrity of any government formed in any manner whatever; and really it does seem to me, that all their reasons may be fairly carried to this position, that inasmuch as any confidence in any men would be unwise, as we can give no power but what may be grossly abused, we had better give none at all, but continue as we are, or resolve into total anarchy at once, of which indeed our present condition falls very little short. What sort of a government would that be which, upon the most certain intelligence that hostilities were meditated against it, could take no method for its defence till after a formal declaration of war, or the enemy's standard was actually fixed upon the shore? The first has for some time been out of fashion, but if it had not, the restraint these gentlemen recommend, would certainly have brought it into disuse with every power who meant to make war upon America. They would be such fools as to give us the only warning we had informed them we would accept of, before we would take any steps to counteract their designs. The absurdity of our being prohibited from preparing to resist an invasion till after it had actually taken place[5] is so glaring, that no man can consider it for a moment without being struck with astonishment to see how rashly, and with how little consideration gentlemen, whose characters are certainly respectable, have suffered themselves to be led away by so delusive an idea. The example of other countries, so far from warranting any such limitation of power, is directly against it. That of England has already been particularly noticed. In our present articles of confederation there is no such restriction. It has been observed by the Federalist, that Pennsylvania and North Carolina appear to be the only States in the Union which have attempted any restraint of the Legislative authority in this particular, and that their restraint appears rather in the light of a caution than a prohibition; but notwithstanding that, Pennsylvania had been obliged to raise forces in the very face of that article of her bill of rights. That great writer from the remoteness of his situation, did not know that North Carolina had equally violated her bill of rights in a similar manner. The Legislature of that State in November, 1785, passed an act for raising 200 men for the protection of a county called Davidson county against hostilities from the Indians; they were to continue for two years from the time of their first rendezvous, unless sooner disbanded by the Assembly, and were to be subject to the same "rules with respect to their government as were established in the time of the late war by the Congress of the United States for the government of the Continental army." These are the very words of the act. Thus, from the examples of the only two countries in the world that I believe ever attempted such a restriction, it appears to be a thing incompatible with the safety of government. Whether their restriction is to be considered as a caution or a prohibition, in less than five years after

---

[5]Those gentlemen who gravely tell us that the militia will be sufficient for this purpose, do not recollect that they themselves do not desire we should rely solely on a militia in case of actual war, and therefore in the case I have supposed they cannot be deemed sufficient even by themselves, for when the enemy landed it would undoubtedly be a time of war, but the misfortune would be, that they would be prepared; we not. Certainly all possible encouragement should be given to the training of our militia, but no man can really believe that they will be sufficient, without the aid of any regular troops, in time of foreign hostility. A powerful militia may make fewer regulars necessary, but will not make it safe to dispense with them altogether.

peace the caution has been disregarded, or the prohibition disobeyed.[6] Can the most credulous or suspicious men require stronger proof of the weakness and impolicy of such restraints?

*   *   *

XI. Objection

"Both the general Legislature and the State Legislatures, have expressly prohibited making *ex post facto* laws, though there never was, nor can be, a legislature but must and will make such laws, when necessity and the public safety require them; which will hereafter be a breach of all the constitutions in the Union, and offer precedents for other innovations."

Answer

My ideas of liberty are so different from those of Mr. Mason, that in my opinion this very prohibition is one of the most valuable parts of the new constitution. *Ex post facto* laws may sometimes be convenient, but that they are ever absolutely necessary I shall take the liberty to doubt, till that necessity can be made apparent. Sure I am, they have been the instrument of some of the grossest acts of tyranny that were ever exercised, and have this never failing consequence, to put the minority in the power of a passionate and unprincipled majority, as to the most sacred things, and the plea of necessity is never wanting where it can be of any avail. This very clause, I think, is worth ten thousand declarations of rights, if this, the most essential right of all, was omitted in them. A man may feel some pride in his security, when he knows that what he does innocently and safely to-day in accordance with the laws of his country, cannot be tortured into guilt and danger to-morrow. But if it should happen, that a great and overruling necessity, acknowledged and felt by all, should make a deviation from this prohibition excusable, shall we not be more safe in leaving the excuse for an extraordinary exercise of power to rest upon the apparent equity of it alone, than to leave the door open to a tyranny it would be intolerable to bear? In the one case, every one must be sensible of its justice, and therefore excuse it; in the other, whether its exercise was just or unjust, its being lawful would be sufficient to command obedience. Nor would a case like that, resting entirely on its own bottom, from a conviction of invincible necessity, warrant an avowed abuse of another authority, where no such necessity existed or could be pretended.

I have now gone through Mr. Mason's objections; one thing still remains to be taken notice of, his prediction, which he is pleased to express in these words: "This government will commence in a moderate aristocracy; it is at present impossible to foresee, whether it will in its operation produce a

---

[6] I presume we are not to be deemed in a state of war whenever any Indian hostilities are committed on our frontiers. If that is the case I don't suppose we have had six years of peace since the first settlement of the country, or shall have for fifty years to come. A distinction between peace and war would be idle indeed, if it can be frittered away by such pretences as those.

monarchy, or a corrupt, oppressive aristocracy; it will most probably vibrate some years between the two, and then terminate in the one or the other." From the uncertainty of this prediction, we may hope that Mr. Mason was not divinely inspired when he made it, and of course that it may as fairly be questioned as any of his particular objections. If my answers to his objections are, in general, solid, a very different government will arise from the new constitution, if the several States should adopt it, as I hope they will. It will not probably be too much to flatter ourselves with, that it may present a spectacle of combined strength in government, and genuine liberty in the people, the world has never yet beheld. In the mean time, our situation is critical to the greatest degree. Those gentlemen who think we may at our ease go on from one convention to another, to try if all objections cannot be conquered by perseverance, have much more sanguine expectations than I can presume to form. There are critical periods in the fate of nations, as well as in the life of man, which are not to be neglected with impunity. I am much mistaken if this is not such a one with us. When we were at the very brink of despair, the late excellent Convention with a unanimity that none could have hoped for, generously discarding all little considerations formed a system of government which I am convinced can stand the nicest examination, if reason and not prejudice is employed in viewing it. With a happiness of thought, which in our present awful situation ought to silence much more powerful objections than any I have heard, they have provided in the very frame of government a safe, easy and unexceptionable method of correcting any errors it may be thought to contain. Those errors may be corrected at leisure; in the mean time the acknowledged advantages likely to flow from this constitution may be enjoyed. We may venture to hold up our head among the other powers of the world. We may talk to them with the confidence of an independent people, having strength to resent insults; and avail ourselves of our natural advantages. We may be assured of once more beholding justice, order and dignity taking place of the present anarchical confusion prevailing almost every where, and drawing upon us universal disgrace. We may hope, by proper exertions of industry, to recover thoroughly from the shock of the late war, and truly to become an independent, great and prosperous people. But if we continue as we now are, wrangling about every trifle, listening to the opinion of a small minority, in preference to a large and most respectable majority of the first men in our country, and among them some of the first in the world, if our minds in short are bent rather on indulging a captious discontent, than bestowing a generous and well-placed confidence in those who we have every reason to believe are entirely worthy of it, we shall too probably present a spectacle for malicious exultation to our enemies, and melancholy dejection to our friends; and the honor, glory and prosperity which were just within our reach, will perhaps be snatched from us for ever.

Marcus

The Letters of a Landholder, 1787-1788*

By Oliver Ellsworth

[Monday, December 10, 1787]

He that is first in his own cause seemeth just; but his neighbor cometh and searcheth him.

To the Landholders and Farmers:

The publication of Col. Mason's reasons for not signing the new Constitution, has extorted some truths that would otherwise in all probability have remained unknown to us all. His reasons, like Mr. Gerry's, are most of them *ex post facto,* have been revised in New Y—k by R. H. L.[1] and by him brought into their present artful and insidious form. The factious spirit of R. H. L., his implacable hatred to General Washington, his well-known intrigues against him in the late war, his attempts to displace him and give the command of the American army to General Lee, is so recent in your minds it is not necessary to repeat them. He is supposed to be the author of most of the scurrility poured out in the New-York papers against the new constitution.

Just at the close of the Convention, whose proceedings in general were zealously supported by Mr. Mason, he moved for a clause that no navigation act should ever be passed but with the consent of two-thirds of both branches; urging that a navigation act might otherwise be passed excluding foreign bottoms from carrying American produce to market, and throw a monopoly of the carrying business into the hands of the eastern states who attend to navigation, and that such an exclusion of foreigners would raise the freight of the produce of the southern states, and for these reasons Mr. Mason would have it in the power of the southern states to prevent any navigation act. This clause, as unequal and partial in the extreme to the southern states, was rejected; because it ought to be left on the same footing with other national concerns, and because no state would have a right to complain of a navigation act which should leave the carrying business equally open to them all. Those who preferred cultivating their lands would do so; those who chose to navigate and become carriers would do that. The loss of this question determined Mr. Mason against the signing the doings of the convention, and is undoubtedly among his reasons as drawn for the southern states; but for the eastern states this reason would not do. It would convince us that Mr. Mason preferred the subjects of every foreign power to the subjects of the United States who live in New-England; even the British who lately ravaged Virginia—that Virginia, my countrymen, where your

---

Essays on the Constitution of the United States (1892), pp. 159–66.
[1]Richard Henry Lee.

460

relations lavished their blood—where your sons laid down their lives to secure to her and us the freedom and independence in which we now rejoice, and which can only be continued to us by a firm, equal and effective union. But do not believe that the people of Virginia are all thus selfish: No, there is a Washington, a Blair, a Madison and a Lee, (not R. H. L.) and I am persuaded there is a majority of liberal, just and federal men in Virginia, who, whatever their sentiments may be of the new constitution, will despise the artful injustice contained in Col. Mason's reasons as published in the Connecticut papers.

*   *   *

There is no Declaration of Rights. Bills of Rights were introduced in England when its kings claimed all power and jurisdiction, and were considered by them as grants to the people. They are insignificant since government is considered as originating from the people, and all the power government now has is a grant from the people. The constitution they establish with powers limited and defined, becomes now to the legislator and magistrate, what originally a bill of rights was to the people. To have inserted in this consitution a bill of rights for the states, would suppose them to derive and hold their rights from the federal government, when the reverse is the case.

There is to be no ex post facto laws. This was moved by Mr. Gerry and supported by Mr. Mason,[2] and is exceptional only as being unnecessary; for it ought not to be presumed that government will be so tyranical, and opposed to the sense of all modern civilians, as to pass such laws: if they should, they would be void.

*   *   *

There is no declaration of any kind to preserve the liberty of the press, etc. Nor is liberty of conscience, or of matrimony, or of burial of the dead, it is enough that congress have no power to prohibit either, and can have no temptation. This objection is answered in that the states have all the power originally, and congress have only what the states grant them.

The judiciary of the United States is so constructed and extended as to absorb and destroy the judiciaries of the several states; thereby rendering law as tedious, intricate and expensive, and justice as unattainable by a great part of the community, as in England; and enable the rich to oppress and ruin the poor. It extends only to objects and cases specified, and wherein the national peace or rights, or the harmony of the states is concerned, and not to controversies between citizens of the same state (except where they claim under grants of different states); and nothing hinders but the supreme federal court may be held in different districts, or in all the states, and that all the cases, except the few in which it has original and not appellate jurisdiction, may in the first instance be had in the state courts and those

[2]This is an error. It was moved by Mason and seconded by Gerry.

trials be final except in cases of great magnitude; and the trials be by jury also in most or all the causes which were wont to be tried by them, as congress shall provide, whose appointment is security enough for their attention to the wishes and convenience of the people. In chancery courts juries are never used, nor are they proper in admiralty courts, which proceed not by municipal laws, which they may be supposed to understand, but by the civil law and law of nations.

Mr. Mason deems the president and senate's power to make treaties dangerous, because they become laws of the land. If the president and his proposed council had this power, or the president alone, as in England and other nations is the case, could the danger be less—or is the representative branch suited to the making of treaties, which are often intricate, and require much negotiation and secrecy? The senate is objected to as having too much power, and bold unfounded assertions that they will destroy any balance in the government, and accomplish what usurpation they please upon the rights and liberties of the people; to which it may be answered, they are elective and rotative, to the mass of the people; the populace can as well balance the senatorial branch there as in the states, and much better than in England, where the lords are hereditary, and yet the commons preserve their weight; but the state governments on which the constitution is built will forever be security enough to the people against aristocratic usurpations: The danger of the constitution is not aristocracy or monarchy, but anarchy.

I intreat you, my fellow citizens, to read and examine the new constitution with candor—examine it for yourselves: you are, most of you, as learned as the objector, and certainly as able to judge of its virtues or vices as he is. To make the objections the more plausible, they are called The objections of the Hon. George Mason, etc. They may possibly be his, but be assured they were not those made in convention, and being directly against what he there supported in one instance ought to caution you against giving any credit to the rest; his violent opposition to the powers given congress to regulate trade, was an open decided preference of all the world to you. A man governed by such narrow views and local prejudices, can never be trusted; and his pompous declaration in the House of Delegates in Virginia that no man was more federal than himself, amounts to no more than this, "Make a federal government that will secure Virginia all her natural advantages, promote all her interests regardless of every disadvantage to the other states, and I will subscribe to it."

It may be asked how I came by my information respecting Col. Mason's conduct in convention, as the doors were shut? To this I answer, no delegate of the late convention will contradict my assertions, as I have repeatedly heard them made by others in presence of several of them, who could not deny their truth. Whether the constitution in question will be adopted by the United States in our day is uncertain; but it is neither aristocracy or monarchy can grow out of it, so long as the present descent of landed estates last, and the mass of the people have, as at present, a tolerable education; and were it ever so perfect a scheme of freedom, when we become ignorant, vicious, idle, and regardless of the education of our children, our liberties will be lost—we shall be fitted for slavery, and it will be an easy business to reduce us to obey one or more tyrants.

ATTACKS BY RICHARD HENRY LEE, ELBRIDGE GERRY, AND LUTHER MARTIN, 1787–1788

Commentary

Aside from Mason's *Objections,* the most important of the Antifederalist writings upon the new Constitution were those by Richard Henry Lee, Elbridge Gerry, and Luther Martin. Next to Mason himself, these three men furnished the opponents of ratification with their most effective arguments. The extracts which follow are those portions of the attacks by Lee, Gerry, and Martin, which bear upon the Bill of Rights issue. Stimulated by these writings, that issue was soon the leading argument of the Antifederalists. As Robert Allen Rutland puts it, "no Bill of Rights" became the main popular chant of the Antifederalists, for that issue was the vulnerable chink in the Federalist armor. The omission of a Bill of Rights became the chief stumbling block to ratification, until the Federalists themselves began to recognize the need for amendments to meet the popular concern.

Richard Henry Lee's *Letters from the Federal Farmer* was perhaps the most effective of the longer arguments against the Constitution. Lee himself was one of the leaders in the struggle for a Bill of Rights. As a member of the Confederation Congress, he had sought unsuccessfully to have that body add a Bill of Rights to the Constitution before it was sent to the states for ratification (*supra* p. 440). In his *Farmer* letters, Lee repeated the call for a Bill of Rights. Letter II, which follows, deals directly with the Bill of Rights issue. There are, Lee insists, "certain unalienable and fundamental rights which . . . should be made the basis of every constitution . . . I still believe a complete federal bill of rights to be very practicable." In Letter IV, he rejects the notion that in the absence of express limitations all powers not delegated are reserved in the people. The Constitution does contain a partial Bill of Rights in Article I, sections 9 and 10. This Bill of Rights ought to be carried further and other essential rights established as part of the fundamental compact. Then he discusses what became the core of the controversy between the Federalists and Antifederalists: the question of how to secure the necessary amendments. He characterizes the idea of adopting the Constitution and obtaining later amendments as "a pernicious idea, it argues a servility of character totally unfit for the support of free government." He continues this theme in Letter V, urging the states "to direct their energies to altering and amending the system proposed before they shall adopt it."

Elbridge Gerry has survived, for most of us, in the name of a disreputable political practice, which took place while he was Governor of Massachusetts. To his contemporaries, he was noteworthy as one of the leading Antifederalists. He was one of the Philadelphia Convention delegates who refused to sign the Constitution, and explained his action in a widely circulated letter to the Massachusetts legislature (from which the relevant extracts follow). Thus Gerry was one of the leaders in the opposition to ratification in the Massachusetts Convention where, though not an official delegate, he was invited to participate in its sessions. After the ratification by Massachusetts, Gerry continued the Antifederalist fight with his *Observations by a Columbian Patriot*. The Antifederal Committee in New York distributed 1,630 copies to its local committees, though the Albany Committee complained that it "was in a style too sublime and florid for the common people in this part of the country." The extracts which follow indicate that this comment was justified. Among Gerry's main points are the lack of securities for basic liberties, notably freedom of the press and from warrants unsupported by evidence. What is needed is a Bill of Rights to guard against dangerous encroachments of power. "The rights of individuals ought to be the primary object of all government, and cannot be too securely guarded by the most explicit declarations in their favor."

Luther Martin, the third of the Antifederalist leaders whose writings were of great influence in the ratification struggle, was one of the leading lawyers of the day. A dissenting member of the Constitutional Convention, he led the opposition to ratification in his home state of Maryland. Martin's letters (published in the *Maryland Journal*) presented his views on the matter. Letter Number II was a reply to a letter by Oliver Ellsworth (signed The Landholder) which had attacked Martin on the Bill of Rights issue, saying, "You sir, had more candour in the Convention . . . there you never signified by any motion or expression whatever, that it stood in need of a bill of rights, or in any wise endangered the trial by jury." Martin answers by asserting that his silence did not prove "that I approved the system in those respects." On the contrary he states that he became convinced of the necessity for "a complete bill of rights . . . prefixed to the Constitution, to serve as a barrier between the general government and the respective states and their citizens." Martin says he actually drafted a Bill of Rights before he left the Convention. He did not introduce it because he was persuaded it would be a vain gesture. (This was uncharacteristic of Martin, but perhaps true in view of the cold reception of the Mason-Gerry motion for a Bill of Rights, [*supra* p. 438] . In Letter Number III, Martin rejects the view that the Constitution be adopted, since subsequent amendments could be secured: "why, I pray you, my fellow citizens, should we not insist upon the necessary amendments being made now . . . ?" Thus, Martin (like Lee) joins issue on what was to become the crucial issue on the Bill of Rights question— that of previous versus subsequent amendments.

Observation Leading to a Fair Examination of the System of Government, 1787*

By Richard Henry Lee

Oct. 9, 1787

Letter II

Dear Sir,

The essential parts of a free and good government are a full and equal representation of the people in the legislature, and the jury trial of the vicinage in the administration of justice—a full and equal representation, is that which possesses the same interests, feelings, opinions, and views the people themselves would were they all assembled—a fair representation, therefore, should be so regulated, that every order of men in the community, according to the common course of elections, can have a share in it—in order to allow professional men, merchants, traders, farmers, mechanics, &c. to bring a just proportion of their best informed men respectively into the legislature, the representation must be considerably numerous—We have about 200 state senators in the United States. and a less number than that of federal representatives cannot, clearly, be a full representation of this people, in the affairs of internal taxation and police, were there but one legislature for the whole union. The representation cannot be equal, or the situation of the people proper for one government only—if the extreme parts of the society cannot be represented as fully as the central—It is apparently impracticable that this should be the case in this extensive country—it would be impossible to collect a representation of the parts of the country five, six, and seven hundred miles from the seat of government.

Under one general government alone, there could be but one judiciary, one supreme and a proper number of inferior courts. I think it would be totally impracticable in this case to preserve a due administration of justice, and the real benefits of the jury trial of the vicinage—there are now supreme courts in each state in the union, and a great number of county and other courts, subordinate to each supreme court—most of these supreme and inferior courts are itinerant, and hold their sessions in different parts every year of their respective states, counties and districts—with all these moving courts, our citizens, from the vast extent of the country, must travel very considerable distances from home to find the place where justice is administered. I am not for bringing justice so near to individuals as to afford them any temptation to engage in law suits; though I think it one of the greatest benefits in a good government, that each citizen should find a court of justice within a reasonable distance, perhaps, within a day's travel of his home; so that, without great inconveniences and enormous expense, he may have the

Pamphlets on the Constitution of the United States, pp. 288–325.

advantages of his witnesses and jury—it would be impracticable to derive these advantages from one judiciary—the one supreme court at most could only set in the centre of the union, and move once a year into the centre of the eastern and southern extremes of it—and, in this case, each citizen, on an average, would travel 150 or 200 miles to find this court—that, however, inferior courts might be properly placed in the different counties, and districts of the union, the appellate jurisdiction would be intolerable and expensive.

If it were possible to consolidate the states, and preserve the features of a free government, still it is evident that the middle states, the parts of the union, about the seat of government, would enjoy great advantages, while the remote states would experience the many inconveniences of remote provinces. Wealth, offices, and the benefits of government would collect in the centre: and the extreme states; and their principal towns, become much less important.

There are other considerations which tend to prove that the idea of one consolidated whole, on free principles, is illfounded—the laws of a free government rest on the confidence of the people, and operate gently—and never can extend the influence very far—if they are executed on free principles, about the centre, where the benefits of the government induce the people to support it voluntarily; yet they must be executed on the principles of fear and force in the extremes—This has been the case with every extensive republic of which we have any accurate account.

There are certain unalienable and fundamental rights, which in forming the social compact, ought to be explicitly ascertained and fixed—a free and enlightened people, in forming this compact, will not resign all their rights to those who govern, and they will fix limits to their legislators and rulers, which will soon be plainly seen by those who are governed, as well as by those who govern: and the latter will know they cannot be passed unperceived by the former, and without giving a general alarm. These rights should be made the basis of every constitution; and if a people be so situated, or have such different opinions that they cannot agree in ascertaining and fixing them, it is a very strong argument against their attempting to form one entire society, to live under one system of laws only. I confess, I never thought the people of these states differed essentially in these respects; they having derived all these rights from one common source, the British systems; and having in the formation of their state constitutions, discovered that their ideas relative to these rights are very similar. However, it is now said that the states differ so essentially in these respects, and even in the important article of the trial by jury, that when assembled in convention, they can agree to no words by which to establish that trial, or by which to ascertain and establish many other of these rights, as fundamental articles in the social compact. If so, we proceed to consolidate the states on no solid basis whatever.

But I do not pay much regard to the reasons given for not bottoming the new constitution on a better bill of rights. I still believe a complete federal bill of rights to be very practicable. Nevertheless I acknowledge the proceedings of the convention furnish my mind with many new and strong reasons, against a complete consolidation of the states. They tend to convince me, that it cannot be carried with propriety very far—that the convention have gone much farther in one respect than they found it practicable to go in another; that is, they propose to lodge in the general government very extensive powers—powers nearly, if not altogether, complete and unlimited, over the purse and the sword. But, in its organization, they furnish the strongest proof that the proper limbs, or parts of a government, to support and execute those powers on proper principles (or in which they can be safely lodged) cannot be formed. These powers must be lodged somewhere in every society; but then they should be lodged where the strength and guardians of the people are collected. They can be wielded, or safely used, in a free country only by an able executive and judiciary, a respectable senate, and a secure, full, and equal representation of the people. I think the principles I have premised or brought into view, are well founded—I think they will not be denied by any fair reasoner. It is in connection with these, and other solid principles, we are to examine the constitution. It is not a few democratic phrases, or a few well formed features, that will prove its merits; or a few small omissions that will produce its rejection among men of sense; they will enquire what are the essential powers in a community, and what are nominal ones; where and how the essential powers shall be lodged to secure government, and to secure true liberty.

In examining the proposed constitution carefully, we must clearly perceive an unnatural separation of these powers from the substantial representation of the people. The state government will exist, with all their governors, senators, representatives, officers and expences; in these will be nineteen twentieths of the representatives of the people; they will have a near connection, and their members an immediate intercourse with the people; and the probability is, that the state governments will possess the confidence of the people, and be considered generally as their immediate guardians.

The general government will consist of a new species of executive, a small senate, and a very small house of representatives. As many citizens will be more than three hundred miles from the seat of this government as will be nearer to it, its judges and officers cannot be very numerous, without making our governments very expensive. Thus will stand the state and the general governments, should the constitution be adopted without any alterations in their organization; but as to powers, the general government will possess all essential ones, at least on paper, and those of the states a mere shadow of power. And therefore, unless the people shall make some great exertions to restore to the state governments their powers in matters of internal police; as the powers to lay and collect, exclusively, internal taxes, to govern the militia, and to hold the decisions of their own judicial courts upon their own laws final, the balance cannot possibly continue long; but the state governments must be annihilated, or continue to exist for no purpose.

It is however to be observed, that many of the essential powers given the national government are not exclusively given; and the general government may have prudence enough to forbear the exercise of those which may still be exercised by the respective states. But this cannot justify the impropriety of giving powers, the exercise of which prudent men will not attempt, and imprudent men will, or probably can, exercise only in a manner destructive of free government. The general government, organized as it is, may be adequate to many valuable objects, and be able to carry its laws into execution on proper principles in several cases; but I think its warmest friends will not contend, that it can carry all the powers proposed to be lodged in it into effect, without calling to its aid a military force, which must very soon destroy all elective governments in the country, produce anarchy, or establish despotism. Though we cannot have now a complete idea of what will be the operations of the proposed system, we may, allowing things to have their common course, have a very tolerable one. The powers lodged in the general government, if exercised by it, must intimately effect the internal police of the states, as well as external concerns; and there is no reason to expect the numerous state governments, and their connections, will be very friendly to the execution of federal laws in those internal affairs, which hitherto have been under their own immediate management. There is more reason to believe, that the general government, far removed from the people, and none of its members elected oftener than once in two years, will be forgot or neglected, and its laws in many cases disregarded, unless a multitude of officers and military force be continually kept in view, and employed to enforce the execution of the laws, and to make the government feared and respected. No position can be truer than this. That in this country either neglected laws, or a military execution of them, must lead to a revolution, and to the destruction of freedom. Neglected laws must first lead to anarchy and confusion; and a military execution of laws is only a shorter way to the same point—despotic government.

Your's, &c.
The Federal Farmer

Oct. 12, 1787

Letter IV
Dear Sir,

It will not be possible to establish in the federal courts the jury trial of the vicinage so well as in the state courts.

Third, there appears to me to be not only a premature deposit of some important powers in the general government—but many of those deposited there are undefined, and may be used to good or bad purposes as honest or designing men shall prevail. By Art. 1, Sec. 2, representatives and direct taxes shall be apportioned among the several states, &c.—same art. sect. 8, the congress shall have powers to lay and collect taxes, duties, &c. for the common defence and general welfare, but all duties, imposts and excises, shall be uniform throughout the United States: By the first recited clause, direct taxes shall be apportioned on the states. This seems to favour the idea suggested by some sensible men and writers that congress, as to direct taxes, will only have power to make requisitions; but the latter clause, power to lay and collect taxes, &c. seems clearly to favour the contrary opinion, and, in my mind, the true one, the congress shall have power to tax immediately individuals, without the intervention of the state legislatures, in fact the first clause appears to me only to provide that each state shall pay a certain portion of the tax, and the latter to provide that congress shall have power to lay and collect taxes, that is to assess upon, and to collect of the individuals in the state, the states quota; but these still I consider as undefined powers, because judicious men understand them differently.

It is doubtful whether the vice-president is to have any qualifications; none are mentioned; but he may serve as president, and it may be inferred, he ought to be qualified therefore as the president; but the qualifications of the president are required only of the person to be elected president. By art. 2, sect. 2, "But the congress may by law vest the appointment of such inferior officers as they think proper in the president alone, in the courts of law, or in the heads of the departments:" Who are inferior officers? May not a congress disposed to vest the appointment of all officers in the president, under this clause, vest the appointment of almost every officer in the president alone, and destroy the check mentioned in the first part of the clause, and lodged in the senate. It is true, this check is badly lodged, but then some check upon the first magistrate in appointing officers, ought it appears by the opinion of the convention, and by the general opinion, to be established in the constitution. By art. 3, sect. 2, the supreme court shall have appellate jurisdiction as to law and facts with such exceptions, &c. to what extent is it intended the exceptions shall be carried—Congress may carry them so far as to annihilate substantially the appellate jurisdiction, and the clause be rendered of very little importance.

4th. There are certain rights which we have always held sacred in the United States, and recognized in all our constitutions, and which, by the adoption of the new constitution in its present form, will be left unsecured. By article 6, the proposed constitution, and the laws of the United States, which shall be made in pursuance thereof; and all treaties made, or which shall be made under the authority of the United States, shall be the supreme law of the land; and the judges in every state shall be bound thereby; anything in the constitution or laws of any state to the contrary notwithstanding.

It is to be observed that when the people shall adopt the proposed constitution it will be their last and supreme act; it will be adopted not by the people of New Hampshire, Massachusetts, &c., but by the people of the United States; and wherever this constitution, or any part of it, shall be incompatible with the ancient customs, rights, the laws or the constitutions heretofore established in the United States, it will entirely abolish them and do them away: And not only this, but the laws of the United States which shall be: made in pursuance of the federal constitution will be also supreme laws, and wherever they shall be incompatible with those customs, rights, laws or constitutions heretofore established, they will also entirely abolish them and do them away.

By the article before recited, treaties also made under the authority of the United States, shall be the supreme law: It is not said that these treaties shall be made in pursuance of the constitution—nor are there any constitutional bounds set to those who shall make them: The president and two-thirds of the senate will be empowered to make treaties indefinitely, and when these treaties shall be made, they will also abolish all laws and state constitutions incompatible with them. This power in the president and senate is absolute, and the judges will be bound to allow full force to whatever rule, article or thing the president and senate shall establish by treaty, whether it be practicable to set any bounds to those who make treaties, I am not able to say; if not, it proves that this power ought to be more safely lodged.

The federal constitution, the laws of congress made in pursuance of the constitution, and all treaties must have full force and effect in all parts of the United States; and all other laws, rights and constitutions which stand in their way must yield: It is proper the national laws should be supreme, and superior to state or district laws; but then the national laws ought to yield to unalienable or fundamental rights—and national laws, made by a few men, should extend only to a few national objects. This will not be the case with the laws of congress: To have any proper idea of their extent, we must carefully examine the legislative, executive and judicial powers proposed to be lodged in the general government, and consider them in connection with a general clause in art. 1, sect. 8, in these words (after enumerating a number of powers) "To make all laws which shall be necessary and proper for carrying into execution the foregoing powers, and all other powers vested by this constitution in the government of the United States, or in any department or officer thereof." The powers of this government as has been observed, extend to internal as well as external objects, and to those objects to which all others are subordinate; it is almost impossible to have a just conception of their powers, or of the extent and number of the laws which may be deemed necessary and proper to carry them into effect, till we shall come to exercise those powers and make the laws. In making laws to carry those powers into effect, it is to be expected, that a wise and prudent congress will pay respect to the opinions of a free people, and bottom their

laws on those principles which have been considered as essential and fundamental in the British, and in our government: But a congress of a different
character will not be bound by the constitution to pay respect to those
principles.

It is said that when people make a constitution, and delegate powers, that
all powers are not delegated by them to those who govern, is reserved in the
people; and that the people, in the present case, have reserved in themselves, and in their state governments, every right and power not expressly
given by the federal constitution to those who shall administer the national
government. It is said, on the other hand, that the people, when they make a
constitution, yield all power not expressly reserved to themselves. The truth
is, in either case, it is mere matter of opinion, and men usually take either
side of the argument, as will best answer their purposes: But the general
presumption being, that men who govern, will in doubtful cases, construe
laws and constitutions most favourably for increasing their own powers; all
wise and prudent people, in forming constitutions, have drawn the line, and
carefully described the powers parted with and the powers reserved. By the
state constitutions, certain rights have been reserved in the people; or rather,
they have been recognized and established in such a manner, that state
legislatures are bound to respect them, and to make no laws infringing upon
them. The state legislatures are obliged to take notice of the bills of rights of
their respective states. The bills of rights, and the state constitutions, are
fundamental compacts only between those who govern, and the people of the
same state.

In the year 1788 the people of the United States made a federal constitution, which is a fundamental compact between them and their federal rulers;
these rulers, in the nature of things, cannot be bound to take notice of any
other compact. It would be absurd for them, in making laws, to look over
thirteen, fifteen, or twenty state constitutions, to see what rights are established as fundamental, and must not be infringed upon, in making laws in
the society. It is true, they would be bound to do it if the people, in their
federal compact, should refer to the state constitutions, recognize all parts
not inconsistent with the federal constitution, and direct their federal rulers
to take notice of them accordingly; but this is not the case, as the plan stands
proposed at present; and it is absurd, to suppose so unnatural an idea is
intended or implied. I think my opinion is not only founded in reason, but I
think it is supported by the report of the convention itself. If there are a
number of rights established by the state constitutions, and which will remain
sacred, and the general government is bound to take notice of them—it must
take notice of one as well as another; and if unnecessary to recognize or
establish one by the federal constitution, it would be unnecessary to recognize or establish another by it. If the federal constitution is to be construed so
far in connection with the state constitution, as to leave the trial by jury in
civil causes, for instance, secured; on the same principles it would have left
the trial by jury in criminal causes, the benefits of the writ of habeas corpus,

&c. secured; they all stand on the same footing; they are the common rights of Americans, and have been recognized by the state constitutions: But the convention found it necessary to recognize or re-establish the benefits of that writ, and the jury trial in criminal cases. As to *expost facto* laws, the convention has done the same in one case, and gone further in another, It is a part of the compact between the people of each state and their rulers, that no *expost facto* laws shall be made. But the convention, by Art. 1, Sect. 10, have put a sanction upon this part even of the state compacts. In fact, the 9th and 10th Sections in Art. 1, in the proposed constitution, are no more nor less, than a partial bill of rights; they establish certain principles as part of the compact upon which the federal legislators and officers can never infringe. It is here wisely stipulated, that the federal legislature shall never pass a bill of attainder, or *expost facto* law; that no tax shall be laid on articles exported, &c. The establishing of one right implies the necessity of establishing another and similar one.

On the whole the position appears to me to be undeniable, that this bill of rights ought to be carried farther, and some other principles established, as a part of this fundamental compact between the people of the United States and their federal rulers.

It is true, we are not disposed to differ much, at present, about religion, but when we are making a constitution, it is to be hoped, for ages and millions yet unborn, why not establish the free exercise of religion, as a part of the national compact. There are other essential rights, which we have justly understood to be the rights of freemen; as freedom from hasty and unreasonable search warrants, warrants not founded on oath, and not issued with due caution, for searching and seizing men's papers, property, and persons. The trials by jury in civil causes, it is said, varies so much in the several states, that no words could be found for the uniform establishment of it. If so, the federal legislation will not be able to establish it by any general laws. I confess I am of opinion it may be established, but not in that beneficial manner in which we may enjoy it, for the reasons beforementioned. When I speak of the jury trial of the vicinage, or the trial of the fact in the neighborhood, I do not lay so much stress upon the circumstance of our being tried by our neighbours: in this enlightened country men may be probably impartially tried by those who do not live very near them: but the trial of facts in the neighbourhood is of great importance in other respects. Nothing can be more essential than the cross examining witnesses, and generally before the triers of the facts in question. The common people can establish facts with much more ease with oral than written evidence; when trials of facts are removed to a distance from the homes of the parties and witnesses, oral evidence becomes intolerably expensive, and the parties must depend on written evidence, which to the common people is expensive and almost useless; it must be frequently taken ex porte, and but very seldom leads to the proper discovery of truth.

The trial by jury is very important in another point of view. It is essential in every free country, that common people should have a part and share of influence, in the judicial as well as in the legislative department. To hold open to them the offices of senators, judges, and offices to fill which an expensive education is required, cannot answer any valuable purposes for them; they are not in a situation to be brought forward and to fill those offices; these, and most other offices of any considerable importance, will be occupied by the few. The few, the well born, &c. as Mr. Adams calls them, in judicial decisions as well as in legislation, are generally disposed, and very naturally too, to favour those of their own description.

The trial by jury in the judicial department, and the collection of the people by their representatives in the legislature, are those fortunate inventions which have procured for them, in this country, their true proportion of influence, and the wisest and most fit means of protecting themselves in the community. Their situation, as jurors and representatives, enables them to acquire information and knowledge in the affairs and government of the society; and to come forward, in turn, as the centinels and guardians of each other. I am very sorry that even a few of our countrymen should consider jurors and representatives in a different point of view, as ignorant, troublesome bodies, which ought not to have any share in the concerns of government.

I confess I do not see in what cases the congress can, with any pretence of right, make a law to suppress the freedom of the press; though I am not clear, that congress is restrained from laying any duties whatever on printing, and from laying duties particularly heavy on certain pieces printed, and perhaps congress may require large bonds for the payment of these duties. Should the printer say, the freedom of the press was secured by the constitution of the state in which he lived, congress might, and perhaps, with great propriety, answer, that the federal constitution is the only compact existing between them and the people; in this compact the people have named no others, and therefore congress, in exercising the powers assigned them, and in making laws to carry them into execution, are restrained by nothing beside the federal constitution, any more than a state legislature is restrained by a compact between the magistrates and people of a county, city, or town of which the people, in forming the state constitution, have taken no notice.

It is not my object to enumerate rights of inconsiderable importance; but there are others, no doubt, which ought to be established as a fundamental part of the national system.

It is worthy of observation, that all treaties are made by foreign nations with a confederacy of thirteen states—that the western country is attached to thirteen states—thirteen states have jointly and severally engaged to pay the public debts. Should a new government be formed of nine, ten, eleven, or twelve states, those treaties could not be considered as binding on the foreign nations who made them. However, I believe the probability to be, that if nine states adopt the constitution, the others will.

It may also be worthy our examination, how far the provision for amending this plan, when it shall be adopted, is of any importance. No measures can be taken towards amendments, unless two-thirds of the congress, or two-thirds of the legislature of the several states shall agree. While power is in the hands of the people, or democratic part of the community, more especially as at present, it is easy, according to the general course of human affairs, for the few influential men in the community, to obtain conventions, alterations in government, and to persuade the common people that they may change for the better, and to get from them a part of the power: But when power is once transferred from the many to the few, all changes become extremely difficult; the government, is this case, being beneficial to the few, they will be exceedingly artful and adroit in preventing any measures which may lead to a change; and nothing will produce it, but great exertions and severe struggles on the part of the common people. Every man of reflection must see, that the change now proposed, is a transfer of power from the many to the few, and the probability is, the artful and ever active aristocracy, will prevent all peaceful measures for changes, unless when they shall discover some favorable moment to increase their own influence. I am sensible, thousands of men in the United States are disposed to adopt the proposed constitution, though they perceive it to be essentially defective, under an idea that amendments of it, may be obtained when necessary. This is a pernicious idea, it argues a servility of character totally unfit for the support of free government; it is very repugnant to that perpetual jealousy respecting liberty, so absolutely necessary in all free states, spoken of by Mr. Dickinson. However, if our countrymen are so soon changed, and the language of 1774, is become odious to them, it will be in vain to use the language of freedom, or to attempt to rouse them to free enquires: But I shall never believe this is the case with them, whatever present appearances may be, till I shall have very strong evidence indeed of it.

Your's, &c.
The Federal Farmer

Oct. 15, 1787

Letter V
Dear Sir,

Thus I have examined the federal constitution as far as a few days leisure would permit. It opens to my mind a new scene; instead of seeing powers cautiously lodged in the hands of numerous legislators, and many magistrates we see all important powers collecting in one centre, where a few men will possess them almost at discretion. And instead of checks in the formation of the government, to secure the rights of the people against the usurpations of those they appoint to govern, we are to understand the equal division of lands among our people, and the strong arm furnished them by nature and situation, are to secure them against those usurpations. If there are advantages in the equal division of our lands, and the strong and manly habits of our people, we ought to establish governments calculated to give duration to them, and not governments which never can work naturally, till that equality of property, and those free and manly habits shall be destroyed: these evidently are not the natural basis of the proposed constitution. No man of reflection, and skilled in the science of goverment, can suppose these will move on harmoniously together for ages, or even for fifty years. As to the little circumstances commented upon, by some writers, with applause—as the age of a representative, of the president, &c.—they have, in my mind, no weight in the general tendency of the system.

There are, however, in my opinion, many good things in the proposed system. It is founded on elective principles, and the deposits of powers in different hands, is essentially right. The guards against those evils we have experienced in some states in legislation are valuable indeed; but the value of every feature in this system is vastly lessened for the want of that one important feature in a free government, a representation of the people. Because we have sometimes abused democracy, I am not among those men who think a democratic branch a nuisance; which branch shall be sufficiently numerous to admit some of the best informed men of each order in the community into the administration of government.

While the radical defects in the proposed system are not so soon discovered, some temptations to each state, and to many classes of men to adopt it, are very visible. It uses the democratic language of several of the state constitutions, particularly that of Massachusetts, the eastern states will receive advantages so far as the regulation of trade, by a bare majority, is committed to it: Connecticut and New Jersey will receive their share of a general impost: The middle states will receive the advantages surrounding the seat of government; The southern states will receive protection, and have their negroes represented in the legislature, and large back countries will soon have a majority in it. This system promises a large field of employment to military gentlemen, and gentlemen of the law; and in case the government shall be executed without convulsions, it will afford security to creditors, to the clergy, salary-men and others depending on money payments. So far as the system promises justice and reasonable advantages, in these respects, it ought to be supported by all honest men; but whenever it promises unequal and improper advantages to any particular states, or orders of men, it ought to be opposed.

I have, in the course of these letters observed, that there are many good things in the proposed constitution, and I have endeavored to point out many important defects in it. I have admitted that we want a federal system—that we have a system presented, which, with several alterations may be made a tolerable good one—I have admitted there is a well founded uneasiness among creditors and mercantile men. In this situation of things, you ask me what I think ought to be done? My opinion in this case is only the opinion of an individual, and so far only as it corresponds with the opinions of the honest and substantial part of the community, is it entitled to consideration. Though I am fully satisfied that the state conventions ought most seriously to direct their exertions to altering and amending the system proposed before they shall adopt it—yet I have not sufficiently examined the subject, or formed an opinion, how far it will be practicable for those conventions to carry their amendments. As to the idea, that it will be in vain for those conventions to attempt amendments, it cannot be admitted; it is impossible to say whether they can or not until the attempt shall be made; and when it shall be determined, by experience, that the conventions cannot agree in amendments, it will then be an important question before the people of the United States, whether they will adopt or not the system proposed in its present form. This subject of consolidating the states is new: and because forty or fifty men have agreed in a system, to suppose the good sense of this country, an enlightened nation, must adopt it without examination, and though in a state of profound peace, without endeavouring to amend those parts they perceive are defective, dangerous to freedom, and destructive of the valuable principles of republican government—is truly humiliating. It is true there may be danger in delay; but there is danger in adopting the system in its present form; and I see the danger in either case will arise principally from the conduct and views of two very unprincipled parties in the United States—two fires, between which the honest and substantial people have long found themselves situated. One party is composed of little insurgents, men in debt, who want no law, and who want a share of the property of others; these are called levellers, Shayites, &c. The other party is composed of a few, but more dangerous men, with their servile dependents; these avariciously grasp at all power and property; you may discover in all the actions of these men, an evident dislike to free and equal government, and they will go systematically to work to change, essentially, the forms of government in this country; these are called aristocrats, m—ites, &c. &c. Between these two parties is the weight of the community; the men of middling property, men not in debt on the one hand, and men, on the other, content with republican governments, and not aiming at immense fortunes, offices, and power. In 1786, the little insurgents, the levellers, came forth, invaded the rights of others, and attempted to establish governments according to their wills. Their movements evidently gave encouragement to the other party, which, in 1787, has taken the political field, and with its fashionable dependants, and the tongue and the pen, is endeavoring to establish in a great haste, a politer kind of government. These two parties, which will probably be opposed or united as it may suit their interests and views, are really insignificant, compared with the solid, free, and independent part of the community. It is not my intention to suggest, that either of these parties, and the real friends of the proposed

constitution, are the same men. The fact is, these aristocrats support and
hasten the adoption of the proposed constitution, merely because they think it
is a stepping stone to their favorite object. I think I am well founded in this
idea; I think the general politics of these men support it, as well as the
common observation among them, That the proffered plan is the best that
can be got at present, it will do for a few years, and lead to something better.
The sensible and judicious part of the community will carefully weigh all
these circumstances; they will view the late convention as a respectable body
of men—America probably never will see an assembly of men, of a like
number, more respectable. But the members of the convention met without
knowing the sentiments of one man in ten thousand in these states respecting
the new ground taken. Their doings are but the first attempts in the most
important scene ever opened. Though each individual in the state conventions will not, probably, be so respectable as each individual in the federal
convention, yet as the state conventions will probably consist of fifteen
hundred or two thousand men of abilities, and versed in the science of
government, collected from all parts of the community and from all orders of
men, it must be acknowledged that the weight of respectability will be in
them—In them will be collected the solid sense and the real political
character of the country. Being revisers of the subject, they will possess
peculiar advantages. To say that these conventions ought not to attempt,
coolly and deliberately, the revision of the system, or that they cannot amend
it, is very foolish or very assuming. If these conventions, after examining the
system, adopt it, I shall be perfectly satisfied, and wish to see men make the
administration of the government an equal blessing to all orders of men. I
believe the great body of our people to be virtuous and friendly to good
government, to the protection of liberty and property; and it is the duty of all
good men, especially of those who are placed as sentinels to guard their
rights—it is their duty to examine into the prevailing politics of parties, and
to disclose them—while they avoid exciting undue suspicions, to lay facts
before the people, which will enable them to form a proper judgment. Men
who wish the people of this country to determine for themselves, and
deliberately to fit the government to their situation, must feel some degree of
indignation at those attempts to hurry the adoption of a system, and to shut
the door against examination. The very attempts create suspicions, that those
who make them have secret views, or see some defects in the system, which,
in the hurry of affairs, they expect will escape the eye of a free people.

What can be the views of those gentlemen in Pennsylvania, who precipitated decisions on this subject? What can be the views of those gentlemen in
Boston, who countenanced the Printers in shutting up the press against a fair
and free investigation of this important system in the usual way. The
members of the convention have done their duty—why should some of them
fly to their states—almost forget a propriety of behavior, and precipitate
measures for the adoption of a system of their own making? I confess

candidly, when I consider these circumstances in connection with the un-guarded parts of the system I have mentioned, I feel disposed to proceed with very great caution, and to pay more attention than usual to the conduct of particular characters. If the constitution presented be a good one, it will stand the test with a well informed people: all are agreed that there shall be state conventions to examine it; and we must believe it will be adopted, unless we suppose it is a bad one, or that those conventions will make false divisions respecting it. I admit improper measures are taken against the adoption of the system as well for it—all who object to the plan proposed ought to point out the defects objected to, and to propose those amendments with which they can accept it, or to propose some other system of govern-ment, that the public mind may be known, and that we may be brought to agree in some system of government, to strengthen and execute the present, or to provide a substitute. I consider the field of enquiry just opened, and that we are to look to the state conventions for ultimate decisions on the subject before us; it is not to be presumed, that they will differ about small amendments, and lose a system when they shall have made it substantially good; but touching the essential amendments, it is to be presumed the several conventions will pursue the most rational measures to agree in and obtain them; and such defects as they shall discover and not remove, they will probably notice, keep them in view as the ground work of future amendments, and in the firm and manly language which every free people ought to use, will suggest to those who may hereafter administer the govern-ment, that it is their expectation, that the system will be so organized by legislative acts, and the government so administered, as to render those defects as little injurious as possible. Our countrymen are entitled to an honest and faithful government; to a government of laws and not of men; and also to one of their chusing—as a citizen of the country, I wish to see these objects secured, and licentious, assuming, and overbearing men res-trained; if the constitution or social compact be vague and unguarded, then we depend wholly upon the prudence, wisdom and moderation of those who manage the affairs of government; or on what, probably, is equally uncertain and precarious, the success of the people oppressed by the abuse of govern-ment, in receiving it from the hands of those who abuse it, and placing it in the hands of those who will use it well.

In every point of view, therefore, in which I have been able, as yet, to contemplate this subject, I can discern but one rational mode of proceeding relative to it: and that is to examine it with freedom and candour, to have state conventions some months hence, which shall examine coolly every article, clause, and word in the system proposed, and to adopt it with such amendments as they shall think fit. How far the state conventions ought to pursue the mode prescribed by the federal convention of adopting or rejec-ting the plan in toto, I leave it to them to determine. Our examination of the subject hitherto has been rather of a general nature. The republican characters in the several states, who wish to make this plan more adequate to security of liberty and property, and to the duration of the principles of a free government, will, no doubt, collect their opinions to certain points, and accurately define those alterations and amendments they wish; if it shall be found they essentially disagree in them, the conventions will then be able to determine whether to adopt the plan as it is, or what will be proper to be done.

Under these impressions, and keeping in view the improper and unadvisable lodgment of powers in the general government, organized as it at present is, touching internal taxes, armies and militia, the elections of its own members, causes between citizens of different states, &c. and the want of a more perfect bill of rights, &c. I drop the subject for the present, and when I shall have leisure to revise and correct my ideas respecting it, and to collect into points the opinions of those who wish to make the system more secure and safe, perhaps I may proceed to point out particularly for your consideration, the amendments which ought to be ingrafted into this system, not only in conformity to my own, but the deliberate opinions of others—you will with me perceive, that the objections to the plan proposed may, by a more leisure examination be set in a stronger point of view, especially the important one, that there is no substantial representation of the people provided for in a government in which the most essential powers, even as to the internal police of the country, is proposed to be lodged.

I think the honest and substantial part of the community will wish to see this system altered, permanency and consistency given to the constitution we shall adopt; and therefore they will be anxious to apportion the powers to the features and organizations of the government, and to see abuse in the exercise of power more effectually guarded against. It is suggested, that state officers, from interested motives will oppose the constitution presented—I see no reason for this, their places in general will not be effected, but new openings to offices and places of profit must evidently be made by the adoption of the constitution in its present form.

Your's, &c.
The Federal Farmer

Elbridge Gerry to the President of the Senate and Speaker of the House of Representatives, Massachusetts, 1787*

Oct. 18, 1787

Gentlemen,

I have the honour to inclose, pursuant to my commission, the constitution proposed by the federal convention.

* *The Records of the Federal Convention of 1787,* Vol. 3, pp. 128-29.

To this system I gave my dissent, and shall submit my objections to the honourable legislature.

It was painful for me, on a subject of such national importance, to differ from the respectable members who signed the constitution: But conceiving as I did, that the liberties of America were not secured by the system, it was my duty to oppose it.

My principal objections to the plan, are, that there is no adequate provision for a representation of the people—that they have no security for the right of election—that some of the powers of the legislature are ambiguous, and others indefinite and dangerous—that the executive is blended with, and will have an undue influence over, the legislature—that the judicial department will be oppressive—that treaties of the highest importance may be formed by the president with the advice of two-thirds of a quorum of the senate—and that the system is without the security of a bill of rights. These are objections which are not local, but apply equally to all the states.

As the convention was called for "the sole and express purpose of revising the articles of confederation, and reporting to congress, and the several legislatures, such alterations and provisions as shall render the federal constitution adequate to the exigencies of government, and the preservation of the union," I did not conceive that these powers extend to the formation of the plan proposed: but the convention being of a different opinion, I acquiesced in it, being fully convinced that to preserve the union, an efficient government was indispensably necessary; and that it would be difficult to make proper amendments to the articles of confederation.

The constitution proposed has few if any federal features; but is rather a system of national government. Nevertheless, in many respects, I think it has great merit, and, by proper amendments, may be adapted to the "exigencies of government, and preservation of liberty."

Observations on the New Constitution and the Federal and State Conventions, 1788*

By Elbridge Gerry

Mankind may amuse themselves with theoretick systems of liberty, and trace its social and moral effects on sciences, virtue, industry and every improvement of which the human mind is capable; but we can only discern its true value by the practical and wretched effects of slavery; and thus dreadfully will they be realized, when the inhabitants of the Eastern States are dragging out a miserable existence, only on the gleanings of their fields; and the Southern, blessed with a softer and more fertile climate, are languishing in hopeless poverty; and when asked, what is become of the flower

*Pamphlets on the Constitution of the United States, pp. 1–23.

of their crop, and the rich produce of their farms—they may answer in the hapless stile of the Man of La Mancha,—"The "steward of my Lord has seized and sent it to Madrid." Or, in the more literal language of truth, the exigencies of government require that the collectors of the revenue should transmit it to the Federal City

Animated with the firmest zeal for the interest of this country, the peace and union of the American States, and the freedom and happiness of a people who have made the most costly sacrifices in the cause of liberty, who have braved the power of Britain, weathered the convulsions of war, and waded thro' the blood of friends and foes to establish their independence and to support the freedom of the human mind; I cannot silently witness this degradation without calling on them, before they are compelled to blush at their own servitude, and to turn back their languid eyes on their lost liberties—to consider, that the character of nations generally changes at the moment of revolution. And when patriotism is discountenanced and publick virtue becomes the ridicule of the sycophant—when every man of liberality, firmness and penetration who cannot lick the hand stretched out to oppress, is deemed an enemy to the State—then is the gulph of despotism set open, and the grades to slavery, though rapid, are scarce perceptible—then genius drags heavily its iron chain—science is neglected, and real merit flies to the shades for security from reproach—the mind becomes enervated, and the national character sinks to a kind of apathy with only energy sufficient to curse the breast that gave it milk, and as an elegant writer observes, "To bewail every new birth as an increase of misery, under a government where the mind is necessarily debased, and talents are seduced to become the panegyrists of usurpation and tyranny." He adds, "that even sedition is not the most indubitable enemy to the publick welfare; but that its most dreadful foe is despotism which always changes the character of nations for the worse, and is productive of nothing but vice, that the tyrant no longer excites to the pursuits of glory or virtue; it is not talents, it is baseness and servility that he cherishes, and the weight of arbitrary power destroys the spring of emulation."[1] If such is the influence of government on the character and manners, and undoubtedly the observation is just, must we not subscribe to the opinion of the celebrated Abbé Mablé? "That there are disagreeable seasons in the unhappy situation of human affairs, when policy requires both the intention and the power of doing mischief to be punished; and when the senate proscribed the memory of Caesar they ought to have put Anthony to death, and extinguished the hopes of Octavius." Self defence is a primary law of nature, which no subsequent law of society can abolish; this primaeval principle, the immediate gift of the Creator, obliges every one to remonstrate against the strides of ambition, and a wanton lust of domination, and to resist the first approaches of tyranny, which at this day threaten to sweep

[1]Helvitius.

away the rights for which the brave sons of America have fought with an heroism scarcely paralleled even in ancient republicks. It may be repeated, they have purchased it with their blood, and have gloried in their independence with a dignity of spirit, which has made them the admiration of philosophy, the pride of America, and the wonder of Europe. It has been observed, with great propriety, that the virtues and vices of a people "when a revolution happens in their government, are the measure of the liberty or slavery they ought to expect. An heroic love for the publick good, a profound reverence for the laws, a contempt of riches, and a noble haughtiness of soul, are the only foundations of a free government."[2] Do not their dignified principles still exist among us? Or are they extinguished in the breasts of Americans, whose fields have been so recently crimsoned to repel the potent arm of a foreign Monarch, who had planted his engines of slavery in every city, with design to erase the vestiges of freedom in this his last asylum. It is yet to be hoped, for the honour of human nature, that no combinations either foreign or domestick have thus darkned this Western hemisphere. On these shores freedom has planted her standard, diped in the purple tide that flowed from the veins of her martyred horoes; and here every uncorrupted American yet hopes to see it supported by the vigour, the justice, the wisdom and unanimity of the people, in spite of the deep-laid plots, the secret intrigues, or the bold effrontery of those interested and avaricious adventurers for place, who intoxicated with the ideas of distinction and preferment have prostrated every worthy principle beneath the shrine of ambition. Yet these are the men who tell us republicanism is dwindled into theory—that we are incapable of enjoying our liberties—and that we must have a master. Let us retrospect the days of our adversity, and recollect who were then our friends; do we find them among the sticklers for aristocratick authority? No, they were generally the same men who now wish to save us from the distractions of anarchy on the one hand, and the jaws of tyranny on the other; where then were the class who now come forth importunately urging that our political salvation depends on the adoption of a system at which freedom spurns? Were not some of them hidden in the corners of obscurity, and others wrapping themselves in the bosom of our enemies for safety? Some of them were in the arms of infancy; and others speculating for fortune, by sporting with public money; while a few, a very few of them were magnanimously defending their country, and raising a character, which I pray heaven may never be sullied by aiding measures derogatory to their former exertions. But the revolutions in principle which time produces among mankind, frequently exhibits the most mortifying instances of human weakness; and this alone can account for the extraordinary appearance of a few names, once distinguished in the honourable walks of patriotism, but now found in the list of the Massachusetts assent to the ratification of a Constitu-

[2] Abbé Mablé.

tion, which, by the undefined meaning of some parts, and the ambiguities of expression in others, is dangerously adapted to the purposes of an immediate aristocratic tyranny; that from the difficulty, if not impracticability of its operation, must soon terminate in the most uncontrouled despotism.

All writers on government agree, and the feelings of the human mind witness the truth of these political axioms, that man is born free and possessed of certain unalienable rights—that government is instituted for the protection, safety and happiness of the people, and not for the profit, honour, or private interest of any man, family, or class of men—That the origin of all power is in the people, and that they have an incontestible right to check the creatures of their own creation, vested with certain powers to guard the life, liberty and property of the community: And if certain selected bodies of men, deputed on these principles, determine contrary to the wishes and expectations of their constituents, the people have an undoubted right to reject their decisions, to call for a revision of their conduct, to depute others in their room, or if they think proper, to demand further time for deliberation on matters of the greatest moment: it therefore is an unwarrantable stretch of authority or influence, if any methods are taken to preclude this peaceful and reasonable mode of enquiry and decision. And it is with inexpressible anxiety, that many of the best friends of the Union of the States—to the peaceable and equal participation of the rights of nature, and to the glory and dignity of this country, behold the insiduous arts, and the strenuous efforts of the partisans of arbitrary power, by their vague definitions of the best established truths, endeavoring to envelope the mind in darkness the concomitant of slavery, and to lock the strong chains of domestic despotism on a country, which by the most glorious and successful struggles is but newly emancipated from the spectre of foreign dominion. But there are certain seasons in the course of human affairs, when Genius, Virtue, and Patriotism, seems to nod over the vices of the times, and perhaps never more remarkably, than at the present period; or we should not see such a passive disposition prevail in some, who we must candidly suppose, have liberal and enlarged sentiments; while a supple multitude are paying a blind and idolatrous homage to the opinions of those who by the most precipitate steps are treading down their dear bought privileges; and who are endeavouring by all the arts of insinuation, and influence, to betray the people of the United States, into an acceptance of a most complicated system of government; marked on the one side with the dark, secret and profound intrigues, of the statesman, long practised in the purlieus of despotism; and on the other, with the ideal projects of young ambition, with its wings just expanded to soar to a summit, which imagination has painted in such gawdy colours as to intoxicate the inexperienced votary, and to send him rambling from State to State, to collect materials to construct the ladder of preferment.

But as a variety of objections to the heterogeneous phantom, have been repeatedly laid before the public by men of the best abilities and intentions;

I will not expatiate long on a Republican form of government, founded on the principles of monarchy—a democratick branch with the features of artistocracy—and the extravagance of nobility pervading the minds of many of the candidates for office, with the poverty of peasantry hanging heavily on them, and insurmountable, from their taste for expence, unless a general provision should be made in the arrangement of the civil list, which may enable them with the champions of their cause to "sail down the new pactolean channel." Some gentlemen, with laboured zeal, have spent much time in urging the necessity of government, from the embarrassments of trade—the want of respectability abroad and confidence of the public engagements at home: These are obvious truths which no one denies; and there are few who do not unite in the general wish for the restoration of public faith, the revival of commerce, arts, agriculture, and industry, under a lenient, peaceable and energetick government: But the most sagacious advocates for the party have not by fair discusion, and rational argumentation, evinced the necessity of adopting this many headed monster; of such motley mixture, that its enemies cannot trace a feature of Democratick or Republican extract; nor have its friends the courage to denominate a Monarchy, an Aristocracy, or an Oligarchy, and the favoured bantling must have passed through the short period of its existence without a name, had not Mr. Wilson, in the fertility of his genius, suggested the happy epithet of a Federal Republic. But I leave the field of general censure on the secresy of its birth, the rapidity of its growth, and the fatal consequences of suffering it to live to the age of maturity, and will particularize some of the most weighty objections to its passing through this continent in a gigantic size. It will be allowed by every one that the fundamental principle of a free government is the equal representation of a free people—And I will first observe with a justly celebrated writer, "That the principal aim of society is to protect individuals in the absolute rights which were vested in them by the immediate laws of nature, but which could not be preserved in peace, without the mutual intercourse which is gained by the institution of friendly and social communities." And when society has thus deputed a certain number of their equals to take care of their personal rights, and the interest of the whole community, it must be considered that responsibility is the great security of integrity and honour; and that annual election is the basis of responsibility,—Man is not immediately corrupted, but power without limitation, or amenability, may endanger the brightest virtue—whereas a frequent return to the bar of their Constituents is the strongest check against the corruptions to which men are liable, either from the intrigues of others of more subtle genius, or the propensities of their own hearts,—and the gentlemen who have so warmly advocated in the late Convention of the Massachusetts, the change from annual to biennial elections; may have been in the same predicament, and perhaps with the same views that Mr. Hutchinson once acknowledged himself, when in a letter to Lord Hillsborough, he observed, "that the grand difficulty of making a change in government against the general bent of the people had caused him to turn his thoughts to a variety of plans, in order to find one that might be executed in spite of opposition," and the first he proposed was that, "instead of annual, the elections should be only once in three years:" but the Minister had not the hardiness to attempt such an innovation, even in the revision of colonial charters: nor has any one ever defended Biennial, Triennial or Septennial Elections, either in the British House of Commons, or in the debates of Provincial assemblies, on general and free principles: but it is unnecessary to dwell long on this article, as the best political writers have supported the principles of annual elections with a precision, that cannot be confuted, though they may be darkned, by the sophistical arguments that have been thrown out with design, to undermine all the barriers of freedom.

2. There is no security in the profered system, either for the rights of conscience or the liberty of the Press: Despotism usually while it is gaining ground, will suffer men to think, say, or write what they please; but when once established, if it is thought necessary to subserve the purposes, of arbitrary power, the most unjust restrictions may take place in the first instance, and an imprimator on the Press in the next, may silence the complaints, and forbid the most decent remonstrances of an injured and oppressed people.

3. There are no well defined limits of the Judiciary Powers, they seem to be left as a boundless ocean, that has broken over the chart of the Supreme Lawgiver, "thus far shalt thou go and no further," and as they cannot be comprehended by the clearest capacity, or the most sagacious mind, it would be an Herculean labour to attempt to describe the dangers with which they are replete.

4. The Executive and the Legislative are so dangerously blended as to give just cause of alarm, and everything relative thereto, is couched in such ambiguous terms—in such vague and indefinite expression, as is a sufficient ground without any objection, for the reprobation of a system, that the authors dare not hazard to a clear investigation.

5. The abolition of trial by jury in civil causes. This mode of trial the learned Judge Blackstone observes, "has been coeval with the first rudiments of civil government, that property, liberty and life, depend on maintaining in its legal force the constitutional trial by jury." He bids his readers pauze, and with Sir Matthew Hale observes, how admirably this mode is adapted to the investigation of truth beyond any other the world can produce. Even the party who have been disposed to swallow, without examination, the proposals of the secret conclave, have started on a discovery that this essential right was curtailed; and shall a privilege, the origin of which may be traced to our Saxon ancestors—that has been a part of the law of nations, even in the fewdatory systems of France, Germany and Italy—and from the earliest records has been held so sacred, both in ancient and modern Britain, that it

could never be shaken by the introduction of Norman customs, or any other conquests or change of government—shall this inestimable privilege be relinquished in America—either thro' the fear of inquisition for unaccounted thousands of public monies in the hands of some who have been officious in the fabrication of the consolidated system, or from the apprehension that some future delinquent possessed of more power than integrity, may be called to a trial by his peers in the hour of investigation.

6. Though it has been said by Mr. Wilson and many others, that a Standing-Army is necessary for the dignity and safety of America, yet freedom revolts at the idea, when the Divan, or the Despot, may draw out his dragoons to suppress the murmurs of a few, who may yet cherish those sublime principles which call forth the exertions, and lead to the best improvements of the human mind. It is hoped this country may yet be governed by milder methods than are usually displayed beneath the bannerets of military law. Standing armies have been the nursery of vice and the bane of liberty from the Roman legions to the establishment of the artful Ximenes, and from the ruin of the Cortes of Spain, to the planting of the British cohorts in the capitals of America: By the edicts of an authority vested in the sovereign power by the proposed constitution, the militia of the country, the bulwark of defence, and the security of national liberty is no longer under the controul of civil authority; but at the rescript of the Monarch, or the aristocracy, they may either be employed to extort the enormous sums that will be necessary to support the civil list—to maintain the regalia of power—and the splendour of the most useless part of the community, or they may be sent into foreign countries for the fulfilment of treaties, stipulated by the President and two-thirds of the Senate.

7. Notwithstanding the delusory promise to guarantee a Republican form of government to every State in the Union. If the most discerning eye could discover any meaning at all in the engagement, there are no resources left for the support of internal government, or the liquidation of the debts of the State. Every source of revenue is in the monopoly of Congress, and if the several legislatures in their enfeebled state, should against their own feelings be necessitated to attempt a dry tax for the payment of their debts, and the support of internal police, even this may be required for the purposes of the general government.

8. As the new Congress are empowered to determine their own salaries, the requisitions for this purpose may not be very moderate, and the drain for public moneys will probably rise past all calculation: and it is to be feared when America has consolidated its despotism, the world will witness the truth of the assertion—"that the pomp of an Eastern monarch may impose on the vulgar who may estimate the force of a nation by the magnificence palaces; but the wise man judges differently, it is by that very magnificence he estimates its weakness. He sees nothing more in the midst of this imposing pomp, where the tyrant sets enthroned, than a sumptuous and mournful

decoration of the dead; the apparatus of a fastuous funeral, in the centre of which is a cold and lifeless lump of unanimated earth, a phantom of power ready to disappear before the enemy, by whom it is despised!''

9. There is no provision for a rotation, nor anything to prevent the perpetuity of office in the same hands for life; which by a little well timed bribery, will probably be done, to the exclusion of men of the best abilities from their share in the offices of government. By this neglect we lose the advantages of that check to the overbearing insolence of office, which by rendering him ineligible at certain periods, keeps the mind of man in equilibrio, and teaches him the feelings of the governed, and better qualifies him to govern in his turn.

10. The inhabitants of the United States, are liable to be draged from the vicinity of their own country, or state, to answer the litigious or unjust suit of an adversary, on the most distant borders of the Continent: in short the appelate jurisdiction of the Supreme Federal Court, includes an unwarrantable stretch of power over the liberty, life, and property of the subject, through the wide Continent of America.

11. One Representative to thirty thousand inhabitants is a very inadequate representation; and every man who is not lost to all sense of freedom to his country, must reprobate the idea of Congress altering by law, or on any pretence whatever, interfering with any regulations for time, places, and manner of choosing our own Representatives.

12. If the sovereignty of America is designed to be elective, the surcumscribing the votes to only ten electors in this State, and the same proportion in all the others, is nearly tantamount to the exclusion of the voice of the people in the choice of their first magistrate. It is vesting the choice solely in an aristocratic junto, who may easily combine in each State to place at the head of the Union the most convenient instrument for despotic sway.

13. A Senate chosen for six years will, in most instances, be an appointment for life, as the influence of such a body over the minds of the people will be coequal to the extensive powers with which they are vested, and they will not only forget, but be forgotten by their constituents—a branch of the Supreme Legislature thus set beyond all responsibility is totally repugnant to every principle of a free government.

14. There is no provision by a bill of rights to guard against the dangerous encroachments of power in too many instances to be named: but I cannot pass over in silence the insecurity in which we are left with regard to warrants unsupported by evidence—the daring experiment of granting writs of assistance in a former arbitrary administration is not yet forgotten in the Massachusetts; nor can we be so ungrateful to the memory of the patriots who counteracted their operation, as so soon after their manly exertions to save us from such a detestable instrument of arbitrary power, to subject ourselves to the insolence of any petty revenue officer to enter our houses,

search, insult, and seize at pleasure. We are told by a gentleman of too much virtue and real probity to suspect he has a design to deceive—"that the whole constitution is a declaration of rights,"—but mankind must think for themselves, and to many very judicious and discerning characters, the whole constitution with very few exceptions appears a perversion of the rights of particular states, and of private citizens. But the gentleman goes on to tell us, "that the primary object is the general government, and that the rights of individuals are only incidentally mentioned, and that there was a clear impropriety in being very particular about them." But, asking pardon for dissenting from such respectable authority, who has been led into several mistakes, more from his prediliction in favour of certain modes of government, than from a want of understanding or veracity. The rights of individuals ought to be the primary object of all government, and cannot be too securely guarded by the most explicit declarations in their favor. This has been the opinion of the Hampdens, the Pyms, and many other illustrious names, that have stood forth in defence of English liberties; and even the Italian master in politicks, the subtle and renouned Machiavel acknowledges, that no republic ever yet stood on a stable foundation without satisfying the common people.

15. The difficulty, if not impracticability, of exercising the equal and equitable powers of government by a single legislature over an extent of territory that reaches from the Mississippi to the Western lakes, and from them to the Atlantic Ocean, is an insuperable objection to the adoption of the new system. Mr. Hutchinson, the great champion for arbitrary power, in the multitude of his machinations to subvert the liberties in this country, was obliged to acknowledge in one of his letters, that, "from the extent of country from north to south, the scheme of one government was impracticable." But if the authors of the present visionary project, can by the arts of deception, precipitation and address, obtain a majority of suffrages in the conventions of the states to try the hazardous experiment, they may then make the same inglorious boast with this insidious politician, who may perhaps be their model, that "the union of the colonies was pretty well broken, and that he hoped to never see it revewed."

16. It is an undisputed fact that not one legislature in the United States had the most distant idea when they first appointed members for a convention, entirely commercial, or when they afterwards authorized them to consider on some amendments of the Federal union, that they would without any warrant from their constituents, presume on so bold and daring a stride, as ultimately to destroy the state governments, and offer a consolidated system, irreversible but on conditions that the smallest degree of penetration must discover to be impracticable.

17. The first appearance of the article which declares the ratification of nine states sufficient for the establishment of the new system, wears the face

of dissension, is a subversion of the union of Confederated States, and tends to the introduction of anarchy and civil convulsions, and may be a means of involving the whole country in blood.

18. The mode in which this constitution is recommended to the people to judge without either the advice of Congress, or the legislatures of the several states is very reprehensible—it is an attempt to force it upon them before it could be thoroughly understood, and may leave us in that situation, that in the first moments of slavery in the minds of the people agitated by the remembrance of their lost liberties, will be like the sea in a tempest, that sweeps down every mound of security.

But it is needless to enumerate other instances, in which the proposed constitution appears contradictory to the first principles which ought to govern mankind; and it is equally so to enquire into the motives that induced to so bold a step as the annihilation of the independence and sovereignty of the thirteen distinct states. They are but too obvious through the whole progress of the business, from the first shutting up the doors of the federal convention and resolving that no member should correspond with gentlemen in the different states on the subject under discussion; till the trivial proposition of recommending a few amendments was artfully ushered into the convention of the Massachusetts. The questions that were then before that honorable assembly were profound and important, they were of such magnitude and extent, that the consequences may run parallel with the existence of the country; and to see them waved and hastily terminated by a measure too absurd to require a serious refutation, raises the honest indignation of every true lover of his country. Nor are they less grieved that the ill policy and arbitrary disposition of some of the sons of America has thus precipitated to the contemplation and discussion of questions that no one could rationally suppose would have been agitated among us, till time had blotted out the principles on which the late revolution was grounded; or till the last traits of the many political tracts, which defended the separation from Britain, and the rights of men were consigned to everlasting oblivion. After the severe conflicts this country has suffered, it is presumed that they are disposed to make every reasonable sacrifice before the altar of peace. But when we contemplate the nature of men and consider them originally on an equal footing, subject to the same feelings, stimulated by the same passions, and recollecting the struggles they have recently made, for the security of their civil rights; it cannot be expected that the inhabitants of the Massachusetts, can be easily lulled into a fatal security, by the declamatory effusions of gentlemen, who, contrary to the experience of all ages would perswade them there is no danger to be apprehended, from vesting discretionary powers in the hands of man, which he may, or may not abuse. The very suggestion, that we ought to trust to the precarious hope of amendments and redress, after we have voluntarily fixed the shackles on our own necks should have awakened to a double degree of caution. This people have not forgotten the artful insinuations of a former Governor, when pleading the unlimited authority of parliament before the legislature of the Massachusetts; nor that his arguments were very similar to some lately urged by gentlemen who boast of opposing his measures, "with halters about their necks."

We were then told by him, in all the soft language of insinuation, that no form of government, of human construction can be perfect—that we had nothing to fear—that we had no reason to complain—that we had only to acquiesce in their illegal claims, and to submit to the requisition of parliament, and doubtless the lenient hand of government would redress all grievances, and remove the oppressions of the people: Yet we soon saw armies of mercenaries encamped on our plains—our commerce ruined—our harbours blockaded—and our cities burnt. It may be replied that this was in consequence of an obstinate defence of our privileges; this may be true; and when the "ultima ratio" is called to aid, the weakest must fall. But let the best informed historian produce an instance when bodies of men were entrusted with power, and the proper checks relinquished, if they were ever found destitute of ingenuity sufficient to furnish pretences to abuse it. And the people at large are already sensible, that the liberties which America has claimed, which reason has justified, and which have been so gloriously defended by the swords of the brave; are not about to fall before the tyranny of foreign conquest; it is native usurpation that is shaking the foundations of peace, and spreading the sable curtain of despotism over the United States. The banners of freedom were erected in the wilds of America by our ancestors, while the wolf prowled for his prey on the one hand, and more savage man on the other; they have been since rescued from the invading hand of foreign power, by the valor and blood of their posterity; and there was reason to hope they would continue for ages to illumine a quarter of the globe, by nature kindly separated from the proud monarchies of Europe, and the infernal darkness of Asiatic slavery. And it is to be feared we shall soon see this country rushing into the extremes of confusion and violence, in consequence of the proceeding of a set of gentlemen, who disregarding the purposes of their appointment, have assumed powers unauthorized by any commission, have unnecessarily rejected the confederation of the United States, and annihilated the sovereignty and independence of the individual governments. The causes which have inspired a few men to assemble for very different purposes with such a degree of temerity as to break with a single stroke the union of America, and disseminate the seeds of discord through the land may be easily investigated, when we survey the partizans of monarchy in the state conventions, urging the adoption of a mode of government that militates with the former professions and exertions of this country, and with all ideas of republicanism, and the equal rights of men.

Passion, prejudice, and error, are characteristics of human nature; and as it cannot be accounted for on any principles of philosophy, religion, or good policy; to these shades in the human character must be attributed the mad zeal of some, to precipitate to a blind adoption of the measures of the late federal convention, without giving opportunity for better information to those who are misled by influence or ignorance into erroneous opinions. Litterary talents may be prostituted and the powers of genius debased to subserve the purposes of ambition or avarice; but the feelings of the heart will dictate the language of truth, and the simplicity of her accents will proclaim the infamy of those, who betray the rights of the people, under the specious, and popular pretence of justice, consolidation, and dignity.

*   *   *

Though the virtues of a Cato could not save Rome, nor the abilities of a Padilla defend the citizens of Castile from falling under the yoke of Charles; yet a Tell once suddenly rose from a little obscure city, and boldly rescued the liberties of his country. Every age has its Bruti and its Decci, as well as its Caesars and Sejani: The happiness of mankind depends much on the modes of government, and the virtues of the governors; and America may yet produce characters who have genius and capacity sufficient to form the manners and correct the morals of the people, and virtue enough to lead their country to freedom, Since their dismemberment from the British empire, America has, in many instances, resembled the conduct of a restless, vigorous, luxurious youth, prematurely emancipated from the authority of a parent, but without the experience necessary to direct him to act with dignity or discretion. Thus we have seen her break the shackles of foreign dominion, and all the blessings of peace restored on the most honourable terms: She acquired the liberty of framing her own laws, choosing her own magistrates, and adopting manners and modes of government the most favourable to the freedom and happiness of society. But how little have we availed ourselves of these superior advantages: The glorious fabric of liberty successfully reared with so much labor and assiduity totters to the foundation, and may be blown away as the bubble of fancy by the rude breath of military combinations, and politicians of yesterday.

It is true this country lately armed in opposition to regal despotism—improverished by the expences of a long war, and unable immediately to fulfil their public or private engagements that appeared in some instances, with a boldness of spirit that seemed to set at defiance all authority, government, or order, on the one hand; while on the other, there has been, not only a secret wish, but an open avowal of the necessity of drawing the reins of government much too taught, not only for a republicanism, but for a wise and limited monarchy. But the character of this people is not averse to a degree of subordination, the truth of this appears from the easy restoration of tranquility, after a dangerous insurrection in one of the states; this also evinces a little necessity of a complete revolution of government throughout the union. But it is a republican principle that the majority should rule; and if a spirit of moderation should be cultivated on both sides, till the voice of the people at large could be fairly heard it should be held sacred. And if, on such a scrutiny, the proposed constitution should appear repugnant to their character and wishes; if they, in the language of a late elegant pen, should acknowledge that "no confusion in my mind, is more terrible to them than the stern disciplined regularity and vaunted police of arbitrary governments, where every heart is depraved by fear, where mankind dare not assume their natural characters, where the free spirit must crouch to the slave in office, where genius must repress her effusions, or like the Egyptian worshippers, offer them in sacrifice to the calves in power, and where the human mind, always in shackles, shrinks from every generous effort." Who would then have the effrontery to say, it ought not to be thrown out with indignation, however some respectable names have appeared to support it. But if after all, on a dispassionate and fair discussion, the people generally give their voices for a voluntary dereliction of their privileges, let every individual who chooses the active scenes of life strive to support the peace and unanimity of his country, though every other blessing may expire—And while the states-man is plodding for power, and the courtier practising the arts of dissimula-tion without check—while the rapacious are growing rich by oppression, and fortune throwing her gifts into the lap of fools, let the sublimer characters, the philosophic lovers of freedom who have wept over her exit, retire to the calm shades of contemplation, there they may look down with pity on the inconsistency of human nature, the revolutions of states, the rise of king-doms, and the fall of empires.

The Letters of Luther Martin, 1788*

Mar. 21, 1788

Number II

To the Citizens of Maryland,

In the recognition which the Landholder professes to make "of what occurred to my advantage," he equally deals in the arts of misrepresentation, as while he was "only the record of the bad," and I am equally obliged from a regard to truth to disclaim his pretended approbation as his avowed censure. He declares that I originated the clause which enacts that "this Constitution and the laws of the United States, which shall be made in pursuance thereof, and all treaties made, or which shall be made, under the authority of the United States, shall be the supreme law of the land, and the judges in every state shall be bound thereby, any thing in the Constitution or the laws of any state to the contrary notwithstanding." To place this matter

*Essays on the Constitution of the United States, pp. 360–77.

in a proper point of view, it will be necessary to state, that as the propositions were reported by the committee of the whole house, a power was given to the general government to negative the laws passed by the state legislatures, a power which I considered as totally inadmissible; in substitution of this I proposed the following clause, which you will find very materially different from the clause adopted by the Constitution, "that the legislative acts of the United States, made by virtue and in pursuance of the articles of the union, and all treaties made and ratified under the authority of the United States, shall be the supreme law of the respective states, so far as those acts or treaties shall relate to the said states or their citizens, and that the judiciaries of the several states shall be bound thereby in their decisions, any thing in the respective laws of the individual states to the contrary notwithstanding." When this clause was introduced, it was not established that inferior continental courts should be appointed for trial of all questions arising on treaties and on the laws of the general government, and it was my wish and hope that every question of that kind would have been determined in the first instance in the courts of the respective states; had this been the case, the propriety and the necessity that treaties duly made and ratified, and the laws of the general government, should be binding on the state judiciaries which were to decide upon them, must be evident to every capacity, while at the same time, if such treaties or laws were inconsistent with our constitution and bill of rights, the judiciaries of this state would be bound to reject the first and abide by the last, since in the form I introduced the clause, notwithstanding treaties and the laws of the general government were intended to be superior to the laws of our state government, where they should be opposed to each other, yet that they were not proposed nor meant to be superior to our constitution and bill of rights. It was afterwards altered and amended (if it can be called an amendment) to the form in which it stands in the system now published, and as inferior continental, and not state courts, are originally to decide on those questions, it is now worse than useless, for being so altered as to render the treaties and laws made under the general government superior to our constitution, if the system is adopted it will amount to a total and unconditional surrender to that government, by the citizens of this state, of every right and privilege secured to them by our constitution, and an express compact and stipulation with the general government that it may, at its discretion, make laws in direct violation of those rights. But on this subject I shall enlarge in a future number.

*   *   *

Thus, my fellow citizens, that candour with which I have conducted myself through the whole of this business obliges me, however reluctantly, and however "mortifying it may be to my vanity," to disavow all "those greater positive virtues" which the Landholder has so obligingly attributed to me in Convention, and which he was so desirous of conferring upon me as to consider the guilt of misrepresentation and falsehood but a trifling sacrifice for that purpose, and to increase my mortification, you will find I am equally compelled to yield up every pretence even to those of a negative nature, which a regard to justice has, as he says, obliged him not to omit. These consist, as he tells us, in giving my entire approbation to the system as to those parts which are said to endanger a trial by jury, and as to its want of a bill of rights, and in having too much candour there to signify that I thought it deficient in either of these respects. But how, I pray, can the Landholder be certain that I deserve this encomium? Is it not possible, as I so frequently exhausted the politeness of the Convention, that some of those marks of fatigue and disgust, with which he intimates I was mortified as oft as I attempted to speak, might at that time have taken place, and have been of such a nature as to attract his attention; or perhaps, as the Convention was prepared to slumber whenever I rose, the Landholder, among others, might have sunk into sleep, and at that very moment might have been feasting his imagination with the completion of his ambitious views, and dreams of future greatness. But supposing I never did declare in Convention that I thought the system defective in those essential points, will it amount to a positive proof that I approved the system in those respects, or that I culpably neglected an indispensable duty? Is it not possible, whatever might have been my insolence and assurance when I first took my seat, and however fond I might be at that time of obtruding my sentiments, that the many rebuffs with which I met, the repeated mortifications I experienced, the marks of fatigue and disgust with which my eyes were sure to be assailed wherever I turned them—one gaping here, another yawning there, a third slumbering in this place, and a fourth snoring in that—might so effectually have put to flight all my original arrogance, that, as we are apt to run into extremes, having at length become convinced of my comparative nothingness, in so august an assembly and one in which the science of government was so perfectly understood, I might sink into such a state of modesty and diffidence as not to be able to muster up resolution enough to break the seal of silence and open my lips even after the rays of light had begun to penetrate my understanding, and in some measure to chase away those clouds of error and ignorance in which it was enveloped on my first arrival? Perhaps had I been treated with a more forbearing indulgence while committing those memorable blunders, for a want of a sufficient knowledge in the science of government, I might, after the rays of light had illuminated my mind, have rendered my country much more important services, and not only assisted in raising some of the pillars, but have furnished the edifice with a new roof of my own construction, rather better calculated for the convenience and security of those who might wish to take shelter beneath it, than that which it at present enjoys. Or even admitting I was not mortified, as I certainly ought to have been, from the Landholder's account of the matter, into a total loss of speech, was it in me, who considered the system, for a variety of reasons, absolutely inconsistent with your political welfare and happiness, a culpable neglect of duty in not endeavouring, and that against every chance of success, to remove one or two defects, when I had before ineffectually endeavoured to clear it of the others, which therefore, I knew must remain? But to be serious, as to what relates to the appellate jurisdiction in the extent given by the system proposed, I am positive there were objections made to it, and as far as my memory will serve me, I think I was in the number of those who actually objected; but I am sure that the objections met with my approbation. With respect to a bill of rights, had the government been formed upon principles truly federal, as I wished it, legislating over and acting upon the states only in their collective or political capacity, and not on individuals, there would have been no need of a bill of rights, as far as related to the rights of individuals, but only as to the rights of states. But the proposed constitution being intended and empowered to act not only on states, but also immediately on individuals; it renders a recognition and a stipulation in favour of the rights both of states and of men, not only proper, but in my opinion absolutely necessary. I endeavoured to obtain a restraint on the powers of the general government, as to standing armies, but it was rejected. It was my wish that the general government should not have the power of suspending the privilege of the writ of habeas corpus, as it appears to me altogether unnecessary, and that the power given to it may and will be used as a dangerous engine of oppression, but I could not succeed. An honorable member from South Carolina most anxiously sought to have a clause inserted securing the liberty of the Press, and repeatedly brought this subject before the Convention, but could not obtain it. I am almost positive he made the same attempt to have a stipulation in favour of liberty of conscience, but in vain. The more the system advanced the more was I impressed with the necessity of not merely attempting to secure a few rights, but of digesting and forming a complete bill of rights, including those of states and of individuals, which should be assented to, and prefixed to the Constitution, to serve as a barrier between the general government and the respective states and their citizens; because the more the system advanced the more clearly it appeared to me that the framers of it did not consider that either states or men had any rights at all, or that they meant to secure the enjoyment of any to either the one or the other; accordingly, I devoted a part of my time to the actuall preparing and draughting such a bill of rights, and had it in readiness before I left the Convention, to have laid it before a committee. I conversed with several members on the subject; they agreed with me on the propriety of the measure, but at the same time expressed their sentiments that it would be impossible to procure its adoption if attempted. A very few days before I left the Convention, I shewed to an honorable member sitting by me a proposition, which I then had in my hand, couched in the following words: "Resolved that a committee be appointed to prepare and report a bill of rights, to be prefixed to the proposed Constitution," and I then would instantly have moved for the appointment of a committee for that purpose, if he would have agreed to second the motion, to do which he hesitated, not as I understand from any objection to the measure, but from a conviction in his own mind that the motion would be in vain.

Thus my fellow citizens, you see that so far from having no objections to the system on this account, while I was at Convention, I not only then thought a bill of rights necessary, but I took some pains to have the subject brought forward, which would have been done, had it not been for the difficulties I have stated. At the same time I declare that when I drew up the motion, and was about to have proposed it to the Convention, I had not the most distant hope it would meet with success. The rejection of the clauses attempted in favour of particular rights, and to check and restrain the dangerous and exorbitant powers of the general government from being abused, had sufficiently taught me what to expect. And from the best judgment I could form while in Convention, I then was, and yet remained, decidedly of the opinion that ambition and interest had so far blinded the understanding of some of the principal framers of the Constitution, that while they were labouring to erect a fabrick by which they themselves might be exalted and benefited, they were rendered insensible to the sacrifice of the freedom and happiness of the states and their citizens, which must, inevitably be the consequence. I most sacredly believe their object is the total abolition and destruction of all state governments, and the erection on their ruins of one great and extensive empire, calculated to aggrandize and elevate its rulers and chief officers far above the common herd of mankind, to enrich them with wealth, and to encircle them with honours and glory, and which according to my judgment on the maturest reflection, must inevitably be attended with the most humiliating and abject slavery of their fellow citizens, by the sweat of whose brows, and by the toil of whose bodies, it can only be effected. And so anxious were its zealous promoters to hasten to a birth this misshapened heterogenous monster of ambition and interest, that, for some time before the Convention rose, upon the least attempt to alter its form, or modify its powers, the most fretful impatience was shown, such as would not have done much honour to a State Assembly, had they been sitting as long a time, and their treasury empty; while it was repeatedly urged on the contrary, but urged in vain, that in so momentous an undertaking, in forming a system for such an extensive continent, on which the political happiness of so many millions, even to the latest ages, may depend, no time could be too long—no thoughts and reflections too great—and that if by continuing six months, or even as many years, we could free the system from all its errors and defects, it would be the best use to which we could possibly devote our time. Thus my fellow citizens am I under necessity of resigning again into the hands of the Landholder, all those virtues both of a positive and negative kind, which from an excess of goodness he bestowed upon me, and give him my full permission to dispose of them hereafter in favour of some other person, who may be more deserving, and to whom they will be more acceptable: at the same time, I must frankly acknowledge, however it may operate as a proof of my dullness and stupidity, that the "ignorance in the science of government" under which I laboured at first was not removed by more than two months close application under those august and enlightened masters of the science with which the Convention abounded, nor was I able to discover during that time, either by my own researches, or by any light borrowed from those luminaries, anything in the history of mankind or in the sentiments of those who have favoured the world with their ideas on government, to warrant or countenance the motley mixture of a system proposed: a system which is an innovation in government of the most extraordinary kind; a system neither wholly federal, nor wholly national—but a strange hotchpotch of both—just so much federal in appearance as to give its advocates in some measure, an opportunity of passing it as such upon the unsuspecting multitude, before they had time and opportunity to examine it, and yet so predominantly national as to put it in the power of its movers, whenever the machine shall be set agoing, to strike out every part that has the appearance of being federal, and to render it wholly and entirely a national government: And if the framing and approving the Constitution now offered to our acceptance, is a proof of knowledge in the science of government, I not only admit, but I glory in my ignorance; and if my rising to speak had such a somnific influence on the Convention as the Landholder represents, I have no doubt the time will come, should this system be adopted, when my countrymen will ardently wish I had never left the Convention, but remained there to the last, daily administering to my associates the salutary opiate. Happy, thrice happy, would it have been for my country, if the whole of that time had been devoted to sleep, or been a blank in our lives, rather than employed in forging its chains. As I fully intended to have returned to the Convention before the completion of its business, my colleagues very probably might, and were certainly well warranted to, give that information the Landholder mentions; but whether the Convention was led to conclude that I "would have honoured the Constitution with my signature had not indispensable business called me away," may be easily determined after stating a few facts. The Landholder admits I was at first against the system—when the compromise took place on the subject of representation, I in the most explicit manner declared in Convention, that though I had concurred in the report, so far as to consent to proceed upon it that we might see what kind of a system might be formed, yet I disclaimed every idea of being bound to give it my assent, but reserved to myself the full liberty of finally giving it my negative, if it appeared to me inconsistent with the happiness of my country. In a desultory conversation which long after took place in Convention, one morning before our honourable president took the chair, he was observing how unhappy it would be should there be such a diversity of sentiment as to cause any of the members to oppose the system when they returned to their states; on that occasion I replied that I was confident no state in the union would more readily accede to a proper system of government than Maryland, but that the system under consideration was of such a nature, that I never could recommend it for acceptance; that I thought the state never ought to adopt it, and expressed my firm belief that it never would.

An honourable member from Pennsylvania objected against that part of the sixth article which requires an oath to be taken by the persons there mentioned, in support of the constitution, observing (as he justly might from the conduct the convention was then pursuing) how little such oaths were regarded. I immediately joined in the objection, but declared my reason to be, that I thought it such a constitution as no friend of his country ought to bind himself to support. And not more than two days before I left Philadelphia, another honourable member from the same state urged most strenuously that the Convention ought to hasten their deliberations to a conclusion, assigning as a reason that the Assembly of Pennsylvania was just then about to meet, and that it would be of the greatest importance to bring the system before that session of the legislature, in order that a Convention of the State might be immediately called to ratify it, before the enemies of the system should have an opportunity of making the people acquainted with their objections, at the same time declaring that if the matter should be delayed and the people have time to hear the variety of objections which would be made to it by its opposers, he thought it doubtful whether that state or any other state in the union would adopt it. As soon as the honourable member took his seat, I rose and observed, that I was precisely of the same opinion, that the people of America never would, nor did I think they ought to, adopt the system, if they had time to consider and understand it; whereas a proneness for novelty and change—a conviction that some alteration was necessary, and a confidence in the members who composed the Convention— might possibly procure its adoption, if brought hastily before them, but that these sentiments induced me to wish that a very different line of conduct should be pursued from that recommended by the honourable member. I wished the people to have every opportunity of information, as I thought it much preferable that a bad system should be rejected at first, than hastily adopted and afterwards be unavailingly repented of. If these were instances of my "high approbation," I gave them in abundance as all the Convention can testify, and continued so to do till I left them. That I expressed great regret at being obliged to leave Philadelphia, and a fixed determination to return if possible before the Convention rose, is certain. That I might declare that I had rather lose an hundred guineas than not to be there at the close of the business is very probable—and it is possible that some who heard me say this, not knowing my reasons, which could not be expressed without a breach of that secrecy to which we were enjoined, might erroneously have concluded that my motive was the gratification of vanity, in having my name enrolled with those of a Franklin and a Washington. As to the first, I cordially join in the tribute of praise so justly paid to the enlightened philosopher and statesman, while the polite, friendly and affectionate treatment myself and my family received from that venerable sage and the worthy family in which he is embosomed, will ever endear him to my heart. The name of Washington is far above my praise. I would to Heaven that on this occasion one more wreath had been added to the number of those which are twined around his amiable brow—that those with which it is already surrounded may flourish with immortal verdure, nor wither or fade till time shall be no more, is my fervent prayer, and may that glory which encircles his head ever shine with undiminished rays. To find myself under the necessity of opposing such illustrious characters, whom I venerated and loved, filled me with regret; but viewing the system in the light I then did, and yet do view it, to have hesitated would have been criminal; complaisance would have been guilt. If it was the idea of my state that whatever a Washington or Franklin approved, was to be blindly adopted, she ought to have spared herself the expence of sending any members to the Convention, or to have instructed them implicitly to follow where they led the way. It was not to have my "name enrolled with the other labourers," that I wished to return to Philadelphia—that sacrifice which I must have made of my principles by putting my name to the Constitution, could not have been effaced by any derivative lustre it could possibly receive from the bright constellation with which it would have been surrounded. My object was in truth the very reverse; as I had uniformly opposed the system in its progress, I wished to have been present at the conclusion, to have then given it my solemn negative, which I certainly should have done, even had I stood single and alone, being perfectly willing to leave it to the cool and impartial investigation both of the present and of future ages to decide who best understood the science of government—who best knew the rights of men and of states, who best consulted the true interest of America, and who most faithfully discharged the trust reposed in them, those who agreed to or those who opposed the new Constitution—and so fully have I made up my own mind on this subject, that as long as the history of mankind shall record the appointment of the late Convention, and the system which has been proposed by them, it is my highest ambition that my name may also be recorded as one who considered the system injurious to my country, and as such opposed it. Having shown that I did not "alter my opinion after I left Philadelphia," and that I acted no "contradictory parts on the great political stage," and therefore that there are none such to reconcile, the reason assigned by the Landholder for that purpose doth not deserve my notice, except only to observe that he shrewdly intimates there is already a Junto established, who are to share in and deal out the offices of this new government at their will and pleasure, and that they have already fixed upon the character who is to be "Deputy Attorney General of the

United States for the State of Maryland." If this is true, it is worth while to inquire of whom this Junto consists, as it might lead to a discovery of the persons for the gratification of whose ambition and interest this system is prepared, and is, if possible, to be enforced, and from the disposition of offices already allotted in the various and numerous departments, we possibly might discover whence proceeds the conviction and zeal of some of its advocates.

Mar. 28, 1788

Number III

To the Citizens of Maryland.

There is, my fellow citizens, scarcely an individual of common understanding, I believe, in this state, who is any ways acquainted with the proposed Constitution, who doth not allow it to be, in many instances, extremely censurable, and that a variety of alterations and amendments are essentially requisite, to render it consistent with a reasonable security for the liberty of the respective states, and their citizens. Aristides,[1] it is true, is an exception from this observation; he declares, that "if the whole matter was left to his discretion, he would not change any part of the proposed Constitution," whether he meant this declaration as a proof of his discretion, I will not say; it will however, readily be admitted, by most, as a proof of his enthusiastic zeal in favour of the system. But it would be injustice to that writer not to observe, that if he is as much mistaken in the other parts of the Constitution, as in that which relates to the judicial department, the Constitution which he is so earnestly recommending to his countrymen, and on which he is lavishing so liberally his commendations, is a thing of his own creation and totally different from that which is offered for your acceptance. He has given us an explanation of the original and appellate jurisdiction of the judiciary of the general government, and of the manner in which he supposes it is to operate—an explanation so inconsistent with the intention of its framers, and so different from its true construction and from the effect which it will have, should the system be adopted, that I could scarce restrain my astonishment at the error, although I was in some measure prepared for it, by his previous acknowledgment that he did not very well understand that part of the system; a circumstance I apprehended he did not recollect at the time when he was bestowing upon it his dying benediction. And if one of our judges, possessed of no common share of understanding, and of extensive acquired knowledge, who, as he informs us, has long made the science of government his peculiar study, so little understands the true import and construction of this Constitution, and that too in a part more particularly within his own province, can it be wondered at that the people in general, whose knowledge in

[1] A reference to Alexander Contee Hanson's pamphlet, written under the pseudonym of Aristides, *infra* p. 540.

subjects of this nature is much more limited and circumscribed, should but imperfectly comprehend the extent, operation and consequences of so complex and intricate a system; and is not this of itself a strong proof of the necessity that it should be corrected and amended, at least so as to render it more clear and comprehensible to those who are to decide upon it, or to be affected by it. But although almost every one agrees the Constitution, as it is, to be both defective and dangerous, we are not wanting in characters who earnestly advise us to adopt it, in its present form, with all its faults, and assure us we may safely rely on obtaining hereafter the amendments that are necessary. But why, I pray you, my fellow citizens, should we not insist upon the necessary amendments being made now, while we have the liberty of acting for ourselves, before the Constitution becomes binding upon us by our assent, as every principle of reason, common sense and safety would dictate? Because, say they, the sentiments of men are so different, and the interests of the different states are so jarring and dissonant, that there is no probability they would agree if alterations and amendments were attempted. Thus with one breath they tell us that the obstacles to any alterations and amendments being agreed to by the states are so insuperable, that it is vain to make the experiment, while in the next they would persuade us it is so certain the states will accede to those which shall be necessary, and that they may be procured even after the system shall be ratified, that we need not hesitate swallowing the poison, from the ease and security of instantly obtaining the antidote—and they seem to think it astonishing that any person should find a difficulty in reconciling the absurdity and contradiction. If it is easy to obtain proper amendments, do not let us sacrifice everything that ought to be dear to freemen, for want of insisting upon its being done, while we have the power. If the obtaining them will be difficult and improbable, for God's sake do not accept of such a form of government as without amendments cannot fail of rendering you mere beasts of burthen, and reducing you to a level with your own slaves, with this aggravating distinction, that you once tasted the blessings of freedom. Those who would wish you to believe that the faults in the system proposed are wholly or principally owing to the difference of state interests, and proceed from that cause, are either imposed upon themselves, or mean to impose upon you. The principal questions, in which the state interests had any material effect, were those which related to representation, and the number in each branch of the legislature, whose concurrence should be necessary for passing navigation acts, or making commercial regulations. But what state is there in the union whose interest would prompt it to give the general government the extensive and unlimited powers it possesses in the executive, legislative and judicial departments together with the powers over the militia, and the liberty of establishing a standing army without any restriction? What state in the union considers it advantageous to its interest that the President should be re-eligible—the members of both houses appointable to offices—the judges capable of holding other offices at the will and pleasure of the government, and that there should be no real responsibility either in the President or in the members of either branch of the Legislature? Or what state is there that would have been averse to a bill of rights, or that would have wished for the destruction of jury trial in a great variety of cases, and in a particular manner in every case without exception where the government itself is interested? These parts of the system, so far from promoting the interest of any state, or states, have an immediate tendency to annihilate all the state governments indiscriminately, and to subvert their rights and the rights of their citizens. To oppose these, and to procure their alteration, is equally the interest of every state in the union. The introduction of these parts of the system must not be attributed to the jarring interests of states, but to a very different source, the pride, the ambition and the interest of individuals. This being the case, we may be enabled to form some judgment of the probability of obtaining a safe and proper system, should we have firmness and wisdom to reject that which is now offered; and also of the great improbability of procuring any amendments to the present system, if we should weakly and inconsiderately adopt it. The bold and daring attempt that has been made to use, for the total annihilation of the states, that power that was delegated for their preservation, will put the different states on their guard. The votaries of ambition and interest being totally defeated in their attempt to establish themselves on the ruins of the States, which they will be if this Constitution is rejected, an attempt in which they had more probability of success from the total want of suspicion in their countrymen than they can have hereafter, they will not hazard a second attempt of the same nature, in which they will have much less chance of success; besides, being once discovered they will not be confided in. The true interest and happiness of the states and their citizens will, therefore, most probably be the object which will be principally sought for by a second Convention, should a second be appointed, which if really aimed at, I cannot think very difficult to accomplish, by giving to the federal government sufficient power for every salutary purpose, while the rights of the states and their citizens should be secure from any imminent danger. But if the arts and influence of ambitious and interested men, even in their present situation, while more on a level with yourselves, and unarmed with any extraordinary powers, should procure you to adopt this system, dangerous as it is admitted to be to your rights, I will appeal to the understanding of every one of you, who will on this occasion give his reason fair play, whether there is not every cause to believe they will, should this government be adopted, with that additional power, consequence and influence it will give them, most easily prevent the necessary alterations which might be wished for, the purpose of which would be directly opposite to their views, and defeat every attempt to procure them. Be assured, whatever obstacles or difficulties may be at this time in the way of obtaining a proper system of government, they will be increased an hundred fold after this system is adopted. Reflect also, I entreat you, my fellow citizens, that the alterations and amendments which are wanted in the present system are of such a nature as to diminish and lessen, to check and restrain the powers of the general government, not to increase and enlarge those powers. If they were of the last kind, we might safely adopt it, and trust to giving greater powers hereafter, like a physician who administers an emetic ex re nata, giving a moderate dose at first, and increasing it afterwards as the constitution of the patient may require. But I appeal to the history of mankind for this truth, that when once power and authority are delegated to a government, it knows how to keep it, and is sufficiently and successfully fertile in expedients for that purpose. Nay more, the whole history of mankind proves that so far from parting with the powers actually delegated to it, government is constantly encroaching on the small pittance of rights reserved by the people to themselves, and gradually wresting them out of their hands until it either terminates in their slavery or forces them to arms, and brings about a revolution. From these observations it appears to me, my fellow citizens, that nothing can be more weak and absurd than to accept of a system that is admitted to stand in need of immediate amendments to render your rights secure—for remember, if you fail in obtaining them, you cannot free yourselves from the yoke you will have placed on your necks, and servitude must, therefore, be your portion. Let me ask you my fellow citizens what you would think of a physician who, because you were slightly indisposed, should bring you a dose which properly corrected with other ingredients might be a salutary remedy, but of itself was a deadly poison, and with great appearance of friendship and zeal, should advise you to swallow it immediately, and trust to accident for those requisites necessary to qualify its malignity, and prevent its destructive effects? Would not you reject the advice, in however friendly a manner it might appear to be given, with indignation, and insist that he should first procure, and properly attempt, the necessary ingredients, since after the fatal draught was once received into your bowels, it would be too late should the antidote prove unattainable, and death must ensue. With the same indignation ought you, my fellow citizens, to reject the advice of those political quacks, who under pretence of healing the disorders of our present government, would urge you rashly to gulp down a constitution, which in its present form, unaltered and unamended, would be as certain death to your liberty, as arsenic could be to your bodies.

OTHER ANTIFEDERALIST WRITINGS, 1787–1788

Commentary

The extracts which follow are from the writings of other Antifederalists in opposition to the Constitution, so far as they bear upon the Bill of Rights issue. The writers are Brutus (a pseudonym used by a Massachusetts Antifederalist), James Winthrop of Massachusetts (*Letters of Agrippa*), Hugh Brackenridge of Pennsylvania (*Cursory Remarks*), and Robert Yates of New York (*Letters of Sydney*). They add little of substance that is new to the constitutional debate. Each attacks the absence of a Bill of Rights, asserting that without one, fundamental rights remain unprotected. "It is a mere fallacy, invented by the deceptive powers of Mr. Wilson, that what rights are not given are reserved." (This Antifederalist argument led directly to the Tenth Amendment—showing that most Americans of that day did not agree with the Supreme Court's later statement [1941], that it is "a truism that all is retained which has not been surrendered," *United States* v. *Darby,* 312 U.S. 100,116.) On the contrary, "whatever is the form of government, a bill of rights is essential to the security of the persons and property of the people." The extreme statement of this view is in the Brackenridge *Remarks.* Winthrop emphasizes the need for amendments and the ones proposed by him bear some resemblance to those conceded by the Federalists and introduced by Hancock in the Massachusetts Convention. This tends to bear out what, to the present-day observer, may be Winthrop's most important point, that his amendments "show how nearly those who are for admitting the system with the necessary alterations, agree with those who are for rejecting this system and amending the confederation." This is, indeed, the chief thing to understand in the post-Constitution movement to secure a Bill of Rights. However far apart they might have been at the beginning, as the ratification struggle went on, the leading Federalists joined their opponents in recognizing the need for a Bill of Rights. It was the Federalist concession on this that secured the votes for ratification in doubtful states—even where, as in New York, the Antifederalists had the Convention majority. Only the extremists in the Antifederalist ranks could cry till the end, with Yates, that if the Constitution is "adopted we may (in imitation of the Carthaginians) say, Delenda vit Americae."

Letters of Brutus, 1788*

No. II

I flatter myself that my last address established this position, that to reduce the thirteen States into one government, would prove the destruction of our liberties.

* Debates and Proceedings in the Convention of the Commonwealth of Massachusetts Held in the Year 1788 (1856), pp. 378–84.

But lest this truth should be doubted by some, I will now proceed to consider its merits.

Though it should be admitted, that the arguments against reducing all the States into one consolidated government, are not sufficient fully to establish this point, yet they will, at least, justify this conclusion, that in forming a Constitution for such a country, great care should be taken to limit and define its powers, adjust its parts, and guard against an abuse of authority. How far attention has been paid to these objects, shall be the subject of future inquiry. When a building is to be erected which is intended to stand for ages, the foundation should be firmly laid. The Constitution proposed to your acceptance is designed, not for yourselves alone, but for generations yet unborn. The principles, therefore, upon which the social compact is founded, ought to have been clearly and precisely stated, and the most express and full declaration of rights to have been made. But on this subject there is almost an entire silence.

If we may collect the sentiments of the people of America, from their own most solemn declarations, they held this truth as self-evident, that all men are by nature free. No one man, therefore, or any class of men, have a right, by the law of nature, or of God, to assume or exercise authority over their fellows. The origin of society, then, is to be sought, not in any natural right which one man has to exercise authority over another, but in the united consent of those who associate. The mutual wants of men at first dictated the propriety of forming societies; and when they were established, protection and defence pointed out the necessity of instituting government. In a state of nature every individual pursues his own interest; in this pursuit it frequently happened, that the possessions or enjoyments of one were sacrificed to the views and designs of another; thus the weak were a prey to the strong, the simple and unwary were subject to impositions from those who were more crafty and designing. In this state of things, every individual was insecure; common interest, therefore, directed that government should be established, in which the force of the whole community should be collected, and under such directions, as to protect and defend every one who composed it. The common good, therefore, is the end of civil government, and common consent, the foundation on which it is established. To effect this end, it was necessary that a certain portion of natural liberty should be surrendered, in order that what remained should be preserved. How great a proportion of natural freedom is necessary to be yielded by individuals, when they submit to government, I shall not inquire. So much, however, must be given, as will be sufficient to enable those to whom the administration of the government is committed, to establish laws for the promoting the happiness of the community, and to carry those laws into effect. But it is not necessary, for this purpose, that individuals should relinquish all their natural rights. Some are of such a nature that they cannot be surrendered. Of this kind are the rights of conscience, the right of enjoying and defending life, &c. Others are not necessary to be resigned in order to attain the end for which government is instituted, these therefore ought not to be given up. To surrender them, would counteract the very end of government, to wit, the common good. From these observations it appears, that in forming a government on its true principles, the foundation should be laid in the manner I before stated, by expressly reserving to the people such of their essential rights as are not necessary to be parted with. The same reasons which at first induced mankind to associate and institute government, will operate to influence them to observe this precaution. If they had been disposed to conform themselves to the rule of immutable righteousness, government would not have been requisite. It was because one part exercised fraud, oppression and violence on the other, that men came together, and agreed that certain rules should be formed to regulate the conduct of all, and the power of the whole community lodged in the hands of rulers to enforce an obedience to them. But rulers have the same propensities as other men; they are as likely to use the power with which they are vested, for private purposes, and to the injury and oppression of those over whom they are placed, as individuals in a state of nature are to injure and oppress one another. It is therefore as proper that bounds should be set to their authority, as that government should have at first been instituted to restrain private injuries.

This principle, which seems so evidently founded in the reason and nature of things, is confirmed by universal experience. Those who have governed, have been found in all ages ever active to enlarge their powers and abridge the public liberty. This has induced the people in all countries, where any sense of freedom remained, to fix barriers against the encroachments of their rulers. The country from which we have derived our origin, is an eminent example of this. Their magna charta and bill of rights have long been the boast, as well as the security of that nation. I need say no more, I presume, to an American, than that this principle is a fundamental one, in all the Constitutions of our own States; there is not one of them but what is either founded on a declaration or bill of rights, or has certain express reservation of rights interwoven in the body of them. From this it appears, that at a time when the pulse of liberty beat high, and when an appeal was made to the people to form Constitutions for the government of themselves, it was their universal sense, that such declarations should make a part of their frames of government. It is, therefore, the more astonishing, that this grand security to the rights of the people is not to be found in this Constitution.

It has been said, in answer to this objection, that such declaration of rights, however requisite they might be in the Constitutions of the States, are not necessary in the general Constitution, because, "in the former case, every thing which is not reserved is given; but in the latter, the reverse of the proposition prevails, and every thing which is not given is reserved." It requires but little attention to discover, that this mode of reasoning is rather specious than solid. The powers, rights and authority, granted to the general government by this Constitution, are as complete, with respect to every object to which they extend, as that of any State government—it reaches to every thing which concerns human happiness—life, liberty, and property are under its control. There is the same reason, therefore, that the exercise of power, in this case, should be restrained within proper limits, as in that of the State governments. To set this matter in a clear light, permit me to instance some of the articles of the bills of rights of the individual States, and apply them to the case in question.

For the security of life, in criminal prosecutions, the bills of rights of most of the States have declared, that no man shall be held to answer for a crime until he is made fully acquainted with the charge brought against him; he shall not be compelled to accuse, or furnish evidence against himself—the witnesses against him shall be brought face to face, and he shall be fully heard by himself or counsel. That it is essential to the security of life and liberty, that trial of facts be in the vicinity where they happen. Are not provisions of this kind as necessary in the general government, as in that of a particular State? The powers vested in the new Congress extend in many cases to life; they are authorized to provide for the punishment of a variety of capital crimes, and no restraint is laid upon them in its exercise, save only, that "the trial of all crimes, except in cases of impeachment, shall be by jury; and such trial shall be in the State where the said crimes shall have been committed." No man is secure of a trial in the county where he is charged to have committed a crime; he may be brought from Niagara to New York, or carried from Kentucky to Richmond for trial for an offence supposed to be committed. What security is there, that a man shall be furnished with a full and plain description of the charges against him? That he shall be allowed to produce all proof he can in his favor? That he shall see the witnesses against him face to face, or that he shall be fully heard in his own defence by himself or counsel?

For the security of liberty it has been declared, "that excessive bail should not be required, nor excessive fines imposed, nor cruel or unusual punishments inflicted. That all warrants, without oath or affirmation, to search suspected places, or seize any person, his papers or property, are grievous and oppressive."

These provisions are as necessary under the general government as under that of the individual States; for the power of the former is as complete to the purpose of requiring bail, imposing fines, inflicting punishments, granting search warrants, and seizing persons, papers, or property, in certain cases, as the other.

For the purpose of securing the property of the citizens, it is declared by all the States, "that in all controversies at law, respecting property, the ancient mode of trial by jury is one of the best securities of the rights of the people, and ought to remain sacred and inviolable."

Does not the same necessity exist of reserving this right under their national compact, as in that of the States? Yet nothing is said respecting it. In the bills of rights of the States it is declared, that a well regulated militia is the proper and natural defence of a free government; that as standing armies in time of peace are dangerous, they are not to be kept up, and that the military should be kept under strict subordination to, and controlled by, the civil power.

The same security is as necessary in this Constitution, and much more so; for the general government will have the sole power to raise and to pay armies, and are under no control in the exercise of it; yet nothing of this is to be found in this new system.

I might proceed to instance a number of other rights, which were as necessary to be reserved, such as, that elections should be free, that the liberty of the press should be held sacred; but the instances adduced are sufficient to prove that this argument is without foundation. Besides, it is evident that the reason here assigned was not the true one, why the framers of this Constitution omitted a bill of rights; if it had been, they would not have made certain reservations, while they totally omitted others of more importance. We find they have, in the ninth section of the first article declared, that the writ of *habeas corpus* shall not be suspended, unless in cases of rebellion, that no bill of attainder, or *ex post facto* law, shall be passed, that no title of nobility shall be granted by the United States, &c. If every thing which is not given is reserved, what propriety is there in these exceptions? Does this Constitution any where grant the power of suspending the *habeas corpus*, to make *ex post facto* laws, pass bills of attainder, or grant titles of nobility? It certainly does not in express terms. The only answer that can be given is, that these are implied in the general powers granted. With equal truth it may be said, that all the powers which the bills of rights guard against the abuse of, are contained or implied in the general ones granted by this Constitution.

So far is it from being true, that a bill of rights is less necessary in the general Constitution than in those of the States, the contrary is evidently the fact. This system, if it is possible for the people of America to accede to it, will be an original compact; and being the last, will, in the nature of things, vacate every former agreement inconsistent with it. For it being a plan of government received and ratified by the whole people, all other forms which are in existence at the time of its adoption, must yield to it. This is expressed in positive and unequivocal terms in the sixth article: "That this Constitution, and the laws of the United States which shall be made in pursuance thereof, and all treaties made, or which shall be made, under the authority of the United States, shall be the supreme law of the land; and the judges in every State shall be bound thereby, any thing in the Constitution, or laws of any State, to the contrary notwithstanding."

"The senators and representatives before-mentioned, and the members of the several State legislatures, and all executive and judicial officers, both of the United States, and in the United States, shall be bound, by oath or affirmation, to support this Constitution."

It is therefore not only necessarily implied thereby, but positively expressed, that the different State Constitutions are repealed and entirely done away, so far as they are inconsistent with this, with the laws which shall be made in pursuance thereof, or with treaties made, or which shall be made, under the authority of the United States. Of what avail will the Constitutions of the respective States be to preserve the rights of its citizens? Should they be plead, the answer would be, the Constitution of the United States, and the laws made in pursuance thereof, is the supreme law, and all legislatures and judicial officers, whether of the General or State governments, are bound by oath to support it. No privilege, reserved by the bills of rights, or secured by the State governments, can limit the power granted by this, or restrain any laws made in pursuance of it. It stands, therefore, on its own bottom, and must receive a construction by itself, without any reference to any other. And hence it was of the highest importance, that the most precise and express declarations and reservations of rights should have been made.

This will appear the more necessary, when it is considered, that not only the Constitution and laws made in pursuance thereof, but all treaties made, under the authority of the United States, are the supreme law of the land, and supersede the Constitutions of all the States. The power to make treaties, is vested in the president, by and with the advice and consent of two-thirds of the senate. I do not find any limitation or restriction to the exercise of this power. The most important article in any Constitution may therefore be repealed, even without a legislative act. Ought not a government, vested with such extensive and indefinite authority, to have been restricted by declaration of rights? It certainly ought.

So clear a point is this, that I cannot help suspecting that persons who attempt to persuade people that such reservations were less necessary under this Constitution than under those of the States, are wilfully endeavoring to deceive, and to lead you into an absolute state of vassalage.

Letters of Agrippa, 1788*

Accredited to James Winthrop

[Tuesday, January 14, 1788]

To the Massachusetts Convention

The question then arises, what is the kind of government best adapted to the object of securing our persons and possessions from violence? I answer, a

*Essays on the Constitution of the United States, pp. 93–122.

Federal Republick. By this kind of government each state reserves to itself the right of making and altering its laws for internal regulation, and the right of executing those laws without any external restraint, while the general concerns of the empire are committed to an assembly of delegates, each accountable to his own constituents. This is the happy form under which we live, and which seems to mark us out as a people chosen of God. No instance can be produced of any other kind of government so stable and energetick as the republican.

*   *   *

Let us now consider the probable effects of a consolidation of the separate states into one mass; for the new system extends so far. Many ingenious explanations have been given of it; but there is this defect, that they are drawn from maxims of the common law, while the system itself cannot be bound by any such maxims. A legislative assembly has an inherent right to alter the common law, and to abolish any of its principles, which are not particularly guarded in the constitution. Any system therefore which appoints a legislature, without any reservation of the rights of individuals, surrenders all power in every branch of legislation to the government. The universal practice of every government proves the justness of this remark; for in every doubtful case it is an established rule to decide in favour of authority. The new system is, therefore, in one respect at least, essentially inferior to our state constitutions. There is no bill of rights, and consequently a continental law may controul any of those principles, which we consider at present as sacred; while not one of those points, in which it is said that the separate governments misapply their power, is guarded. Tender acts and the coinage of money stand on the same footing of a consolidation of power. It is a mere fallacy, invented by the deceptive powers of Mr. Wilson, that what rights are not given are reserved. The contrary has already been shewn. But to put this matter of legislation out of all doubt, let us compare together some parts of the book; for being an independent system, this is the only way to ascertain its meaning.

In article III, section 2, it is declared, that "the judicial power shall extend to all cases in law and equity arising under this constitution, the laws of the United States, and treaties made or which shall be made under their authority." Among the cases arising under this new constitution are reckoned, "all controversies between citizens of different states," which include all kinds of civil causes between those parties. The giving Congress a power to appoint courts for such a purpose is as much, there being no stipulation to the contrary, giving them power to legislate for such causes, as giving them a right to raise an army, is giving them a right to direct the operations of the army when raised. But it is not left to implication. The last clause of article I, section 8, expressly gives them power "to make all laws which shall be needful and proper for carrying into execution the foregoing powers, all other powers vested by this constitution in the government of the United States, or in any department or officer thereof." It is, therefore, as plain as words can make it, that they have a right by this proposed form to legislate for all kinds of causes respecting property between citizens of different states. That this power extends to all cases between citizens of the same state, is evident from the sixth article, which declares all continental laws and treaties to be the supreme law of the land, and that all state judges are bound thereby, "anything in the constitution or laws of any state to the contrary notwithstanding." If this is not binding the judges of the separate states in their own office, by continental rules, it is perfect nonsense. There is then a complete consolidation of the legislative powers in all cases respecting property. This power extends to all cases between a state and citizens of another state. Hence a citizen, possessed of the notes of another state, may bring his action, and there is no limitation that the execution shall be levied on the publick property of the state; but the property of individuals is liable. This is a foundation for endless confusion and discord. The right to try causes between a state and citizens of another state, involves in it all criminal causes; and a man who has accidentally transgressed the laws of another state, must be transported, with all his witnesses, to a third state, to be tried. He must be ruined to prove his innocence. These are necessary parts of the new system, and it will never be complete till they are reduced to practice. They effectually prove a consolidation of the states, and we have before shewn the ruinous tendency of such a measure.

By sect. 8 of article I, Congress are to have the unlimited right to regulate commerce, external and internal, and may therefore create monopolies which have been universally injurious to all the subjects of the countries that have adopted them, excepting the monopolists themselves. They have also the unlimited right to imposts and all kinds of taxes, as well to levy as to collect them. They have indeed very nearly the same powers claimed formerly by the British parliament. Can we have so soon forgot our glorious struggle with that power, as to think a moment of surrendering it now? It makes no difference in principle whether the national assembly was elected for seven years or for six. In both cases we should vote to great disadvantage, and therefore ought never to agree to such an article. Let us make provision for the payment of the interest of our part of the debt, and we shall be fairly acquitted. Let the fund be an impost on our foreign trade, and we shall encourage our manufactures. But if we surrender the unlimited right to regulate trade, and levy taxes, imposts will oppress our foreign trade for the benefit of other states, while excises and taxes will discourage our internal industry. The right to regulate trade, without any limitations, will, as certainly as it is granted, transfer the trade of this state to Pennsylvania. That will be the seat of business and of wealth, while the extremes of the empire will, like Ireland and Scotland, be drained to fatten an overgrown capital. Under our present equal advantages, the citizens of this state come in for their full share of commercial profits. Surrender the rights of taxation and commercial regulation, and the landed states at the southward will all be interested in draining our resources; for whatever can be got by impost on our trade and excises on our manufactures, will be considered as so much saved to a state inhabited by planters. All savings of this sort ought surely to be made in favour of our own state; and we ought never to surrender the unlimited powers of revenue and trade to uncommercial people. If we do, the glory of the state from that moment departs, never to return.

The safety of our constitutional rights consists in having the business of governments lodged in different departments, and in having each part well defined. By this means each branch is kept within the constitutional limits. Never was a fairer line of distinction than what may be easily drawn between the continental and state governments. The latter provide for all cases, whether civil or criminal, that can happen ashore, because all such causes must arise within the limits of some state. Transactions between citizens may all be fairly included in this idea even although they should arise in passing by water from one state to another. But the intercourse between us and foreign nations properly forms the department of Congress. They should have the power of regulating trade under such limitations as should render their laws equal. They should have the right of war and peace, saving the equality of rights, and the territory of each state. But the power of naturalization and internal regulation should not be given them. To give my scheme a more systematick appearance, I have thrown it into the form of a resolve which is submitted to your wisdom for amendment, but not as being perfect.

Resolved, that the form of government proposed by the federal convention, lately held in Philadelphia, be rejected on the part of this commonwealth; and that our delegates in Congress are hereby authorised to propose on the part of this commonwealth, and, if the other states for themselves agree thereto, to sign an article of confederation, as an addition to the present articles, in the form following, provided such agreement be made on or before the first day of January, which will be in the year of our Lord 1790; the said article shall have the same force and effect as if it had been inserted in the original confederation, and is to be construed consistently with the clause in the former articles, which restrains the United States from exercising such powers as are not expressly given.

XIV. The United States shall have power to regulate, whether by treaty, ordinance or law, the intercourse between these states and foreign dominions and countries, under the following restrictions. No treaty, ordinance, or law shall give a preference to the ports of one state over those of another; nor 2d. impair the territory or internal authority of any state; nor 3d. create any monopolies or exclusive companies; nor 4th. naturalize any foreigners. All their imposts and prohibitions shall be confined to foreign produce and manufactures imported, and to foreign ships trading in our harbours. All imposts and confiscations shall be to the use of the state where they shall accrue, excepting only such branches of impost as shall be assigned by the separate states to Congress for a fund to defray the interest of their debt, and their current charges. In order the more effectually to execute this and the former articles, Congress shall have authority to appoint courts, supreme and subordinate, with power to try all crimes, not relating to state securities, between any foreign state, or subject of such state, actually residing in a foreign country, and not being an absentee or person who has alienated himself from these states on the one part, and any of the United States or citizens thereof on the other part; also all causes in which foreign ambassadours or other foreign ministers resident here shall be immediately concerned, respecting the jurisdiction or immunities only. And the Congress shall have authority to execute the judgment of such courts by their own affairs. Piracies and felonies committed on the high seas shall also belong to the department of Congress for them to define, try, and punish, in the same manner as the other causes shall be defined, tried, and determined. All the before-mentioned causes shall be tried by jury and in some sea-port town. And it is recommended to the general court at their next meeting to provide and put Congress in possession of funds arising from foreign imports and ships sufficient to defray our share of the present annual expenses of the continent.

Such a resolve, explicitly limiting the powers granted, is the farthest we can proceed with safety. The scheme of accepting the report of the Convention, and amending it afterwards, is merely delusive. There is no intention among those who make the proposition to amend it at all. Besides, if they have influence enough to get it accepted in its present form, there is no probability that they will consent to an alteration when possessed of an unlimited revenue. It is an excellence in our present confederation, that it is extremely difficult to alter it. An unanimous vote of the states is required. But this newly proposed form is founded in injustice, as it proposes that a fictitious consent of only nine states shall be sufficient to establish it. Nobody can suppose that the consent of a state is any thing more than a fiction, in the view of the federalists, after the mobbish influence used over the Pennsylvania convention. The two great leaders of the plan, with a modesty of Scotsmen, placed a rabble in the gallery to applaud their speeches, and thus supplied their want of capacity in the argument. Repeatedly were Wilson and Mr. Kean worsted in the argument by the plain good sense of Findly and Smilie. But reasoning or knowledge had little to do with the federal party. Votes were all they wanted, by whatever means obtained. Means not less criminal have been mentioned among us. But votes that are bought can never justify a treasonable conspiracy. Better, far better, would it be to reject the whole and remain in possession of present advantages. The authority of Congress to decide disputes between states is sufficient to prevent their recurring to hostility: and their different situation, wants and produce is a sufficient foundation for the most friendly intercourse. All the arts of delusion and legal chicanery will be used to elude your vigilance, and obtain a majority. But keeping the constitution of the state and the publick interest in view, will be your safety.

*   *   *

From this general view of the state of mankind it appears that all the powers of government originally reside in the body of the people; and that when they appoint certain persons to administer the government, they delegate all the powers of government not expressly reserved. Hence it appears that a constitution does not in itself imply any more than a declaration of the relation which the different parts of the government bear to each other, but does not in any degree imply security to the rights of individuals. This has been the uniform practice. In all doubtful cases the decision is in favour of the government. It is therefore impertinent to ask by what right government exercises powers not expressly delegated. Mr. Wilson, the great oracle of federalism, acknowledges, in his speech to the Philadelphians,[1] the truth of these remarks, as they respect the state governments, but attempts to set up a distinction between them and the continental government. To anybody who will be at the trouble to read the new system, it is evidently in the same situation as the state constitutions now possess. It is a compact among the people for the purposes of government, and not a compact between states. It begins in the name of the people, and not of the states.

It has been shown in the course of this paper, that when people institute government, they of course delegate all rights not expressly reserved. In our state constitution the bill of rights consists of thirty articles. It is evident therefore that the new constitution proposes to delegate greater powers than are granted to our own government, sanguine as the person was who denied it. The complaints against the separate governments, even by the friends of the new plan, are not that they have not power enough, but that they are disposed to make a bad use of what power they have. Surely then they reason badly, when they purpose to set up a government possess'd of much more extensive powers than the present, and subject to much smaller checks.

Bills of rights, reserved by authority of the people, are, I believe, peculiar to America. A careful observance of the abuse practised in other countries has had its just effect by inducing our people to guard against them. We find the happiest consequences to flow from it. The separate governments know their powers, their objects, and operations. We are therefore not perpetually tormented with new experiments. For a single instance of abuse among us there are thousands in other countries. On the other hand, the people know their rights, and feel happy in the possession of their freedom; both civil and political. Active industry is the consequence of their security, and within one

[1] Delivered Oct. 6, 1787, *infra* p. 528.

year the circumstances of the state and of individuals have improved to a degree never before known in this commonwealth. Though our bill of rights does not, perhaps, contain all the cases in which power might be safely reserved, yet it affords a protection to the persons and possessions of individuals not known in any foreign country. In some respects the power of government is a little too confined. In many other countries we find the people resisting their governours for exercising their power in an unaccustomed mode. But for want of a bill of rights the resistance is always, by the principles of their government, a rebellion which nothing but success can justify. In our constitution we have aimed at delegating the necessary powers of government and confining their operation to beneficial purposes. At present we appear to have come very near the truth. Let us therefore have wisdom and virtue enough to preserve it inviolate. It is a stale contrivance, to get the people into a passion, in order to make them sacrifice their liberty. Repentance always comes, but it comes too late. Let us not flatter ourselves that we shall always have good men to govern us. If we endeavour to be like other nations we shall have more bad men than good ones to exercise extensive powers. That circumstance alone will corrupt them. While they fancy themselves the viceregents of God, they will resemble him only in power, but will always depart from his wisdom and goodness.

[Tuesday, February 5, 1788]

To the Massachusetts Convention

In my last address I ascertained, from historical records, the following principles: that, in the original state of government, the whole power resides in the whole body of the nation, that when a people appoint certain persons to govern them, they delegate their whole power; that a constitution is not in itself a bill of rights; and that, whatever is the form of government, a bill of rights is essential to the security of the persons and property of the people. It is an idea favourable to the interest of mankind at large, that government is founded in compact. Several instances may be produced of it, but none is more remarkable than our own. In general, I have chosen to apply to such facts as are in the reach of my readers. For this purpose I have chiefly confined myself to examples drawn from the history of our own country, and to the Old Testament. It is in the power of every reader to verify examples thus substantiated. Even in the remarkable arguments on the fourth section, relative to the power over election I was far from stating the worst of it, as it respects the adverse party. A gentleman, respectable in many points, but more especially for his systematick and perspicuous reasoning in his profession, has repeatedly stated to the Convention, among his reasons in favour of that section, that the Rhode Island assembly have for a considerable time past had a bill lying on their table for altering the manner of elections for representatives in that state. He has stated it with all the zeal of a person who believed his argument to be a good one. But surely a bill lying on a table can never be considered as any more than an intention to pass it, and nobody pretends that it ever actually did pass. It is in strictness only the intention of a part of the assembly, for nobody can aver that it ever will pass. I write not with an intention to deceive, but that the whole argument may be stated fairly. Much eloquence and ingenuity have been employed in shewing that side of the argument in favor of the proposed constitution, but it ought to be considered that if we accept it upon mere verbal explanations, we shall find ourselves deceived. I appeal to the knowledge of every one, if it does not frequently happen, that a law is interpreted in practice very differently from the intention of the legislature. Hence arises the necessity of acts to amend and explain former acts. This is not an inconvenience in the common and ordinary business of legislation, but is a great one in a constitution. A constitution is a legislative act of the whole people. It is an excellence that it should be permanent, otherwise we are exposed to perpetual insecurity from the fluctuation of government. We should be in the same situation as under absolute government, sometimes exposed to the pressure of greater, and sometimes unprotected by the weaker power in the sovereign.

It is now generally understood that it is for the security of the people that the powers of the government should be lodged in different branches. By this means publick business will go on when they all agree, and stop when they disagree. The advantage of checks in government is thus manifested where the concurrence of different branches is necessary to the same act, but the advantage of a division of business is advantageous in other respects. As in every extensive empire, local laws are necessary to suit the different interests, no single legislature is adequate to the business. All human capacities are limited to a narrow space, and as no individual is capable of practising a great variety of trades, no single legislature is capable of managing all the variety of national and state concerns. Even if a legislature was capable of it, the business of the judicial department must, from the same cause, be slovenly done. Hence arises the necessity of a division of the business into national and local. Each department ought to have all the powers necessary for executing its own business, under such limitations as tend to secure us from any inequality in the operations of government. I know it is often asked against whom in a government by representation is a bill of rights to secure us? I answer, that such a government is indeed a government by ourselves; but as a just government protects all alike, it is necessary that the sober and industrious part of the community should be defended from the rapacity and violence of the vicious and idle. A bill of rights, therefore, ought to set forth the purposes for which the compact is made, and serves to secure the minority against the usurpation and tyranny of the majority. It is a just observation of his excellency, doctor Adams, in his learned defence of the American constitutions that unbridled passions produce the same effect, whether in a king, nobility, or a mob. The experience of all mankind has proved the prevalence of a disposition to use power wantonly. It is therefore as necessary to defend an individual against the majority in a republick as against the king in a monarchy. Our state constitution has wisely guarded this point. The present confederation has also done it.

I confess that I have yet seen no sufficient reason for not amending the confederation, though I have weighed the argument with candour; I think it would be much easier to amend it than the new constitution. But this is a point on which men of very respectable character differ. There is another point in which nearly all agree, and that is, that the new constitution would be better in many respects if it had been differently framed. Here the question is not so much what the amendments ought to be, as in what manner they shall be made, whether they shall be made as conditions of our accepting the constitution, or whether we shall first accept it, and then try to amend it. I can hardly conceive that it should seriously be made a question. If the first question, whether we will receive it as it stands, be negatived, as it undoubtedly ought to be, while the conviction remains that amendments are necessary; the next question will be, what amendments shall be made? Here permit an individual, who glories in being a citizen of Massachusetts, and who is anxious that her character may remain undiminished, to propose such articles as appear to him necessary for preserving the rights of the state. He means not to retract anything with regard to the expediency of amending the old confederation, and rejecting the new one totally; but only to make a proposition which he thinks comprehends the general idea of all parties. If the new constitution means no more than the friends of it acknowledge, they certainly can have no objection to affixing a declaration in favor of the rights of states and of citizens, especially as a majority of the states have not yet voted upon it.

Resolved, that the constitution lately proposed for the United States be received only upon the following conditions:

1. Congress shall have no power to alter the time, place or manner of elections, nor any authority over elections, otherwise than by fining such state as shall neglect to send its representatives or senators, a sum not exceeding the expense of supporting its representatives or senators one year.

2. Congress shall not have the power of regulating the intercourse between the states, nor to levy any direct tax on polls or estates, or any excise.

3. Congress shall not have power to try causes between a state and citizens of another state, nor between citizens of different states; nor to make any laws relative to the transfer of property between those parties, nor any other matter which shall originate in the body of any state.

4. It shall be left to every state to make and execute its own laws, except laws impairing contracts, which shall not be made at all.

5. Congress shall not incorporate any trading companies, nor alienate the territory of any state. And no treaty, ordinance or law of the United States shall be valid for these purposes.

6. Each state shall have the command of its own militia.

7. No continental army shall come within the limits of any state, other than garrison to guard the publick stores, without the consent of such states in time of peace.

8. The president shall be chosen annually and shall serve but one year, and shall be chosen successively from the different states, changing every year.

9. The judicial department shall be confined to cases in which ambassadours are concerned, to cases depending upon treaties, to offences committed upon the high seas, to the capture of prizes, and to cases in which a foreigner residing in some foreign country shall be a party, and an American state or citizen shall be the other party, provided no suit shall be brought upon a state note.

10. Every state may emit bills of credit without making them a tender, and may coin money, of silver, gold or copper, according to the continental standard.

11. No powers shall be exercised by Congress or the president but such as are expressly given by this constitution and not excepted against by this declaration. And any officer of the United States offending against an individual state shall be held accountable to such state, as any other citizen would be.

12. No officer of Congress shall be free from arrest for debt [but] by authority of the state in which the debt shall be due.

13. Nothing in this constitution shall deprive a citizen of any state of the benefit of the bill of rights established by the constitution of the state in which he shall reside, and such bill of rights shall be considered as valid in any court of the United States where they shall be pleaded.

14. In all those causes which are triable before the continental courts, the trial by jury shall be held sacred."

These at present appear to me the most important points to be guarded. I have mentioned a reservation of excise to the separate states, because it is necessary, that they should have some way to discharge their own debts, and because it is placing them in an humiliating & disgraceful situation to depute them to transact the business of international government without the means to carry it on. It is necessary also, as a check on the national government, for it has hardly been known that any government having the powers of war, peace, and revenue, has failed to engage in needless and wanton expense. A reservation of this kind is therefore necessary to preserve the importance of the state governments: without this the extremes of the empire will in a very short time sink into the same degradation and contempt with respect to the middle state as Ireland, Scotland, & Wales, are in with regard to England. All the men of genius and wealth will resort to the seat of government, that will be center of revenue, and of business, which the extremes will be drained to supply.

This is not mere vision, it is justified by the whole course of things. We shall, therefore, if we neglect the present opportunity to secure ourselves, only increase the number of proofs already too many, that mankind are incapable of enjoying their liberty. I have been the more particular in stating the amendments to be made, because many gentlemen think it would be preferable to receive the new system with corrections. I have by this means brought the corrections into one view, and shown several of the principal points in which it is unguarded. As it is agreed, at least professedly, on all sides, that those rights should be guarded, it is among the inferior questions in what manner it is done, provided it is absolutely and effectually done. For my own part, I am fully of opinion that it would be best to reject this plan, and pass an explicit resolve, defining the powers of Congress to regulate the intercourse between us and foreign nations, under such restrictions as shall render their regulations equal in all parts of the empire. The impost, if well collected, would be fully equal to the interest of the foreign debt, and the current charges of the national government. It is evidently for our interest that the charges should be as small as possible. It is also for our interest that the western lands should, as fast as possible, be applied to the purpose of paying the home debt. Internal taxation and that fund have already paid two-thirds of the whole debt, notwithstanding the embarrassments usual at the end of a war.

We are now rising fast above our difficulties; everything at home has the appearance of improvement, government is well established, manufactures increasing rapidly, and trade expanding. Till since the peace we never sent a ship to India, and the present year, it is said, sends above a dozen vessels from this state only, to the countries round the Indian ocean. Vast quantities of our produce are exported to those countries. It has been so much the practice of European nations to farm out this branch of trade, that we ought to be exceedingly jealous of our right. The manufactures of the state probably exceed in value one million pounds for the last year. Most of the useful and some ornamental fabricks are established. There is great danger of these improvements being injured unless we practice extreme caution at setting out. It will always be for the interest of the southern states to raise a revenue from the more commercial ones. It is said that the consumer pays it. But does not a commercial state consume more foreign goods than a landed one? The people are more crowded, and of consequence the land is less able to support them. We know it is to be a favourite system to raise the money where it is. But the money is to be expended at another place, and is therefore so much withdrawn annually from our stock. This is a single instance of the difference of interest; it would be very easy to produce others. Innumerable as the differences of manners, and these produce differences in the laws. Uniformity in legislation is of no more importance than in religion. Yet the framers of this new constitution did not even think it necessary that the president should believe that there is a God, although they require an oath of him. It would be easy to shew the propriety of a general declaration upon that subject. But this paper is already extended to so far [sic].

Another reason which I had in stating the amendments to be made, was to shew how nearly those who are for admitting the system with the necessary alterations, agree with those who are for rejecting this system and amending the confederation. In point of convenience, the confederation amended would be infinitely preferable to the proposed constitution. In amending the former, we know the powers granted, and are subject to no perplexity; but in reforming the latter, the business is excessively intricate, and great part of the checks on Congress are lost. It is to be remembered too, that if you are so far charmed with eloquence, and misled by fair representations and charitable constructions, as to adopt an undefined system, there will be no saying afterwards that you were mistaken, and wish to correct it. It will then be the constitution of our country, and entitled to defence. If Congress should chuse to avail themselves of a popular commotion to continue in being, as the fourth section justifies, and as the British parliament has repeatedly done, the only answer will be, that it is the constitution of our country, and the people chose it. It is therefore necessary to be exceedingly critical. Whatsoever way shall be chosen to secure our rights, the same resolve ought to contain the whole system of amendment. If it is rejected, the resolve should contain the amendations of the old system; and if accepted, it should contain the corrections of the new one.

Cursory Remarks, 1788*

By Hugh Henry Brackenridge

It is not my intention to enter largely into a consideration of this plan of government, but to suggest some ideas in addition to, and of the same nature with, those already made, showing the imperfections and the danger of it.

The first thing that strikes a diligent observer, is the want of precaution with regard to the sex of the president. Is it provided that he shall be of the male gender? The Salii, a tribe of the Burgundians, in the 11th century, excluded females from the sovereignty. Without a similar exclusion, what shall we think, if, in progress of time, we should come to have an old woman at the head of our affairs? But what security have we that he shall be a white man? What would be the national disgrace if he should be elected from one of the southern states, and a vile negro should come to rule over us? Treaties would then be formed with the tribes of Congo and Loango, instead of the civilized nations of Europe. But is there any security that he shall be a

Essays on the Constitution of the United States, pp. 319–21.

freeman? Who knows but the electors at a future period, in days of corruption, may pick up a man-servant, a convict perhaps, and give him the dominion? Is any care taken that he shall be of perfect parts? Shall we, in affairs of a civil nature, leave a door open to lame men, bastards, eunuchs, and the devil knows what?

A senate is the next great constituent part of the government; and yet there is not a word said with regard to the ancestry of any of them; whether they should be altogether Irish, or only Scots Irish. If any of them have been in the war of the White Boys, the Heart of Oak, or the like, they may overturn all authority, and make Shilelah the supreme law of the land.

The house of representatives is to be so large, that it can never be built. They may begin it, but it can never be finished. Ten miles square! Babylon itself, unless the suburbs are taken into view, was not of greater extent.

But what avails it to dwell on these things? The want of a bill of rights is the great evil. There was no occasion for a bill of wrongs; for there will be wrongs enough. But oh! a bill of rights! What is the nature of a bill of rights? "It is a schedule or inventory of those powers which Congress do not possess." But if it is clearly ascertained what powers they have, what need of a catalogue of those powers they have not? Ah! there is the mistake. A minister preaching, undertook, first, to show what was in his text; second, what was not in it. When it is specified what powers are given, why not also what powers are not given? A bill of rights is wanting, and all those things which are usually secured under it—

1. The rights of conscience are swept away. The Confession of Faith, the Prayer Book, the Manual and Pilgrim's Progress are to go. The psalms of Watts, I am told, are the only thing of the kind that is to have any quarter at all.

2. The liberty of the press—that is gone at the first stroke. Not so much as an advertisement for a stray horse, or a runaway negro, can be put in any of the gazettes.

3. The trial by jury—that is knocked in the head, and all that worthy class of men, the lawyers, who live by haranguing and bending the juries, are demolished.

I would submit it to any candid man, if in this constitution there is the least provision for the privilege of shaving the beard? or is there any mode laid down to take the measure of a pair of breeches? Whence is it then, that men of learning seem so much to approve, while the ignorant are against it? The cause is perfectly apparent, viz., that reason is an erring guide, while instinct, which is the governing principle of the untaught, is certain. Put a pig in a poke, carry it half a day's journey through woods and by-ways, let it out, and it will run home without deviation. Could Dr. Franklin do this? What reason have we then to suppose that his judgment, or that of Washington, could be equal to that of Mr. Smilie[1] in state affairs?

[1]John Smilie, a prominent Anti-Federalist.

Were it not on this principle that we are able to account for it, it might be thought strange that old Livingston,[2] of the Jersies, could be so hoodwinked as to give his sanction to such a diabolical scheme of tyranny amongst men—a constitution which may well be called hell-born. For if all the devils in Pandemonium had been employed about it, they could not have made a worse.

Neil MacLaughlin, a neighbor of mine, who has been talking with Mr. Findley, says that under this constitution all weavers are to be put to death. What have these innocent manufacturers done that they should be proscribed?

Let other states think what they will of it, there is one reason why every Pennsylvanian should execrate this imposition upon mankind. It will make his state most probably the seat of government, and bring all the officers, and cause a great part of the revenue to be expended here. This must make the people rich, enable them to pay their debts, and corrupt their morals. Any citizen, therefore, on the Delaware and Susquehannah waters, ought to be hanged and quartered, that would give it countenance.

I shall content myself at present with these strictures, but shall continue them from time to time as occasion may require.

Letters of Sydney, 1788*

By Robert Yates

To the Citizens of the State of New York

Although a variety of objections to the proposed new constitution for the government of the United States have been laid before the public by men of the best abilities, I am led to believe that representing it in a point of view which has escaped their observation may be of use, that is, by comparing it with the constitution of the State of New York.

The following contrast is therefore submitted to the public, to show in what instances the powers of the state government will be either totally or partially absorbed, and enable us to determine whether the remaining powers will, from those kind of pillars, be capable of supporting the mutilated fabric of a government, which even the advocates for the new constitution admit excels "the boasted models of Greece or Rome, and those of all other nations, in having precisely marked out the power of the government and the rights of the people."

It may be proper to premise that the pressure of necessity and distress (and not corruption) had a principal tendency to induce the adoption of the state constitutions and the existing confederation, that power was even then

---

[2]William Livingston.

Essays on the Constitution of the United States, pp. 297–314.

vested in the rulers with the greatest caution, and that, as from every circumstance we have reason to infer that the new constitution does not originate from a pure source, we ought deliberately to trace the extent and tendency of the trust we are about to repose, under the conviction that a reassumption of that trust will at least be difficult, if not impracticable. If we take a retrospective view of the measures of Congress who have their secret journals, the conduct of their officers, at home and abroad, acting under an oath of secrecy, as well as of individuals who were intimately connected with them, from the year 1780 to the last convention, who also acted under an injunction of secrecy (and whose journals have not been published even to this day, but will no doubt continue buried in the dark womb of suspicious secrecy), we can scarcely entertain a doubt but that a plan has long since been framed to subvert the confederation; that that plan has been matured with the most persevering industry and unremitted attention, and that the objects expressed in the preamble to the constitution, that is "to promote the general welfare and secure the blessings of liberty to ourselves and our posterity," were merely the ostensible, and not the real reasons of its framers. That necessity and danger have been the moving causes to the establishment of the confederation will appear from the words of Congress recommending its formation to the several legislatures which are "under a conviction of the absolute necessity of uniting all our councils and all our strength to maintain our common liberties. Let them be examined with liberality becoming brethren and fellow citizens, surrounded by the same iminent dangers, contending for the same illustrious prize, and deeply interested in being forever bound and connected together by the ties the most intimate and indissoluble."

That these principles equally applied to the formation of our state constitution no person can seriously doubt who recollects the rapid progress of the British troops in this state and in Jersey in the year 1776, and the despondence which prevailed among the people on that occasion. The convention of this state, about that period, in explaining to the people the justice of the American cause, addressed them as follows: "You and all men were created free and authorised to establish civil government for the preservation of our rights against civil oppression, and the security of that freedom which God had given you, against the rapacious hand of tyranny and lawless power. If then God hath given us freedom, are we not responsible to him for that as well as other talents? If it is our birth-right, let us not sell it for a mess of pottage, nor suffer it to be torn from us by the hand of violence."

The omission of a bill of rights in this State has given occasion to an inference that the omission was equally warrantable in the constitution for the United States. On this it may be necessary to observe that while the constitution of this State was in agitation, there appeared doubts upon the propriety of the measure, from the peculiar situation in which the country then was; our connection with Britain dissolved, and her government formally renounced—no substitute devised—all the powers of government avowedly temporary, and solely calculated for defence; it was urged by those in favor of a bill of rights that the power of the rulers ought to be circumscribed, the better to protect the people at large from the oppression and usurpation of their rulers. The English peitition of rights, in the reign of Charles the First, and the bill of rights in the reign of king William, were mentioned as examples to support their opinions. Those in opposition admitted that in established governments, which had an implied constitution, a declaration of rights might be necessary to prevent the usurpation of ambitious men, but that was not our situation, for upon the declaration of independence it had become necessary that the exercise of every kind of authority "under the former government should be totally suppressed, and all the power of government exerted under the authority of the people of the colonies;" that we could not suppose that we had an existing constitution or form of government, express or implied, and therefore our situation resembled a people in a state of nature, who are preparing "to institute a government, laying its foundation on such principles, and organizing its powers in such form as to them shall seem most likely to effect their safety and happiness," and as such, the constitution to be formed would operate as a bill of rights.

These and the like considerations operated to induce the convention of New York to dismiss the idea of a bill of rights, and the more especially as the legislative state officers being elected by the people at short periods, and thereby rendered from time to time liable to be displaced in case of malconduct. But these reasons will not apply to the general government, because it will appear in the sequel that the state governments are considered in it as mere dependencies, existing solely by its toleration, and possessing powers of which they may be deprived whenever the general government is disposed so to do. If then the powers of the state governments are to be totally absorbed, in which all agree and only differ as to the mode, whether it will be effected by a rapid progression, or by as certain, but slower, operations: what is to limit the oppression of the general government? Where are the rights, which are declared to be incapable of violation? And what security have people against the wantor oppression of unprincipled governors? No constitutional redress is pointed out, and no express declaration is contained in it, to limit the boundaries of their rulers; beside which the mode and period of their being elected tends to take away their responsibility to the people over whom they may, by the power of the purse and the sword, domineer at discretion; nor is there a power on earth to tell them, What dost thou? or, Why dost thou so?

I shall now proceed to compare the constitution of the state of New York with the proposed federal government, distinguishing the paragraphs in the former, which are rendered nugatory by the latter; those which are in a great measure enervated, and such as are in the discretion of the general government to permit or not.

*   *   *

From this contrast it appears that the general government, when compleatly organized, will absorb all those powers of the state which the framers of its constitution had declared should be only exercised by the representatives of the people of the state; that the burthens and expence of supporting a state establishment will be perpetuated; but its operations to ensure or contribute to any essential measures promotive of the happiness of the people may be totally prostrated, the general government arrogating to itself the right of interfering in the most minute objects of internal police, and the most trifling domestic concerns of every state, by possessing a power of passing laws "to provide for the general welfare of the United States," which may affect life, liberty and property in every modification they may think expedient, unchecked by cautionary reservations, and unrestrained by a declaration of any of those rights which the wisdom and prudence of America in the year 1776 held ought to be at all events protected from violation.

In a word, the new constitution will prove finally to dissolve all the power of the several state legislatures, and destroy the rights and liberties of the people; for the power of the first will be all in all, and of the latter a mere shadow and form without substance, and if adopted we may (in imitation of the Carthaginians) say, Delenda vit Americae.

LEADING FEDERALIST WRITINGS, 1787–1788

Commentary

Historically, there is nothing as irrelevant as a lost constitutional cause—particularly one that was lost centuries ago. We tend today to ignore the writings of the Antifederalists and concentrate instead on what we consider the statesmanlike essays of their opponents; for it is hard for us to find merit in a political view which we consider so plainly wrong as that of opposition to the Constitution. The same should not, however, be true of the controversy over the absence of a Bill of Rights. Here, the Antifederalists had the stronger case and their opponents were on the defensive from the beginning. It was, indeed, not until the Federalists yielded in their rigid opposition on Bill of Rights amendments that ratification of the Constitution was assured.

On the Bill of Rights issue, it is the Antifederalist writings which are the more interesting and even the more influential. That is why (in our presentation) more emphasis has been devoted to the Antifederalist attacks upon the absence of a Bill of Rights than to the Federalist defenses of the Constitution on that issue. At this point, we shall balance the picture somewhat by presenting extracts from some of the leading Federalist writings on the Bill of Rights issue. The authors of the addresses, letters, and essays which follow are James Wilson of Pennsylvania, James Sullivan of Massachusetts, Roger Sherman of Connecticut, Alexander Contee Hanson of Maryland, John Dickinson of Delaware, and Hugh Williamson of North Carolina.

Of these the most important was the *Address* by James Wilson (the future Supreme Court Justice and possessor of perhaps the best legal mind in the Constitutional Convention itself). Three weeks after that Convention adjourned, Wilson delivered his speech to a meeting in Philadelphia. His talk, published in pamphlet form, had great influence and set the theme for what may be called the classic Federalist defense on the Bill of Rights issue (later given definitive form by Hamilton in *The Federalist*), based upon the distinction between delegated and reserved powers. Whatever power is not given to the Federal Government is reserved; and this "will furnish an answer to those who think the omission of a bill of rights, a defect in the proposed constitution." The Congress has no power to interfere with a liberty-like freedom of the press. Hence, explicit protection of such a right is unnecessary; "it would have been superfluous and absurd, to have stipulated with a federal body of our own creation, that we are not divested either by the intention or the act that has brought that body into existence." Wilson was to repeat this argument in the Pennsylvania Ratifying Convention (*infra* p. 631) and it was to become the standard Federalist answer on the Bill of Rights issue.

Of the other Federalist writers, from whom extracts follow, the ones who had the most popular impact were Roger Sherman and John Dickinson, both leaders in the struggle for Independence, the Confederation Congress, and the Philadelphia Convention. It had been Sherman who alone had expressed opposition to the Mason-Gerry effort to add a Bill of Rights to the Constitution and his *Letters of a Countryman* repeated his opposition (expressed perhaps in more extreme form than by any other Federalist of his stature). Dickinson had particular weight as the author of the Revolutionary *Letters of a Pennsylvania Farmer* (which, in William Pierce's famous character sketches of delegates to the federal Convention, made him "one of the most important characters in the United States"). The other writers were of importance in the ratification contests in their states. The extracts from their writings which follow add little that is new to the debate on the Bill of Rights issue. But they do illustrate the approach of Federalist writers to the weakest aspect of their case.

An Address to a Meeting of the Citizens of Philadelphia, 1787*

By James Wilson

Having received the honour of an appointment to represent you in the late convention, it is, perhaps, my duty to comply with the request of many gentlemen, whose characters and judgments I sincerely respect, and who have urged that this would be a proper occasion to lay before you any information, which will serve to elucidate and explain the principles and arrangements of the constitution that has been submitted to the consideration of the United States. I confess that I am unprepared for so extensive and so important a disquisition: but the insidious attempts, which are clandestinely and industriously made to pervert and destroy the new plan, induce me the more readily to engage in its defence: and the impressions of four months constant attendance to the subject, have not been so easily effaced, as to leave me without an answer to the objections which have been raised.

It will be proper, however, before I enter into the refutation of the charges that are alleged, to mark the leading discrimination between the state constitutions, and the constitution of the United States. When the people established the powers of legislation under their separate governments, they invested their representatives with every right and authority which they did not in explicit terms reserve: and therefore upon every question, respecting the jurisdiction of the house of assembly, if the frame of government is silent, the jurisdiction is efficient and complete. But in delegating federal

*Pamphlets on the Constitution of the United States, pp. 155–61.

powers, another criterion was necessarily introduced: and the congressional authority is to be collected, not from tacit implication, but from the positive grant, expressed in the instrument of union. Hence, it is evident, that in the former case, everything which is not reserved, is given: but in the latter, the reverse of the proposition prevails, and every thing which is not given, is reserved. This distinction being recognized, will furnish an answer to those who think the omission of a bill of rights, a defect in the proposed constitution: for it would have been superfluous and absurd, to have stipulated with a federal body of our own creation, that we should enjoy those privileges, of which we are not divested either by the intention or the act that has brought that body into existence. For instance, the liberty of the press, which has been a copious subject of declamation and opposition: what controul can proceed from the federal government, to shackle or destroy that sacred palladium of national freedom? If, indeed, a power similar to that which has been granted for the regulation of commerce, had been granted to regulate literary publications, it would have been as necessary to stipulate that the liberty of the press should be preserved inviolate, as that the impost should be general in its operation. With respect, likewise, to the particular district of ten miles, which is to be the seat of government, it will undoubtedly be proper to observe this salutary precaution, as there the legislative power will be vested in the president, senate, and house of representatives of the United States. But this could not be an object with the convention: for it must naturally depend upon a future compact; to which the citizens immediately interested, will, and ought to be parties: and there is no reason to suspect, that so popular a privilege will in that case be neglected. In truth, then, the proposed system possesses no influence whatever upon the press; and it would have been merely nugatory, to have introduced a formal declaration upon the subject; nay, that very declaration might have been construed to imply that some degree of power was given, since we undertook to define its extent.

Another objection that has been fabricated against the new constitution, is expressed in this disingenuous form—"the trial by jury is abolished in civil cases." I must be excused, my fellow citizens, if, upon this point, I take advantage of my professional experience, to detect the futility of the assertion. Let it be remembered, then, that the business of the federal constitution was not local, but general—not limited to the views and establishments of a single state, but co-extensive with the continent, and comprehending the views and establishments of thirteen independent sovereignties. When, therefore, this subject was in discussion, we were involved in difficulties, which pressed on all sides, and no precedent could be discovered to direct our course. The cases open to a jury, differed in the different states; it was therefore impracticable, on that ground, to have made a general rule. The want of uniformity would have rendered any reference to the practice of the states idle and useless: and it could not, with any propriety, be said, that "the trial by jury shall be as heretofore:" since there has never existed any federal system of jurisprudence, to which the declaration could relate. Besides, it is not in all cases that the trial by jury is adopted in civil questions: for causes depending in courts of admiralty, such as relate to maritime captures, and such as are agitated in the courts of equity, do not require the intervention of that tribunal. How, then, was the line of discrimination to be drawn? The convention found the task too difficult for them: and they left the business as it stands—in the fullest confidence, that no danger could possibly ensue, since the proceedings of the supreme court are to be regulated by the congress, which is a faithful representation of the people: and the oppression of government is effectually barred, by declaring that in all criminal cases, the trial by jury shall be preserved.

This constitution, it has been further urged, is of a pernicious tendency, because it tolerates a standing army in the time of peace. This has always been a popular topic of declamation: and yet I do not know a nation in the world, which has not found it necessary and useful to maintain the appearance of strength in a season of the most profound tranquility. Nor is it a novelty with us; for under the present articles of confederation, congress certainly possesses this reprobated power: and the exercise of it is proved at this moment by the cantonments along the banks of the Ohio. But what would be our national situtation, where it otherwise? Every principle of policy must be subverted, and the government must declare war before they are prepared to carry it on. Whatever may be the provocation, however important the object in view, and however necessary dispatch and secrecy may be, still the declaration must precede the preparation, and the enemy will be informed of your intention, not only before you are equipped for an attack, but even before you are fortified for a defence. The consequence is too obvious to require any further delineation; and no man, who regards the dignity and safety of his country, can deny the necessity of a military force, under the controul, and with the restrictions which the new constitution provides.

Perhaps there never was a charge made with less reason, than that which predicts the institution of a baneful aristocracy in the federal senate. This body branches into two characters, the one legislative, and the other executive. In its legislative character, it can effect no purpose without the co-operation of the house of representatives: and in its executive character, it can accomplish no object, without the concurrence of the president. Thus fettered, I do not know any act which the senate can of itself perform: and such dependence necessarily precludes every idea of influence and superiority. But I will confess, that in the organization of this body, a compromise between contending interests is discernible: and when we reflect how various are the laws, commerce, habits, population, and extent of the confederated states, this evidence of mutual concession and accommodation ought rather to command a generous applause, than to excite jealousy and reproach. For my part, my admiration can only be equalled by my astonishment, in beholding so perfect a system formed from such heterogenous materials.

The next accusation I shall consider, is that which represents the federal constitution as not only calculated, but designedly framed, to reduce the state governments to mere corporations, and eventually to annihilate them. Those who have employed the term corporation, upon this occasion, are not perhaps aware of its extent. In common parlance, indeed, it is generally applied to petty associations for the ease and conveniency of a few individuals; but in its enlarged sense, it will comprehend the government of Pennsylvania, the existing union of the states, and even this projected system is nothing more than a formal act of incorporation. But upon what pretence can it be alleged that it was designed to annihilate the state governments? For, I will undertake to prove that upon their existence depends the existence of the federal plan. For this purpose, permit me to call your attention to the manner in which the president, senate, and house of representatives, are proposed to be appointed. The president is to be chosen by electors, nominated in such manner as the legislature of each state may direct; so that if there is no legislature, there can be no senate. The house of representatives is to be composed of members chosen every second year by the people of the several states, and the electors in each state shall have the qualifications requisite to electors of the most numerous branch of the state legislature—unless, therefore, there is a state legislature, that qualification cannot be ascertained, and the popular branch of the federal constitution must likewise be extinct. From this view, then, it is evidently absurd to suppose, that the annihilation of the separate governments will result from their union; or, that, having that intention, the authors of the new system would have bound their connection with such indissoluble ties. Let me here advert to an arrangement highly advantageous; for you will perceive, without prejudice to the powers of the legislature in the election of senators, the people at large will acquire an additional privilege in returning members to the house of representatives— whereas, by the present confederation, it is the legislature alone that appoints the delegates to congress.

The power of direct taxation has likewise been treated as an improper delegation to the federal government; but when we consider it as the duty of that body to provide for the national safety, to support the dignity of the union, and to discharge the debts contracted upon the collective faith of the states, for their common benefit, it must be acknowledged that those, upon whom such important obligations are imposed, ought, in justice and in policy, to possess every means requisite for a faithful performance of their trust. But why should we be alarmed with visionary evils? I will venture to predict, that the great revenue of the United States must, and always will, be raised by impost; for, being at once less obnoxious, and more productive, the interest of the government will be best promoted by the accommodation of the people. Still, however, the object of direct taxation should be within reach in all cases of emergency; and there is no more reason to apprehend oppression in the mode of collecting a revenue from this resource, than in the form of impost, which, by universal assent, is left to the authority of the federal government. In either case, the force of civil constitutions will be adequate to the purpose; and the dread of military violence, which has been assiduously disseminated, must eventually prove the mere effusion of a wild imagination, or a factious spirit. But the salutary consequences that must flow from thus enabling the government to relieve and support the credit of the union, will afford another answer to the objections upon this ground. The state of Pennsylvania, particularly, which has encumbered itself with the assumption of a great proportion of the public debt, will derive considerable relief and advantage; for, as it was the imbecility of the present confederation, which gave rise to the funding law, that law must naturally expire, when a complete and energetic federal system shall be substituted—the state will then be discharged from an extraordinary burden, and the national creditor will find it to be to his interest to return to his original security.

After all, my fellow-citizens, it is neither extraordinary nor unexpected, that the constitution offered to your consideration, should meet with opposition. It is the nature of man to pursue his own interest, in preference to the public good; and I do not mean to make any personal reflection, when I add, that it is the interest of a very numerous, powerful, and respectable body, to counteract and destroy the excellent work produced by the late convention. All the officers of government, and all the appointments for the administration of justice and the collection of the public revenue, which are transferred from the individual to the aggregate sovereignty of the states, will necessarily turn the stream of influence and emolument into a new channel. Every person, therefore, who either enjoys, or expects to enjoy a place of profit under the present establishment, will object to the proposed innovation? not, in truth, because it is injurious to the liberties of his country, but because it effects his schemes of wealth and consequence. I will confess, indeed, that I am not a blind admirer of this plan of government, and that there are some parts of it, which, if my wish had prevailed, would certainly have been altered. But, when I reflect how widely men differ in their opinions, and that every man (and the observation applies likewise to every state) has an equal pretension to assert his own, I am satisfied that anything nearer to perfection could not have been accomplished. If there are errors, it should be remembered, that the seeds of reformation are sown in the work itself, and the concurrence of two thirds of the congress may at any time introduce alterations and amendments. Regarding it, then, in every point of view, with a candid and disinterested mind, I am bold to assert, that it is the best form of Government which has ever been offered to the World.

Letters of Cassius, 1787*

By James Sullivan

[December 14, 1787]

In some former publications, I have confined myself chiefly to pointing out the views of the opposers to the plan of federal government; the reason why I did not enter particularly into the merits of the new constitution is, that I conceived if it was candidly read, and properly attended to, that alone would be sufficient to recommend it to the acceptance of every rational and thinking mind that was interested in the happiness of the United States of America. Some babblers of the opposition junto have, however, complained that nothing has been said, except in general terms, in favour of the federal constitution; in consequence of this, incompetent as I am to the undertaking, I have been induced to lay the following remarks before the publick.

Sect. first, of the new constitution, says,

"All legislative powers Herein Granted shall be vested in a congress of the United States."

I beg the reader to pay particular attention to the words herein granted, as perhaps there may be occasion for me to recur to them more than once in the course of my observations.

The second section of the federal constitution says, that the members of the house of representatives shall be chosen every second year, and the electors shall have the qualifications required for electors of the most numerous branch of the state legislature. Some have made objections to the time for which the representatives are to be chosen; but it is to be considered, that the convention, in this particular, meant to accommodate the time for which the representatives should stand elected, to the constitutions of the different states. If it had been provided, that the time should have been of shorter duration, would not a citizen of Maryland or South-Carolina had reason to murmur?

The weakness the anti-federalists discover in insinuating that the federal government will have it in their power to establish a despotick government, must be obvious to every one; for the time for which they are elected is so short, as almost to preclude the possibility of their effecting plans for enslaving so vast an empire as the United States of America, even if they were so base as to hope for anything of the kind. The representatives of the people would also be conscious, that their good conduct alone, would be the only thing which could influence a free people to continue to bestow on them their suffrages: the representatives of the people would not, moreover, dare to act

*Essays on the Constitution of the United States, p. 25–48.

contrary to the instructions of their constituents; and if any one can suppose that they would, I would ask them, why such clamour is made about a bill of rights, for securing the liberties of the subject? for if the delegates dared to act contrary to their instructions, would they be afraid to encroach upon a bill of rights? If they determined among themselves to use their efforts to effect the establishment of an aristocratical or despotick government, would a bill of rights be any obstacle to their proceedings? If they were guilty of a breach of trust in one instance, they would be so in another.

The second section also says, no person shall be elected a representative who shall not have been seven years an inhabitant of the United States. This clause effectually confounds all the assertions of the anti-federalists, respecting the representatives not being sufficiently acquainted with the different local interests of their constituents; for a representative, qualified as the constitution directs, must be a greater numbskull than a Vox Populi or an Agrippa, not to have a knowledge of the different concerns of the Confederation.

The objection that the representation will not be sufficient, is weak in the highest degree. It is supposed, that there are sufficient inhabitants in the state of Massachusetts to warrant the sending of six delegates, at least, to the new Congress—To suppose that three gentlemen, of the first characters and abilities, were inadequate to represent the concerns of this state in a just manner, would be absurd in the highest degree, and contradictory to reason and common sense. The weakness of the anti-federalists, in regard to the point just mentioned, sufficiently shews their delinquency with respect to rational argument. They have done nothing more than barely to assert, that the representation would not be sufficient: it is a true saying, that assertions are often the very reverse of facts.

Sect. third, of the new constitution, says, each state shall choose two senators, &c. The liberalty of this clause is sufficient, any reasonable person would suppose, to damp all opposition.

Can any thing be more consistent with the strictest principles of republicanism?

Each state is here upon an equal footing; for the house of representatives can of themselves do nothing without the concurrence of the senate.

The third section further provides, that the senate shall choose their own officers. This is so congenial with the constitution of our own state, that I need not advance any argument to induce the free citizens of Massachusetts to approbate it. And those who oppose this part of the federal plan, act in direct opposition to what the anti-federalists often profess, for the excellency of our constitution has been their favourite theme.

The third section also provides, that the senate shall have the sole power to try all impeachments. This clause seems to be peculiarly obnoxious to anti-federal sycophants.

They have declared it to be arbitrary and tyrannical in the highest degree. But, fellow-citizens, your own good sense will lead you to see the folly and weakness contained in such assertions. You have experienced the tyranny of such a government; that under which you now live is an exact model of it. In Massachusetts, the house of representatives impeach, and the senate try, the offender.

That part of the proposed form of government, which is to be styled the senate, will not have it in their power to try any person, without the consent of two-thirds of the members.

In this respect, therefore, the new constitution is not more arbitrary than the constitution of this state. This clause does not, therefore, savour in the least of any thing more arbitrary than what has already been experienced: so that the horrours the anti-federal junto pretend to anticipate on that head, must sink into nothing. Besides, when the house of representatives have impeached, and the senate tried any one, and found him guilty of the offence for which he is impeached, they can only disqualify him from holding any office of power and trust in the United States: and after that he comes within the jurisdiction of the law of the land.

How such a proceeding can be called arbitrary, or thought improper, I cannot conceive. I leave it to the gentlemen in opposition to point out the tyranny of such conduct, and explain the horrid tendency it will have, for the government of the United States to determine whether any one or more of their own body are worthy to continue in the station to which they were elected.

Another clause, which the anti-federal junto labour to prove to be arbitrary and tyrannical, is contained in the fourth section, which provides, that the time and place for electing senators and representatives shall be appointed by the different state legislatures, except Congress shall at any time make a law to alter such regulation in regard to the place of choosing representatives. The former part of this clause, gives not the least opportunity for a display of anti-federal scandal, and the latter, only by misrepresentation, and false construction, is by them made a handle of. What is intended, by saying that Congress shall have power to appoint the place for electing representatives, is, only to have a check upon the legislature of any state, if they should happen to be composed of villains and knaves, as is the case in a sister state; and should take upon themselves to appoint a place for choosing delegates to send to Congress; which place might be the most inconvenient in the whole state; and for that reason be appointed by the legislature, in order to create a disgust in the minds of the people against the federal government, if they themselves should dislike it. The weakness of their arguments on this head, must therefore be obvious to every attentive mind.

There is one thing, however, which I might mention, as a reason why the opposition junto dread the clause a forementioned—they may suppose, that

Congress, when the people are assembled for the choice of their rulers, in the place they have appointed, will send their terrible standing army (which I shall speak of in its place) and, Cesar Borgia like, massacre the whole, in order to render themselves absolute. This is so similar to many of the apprehensions they have expressed, that I could not pass it by unnoticed. Indeed the chief of their productions abound with improbabilities and absurdities of the like kind; for having nothing reasonable to alledge against a government founded on the principles of staunch republicanism, and which, if well supported, will establish the glory and happiness of our country. They resort to things the most strange and fallacious, in order to blind the eyes of the unsuspecting and misinformed.

*   *   *

On what grounds can the opposers to the new plan found their assertions that Congress will have it in their power to make what laws they please, and what alterations they think proper in the constitution, after the people have adopted it? The constitution expressly says, that any alterations in the constitution must be ratified by three-fourths of the states. The 5th article also provides, that the states may propose any alterations which they see fit, and that Congress shall take measures for having them carried into effect.

If this article does not clearly demonstrate that all power is in the hands of the people, then the language by which we convey our ideas, is shockingly inadequate to its intended purposes, and as little to be understood by us, as Hebrew to the most illiterate.

The 6th section provides, that this constitution, and the laws which shall be made in pursuance thereof, and all treaties made, or which shall be made, in pursuance thereof, under the authority of the United States, shall be the supreme law of the land, and the judges in every state shall be bound thereby, anything in the constitution or laws of any state to the contrary notwithstanding.

This is the article, my countrymen, which knaves and blockheads have so often dressed up in false colours, and requested your attention to the construction of it. Adopt not a constitution, say they, which stipulates that the laws of Congress shall be the supreme law of the land—or, in other words, they request of you not to obey laws of your own making. This is the article which they say is so arbitrary and tyrannical, that unless you have a bill of rights to secure you, you are ruined forever.

But in the name of common sense I would ask, of what use would be a bill of rights, in the present case? . . . It can only be to resort to when it is supposed that Congress have infringed the unalienable rights of the people: but would it not be much easier to resort to the federal constitution, to see if therein power is given to Congress to make the law in question? If such power is not given, the law is in fact a nullity, and the people will not be bound thereby. For let it be remembered, that such laws, and such only, as are founded on this constitution, are to be the common law of the land;—

and it would be absurd indeed, if the laws which are granted in the constitution, were not to be, without reserve, the supreme law of the land. To give Congress power to make laws for the Union, and then to say they should not have force throughout the Union, would be glaringly inconsistent: —Such an inconsistency, however, has hitherto been the evil which the whole continent have complained of, and which the new constitution is designed to remedy.—Let us reverse the proposition, and see how it will then stand.—This constitution, and the laws of the United States which shall be made in pursuance thereof, and all treaties made, or which shall be made under their authority, shall not be the supreme law of the land—and the judges in the several states shall not be bound thereby.—This is exactly what the anti-federalists wish to be the case; this, and in this alone would they glory.—But, fellow citizens, you will discern the excellency of the aforementioned clause; you will perceive that it is calculated, wisely calculated, to support the dignity of this mighty empire, to restore publick and private credit, and national confidence.

Article IV. further provides, That the senators and representatives before mentioned, and the members of the several state legislatures and all executive and judicial officers, both of the United States and of the several states, shall be bound, by oath or affirmation, to support this constitution; but no religious test shall ever be required as a qualification to any office or publick trust under the United States.

Thus, my fellow-citizens, we see that our rulers are to be bound by the most sacred ties, to support our rights and liberties, to secure to us the full enjoyment of every privilege which we can wish for; they are bound by the constitution to guarantee to us a republican form of government in its fullest extent; and what is there more that we can wish for?

Thus the people of the United States, "in order to form a more perfect Union, establish justice, insure domestick tranquillity, provide for the common defence, promote the general welfare, and secure the blessings of liberty to ourselves and our posterity," have appointed a federal convention to "ordain and establish," with the concurrence of the people, a constitution for the United States of America. That federal convention have assembled together, and after a full investigation of the different concerns of the Union, have proposed a form of government, calculated to support, and transmit, inviolate, to the latest posterity, all the blessings of civil and religious liberty.

Citizens of Massachusetts! consider, O consider well, these important matters, and weigh them deliberately in the scale of reason! Consider at what a vast expense of toil, difficulty, treasure and blood, you have emancipated yourselves from the yoke of bondage, and established yourselves an independent people! Consider that those immortal characters, who first planned the event of the revolution, and with arms in their hands stepped forth in the glorious cause of human nature, have now devised a plan for supporting your freedom, and increasing your strength, your power and happiness.

Will you then, O my countrymen! listen to the mad dictates of men, who are aiming, by every artifice and falsehood, which the emissaries of hell can invent, to effect your total destruction and overthrow? who wish to ascend the chariot of anarchy, and ride triumphant over your smoking ruins, which they hope to effect, by their more than hellish arts: in your misery they hope to glory, and establish their own greatness "on their country's ruin."

If they can effect this, they will laugh at your calamity, and mock your misfortunes—the language of each brother in iniquity, when they meet, will be, "hail damn'd associates," see our high success!

Think, O my countrymen! think, before it is too late! The important moment approaches, when these states must, by the most wise of all conduct, forever establish their glory and happiness, on the firmest basis, by adopting the constitution, or by the most foolish and inconsistent of all conduct, in rejecting it, entail on themselves and on their posterity, endless infamy.

> There is a tide in the affairs of men,
> Which taken at the flood, leads on to fortune;
> Omitted, all the voyage of their life
> Is bound in shallowness.

If you embrace not the golden moment now before you, and refuse to receive that which only can establish the dignity of your towering Eagle, this and generations yet unborn, will curse, with an anathema, your dying fame, and breathe, with imprecations and just indignation, vengeance and insults on your sleeping ashes! But should you, on the contrary, with energy and vigour, push your fortune, and, with earnestness and gratitude, clasp to your arms this great blessing which Heaven has pointed to your view, posterity, made happy by your wisdom and exertions, will honour and revere your memories. Secure in their prosperity, they will weep for joy, that Heaven had given them—Fathers!

Letters of a Countryman, 1787*

By Roger Sherman

[November 22, 1787]

To the People of Connecticut

It is fortunate that you have been but little distressed with that torrent of impertinence and folly, with which the newspaper politicians have over whelmed many parts of our country.

It is enough that you should have heard, that one party has seriously urged, that we should adopt the New Constitution because it has been

Essays on the Constitution of the United States, pp. 218–21.

approved by Washington and Franklin: and the other, with all the solemnity of apostolic address to Men, Brethren, Fathers, Friends and Countrymen, have urged that we should reject, as dangerous, every clause thereof, because that Washington is more used to command as a soldier, than to reason as a politician—Franklin is old, others are young—and Wilson is haughty. You are too well informed to decide by the opinion of others, and too independent to need a caution against undue influence.

Of a very different nature, tho' only one degree better than the other reasoning, is all that sublimity of nonsense and alarm, that has been thundered against it in every shape of metaphoric terror, on the subject of a bill of rights, the liberty of the press, rights of conscience, rights of taxation and election, trials in the vicinity, freedom of speech, trial by jury, and a standing army. These last are undoubtedly important points, much too important to depend on mere paper protection. For, guard such privileges by the strongest expressions, still if you leave the legislative and executive power in the hands of those who are or may be disposed to deprive you of them—you are but slaves. Make an absolute monarch—give him the supreme authority, and guard as much as you will by bills of rights, your liberty of the press, and trial by jury;—he will find means either to take them from you, or to render them useless.

The only real security that you can have for all your important rights must be in the nature of your government. If you suffer any man to govern you who is not strongly interested in supporting your privileges, you will certainly lose them. If you are about to trust your liberties with people whom it is necessary to bind by stipulation, that they shall not keep a standing army, your stipulation is not worth even the trouble of writing. No bill of rights ever yet bound the supreme power longer than the honeymoon of a new married couple, unless the rulers were interested in preserving the rights; and in that case they have always been ready enough to declare the rights, and to preserve them when they were declared. The famous English Magna Charta is but an act of parliament, which every subsequent parliament has had just as much constitutional power to repeal and annul, as the parliament which made it had to pass it at first. But the security of the nation has always been, that their government was so formed, that at least one branch of their legislature must be strongly interested to preserve the rights of the nation.

You have a bill of rights in Connecticut (i.e.) your legislature many years since enacted that the subjects of this state should enjoy certain privileges. Every assembly since that time, could, by the same authority, enact that the subjects should enjoy none of those privileges; and the only reason that it has not long since been so enacted, is that your legislature were as strongly interested in preserving those rights as any of the subjects; and this is your only security that it shall not be so enacted at the next session of assembly: and it is security enough.

Your General Assembly under your present constitution are supreme. They may keep troops on foot in the most profound peace, if they think proper. They have heretofore abridged the trial by jury in some cases, and they can again in all. They can restrain the press, and may lay the most burdensome taxes if they please, and who can forbid? But still the people are perfectly safe that not one of these events shall take place so long as the members of the General Assembly are as much interested, and interested in the same manner, as the other subjects.

On examining the new proposed constitution, there can be no question but that there is authority enough lodged in the proposed Federal Congress, if abused, to do the greatest injury. And it is perfectly idle to object to it, that there is no bill of rights, or to propose to add to it a provision that a trial by jury shall in no case be omitted, or to patch it up by adding a stipulation in favor of the press, or to guard it by removing the paltry objection to the right of Congress to regulate the time and manner of elections.

If you cannot prove by the best of all evidence, viz., by the interest of the rulers, that this authority will not be abused, or at least that those powers are not more likely to be abused by the Congress, than by those who now have the same powers, you must by no means adopt the constitution: —No, not with all the bills of rights and with all the stipulations in favor of the people that can be made.

But if the members of Congress are to be interested just as you and I are, and just as the members of our present legislatures are interested, we shall be just as safe, with even supreme power (if that were granted) in Congress, as in the General Assembly. If the members of Congress can take no improper step which will not affect them as much as it does us, we need not apprehend that they will usurp authorities not given them to injure that society of which they are a part.

The sole question, (so far as any apprehension of tyranny and oppression is concerned) ought to be, how are Congress formed? how far have you a control over them? Decide this, and then all the questions about their power may be dismissed for the amusement of those politicians whose business it is to catch flies, or may occasionally furnish subjects for George Bryan's Pomposity, or the declamations of Cato—An Old Whig—Son of Liberty—Brutus—Brutus junior—An Officer of the Continental Army,—the more contemptible Timoleon, and the residue of that rabble of writers.

Address on the Proposed Plan of a Federal Government, 1788*

By Aristides (Alexander Contee Hanson)

It is my intention, with all possible plainness, to examine the proposed plan of a Federal Government. Its enemies and its advocates have laid

*Pamphlets on the Constitution of the United States, pp. 219-57.

particular stress on the names, wherewith it is subscribed. As one side would obtain your implicit assent, by a reference to characters, and as the other would defeat measures by exciting your jealousy of men, permit me, in the first place, to make some general observations on the persons who composed the late memorable convention.

In general, they had been distinguished by their talents and services. They were not principally the men to whom the idea of the convention first suggested itself, and it is notorious that, in general, they accepted their appointments with reluctance. It would seem, however, according to some vague insinuations, that, no sooner did they find themselves convened, than their natures changed; and fatally have they combined for the destruction of your liberties. Now this altogether shocks my faith. I should sooner imagine that the sacredness of the trust, the unparalleled grandeur of the occasion, and the fellowship of the great and good, might have elevated the soul of the most abandoned wretch, had it been possible for such to obtain a seat in that illustrious assemblage.

If those, who would inspire suspicion and distrust, can suggest any precise idea, it must be this, that the members of the convention will be elected into the first federal congress, and there combining again will compose a body capable of bearing down all opposition to their own aggrandisement.

By their scheme, however, thus deeply concerted, the house of representatives is to be chosen by the people once in two years; and if they have acted so as to warrant any reasonable apprehension of their designs, it will be easy at any time, to prevent their election. The truth is, that very few of them either wish to be elected, or would consent to serve, either in that house, or in the senate. I have exercised my imagination to devise in what manner they or any other men, supposing them to bear full sway in both houses, could erect this imaginary fabric of power. I request any person to point out any law, or system of laws, that could be possibly contrived for that purpose, obtain the final assent of each branch, and be carried into effect, contrary to the interests and wishes of a free, intelligent, prying people, accustomed to the most unbounded freedom of inquiry. To begin by an attempt to restrain the press, instead of promoting their designs, would be the most effectual thing to prevent them.

I am apprized of the almost universal disposition for the increase and abuse of authority. But if we are to withhold power because there is a possibility of its perversion, we must abolish government, and submit to those evils, which it was intended to prevent. The perfection of political science consists chiefly in providing mutual checks amongst the several departments of power, preserving at the same time, the dependance of the greatest on the people. I speak with reference to a single government. The necessity of another species of government, for the mutual defence and protection of these American states, no man of sense and honesty, that I know of, has ever yet denied.

The convention had the above principle constantly in their view. They have contrived, that it shall be extremely difficult, if not altogether impracticable, for any person to exceed or abuse his lawful authority. There is nothing in their plan like the cloathing of individuals with power, for their own gratification. Every delegation, and every advantage that may be derived to individuals, has a strict reference to the general good.

To examine their constitution, by article and section, would be a painful and needless undertaking. I shall endeavor to answer such objections, as I have already heard, to anticipate others; to point out some advantages not generally known; and to correct certain errors, with respect to construction.

*   *   *

The institution of the trial by jury has been sanctified by the experience of ages. It has been recognised by the constitution of every state in the union. It is deemed the birthright of Americans; and it is deemed, that liberty cannot subsist without it. The proposed plan expressly adopts it, for the decision of all criminal accusations, except impeachment; and is silent with respect to the determination of facts in civil causes.

The inference, hence drawn by many, is not warranted by the premises. By recognizing the jury trial in criminal cases, the constitution effectually provides, that it shall prevail, so long as the constitution itself shall remain unimpaired and unchanged. But, from the great variety of civil cases, arising under this plan of government it would be unwise and impolite to say aught about it in regard to these. Is there not a great variety of cases, in which this trial is taken away in each of the states? Are there not many more cases, where it is denied in England? For the convention to ascertain in what cases it shall prevail, and in what others it may be expedient to prefer other modes was impracticable. On this subject a future congress is to decide; and I see no foundation under Heaven for the opinion that congress will despise the known prejudices and inclination of their countrymen. A very ingenious writer of Philadelphia has mentioned the objections without deigning to refute that, which he conceives to have originated in "sheer malice."

I proceed to attack the whole body of anti-federalists in their strong hold. The proposed constitution contains no bill of rights.

Consider again the nature and intent of a federal republic. It consists of an assemblage of distinct states, each completely organized for the protection of its own citizens, and the whole consolidated, by express compact, under one head, for the general welfare and common defence.

Should the compact authorize the sovereign, or head to do all things it may think necessary and proper, then there is no limitation to its authority; and the liberty of each citizen in the union has no other security, than the sound policy, good faith, virtue, and perhaps proper interests, of the head.

When the compact confers the aforesaid general power, making nevertheless some special reservations and exceptions, then is the citizen protected further, so far as these reservations and exceptions shall extend.

But, when the compact ascertains and defines the power delegated to the federal head, then cannot this government, without manifest usurpation, exert any power not expressly, or by necessary implication, conferred by the compact.

This doctrine is so obvious and plain, that I am amazed any good man should deplore the omission of a bill of rights.

When we were told, that the celebrated Mr. Wilson had advanced this doctrine in effect, it was said, Mr. Wilson would not dare to speak thus to a Constitutionalist. With talents inferior to that gentleman's, I will maintain the doctrine against any Constitutionalist who will condescend to enter the lists, and behave like a gentleman.

It is, however, the idea of another most respectable character, that, as a bill of rights could do no harm, and might quiet the minds of many good people, the convention would have done well to indulge them. With all due deference, I apprehend, that a bill of rights might not be this innocent quieting instrument. Had the convention entered on the work, they must have comprehended within it everything, which the citizens of the United States claim as a natural or a civil right. An omission of a single article would have caused more discontent, than is either felt or pretended, on the present occasion. A multitude of articles might be the source of infinite controversy, by clashing with the powers intended to be given. To be full and certain, a bill of rights might have cost the convention more time, than was expended on their other work. The very appearance of it might raise more clamour than its omission,—I mean from those who study pretexts for condemning the whole fabric of the constitution. "What! (might they say) did these exalted spirits imagine, that the natural rights of mankind depend on their gracious concession. If indeed they possessed that tyrannic sway, which, the kings of England had once usurped, we might humbly thank them for their magna charta, defective as it is. As that is not the case, we will not suffer it to be understood, that their new-fangled federal head shall domineer with the powers not excepted by their precious bill of rights. What! if the owner of 1,000 acres of land thinks proper to fell one half, is it necessary to take a release from the vendee of the other half? Just as necessary is it for the people to have a grant of their natural rights from a government which derives everything it has, from the grant of the people."

The restraints laid on the state legislatures will tend to secure domestic tranquility, more than all the bills, or declarations, of rights, which human policy could devise. It is very justly asserted, that the plan contains an avowal of many rights. It provides that no man, shall suffer by expost facto laws or bills of attainder. It declares, that gold and silver only shall be a tender for specie debts; and that no law shall impair the obligation of a contract.

I have here perhaps touched a string, which secretly draws together many of the foes to the plan. Too long have we sustained evils, resulting from injudicious emissions of paper, and from the operation of tender laws. To bills of credit as they are now falsely called, may we impute the entire loss of confidence between men. Hence it is, that specie has, in a great degree, ceased its proper office, and been confined to speculations, baneful to the public, and enriching a few enterprising sharp-sighted men, at the expence not only of the ignorant, slothful, and needy, but of their country's best benefactors. Hence chiefly are the bankruptcies throughout America, and the disreputable ruinous state of our commerce. Hence is it principally, that America hath lost its credit abroad, and American faith become a proverb. The convention plainly saw, that nothing short of a renunciation of the right to emit bills of credit could produce that grand consummation of policy, the restoration of public and private faith.

Were it possible for the nations abroad to suppose Great Britain would emit bills on the terms whereon they have issued in America, how soon would the wide arch of that mighty empire tumble into ruins? In no other country in the universe has prevailed the idea of supplying, by promissory notes, the want of coin, for commerce and taxes.

*   *   *

With a view to defeat totally the plan, another general convention is proposed; not with the power of giving a finishing hand to a constitution; but again to consider objections, to strike out, to add, and again to make their report to the several states.

In this way, there can never be an end. We must at last return to this, that whatever is agreed on, by the assembly appointed to propose, must be either adopted in the whole, or in the whole rejected.

The idea of a new convention is started by some men, with the vain expectation of having amendments made to suit a particular state, or to advance their own selfish views. Were this fatal idea adopted; I should bid a last adieu to that elevated hope, which now inspires me, of living under the happiest form of government which the sun ever beheld. Recollect again and again, that almost every state in the union made a determined point of delegating its first characters to this grand convention. Reflect upon the time spent in the arduous work, and the sacrifices which those distinguished persons made to their country. Should the same men be deputed again, would they not, think you, with the same unanimity, subscribe and recommend the same plan? So far as I have been informed, those members, who, in the progression of the plan, had opposed certain parts, and yet afterwards subscribed cheerfully to the whole, have, with the candour which becomes them, acknowledged their errors in debate. Even an illustrious character, who was of the minority, consisting only of three, I have been told, has since regretted his refusal.

Suppose then a second convention, with a different choice of delegates. These too would either speedily subscribe, or they might propose some other system, to be debated, paragraph by paragraph, in thirteen different assemblies; and then there would be the same probability of a mutilated plan; or they would propose something, to be adopted or rejected in the whole; and there would be the same necessity of another convention. Besides, as the second convention, if it consist of different men, must inevitably be inferior to the first, there is little probability that their world will be superior. Never again, in an assembly constituted as that was, will there be found the same liberality of sentiment, "the same spirit of amity, and the same mutual deference and concession."

If it be contended, that the second, being possessed of the various objections from the several states, must be better able to determine, I would ask, what conduct this second convention should adopt? Are they to take the proposed plan, and strike out every thing objected to by nine states? Or may they likewise adopt and recommend the entire plan? In short, to appoint a second convention, merely to consult and propose, would be the most absurd expedient, that ever, in a matter of this amazing magnitude, was proposed. Does any man then entertain the thought of another kind of convention, invested with full powers to consult, amend, adopt, and confirm? A scheme like this was never yet, I trust, in agitation. But, if it were, I would propose this single question. Whether is it better to amend, before it be tried, that plan, which may be termed the result of the wisdom of America, or leave it to be amended, at leisure, as mature experience shall direct?

*   *   *

An aristocracy can perhaps subsist with only a moderate extent of territory and population, But it is a farce to talk of an aristocracy; when there are two branches, so differently formed; when the members of each are chosen for a reasonable term; and when their reappointment depends on the good opinion of their countrymen. It is not in nature that a man with the least portion of common sense can believe the people of America will consent to such a deplorable change in their constitution, as shall confine all power to a few noble families, or that, without their consent, the change will be effected, by internal policy, or force.

Whilst mankind shall believe freedom to be better than slavery; whilst our lands shall be generally distributed, and not held by a few insolent barons, on the debasing terms of vassalage; whilst we shall teach our children to read and write; whilst the liberty of the press, that grand palladium, which tyrants are compelled to respect, shall remain; whilst a spark of public love shall animate even a small part of the people; whilst even self-love shall be the general ruling principle; so long will it be impossible for an aristocracy to arise from the proposed plan. Should Heaven, in its wrath, inflict blindness on the people of America; should they reject this fair offer of permanent safety and happiness; to predict what species of government shall at last spring from disorder, is beyond the short reach of political foresight.

Believe me, my fellow citizens, that no overweening self conceit, no vain ambition, no restless meddling spirit, has produced this address. Long had I waited to see this vast question treated, as it deserves; and the publication disseminated in my native state. Many judicious observations had appeared in newspapers and handbills. But no publication, that I have seen, has gone fully into the merits, considered the objections, and explained that, which is doubtful and obscure. On this account I, at length, made the attempt. That my performance is equal to my wishes, I can by no means believe. I have, however, a consolation in reflecting, that it will be difficult for any man to demonstrate, that, in this business, I have a particular interest. In many of my remarks, I have been anticipated by writings, which I have seen; and I have collected materials, wherever I could find them. Could I be convinced, that I have said nothing, which had not before been said or thought by thousands, the reflection would yield far less mortification than pleasure.

Letters of Fabius, 1788*

By John Dickinson

Letter IV

Another question remains. How are the contributed rights to be managed? The resolution has been in great measure anticipated, by what has been said concerning the system proposed. Some few reflections may perhaps finish it.

If it be considered separately, a constitution is the organization of the contributed rights in society. Government is the exercise of them. It is intended for the benefit of the governed; of course can have no just powers but what conduce to that end: and the awfulness of the trust is demonstrated in this—that it is founded on the nature of man, that is, on the will of his Maker, and is therefore sacred. It is then an offence against Heaven, to violate that trust.

If the organization of a constitution be defective, it may be amended,

A good constitution promotes, but not always produces a good administration.

The government must never be lodged in a single body. From such an one, with an unlucky composition of its parts, rash, partial, illegal, and when intoxicated with success, even cruel, insolent and contemptible edits, may at

*Pamphlets on the Constitution of the United States, pp. 181–87.

times be expected. By these, if other mischiefs do not follow, the national dignity may be impaired.

Several inconveniences might attend a division of the government into two bodies, that probably would be avoided in another arrangement.

The judgment of the most enlightened among mankind, confirmed by multiplied experiments, points out the propriety of government being committed to such a number of great departments, as can be introduced without confusion, distinct in office, and yet connected in operation. It seems to be agreed, that three or four of these departments are a competent number.

Such a repartition appears well calculated to express the sense of the people, and to encrease the safety and repose of the governed, which with the advancement of their happiness in other respects, are the objects of government; as thereby there will be more obstructions interposed; against errors, feuds, and frauds, in the administration, and the extraordinary interference of the people need be less frequent. Thus, wars, tumults, and uneasinesses, are avoided. The departments so constituted, may therefore be said to be balanced.

But, notwithstanding, it must be granted, that a bad administration may take place. What is then to be done? The answer is instantly found—Let the Fasces be lowered before—the supreme sovereignty of the people. It is their duty to watch, and their right to take care, that the constitution be preserved; or in the Roman phrase on perilous occasions—to provide, that the republic receive no damage.

Political bodies are properly said to be balanced, with respect to this primary origination and ultimate destination, not to any intrinsic or constitutional properties. It is the power from which they proceed, and which they serve, that truly and of right balances them.

But, as a good constitution not always produces a good administration, a defective one not always excludes it. Thus in governments very different from those of United America, general manners and customs, improvement in knowledge, and the education and disposition of princes, not unfrequently soften the features, and qualify the defects. Jewels of value are substituted, in the place of the rare and genuine orient of highest price and brightest lustre: and though the sovereigns cannot even in their ministers, be brought to account by the governed, yet there are instances of their conduct indicating a veneration for the rights of the people, and an internal conviction of the guilt that attends their violation. Some of them appear to be fathers of their countries. Revered princes! Friends of mankind! May peace be in their lives—and in their deaths—Hope.

By this superior will of the people, is meant a reasonable, not a distracted will. When frenzy seizes the mass, it would be equal madness to think of their happiness, that is, of their freedom. They will infallibly have a Philip or a Caesar, to bleed them into soberness of mind. At present we are cool: and let us attend to our business.

Our government under the proposed confederation, will be guarded by a repetition of the strongest cautions against excesses. In the senate the sovereignties of the several states will be equally represented; in the house of representatives, the people of the whole union will be equally represented; and, in the president, and the federal independent judges, so much concerned in the execution of the laws, and in the determination of their constitutionality, the sovereignties of the several states and the people of the whole union, may be considered as conjointly represented.

Where was there ever and where is there now upon the face of the earth, a government so diversified and attempered? If a work formed with so much deliberation, so respectful and affectionate an attention to the interests, feelings, and sentiments of all United America, will not satisfy, what would satisfy all United America?

It seems highly probable, that those who would reject this labour of public love, would also have rejected the Heaven-taught institution of trial by jury, had they been consulted upon its establishment. Would they not have cried out, that there never was framed so detestable, so paltry, and so tyrannical a device for extinguishing freedom, and throwing unbounded domination into the hands of the king and barons, under a contemptible pretence of preserving it? "What! Can freedom be preserved by imprisoning its guardians? Can freedom be preserved, by keeping twelve men closely confined without meat, drink, fire, or candle, until they unanimously agree, and this to be innumerably repeated? Can freedom be preserved, by thus delivering up a number of freemen to a monarch and an aristocracy, fortified by dependant and obedient judges and officers, to be shut up, until under duress they speak as they are ordered? Why cannot the twelve jurors separate, after hearing the evidence, return to their respective homes, and there take time, and think of the matter at their ease? Is there not a variety of ways, in which causes have been, and can be tried, without this tremendous, unprecedented inquisition? Why then is it insisted on; but because the fabricators of it know that it will, and intend that it shall reduce the people to slavery? Away with it— Freemen will never be enthralled by so insolent, so execrable, so pitiful a contrivance."

Happily for us our ancestors thought otherwise. They were not so over-nice and curious, as to refuse blessings, because, they might possibly be abused.

They perceived, that the uses included were great and manifest. Perhaps they did not foresee, that from this acorn, as it were, of their planting, would be produced a perpetual vegetation of political energies, that "would secure the just liberties of the nation for a long succession of ages, and elevate it to the distinguished rank it has for several centuries held. As to abuses, they trusted to their own spirit for preventing or correcting them: And worthy is it of deep consideration by every friend of freedom, that abuses that seem to be but "trifles," may be attended by fatal consequences. What can be "trifling," that diminishes or detracts from the only defence, that ever was found against "open attacks and secret machinations?" This establishment originates from a knowledge of human nature. With a superior force, wisdom, and benevolence united, it rives the difficulties concerning administration of justice, that have distressed, or destroyed the rest of mankind. It reconciles contradictions—vastness of power, with safety of private station. It is ever new, and always the same.

Trial by jury and the dependence of taxation upon representation, those corner stones of liberty, were not obtained by a bill of rights, or any other records, and have not been and cannot be preserved by them. They and all other rights must be preserved, by soundness of sense and honesty of heart. Compared with these, what are a bill of rights, or any characters drawn upon paper or parchment, those frail remembrances? Do we want to be reminded, that the sun enlightens, warms, invigorates, and cheers? or how horrid it would be, to have his blessed beams intercepted, by our being thrust into mines or dungeons? Liberty is the sun of society. Rights are the beams.

"It is the duty which every man owes to his country, his friends, his posterity, and himself, to maintain to the utmost of his power this valuable palladium in all its rights; to restore to its its ancient dignity, if at all impaired by the different value of property, or otherwise deviated from its first institution; to amend it, wherever it is defective; and above all to guard with the most jealous circumspection against the new and arbitrary methods of trial, which, under a variety of plausible pretences, may in time imperceptibly undermine this best preservative of liberty." Trial by Jury is our birth-right; and tempted to his own ruin, by some seducing spirit, must be the man, who in opposition to the genius of United America, shall dare to attempt its subversion.

In the proposed confederation, it is preserved inviolable in criminal cases, and cannot be altered in other respects, but when United America demands it.

There seems to be a disposition in men to find fault, no difficult matter, rather than to act as they ought. The works of creation itself have been objected to: and one learned prince declared, that if he had been consulted, they would have been improved. With what book has so much fault been found, as with the Bible? Perhaps, principally, because it so clearly and strongly enjoins men to do right. How many, how plausible objections have been made against it, with how much ardor, with how much pains? Yet, the book has done more good than all the books in the world; would do much more, if duly regarded; and might lead the objectors against it to happiness, if they would value it as they should.

When objections are made to a system of high import, should they not be weighed against the benefits? Are these great, positive, immediate? Is there a chance of endangering them by rejection or delay? May they not be attained without admitting the objections at present, supposing the objections to be well founded? If the objections are well founded, may they not be hereafter admitted, without danger, disgust, or inconvenience? Is the system so formed, that they may be thus admitted? May they not be of less efficiency, than they are thought to be by their authors? are they not designed to hinder evils, which are generally deemed to be sufficiently provided against? May not the admission of them prevent benefits, that might otherwise be obtained? In political affairs, is it not more safe and advantageous, for all to agree in measures that may not be best, than to quarrel among themselves, what are best?

When questions of this kind with regard to the plan proposed, are calmly considered, it seems reasonable to hope, that every faithful citizen of United America, will make up his mind, with much satisfaction to himself, and advantage to his country.

Remarks on the New Plan of Government, 1788*

By Hugh Williamson

Though I am conscious that a subject of the greatest magnitude must suffer in the hands of such an advocate, I cannot refuse, at the request of my fellow-citizens, to make some observations on the new plan of government.

It seems to be generally admitted, that the system of government which has been proposed by the late convention, is well calculated to relieve us from many of the grievances under which we have been laboring. If I might express my particular sentiments on this subject, I should describe it as more free and more perfect than any form of government that has ever been adopted by any nation; but I would not say it has no faults. Imperfection is inseparable from every device. Several objections were made to this system by two or three very respectable characters in the convention, which have been the subject of much conversation; and other objections, by citizens of this state, have lately reached our ears. It is proper you should consider of these objections. They are of two kinds; they respect the things that are in the system, and the things that are not in it. We are told that there should have been a section for securing the trial by Jury in civil cases, and the liberty of the press: that there should also have been a declaration of rights. In the new system, it is provided, that "the trial of all crimes, except in cases of impeachment, shall be by jury," but this provision could not possibly be extended to all civil cases. For it is well known that the trial by jury is not general and uniform throughout the United States, either in cases of admiralty or of chancery; hence it becomes necessary to submit the question to the general Legislature, who might accommodate their laws on this occasion to

Essays on the Constitution of the United States, pp. 395–406.

the desires and habits of the nation. Surely there is no prohibition in a case that is untouched.

We have been told that the liberty of the press is not secured by the new Constitution. Be pleased to examine the Plan, and you will find that the liberty of the press and the laws of Mahomet are equally affected by it. The new government is to have the power of protecting literary property; the very power which you have by a special act delegated to the present congress. There was a time in England, when neither book, pamphlet, nor paper could be published without a license from government. That restraint was finally removed in the year 1694 and, by such removal, their press became perfectly free, for it is not under the restraint of any license. Certainly the new government can have no power to impose restraints. The citizens of the United States have no more occasion for a second declaration of rights, than they have for a section in favour of the press. Their rights, in the several states, have long since been explained and secured by particular declarations, which make a part of their several constitutions. It is granted, and perfectly understood, that under the government of the assemblies of the states, and under the government of the congress, every right is reserved to the individual which he has not expressly delegated to this, or that legislature. The other objections that have been made to the new plan of government, are: That it absorbs the powers of the several states; that the national judiciary is too extensive; that a standing army is permitted; that congress is allowed to regulate trade; that the several states are prevented from taxing exports for their own benefit.

When Gentlemen are pleased to complain, that little power is left in the hands of the separate states, they should be advised to cast an eye upon the large code of laws, which have passed in this state since the peace. Let them consider how few of those laws have been framed for the general benefit of the nation. Nine out of ten of them are domestic; calculated for the sole use of this state or of particular citizens. There must still be use for such laws, though you should enable the congress to collect a revenue for national purposes; and the collection of that revenue includes the chief of the new powers, which are now to be committed to the congress.

Hitherto you have delegated certain powers to the Congress, and other powers to the Assemblies of the states. The portion that you have delegated to Congress, is found to have been useless, because it is too small: and the powers that are committed to the Assemblies of the several states are also found to be absolutely ineffectual for national purposes, because they can never be so managed as to operate in concert. Of what use is that small portion of reserve powers? It neither makes you respectable nor powerful. The consequence of such reservation is national contempt abroad, and a state of dangerous weakness at home. What avails the claim of power, which appears to be nothing better than the empty whistling of a name? The

Congress will be chosen by yourselves, as your members of Assembly are. They will be creatures of your hands, and subject to your advice. Protected and cherished by the small addition of power which you shall put into their hands, you may become a great and respectable nation.

It is complained that the powers of the national judiciary are too extensive. This objection appears to have the greatest weight in the eyes of gentlemen who have not carefully compared the powers which are to be delegated, with those that had been formerly delegated to Congress. The powers now to be committed to the national legislature, as they are detailed in the 8th section of the first article, have already been chiefly delegated to the Congress, under one form or another, except those which are contained in the first paragraph of that section. And the objects that are now to be submitted to the supreme judiciary, or to the inferior courts, are those which naturally arise from the constitutional laws of Congress. If there is a single new case that can be exceptional, it is that between a Foreigner and a Citizen, or that between the Citizens of different States. These cases may come up by appeal. It is provided in this system, that there shall be no fraudulent tender in the payments of debts. Foreigners with whom we have treaties will trust our citizens on the faith of this engagement; and the citizens of different states will do the same. If the Congress had a negative on the laws of the several states, they would certainly prevent all such laws as might endanger the honor or peace of the nation, by making a tender of base money; but they have no such power, and it is at least possible that some state may be found in this union, disposed to break the constitution, and abolish private debts by such tenders. In these cases the courts of the offending state would probably decide according to its own laws. The foreigner would complain, and the nation might be involved in war for the support of such dishonest measures. It is not better to have a court of appeals in which the judges can only be determined by the laws of the nation? This court is equally to be desired by the citizens of different states. But we are told that justice will be delayed, and the poor will be drawn away by the rich to a distant court. The authors of this remark have not fully considered the question, else they must have recollected that the poor of this country have little to do with foreigners or with the citizens of distant states. They do not consider that there may be an inferior court in every state; nor have they recollected that the appeals being with such exceptions, and under such regulations as Congress shall make, will never be permitted for trifling sums or under trivial pretences, unless we can suppose that the national legislature shall be composed of knaves and fools. The line that separates the powers of the national legislature from those of the several states is clearly drawn. The several states reserve every power that can be exercised for the particular use and comfort of the state. They do not yield a single power which is not absolutely necessary to the safety and prosperity of the nation, nor one that could be employed to any effect in the hands of particular states. The powers of judiciary naturally arise from those of the legislature. Questions that are of a national concern, and those cases which are determinable by the general laws of the nation, are to be referred to the national judiciary; but they have not anything to do with a single case either civil or criminal which respects the private and particular concerns of a state or its citizens.

*   *   *

When you refer the proposed system to the particular circumstances of North Carolina, and consider how she is to be affected by this plan, you must find the utmost reason to rejoice in the prospect of better times. This is a sentiment that I have ventured with the greater confidence, because it is the general opinion of my late honourable colleagues, and I have the utmost reliance in their superior abilities. But if our constituents shall discover faults where we could not see any—or if they shall suppose that a plan is formed for abridging their liberties, when we imagined that we had been securing both liberty and property on a more stable foundation—if they perceive that they are to suffer a loss, where we thought they must rise from a misfortune—they will, at least do us the justice to charge those errors to the head, and not to the heart.

The proposed system is now in your hands, and with it the fate of your country. We have a common interest for we are embarked in the same vessel. At present she is in a sea of trouble, without sails, oars, or pilot; ready to be dashed to pieces by every flaw of wind. You may secure a port, unless you think it better to remain at sea. If there is any man among you that wishes for troubled times and fluctuating measures, that he may live by speculations, and thrive by the calamities of the state, this government is not for him.

If there is any man who envies the prosperity of a native citizen—who wishes that we should remain without native merchants or seamen, without shipping, without manufactures, without commerce—poor and contemptible, the tributaries of a sovereign country—this government is not for him.

And if there is any man who has never been reconciled to our independence, who wishes to see us degraded and insulted abroad, oppressed by anarchy at home, and torn into pieces by factions—incapable of resistance, and ready to become a prey to the first invader—this government is not for him.

But it is a government, unless I am greatly mistaken, that gives the fairest promise of being firm and honourable; safe from foreign invasion or domestic sedition—a government by which our commerce must be protected and enlarged; the value of our produce and of our lands must be increased; the labourer and the mechanic must be encouraged and supported. It is a form of government that is perfectly fitted for protecting liberty and property, and for cherishing the good citizen and honest man.

ADDRESSES BY JOHN JAY AND MELANCTON SMITH, 1788

Commentary

As will be seen (*infra* p. 852) what was in many ways the most closely contested of the struggles for ratification of the federal Consitution occurred in New York. Two of the opposing leaders in the New York contest were John Jay (Federalist) and Melancton Smith (Antifederalist). They both wrote influential Addresses on ratification to the people of their state, which illustrate the arguments used on both sides in what became the last of the important ratification contests. By this time, the issue was no longer one of whether there should be a Bill of Rights (though Jay does lamely repeat the Federalist theme that a Bill of Rights is unnecessary), but one of how to accomplish the required guarantees for individual rights. Jay rejects the notion of a second Convention to accomplish the needed changes. (The threat of such a Convention had become the leading Antifederalist threat.) The main thing, says Jay, is to accept the present plan as the best available, and work for amendments in the manner specified in the Constitution.

Smith, on the contrary, urges the need for amendments as a condition of ratification. He recognizes that the Federalists themselves had come to concede the need for amendments, but warns against accepting their view that amendments will come afterwards, "provided they will first agree to accept the proferred system as it is." He ridicules the idea that those in power under the new system will consent to limitations upon their authority: "the idea of receiving a form radically defective, under the notion of making the necessary amendments, is evidently absurd." To the Federalists who now say, "adopt it first, and then amend it. I ask, why not amend and then adopt it?" Smith then adds a Postscript as a direct reply to the Jay Address. Much of it is devoted to the Bill of Rights issue and a rejection of the Federalist view that a Bill of Rights is not necessary. The views thus stated by Smith were repeated by his Antifederalist colleagues in the New York ratification debates, particularly on the need for previous amendments as a condition for ratification. In the end, however, Smith himself was one of the leaders who defected to the Federalists on the issue of previous versus subsequent amendments. That alone, as it turned out, enabled New York to ratify the Constitution.

Address to the People of New York on the Constitution, 1788*

By John Jay

There are times and seasons, when general evils spread general alarm and uneasiness, and yet arise from causes too complicated, and too little under-

Pamphlets on the Constitution of the United States, pp. 67–85.

stood by many, to produce an unanimity of opinions respecting their remedies. Hence it is, that on such occasions, the conflict of arguments too often
excites a conflict of passions, and introduces a degree of discord and animosity, which, by agitating the public mind dispose it to precipitation and
extravagance. They who on the ocean have been unexpectedly enveloped
with tempests, or suddenly entangled among rocks and shoals, know the
value of that serene, self-possession and presence of mind, to which in such
cases they owed their preservation; nor will the heroes who have given us
victory and peace, hesitate to acknowledge that we are as much indebted for
those blessings to the calm prevision, and cool intrepidity which planned and
conducted our military measures, as to the glowing animation with which
they were executed.

While reason retains her rule, while men are as ready to receive as to give
advice, and as willing to be convinced themselves, as to convince others,
there are few political evils from which a free and enlightened people cannot
deliver themselves. It is unquestionably true, that the great body of the
people love their country, and wish it prosperity; and this observation is
particularly applicable to the people of a free country, for they have more
and stronger reasons for loving it than others. It is not therefore to vicious
motives that the unhappy divisions which sometimes prevail among them are
to be imputed; the people at large always mean well, and although they may
on certain occasions be misled by the counsels, or injured by the efforts of
the few who expect more advantage from the wreck, than from the preservation of national prosperity, yet the motives of these few, are by no means to
be confounded with those of the community in general.

That such seeds of discord and danger have been disseminated and begin
to take root in America, as unless eradicated will soon poison our gardens
and our fields, is a truth much to be lamented; and the more so, as their
growth rapidly increases, while we are wasting the season in honestly but
imprudently disputing, not whether they shall be pulled up, but by whom, in
what manner, and with what instruments, the work shall be done.

When the king of Great Britain, misguided by men who did not merit his
confidence, asserted the unjust claim of binding us in all cases whatsoever,
and prepared to obtain our submission by force, the object which engrossed
our attention, however important, was nevertheless plain and simple, "What
shall we do?" was the question—the people answered, let us unite our
counsels and our arms. They sent Delegates to Congress, and soldiers to the
field. Confiding in the probity and wisdom of Congress, they received their
recommendations as if they had been laws: and that ready acquiesence in
their advice enabled those patriots to save their country. Then there was
little leisure or disposition for controversy respecting the expediency of
measures—hostile fleets soon filled our ports, and hostile armies spread
desolation on our shores. Union was then considered as the most essential of
human means and we almost worshipped it with as much fervor, as pagans
in distress formerly implored the protection of their tutelar deities. That

union was the child of wisdom—heaven blessed it, and it wrought out our political salvation.

That glorious war was succeeded by an advantageous peace. When danger disappeared, ease, tranquility, and a sense of security loosened the bands of union; and Congress and soldiers and good faith depreciated with their apparent importance. Recommendations lost their influence, and requisitions were rendered nugatory, not by their want of propriety, but by their want of power. The spirit of private gain expelled the spirit of public good, and men became more intent on the means of enriching and aggrandizing themselves, than of enriching and aggrandizing their country. Hence the war-worn veteran, whose reward for toils and wounds existed in written promises, found Congress without the means, and too many of the States without the disposition, to do him justice. Hard necessity compelled him, and others under similar circumstances, to sell their honest claims on the public for a little bread; and thus unmerited misfortunes and patriotic distresses became articles of speculation and commerce.

These and many other evils, too well known to require enumeration, imperceptibly stole in upon us, and acquired an unhappy influence on our public affairs. But such evils, like the worst of weeds, will naturally spring up in so rich a soil; and a good Government is as necessary to subdue the one, as an attentive gardner or husbandman is to destroy the other—Even the garden of Paradise required to be dressed, and while men continue to be constantly impelled to error and to wrong by innumerable circumstances and temptations, so long will society experience the unceasing necessity of government.

It is a pity that the expectations which actuated the authors of the existing confederation, neither have nor can be realized: accustomed to see and admire the glorious spirit which moved all ranks of people in the most gloomy moments of the war, observing their steadfast attachment to Union, and the wisdom they so often manifested both in choosing and confiding in their rulers, those gentlemen were led to flatter themselves that the people of America only required to know what ought to be done, to do it. This amiable mistake induced them to institute a national government in such a manner, as though very fit to give advice, was yet destitute of power, and so constructed as to be very unfit to be trusted with it. They seem not to have been sensible that mere advice is a sad substitute for laws; nor to have recollected that the advice even of the allwise and best of Beings, has been always disregarded by a great majority of all the men that ever lived.

Experience is a severe preceptor, but it teaches useful truths, and however harsh, is always honest—Be calm and dispassionate, and listen to what it tells us.

Prior to the revolution we had little occasion to inquire or know much about national affairs, for although they existed and were managed, yet they were managed for us, but not by us. Intent on our domestic concerns, our internal legislative business, our agriculture, and our buying and selling, we were seldom anxious about what passed or was doing in foreign Courts. As we had nothing to do with that department of policy, so the affairs of it were not detailed to us, and we took as little pains to inform ourselves, as others did to inform us of them. War, and peace, alliances, and treaties, and commerce, and navigation, were conducted and regulated without our advice or controul. While we had liberty and justice, and in security enjoyed the fruits of our "vine and fig tree," we were in general too content and too much occupied, to be at the trouble of investigating the various political combinations in this department, or to examine and perceive how exceedingly important they often were to the advancement and protection of our prosperity. This habit and turn of thinking affords one reason why so much more care was taken, and so much more wisdom displayed, in forming our State Governments, than in forming our Federal or national one.

By the Confederation as it now stands, the direction of general and national affairs is committed to a single body of men, viz. the Congress. They may make war, but are not empowered to raise men or money to carry it on. They may make peace, but without power to see the terms of it observed— They may form alliances, but without ability to comply with the stipulations on their part—They may enter into treaties of commerce, but without power to enforce them at home or abroad—They may borrow money, but without having the means of repayment—They may partly regulate commerce, but without authority to execute their ordinances—They may appoint ministers and other officers of trust, but without power to try or punish them for misdemeanors—They may resolve, but cannot execute either with dispatch or with secrecy—In short, they may consult, and deliberate, and recommend, and make requisitions, and they who please, may regard them.

From this new and wonderful system of Government, it has come to pass, that almost every national object of every kind, is at this day unprovided for; and other nations taking the advantage of its imbecility, are daily multiplying commercial restraints upon us. Our fur trade is gone to Canada, and British garrisons keep the keys of it. Our shipyards have almost ceased to disturb the repose of the neighborhood by the noise of the axe and hammer; and while foreign flags fly triumphantly above our highest houses, the American Stars seldom do more than shed a few feeble rays about the humble masts of river sloops and coasting schooners. The greater part of our hardy seamen, are plowing the ocean in foreign pay; and not a few of our ingenious shipwrights are now building vessels on alien shores. Although our increasing agriculture and industry extend and multiply our productions, yet they constantly diminish in value; and although we permit all nations to fill our country with their merchandises, yet their best markets are shut against us. Is there an English, or a French, or a Spanish island or port in the West-Indies, to which an American vessel can carry a cargo of flour for sale? Not one. The Algerines exclude us from the Mediterranean, and adjacent countries;

and we are neither able to purchase, nor to command the free use of those seas. Can our little towns or larger cities consume the immense productions of our fertile country? or will they without trade be able to pay a good price for the proportion which they do consume? The last season gave a very unequivocal answer to these questions—What numbers of fine cattle have returned from this city to the country for want of buyers? What great quantities of salted and other provisions still lie useless in the stores? To how much below the former price, is our corn, and wheat and flour and lumber rapidly falling? Our debts remain undiminished, and the interest on them accumulating—our credit abroad is nearly extinguished, and at home un-restored—they who had money have sent it beyond the reach of our laws, and scarcely any man can borrow of his neighbor. Nay, does not experience also tell us, that it is as difficult to pay as to borrow? That even our houses and lands cannot command money—that law suits and usurious contracts abound—that our farms sell on executions for less than half their value, and that distress in various forms, and in various ways, is approaching fast to the doors of our best citizens.

These things have been gradually coming upon us ever since the peace—they have been perceived and proclaimed, but the universal rage and pursuit of private gain conspired with other causes, to prevent any proper efforts being made to meliorate our condition by due attention to our national affairs, until the late Convention was convened for that purpose. From the result of their deliberations, the States expected to derive much good, and should they be disappointed, it will probably be not less their misfortune than their fault. That Convention was in general composed of excellent and tried men—men who had become conspicuous for their wisdom and public services, and whose names and characters will be venerated by posterity. Generous and candid minds cannot perceive without pain, the illiberal manner in which some have taken the liberty to treat them; nor forbear to impute it to impure and improper motives, zeal for public good, like zeal for religion, may sometimes carry men beyond the bounds of reason, but it is not conceivable, that on this occasion, it should find means so to inebriate any candid American, as to make him forget what he owed to truth and to decency, or induce him either to believe or to say, that the almost unanimous advice of the Convention, proceeded from a wicked combination and conspiracy against the liberties of their country. This is not the temper with which we should receive and consider their recommendations, nor the treatment that would be worthy either of us or them. Let us continue careful therefore that facts do not warrant historians to tell future generations, that envy, malice and uncharitableness pursued our patriotic benefactors to their graves, and that not even pre-eminence in virtue, nor lives devoted to the public, could shield them from obloquy and detraction. On the contrary, let our bosoms always retain a sufficient degree of honest indignation to disappoint and discourage those who expect our thanks or applause for calumiating our most faithful and meritorious friends.

The Convention concurred in opinion with the people, that a national government, competent to every national object, was indispensibly necessary; and it was as plain to them, as it now is to all America, that the present confederation does not provide for such a government. These points being agreed, they proceeded to consider how and in what manner such a government could be formed, as on the one hand, should be sufficiently energetic to raise us from our prostrate and distressed situation, and on the other be perfectly consistent with the liberties of the people of every State. Like men to whom the experience of other ages and countries had taught wisdom, they not only determined that it should be erected by, and depend on the people; but remembering the many instances in which governments vested solely in one man, or one body of men, had degenerated into tyrannies, they judged it most prudent that the three great branches of power should be committed to different hands, and therefore that the executive should be separated from the legislative, and the judicial from both. Thus far the propriety of their work is easily seen and understood, and therefore is thus far almost universally approved—for no one man or thing under the sun ever yet pleased every body.

The next question was, what particular powers should be given to these three branches? Here the different views and interests of the different states, as well as the different abstract opinions of their members on such points, interposed many difficulties. Here the business became complicated, and presented a wide field for investigation; too wide for every eye to take a quick and comprehensive view of it.

It is said that "in a multitude of counsellors there is safety," because in the first place, there is greater security for probity; and in the next, if every member cast in only his mite of information and argument, their joint stock of both will thereby become greater than the stock possessed by any one single man out of doors. Gentlemen out of doors therefore should not be hasty in condemning a system, which probably rests on more good reasons than they are aware of, especially when formed under such advantages, and recommended by so many men of distinguished worth and abilities.

The difficulties before mentioned occupied the Convention a long time and it was not without mutual concessions that they were at last surmounted. These concessions serve to explain to us the reason why some parts of the system please in some states, which displease in others; and why many of the objections which have been made to it, are so contradictory and inconsistent with one another. It does great credit to the temper and talents of the Convention, that they were able so to reconcile the different views and interests of the different States, and the clashing opinions of their members as to unite with such singular and almost perfect unanimity in any plan whatever, on a subject so intricate and perplexed. It shews that it must have been thoroughly discussed and understood; and probably if the community at large had the same lights and reasons before them, they would, if equally candid and uninfluenced, be equally unanimous.

It would be arduous, and indeed impossible, to comprise within the limits of this address, a full discussion of every part of the plan. Such a task would require a volume, and few men have leisure or inclination to read volumes on any subject. The objections made to it are almost without number, and many of them without reason—some of them are real and honest, and others merely ostensible. There are friends to Union and a national Government who have serious doubts, who wish to be informed, and to be convinced; and there are others who, neither wishing for union, nor any national Government at all, will oppose and object to any plan that can be contrived.

We are told, among other strange things, that the liberty of the press is left insecure by the proposed Constitution, and yet that Constitution says neither more nor less about it, than the Constitution of the State of New York does. We are told that it deprives us of trial by jury, whereas the fact is, that it expressly secures it in certain cases, and takes it away in none—it is absurd to construe the silence of this, or of our own constitution, relative to a great number of our rights, into a total extinction of them—silence and blank paper neither grant nor take away anything. Complaints are also made that the proposed constitution is not accompanied by a bill of rights; and yet they who would make these complaints, know and are content that no bill of rights accompanied the Constitution of this State. In days and countries, where Monarchs and their subjects were frequently disputing about prerogative and privileges, the latter often found it necessary, as it were to run out the line between them, and oblige the former to admit by solemn acts, called bills of rights, that certain enumerated rights belonged to the people, and were not comprehended in the royal prerogative. But thank God we have no such disputes—we have no Monarchs to contend with, or demand admission from—the proposed Government is to be the government of the people—all its officers are to be their officers, and to exercise no rights but such as the people commit to them. The Constitution only serves to point out that part of the people's business, which they think proper by it to refer to the management of the persons therein designated—those persons are to receive that business to manage, not for themselves and as their own, but as agents and overseers for the people to whom they are constantly responsible, and by whom only they are to be appointed.

But the design of this address is not to investigate the merits of the plan, nor of the objections to it. They who seriously contemplate the present state of our affairs will be convinced that other considerations of at least equal importance demand their attention. Let it be admitted that this plan, like everything else devised by man, has its imperfections: That it does not please every body is certain and there is little reason to expect one that will. It is a question of great moment to you, whether the probability of your being able seasonably to obtain a better, is such as to render it prudent and advisable to reject this, and run the risque. Candidly to consider this question is the design of this address.

As the importance of this question must be obvious to every man, whatever his private opinions respecting it may be, it becomes us all to treat it in that calm and temperate manner, which a subject so deeply interesting to the future welfare of our country and prosperity requires. Let us therefore as much as possible repress and compose that irritation in our minds, which to warm disputes about it may have excited. Let us endeavour to forget that this or that man, is on this or that side; and that we ourselves, perhaps without sufficient reflection, have classed ourselves with one or the other party. Let us remember that this is not a matter to be regarded as a matter that only touches our local parties, but as one so great, so general, and so extensive in its future consequences to America, that for our deciding upon it according to the best of our unbiassed judgment, we must be highly responsible both here and hereafter.

The question now before us now naturally leads to three enquiries:

1. Whether it is probable that a better plan can be obtained?

2. Whether, if attainable, it is likely to be in season?

3. What would be our situation, if after rejecting this, all our efforts to obtain a better should prove fruitless?

The men, who formed this plan are Americans, who had long deserved and enjoyed our confidence, and who are as much interested in having a good government as any of us are, or can be. They were appointed to that business at a time when the States had become very sensible of the derangement of our national affairs, and of the impossibility of retrieving them under the existing Confederation. Although well persuaded that nothing but a good national government could oppose and divert the tide of evils that was flowing in upon us, yet those gentlemen met in Convention with minds perfectly unprejudiced in favour of any particular plan. The minds of their Constituents were at that time equally unbiased, cool and dispassionate. All agreed in the necessity of doing something, but no one ventured to say decidedly what precisely ought to be done—opinions were then fluctuating and unfixed, and whatever might have been the wishes of a few individuals, yet while the Convention deliberated, the people remained in silent suspence. Neither wedded to favourite systems of their own, nor influenced by popular ones abroad, the members were more desirous to receive light from, than to impress their private sentiments on, one another. These circumstances naturally opened the door to that spirit of candour, of calm enquiry, of mutual accommodation, and mutual respect, which entered into the Convention with them, and regulated their debates and proceedings.

The impossibility of agreeing upon any plan that would exactly quadrate with the local policy and objects of every State, soon became evident; and they wisely thought it better mutually to concede, and accommodate, and in that way to fashion their system as much as possible by the circumstances and wishes of different States, than by pertinaciously adhering, each to his own ideas, oblige the Convention to rise without doing anything. They were sensible that obstacles arising from local circumstances, would not cease while those circumstances continued to exist; and so far as those circumstances depended on differences of climate, productions, and commerce, that no change was to be expected. They were likewise sensible that on a subject so comprehensive, and involving such a variety of points and questions, the most able, the most candid, and the most honest men will differ in opinion. The same proposition seldom strikes many minds exactly in the same point of light; different habits of thinking, different degrees and modes of education, different prejudices and opinions early formed and long entertained, conspire with a multitude of other circumstances, to produce among men a diversity and contrariety of opinions on questions of difficulty. Liberality therefore as well as prudence, induced them to treat each other's opinions with tenderness, to argue without asperity, and to endeavor to convince the judgment without hurting the feelings of each other. Although many weeks were passed in these discussions, some points remained, on which a unison of opinions could not be effected. Here again that same happy disposition to unite and conciliate, induced them to meet each other; and enabled them, by mutual concessions, finally to complete and agree to the plan they have recommended, and that too with a degree of unanimity which, considering the variety of discordant views and ideas, they had to reconcile, is really astonishing.

They tell us very honestly that this plan is the result of accommodation— they do not hold it up as the best of all possible ones, but only as the best which they could unite in, and agree to. If such men, appointed and meeting under such auspicious circumstances, and so sincerely disposed to conciliation, could go no further in their endeavors to please every State, and every body, what reason have we at present to expect any system that would give more general satisfaction?

Suppose this plan to be rejected, what measures would you propose for obtaining a better? Some will answer, let us appoint another Convention, and as everything has been said and written that can well be said and written on the subject, they will be better informed than the former one was, and consequently be better able to make and agree upon a more eligible one.

This reasoning is fair, and as far as it goes has weight; but it nevertheless takes one thing for granted, which appears very doubtful; for although the new Convention might have more information, and perhaps equal abilities, yet it does not from thence follow that they would be equally disposed to agree. The contrary of this position is the most probable. You must have observed that the same temper and equanimity which prevailed among the people on the former occasion, no longer exists. We have unhappily become divided into parties; and this important subject has been handled with such indiscreet and offensive acrimony, and with so many little unhandsome artifices and misrepresentations, that pernicious heats and animosities have been kindled, and spread their flames far and wide among us. When therefore it becomes a question who shall be deputed to the new Convention; we cannot flatter ourselves that the talents and integrity of the candidates will determine who shall be elected. Federal electors will vote for Federal deputies, and anti-Federal electors for anti-Federal ones. Nor will either party prefer the most moderate of their adherents, for as the most staunch and active partizans will be the most popular, so the men most willing and able to carry points, to oppose, and divide, and embarrass their opponents, will be chosen. A Convention formed at such a season, and of such men, would be but too exact an epitome of the great body that named them. The same party views, the same propensity to opposition, the same distrusts and jealousies, and the same unaccommodating spirit which prevail without, would be concentred and ferment with still greater violence within. Each deputy would recollect who sent him, and why he was sent; and be too apt to consider himself bound in honor, to contend and act vigorously under the standard of his party, and not hazard their displeasure by prefering compromise to victory. As vice does not sow the seeds of virtue, so neither does passion cultivate the fruits of reason. Suspicions and resentments create no disposition to conciliate, nor do they infuse a desire of making partial and personal objects bend to general union and the common good. The utmost efforts of that excellent disposition were necessary to enable the late Convention to perform their task; and although contrary causes sometimes operate similar effects, yet to expect that discord and animosity should produce the fruits of confidence and agreement, is to expect "grapes from thorns, and figs from thistles."

The States of Georgia, Delaware, Jersey, and Connecticut, have adopted the present plan with unexampled unanimity; they are content with it as it is, and consequently their deputies, being apprized of the sentiments of their Constituents, will be little inclined to make alterations, and cannot be otherwise than averse to changes which they have no reason to think would be agreeable to their people—some other States, tho' less unanimous, have nevertheless adopted it by very respectable majorities; and for reasons so evidently cogent, that even the minority in one of them, have nobly pledged themselves for its promotion and support. From these circumstances, the new Convention would derive and experience difficulties unknown to the former. Nor are these the only additional difficulties they would have to encounter. Few are ignorant that there has lately sprung up a sect of politicans who teach and profess to believe that the extent of our nation is too great for the superintendance of one national Government, and on that principle argue that it ought to be divided into two or three. This doctrine, however mischievous in its tendency and consequences, has its advocates; and, should any of them be sent to the Convention, it will naturally be their policy rather to cherish than to prevent divisions; for well knowing that the institution of any national Government, would blast their favourite system, no measures that lead to it can meet with their aid or approbation.

Nor can we be certain whether or not any and what foreign influence would, on such an occasion, be indirectly exerted, nor for what purposes—delicacy forbids an ample discussion of this question. Thus much may be said, without error or offence, viz. That such foreign nations as desire the prosperity of America, and would rejoice to see her become great and powerful, under the auspices of a Government wisely calculated to extend her commerce, to encourage her navigation and marine, and to direct the whole weight of her power and resources as her interest and honour may require, will doubtless be friendly to the Union of the States, and to the establishment of a Government able to perpetuate, protect and dignify it. Such other foreign nations, if any such there be, who, jealous of our growing importance, and fearful that our commerce and navigation should impair their own—who behold our rapid population with regret, and apprehend that the enterprising spirit of our people, when seconded by power and probability of success, may be directed to objects not consistent with their policy or interests, cannot fail to wish that we may continue a weak and a divided people.

These considerations merit much attention, and candid men will judge how far they render it probable that a new Convention would be able either to agree in a better plan, or with tolerable unanimity, in any plan at all. Any plan forcibly carried by a slender majority, must expect numerous opponents among the people, who, especially in their present temper, would be more inclined to reject than adopt any system so made and carried. We should in such case again see the press teeming with publications for and against it; for as the minority would take pains to justify their dissent, so would the majority be industrious to display the wisdom of their proceedings. Hence new divisions, new parties, and new distractions would ensue, and no one can foresee or conjecture when or how they would terminate.

Let those who are sanguine in their expectations of a better plan from a new Convention, also reflect on the delays and risque to which it would expose us. Let them consider whether we ought, by continuing much longer in our present humiliated condition, to give other nations further time to perfect their restrictive systems of commerce, to reconcile their own people to them, and to fence and guard and strengthen them by all those regulations and contrivances in which a jealous policy is ever fruitful. Let them consider whether we ought to give further opportunities to discord to alienate the hearts of our citizens from one another, and thereby encourage new Cromwells to bold exploits. Are we certain that our foreign creditors will continue patient, and ready to proportion their forbearance to our delays? Are we sure that our distresses, dissentions and weakness will neither invite hostility nor insult? If they should, how ill prepared shall we be for defence! without Union, without Government, without money, and without credit!

It seems necessary to remind you, that some time must yet elapse, before all the States will have decided on the present plan. If they reject it, some time must also pass before the measure of a new Convention, can be brought about and generally agreed to. A further space of time will then be requisite to elect their deputies, and send them on to Convention. What time they may expend when met, cannot be divined, and it is equally uncertain how much time the several States may take to deliberate and decide on any plan they may recommend—if adopted, still a further space of time will be necessary to organize and set it in motion: —In the mean time our affairs are daily going on from bad to worse, and it is not rash to say that our distresses are accumulating like compound interest.

But if for the reasons already mentioned, and others that we cannot now perceive, the new Convention, instead of producing a better plan, should give us only a history of their disputes, or should offer us one still less pleasing than the present, where should we be then? The old Confederation has done its best, and cannot help us; and is now so relaxed and feeble, that in all probability it would not survive so violent a shock. Then "to your tents Oh Israel!" would be the word. Then every band of union would be severed. Then every State would be a little nation, jealous of its neighbors, and anxious to strengthen itself by foreign alliances, against its former friends. Then farewell to fraternal affection, unsuspecting intercourse; and mutual participation in commerce, navigation and citizenship. Then would arise mutual restrictions and fears, mutual garrisons,—and standing armies, and all those dreadful evils which for so many ages plagued England, Scotland, Wales, and Ireland, while they continued disunited, and were played off against each other.

Consider my fellow citizens what you are about, before it is too late— consider what in such an event would be your particular case. You know the geography of your State, and the consequences of your local position. Jersey and Connecticut, to whom your impost laws have been unkind—Jersey and Connecticut, who have adopted the present plan, and expect much good from it—will impute its miscarriage and all the consequent evils to you. They now consider your opposition as dictated more by your fondness for your impost, than for those rights to which they have never been behind you in attachment. They cannot, they will not love you—they border upon you, and are your neighbors; but you will soon cease to regard their neighborhood as a blessing. You have but one port and outlet to your commerce, and how you are to keep that outlet free and uninterrupted, merits consideration. What advantage Vermont in combination with others, might take of you, may easily be conjectured; nor will you be at a loss to perceive how much reason the people of Long Island, whom you cannot protect, have to deprecate being constantly exposed to the depredations of every invader.

These are short hints—they ought not to be more developed—you can easily in your own mind dilate and trace them through all their relative circumstances and connections.—Pause then for a moment, and reflect whether the matters you are disputing about, are of sufficient moment to justify your running such extravagant risques. Reflect that the present plan comes recommended to you by men and fellow citizens who have given you the highest proofs that men can give, of their justice, their love for liberty and their country of their prudence, of their application, and of their talents. They tell you it is the best that they could form; and that in their opinion, it is necessary to redeem you from those calamities which already begin to be heavy upon us all. You find that not only those men, but others of similar characters, and of whom you have also had very ample experience, advise you to adopt it. You find that whole States concur in the sentiment, and among them are your next neighbors; both whom have shed much blood in the cause of liberty, and have manifested as strong and constant a predilection for a free Republican Government as any State in the Union, and perhaps in the world. They perceive not those latent mischiefs in it, with which some double-sighted politicians endeavor to alarm you. You cannot but be sensible that this plan or constitution will always be in the hands and power of the people, and that if on experiment, it should be found defective or incompetent, they may either remedy its defects, or substitute another in its room. The objectionable parts of it are certainly very questionable, for otherwise there would not be such a contrariety of opinions about them. Experience will better determine such questions than theoretical arguments, and so far as the danger of abuses is urged against the institution of a Government, remember that a power to do good, always involves a power to do harm. We must in the business of Government as well as in all other business, have some degree of confidence, as well as a great degree of caution. Who on a sick bed would refuse medicines from a physician, merely because it is as much in his power to administer deadly poisons, as salutary remedies.

*   *   *

Address to the People of New York on the Necessity of Amendments to the Constitution, 1788*

By Melancton Smith

The advocates for the proposed new constitution, having been beaten off the field of argument, on its merits, have now taken new ground. They admit it is liable to well-founded objections—that a number of its articles ought to be amended; that if alterations do not take place, a door will be left open for an undue administration, and encroachments on the liberties of the people; and many of them go as far as to say, if it should continue for any considerable period, in its present form, it will lead to a subversion of our

*Pamphlets on the Constitution of the United States, pp. 89–115.

equal republican forms of government. But still, although they admit this, they urge that it ought to be adopted, and that we should confide in procuring the necessary alterations after we have received it. Most of the leading characters, who advocate its reception, now profess their readiness to concur with those who oppose, in bringing about the most material amendments contended for, provided they will first agree to accept the proffered system as it is. These concessions afford strong evidence, that the opposers of the constitution have reason on their side, and that they have not been influenced, in the part they have taken, by the mean and unworthy motives of selfish and private interests with which they have been illiberally charged.— As the favourers of the constitution seem, if their professions are sincere, to be in a situation similiar to that of Agrippa, when he cried out upon Paul's preaching—"almost thou persuadest me to be a christian," I cannot help indulging myself in expressing the same wish which St. Paul uttered on that occasion, "Would to God you were not only almost, but altogether such an one as I am." But alas, as we hear no more of Agrippa's christianity after this interview with Paul, so it is much to be feared, that we shall hear nothing of amendments from most of the warm advocates for adopting the new government, after it gets into operation. When the government is once organized, and all the offices under it filled, the inducements which our great men will have to support it, will be much stronger than they are now to urge its reception. Many of them will then hold places of great honour and emolument, and others will then be candidates for such places. It is much harder to relinquish honours or emoluments, which we have in possession, than to abandon the pursuit of them, while the attainment is held in a state of uncertainty. The amendments contended for as necessary to be made, are of such a nature, as will tend to limit and abridge a number of the powers of the government. And is it probable, that those who enjoy these powers will be so likely to surrender them after they have them in possession, as to consent to have them restricted in the act of granting them? Common sense says they will not.

When we consider the nature and operation of government, the idea of receiving a form radically defective, under the notion of making the necessary amendments, is evidently absurd.

Government is a compact entered into by mankind, in a state of society, for the promotion of their happiness. In forming this compact, common sense dictates, that no articles should be admitted that tend to defeat the end of its institution. If any such are proposed, they should be rejected. When the compact is once formed and put into operation, it is too late for individuals to object. The deed is executed—the conveyance is made—and the power of reassuming the right is gone, without the consent of the parties. Besides, when a government is once in operation, it acquires strength by habit, and stability by exercise. If it is tolerably mild in its administration, the people sit down easy under it, be its principles and forms ever so repugnant to the maxims of liberty. It steals, by insensible degrees, one right from the people after another, until it rivets its powers so as to put it beyond the ability of the community to restrict or limit it. The history of the world furnishes many instances of a people's increasing the powers of their rulers by persuasion, but I believe it would be difficult to produce one in which the rulers have been persuaded to relinquish their powers to the people. Wherever this has taken place, it has always been the effect of compulsion. These observations are so well-founded, that they are become a kind of axioms in politics; and the inference to be drawn from them is equally evident, which is this,—that, in forming a government, care should be taken not to confer powers which it will be necessary to take back; but if you err at all, let it be on the contrary side, because it is much easier, as well as safer, to enlarge the powers of your rulers, if they should prove not sufficiently extensive, than it is to abridge them if they should be too great.

It is agreed, the plan is defective—that some of the powers granted, are dangerous—others not well defined—and amendments are necessary. Why then not amend it? why not remove the cause of danger, and, if possible, even the apprehension of it? The instrument is yet in the hands of the people; it is not signed, sealed, and delivered, and they have power to give it any form they please.

But it is contended, adopt it first, and then amend it. I ask, why not amend, and then adopt it? Most certainly the latter mode of proceeding is more consistent with our ideas of prudence in the ordinary concerns of life. If men were about entering into a contract respecting their private concerns, it would be highly absurd in them to sign and seal an instrument containing stipulations which are contrary to their interests and wishes, under the expectation, that the parties, after its execution, would agree to make alterations agreeable to their desire. They would insist upon the exceptionable clauses being altered before they would ratify the contract. And is a compact for the government of ourselves and our posterity of less moment than contracts between individuals? Certainly not. But to this reasoning, which at first view would appear to admit of no reply, a variety of objections are made, and a number of reasons urged for adopting the system, and afterwards proposing amendments. Such as have come under my observation, I shall state, and remark upon.

It is insisted, that the present situation of our country is such, as not to admit of a delay in forming a new government, or of time sufficient to deliberate and agree upon the amendments which are proper, without involving ourselves in a state of anarchy and confusion.

On this head, all the powers of rhetoric, and arts of description, are employed to paint the condition of this country, in the most hideous and frightful colors. We are told, that agriculture is without encouragement; trade is languishing; private faith and credit are disregarded, and public credit is prostrate; that the laws and magistrates are contemned and set at naught;

that a spirit of licentiousness is rampant, and ready to break over every bound set to it by the government, that private embarrassments and distresses invade the house of every man of middling property, and insecurity threatens every man in affluent circumstances: in short, that we are in a state of the most grievous calamity at home, and that we are contemptible abroad, the scorn of foreign nations, and the ridicule of the world. From this high-wrought picture, one would suppose that we were in a condition the most deplorable of any people upon earth. But suffer me, my countrymen, to call your attention to a serious and sober estimate of the situation in which you are placed, while I trace the embarrassments under which you labor, to their true sources. What is your condition? Does not every man sit under his own vine and under his own fig-tree, having none to make him afraid? Does not every one follow his calling without impediments and receive the reward of his well-earned industry? The farmer cultivates his land, and reaps the fruit which the bounty of heaven bestows on his honest toil. The mechanic is exercised in his art, and receives the reward of his labour. The merchant drives his commerce, and none can deprive him of the gain he honestly acquires; all classes and callings of men amongst us are protected in their various pursuits, and secured by the laws in the possession and enjoyment of the property obtained in those pursuits. The laws are as well executed as they ever were, in this or any other country. Neither the hand of private violence, nor the more to be dreaded hand of legal oppression, are reached out to distress us.

*　　　*　　　*

But it is said that if we postpone the ratification of this system until the necessary amendments are first incorporated, the consequence will be a civil war among the states. On this head weak minds are alarmed with being told, that the militia of Connecticut and Massachusetts, on the one side, and of New Jersey and Pennsylvania on the other, will attack us with hostile fury; and either destroy us from the face of the earth, or at best divide us between the two states adjoining on either side. The apprehension of danger is one of the most powerful incentives to human action, and is therefore generally excited on political questions: But still, a prudent man, though he foreseeth the evil and avoideth it, yet he will not be terrified by imaginary dangers. We ought therefore to enquire what ground there is to fear such an event?— There can be no reason to apprehend, that the other states will make war with us for not receiving the constitution proposed, until it is amended, but from one of the following causes: either that they will have just cause to do it, or that they have a disposition to do it. We will examine each of these: That they will have no just cause to quarrel with us for not acceding, is evident, because we are under no obligation to do it, arising from any existing compact or previous stipulation. The confederation is the only compact now existing between the states: By the terms of it, it cannot be changed without the consent of every one of the parties to it. Nothing therefore can be more unreasonable than for part of the states to claim of the others, as matter of right, an accession to a system to which they have material objections. No war can therefore arise from this principle, but on the contrary, it is to be presumed, it will operate strongly the opposite way. The states will reason on the subject in the following manner: On this momentuous question, every state has an indubitable right to judge for itself: This is secured to it by solemn compact, and if any of our sister states disagree with us upon the question, we ought to attend to their objections, and accommodate ourselves as far as possible to the amendments they propose.

*   *   *

It is further urged we must adopt this plan because we have no chance of getting a better. This idea is inconsistent with the principles of those who advance it. They say, it must be altered, but it should be left until after it is put in operation. But if this objection is valid, the proposal of altering, after it is received, is mere delusion.

It is granted, that amendments ought to be made; that the exceptions taken to the constitution, are grounded on just principles, but it is still insisted, that alterations are not to be attempted until after it is received: But why not? Because it is said, there is no probability of agreeing in amendments previous to the adoption, but they may be easily made after it. I wish to be informed what there is in our situation or circumstances that renders it more probable that we shall agree in amendments better after, than before submitting to it? No good reason has as yet been given; it is evident none can be given: On the contrary, there are several considerations which induce a belief, that alterations may be obtained with more ease before than after its reception, and if so, every one must agree it is much the safest. The importance of preserving an union, and of establishing a government equal to the purpose of maintaining that union, is a sentiment deeply impressed on the mind of every citizen of America. It is now no longer doubted, that the confederation, in its present form, is inadequate to that end: Some reform in our government must take place: In this, all parties agree: It is therefore to be presumed, that this object will be pursued with ardour and perseverance, until it is attained by all parties. But when a government is adopted that promises to effect this, we are to expect the ardour of many, yea, of most people, will be abated: their exertions will cease or be languid, and they will sit down easy, although they may see that the constitution which provides for this, does not sufficiently guard the rights of the people, or secure them against the encroachments of their rulers. The great end they had in view, the security of the union, they will consider effected, and this will divert their attention from that which is equally interesting, safety to their liberties.

Besides, the human mind cannot continue intensely engaged for any great length of time upon one object. As after a storm, a calm generally succeeds, so after the minds of a people have been ardently employed upon a subject, especially upon that of government, we commonly find that they become cool and inattentive: Add to this that those in the community who urge the adoption of this system, because they hope to be raised above the common level of their fellow citizens; because they expect to be among the number of the few who will be benefitted by it, will more easily be induced to consent to the amendments before it is received than afterwards. Before its reception they will be inclined to be pliant and condescending; if they cannot obtain all they wish, they will consent to take less. They will yield part to obtain the rest. But when the plan is once agreed to, they will be tenacious of every power, they will strenuously contend to retain all they have got; this is natural to human nature, and it is consonant to the experience of mankind. For history affords us no examples of persons once possessed of power resigning it willingly.

The reasonings made use of to persuade us, that no alterations can be agreed upon previous to the adoption of the system, are as curious as they are futile. It is alledged, that there was great diversity of sentiments in forming the proposed constitution; that it was the effect of mutual concessions and a spirit of accommodation, and from hence it is inferred, that farther changes cannot be hoped for. I should suppose that the contrary inference was the fair one. If the convention, who framed this plan, were possessed of such a spirit of moderation and condescension, as to be induced to yield to each other certain points, and to accommodate themselves to each other's opinions, and even prejudices, there is reason to expect, that this same spirit will continue and prevail in a future convention, and produce an union of sentiments on the points objected to. There is more reason to hope for this, because the subject has received a full discussion, and the minds of the people much better known than they were when the convention sat. Previous to the meeting of the convention, the subject of a new form of government had been little thought of, and scarcely written upon at all. It is true, it was the general opinion, that some alterations were requisite in the federal system. This subject had been contemplated by almost every thinking man in the union. It had been the subject of many well-written essays, and it was the anxious wish of every true friend to America. But it was never in the contemplation of one in a thousand of those who had reflected on the matter, to have an entire change in the nature of our federal government—to alter it from a confederation of states, to that of one entire government, which will swallow up that of the individual states. I will venture to say, that the idea of a government similar to the one proposed, never entered the minds of the legislatures who appointed the convention, and of but very few of the members who composed it, until they had assembled and heard it proposed in that body: much less had the people any conception of such a plan until after it was promulgated. While it was agitated, the debates of the convention were kept an impenetrable secret, and no opportunity was given for well informed men to offer their sentiments upon the subject. The system was therefore never publicly discussed, nor indeed could be, because it was not known to the people until after it was proposed. Since that, it has been the object of universal attention—it has been thought of by every reflecting man—been discussed in a public and private manner, in conversation and in print; its defects have been pointed out, and every objection to it stated; able advocates have written in its favour, and able opponents have written against it. And what is the result? It cannot be denied but that the general opinion is, that it contains material errors, and requires important amendments. This then being the general sentiment, both of the friends and foes of the system, can it be doubted, that another convention would concur in such amendments as would quiet the fears of the opposers, and effect a great degree of union on the subject? An event most devoutly to be wished. But it is farther said, that there can be no prospects of procuring alterations before it is acceded to, because those who oppose it do not agree among themselves with respect to the amendments that are necessary. To this I reply, that this may be urged against attempting alterations after it is received, with as much force as before; and therefore, if it concludes anything, it is that we must receive any system of government proposed to us, because those who object to it do not entirely concur in their objections. But the assertion is not true to any considerable extent. There is a remarkable uniformity in the objections made to the constitution, on the most important points. It is also worthy of notice, that very few of the matters found fault with in it, are of a local nature, or such as affect any particular state; on the contrary, they are such as concern the principles of general liberty, in which the people of New Hampshire, New York and Georgia are equally interested.

It would be easy to shew, that in the leading and most important objections that have been made to the plan, there has been and is an entire concurrence of opinion among writers, and in public bodies throughout the United States.

I have not time to fully illustrate this by a minute narration of particulars; but to prove that this is the case, I shall adduce a number of important instances.

It has been objected to that the new system, that it is calculated to, and will effect such a consolidation of the States, as to supplant and overturn the state governments. In this the minority of Pennsylvania, the opposition in Massachusetts, and all the writers of any ability or note in Philadelphia, New York, and Boston concur. It may be added, that this appears to have been the opinion of the Massachusetts convention, and gave rise to that article in the amendments proposed, which confines the general government to the exercise only of powers expressly given.

It has been said that the representation in the general legislature is too small to secure liberty, or to answer the intention of representation. In this there is an union of sentiments in the opposers.

The constitution has been opposed, because it gives to the legislature an unlimited power of taxation both with respect to direct and indirect taxes, a right to lay and collect taxes, duties, imposts and excises of every kind and description, and to any amount. In this there has been as general a concurrence of opinion as in the former.

The opposers to the constitution have said that it is dangerous, because the judicial power may extend to many cases which ought to be reserved to the decision of the State courts, and because the right of trial by jury is not secured in the judicial courts of the general government, in civil cases. All the opposers are agreed in this objection.

The power of the general legislature to alter and regulate the time, place and manner of holding elections, has been stated as an argument against the adoption of the system. It has been argued that this power will place in the hands of the general government, the authority, whenever they shall be disposed, and a favorable opportunity offers, to deprive the body of the people in effect, of all share in the government. The opposers to the constitution universally agree in this objection, and of such force is it, that most of its ardent advocates admit its validity, and those who have made attempts to vindicate it, have been reduced to the necessity of using the most trifling arguments to justify it.

The mixture of legislative, judicial, and executive powers in the senate; the little degree of responsibility under which the great officers of government will be held; and the liberty granted by the system to establish and maintain a standing army without any limitation or restriction, are also objected to the constitution; and in these there is a great degree of unanimity of sentiment in the opposers.

From these remarks it appears, that the opponents to the system accord in the great and material points on which they wish amendments. For the truth of the assertion, I appeal to the protest of the minority of the convention of Pennsylvania, to all the publications against the constitution, and to the debates of the convention of Massachusetts. As a higher authority than these, I appeal to the amendments proposed by the Massachusetts; these are to be considered as the sense of that body upon the defects of the system. And it is a fact, which I will venture to assert, that a large majority of the convention were of opinion, that a number of additional alterations ought to be made. Upon reading the articles which they propose as amendments, it will appear that they object to indefinite powers in the legislature—to the power of laying direct taxes—to the authority of regulating elections—to the extent of the judicial powers, both as it respects the inferior court and the appellate jurisdiction—to the smallness of the representation, &c.—It is admitted that some writers have advanced objections that others have not noticed—that exceptions have been taken by some, that have not been insisted upon by others, and it is probable, that some of the opponents may approve what others will reject. But still these difference are on matters of small importance, and of such a nature as the persons who hold different opinions will not be tenacious of. Perfect uniformity of sentiment on so great a political subject is not to be expected. Every sensible man is impressed with this idea and is therefore prepared to make concessions and accommodate on matters of small importance. It is sufficient that we agree in the great leading principles, which relate to the preservation of public liberty and private security. And on these I will venture to affirm we are as well agreed, as any people ever were on a question of this nature. I dare pronounce that were the principal advocates for the proposed plan to write comments upon it, they would differ more in the sense they would give the constitution, than those who oppose it do, in the amendments they would wish. I am justified in this opinion, by the sentiments advanced by the different writers in favour of the constitution.

*   *   *

Postscript

Since the foregoing pages have been put to the press, a pamphlet has appeared, entitled, "An address to the people of the state of New York, on the subject of the new constitution, &c." Upon a cursory examination of this performance (for I have not had time to give it more than a cursory examination) it appears to contain little more than declamation and observations that have been often repeated by the advocates of the new constitution.

An attentive reader will readily perceive, that almost everything deserving the name of an argument in this publication, has received consideration, and, I trust, a satisfactory answer in the preceding remarks, so far as they apply to prove the necessity of an immediate adoption of the plan, without amendments.

I shall therefore only beg the patience of my readers, while I make a few very brief remarks on this piece.

The author introduces his observations with a short history of the revolution, and of the establishment of the present existing federal government. He draws a frightful picture of our condition under the present confederation. The whole of what he says on that head, stripped of its artificial colouring, amounts to this, that the existing system is rather commendatory than coercive, or that Congress have not in most cases, the power of enforcing their own resolves. This he calls "a new and wonderful system." However "wonderful" it may seem, it certainly is not "new." For most of the federal governments that have been in the world, have been of the same nature. The united Netherlands are governed on the same plan. There are other governments also now existing, which are in a similar condition with our's, with regard to several particulars, on account of which this author denominates it "new and wonderful." The king of Great Britain "may make war; but has not power to raise money to carry it on." He may borrow money, but it is without the means of repayment, &c. For these he is dependent on his parliament. But it is needless to add on this head, because it is admitted that the powers of the general government ought to be increased in several of the particulars this author instances. But these things are mentioned to shew, that the outcry made against the confederation, as being a system new, unheard of, and absurd, is really without foundation.

The author proceeds to depicture our present condition in the high-wrought strains common to his party. I shall add nothing to what I have said on this subject in the former part of this pamphlet, but will only observe, that his imputing our being kept out of the possession of the western posts, and our want of peace with the Algerines, to the defects in our present government, is much easier said than proved. The British keep possession of these posts, because it subserves their interest, and probably will do so, until they perceive that we have gathered strength and resources sufficient to assert our rights with the sword. Let our government be what it will, this cannot be done without time and patience. In the present exhausted situation of the country, it would be madness in us, had we ever so perfect a government, to commence a war for the recovery of these posts. With regard to the Algerines, there are but two ways in which their ravages can be prevented. The one is, by a successful war against them, and the other is by treaty, The powers of Congress under the confederation are completely competent either to declare war against them, or to form treaties. Money, it is true, is necessary to do both these. This only brings us to this conclusion, that the great defect in our present government, is the want of powers to provide money for the public exigencies. I am willing to grant reasonable powers, on this score, but not unlimited ones; commercial treaties may be made under the present powers of Congress. I am persuaded we flatter ourselves with advantages which will result from them, that will never be realized. I know of no benefits that we receive from any that have yet been formed.

This author tells us, "it is not his design to investigate merits of the plan, nor of the objections made to it." It is well he did not undertake it, for if he had, from the specimen he has given, the cause he assumes would not have probably gained much strength by it.

He however takes notice of two or three of the many objections brought against the plan.

"We are told, (says he) among other strange things, that the liberty of the press is left insecure by the proposed constitution, and yet that constitution says neither more nor less about it, than the constitution of the state of New York does. We are told it deprives us of trial by jury, whereas the fact is, that it expressly secures it in certain cases, and takes it away in none, &c. it is absurd to construe the silence of this, or of our own constitution relative to a great number of our rights into a total extinction of them; silence and a blank paper neither grant nor take away anything."

It may be a strange thing to this author to hear the people of America anxious for the preservation of their rights, but those who understand the true principles of liberty, are no strangers to their importance. The man who supposes the constitution, in any part of it, is like a blank piece of paper, has very erroneous ideas of it. He may be assured every clause has a meaning, and many of them such extensive meaning, as would take a volume to unfold. The suggestion, that the liberty of the press is secure, because it is not in express words spoken of in the constitution, and that the trial by jury is not taken away, because it is not said in so many words and letters it is so, is puerile and unworthy of a man who pretends to reason. We contend, that by the indefinite powers granted to the general government, the liberty of the press may be restricted by duties, &c. and therefore the constitution ought to have stipulated for its freedom. The trial by jury, in all civil cases is left at the discretion of the general government, except in the supreme court on the appelate jurisdiction, and in this I affirm it is taken away, not by express words, but by fair and legitimate construction and inference; for the supreme court have expressly given them an appelate jurisdiction, in every case to which their powers extend (with two or three exceptions)) both as to law and fact. The court are the judges; every man in the country, who has served as a juror, knows, that there is a difference between the court and the jury, and that the lawyers in their pleading, make the distinction. If the court, upon appeals, are to determine both the law and the fact, there is no room for a jury, and the right of trial in this mode is taken away.

The author manifests levity in referring to the constitution of this state, to show that it was useless to stipulate for the liberty of the press, or to insert a bill of rights in the constitution. With regard to the first, it is perhaps an imperfection in our constitution that the liberty of the press is not expressly reserved; but still there was not equal necessity of making this reservation in our State as in the general Constitution, for the common and statute law of England, and the laws of the colony are established, in which this privilege is fully defined and secured. It is true, a bill of rights is not prefixed to our constitution, as it is in that of some of the states; but still this author knows, that many essential rights are reserved in the body of it; and I will promise, that every opposer of this system will be satisfied, if the stipulations that they contend for are agreed to, whether they are prefixed, affixed, or inserted in the body of the constitution, and that they will not contend which way this is done, if it be but done. I shall add but one remark, and that is upon the hackneyed argument introduced by the author, drawn from the character and ability of the framers of the new constitution. The favourers of this system are not very prudent in bringing this forward. It provokes to an investigation of characters, which is an invidious task. I do not wish to detract from their merits, but I will venture to affirm, that twenty assemblies of equal number might be collected, equally respectable both in point of ability, integrity and patriotism. Some of the characters which compose it I revere; others I consider as of small consequence, and a number are suspected of being great public defaulters, and to have been guilty of notorious peculation and fraud, with regard to public property in the hour of our distress. I will not descend to personalities, nor would I have said so much on the subject, had it not been in self defence. Let the constitution stand on its own merits. If it be good, it stands not in need of great men's names to support it. If it be bad, their names ought not to sanction it.

THE FEDERALIST, 1788

Commentary

The most famous of the Federalist writings on the Bill of Rights issue is Alexander Hamilton's essay in No. 84 of *The Federalist*. Here we have the definitive version of the standard Federalist answer to the claim that the new Constitution was defective because it lacked a Bill of Rights. Hamilton admits that one of the most considerable "objections is that the plan of the convention contains no bill of rights." To this, he answers that a Bill of Rights is unnecessary under a Constitution such as that drafted at Philadelphia ("here, in strictness, the people surrender nothing; and as they retain everything they have no need of particular reservations") and dangerous, since it would contain exceptions to powers not granted and afford a basis for claiming more than was granted. ("For why declare that things shall not be done which there is no power to do?") In No. 85, Hamilton deals with the issue of previous versus subsequent amendments. He takes up the Antifederalist claim that the Constitution should be perfected by amendments before it is irrevocably adopted. "It appears to me susceptible of absolute demonstration that it will be far more easy to obtain subsequent than previous amendments to the Constitution." The argument was aimed directly at the Antifederalists, particularly Melancton Smith, whose ultimate willingness to settle for a Bill of Rights through subsequent amendments enabled the New York Federalists to secure the votes needed for ratification (*infra* p. 854). It may well be true that *The Federalist* itself contributed little to that result. Nos. 84 and 85 appeared in book form on May 28, 1788, but were not printed in newspapers (except for a small part of 84) until after the New York Ratifying Convention had adjourned. The Hamilton reasoning (though now accepted as the classic state paper on the matter) may thus have appeared in the popular press too late to influence the Convention for which it was written.

The Federalist No. 84, 1788*

To the People of the State of New-York.

    In the course of the foregoing review of the constitution I have taken notice of, and endeavoured to answer, most of the objections which have

*H. C. Syrett, ed., *The Papers of Alexander Hamilton* (1962), Vol. 5, pp. 702–13. J. and A. McLean, *The Federalist*, II, 344–57, published on May 28, 1788, numbered 84. In *The* [New York] *Independent Journal or the General Advertiser* this essay was begun on July 16, continued on July 26, concluded on August 9, and is numbered 83. In *The New-York Packet* it was begun on July 29, continued on August 8, concluded on August 12, and is numbered 84.

appeared against it. There however remain a few which either did not fall naturally under any particular head, or were forgotten in their proper places. These shall now be discussed; but as the subject has been drawn into great length, I shall so far consult brevity as to comprise all my observations on these miscellaneous points in a single paper.

The most considerable of these remaining objections is, that the plan of the convention contains no bill of rights. Among other answers given to this, it has been upon different occasions remarked, that the constitutions of several of the states are in a similar predicament. I add, that New-York is of this number. And yet the opposers of the new system in this state, who profess an unlimited admiration for its constitution, are among the most intemperate partizans of a bill of rights. To justify their zeal in this matter, they alledge two things; one is, that though the constitution of New-York has no bill of rights prefixed to it, yet it contains in the body of it various provisions in favour of particular privileges and rights, which in substance amount to the same thing; the other is, that the constitution adopts in their full extent the common and statute law of Great-Britain, by which many other rights not expressed in it are equally secured.

To the first I answer, that the constitution proposed by the convention contains, as well as the constitution of this state, a number of such provisions.

Independent of those, which relate to the structure of the government, we find the following: Article I. section 3. clause 7. "Judgment in cases of impeachment shall not extend further than to removal from office, and disqualification to hold and enjoy any office of honour, trust or profit under the United States; but the party convicted shall nevertheless be liable and subject to indictment, trial, judgment and punishment, according to law." Section 9. of the same article, clause 2. "The privilege of the writ of habeas corpus shall not be suspended, unless when in cases of rebellion or invasion the public safety may require it." Clause 3. "No bill of attainder or ex post facto law shall be passed." Clause 7. "No title of nobility shall be granted by the United States: And no person holding any office of profit or trust under them, shall, without the consent of congress, accept of any present, emolument, office or title, of any kind whatever, from any king, prince or foreign state." Article III. section 2. clause 3. "The trial of all crimes, except in cases of impeachment, shall be by jury; and such trial shall be held in the state where the said crimes shall have been committed; but when not committed within any state, the trial shall be at such place or places as the congress may by law have directed." Section 3, of the same article, "Treason against the United States shall consist only in levying war against them, or in adhering to their enemies, giving them aid and comfort. No person shall be convicted of treason unless on the testimony of two witness to the same overt act, or on confession in open court." And clause 3, of the same section. "The congress shall have power to declare the punishment of treason, but no attainder of treason shall work corruption of blood, or forfeiture, except during the life of the person attainted."

It may well be a question whether these are not upon the whole, of equal importance with any which are to be found in the constitution of this state. The establishment of the writ of habeas corpus, the prohibition of ex post facto laws, and of Titles of Nobility, to which we have no corresponding provisions in our constitution, are perhaps greater securities to liberty and republicanism than any it contains. The creation of crimes after the commission of the fact, or in other words, the subjecting of men to punishment for things which, when they were done, were breaches of no law, and the practice of arbitrary imprisonments have been in all ages the favourite and most formidable instruments of tyranny. The observations of the judicious Blackstone in reference to the latter, are well worthy of recital. "To bereave a man of life (says he) or by violence to confiscate his estate, without accusation or trial, would be so gross and notorious an act of despotism, as must at once convey the alarm of tyranny throughout the whole nation; but confinement of the person by secretly hurrying to goal, where his sufferings are unknown or forgotten, is a less public, a less striking, and therefore a more dangerous engine of arbitrary government." And as a remedy for this fatal evil, he is every where peculiarly emphatical in his encomiums on the habeas corpus act, which in one place he calls "the bulwark of the British constitution."

Nothing need be said to illustrate the importance of the prohibition of titles of nobility. This may truly be denominated the corner stone of republican government; for so long as they are excluded, there can never be serious danger that the government will be any other than that of the people.

To the second, that is, to the pretended establishment of the common and statute law by the constitution, I answer, that they are expressly made subject "to such alterations and provisions as the legislature shall from time to time make concerning the same." They are therefore at any moment liable to repeal by the ordinary legislative power, and of course have no constitutional sanction. The only use of the declaration was to recognize the ancient law, and to remove doubts which might have been occasioned by the revolution. This consequently can be considered as no part of a declaration of rights, which under our constitutions must be intended as limitations of the power of the government itself.

It has been several times truly remarked, that bills of rights are in their origin, stipulations between kings and their subjects, abridgments of prerogative in favor of privilege, reservations of rights not surrendered to the prince. Such was Magna Charta, obtained by the Barons, sword in hand, from king John. Such were the subsequent confirmations of that charter by subsequent princes. Such was the petition of right assented to by Charles the First, in the beginning of his reign. Such also was the declaration of right presented by the lords and commons to the prince of Orange in 1688, and afterwards thrown into the form of an act of parliament, called the bill of rights. It is evident, therefore, that according to their primitive signification, they have no application to constitutions professedly founded upon the power of the people, and executed by their immediate representatives and servants. Here, in strictness, the people surrender nothing, and as they retain every thing, they have no need of particular reservations. "We the people of the United States, to secure the blessings of liberty to ourselves and our posterity, do ordain and establish this constitution for the United States of America." Here is a better recognition of popular rights than volumes of those aphorisms which make the principal figure in several of our state bills of rights, and which would sound much better in a treatise of ethics than in a constitution of government.

But a minute detail of particular rights is certainly far less applicable to a constitution like that under consideration, which is merely intended to regulate the general political interests of the nation, than to a constitution which has the regulation of every species of personal and private concerns. If therefore the loud clamours against the plan of the convention on this score, are well founded, no epithets of reprobation will be too strong for the constitution of this state. But the truth is, that both of them contain all, which in relation to their objects, is reasonably to be desired.

I go further, and affirm that bills of rights, in the sense and in the extent in which they are contended for, are not only unnecessary in the proposed constitution, but would even be dangerous. They would contain various exceptions to powers which are not granted; and on this very account, would afford a colourable pretext to claim more than were granted. For why declare that things shall not be done which there is no power to do? Why for instance, should it be said, that the liberty of the press shall not be restrained, when no power is given by which restrictions may be imposed? I will not contend that such a provision would confer a regulating power; but it is evident that it would furnish, to men disposed to usurp, a plausible pretence for claiming that power. They might urge with a semblance of reason, that the constitution ought not to be charged with the absurdity of providing against the abuse of an authority, which was not given, and that the provision against restraining the liberty of the press afforded a clear implication, that a power to prescribe proper regulations concerning it, was intended to be vested in the national government. This may serve as a specimen of the numerous handles which would be given to the doctrine of constructive powers, by the indulgence of an injudicious zeal for bills of rights.

On the subject of the liberty of the press, as much has been said, I cannot forbear adding a remark or two: In the first place, I observe that there is not a syllable concerning it in the constitution of this state, and in the next, I contend that whatever has been said about it in that of any other state, amounts to nothing. What signifies a declaration that "the liberty of the press shall be inviolably preserved?" What is the liberty of the press? Who can give it any definition which would not leave the utmost latitude for evasion?

I hold it to be impracticable; and from this, I infer, that its security, whatever fine declarations may be inserted in any constitution respecting it, must altogether depend on public opinion, and on the general spirit of the people and of the government.[1] And here, after all, as intimated upon another occasion, must we seek for the only solid basis of all our rights.

There remains but one other view of this matter to conclude the point. The truth is, after all the declamation we have heard, that the constitution is itself in every rational sense, and to every useful purpose, a Bill of Rights. The several bills of rights, in Great-Britain, form its constitution, and conversely the constitution of each state is its bill of rights. And the proposed constitution, if adopted, will be the bill of rights of the union. Is it one object of a bill of rights to declare and specify the political privileges of the citizens in the structure and administration of the government? This is done in the most ample and precise manner in the plan of the convention, comprehending various precautions for the public security, which are not to be found in any of the state constitutions. Is another object of a bill of rights to define certain immunities and modes of proceeding, which are relative to personal and private concerns? This we have seen has also been attended to, in a variety of cases, in the same plan. Adverting therefore to the substantial meaning of a bill of rights, it is absurd to allege that it is not to be found in the work of the convention. It may be said that it does not go far enough, though it will not be easy to make this appear; but it can with no propriety be contended that there is no such thing. It certainly must be immaterial what mode is observed as to the order of declaring the rights of the citizens, if they are to be found in any part of the instrument which establishes the government. And hence it must be apparent that much of what has been said on this subject rests merely on verbal and nominal distinctions, which are entirely foreign from the substance of the thing.

Another objection, which has been made, and which from the frequency of its repetition it is to be presumed is relied on, is of this nature: It is improper (say the objectors) to confer such large powers, as are proposed, upon the national government; because the seat of that government must of

[1]To show that there is a power in the constitution by which the liberty of the press may be affected, recourse has been had to the power of taxation. It is said that duties may be laid upon publications so high as to amount to a prohibition. I know not by what logic it could be maintained that the declarations in the state constitutions, in favour of the freedom of the press, would be a constitutional impediment to the imposition of duties upon publications by the state legislatures. It cannot certainly be pretended that any degree of duties, however low, would be an abrigement of the liberty of the press. We know that newspapers are taxed in Great-Britain, and yet it is notorious that the press no where enjoys greater liberty than in that country. And if duties of any kind may be laid without a violation of that liberty, it is evident that the extent must depend on legislative discretion, regulated by public opinion; so that after all, general declarations respecting the liberty of the press will give it no greater security than it will have without them. The same invasions of it may be effected under the state constitutions which contain those declarations through the means of taxation, as under the proposed constitution which has nothing of the kind. It would be quite as significant to declare that government ought to be free, that taxes ought not to be excessive &c., as that the liberty of the press ought not to be restrained.

necessity be too remote from many of the states to admit of a proper knowledge on the part of the constituent, of the conduct of the representative body. This argument, if it proves any thing, proves that there ought to be no general government whatever. For the powers which it seems to be agreed on all hands, ought to be vested in the union, cannot be safely intrusted to a body which is not under every requisite controul. But there are satisfactory reasons to shew that the objection is in reality not well founded. There is in most of the arguments which relate to distance a palpable illusion of the imagination. What are the sources of information by which the people in Montgomery county must regulate their judgment of the conduct of their representatives in the state legislature? Of personal observation they can have no benefit. This is confined to the citizens on the spot. They must therefore depend on the information of intelligent men, in whom they confide—and how must these men obtain their information? Evidently from the complection of public measures, from the public prints, from correspondences with their representatives, and with other persons who reside at the place of their deliberation. This does not apply to Montgomery county only, but to all the counties, at any considerable distance from the seat of government.

It is equally evident that the same sources of information would be open to the people, in relation to the conduct of their representatives in the general government; and the impediments to a prompt communication which distance may be supposed to create, will be overballanced by the effects of the vigilance of the state governments. The executive and legislative bodies of each state will be so many centinels over the persons employed in every department of the national administration; and as it will be in their power to adopt and pursue a regular and effectual system of intelligence, they can never be at a loss to know the behaviour of those who represent their constituents in the national councils, and can readily communicate the same knowledge to the people. Their disposition to apprise the community of whatever may prejudice its interests from another quarter, may be relied upon, if it were only from the rivalship of power. And we may conclude with the fullest assurance, that the people, through that channel, will be better informed of the conduct of their national representatives, than they can be by any means they now possess of that of their state representatives.

It ought also to be remembered, that the citizens who inhabit the country at and near the seat of government, will in all questions that affect the general liberty and prosperity, have the same interest with those who are at a distance; and that they will stand ready to sound the alarm when necessary, and to point out the actors in any pernicious project. The public papers will be expeditious messengers of intelligence to the most remote inhabitants of the union.

Among the many extraordinary objections which have appeared against the proposed constitution, the most extraordinary and the least colourable one, is derived from the want of some provision respecting the debts due to the United States. This has been represented as a tacit relinquishment of those debts, and as a wicked contrivance to screen public defaulters. The newspapers have teemed with the most inflammatory railings on this head; and yet there is nothing clearer than that the suggestion is entirely void of foundation, and is the offspring of extreme ignorance or extreme dishonesty. In addition to the remarks I have made upon the subject in another place, I shall only observe, that as it is a plain dictate of common sense, so it is also an established doctrine of political law, that "States neither lose any of their rights, nor are discharged from any of their obligations by a change in the form of their civil government.

The last objection of any consequence which I at present recollect, turns upon the article of expence. If it were even true that the adoption of the proposed government would occasion a considerable increase of expence, it would be an objection that ought to have no weight against the plan. The great bulk of the citizens of America, are with reason convinced that union is the basis of their political happiness. Men of sense of all parties now, with few exceptions, agree that it cannot be preserved under the present system, nor without radical alterations; that new and extensive powers ought to be granted to the national head, and that these require a different organization of the federal government, a single body being an unsafe depository of such ample authorities. In conceding all this, the question of expence must be given up, for it is impossible, with any degree of safety, to narrow the foundation upon which the system is to stand. The two branches of the legislature are in the first instance, to consist of only sixty-five persons, which is the same number of which congress, under the existing confederation, may be composed. It is true that this number is intended to be increased; but this is to keep pace with the increase of the population and resources of the country. It is evident, that a less number would, even in the first instance, have been unsafe; and that a continuance of the present number would, in a more advanced stage of population, be a very inadequate representation of the people.

Whence is the dreaded augmentation of expence to spring? One source pointed out, is the multiplication of offices under the new government. Let us examine this a little.

It is evident that the principal departments of the administration under the present government, are the same which will be required under the new. There are now a secretary at war, a secretary for foreign affairs, a secretary for domestic affairs, a board of treasury consisting of three persons, a treasurer, assistants, clerks, &c. These offices are indispensable under any system, and will suffice under the new as well as under the old. As to ambassadors and other ministers and agents in foreign countries, the proposed constitution can make no other difference, than to render their characters, where they reside, more respectable, and their services more useful. As to persons to be employed in the collection of the revenues, it is unquestionably true that these will form a very considerable addition to the number of federal officers; but it will not follow, that this will occasion an increase of public expence. It will be in most cases nothing more than an exchange of state officers for national officers. In the collection of all duties, for instance, the persons employed will be wholly of the latter description. The states individually will stand in no need of any for this purpose. What difference can it make in point of expence, to pay officers of the customs appointed by the state, or those appointed by the United States? There is no good reason to suppose, that either the number or the salaries of the latter, will be greater than those of the former.

Where then are we to seek for those additional articles of expence which are to swell the account to the enormous size that has been represented to us? The chief item which occurs to me, respects the support of the judges of the United States. I do not add the president, because there is now a president of congress, whose expences may not be far, if any thing, short of those which will be incurred on account of the president of the United States. The support of the judges will clearly be an extra expence, but to what extent will depend on the particular plan which may be adopted in practice in regard to this matter. But it can upon no reasonable plan amount to a sum which will be an object of material consequence.

Let us now see what there is to counterballance any extra expences that may attend the establishment of the proposed government. The first thing that presents itself is, that a great part of the business, which now keeps congress sitting through the year, will be transacted by the president. Even the management of foreign negociations will naturally devolve upon him according to general principles concerted with the senate, and subject to their final concurrence. Hence it is evident, that a portion of the year will suffice for the session of both the senate and the house of representatives: We may suppose about a fourth for the latter, and a third or perhaps a half for the former. The extra business of treaties and appointments may give this extra occupation to the senate. From this circumstance we may infer, that until the house of representatives shall be increased greatly beyond its present number, there will be a considerable saving of expence from the difference between the constant session of the present, and the temporary session of the future congress.

But there is another circumstance, of great importance in the view of the economy. The business of the United States has hitherto occupied the state legislatures as well as congress. The latter has made requisitions which the former have had to provide for. Hence it has happened that the sessions of the state legislatures have been protracted greatly beyond what was necessary for the execution of the mere local business of the states. More than half their time has been frequently employed in matters which related to the United States. Now the members who compose the legislatures of the several states amount to two thousand and upwards; which number has hitherto performed what under the new system will be done in the first instance by sixty-five persons, and probably at no future period by above a fourth or a fifth of that number. The congress under the proposed government will do all the business of the United States themselves, without the intervention of the state legislatures, who thenceforth will have only to attend to the affairs of their particular states, and will not have to sit in any proportion as long as they have heretofore done. This difference, in the time of the sessions of the state legislatures, will be all clear gain, and will alone form an article of saving, which may be regarded as an equivalent for any additional objects of expence that may be occasioned by the adoption of the new system.

The result from these observations is, that the sources of additional expence from the establishment of the proposed constitution are much fewer than may have been imagined, that they are counterbalanced by considerable objects of saving, and that while it is questionable on which side the scale will preponderate, it is certain that a government less expensive would be incompetent to the purposes of the union.

Publius

The Federalist No. 85, 1788*

To the People of the State of New-York.

According to the formal division of the subject of these papers, announced in my first number, there would appear still to remain for discussion, two points, "the analogy of the proposed government to your own state constitution," and "the additional security, which its adoption will afford to republican government, to liberty and to property." But these heads have been so fully anticipated and exhausted in the progress of the work, that it would now scarcely be possible to do any thing more than repeat, in a more dilated form, what has been heretofore said; which the advanced stage of the question, and the time already spent upon it conspire to forbid.

It is remarkable, that the resemblance of the plan of the convention to the act which organizes the government of this state holds, not less with regard to many of the supposed defects, than to the real excellencies of the former. Among the pretended defects, are the re-eligibility of the executive, the want of a council, the omission of a formal bill of rights, the omission of a provision respecting the liberty of the press: These and several others, which have been noted in the course of our inquiries, are as much chargeable on the existing constitution of this state, as on the one proposed for the Union. And a man must have slender pretensions to consistency, who can rail at the latter for imperfections which he finds no difficulty in excusing in the former.

The Papers of Alexander Hamilton, Vol. 5, pp. 714–21. J. and A. McLean, *The Federalist,* II, 357–65, published May 28, 1788, numbered 85. In *The* [New York] *Independent Journal or the General Advertiser* this essay was begun on August 13 and concluded on August 16 and is numbered 84. In *The New-York Packet* it appeared on August 14 and is numbered 85.

Nor indeed can there be a better proof of the insincerity and affectation of some of the zealous adversaries of the plan of the convention among us, who profess to be the devoted admirers of the government under which they live, than the fury with which they have attacked that plan, for matters in regard to which our own constitution is equally, or perhaps more vulnerable.

The additional securities to republican government, to liberty and to property, to be derived from the adoption of the plan under consideration, consist chiefly in the restraints which the preservation of the union will impose on local factions and insurrections, and on the ambition of powerful individuals in single states, who might acquire credit and influence enough, from leaders and favorites, to become the despots of the people; in the diminution of the opportunities to foreign intrigue, which the dissolution of the confederacy would invite and facilitate; in the prevention of extensive military establishments, which could not fail to grow out of wars between the states in a disunited situation; in the express guarantee of a republican form of government to each; in the absolute and universal exclusion of titles of nobility; and in the precautions against the repetition of those practices on the part of the state governments, which have undermined the foundations of property and credit, have planted mutual distrust in the breasts of all classes of citizens, and have occasioned an almost universal prostration of morals.

Thus have I, my fellow citizens, executed the task I had assigned to myself; with what success, your conduct must determine. I trust at least you will admit, that I have not failed in the assurance I gave you respecting the spirit with which my endeavours should be conducted. I have addressed myself purely to your judgments, and have studiously avoided those asperities which are too apt to disgrace political disputants of all parties, and which have been not a little provoked by the language and conduct of the opponents of the constitution. The charge of a conspiracy against the liberties of the people, which has been indiscriminately brought against the advocates of the plan, has something in it too wanton and too malignant not to excite the indignation of every man who feels in his own bosom a refutation of the calumny. The perpetual changes which have been rung upon the wealthy, the well-born and the great, have been such as to inspire the disgust of all sensible men. And the unwarrantable concealments and misrepresentations which have been in various ways practiced to keep the truth from the public eye, have been of a nature to demand the reprobation of all honest men. It is not impossible that these circumstance may have occasionally betrayed me into intemperances of expression which I did not intend: It is certain that I have frequently felt a struggle between sensibility and moderation, and if the former has in some instances prevailed, it must be my excuse that it has been neither often nor much.

Let us now pause and ask ourselves whether, in the course of these papers, the proposed constitution has not been satisfactorily vindicated from the aspersions thrown upon it, and whether it has not been shewn to be worthy of the public approbation, and necessary to the public safety and prosperity. Every man is bound to answer these questions to himself, according to the best of his conscience and understanding, and to act agreeably to the genuine and sober dictates of his judgment. This is a duty, from which nothing can give him a dispensation. 'Tis one that he is called upon, nay, constrained by all the obligations that form the bands of society, to discharge sincerely and honestly. No partial motive, no particular interest, no pride of opinion, no temporary passion or prejudice, will justify to himself, to his country or to his posterity, an improper election of the part he is to act. Let him beware of an obstinate adherence to party. Let him reflect that the object upon which he is to decide is not a particular interest of the community, but the very existence of the nation. And let him remember that a majority of America has already given its sanction to the plan, which he is to approve or reject.

I shall not dissemble, that I feel an intire confidence in the arguments, which recommend the proposed system to your adoption; and that I am unable to discern any real force in those by which it has been opposed. I am persuaded, that it is the best which our political situation, habits and opinions will admit, and superior to any the revolution has produced.

Concessions on the part of the friends of the plan, that it has not a claim to absolute perfection, have afforded matter of no small triumph to its enemies. Why, say they, should we adopt an imperfect thing? Why not amend it, and make it perfect before it is irrevocably established? This may be plausible enough, but it is only plausible. In the first place I remark, that the extent of these concessions has been greatly exaggerated. They have been stated as amounting to an admission, that the plan is radically defective; and that, without material alterations, the rights and the interests of the community cannot be safely confided to it. This, as far as I have understood the meaning of those who make the concessions, is an intire perversion of their sense. No advocate of the measure can be found who will not declare as his sentiment, that the system, though it may not be perfect in every part, is upon the whole a good one, is the best that the present views and circumstances of the country will permit, and is such an one as promises every species of security which a reasonable people can desire.

I answer in the next place, that I should esteem it the extreme of imprudence to prolong the precarious state of our national affairs, and to expose the union to the jeopardy of successive experiments, in the chimerical pursuit of a perfect plan. I never expect to see a perfect work from imperfect man. The result of the deliberations of all collective bodies must necessarily be a compound as well of the errors and prejudices, as of the good sense and wisdom of the individuals of whom they are composed. The compacts which are to embrace thirteen distinct states, in a common bond of amity and union, must as necessarily be a compromise of as many dissimilar interests and inclinations. How can perfection spring from such materials?

The reasons assigned in an excellent little pamphlet lately published in this city[1] are unanswerable to shew the utter improbability of assembling a new convention, under circumstances in any degree so favourable to a happy issue, as those in which the late convention met, deliberated and concluded. I will not repeat the arguments there used, as I presume the production itself has had an extensive circulation. It is certainly well worthy the perusal of every friend to his country. There is however one point of light in which the subject of amendments still remains to be considered; and in which it has not yet been exhibited to public view. I cannot resolve to conclude, without first taking a survey of it in this aspect.

It appears to me susceptible of absolute demonstration, that it will be far more easy to obtain subsequent than previous amendments to the constitution. The moment an alteration is made in the present plan, it becomes, to the purpose of adoption, a new one, and must undergo a new decision of each state. To its complete establishment throughout the union, it will therefore require the concurrence of thirteen states. If, on the contrary, the constitution proposed should once be ratified by all the states as it stands, alterations in it may at any time be affected by nine states. Here then the chances are as thirteen to nine[2] in favour of subsequent amendments, rather than of the original adoption of an intire system.

This is not all. Every constitution for the United States must inevitably consist of a great variety of particulars, in which thirteen independent states are to be accommodated in their interests or opinions of interest. We may of course expect to see, in any body of men charged with its original formation, very different combinations of the parts upon different points. Many of those who form the majority on one question may become the minority on a second, and an association dissimilar to either may constitute the majority on a third. Hence the necessity of moulding and arranging all the particulars which are to compose the whole in such a manner as to satisfy all the parties to the compact; and hence also an immense multiplication of difficulties and casualties in obtaining the collective assent to a final act. The degree of that multiplication must evidently be in a ratio to the number of particulars and the number of parties.

But every amendment to the constitution, if once established, would be a single proposition, and might be brought forward singly. There would then be no necessity for management or compromise, in relation to any other point, no giving nor taking. The will of the requisite number would at once bring the matter to a decisive issue. And consequently whenever nine or rather ten states, were united in the desire of a particular amendment, that amendment must infallibly take place. There can therefore be no comparison

---

[1] Intitled "An Address to the people of the state of New-York," *supra* p. 554.
[2] It may rather be said ten for though two-thirds may set on foot the measure, three-fourths must ratify.

between the facility of effecting an amendment, and that of establishing in the first instance a complete constitution.

In opposition to the probability of subsequent amendments it has been urged, that the persons delegated to the administration of the national government, will always be disinclined to yield up any portion of the authority of which they were once possessed. For my own part I acknowledge a thorough conviction that any amendments which may, upon mature consideration, be thought useful, will be applicable to the organization of the government, not to the mass of its powers; and on this account alone, I think there is no weight in the observation just stated. I also think there is little weight in it on another account. The intrinsic difficulty of governing thirteen states at any rate, independent of calculations upon an ordinary degree of public spirit and integrity, will, in my opinion, constantly impose on the national rulers the necessity of a spirit of accommodation to the reasonable expectations of their constituents. But there is yet a further consideration, which proves beyond the possibility of doubt, that the observation is futile. It is this, that the national rulers, whenever nine states concur, will have no option upon the subject. By the fifth article of the plan the congress will be obliged, "on the application of the legislatures of two-thirds of the states, (which at present amounts to nine) to call a convention for proposing amendments, which shall be valid to all intents and purposes, as part of the constitution, when ratified by the legislatures of three-fourths of the states, or by conventions in three-fourths thereof." The words of this article are peremptory. The Congress "shall call a convention." Nothing in this particular is left to the discretion of that body. And of consequence all the declamation about their disinclination to a change, vanishes in air. Nor however difficult it may be supposed to unite two-thirds or three-fourths of the state legislatures, in amendments which may affect local interest, can there be any room to apprehend any such difficulty in a union on points which are merely relative to the general liberty or security of the people. We may safely rely on the disposition of the state legislatures to erect barriers against the encroachments of the national authority.

If the foregoing argument is a fallacy, certain it is that I am myself deceived by it; for it is, in my conception, one of those rare instances in which a political truth can be brought to the test of mathematical demonstration. Those who see the matter in the same light with me, however zealous they may be for amendments, must agree in the propriety of a previous adoption, as the most direct road to their own object.

The zeal for attempts to amend, prior to the establishment of the constitution, must abate in every man, who, is ready to accede to the truth of the following observations of a writer, equally solid and ingenious: "To balance a large state or society (says he) whether monarchical or republican, on general laws, is a work of so great difficulty, that no human genius, however comprehensive, is able by the mere dint of reason and reflection, to effect it.

The judgments of many must unite in the work: experience must guide their labour: Time must bring it to perfection: And the feeling of inconveniences must correct the mistakes which they inevitably fall into, in their first trials and experiments."[3] These judicious reflections contain a lesson of moderation to all the sincere lovers of the union, and ought to put them upon their guard against hazarding anarchy, civil war, a perpetual alienation of the states from each other, and perhaps the military despotism of a victorious demagogue, in the pursuit of what they are not likely to obtain, but from time and experience. It may be in me a defect of political fortitude, but I acknowledge, that I cannot entertain an equal tranquillity with those who affect to treat the dangers of a longer continuance in our present situation as imaginary. A nation without a national government is, in my view, an awful spectacle. The establishment of a constitution, in time of profound peace, by the voluntary consent of a whole people, is a prodigy, to the completion of which I look forward with trembling anxiety. I can reconcile it to no rules of prudence to let go the hold we now have, in so arduous an enterprise, upon seven out of the thirteen states; and after having passed over so considerable a part of the ground to recommence the course. I dread the more the consequences of new attempts, because I know that powerful individuals, in this and in other states, are enemies to a general national government, in every possible shape.

Publius

---

[3]Hume's *Essays,* Vol. I, p. 128. The rise of arts and sciences.

THOMAS JEFFERSON–JAMES MADISON CORRESPONDENCE, 1787–1789

Commentary

Among the most influential writings on the new Constitution (at least in their impact on the movement to secure a federal Bill of Rights) were letters written by Jefferson and Madison to each other and also some letters by them to others. The correspondence between Jefferson and Madison was important for two reasons: 1) each influenced the other's thinking (particularly the case in the evolution of Madison's thinking on a Bill of Rights, with Jefferson's unfailing emphasis on the need for one converting Madison's original lukewarm attitude to one of support); and 2) the wide publicity given to some of the letters had great impact on the ratification debates. (Jefferson's views were widely used in the debates and his February, 1788, statements that nine states should ratify and four reject, until a Bill of Rights was added, was strongly relied upon by the Antifederalists who urged ratification conditioned upon previous amendments—even, as we shall see, after Jefferson modified his view in favor of the Massachusetts approach of ratification with recommendatory amendments.)

The Jefferson-Madison correspondence which follows begins with Madison's letter of October 24, 1787, in which he tells Jefferson (then in Paris as Minister to France) about the result of the Philadelphia Convention. The letter is a masterful summary both of the work of the Convention and of the new Constitution. For our purposes, the letter is important because it started the exchange of views on the Constitution between the two men, and because of the summary at the letter's end of the probable reception of the new document, with emphasis on those objecting to the Constitution (particularly Mason, who "considers the want of a Bill of Rights as a fatal objection").

Jefferson answered in his oft-quoted letter of December 20, where he stated his general approval of the Constitution, but went on: "I will now add what I do not like. First the omission of a bill of rights providing clearly and without the aid of sophisms" for essential freedoms (he names religion, press, habeas corpus, jury trial, among others). In a famous passage, he asserts "that a bill of rights is what the people are entitled to against every government on earth, general or particular, and what no just government should refuse, or rest on inference." Jefferson specifically rejects the argument of James Wilson (*supra* p. 528.) that a Bill of Rights is not necessary because the Federal Government has only the powers delegated to it as "surely gratis dictum."

Then, in his letter to Madison of February 6, 1788, as well as in the contemporaneous letters to William Smith and Alexander Donald, which also follow, Jefferson makes his suggestion, already referred to, that nine states should accept, and four reject, the Constitution, as "the latter will oblige them to offer a declaration of rights in order to complete the union . . . and cure it's principal defect." In his letter to Donald (as well as that to Dumas) Jefferson repeats the essentials of a Bill of Rights.

The next letter is Madison's important letter of October 17, 1788, in which he indicates a shift toward the Jefferson view on the need for a Bill of Rights. He states that he does not fully accept the Wilson argument that all powers not granted are reserved. "My own opinion has always been in favor of a bill of rights," though "I have not viewed it in an important light." He fears a Bill of Rights may not be effective (he calls it a "parchment barrier"). But he concedes that desirable ends may be served by a Bill of Rights. Should danger of "subversion of liberty . . . exist at all, it is prudent to guard against it, especially when the precaution can do no injury." By implication, he states his support for a Bill of Rights—if not "for any other reason than that it is anxiously desired by others" (presumably Jefferson in particular).

With his October 17 letter, Madison enclosed a pamphlet containing the proposed amendments recommended by the states. This may well have induced Jefferson to come out in favor of the Massachusetts approach as the best practical method of obtaining both the Constitution and a Bill of Rights. In his March 13, 1789, letter to Francis Hopkinson, Jefferson explains how his first opinion in favor of rejection by four states changed "the moment I saw the much better plan of Massachusetts and which had never occurred to me." He states acutely that "the majority of the United States are of my opinion," recognizing that after other states had followed the Massachusetts approach not only the Antifederalists, but also "a very responsible proportion of the federalists think that such a declaration should now be annexed." (On Jefferson's approval of the Massachusetts approach, see also *infra* p. 728.)

Also included is Jefferson's letter to Madison of March 15, 1789, because it is in reply to Madison's letter of October 17, 1788, particularly to Madison's assertion that a Bill of Rights will be ineffective. Jefferson states that this is not true, for Madison omits to mention, in his arguments, "one which has great weight with me, the legal check which [a Bill of Rights] puts into the hands of the judiciary." The Jefferson assertion on the matter led Madison to emphasize, when he later presented his draft of the Bill of Rights to Congress, that the courts would enforce the limitations imposed in his proposed amendments (*infra* p. 1009).

Madison to Jefferson, 1787*

New York, Oct. 24, 1787
Dear Sir,
Your favor of June 20 has been already acknowledged. The last Packet from France brought me that of August 2d. I have recd. also by the *Mary*

*The Writings of James Madison, Vol. 5, pp. 17–41.

Capt. Howland the three Boxes for W. H.,[1] B. F.[2] and myself. The two first have been duly forwarded. The contents of the last are a valuable addition to former literary remittances and lay me under additional obligations, which I shall always feel more strongly than I express. The articles for Congress have been delivered & those for the two Universities and for General Washington have been forwarded, as have been the various letters for your friends in Virginia and elsewhere. The parcel of rice referred to in your letter to the Delegates of S. Carolina has met with some accident. No account whatever can be gathered concerning it. It probably was not shipped from France. Ubbo's book I find was not omitted as you seem to have apprehended. The charge for it however is, which I must beg you to supply. The duplicate vol of the Encyclopedie, I left in Virginia, and it is uncertain when I shall have an opportunity of returning it. Your Spanish duplicates will I fear be hardly vendible. I shall make a trial whenever a chance presents itself. A few days ago I recd. your favor of 15 of Augst. via L'Orient & Boston. The letters inclosed along with it were immediately sent to Virga.

You will herewith receive the result of the Convention, which continued its session till the 17th of September. I take the liberty of making some observations on the subject, which will help to make up a letter, if they should answer no other purpose.

It appeared to be the sincere and unanimous wish of the Convention to cherish and preserve the Union of the States. No proposition was made, no suggestion was thrown out, in favor of a partition of the Empire into two or more Confederacies.

It was generally agreed that the objects of the Union could not be secured by any system founded on the principle of a confederation of Sovereign States. A voluntary observance of the federal law by all the members could never be hoped for. A compulsive one could evidently never be reduced to practice, and if it could, involved equal calamities to the innocent & the guilty, the necessity of a military force both obnoxious & dangerous, and in general a scene resembling much more a civil war than the administration of a regular Government.

Hence was embraced the alternative of a Government which instead of operating, on the States, should operate without their intervention on the individuals composing them; and hence the change in the principle and proportion of representation.

This ground-work being laid, the great objects which presented themselves were 1. to unite a proper energy in the Executive, and a proper stability in the Legislative departments, with the essential characters of Republican Government. 2. to draw a line of demarkation which would give to the General Government every power requisite for general purposes, and leave to the States every power which might be most beneficially administered by

[1]William Hay in Richmond.
[2]Benjamin Franklin.

them. 3. to provide for the different interests of different parts of the Union. 4. to adjust the clashing pretensions of the large and small States. Each of these objects was pregnant with difficulties. The whole of them together formed a task more difficult than can be well conceived by those who were not concerned in the execution of it. Adding to these considerations the natural diversity of human opinions on all new and complicated subjects, it is impossible to consider the degree of concord which ultimately prevailed as less than a miracle.

The first of these objects, as respects the Executive, was peculiarly embarrassing. On the question whether it should consist of a single person, or a plurality of co-ordinate members, on the mode of appointment, on the duration in office, on the degree of power, on the re-eligibility, tedious and reiterated discussions took place. The plurality of co-ordinate members had finally but few advocates. Governour Randolph was at the head of them. The modes of appointment proposed were various, as by the people at large—by electors chosen by the people—by the Executives of the States— by the Congress, some preferring a joint ballot of the two Houses—some a separate concurrent ballot, allowing to each a negative on the other house— some, a nomination of several candidates by one House, out of whom a choice should be made by the other. Several other modifications were started. The expedient at length adopted seemed to give pretty general satisfaction to the members. As to the duration in office, a few would have preferred a tenure during good behaviour—a considerable number would have done so in case an easy & effectual removal by impeachment could be settled. It was much agitated whether a long term, seven years for example, with a subsequent & perpetual ineligibility, or a short term with a capacity to be re-elected, should be fixed. In favor of the first opinion were urged the danger of a gradual degeneracy of re-elections from time to time, into first a life and then a hereditary tenure, and the favorable effect of an incapacity to be reappointed on the independent exercise of the Executive authority. On the other side it was contended that the prospect of necessary degradation would discourage the most dignified characters from aspiring to the office, would take away the principal motive to ye. faithful discharge of its duties—the hope of being rewarded with a reappointment would stimulate ambition to violent efforts for holding over the Constitutional term—and instead of producing an independent administration, and a firmer defence of the constitutional rights of the department, would render the officer more indifferent to the importance of a place which he would soon be obliged to quit forever, and more ready to yield to the encroachmts. of the Legislature of which he might again be a member. The questions concerning the degree of power turned chiefly on the appointment to offices, and the controul on the Legislature. An absolute appointment to all offices—to some offices—to no offices, formed the scale of opinions on the first point. On the second, some contended for an absolute negative, as the only possible mean of reducing to practice

the theory of a free Government which forbids a mixture of the Legislative &
Executive powers. Others would be content with a revisionary power, to be
overruled by three fourths of both Houses. It was warmly urged that the
judiciary department should be associated in the revision. The idea of some
was that a separate revision should be given to the two departments—that if
either objected two thirds, if both, three fourths, should be necessary to
overrule.

In forming the Senate, the great anchor of the Government the questions,
as they came within the first object, turned mostly on the mode of appointment, and the duration of it. The different modes proposed were 1. by the
House of Representatives. 2. by the Executive. 3. by electors chosen by the
people for the purpose. 4. by the State Legislatures. On the point of duration, the propositions descended from good behavior to four years, through
the intermediate terms of nine, seven, six, & five years. The election of the
other branch was first determined to be triennial, and afterwards reduced to
biennial.

The second object, the due partition of power between the General & local
Governments, was perhaps of all, the most nice and difficult. A few contended for an entire abolition of the States; Some for indefinite power of Legislation in the Congress, with a negative on the laws of the States; some for such
a power without a negative; some for a limited power of legislation, with
such a negative; the majority finally for a limited power without the negative. The question with regard to the negative underwent repeated discussions, and was finally rejected by a bare majority. As I formerly intimated
to you my opinion in favor of this ingredient, I will take this occasion of
explaining myself on the subject. Such a check on the States appears to me
necessary 1. to prevent encroachments on the General authority. 2. to
prevent instability and injustice in the legislation of the States.

1. Without such a check in the whole over the parts, our system involves
the evil of imperia in imperio. If a compleat supremacy somewhere is not
necessary in every Society, a controuling power at least is so, by which the
general authority may be defended against encroachments of the subordinate
authorities, and by which the latter may be restrained from encroachments
on each other. If the supremacy of the British Parliament is not necessary as
has been contended, for the harmony of that Empire; it is evident I think that
without the royal negative or some equivalent controul, the unity of the
system would be destroyed. The want of some such provision seems to have
been mortal to the antient Confederacies, and to be the disease of the
modern. Of the Lycian confederacy little is known. That of the
Amphyctions is well known to have been rendered of little use whilst it
lasted, and in the end to have been destroyed, by the predominance of the
local over the federal authority. The same observation may be made, on the
authority of Polybius, with regard to the Achaean League. The Helvetic
System scarcely amounts to a confederacy, and is disguised by too many

peculiarities, to be a ground of comparison. The case of the United Netherlands is in point. The authority of a Stadtholder, the influence of a Standing
Army, the common interest in the conquered possessions, the pressure of
surrounding danger, the guarantee of foreign powers, are not sufficient to
secure the authority and interest of the generality agst. the anti-federal
tendency of the provincial sovereignties. The German Empire is another
example. A Hereditary chief with vast independent resources of wealth and
power, a federal Diet, with ample parchment authority, a regular Judiciary
establishment, the influence of the neighbourhood of great & formidable
Nations have been found unable either to maintain the subordination of the
members, or to prevent their mutual contests & encroachments. Still more to
the purpose is our own experience both during the war and since the peace.
Encroachments of the States on the general authority, sacrifices of national to
local interests, interferences of the measures of different States, form a great
part of the history of our political system. It may be said that the new
Constitution is founded on different principles, and will have a different
operation. I admit the difference to be material. It presents the aspect rather
of a feudal system of republics, if such a phrase may be used, than of a
Confederacy of independent States. And what has been the progress and
event of the feudal Constitutions? In all of them a continual struggle between
the head and the inferior members, until a final victory has been gained in
some instances by one, in others, by the other of them. In one respect indeed
there is a remarkable variance between the two cases. In the feudal system
the sovereign, though limited, was independent; and having no particular
sympathy of interests with the Great Barons, his ambition had as full play as
theirs in the mutual projects of usurpation. In the American Constitution The
general authority will be derived entirely from the subordinate authorities.
The Senate will represent the States in their political capacity; the other
House will represent the people of the States in their individual capacy. The
former will be accountable to their constituents at moderate, the latter at
short periods. The President also derives his appointment from the States,
and is periodically accountable to them. This dependence of the General on
the local authorities, seems effectually to guard the latter against any dangerous encroachments of the former; whilst the latter, within their respective
limits, will be continually sensible of the abridgement of their power, and be
stimulated by ambition to resume the surrendered portion of it. We find the
representatives of Counties and Corporations in the Legislatures of the
States, much more disposed to sacrifice the aggregate interest, and even
authority, to the local views of their constituents, than the latter to the
former. I mean not by these remarks to insinuate that an esprit de corps will
not exist in the National Government or that opportunities may not occur of
extending its jurisdiction in some points. I mean only that the danger of
encroachments is much greater from the other side, and that the impossibility
of dividing powers of legislation, in such a manner, as to be free from

different constructions by different interests, or even from ambiguity in the judgment of the impartial, requires some such expedient as I contend for. Many illustrations might be given of this impossibility. How long has it taken to fix, and how imperfectly is yet fixed the legislative power of corporations, though that power is subordinate in the most compleat manner? The line of distinction between the power of regulating trade and that of drawing revenue from it, which was once considered the barrier of our liberties, was found on fair discussion, to be absolutely undefinable. No distinction seems to be more obvious than that between spiritual and temporal matters. Yet wherever they have been made objects of Legislation, they have clashed and contended with each other, till one or the other has gained the supremacy. Even the boundaries between the Executive, Legislative, & Judiciary powers, though in general so strongly marked in themselves, consist in many instances of mere shades of difference. It may be said that the Judicial authority, under our new system will keep the States within their proper limits, and supply the place of a negative on their laws. The answer is, that it is more convenient to prevent the passage of a law than to declare it void after it is passed; that this will be particularly the case, where the law aggrieves individuals, who may be unable to support an appeal agst. a State to the supreme Judiciary; that a State which would violate the Legislative rights of the Union, would not be very ready to obey a Judicial decree in support of them, and that a recurrence to force, which, in the event of disobedience would be necessary, is an evil which the new Constitution meant to exclude as far as possible.

2. A constitutional negative on the laws of the States seems equally necessary to secure individuals agst. encroachments on their rights. The mutability of the laws of the States is found to be a serious evil. The injustice of them has been so frequent and so flagrant as to alarm the most stedfast friends of Republicanism. I am persuaded I do not err in saying that the evils issuing from these sources contributed more to that uneasiness which produced the Convention, and prepared the Public mind for a general reform, than those which accrued to our national character and interest from the inadequacy of the Confederation to its immediate objects. A reform therefore which does not make provision for private rights, must be materially defective. The restraints agst. paper emissions, and violations of contracts are not sufficient. Supposing them to be effectual as far as they go, they are short of the mark. Injustice may be effected by such an infinitude of legislative expedients, that where the disposition exists it can only be controuled by some provision which reaches all cases whatsoever. The partial provision made, supposes the disposition which will evade it. It may be asked how private rights will be more secure under the Guardianship of the General Government than under the State Governments, since they are both founded on the republican principle which refers the ultimate decision to the will of the majority, and are distinguished rather by the extent within which

they will operate, than by any material difference in their structure. A full discussion of this question would, if I mistake not, unfold the true Principles of Republican Government, and prove in contradiction to the concurrent opinions of the theoretical writers, that this form of Government, in order to effect its purposes, must operate not within a small but an extensive sphere. I will state some of the ideas which have occurred to me on the subject. Those who contend for a simple Democracy, or a pure republic, actuated by the sense of the majority, and operating within narrow limits, assume or suppose a case which is altogether fictitious. They found their reasoning on the idea, that the people composing the Society, enjoy not only an equality of political rights; but that they have all precisely the same interests, and the same feelings in every respect. Were this in reality the case, their reasoning would be conclusive. The interest of the majority would be that of the minority also; the decisions could only turn on mere opinion concerning the good of the whole, of which the major voice would be the safest criterion; and within a small sphere, this voice could be most easily collected, and the public affairs most accurately managed. We know however that no society ever did or can consist of so homogeneous a mass of Citizens. In the savage state indeed, an approach is made towards it; but in that state little or no Government is necessary. In all civilized societies, distinctions are various and unavoidable. A distinction of property results from that very protection which a free Government gives to unequal faculties of acquiring it. There will be rich and poor; creditors and debtors; a landed interest, a monied interest, a mercantile interest, a manufacturing interest. These classes may again be subdivided according to the different productions of different situations & soils, & according to different branches of commerce and of manufactures. In addition to these natural distinctions, artificial ones will be founded, on accidental differences in political, religious, or other opinions, or an attachment to the persons of leading individuals. However erroneous or ridiculous these grounds of dissention and faction may appear to the enlightened Statesman or the benevolent philosopher, the bulk of mankind who are neither Statesmen nor Philosophers, will continue to view them in a different light. It remains then to be enquired whether a majority having any common interest, or feeling any common passion, will find sufficient motives to restrain them from oppressing the minority. An individual is never allowed to be a judge or even a witness, in his own cause. If two individuals are under the bias of interest or enmity agst. a third, the rights of the latter could never be safely referred to the majority of the three. Will two thousand individuals be less apt to oppress one thousand, or two hundred thousand one hundred thousand? Three motives only can restrain in such cases: 1. a prudent regard to private or partial good, as essentially involved in the general and permanent good of the Whole. This ought no doubt to be sufficient of itself. Experience however shews that it has little effect on individuals, and perhaps still less on a collection of individuals, and least of all on a majority with the public authority in their hands. If the former are ready to forget that honesty is the best policy; the last do more. They often proceed on the converse of the maxim, that whatever is politic is honest. 2. respect for character. This motive is not found sufficient to restrain individuals from injustice. And loses its efficacy in proportion to the number which is to divide the pain or the blame. Besides as it has reference to public opinion, which is that of the majority, the standard is fixed by those whose conduct is to be measured by it. 3. Religion. The inefficacy of this restraint on individuals is well known. The conduct of every popular Assembly, acting on oath, the strongest of religious ties, shews that individuals join without remorse in acts agst. which their consciences would revolt, if proposed to them separately in their closets. When Indeed Religion is kindled into enthusiasm, its force like that of other passions is increased by the sympathy of a multitude. But enthusiasm is only a temporary state of Religion, and whilst it lasts will hardly be seen with pleasure at the helm. Even in its coolest state, it has been much oftener a motive to oppression than a restraint from it. If then there must be different interests and parties in society; and a majority when united by a common interest or passion cannot be restrained from oppressing the minority, what remedy can be found in a republican Government, where the majority must ultimately decide, but that of giving such an extent to its sphere, that no common interest or passion will be likely to unite a majority of the whole number in an unjust pursuit. In a large Society, the people are broken into so many interests and parties, that a common sentiment is less likely to be felt, and the requisite concert less likely to be formed, by a majority of the whole. The same security seems requisite for the civil as for the religious rights of individuals. If the same sect form a majority and have the power, other sects will be sure to be depressed. Divide et impera, the reprobated axiom of tyranny, is under certain qualifications, the only policy, by which a republic can be administered on just principles. It must be observed however that this doctrine can only hold within a sphere of a mean extent. As in too small a sphere oppressive combinations may be too easily formed agst. the weaker party; so in too extensive a one, a defensive concert may be rendered too difficult against the oppression of those entrusted with the administration. The great desideratum in Government is, so to modify the sovereignty as that it may be sufficiently neutral between different parts of the Society to controul one part from invading the rights of another, and at the same time sufficiently controuled itself, from setting up an interest adverse to that of the entire Society. In absolute monarchies, the Prince may be tolerably neutral towards different classes of his subjects but may sacrifice the happiness of all to his personal ambition or avarice. In small republics, the sovereign will is controuled from such a sacrifice of the entire Society, but is not sufficiently neutral towards the parts composing it. In the extended Republic of the United States, the General Government would hold a pretty even balance between the parties of particular States, and be at the same time sufficiently restrained by its dependence on the community, from betraying its general interests.

Begging pardon for this immoderate digression I return to the third object above mentioned, the adjustments of the different interests of different parts of the Continent. Some contended for an unlimited power over trade including exports as well as imports, and over slaves as well as other imports; some for such a power, provided the concurrence of two thirds of both Houses were required; Some for such a qualification of the power, with an exemption of exports and slaves, others for an exemption of exports only. The result is seen in the Constitution. S. Carolina & Georgia were inflexible on the point of the slaves.

The remaining object created more embarrassment, and a greater alarm for the issue of the Convention than all the rest put together. The little States insisted on retaining their equality in both branches, unless a compleat abolition of the State Governments should take place; and made an equality in the Senate a sine qua non. The large States on the other hand urged that as the new Government was to be drawn principally from the people immediately and was to operate directly on them, not on the States; and consequently as the States wd. lose that importance which is now proportioned to the importance of their voluntary compliances with the requisitions of Congress, it was necessary that the representation in both Houses should be in proportion to their size. It ended in the compromise which you will see, but very much to the dissatisfaction of several members from the large States.

It will not escape you that three names only from Virginia are subscribed to the Act. Mr. Wythe did not return after the death of his lady. Docr. M'Clurg left the Convention some time before the adjournment. The Governour and Col. Mason refused to be parties to it. Mr. Gerry was the only other member who refused. The objections of the Govr. turn principally on the latitude of the general powers, and on the connection established between the President and the Senate. He wished that the plan should be proposed to the States with liberty to them to suggest alterations which should all be referred to another general Convention, to be incorporated into the plan as far as might be judged expedient. He was not inveterate in his opposition, and grounded his refusal to subscribe pretty much on his unwillingness to commit himself, so as not to be at liberty to be governed by further lights on the subject. Col. Mason left Philada. in an exceeding ill humour indeed. A number of little circumstances arising in part from the impatience which prevailed towards the close of the business, conspired to whet his acrimony. He returned to Virginia with a fixed disposition to prevent the adoption of the plan if possible. He considers the want of a Bill of Rights as a fatal objection. His other objections are to the substitution of the Senate in place of an Executive Council & to the powers vested in that body—to the powers of the Judiciary—to the vice President being made President of the Senate—to the smallness of the number of Representatives—to the restriction on the States with regard to ex post facto laws—and most of all probably to the power of regulating trade, by a majority only of each House. He has some other lesser objections. Being now under the necessity of justifying his refusal to sign, he will of course muster every possible one. His conduct has given great umbrage to the County of Fairfax, and particularly to the Town of Alexandria. He is already instructed to promote in the assembly the calling of a Convention, and will probably be either not deputed to the Convention, or be tied up by express instructions. He did not object in general to the powers vested in the National Government, so much as to the modification. In some respects he admitted that some further powers would have improved the system. He acknowledged in particular that a negative on the State laws, and the appointment of the State Executive ought to be ingredients; but supposed that the public mind would not now bear them, and that experience would hereafter produce these amendments.

The final reception which will be given by the people at large to the proposed system cannot yet be decided. The Legislature of N. Hampshire was sitting when it reached that State and was well pleased with it. As far as the sense of the people there has been expressed, it is generally favorable. Boston is warm and almost unanimous in embracing it. The impression on the country is not yet known. No symptoms of disapprobation have appeared. The Legislature of that State is now sitting, through which the sense of the people at large will soon be promulged with tolerable certainty. The paper money faction in R. Island is hostile. The other party zealously attached to it. Its passage through Connecticut is likely to be very smooth and easy. There seems to be less agitation in this State N. York than anywhere. The discussion of the subject seems confined to the Newspapers. The principal characters are known to be friendly. The Governour's party which has hitherto been the popular & most numerous one, is supposed to be on the opposite side; but considerable reserve is practiced, of which he sets the example. N. Jersey takes the affirmative side of course. Meetings of the people are declaring their approbation and instructing their representatives. Penna. will be divided. The City of Philada., the Republican party, the Quakers, and most of the Germans espouse the Constitution. Some of the Constitutional leaders, backed by the Western Country will oppose. An unlucky ferment on the subject in their Assembly just before its late adjournment has irritated both sides, particularly the opposition, and by redoubling the exertions of that party may render the event doubtful. The voice of Maryland I understand from pretty good authority, is, as far as it has been declared, strongly in favor of the Constitution. Mr. Chase is an enemy, but the Town of Baltimore which he now represents, is warmly attached to it, and will shackle him as far as it can. Mr. Paca will probably be, as usual, in the politics of Chase. My information from Virginia is as yet extremely imperfect. I have a letter from Genl. Washington which speaks favorably of the impression within a circle of some extent; and another from Chancellor Pendleton which expresses his full acceptance of the plan, and the popularity of it in his district, I am told also that Innes and Marshall are patrons of it. In the opposite scale are Mr. James Mercer, Mr. R. H. Lee, Docr. Lee and their connections of course, Mr. M. Page according to Report, and most of the Judges & Bar of the general Court. The part which Mr. Henry will take is unknown here. Much will depend on it. I had taken it for granted from a variety of circumstances that he wd. be in the opposition, and still think that will be the case. There are reports however which favor a contrary supposition. From the States South of Virginia nothing has been heard. As the deputation from S. Carolina consisted of some of its weightiest characters, who have returned unanimously zealous in favor of the Constitution, it is probable that State will readily embrace it. It is not less probable that N. Carolina will follow the example unless that of Virginia should counterbalance it. Upon the whole, although, the public mind will not be fully known, nor finally settled, for a considerable time, appearances at present augur a more prompt, and general adoption of the plan than could have been well expected.

When the plan came before Congress for their sanction, a very serious effort was made by R. H. Lee & Mr. Dane, from Massts. to embarrass it. It was first contended that Congress could not properly give any positive countenance to a measure which had for its object the subversion of the Constitution under which they acted. This ground of attack failing, the former gentleman urged the expediency of sending out the plan with amendments, & proposed a number of them corresponding with the objections of Col. Mason. This experiment had still less effect. In order however to obtain unanimity it was necessary to couch the resolution in very moderate terms.

Mr. Adams has recd. permission to return, with thanks for his services. No provision is made for supplying his place, or keeping up any representation there. Your reappointment for three years will be notified from the office of F. Affrs. It was made without a negative, eight States being present. Connecticut, notwithstanding put in a blank ticket, the sense of that State having been declared against embassies. Massachusts. betrayed some scruple on like ground. Every personal consideration was avowed, & I believe with sincerity, to have militated against these scruples. It seems to be understood that letters to & from the foreign Ministers of the U.S. are not free of Postage; but that the charge is to be allowed in their accounts.

The exchange of our French for Dutch Creditors has not been countenanced either by Congress or the Treasury Board. The paragraph in your last letter to Mr. Jay, on the subject of applying a loan in Holland to the discharge of the pay due to the foreign officers has been referred to the Board since my arrival here. No report has yet been made. But I have little idea that the proposition will be adopted. Such is the state & prospect of our fiscal department, that any new loan however small, that should now be made, would probably subject us to the reproach of premeditated deception. The balance of Mr. Adams's last loan will be wanted for the interest due in Holland, and with all the income here, will it is feared, not save our credit in Europe from farther wounds. It may well be doubted whether the present Government can be kept alive during the ensuing year, or until the new one may take its place.

Upwards of 100,000 Acres of the lands of the U.S. have been disposed of in open market. Five millions of unsurveyed have been sold by private contract to a N. England company, at 2/3 of a dollar per Acre, payment to be made in the principal of the public securities. A negotiation is nearly closed with a N. Jersey company for two millions more on like terms, and another commenced with a company of this City for four millions. Col. Carrington writes more fully on this subject.

You will receive herewith the desired information from Alderman Broome in the case of Mr. Burke, also the Virga. Bill on Crimes & punishments. Sundry alterations having been made in conformity to the sense of the House in its latter stages, it is less accurate & methodical than it ought to have been. To these papers I add a Speech of Mr. C. P. on the Mississippi business. It is printed under precautions of secrecy, but surely could not have been properly exposed to so much risk of publication. You will find also among the pamphlets & papers I send by Comodore Jones, another printed speech of the same Gentleman. The Museum[?], Magazine, & Philada. Gazettes will give you a tolerable idea of the objects of present attention.

The summer crops in the Eastern & Middle States have been extremely plentiful. Southward of Virga. They differ in different places. On the whole I do not know that they are bad in that region. In Virginia the drought has been unprecedented, particularly between the falls of the Rivers & the Mountains. The crops of Corn are in general alarmingly short. In Orange I find there will be scarcely subsistence for the inhabitants. I have not heard from Albemarle. The crops of Tobo. are every where said to be pretty good in point of quantity, & the quality unusually fine. The crops of wheat were also in general excellent in quality & tolerable in quantity.

Novr. 1. Commodore Paul Jones having preferred another vessel to the packet, has remained here till this time. The interval has produced little necessary to be added to the above. The Legislature of Massts. has it seems taken up the act of the Convention, and has appointed or probably will appoint an early day for its State Convention. There are letters also from Georgia which denote a favorable disposition. I am informed from Richmond that the New Election-law from the Revised Code produced a pretty full House of Delegates, as well as a Senate, on the first day. It had previously had equal effect in producing full meetings of the freeholders for the County elections. A very decided majority of the Assembly is said to be zealous in favor of the New Constitution. The same is said of the Country at large. It appears however that individuals of great weight both within & without the Legislature are opposed to it. A letter I just have from Mr. A. Stuart, names Mr. Henry, Genl. Nelson, W. Nelson, the family of Cabels, St. George Tucker, John Taylor, and the Judges of the Genl. Court except P. Carrington. The other opponents he describes as of too little note to be mentioned, which gives a negative information of the Characters on the other side. All are agreed that the plan must be submitted to a Convention.

We hear from Georgia that that State is threatened with a dangerous war with the Creek Indians. The alarm is of so serious a nature that law-martial has been proclaimed, and they are proceeding to fortify even the Town of Savannah. The idea there is, that the Indians derive their motives as well as their means from their Spanish neighbours. Individuals complain also that their fugitive slaves are encouraged by East Florida. The policy of this is explained by supposing that it is considered as a discouragement to the Georgians to form settlements near the Spanish boundaries.

There are but few States on the spot here which will survive the expiration of the federal year, and it is extremely uncertain when a Congress will again be formed. We have not yet heard who are to be in the appointment of Virginia for the next year.

With the most affectionate attachment I remain

Jefferson to Madison, 1787*

Paris, Dec. 20, 1787

Dear Sir,

My last to you was of Oct. 8 by the Count de Moustier. Yours of July 18. Sep. 6. and Oct. 24. have been successively received, yesterday, the day before and three or four days before that. I have only had time to read the letters, the printed papers communicated with them, however interesting, being obliged to lie over till I finish my dispatches for the packet, which dispatches must go from hence the day after tomorrow. I have much to thank you for. First and most for the cyphered paragraph respecting myself. These little informations are very material towards forming my own decisions. I would be glad even to know when any individual member thinks I have gone wrong in any instance. If I know myself it would not excite ill blood in me, while it would assist to guide my conduct, perhaps to justify it, and to keep me to my duty, alert. I must thank you too for the information in Thos. Burke's case, tho' you will have found by a subsequent letter that I

*J. P. Boyd, ed., *The Papers of Thomas Jefferson* (1958), Vol. 12, pp. 438–42.

have asked of you a further investigation of that matter. It is to gratify the lady who is at the head of the Convent wherein my daughters are, and who, by her attachment and attention to them, lays me under great obligations. I shall hope therefore still to receive from you the result of the further enquiries my second letter had asked.—The parcel of rice which you informed me had miscarried accompanied my letter to the Delegates of S. Carolina. Mr. Bourgoin was to be the bearer of both and both were delivered together into the hands of his relation here who introduced him to me, and who at a subsequent moment undertook to convey them to Mr. Bourgoin. This person was an engraver particularly recommended to Dr. Franklin and Mr. Hopkinson. Perhaps he may have mislaid the little parcel of rice among his baggage. I am much pleased that the sale of Western lands is so successful. I hope they will absorb all the Certificates of our Domestic debt speedily in the first place, and that then offered for cash they will do the same by our foreign one.

The season admitting only of operations in the Cabinet, and these being in a great measure secret, I have little to fill a letter. I will therefore make up the deficiency by adding a few words on the Constitution proposed by our Convention. I like much the general idea of framing a government which should go on of itself peaceably, without needing continual recurrence to the state legislatures. I like the organization of the government into Legislative, Judiciary and Executive. I like the power given the Legislature to levy taxes; and for that reason solely approve of the greater house being chosen by the people directly. For tho' I think a house chosen by them will be very illy qualified to legislate for the Union, for foreign nations &c. yet this evil does not weigh against the good of preserving inviolate the fundamental principle that the people are not to be taxed but by representatives chosen immediately by themselves. I am captivated by the compromise of the opposite claims of the great and little states, of the latter to equal, and the former to proportional influence. I am much pleased too with the substitution of the method of voting by persons, instead of that of voting by states: and I like the negative given to the Executive with a third of either house, though I should have liked it better had the Judiciary been associated for that purpose, or invested with a similar and separate power. There are other good things of less moment. I will now add what I do not like. First the omission of a bill of rights providing clearly and without the aid of sophisms for freedom of religion, freedom of the press, protection against standing armies, restriction against monopolies, the eternal and unremitting force of the habeas corpus laws, and trials by jury in all matters of fact triable by the laws of the land and not by the law of Nations. To say, as Mr. Wilson does that a bill of rights was not necessary because all is reserved in the case of the general government which is not given, while in the particular ones all is given which is not reserved might do for the Audience to whom it was addressed, but is surely gratis dictum, opposed by strong inferences from the body of the instrument, as well as from the omission of the clause of our present confederation which had declared that in express terms. It was a hard conclusion to say because there has been no uniformity among the states as to the cases triable by jury, because some have been so incautious as to abandon this mode of trial, therefore the more prudent states shall be reduced to the same level of calamity. It would have been much more just and wise to have concluded the other way that as most of the states had judiciously preserved this palladium, those who had wandered should be brought back to it, and to have established general right instead of general wrong. Let me add that a bill of rights is what the people are entitled to against every government on earth, general or particular, and what no just government should refuse, or rest on inference. The second feature I dislike, and greatly dislike, is the abandonment in every instance of the necessity of rotation in office, and most particularly in the case of the President. Experience concurs with reason in concluding that the first magistrate will always be re-elected if the constitution permits it. He is then an officer for life. This once observed it becomes of so much consequence to certain nations to have a friend or a foe at the head of our affairs that they will interfere with money and with arms. A Galloman or an Angloman will be supported by the nation he befriends. If once elected, and at a second or third election outvoted by one or two votes, he will pretend false votes, foul play, hold possession of the reins of government, be supported by the states voting for him, especially if they are the central ones lying in a compact body themselves and separating their opponents: and they will be aided by one nation of Europe, while the majority are aided by another. The election of a President of America some years hence will be much more interesting to certain nations of Europe than ever the election of a king of Poland was. Reflect on all the instances in history antient and modern, of elective monarchies, and say if they do not give foundation for my fears, the Roman emperors, the popes, while they were of any importance, the German emperors till they become hereditary in practice, the kings of Poland, the Deys of the Ottoman dependancies. It may be said that if elections are to be attended with these disorders, the seldomer they are renewed the better. But experience shews that the only way to prevent disorder is to render them uninteresting by frequent changes. An incapacity to be elected a second time would have been the only effectual preventative. The power of removing him every fourth year by the vote of the people is a power which will not be exercised. The king of Poland is removeable every day by the Diet, yet he is never removed. Smaller objections are the Appeal in fact as well as law, and the binding all persons Legislative, Executive and Judiciary by oath to maintain that constitution. I do not pretend to decide what would be the best method of procuring the establishment of the manifold good things in this constitution, and of getting rid of the bad. Whether by adopting it in hopes of future amendment, or, after it has been duly weighed and canvassed by the people, after seeing the parts they generally dislike, and those they generally approve, to say to them 'We see now what you wish. Send together your deputies again, let them frame a constitution for you omitting what you have condemned, and establishing the powers you approve. Even these will be a great addition to the energy of your government,'—At all events I hope you will not be discouraged from other trials, if the present one should fail of it's full effect. I have thus told you freely what I like and dislike: merely as a matter of curiosity for I know your own judgment has been formed on all these points after having heard every thing which could be urged on them. I own I am not a friend to a very energetic government. It is always oppressive. The late rebellion in Massachusets has given more alarm than I think it should have done. Calculate that one rebellion in 13 states in the course of 11 years, is but one for each state in a century and a half. No country should be so long without one. Nor will any degree of power in the hands of government prevent insurrections. France with all it's despotism, and two or three hundred thousand men always in arms has had three insurrections in the three years I have been here in every one of which greater numbers were engaged than in Massachusets and a great deal more blood was spilt. In Turkey, which Montesquieu supposes more despotic, insurrections are the events of every day. In England, where the hand of power is lighter than here, but heavier than with us they happen every half dozen years. Compare again the ferocious depredations of their insurgents with the order, the moderation and the almost self extinguishment of ours. After all, it is my principle that the will of the Majority should always prevail. If they approve the proposed Convention in all it's parts, I shall concur in it chearfully, in hopes that they will amend it whenever they shall find it work wrong. I think our governments will remain virtuous for many centuries; as long as they are chiefly agricultural; and this will be as long as there shall be vacant lands in any part of America. When they get piled upon one another in large cities, as in Europe, they will become corrupt as in Europe. Above all things I hope the education of the common people will be attended to; convinced that on their good sense we may rely with the most security for the preservation of a due degree of liberty. I have tired you by this time with my disquisitions and will therefore only add assurances of the sincerity of those sentiments of esteem and attachment with which I am Dear Sir your affectionate friend & servant,

P.S. The instability of our laws is really an immense evil. I think it would be well to provide in our constitutions that there shall always be a twelvemonth between the ingrossing a bill and passing it: that it should then be offered to it's passage without changing a word: and that if circumstances should be thought to require a speedier passage, it should take two thirds of both houses instead of a bare majority.

Jefferson to William Stephens Smith, 1788*

Paris, Feb. 2, 1788

Dear Sir,

Mr. Payne happened to be present when I received your favour of January 16. I read to him that part which stated the circumstances of your delivery of the letter of Dec. 3 to Mr. Littlepage and of the place where he put it for greater care. Payne conjectured what had happened, that it's separation from the common mass of letters had occasioned it to be over-looked. He repeated the circumstances to Littlepage on his return to his lodgings, and he immediately re-examined and found the letter, which I now have. I inclose you your press copies, with a supplement to our account, as far as my memorandum book or an examination of our letters enable me to make it out. You will be so good as to examine and correct the new articles where they need it, and whatever balance may remain, Mr. Trumbul will receive and employ it for me. With respect to Mr. Adams's picture, I must again press it to be done by Brown, because Trumbul does not paint of the size of the life, and could not be asked to hazard himself on it. I have sent to Florence for those of Columbus (if it exists) of Americus Vesputius, Magel-lan &c. and I must not be disappointed of Mr. Adams's. When done, Mr. Trumbul will receive and forward it to me. Be so good also as to let me know who undertook the map of S. America, and even to get from him some acknolegement in writing, of what he is to do. I am glad to learn by letters which come down to the 20th. of December that the new constitution will undoubtedly be received by a sufficiency of the states to set it a going. Were I in America, I would advocate it warmly till nine should have adopted, and then as warmly take the other side to convince the remaining four that they ought not to come into it till the declaration of rights is annexed to it. By this means we should secure all the good of it, and procure so respectable an opposition as would induce the accepting states to offer a bill of rights. This would be the happiest turn the thing could take. I fear much the effects of the perpetual re-eligibility of the President. But it is not thought of in America, and have therefore no prospect of a change of that article. But I own it astonishes me to find such a change wrought in the opinions of our countrymen since I left them, as that threefourths of them should be con-tented to live under a system which leaves to their governors the power of taking from them the trial by jury in civil cases, freedom of religion, freedom of the press, freedom of commerce, the habeas corpus laws, and of yoking them with a standing army. This is a degeneracy in the principles of liberty to which I had given four centuries instead of four years. But I hope it will all come about. We are now vibrating between too much and too little government, and the pendulum will rest finally in the middle. Adieu, yours affectionately,

*The Papers of Thomas Jefferson, Vol. 12, pp. 557–58.

Jefferson to Madison, 1788*

Paris, Feb. 6, 1788

Dear Sir,

I wrote you last on the 20th. of December since which your's of the same day and of the 9th. have come to hand. The apples and cranberries you were so kind as to send at the same time were all spoiled when they arrived at Havre, so that probably those articles will not keep during the passage. The box of plants is arrived at the Custom house here, but I shall probably not receive them till after I shall have sealed my letter. They are well chosen, as to the species, for this country. I wish there had been some willow oaks (Quercus Phellos Linnaei) among them, either the plants or acorns, as that tree is much desired here, and absolutely unknown. As the red-birds and opossums are not to be had at New York, I will release you from the trouble of procuring them elsewhere. This trouble, with the incertainty of their coming safe, is more than the importance of the object will justify. You omitted to inclose Prince's catalogue of plants which your letter mentions to have been inclosed. I send herewith two small boxes, one addressed to Mr. Drayton to the care of the S. Carola. delegates, with a letter. Will you be so good as to ask those gentlemen to forward the letter and box without delay. The box contains cork acorns, and Sulla, which should arrive at their destination as quick as possible. The other box is addressed to you, and contains, cork acorns, Sulla, and peas. The two first articles are to be forwarded to Monticello to Colo. Nicholas Lewis, taking thereout what proportion of them you please for yourself. The peas are brought me from the South of France and are said to be valuable. Considering the season of the year I think it would be best to sow them at New York, and to send the produce on next winter to such persons as you please in Virginia, in order to try whether they are any of them better than what we already have. The Sulla is a species of St. foin which comes from Malta, and is proof against any degree of drought. I have raised it in my garden here, and find it a luxuriant and precious plant. I inclose you the bills of lading for the three boxes of books which ought to have gone last fall, but are only lately gone by the Juno Capt. Jenkins. Your pedometer is done, and I now wait only for some trusty passenger to take charge of it. I hope there will be one in the March packet. It cost 300. livres. Your watch you will have received by the Ct. de Moustier. With respect to the Mercures de France always forwarded to you for Bannister, I must beg you never to let them go so as to subject him to postage for them.

I am glad to hear that the new constitution is received with favor. I sincerely wish that the 9 first conventions may receive, and the 4. last reject

The Papers of Thomas Jefferson, Vol. 12, pp. 568–69.

it. The former will secure it finally, while the latter will oblige them to offer a declaration of rights in order to complete the union. We shall thus have all it's good, and cure it's principal defect. You will of course be so good as to continue to mark to me it's progress. I will thank you also for as exact a state as you can procure me of the impression made on the sum of our domestic debt by the sale of lands, and by federal and state exertions in any other manner. I have not yet heard whether the law passed in Virginia for prohibiting the importation of brandies. If it did, the late arret here for encouraging our commerce will be repealed. The minister will be glad of such a pretext to pacify the opposition. I do not see that there are at present any strong symptoms of rupture among the Western powers of Europe. Domestic effervescence and the want of money shackle all the movements of this court. Their prevailing sentiments are total distrust of England, disgust towards the k. of Prussia, jealousy of the two empires, and I presume I may add a willingness to restore the affairs of the Dutch patriots, if it can be done without war.

I will beg the favor of you to send me a copy of the American philosophical transactions, both the 1st. and 2d. volumes, by the first packet and to accept assurances of the sincere esteem with which I am dear Sir your affectionate friend & servant,

P.S. Among the copies of my Notes to be sent to S. Carolina, be so good as to forward one for Mr. Kinlock whom I think I omitted to name in the list.

Jefferson to Alexander Donald, 1788*

Paris, Feb. 7, 1788

Dear Sir,

I received duly your friendly letter of Nov. 12. By this time you will have seen published by Congress the new regulation obtained from this court in favor of our commerce. I should have made them known to you at the same time but that there is a sort of decency which requires that first communications should be made to government. You will observe that the arrangement relative to tobacco is a continuation of the order of Berni for five years, only leaving the price to be settled between the buyer and seller. You will see too that all contracts for tobacco are forbidden till it arrives in France. Of course your proposition for a contract is precluded. I fear the prices here will be low, especially if the market be crowded. You should be particularly attentive to the article which requires that the tobacco should come in French or American bottoms, as this article will in no instance be departed from.

I wish with all my soul that the nine first Conventions may accept the new

*The Papers of Thomas Jefferson, Vol. 12, pp. 570–72.

Constitution, because this will secure to us the good it contains, which I think great and important. But I equally wish that the four latest conventions, whichever they be, may refuse to accede to it till a declaration of rights be annexed. This would probably command the offer of such a declaration, and thus give to the whole fabric, perhaps as much perfection as any one of that kind ever had. By a declaration of rights I mean one which shall stipulate freedom of religion, freedom of the press, freedom of commerce against monopolies, trial by juries in all cases, no suspensions of the habeas corpus, no standing armies. These are fetters against doing evil which no honest government should decline. There is another strong feature in the new constitution which I as strongly dislike. That is the perpetual re-eligibility of the President. Of this I expect no amendment at present because I do not see that any body has objected to it on your side the water. But it will be productive of cruel distress to our country even in your day and mine. The importance to France and England to have our government in the hands of a Friend or a foe, will occasion their interference by money, and even by arms. Our President will be of much more consequence to them than a king of Poland. We must take care however that neither this nor any other objection to the new form produce a schism in our union. That would be an incurable evil, because near friends falling out never reunite cordially; whereas, all of us going together, we shall be sure to cure the evils of our new constitution, before they do great harm. The box of books I had taken the liberty to address to you is but just gone from Havre for New York. I do not see at present any symptoms strongly indicating war. It is true that the distrust existing between the two courts of Versailles and London is so great that they can scarcely do business together. However the difficulty and doubt of obtaining money makes both afraid to enter into war. The little preparations for war, which we see, are the effect of distrust rather than of a design to commence hostilities. However, in such a state of mind, you know small things may produce a rupture. So that tho peace is rather probable, war is very possible.

Your letter has kindled all the fond recollections of antient times, recollections much dearer to me than any thing I have known since. There are minds which can be pleased by honors and preferments, but I see nothing in them but envy and enmity. It is only necessary to possess them to know how little they contribute to happiness, or rather how hostile they are to it. No attachments soothe the mind so much as those contracted in early life: nor do I recollect any societies which have given me more pleasure than those of which you have partaken with me. I had rather be shut up in a very modest cottage, with my books, my family and a few old friends, dining on simple bacon, and letting the world roll on as it liked, than to occupy the most splendid post which any human power can give. I shall be glad to hear from you often. Give me the small news as well as the great. Tell Dr. Currie that I believe I am indebted to him a letter, but that, like the mass of my countrymen I am not at this moment able to pay all my debts: the post being to depart in an hour, and the last stroke of a pen I am able to send by it being that which assures you of the sentiments of esteem and attachment with which I am dear Sir your affectionate friend & servt.,

Jefferson to C. W. F. Dumas, 1788*

Paris, Feb. 12, 1788

Sir,

I have duly received your favor of the 5th. inst. inclosing that for Mr. Jay. The packet was gone, as I presume: but I have another occasion of forwarding it securely. Your attentions to the Leyden gazette are in my opinion very useful. The paper is much read and respected. It is the only one I know in Europe which merits respect. Your publications in it will tend to reestablish that credit which the solidity of our affairs deserve. With respect to the sale of lands, we know that two sales of 5. millions and 2. millions of acres have been made. Another was begun for 4. millions, which in the course of the negociation may have been reduced to 3. millions as you mention. I have not heard that this sale is absolutely concluded, but there is reason to presume it. Stating these sales at two thirds of a dollar the acre and allowing for 3. or 400,000 acres sold at public sale and a very high price, we may say they have absorbed 7. millions of dollars of the domestic federal debt. The states by taxation and otherwise have absorbed 11. millions more: so that that debt stands now at about 10. millions of dollars and will probably be all absorbed in the course of the next year. There will remain then our foreign debt between 10 and 12. millions, including interest. The sale of lands will then go on for the paiment of this. But as this paiment must be in cash, not in public effects, the lands must be sold cheaper. The demand too will probably be less brisk. So we may suppose this will be longer paying off than the domestic debt. With respect to the new government, 9. or 10. states will probably have accepted it by the end of this month. The others may oppose it. Virginia I think will be of this number. Besides other objections of less moment, she will insist on annexing a bill of rights to the new constitution, i.e. a bill wherein the government shall declare that 1. Religion shall be free. 2. Printing presses free. 3. Trials by jury preserved in all cases. 4. No monopolies in commerce. 5. No standing army. Upon receiving this bill of rights, she will probably depart from her other objections; and this bill is so much of the interest of all the states that I presume they will offer it, and thus our constitution be amended and our union closed by the end of the present year. In this way there will have been opposition enough to do good,

* *The Papers of Thomas Jefferson*, Vol. 12, pp. 583–84.

and not enough to do harm. I have such reliance on the good sense of the body of the people and the honesty of their leaders, that I am not afraid of their letting things go wrong to any length in any case. Wishing you better health, and much happiness I have the honor to be with sentiments of the most perfect esteem and respect Sir your most obedient and most humble servt.,

Madison to Jefferson, 1788*

New York, Oct. 17, 1788

Dear Sir,

I have written a number of letters to you since my return here, and shall add this by another casual opportunity just notified to me by Mr. St. John. Your favor of July 31 came to hand the day before yesterday. The pamphlets of the Marquis Condorcet & Mr. Dupont referred to in it have also been received. Your other letters inclosed to the Delegation have been and will be disposed of as you wish; particularly those to Mr. Eppes & Col. Lewis.

Nothing has been done on the subject of the outfit, there not having been a Congress of nine States for some time, nor even of seven for the last week. It is pretty certain that there will not again be a quorum of either number within the present year, and by no means certain that there will be one at all under the old Confederation. The Committee finding that nothing could be done have neglected to make a report as yet. I have spoken with a member of it in order to get one made, that the case may fall of course and in a favorable shape within the attention of the New Government. The fear of a precedent will probably lead to an allowance for a limited time of the salary, as enjoyed originally by foreign ministers, in preference to a separate allowance for outfit. One of the members of the treasury board, who ought, if certain facts have not escaped his memory, to witness the reasonableness of your calculations, takes occasion I find to impress a contrary idea. Fortunately his influence will not be a very formidable obstacle to right.

The States which have adopted the New Constitution are all proceeding to the arrangements for putting it into action in March next. Pennsylva. alone has as yet actually appointed deputies & that only for the Senate. My last mention that these were Mr. R. Morris & a Mr. McClay. How the other elections there & elsewhere will run is matter of uncertainty. The Presidency alone unites the conjectures of the public. The vice president is not at all marked out by the general voice. As the President will be from a Southern State, it falls almost of course for the other part of the Continent to supply the next in rank. South Carolina may however think of Mr. Rutledge unless

* The Writings of James Madison, Vol. 5, pp. 269–75.

it should be previously discovered that votes will be wasted on him. The only candidates in the Northern States brought forward with their known consent are Handcock and Adams, and between these it seems probable the question will lie. Both of them are objectionable & would I think be postponed by the general suffrage to several others if they would accept the place. Handcock is weak ambitious a courtier of popularity, given to low intrigue, and lately reunited by a factious friendship with S. Adams. F. Adams has made himself obnoxious to many, particularly in the Southern States by the political principles avowed in his book. Others recollecting his cabal during the war against general Washington, knowing his extravagant self-importance, and considering his preference of an unprofitable dignity to some place of emolument better adapted to private fortune as a proof of his having an eye to the presidency, conclude that he would not be a very cordial second to the General, and that an impatient ambition might even intrigue for a premature advancement. The danger would be the greater if particular factious characters, as may be the case, should get into the public councils. Adams it appears, is not unaware of some of the obstacles to his wish, and thro a letter to Smith has thrown out popular sentiments as to the proposed president.

The little pamphlet herewith inclosed will give you a collective view of the alterations which have been proposed for the new Constitution. Various and numerous as they appear they certainly omit many of the true grounds of opposition. The articles relating to Treaties, to paper money, and to contracts, created more enemies than all the errors in the System positive & negative put together. It is true nevertheless that not a few, particularly in Virginia have contended for the proposed alterations from the most honorable & patriotic motives; and that among the advocates for the Constitution there are some who wish for further guards to public liberty & individual rights. As far as these may consist of a constitutional declaration of the most essential rights, it is probable they will be added; though there are many who think such addition unnecessary, and not a few who think it misplaced in such a Constitution. There is scarce any point on which the party in opposition is so much divided as to its importance and its propriety. My own opinion has always been in favor of a bill of rights; provided it be so framed as not to imply powers not meant to be included in the enumeration. At the same time I have never thought the omission a material defect, nor been anxious to supply it even by subsequent amendment, for any other reason than that it is anxiously desired by others. I have favored it because I supposed it might be of use, and if properly executed could not be of disservice. I have not viewed it in an important light—1. because I conceive that in a certain degree, though not in the extent argued by Mr. Wilson, the rights in question are reserved by the manner in which the federal powers are granted. 2. because there is great reason to fear that a positive declaration of some of the most essential rights could not be obtained in the requisite latitude. I am sure that the rights of conscience in particular, if submitted to public definition would be narrowed much more than they are likely ever to be by an assumed power. One of the objections in New England was that the Constitution by prohibiting religious tests, opened a door for Jews Turks & infidels. 3. because the limited powers of the federal Government and the jealousy of the subordinate Governments, afford a security which has not existed in the case of the State Governments, and exists in no other. 4. because experience proves the inefficacy of a bill of rights on those occasions when its controul is most needed. Repeated violations of these parchment barriers have been committed by overbearing majorities in every State. In Virginia I have seen the bill of rights violated in every instance where it has been opposed to a popular current. Notwithstanding the explicit provision contained in that instrument for the rights of Conscience, it is well known that a religious establishment wd. have taken place in that State, if the Legislative majority had found as they expected, a majority of the people in favor of the measure; and I am persuaded that if a majority of the people were now of one sect, the measure would still take place and on narrower ground than was then proposed, notwithstanding the additional obstacle which the law has since created. Wherever the real power in a Government lies, there is the danger of oppression. In our Governments the real power lies in the majority of the Community, and the invasion of private rights is chiefly to be apprehended, not from acts of Government contrary to the sense of its constituents, but from acts in which the Government is the mere instrument of the major number of the Constituents. This is a truth of great importance, but not yet sufficiently attended to; and is probably more strongly impressed on my mind by facts, and reflections suggested by them, than on yours which has contemplated abuses of power issuing from a very different quarter. Wherever there is an interest and power to do wrong, wrong will generally be done, and not less readily by a powerful & interested party than by a powerful and interested prince. The difference so far as it relates to the superiority of republics over monarchies, lies in the less degree of probability that interest may prompt more abuses of power in the former than in the latter; and in the security in the former agst. an oppression of more than the smaller part of the Society, whereas in the former [latter] it may be extended in a manner to the whole. The difference so far as it relates to the point in question—the efficacy of a bill of rights in controuling abuses of power—lies in this: that in a monarchy the latent force of the nation is superior to that of the Sovereign, and a solemn charter of popular rights must have a great effect, as a standard for trying the validity of public acts, and a signal for rousing & uniting the superior force of the community; whereas in a popular Government, the political and physical power may be considered as vested in the same hands, that is in a majority of the people, and, consequently the tyrannical will of the Sovereign is not [to] be controuled by the dread of an appeal to any other force within the community. What use then it may be asked can a bill of rights serve in popular Governments? I answer the two following which, though less essential than in other Governments, sufficiently recommend the precaution: 1. The political truths declared in that solemn manner acquire by degrees the character of fundamental maxims of free Government, and as they become incorporated with the national sentiment, counteract the impulses of interest and passion. 2. Altho. it be generally true as above stated that the danger of oppression lies in the interested majorities of the people rather than in usurped acts of the Government, yet there may be occasions on which the evil may spring from the latter source; and on such, a bill of rights will be a good ground for an appeal to the sense of the community. Perhaps too there may be a certain degree of danger, that a succession of artful and ambitious rulers may by gradual & well timed advances, finally elect an independent Government on the subversion of liberty. Should this danger exist at all, it is prudent to guard agst. it, especially when the precaution can do no injury. At the same time I must own that I see no tendency in our Governments to danger on that side. It has been remarked that there is a tendency in all Governments to an augmentation of power at the expence of liberty. But the remark as usually understood does not appear to me well founded. Power when it has attained a certain degree of energy and independence goes on generally to further degrees. But when below that degree, the direct tendency is to further degrees of relaxation, until the abuses of liberty beget a sudden transition to an undue degree of power. With this explanation the remark may be true; and in the latter sense only is it, in my opinion applicable to the Governments in America. It is a melancholy reflection that liberty should be equally exposed to danger whether the Government have too much or too little power, and that the line which divides these extremes should be so inaccurately defined by experience.

Supposing a bill of rights to be proper the articles which ought to compose it, admit of much discussion. I am inclined to think that absolute restrictions in cases that are doubtful, or where emergencies may overrule them, ought to be avoided. The restrictions however strongly marked on paper will never be regarded when opposed to the decided sense of the public, and after repeated violations in extraordinary cases they will lose even their ordinary efficacy. Should a Rebellion or insurrection alarm the people as well as the Government, and a suspension of the Hab. Corp. be dictated by the alarm, no written prohibitions on earth would prevent the measure. Should an army in time of peace be gradually established in our neighborhood by Britn. or Spain, declarations on paper would have as little effect in preventing a standing force for the public safety. The best security agst. these evils is to remove the pretext for them. With regard to Monopolies, they are justly classed among the greatest nuisances in Government. But is it clear that as encouragements to literary works and ingenious discoveries, they are not too valuable to be wholly renounced? Would it not suffice to reserve in all cases a right to the public to abolish the privilege at a price to be specified in the grant of it? Is there not also infinitely less danger of this abuse in our Governments than in most others? Monopolies are sacrifices of the many to the few. Where the power is in the few it is natural for them to sacrifice the many to their own partialities and corruptions. Where the power as with us is in the many not in the few the danger cannot be very great that the few will be thus favored. It is much more to be dreaded that the few will be unnecessarily sacrificed to the many.

I inclose a paper containing the late proceedings in Kentucky. I wish the ensuing Convention may take no step injurious to the character of the district, and favorable to the views of those who wish ill to the U. States. One of my late letters communicated some circumstances which will not fail to occur on perusing the objects of the proposed Convention in next month. Perhaps however there may be less connection between the two cases than at first one is ready to conjecture.

I am, Dr. sir with the sincerest esteem & affectn.,

Jefferson to Francis Hopkinson, 1789*

Paris, Mar. 13, 1789

Dear Sir,

Since my last, which was of Dec. 21. yours of Dec. 9. and 21. are received. Accept my thanks for the papers and pamphlets which accompanied them, and mine and my daughter's for the book of songs. I will not tell you how much they have pleased us nor how well the last of them merits praise for it's pathos, but relate a fact only, which is that while my elder daughter was playing it on the harpsichord, I happened to look towards the fire and saw the younger one all in tears. I asked her if she was sick? She said "no; but the tune was so mournful." The Editor of the Encyclopedie has published something as to an advanced price on his future volumes, which I understand alarms the subscribers. It was in a paper which I do not take and therefore I have not yet seen it, nor can say what it is. I hope that by this time you have ceased to make wry faces about your vinegar, and that you have received it safe and good. You say that I have been dished up to you as an antifederalist, and ask me if it be just. My opinion was never worthy enough of notice to merit citing: but since you ask it I will tell it you. I am not a Federalist, because I never submitted the whole system of my opinions to the creed of any party of men whatever in religion, in philosophy, in politics, or in any thing else where I was capable of thinking for myself. Such an addiction is the last degradation of a free and moral agent. If I could not go to heaven but with a party, I would not go there at all. Therefore I

*The Papers of Thomas Jefferson, Vol. 14, pp. 649–51.

protest to you I am not of the party of federalists. But I am much farther from that of the Antifederalists. I approved from the first moment, of the great mass of what is in the new constitution, the consolidation of the government, the organisation into Executive, legislative and judiciary, the subdivision of the legislative, the happy compromise of interests between the great and little states by the different manner of voting in the different houses, the voting by persons instead of states, the qualified negative on laws given to the Executive which however I should have liked better if associated with the judiciary also as in New York, and the power of taxation. I thought at first that the latter might have been limited. A little reflection soon convinced me it ought not to be. What I disapproved from the first moment also was the want of a bill of rights to guard liberty against the legislative as well as executive branches of the government, that is to say to secure freedom in religion, freedom of the press, freedom from monopolies, freedom from unlawful imprisonment, freedom from a permanent military, and a trial by jury in all cases determinable by the laws of the land. I disapproved also the perpetual reeligibility of the President. To these points of disapprobation I adhere. My first wish was that the 9. first conventions might accept the constitution, as the means of securing to us the great mass of good it contained, and that the 4. last might reject it, as the means of obtaining amendments. But I was corrected in this wish the moment I saw the much better plan of Massachusets and which had never occurred to me. With respect to the declaration of rights I suppose the majority of the United states are of my opinion: for I apprehend all the antifederalists, and a very respectable proportion of the federalists think that such a declaration should now be annexed. The enlightened part of Europe have given us the greatest credit for inventing this instrument of security for the rights of the people, and have been not a little surprised to see us so soon give it up. With respect to the re-eligibility of the president, I find myself differing from the majority of my countrymen, for I think there are but three states of the 11. which have desired an alteration of this. And indeed, since the thing is established, I would wish it not to be altered during the life of our great leader, whose executive talents are superior to those I beleive of any man in the world, and who alone by the authority of his name and the confidence reposed in his perfect integrity, is fully qualified to put the new government so under way as to secure it against the efforts of opposition. But having derived from our error all the good there was in it I hope we shall correct it the moment we can no longer have the same person at the helm. These, my dear friend, are my sentiments, by which you will see I was right in saying I am neither federalist nor antifederalist; that I am of neither party, nor yet a trimmer between parties. These my opinions I wrote within a few hours after I had read the constitution, to one or two friends in America. I had not then read one single word printed on the subject. I never had an opinion in politics or religion which I was afraid to own. A costive reserve on these subjects might have procured me more esteem from some people, but less from myself. My great wish is to go on in a strict but silent performance of my duty: to avoid attracting notice and to keep my name out of newspapers, because I find the pain of a little censure, even when it is unfounded, is more acute than the pleasure of much praise. The attaching circumstance of my present office is that I can do it's duties unseen by those for whom they are done. You did not think, by so short a phrase in your letter, to have drawn on yourself such an egoistical dissertation. I beg your pardon for it, and will endeavor to merit that pardon by the constant sentiments of esteem & attachment with which I am Dear Sir, Your sincere friend & servant,

P.S. Affectionate respects to Dr. Franklin Mr. Rittenhouse, their and your good families.

Jefferson to Madison, 1789*

Paris, Mar. 15, 1789

Dear Sir,

I wrote you last on the 12th. of Jan. since which I have received yours of Octob. 17. Dec. 8. and 12. That of Oct. 17. came to hand only Feb. 23. How it happened to be four months on the way, I cannot tell, as I never knew by what hand it came. Looking over my letter of Jan. 12th I remark an error of the word 'probable' instead of 'improbable,' which doubtless however you had been able to correct. Your thoughts on the subject of the Declaration of rights in the letter of Oct. 17. I have weighed with great satisfaction. Some of them had not occurred to me before, but were acknoleged just in the moment they were presented to my mind. In the arguments in favor of a declaration of rights, you omit one which has great weight with me, the legal check which it puts into the hands of the judiciary. This is a body, which if rendered independent, and kept strictly to their own department merits great confidence for their learning and integrity. In fact what degree of confidence would be too much for a body composed of such men as Wythe, Blair, and Pendleton? On characters like these the 'civium ardor prava jubentium' would make no impression. I am happy to find that on the whole you are a friend to this amendment. The Declaration of rights is like all other human blessings alloyed with some inconveniences, and not accomplishing fully it's object. But the good in this instance vastly overweighs the evil. I cannot refrain from making short answers to the objections which your letter states to have been raised. 1. That the rights in question are reserved by the manner in which the federal powers are granted. Answer. A constitutive act may certainly be so formed as to need no declaration of

*The Papers of Thomas Jefferson, Vol. 14, pp. 659–62.

rights. The act itself has the force of a declaration as far as it goes: and if it goes to all material points nothing more is wanting. In the draught of a constitution which I had once a thought of proposing in Virginia, and printed afterwards, I endeavored to reach all the great objects of public liberty, and did not mean to add a declaration of rights. Probably the object was imperfectly executed: but the deficiencies would have been supplied by others in the course of discussion. But in a constitutive act which leaves some precious articles unnoticed, and raises implications against others, a declaration of rights becomes necessary by way of supplement. This is the case of our new federal constitution. This instrument forms us into one state as to certain objects, and gives us a legislative and executive body for these objects. It should therefore guard us against their abuses of power within the field submitted to them. 2. A positive declaration of some essential rights could not be obtained in the requisite latitude. Answer. Half a loaf is better than no bread. If we cannot secure all our rights, let us secure what we can. 3. The limited powers of the federal government and jealousy of the subordinate governments afford a security which exists in no other instance. Answer. The first member of this seems resolvable into the 1st. objection before stated. The jealousy of the subordinate governments is a precious reliance. But observe that those governments are only agents. They must have principles furnished them whereon to found their opposition. The declaration of rights will be the text whereby they will try all the acts of the federal government. In this view it is necessary to the federal government also: as by the same text they may try the opposition of the subordinate governments. 4. Experience proves the inefficacy of a bill of rights. True. But tho it is not absolutely efficacious under all circumstances, it is of great potency always, and rarely inefficacious. A brace the more will often keep up the building which would have fallen with that brace the less. There is a remarkeable difference between the characters of the Inconveniencies which attend a Declaration of rights, and those which attend the want of it. The inconveniences of the Declaration are that it may cramp government in it's useful exertions. But the evil of this is shortlived, moderate, and reparable. The inconveniencies of the want of a Declaration are permanent, afflicting and irreparable: they are in constant progression from bad to worse. The executive in our governments is not the sole, it is scarcely the principal object of my jealousy. The tyranny of the legislatures is the most formidable dread at present, and will be for long years. That of the executive will come in it's turn, but it will be at a remote period. I know there are some among us who would now establish a monarchy. But they are inconsiderable in number and weight of character. The rising race are all republicans. We were educated in royalism: no wonder if some of us retain that idolatry still. Our young people are educated in republicanism. An apostacy from that to royalism is unprecedented and impossible. I am much pleased with the prospect that a declaration of rights will be added: and hope it will be done in that way which will not endanger the whole frame of the government, or any essential part of it.

I have hitherto avoided public news in my letters to you, because your situation ensured you a communication of my letters to Mr. Jay. This circumstance being changed, I shall in future indulge myself in these details to you. There had been some slight hopes that an accomodation might be effected between the Turks and two empires. But these hopes do not strengthen, and the season is approaching which will put an end to them for another campaign at least. The accident to the king of England has had great influence on the affairs of Europe. His mediation joined with that of Prussia would certainly have kept Denmark quiet, and so have left the two empires in the hands of the Turks and Swedes. But the inactivity to which England is reduced, leaves Denmark more free, and she will probably go on in opposition to Sweden. The K. of Prussia too had advanced so far that he can scarcely retire. This is rendered the more difficult by the troubles he has excited in Poland. He cannot well abandon the party he had brought forward there. So that it is very possible he may be engaged in the ensuing campaign. France will be quiet this year, because this year at least is necessary for settling her future constitution. The States will meet the 27th. of April: and the public mind will I think by that time be ripe for a just decision of the Question whether they shall vote by orders or persons. I think there is a majority of the nobles already for the latter. If so, their affairs cannot but go on well. Besides settling for themselves a tolerably free constitution, perhaps as free as or as the nation is as yet prepared to bear, they will fund their public debts. This will give them such a credit as will enable them to borrow any money they may want, and of course to take the feild again when they think proper. And I believe they mean to take the feild as soon as they can. The pride of every individual in the nation suffers under the ignominies they have lately been exposed to: and I think the states general will give money for a war to wipe off the reproach. There have arisen new bickerings between this court and that of the Hague, and the papers which have passed shew the most bitter acrimony rankling at the heart of this ministry. They have recalled their Ambassador from the Hague without appointing a successor. They have given a note to the Diet of Poland which shews a disapprobation of their measures. The insanity of the King of England has been fortunate for them as it given them time to put their house in order. The English papers tell you the king is well: and even the English ministry say so. They will naturally set the best foot foremost: and they guard his person so well that it is difficult for the public to contradict them. The king is probably better, but not well by a great deal. 1. He has been bled, and judicious physicians say that in his exhausted state nothing could have induced a recurrence to bleeding but symptoms of relapse. 2. The Prince of Wales tells the Irish deputation he will give them a definitive answer in some days: but if the king had been well he could have given it at once. 3. They talk of passing a standing law for providing a regency in similar cases. They apprehend then they are not yet clear of the danger of wanting a regency. 4. They have carried the king to church: but it was his private chapel. If he be well, why do not they shew him publicly to the nation, and raise them from that consternation into which they have been thrown by the prospect of being delivered over to the profligate hands of the prince of Wales. In short, judging from little facts which escape in spite of their teeth, we may say the king is better, but not well. Possibly he is getting well; but still, time will be wanting to satisfy even the ministry that it is not merely a lucid interval. Consequently they cannot interrupt France this year in the settlement of her affairs, and after this year it will be too late.

As you will be in a situation to know when the leave of absence will be granted me which I have asked, will you be so good as to communicate it by a line to Mr. Lewis and Mr. Eppes? I hope to see you in the summer, and that if you are not otherwise engaged, you will encamp with me at Monticello for a while. I am with great and sincere attachment Dear sir Your affectionate friend & servt,